Nine

Great

Plays

FROM AESCHYLUS TO ELIOT

Revised Edition

EDITED BY Leonard F. Dean
UNIVERSITY OF CONNECTICUT

Ottemiller

Harcourt, Brace & World, Inc.
NEW YORK · BURLINGAME

Copyright, 1950, © *1956, by Harcourt, Brace & World, Inc.*

PRINTED IN THE UNITED STATES OF AMERICA

Contents

Contents

In the Present Edition

Prefatory Note
to the Revised Edition

NINE GREAT PLAYS has been revised, first of all, to include desirable material which was not available in 1950. Shaw's plays may now be reprinted in anthologies, and *Pygmalion,* probably his most popular play, has been substituted for *The Emperor Jones.* Morris Bishop's lively and expert translation of Molière's *The Would-Be Invalid* replaces the older prose translation of *The Misanthrope.* In addition to their intrinsic merits, these two newcomers to the volume extend its representation of comedy. Other changes have been made in answer to suggestions from some of the many teachers and students who have used the original edition during the past four years. The much-admired translation by Dudley Fitts and Robert Fitzgerald of *Oedipus Rex* has been substituted for Yeats' version of the play because it presents Sophocles' choruses in full rather than in condensed form. Finally, Ibsen's *An Enemy of the People* replaces *The Wild Duck* because many teachers find the former play particularly timely and effective in the classroom.

Preface
to the Original Edition

MOST OF the plays in this volume chose themselves. MacNeice's translation of Aeschylus' *Agamemnon* and Yeats' version of Sophocles' *King Oedipus* provided the happy combination of the greatest Greek tragedies with brilliant modern poetry. Once it was decided not to include Shakespeare because his plays are readily available, Ben Jonson was an obvious choice. His *Volpone,* Molière's *The Misanthrope,* and Congreve's *The Way of the World* represent Elizabethan and seventeenth-century comedy at its finest. The selection of the modern plays was less easy, but given the importance of social and psychological drama in our time and the unavailability of Shaw's plays, there was little question that Ibsen, Chekhov, and O'Neill should be represented. As the last play, we were fortunate to be able to include the most distinguished modern poetic drama, T. S. Eliot's *Murder in the Cathedral.* These nine plays, representing a variety of types, are so notable both intrinsically and historically and so generally significant that they should constitute a valuable text for many kinds of courses in which drama is studied.

General Introduction

THE NINE plays in this volume, ranging from Greek to modern, are recognized artistic achievements. The emphasis in the introductions to the individual plays will be on their artistry, on ways of getting at meaning through attention to the inner significance of character, plot, language, and structure. The separate introductions will be kept short to avoid the implication that there is any substitute for an alert and sympathetic reading of the plays themselves, and because topics which apply to more than one play can best be handled in a general introduction. Among those topics are the relation of the plays to the theater and to society, and some of the terms or concepts that are useful in discussing drama of any period.

From one view, a play is a self-contained work of art; from another view, it is a symbol which concentrates and interprets the society in which it is created. Between the play and society is the theater, which in its own conventions and function reflects a particular culture. This is easiest to see in drama that is distant from our own. The Greek plays contained in this volume were clearly an integral part of Athenian civic and religious life. They were written by Aeschylus and Sophocles for the City Dionysia, a national festival held in Athens during the early spring. The arrangements for the festival were made by the highest state official; he selected the plays, the actors, and the wealthy citizens who bore the cost. The festival lasted for a week and included a variety of religious and dramatic performances which caught up not only the citizens of Athens but also representatives from the ten Attic tribes.

It was a moment of political and cultural unity. The tragedies, in sets of three, began at dawn on successive days. Their materials were the familiar stories about legendary heroes, and their pattern reflected the career of Dionysus. Like other gods of fertility, his career follows the symbolic curve of the year, passing from fruitful summer through winter to the season of death and rebirth in the spring. Since the theme of the plays, mirroring the Dionysiac pattern, was the rejuvenation of the community, the participants were subordinated rather than individualized as they are likely to be today. The actors wore masks and long flowing robes; their acting was symbolic rather than realistic.

The audience from an amphitheater in the southeastern slope of the Acropolis looked down on a circle sixty-five feet in diameter with an altar in its center. Near the circle a seat of honor was occupied by the priest of Dionysus, and an image of the god was brought to each play. The members of the chorus performed in the circle, where they symbolically acted out the audience's supplication for understanding and divine favor. The attention of audience and chorus was on the action of the chief persons in the play, who moved between the circle and a raised place beyond it in front of a temple. These chief persons, the great figures of Greek myth and legend, were a projection in heroic size of the community with all its human limitations and possibilities. Their actions, as has been noticed, reflected the career of Dionysus. The clearest example is that of Oedipus. The reader will see him at the beginning of Sophocles' play in the summer of his strength. There follows the harsh season in which he learns his mortal limitation and in which society suffers from plague and loss of fertility. But his death at Colonus is also a rebirth, an assertion of value and rejuvenation when man understands his true nature. This pattern, with its passage from misunderstood achievement through disillusionment to insight, is commonly implied by the term tragedy. In the Greek representations of the pattern, and in the more familiar Christian version, the final insight is a paradox which fruitfully unites mankind and god. With the tragic hero we lose our life in order to find it and to bring another season of grace to the community.

The third play in this volume, Ben Jonson's *Volpone,* was performed on the stage of the Globe Theater in London at the beginning of the seventeenth century. The Globe was a privately owned business in a predominantly middle-class commercial city of about 200,000, but in some ways it was closer to the Athenian national amphitheater than to a modern playhouse. Its owners (Shakespeare was one) were themselves engaged in the theatrical arts; its actors were sponsored by the royal government; and it mirrored the basic social and religious beliefs of the community, even though some preachers and city officials frowned on it. The building was a wooden structure, closed on all sides but still open to the sky. The stage, a bare wooden platform, extended well into the area in which the audience stood; that feature and the absence of a front curtain and footlights promoted a greater intimacy between players and spectators than is customary today. A priest or a divine image in the Greek manner would have been out of place in this theater, but the trapdoor in the stage was still accepted on occasion as an entrance to the underworld of spirits, the balcony above the back of the stage as an approach to heaven; and the whole stage thus reflected a culture which thought of man as part angel and part animal, "caught in strange odds between the earth and sky." A fundamental source of drama in such a society was the conflict between religious ideals and worldly practice. The material in *Volpone* would have only documentary interest for spectators who accepted money-making and shrewdness without much question; in 1606, however, such material was at the tense center of a society moving from medieval religion toward modern secularism.

Artistically considered, the Globe was also between the Acropolis and the conventional modern theater. The absence of painted sets and electric lighting meant a neutral, flexible stage where language was crucially important and where symbolism was still an accepted and necessary convention. Characters could range from personified abstractions to complex individuals; their thoughts and feelings could be expressed in a richer language than actual conversation. Verbal descriptions of setting could be varied to reinforce changes in mood, and the location of action could be altered at a word to

permit rapid contrasts as a means of developing plot and theme. These and other freedoms from photographic realism were opportunities for a gifted writer like Jonson in his dramatization of basic social problems during a period of change.

In contrast to the Globe the theaters of Molière and Congreve were closed to the sky, ornately decorated, equipped with painted sets, and lighted with handsome candelabra. Though *The Would-Be Invalid* (1673) and *The Way of the World* (1700) are not far in time from *Volpone,* their different theaters suggest the different societies which they symbolize. The basic problems in the societies around Louis XIV of France and Charles II of England were not the relations of man and God, of religious idealism and worldly practice, but of men and women in a momentarily stable society of aristocratic refinement. The drama which mirrored this society was the comedy of manners. Comedy may range from slapstick or farce to a tableau of pure joy, but it is characteristically a criticism of the existing order of things. Tragedy reveals potential perfection in the midst of disaster; it makes us feel what we might be. Comedy is more intellectual and immediate. The comedy of manners dramatizes the ways in which high society falls short of its own code, and then at its best it goes on to show how the code itself is limited. Since comedy is concerned with present behavior rather than with ideal possibilities, its surface is likely to be realistic; but since its aim is correction, it may employ the artifices and indirection of satire. The plot, for example, may be altered from strict realism in order to maneuver the characters into positions that will reveal their deficiencies. Certain facts that would normally resolve the action may be withheld so that artificially limited choices are debated more thoroughly than in actual life. By such means the comedy of manners reflects a closed aristocratic society, points out lapses from rationally approved behavior, and reaches the outer limits of the accepted code in considering the status of such seeming misfits as the sincere lover.

When the realistic living-room sets of Ibsen's plays, two hundred years later, are approached through a chronological review of the theater, they are seen, like their theatrical predecessors, to be the projection of a particular culture. The faithful stage reproduction

of middle-class interiors to which most of us are still accustomed was the circle within which Ibsen's explorations had to be conducted. His audience watched, as we are still likely to, with the assumption that it was spying on people who were acting and talking in a perfectly natural way. The evidence and conclusions on such a stage must appear to come from the spectators' own everyday life. The action is serious but it cannot be called tragic in the Greek or Elizabethan sense, since the basic issue is no longer the relation of man to God. The focus in the modern play as in modern life is on man alone, on his social and psychological activities. The term "problem play" conveys most of these characteristics, and they are well illustrated in *An Enemy of the People*. The modern problem play is also likely to seem realistic because it reflects recent interest in the subconscious mind and in states of feeling that are not directly expressed by surface actions. The reader will see evidence of this in *The Cherry Orchard*. The surface of Chekhov's play is realistic enough, but it is used to express a more important inner action, the feelings of the characters about social change. Shaw was a close student of Ibsen and Chekhov, as the reader of *Pygmalion* will discover. His stage was essentially the same as Ibsen's, and his prevailing purpose, as he remarked at the beginning of his career, was to employ the comic art of Molière to spread enlightened good sense about crucial social problems. The last play in this volume, T. S. Eliot's *Murder in the Cathedral,* with its bare stage, abstract characterization, and poetic language, is a deliberate attempt to recover the symbolic expressiveness of the Greek and Elizabethan theaters and their belief in a mystery beyond psychology.

A review of the relationships between the drama and its changing theater and social context suggests that plays gain in meaning when they are recognized to have lines going out into widening circles of experience and when they are understood to interpret that experience through varying artistic conventions. Such a review may help to suggest the right demands for the reader to make on these plays, the demands that the plays are designed to satisfy most fruitfully.

Aeschylus

AGAMEMNON

T HE *Agamemnon* is the first of three related plays (the *Oresteia*) that tell a part of the following story. King Atreus banished his brother Thyestes, who had plotted against him and had seduced his wife. Later, pretending to be reconciled, Atreus recalled Thyestes and entertained him at a feast. When Thyestes learned that he was eating the bodies of his own sons he cursed the family of Atreus, and then returned to exile, where he died. One son, Aegisthus, survived to avenge him. Atreus' son, Agamemnon, succeeded to the throne, and he was chosen to lead the forces against Troy to avenge the theft of Helen, the wife of his brother Menelaus. On his way, Agamemnon killed his daughter Iphigenia as a sacrifice in order to gain the help of the gods for the expedition. During Agamemnon's absence, Aegisthus seduced Clytemnestra, Agamemnon's wife, and aided her in killing Agamemnon on his return. They were later killed by Agamemnon's son Orestes.

Thus summarized, this story of lust and violence appears to have little meaning for normal people today. On the surface it appears to be a case study of degenerates. It must be admitted, furthermore, that as sheer narrative the *Agamemnon* is inefficient; and for its original spectators it did not even have the elementary attraction of suspense and surprise, since they knew the story in advance.

A second look at the plot, however, reveals a meaningful pattern. Running through the particular circumstances is a sequence of justified wrongs: every evil deed is properly punished, and yet every punishment becomes a new crime demanding fresh vengeance. When the plot is generalized in this fashion, there is no longer any question about its significance. Our impulse, in fact, may now be to

turn to the last act and find at once the formula that will release men from the chain of evil duty, from wars-to-end-wars that only breed more violence, from well-meant solutions that only breed more problems. But the meaning of *Agamemnon* and its companion plays is not to be found in a detachable formula at the end of the trilogy; it is available only to the extent that one submits attentively to the symbolic experience through which Aeschylus defines and resolves the great issues of his story. The remarks that follow are an attempt to suggest the deeper meaning of a few illustrative incidents.

The definition of issues is begun in the first speech of the play. The speaker, a watchman, is unnecessary in terms of plot (the beacon signal and the arrival of the army could have been announced in other ways), but his character and his attitude toward events is important. He is a simple man of good heart. The ten-year watch has been hard and lonely, yet he has stuck to it like a faithful dog. Filled with natural relief at the sight of the beacon, he puts a good and simple interpretation on the homecoming—now everyone, and especially the queen, will rejoice. Then he checks himself with the dark hint that there is something evil within the palace, but he will say no more, an ox is on his tongue. *He* knows when to be quiet; *he* wasn't born yesterday. We smile at his naive slyness. Whether we know the plot in advance or not, we soon realize that he is certain to be hurt by events that he cannot understand or escape, no matter how small and quiet he may be. We begin to sense that we, too, are watchmen. The great actions of our own time go by too fast, they are dark and ominous, and we hope all will turn out well if we behave ourselves and do not openly name the evil thing. The play, though, will not let us take this role. Its business is to name and exorcise the evil thing. The naming or defining has begun with the characterization of the watchman. Although we like his good-hearted simplicity, we know the real reason why he has been posted by the queen, and that shocking knowledge contrasts the characters of the two and makes us feel superior to both of them.

The character of the watchman expands, in the next scene, into the character of the chorus. The members of the chorus are old men,

too old for fighting and never able to take clear, positive action. They cannot be Agamemnons; they can only watch and try to understand. In their desperate effort to reduce the danger and mystery of what they are watching, they try to apply the sayings of the wise, and they are eager to hear everyone's explanation. But they always hesitate, even when they stand with Cassandra and hear her true account of the murder that is taking place inside the palace. Apollo had given her the power of prophecy or insight, but because she could not fully submit to him and become one with his divinity, he added the curse that she should never be believed. The chorus act out this curse. They are convinced of her powers, yet they cannot face the truth. Their hesitation suggests that men have better information than that on which they act, that they do not usually live up to their possibilities.

In contrast with the chorus is Agamemnon, who does act. The significance of his choice and manner of action is shown in various ways, and most strikingly in the sacrifice of his daughter and in his homecoming. When Iphigenia is suddenly seized, gagged, carried to the altar and killed, we are shocked at innocence being thus manhandled. She is not permitted to speak, except with her eyes (after all, who is she, a child, to question an adult decision?), but the destruction of what she represents makes us understand the cost to Agamemnon's personality in his choosing to become an effective man of action. And yet what would we have him do? The rape of Helen must be avenged, and only a hardened leader can take Troy. Again the question is posed: How can one crime be punished without the commission of another?

That Agamemnon is not an instrument of perfect justice is implied by the sacrifice and by the Herald's account of the war; the nature of his imperfection is defined through the way he behaves at his homecoming. Somewhat surprisingly, he is not hard and arrogant, but instead, merely superficial. His complacency and obtuseness are intensified for us by our own awareness of the intrigue which surrounds him and of the moral issues which are at stake. It is appropriate that he should be tricked by a gross appeal to his manliness at the moment when he is least truly a man. His slayer, Clytemnestra, is also deficient in self-knowledge, even though she

is his superior in cunning. At the conclusion of the play she asserts that her action has brought the chain of violence to an end, that true order has now been established. The evidence of the play, however, proves that her assertion is wishful thinking and that she has not earned the right to make it. Her motives have always been those of narrow self-interest; she has consequently reduced everything to her own size while at the same time publicly professing to subordinate herself to larger values. A striking example is her speech of welcome to Agamemnon, in which she plays a role that is the opposite of her true character. She begins in the tone of a modest, sheltered woman whose intense emotion overcomes her natural shyness and forces her to open her heart in public. What follows is a remarkably accurate and circumstantial account of how a truly loving wife might feel while her husband was at war, but we are continually reminded (as by her dreams of Agamemnon's death) that it is a diabolical fiction. Her immoral sophistication is in constant contrast with the simplicity of the watchman and the chorus.

Although the basic issues raised by *Agamemnon* have not been resolved at the conclusion, the play is self-contained in the sense that it has defined the form which the resolution must take. The assumptions established by *Agamemnon* demand a conclusion in which the simple heart and the rational mind will be one, in which the letter of the law and the spirit of compassionate understanding will be harmonized, in which a crime is finally punished by a pure avenger. The two plays which follow *Agamemnon* present such a conclusion. Orestes kills his mother not from self-interest but as an instrument of justice. After a period of expiation, he is tried in Athens. The vote of the human jury is a tie; the issue is resolved only by Apollo taking on himself the guilt of everyman, and by the union of the merciful wisdom of Athena with the mechanical and traditional justice of the Furies.

Aeschylus, competing in the Athenian dramatic festival for the last time in the year 458 B.C., won the prize with this trilogy, which proposed to his countrymen not a rigid and uncritical defense of the Athenian way of life, but rather a permanent ideal of justice.

AGAMEMNON

TRANSLATED BY LOUIS MACNEICE

Characters

WATCHMAN

CHORUS OF OLD MEN OF THE CITY

CLYTEMNESTRA

HERALD

AGAMEMNON

CASSANDRA

AEGISTHUS

SCENE—*A space in front of the palace of Agamemnon in Argos.
Night. A* WATCHMAN *on the roof of the palace.*

WATCH. The gods it is I ask to release me from this watch
A year's length now, spending my nights like a dog,
Watching on my elbow on the roof of the sons of Atreus
So that I have come to know the assembly of the nightly stars
Those which bring storm and those which bring summer to
men,
The shining Masters riveted in the sky—
I know the decline and rising of those stars.
And now I am waiting for the sign of the beacon,
The flame of fire that will carry the report from Troy,

THE AGAMEMNON of Aeschylus, translated by Louis MacNeice. Reprinted by per
mission of Faber and Faber Ltd., Publishers.

News of her taking. Which task has been assigned me   10
By a woman of sanguine heart but a man's mind.
Yet when I take my restless rest in the soaking dew,
My night not visited with dreams—
For fear stands by me in the place of sleep
That I cannot firmly close my eyes in sleep—
Whenever I think to sing or hum to myself
As an antidote to sleep, then every time I groan
And fall to weeping for the fortunes of this house
Where not as before are things well ordered now.
But now may a good chance fall, escape from pain,   20
The good news visible in the midnight fire.

[*Pause. A light appears, gradually increasing, the light of the
beacon.*]

Ha! I salute you, torch of the night whose light
Is like the day, an earnest of many dances
In the city of Argos, celebration of Peace.
I call to Agamemnon's wife; quickly to rise
Out of her bed and in the house to raise
Clamour of joy in answer to this torch
For the city of Troy is taken—
Such is the evident message of the beckoning flame.
And I myself will dance my solo first   30
For I shall count my master's fortune mine
Now that this beacon has thrown me a lucky throw.
And may it be when he comes, the master of this house,
That I grasp his hand in my hand.
As to the rest, I am silent. A great ox, as they say,
Stands on my tongue. The house itself, if it took voice,
Could tell the case most clearly. But I will only speak
To those who know. For the others I remember nothing.

[*Enter* CHORUS OF OLD MEN. *During the following chorus the
day begins to dawn.*]

CHOR. The tenth year it is since Priam's high
Adversary, Menelaus the king   40
And Agamemnon, the double-throned and sceptred

Yoke of the sons of Atreus
Ruling in fee from God,
From this land gathered an Argive army
On a mission of war a thousand ships,
Their hearts howling in boundless bloodlust
In eagles' fashion who in lonely
Grief for nestlings above their homes hang
Turning in cycles
Beating the air with the oars of their wings,   50
   Now to no purpose
     Their love and task of attention.

But above there is One,
Maybe Pan, maybe Zeus or Apollo,
Who hears the harsh cries of the birds
Guests in his kingdom,
Wherefore, though late, in requital
He sends the Avenger.
Thus Zeus our master
Guardian of guest and of host   60
Sent against Paris the sons of Atreus
For a woman of many men
Many the dog-tired wrestlings
Limbs and knees in the dust pressed—
   For both the Greeks and Trojans
     An overture of breaking spears.

Things are where they are, will finish
In the manner fated and neither
Fire beneath nor oil above can soothe
The stubborn anger of the unburnt offering.   70
As for us, our bodies are bankrupt,
The expedition left us behind
And we wait supporting on sticks
Our strength—the strength of a child;
For the marrow that leaps in a boy's body

Is no better than that of the old
For the War God is not in his body;
While the man who is very old
And his leaf withering away
Goes on the three-foot way   80
No better than a boy, and wanders
A dream in the middle of the day.

But you, daughter of Tyndareus,
Queen Clytemnestra,
What is the news, what is the truth, what have you learnt,
On the strength of whose word have you thus
Sent orders for sacrifice round?
All the gods, the gods of the town,
Of the worlds of Below and Above,
By the door, in the square,   90
Have their altars ablaze with your gifts,
From here, from there, all sides, all corners,
Sky-high leap the flame-jets fed
By gentle and undeceiving
Persuasion of sacred unguent,
Oil from the royal stores.
Of these things tell
That which you can, that which you may,
Be healer of this our trouble
Which at times torments with evil   100
Though at times by propitiations
A shining hope repels
The insatiable thought upon grief
Which is eating away our hearts.

Of the omen which powerfully speeded
That voyage of strong men, by God's grace even I
Can tell, my age can still
Be galvanized to breathe the strength of song,
To tell how the kings of all the youth of Greece
Two-throned but one in mind   110

Were launched with pike and punitive hand
Against the Trojan shore by angry birds.
Kings of the birds to our kings came,
One with a white rump, the other black,
Appearing near the palace on the spear-arm side
Where all could see them,
Tearing a pregnant hare with the unborn young
Foiled of their courses.
    Cry, cry upon Death; but may the good prevail.

But the diligent prophet of the army seeing the sons   120
Of Atreus twin in temper knew
That the hare-killing birds were the two
Generals, explained it thus—
"In time this expedition sacks the town
Of Troy before whose towers
By Fate's force the public
Wealth will be wasted.
Only let not some spite from the gods benight the bulky
    battalions,
The bridle of Troy, nor strike them untimely;
For the goddess feels pity, is angry   130
With the winged dogs of her father
Who killed the cowering hare with her unborn young;
Artemis hates the eagles' feast."
    Cry, cry upon Death; but may the good prevail.

"But though you are so kind, goddess,
To the little cubs of lions
And to all the sucking young of roving beasts
In whom your heart delights,
Fulfil us the signs of these things,
The signs which are good but open to blame,   140
And I call on Apollo the Healer
That his sister raise not against the Greeks
Unremitting gales to baulk their ships,

Hurrying on another kind of sacrifice, with no feasting,
Barbarous building of hates and disloyalties
Grown on the family. For anger grimly returns
Cunningly haunting the house, avenging the death of a child,
    never forgetting its due."
So cried the prophet—evil and good together,
Fate that the birds foretold to the king's house.
In tune with this   150
   Cry, cry upon Death; but may the good prevail.

Zeus, whoever He is, if this
Be a name acceptable,
By this name I will call him.
There is no one comparable
When I reckon all of the case
Excepting Zeus, if ever I am to jettison
The barren care which clogs my heart.

Not He who formerly was great
With brawling pride and mad for broils   160
Will even be said to have been.
And He who was next has met
His match and is seen no more,
But Zeus is the name to cry in your triumph-song
And win the prize for wisdom.

Who setting us on the road
Made this a valid law—
   "That men must learn by suffering."
Drop by drop in sleep upon the heart
Falls the laborious memory of pain,   170
Against one's will comes wisdom;
The grace of the gods is forced on us
   Throned inviolably.

159. He: Ouranos. **162. He:** Cronus.

So at that time the elder
Chief of the Greek ships
Would not blame any prophet
Nor face the flail of fortune;
For unable to sail, the people
Of Greece were heavy with famine,
Waiting in Aulis where the tides   180
  Flow back, opposite Chalcis.

But the winds that blew from the Strymon,
Bringing delay, hunger, evil harbourage,
Crazing men, rotting ships and cables,
By drawing out the time
Were shredding into nothing the flower of Argos,
When the prophet screamed a new
Cure for that bitter tempest
And heavier still for the chiefs,
Pleading the anger of Artemis so that the sons of Atreus   190
Beat the ground with their sceptres and shed tears.

Then the elder king found voice and answered:
"Heavy is my fate, not obeying,
And heavy it is if I kill my child, the delight of my house,
And with a virgin's blood upon the altar
Make foul her father's hands.
Either alternative is evil.
How can I betray the fleet
And fail the allied army?
It is right they should passionately cry for the winds to be
    lulled   200
By the blood of a girl. So be it. May it be well."

182. Strymon: modern Struma, a river flowing through southwestern Bulgaria and northern Greece, and formerly the boundary between Macedonia and Thrace. The winds were blowing from the northeast toward Aulis on Euripus Strait in Boeotia, where the Greek fleet was assembled.

But when he had put on the halter of Necessity
Breathing in his heart a veering wind of evil
Unsanctioned, unholy, from that moment forward
He changed his counsel, would stop at nothing.
For the heart of man is hardened by infatuation,
A faulty adviser, the first link of sorrow.
Whatever the cause, he brought himself to slay
His daughter, an offering to promote the voyage
To a war for a runaway wife.   210

Her prayers and her cries of father,
Her life of a maiden,
Counted for nothing with those militarists;
But her father, having duly prayed, told the attendants
To lift her, like a goat, above the altar
With her robes falling about her,
To lift her boldly, her spirit fainting,
And hold back with a gag upon her lovely mouth
By the dumb force of a bridle
The cry which would curse the house.   220
Then dropping on the ground her saffron dress,
Glancing at each of her appointed
Sacrificers a shaft of pity,
Plain as in a picture she wished
To speak to them by name, for often
At her father's table where men feasted
She had sung in celebration for her father
With a pure voice, affectionately, virginally,
The hymn for happiness at the third libation.
The sequel to this I saw not and tell not   230
But the crafts of Calchas gained their object.
To learn by suffering is the equation of Justice; the Future
Is known when it comes, let it go till then.
To know in advance is to sorrow in advance.
The facts will appear with the shining of the dawn.

[*Enter* CLYTEMNESTRA.]

But may good, at the least, follow after
As the queen here wishes, who stands
Nearest the throne, the only
Defence of the land of Argos.

LEADER OF THE CHORUS. I have come, Clytemnestra, reverencing your
authority. 240
For it is right to honour our master's wife
When the man's own throne is empty.
But you, if you have heard good news for certain, or if
You sacrifice on the strength of flattering hopes,
I would gladly hear. Though I cannot cavil at silence.

CLYT. Bearing good news, as the proverb says, may Dawn
Spring from her mother Night.
You will hear something now that was beyond your hopes.
The men of Argos have taken Priam's city.

LEAD. What! I cannot believe it. It escapes me. 250

CLYT. Troy in the hands of the Greeks. Do I speak plain?

LEAD. Joy creeps over me, calling out my tears.

CLYT. Yes. Your eyes proclaim your loyalty.

LEAD. But what are your grounds? Have you a proof of it?

CLYT. There is proof indeed—unless God has cheated us.

LEAD. Perhaps you believe the inveigling shapes of dreams?

CLYT. I would not be credited with a dozing brain!

LEAD. Or are you puffed up by Rumour, the wingless flyer?

CLYT. You mock my common sense as if I were a child.

LEAD. But at what time was the city given to sack? 260

CLYT. In this very night that gave birth to this day.

LEAD. What messenger could come so fast?

CLYT. Hephaestus, launching a fine flame from Ida,
Beacon forwarding beacon, despatch-riders of fire,
Ida relayed to Hermes' cliff in Lemnos
And the great glow from the island was taken over third

263. **Hephaestus:** Vulcan, god of fire. The beacons were lighted on Mt. Ida, below Troy, then northwest on the island of Lemnos, on Mt. Athos at the tip of the Acte peninsula in Chalcidice, and so across the Aegean and south on the heights named through Greece to Argos.

By the height of Athos that belongs to Zeus,
And towering then to straddle over the sea
The might of the running torch joyfully tossed
The gold gleam forward like another sun,   270
Herald of light to the heights of Mount Macistus,
And he without delay, nor carelessly by sleep
Encumbered, did not shirk his intermediary role,
His farflung ray reached the Euripus' tides
And told Messapion's watchers, who in turn
Sent on the message further
Setting a stack of dried-up heather on fire.
And the strapping flame, not yet enfeebled, leapt
Over the plain of Asopus like a blazing moon
And woke on the crags of Cithaeron   280
Another relay in the chain of fire.
The light that was sent from far was not declined
By the look-out men, who raised a fiercer yet,
A light which jumped the water of Gorgopis
And to Mount Aegiplanctus duly come
Urged the reveille of the punctual fire.
So then they kindle it squanderingly and launch
A beard of flame big enough to pass
The headland that looks down upon the Saronic gulf,
Blazing and bounding till it reached at length   290
The Arachnaean steep, our neighbouring heights;
And leaps in the latter end on the roof of the sons of Atreus
Issue and image of the fire on Ida.
Such was the assignment of my torch-racers,
The task of each fulfilled by his successor,
And victor is he who ran both first and last.
Such is the proof I offer you, the sign
My husband sent me out of Troy.

LEAD. To the gods, queen, I shall give thanks presently.
But I would like to hear this story further,   300
To wonder at it in detail from your lips.

CLYT. The Greeks hold Troy upon this day.
   The cries in the town I fancy do not mingle.
   Pour oil and vinegar into the same jar,
   You would say they stand apart unlovingly;
   Of those who are captured and those who have conquered
   Distinct are the sounds of their diverse fortunes,
   For *these* having flung themselves about the bodies
   Of husbands and brothers, or sons upon the bodies
   Of aged fathers from a throat no longer   310
   Free, lament the fate of their most loved.
   But *those* a night's marauding after battle
   Sets hungry to what breakfast the town offers
   Not billeted duly in any barracks order
   But as each man has drawn his lot of luck.
   So in the captive homes of Troy already
   They take their lodging, free of the frosts
   And dews of the open. Like happy men
   They will sleep all night without sentry.
   But if they respect duly the city's gods,   320
   Those of the captured land and the sanctuaries of the gods,
   They need not, having conquered, fear reconquest.
   But let no lust fall first upon the troops
   To plunder what is not right, subdued by gain,
   For they must still, in order to come home safe,
   Get round the second lap of the doubled course.
   So if they return without offence to the gods
   The grievance of the slain may learn at last
   A friendly talk—unless some fresh wrong falls.
   Such are the thoughts you hear from me, a woman.   330
   But may the good prevail for all to see.
   We have much good. I only ask to enjoy it.
LEAD. Woman, you speak with sense like a prudent man.
   I, who have heard your valid proofs, prepare
   To give the glory to God.
   Fair recompense is brought us for our troubles.

                    [CLYTEMNESTRA *goes back into the palace.*]

CHOR. O Zeus our king and Night our friend
 Donor of glories,
 Night who cast on the towers of Troy
 A close-clinging net so that neither the grown   340
 Nor any of the children can pass
 The enslaving and huge
 Trap of all-taking destruction.
 Great Zeus, guardian of host and guest,
 I honour who has done his work and taken
 A leisured aim at Paris so that neither
 Too short nor yet over the stars
  He might shoot to no purpose.

 From Zeus is the blow they can tell of,
 This at least can be established,
 They have fared according to his ruling. For some
 Deny that the gods deign to consider those among men
 Who trample on the grace of inviolate things;
 It is the impious man says this,
 For Ruin is revealed the child
 Of not to be attempted actions
 When men are puffed up unduly
 And their houses are stuffed with riches.   10
 Measure is the best. Let danger be distant,
 This should suffice a man
 With a proper part of wisdom.
  For a man has no protection
  Against the drunkenness of riches
  Once he has spurned from his sight
  The high altar of Justice.

 Sombre Persuasion compels him,
 Intolerable child of calculating Doom;
 All cure is vain, there is no glozing it over   20
 But the mischief shines forth with a deadly light
 And like bad coinage

By rubbings and frictions
He stands discoloured and black
Under the test—like a boy
Who chases a winged bird.
He has branded his city for ever.
His prayers are heard by no god.
Who makes such things his practice
The gods destroy him.   30
    This way came Paris
    To the house of the sons of Atreus
    And outraged the table of friendship
    Stealing the wife of his host.

Leaving to her countrymen clanging of
Shields and of spears and
Launching of warships
And bringing instead of a dowry destruction to Troy
Lightly she was gone through the gates daring
Things undared. Many the groans   40
Of the palace spokesmen on this theme—
"O the house, the house, and its princes,
O the bed and the imprint of her limbs;
One can see him crouching in silence
Dishonoured and unreviling."
Through desire for her who is overseas, a ghost
Will seem to rule the household.
    And now her husband hates
    The grace of shapely statues;
    In the emptiness of their eyes   50
    All their appeal is departed.

But appearing in dreams persuasive
Images come bringing a joy that is vain,
Vain for when in fancy he looks to touch her—
Slipping through his hands the vision
Rapidly is gone

Following on wings the walks of sleep.
Such are his griefs in his house on his hearth,
Such as these and worse than these,
But everywhere through the land of Greece which men have
  left   60
Are mourning women with enduring hearts
To be seen in all houses; many
Are the thoughts which stab their hearts;
 For those they sent to war
 They know, but in place of men
 That which comes home to them
 Is merely an urn and ashes.

But the money-changer War, changer of bodies,
Holding his balance in the battle
Home from Troy refined by fire   70
Sends back to friends the dust
That is heavy with tears, stowing
A man's worth of ashes
In an easily handled jar.
And they wail speaking well of the men how that one
Was expert in battle, and one fell well in the carnage—
But for another man's wife.
Muffled and muttered words;
And resentful grief creeps up against the sons
Of Atreus and their cause.   80
 But others there by the wall
 Entombed in Trojan ground
 Lie, handsome of limb,
 Holding and hidden in enemy soil.

Heavy is the murmur of an angry people
Performing the purpose of a public curse;
There is something cowled in the night
That I anxiously wait to hear.
For the gods are not blind to the

Murderers of many and the black   90
Furies in time
When a man prospers in sin
By erosion of life reduce him to darkness,
Who, once among the lost, can no more
Be helped. Over-great glory
Is a sore burden. The high peak
Is blasted by the eyes of Zeus.
  I prefer an unenvied fortune,
  Not to be a sacker of cities
  Nor to find myself living at another's   100
  Ruling, myself a captive.

AN OLD MAN. From the good news' beacon a swift
  Rumour is gone through the town.
  Who knows if it be true
  Or some deceit of the gods?

ANOTHER O.M. Who is so childish or broken in wit
  To kindle his heart at a new-fangled message of flame
  And then be downcast
  At a change of report?

ANOTHER O.M. It fits the temper of a woman   110
  To give her assent to a story before it is proved.

ANOTHER O.M. The over-credulous passion of women expands
  In swift conflagration but swiftly declining is gone
  The news that a woman announced.

LEAD. Soon we shall know about the illuminant torches,
  The beacons and the fiery relays,
  Whether they were true or whether like dreams
  That pleasant light came here and hoaxed our wits.
  Look: I see, coming from the beach, a herald
  Shadowed with olive shoots; the dust upon him,   120
  Mud's thirsty sister and colleague, is my witness
  That he will not give dumb news nor news by lighting
  A flame of fire with the smoke of mountain timber;
  In words he will either corroborate our joy—

But the opposite version I reject with horror.
To the good appeared so far may good be added.
ANOTHER SPEAKER. Whoever makes other prayers for this our city,
    May he reap himself the fruits of his wicked heart.
    [*Enter the* HERALD, *who kisses the ground before speaking.*]
HER. Earth of my fathers, O the earth of Argos,
    In the light of the tenth year I reach you thus   130
    After many shattered hopes achieving one,
    For never did I dare to think that here in Argive land
    I should win a grave in the dearest soil of home;
    But now hail, land, and hail, light of the sun,
    And Zeus high above the country and the Pythian king—
    May he no longer shoot his arrows at us
    (Implacable long enough beside Scamander)
    But now be saviour to us and be healer,
    King Apollo. And all the Assembly's gods
    I call upon, and him my patron, Hermes,   140
    The dear herald whom all heralds adore,
    And the Heroes who sped our voyage, again with favour
    Take back the army that has escaped the spear.
    O cherished dwelling, palace of royalty,
    O august thrones and gods facing the sun,
    If ever before, now with your bright eyes
    Gladly receive your king after much time,
    Who comes bringing light to you in the night time,
    And to all these as well—King Agamemnon.
    Give him a good welcome as he deserves,   150
    Who with the axe of judgment-awarding God
    Has smashed Troy and levelled the Trojan land;
    The altars are destroyed, the seats of the gods,
    And the seed of all the land is perished from it.
    Having cast this halter round the neck of Troy
    The King, the elder son of Atreus, a blessed man,
    Comes, the most worthy to have honour of all
    Men that are now. Paris nor his guilty city
    Can boast that the crime was greater than the atonement.

Convicted in a suit for rape and robbery   160
He has lost his stolen goods and with consummate ruin
Mowed down the whole country and his father's house.
The sons of Priam have paid their account with interest.
LEAD. Hail and be glad, herald of the Greek army.
HER. Yes. Glad indeed! So glad that at the gods' demand
I should no longer hesitate to die.
LEAD. Were you so harrowed by desire for home?
HER. Yes. The tears come to my eyes for joy.
LEAD. Sweet then is the fever which afflicts you.
HER. What do you mean? Let me learn your drift.   170
LEAD. Longing for those whose love came back in echo.
HER. Meaning the land was homesick for the army?
LEAD. Yes. I would often groan from a darkened heart.
HER. This sullen hatred—how did it fasten on you?
LEAD. I cannot say. Silence is my stock prescription.
HER. What? In your masters' absence were there some you feared?
LEAD. Yes. In your phrase, death would now be a gratification.
HER. Yes, for success is ours. These things have taken time.
Some of them we could say have fallen well,
While some we blame. Yet who except the gods   180
Is free from pain the whole duration of life?
If I were to tell of our labours, our hard lodging,
The sleeping on crowded decks, the scanty blankets,
Tossing and groaning, rations that never reached us—
And the land too gave matter for more disgust,
For our beds lay under the enemy's walls.
Continuous drizzle from the sky, dews from the marshes,
Rotting our clothes, filling our hair with lice.
And if one were to tell of the bird-destroying winter
Intolerable from the snows of Ida   190
Or of the heat when the sea slackens at noon
Waveless and dozing in a depressed calm—
But why make these complaints? The weariness is over;
Over indeed for some who never again
Need even trouble to rise.

Why make a computation of the lost?
Why need the living sorrow for the spites of fortune?
I wish to say a long goodbye to disasters.
For us, the remnant of the troops of Argos,
The advantage remains, the pain can not outweigh it;   200
So we can make our boast to this sun's light,
Flying on words above the land and sea:
"Having taken Troy the Argive expedition
Has nailed up throughout Greece in every temple
These spoils, these ancient trophies."
Those who hear such things must praise the city
And the generals. And the grace of God be honoured
Which brought these things about. You have the whole story.
LEAD. I confess myself convinced by your report.
Old men are always young enough to learn.   210
                    [*Enter* CLYTEMNESTRA *from the palace.*]
This news belongs by right first to the house
And Clytemnestra—though I am enriched also.
CLYT. Long before this I shouted at joy's command
At the coming of the first night-messenger of fire
Announcing the taking and capsizing of Troy.
And people reproached me saying, "Do mere beacons
Persuade you to think that Troy is already down?
Indeed a woman's heart is easily exalted."
Such comments made me seem to be wandering but yet
I began my sacrifices and in the women's fashion   220
Throughout the town they raised triumphant cries
And in the gods' enclosures
Lulling the fragrant, incense-eating flame.
And now what need is there for you to tell me more?
From the King himself I shall learn the whole story.
But how the best to welcome my honoured lord
I shall take pains when he comes back—For what
Is a kinder light for a woman to see than this,
To open the gates to her man come back from war
When God has saved him? Tell this to my husband,   230

To come with all speed, the city's darling;
May he returning find a wife as loyal
As when he left her, watchdog of the house,
Good to *him* but fierce to the ill-intentioned,
And in all other things as ever, having destroyed
No seal or pledge at all in the length of time.
I know no pleasure with another man, no scandal,
More than I know how to dye metal red.
Such is my boast, bearing a load of truth,   239
A boast that need not disgrace a noble wife.   [*Exit.*]

LEAD. Thus has she spoken; if you take her meaning,
Only a specious tale to shrewd interpreters.
But do you, herald, tell me; I ask after Menelaus
Whether he will, returning safe preserved,
Come back with you, our land's loved master.

HER. I am not able to speak the lovely falsehood
To profit you, my friends, for any stretch of time.

LEAD. But if only the true tidings could be also good!
It is hard to hide a division of good and true.

HER. The prince is vanished out of the Greek fleet,   250
Himself and ship. I speak no lie.

LEAD. Did he put forth first in the sight of all from Troy,
Or a storm that troubled all sweep him apart?

HER. You have hit the target like a master archer,
Told succinctly a long tale of sorrow.

LEAD. Did the rumours current among the remaining ships
Represent him as alive or dead?

HER. No one knows so as to tell for sure
Except the sun who nurses the breeds of earth.

LEAD. Tell me how the storm came on the host of ships   260
Through the divine anger, and how it ended.

HER. Day of good news should not be fouled by tongue
That tells ill news. To each god his season.
When, despair in his face, a messenger brings to a town
The hated news of a fallen army—
One general wound to the city and many men

Outcast, outcursed, from many homes
By the double whip which War is fond of,
Doom with a bloody spear in either hand,
One carrying such a pack of grief could well   270
Recite this hymn of the Furies at your asking.
But when our cause is saved and a messenger of good
Comes to a city glad with festivity,
How am I to mix good news with bad, recounting
The storm that meant God's anger on the Greeks?
For they swore together, those inveterate enemies,
Fire and sea, and proved their alliance, destroying
The unhappy troops of Argos.
In night arose ill-waved evil,
Ships on each other the blasts from Thrace   280
Crashed colliding, which butting with horns in the violence
Of big wind and rattle of rain were gone
To nothing, whirled all ways by a wicked shepherd.
But when there came up the shining light of the sun
We saw the Aegean sea flowering with corpses
Of Greek men and their ships' wreckage.
But for us, our ship was not damaged,
Whether someone snatched it away or begged it off,
Some god, not a man, handling the tiller;
And Saving Fortune was willing to sit upon our ship   290
So that neither at anchor we took the tilt of waves
Nor ran to splinters on the crag-bound coast.
But then having thus escaped death on the sea,
In the white day, not trusting our fortune,
We pastured this new trouble upon our thoughts,
The fleet being battered, the sailors weary,
And now if any of *them* still draw breath,
They are thinking no doubt of us as being lost
And we are thinking of them as being lost.
May the best happen. As for Menelaus   300
The first guess and most likely is a disaster.
But still—if any ray of sun detects him

Alive, with living eyes, by the plan of Zeus
Not yet resolved to annul the race completely,
There is some hope then that he will return home.
So much you have heard. Know that it is the truth. [*Exit.*]

CHOR. Who was it named her thus
    In all ways appositely
    Unless it was Someone whom we do not see,
    Fore-knowing fate 310
    And plying an accurate tongue?
    Helen, bride of spears and conflict's
    Focus, who as was befitting
    Proved a hell to ships and men,
    Hell to her country, sailing
    Away from delicately-sumptuous curtains,
    Away on the wind of a giant Zephyr,
    And shielded hunters mustered many
    On the vanished track of the oars,
    Oars beached on the leafy 320
    Banks of a Trojan river
    For the sake of bloody war.

    But on Troy was thrust a marring marriage
    By the Wrath that working to an end exacts
    In time a price from guests
    Who dishonoured their host
    And dishonoured Zeus of the Hearth,
    From those noisy celebrants
    Of the wedding hymn which fell
    To the brothers of Paris 330
    To sing upon that day.
    But learning this, unlearning that,
    Priam's ancestral city now
    Continually mourns, reviling
    Paris the fatal bridegroom.
    The city has had much sorrow,

Much desolation in life,
From the pitiful loss of her people.

So in his house a man might rear
A lion's cub caught from the dam   340
In need of suckling,
In the prelude of its life
Mild, gentle with children,
For old men a playmate,
Often held in the arms
Like a new-born child,
Wheedling the hand,
Fawning at belly's bidding.

But matured by time he showed
The temper of his stock and payed   350
Thanks for his fostering
With disaster of slaughter of sheep
Making an unbidden banquet
And now the house is a shambles,
Irremediable grief to its people,
Calamitous carnage;
For the pet they had fostered was sent
By God as a priest of Ruin.

So I would say there came
To the city of Troy   360
A notion of windless calm,
Delicate adornment of riches,
Soft shooting of the eyes and flower
Of desire that stings the fancy.
But swerving aside she achieved
A bitter end to her marriage,
Ill guest and ill companion,
Hurled upon Priam's sons, convoyed

By Zeus, patron of guest and host,
Dark angel dowered with tears. 370

Long current among men an old saying
Runs that a man's prosperity
When grown to greatness
Comes to the birth, does not die childless—
His good luck breeds for his house
Distress that shall not be appeased.
I only, apart from the others,
Hold that the unrighteous action
Breeds true to its kind,
Leaves its own children behind it. 380
But the lot of a righteous house
Is a fair offspring always.

Ancient self-glory is accustomed
To bear to light in the evil sort of men
A new self-glory and madness,
Which sometime or sometime finds
The appointed hour for its birth,
And born therewith is the Spirit, intractable, unholy, irresistible,
The reckless lust that brings black Doom upon the house,
A child that is like its parents. 390

But Honest Dealing is clear
Shining in smoky homes,
Honours the god-fearing life.
Mansions gilded by filth of hands she leaves,
Turns her eyes elsewhere, visits the innocent house,
Not respecting the power
Of wealth mis-stamped with approval,
But guides all to the goal.

[*Enter* AGAMEMNON *and* CASSANDRA *on chariots.*]

CHOR. Come then my King, stormer of Troy,
Offspring of Atreus, 400

How shall I hail you, how give you honour
Neither overshooting nor falling short
  Of the measure of homage?
There are many who honour appearance too much
Passing the bounds that are right.
To condole with the unfortunate man
Each one is ready but the bite of the grief
  Never goes through to the heart.
And they join in rejoicing, affecting to share it,
Forcing their face to a smile.   410
But he who is shrewd to shepherd his sheep
Will fail not to notice the eyes of a man
Which seem to be loyal but lie,
  Fawning with watery friendship.
Even you, in my thought, when you marshalled the troops
For Helen's sake, I will not hide it,
Made a harsh and ugly picture,
Holding badly the tiller of reason,
Paying with the death of men
  Ransom for a willing whore.   420
But now, not unfriendly, not superficially,
I offer my service, well-doers' welcome.
In time you will learn by inquiry
Who has done rightly, who transgressed
  In the work of watching the city.
AGAM. First to Argos and the country's gods
My fitting salutations, who have aided me
To return and in the justice which I exacted
From Priam's city. Hearing the unspoken case
The gods unanimously had cast their vote   430
Into the bloody urn for the massacre of Troy;
But to the opposite urn
Hope came, dangled her hand, but did no more.
Smoke marks even now the city's capture.
Whirlwinds of doom are alive, the dying ashes
Spread on the air the fat savour of wealth.

For these things we must pay some memorable return
To Heaven, having exacted enormous vengeance
For wife-rape; for a woman
The Argive monster ground a city to powder,   440
Sprung from a wooden horse, shield-wielding folk,
Launching a leap at the setting of the Pleiads,
Jumping the ramparts, a ravening lion,
Lapped its fill of the kingly blood.
To the gods I have drawn out this overture
But as for your concerns, I bear them in my mind
And say the same, you have me in agreement.
To few of men does it belong by nature
To congratulate their friends unenviously,
For a sullen poison fastens on the heart,   450
Doubling the pain of a man with this disease;
He feels the weight of his own griefs and when
He sees another's prosperity he groans.
I speak with knowledge, being well acquainted
With the mirror of comradeship—ghost of a shadow
Were those who seemed to be so loyal to me.
Only Odysseus, who sailed against his will,
Proved, when yoked with me, a ready tracehorse;
I speak of him not knowing if he is alive.
But for what concerns the city and the gods   460
Appointing public debates in full assembly
We shall consult. That which is well already
We shall take steps to ensure it remain well.
But where there is need of medical remedies,
By applying benevolent cautery or surgery
We shall try to deflect the dangers of disease.
But now, entering the halls where stands my hearth,
First I shall make salutation to the gods
Who sent me a far journey and have brought me back.
And may my victory not leave my side.   470
[*Enter* CLYTEMNESTRA, *followed by women slaves carrying purple tapestries.*]

CLYT. Men of the city, you the aged of Argos,
  I shall feel no shame to describe to you my love
  Towards my husband. Shyness in all of us
  Wears thin with time. Here are the facts first hand.
  I will tell you of my own unbearable life
  I led so long as this man was at Troy.
  For first that the woman separate from her man
  Should sit alone at home is extreme cruelty,
  Hearing so many malignant rumours—First
  Comes one, and another comes after, bad news to worse,   480
  Clamour of grief to the house. If Agamemnon
  Had had so many wounds as those reported
  Which poured home through the pipes of hearsay, then—
  Then he would be gashed fuller than a net has holes!
  And if only he had died . . . as often as rumour told us,
  He would be like the giant in the legend,
  Three-bodied. Dying once for every body,
  He should have by now three blankets of earth above him—
  All that above him; I care not how deep the mattress under!
  Such are the malignant rumours thanks to which   490
  They have often seized me against my will and undone
  The loop of a rope from my neck.
  And this is why our son is not standing here,
  The guarantee of your pledges and mine,
  As he should be, Orestes. Do not wonder;
  He is being brought up by a friendly ally and host,
  Strophius the Phocian, who warned me in advance
  Of dubious troubles, both your risks at Troy
  And the anarchy of shouting mobs that might
  Overturn policy, for it is born in men   500
  To kick the man who is down.
  This is not a disingenuous excuse.
  For me the outrushing wells of weeping are dried up,
  There is no drop left in them.
  My eyes are sore from sitting late at nights
  Weeping for you and for the baffled beacons,

Never lit up. And, when I slept, in dreams
I have been waked by the thin whizz of a buzzing
Gnat, seeing more horrors fasten on you
Than could take place in the mere time of my dream.   510
Having endured all this, now, with unsorrowed heart
I would hail this man as the watchdog of the farm,
Forestay that saves the ship, pillar that props
The lofty roof, appearance of an only son
To a father or of land to sailors past their hope,
The loveliest day to see after the storm,
Gush of well-water for the thirsty traveller.
Such are the metaphors I think befit him,
But envy be absent. Many misfortunes already
We have endured. But now, dear head, come down   520
Out of that car, not placing upon the ground
Your foot, O King, the foot that trampled Troy.
Why are you waiting, slaves, to whom the task is assigned
To spread the pavement of his path with tapestries?
At once, at once let his way be strewn with purple
That Justice lead him toward his unexpected home.
The rest a mind, not overcome by sleep
Will arrange rightly, with God's help, as destined.

AGAM. Daughter of Leda, guardian of my house,
You have spoken in proportion to my absence.   530
You have drawn your speech out long. Duly to praise me,
That is a duty to be performed by others.
And further—do not by women's methods make me
Effeminate nor in barbarian fashion
Gape ground-grovelling acclamations at me
Nor strewing my path with cloths make it invidious.
It is the gods should be honoured in this way.
But being mortal to tread embroidered beauty
For me is no way without fear.
I tell you to honour me as a man, not god.   540
Footcloths are very well—Embroidered stuffs
Are stuff for gossip. And not to think unwisely

Is the greatest gift of God. Call happy only him
Who has ended his life in sweet prosperity.
I have spoken. This thing I could not do with confidence.

CLYT. Tell me now, according to your judgment.

AGAM. I tell you you shall not override my judgment.

CLYT. Supposing you had feared something . . .
Could you have vowed to God to do this thing?

AGAM. Yes. If an expert had prescribed that vow.   550

CLYT. And how would Priam have acted in your place?

AGAM. He would have trod the cloths, I think, for certain.

CLYT. Then do not flinch before the blame of men.

AGAM. The voice of the multitude is very strong.

CLYT. But the man none envy is not enviable.

AGAM. It is not a woman's part to love disputing.

CLYT. But it is a conqueror's part to yield upon occasion.

AGAM. You think such victory worth fighting for?

CLYT. Give way. Consent to let me have the mastery.

AGAM. Well, if such is your wish, let someone quickly loose   560
My vassal sandals, underlings of my feet,
And stepping on these sea-purples may no god
Shoot me from far with the envy of his eye.
Great shame it is to ruin my house and spoil
The wealth of costly weavings with my feet.
But of this matter enough. This stranger woman here
Take in with kindness. The man who is a gentle master
God looks on from far off complacently.
For no one of his will bears the slave's yoke.
This woman, of many riches being the chosen   570
Flower, gift of the soldiers, has come with me.
But since I have been prevailed on by your words
I will go to my palace home, treading on purples.

> [*He dismounts from the chariot and begins to walk up
> the tapestried path. During the following speech he
> enters the palace.*]

CLYT. There is the sea and who shall drain it dry? It breeds
Its wealth in silver of plenty of purple gushing

And ever-renewed, the dyeings of our garments.
The house has its store of these by God's grace, King.
This house is ignorant of poverty
And I would have vowed a pavement of many garments
Had the palace oracle enjoined that vow   580
Thereby to contrive a ransom for his life.
For while there is root, foliage comes to the house
Spreading a tent of shade against the Dog Star.
So now that you have reached your hearth and home
You prove a miracle—advent of warmth in winter;
And further this—even in the time of heat
When God is fermenting wine from the bitter grape,
Even then it is cool in the house if only
Its master walk at home, a grown man, ripe.
O Zeus the Ripener, ripen these my prayers;   590
Your part it is to make the ripe fruit fall.

[*She enters the palace.*]

CHOR. Why, why at the doors
  Of my fore-seeing heart
  Does this terror keep beating its wings?
  And my song play the prophet
  Unbidden, unhired—
  Which I cannot spit out
  Like the enigmas of dreams
  Nor plausible confidence
  Sit on the throne of my mind?   600
  It is long time since
  The cables let down from the stern
  Were chafed by the sand when the seafaring army started for
    Troy.

  And I learn with my eyes
  And witness myself their return;
  But the hymn without lyre goes up,
  The dirge of the Avenging Fiend,

In the depths of my self-taught heart
Which has lost its dear
Possession of the strength of hope.   610
But my guts and my heart
Are not idle which seethe with the waves
Of trouble nearing its hour.
But I pray that these thoughts
May fall out not as I think
    And not be fulfilled in the end.

Truly when health grows much
It respects not limit; for disease,
Its neighbour in the next door room,
Presses upon it.   620
A man's life, crowding sail,
Strikes on the blind reef:
But if caution in advance
Jettison part of the cargo
With the derrick of due proportion,
The whole house does not sink,
Though crammed with a weight of woe
The hull does not go under.
The abundant bounty of God
And his gifts from the year's furrows   630
Drive the famine back.

But when upon the ground there has fallen once
The black blood of a man's death,
Who shall summon it back by incantations?
Even Asclepius who had the art
To fetch the dead to life, even to him
Zeus put a provident end.
But, if of the heaven-sent fates
One did not check the other,
Cancel the other's advantage,   640

My heart would outrun my tongue
In pouring out these fears.
But now it mutters in the dark,
Embittered, no way hoping
To unravel a scheme in time
  From a burning mind.

[CLYTEMNESTRA *appears in the door of the palace.*]

CLYT. Go in too, you; I speak to you, Cassandra,
  Since God in his clemency has put you in this house
  To share our holy water, standing with many slaves
  Beside the altar that protects the house,   650
  Step down from the car there, do not be overproud.
  Heracles himself they say was once
  Sold, and endured to eat the bread of slavery.
  But should such a chance inexorably fall,
  There is much advantage in masters who have long been rich.
  Those who have reaped a crop they never expected
  Are in all things hard on their slaves and overstep the line.
  From us you will have the treatment of tradition.

LEAD. You, it is you she has addressed, and clearly.
  Caught as you are in these predestined toils   660
  Obey her if you can. But should you disobey . . .

CLYT. If she has more than the gibberish of the swallow,
  An unintelligible barbaric speech,
  I hope to read her mind, persuade her reason.

LEAD. As things now stand for you, she says the best.
  Obey her; leave that car and follow her.

CLYT. I have no leisure to waste out here, outside the door.
  Before the hearth in the middle of my house
  The victims stand already, wait the knife.
  You, if you will obey me, waste no time.   670
  But if you cannot understand my language—

                            [*To* CHORUS LEADER]

  You make it plain to her with the brute and voiceless hand.

LEAD. The stranger seems to need a clear interpreter.
  She bears herself like a wild beast newly captured.

CLYT. The fact is she is mad, she listens to evil thoughts,
        Who has come here leaving a city newly captured
        Without experience how to bear the bridle
        So as not to waste her strength in foam and blood.
        I will not spend more words to be ignored.

                                        [*She re-enters the palace.*]

CHOR. But I, for I pity her, will not be angry.   680
        Obey, unhappy woman. Leave this car.
        Yield to your fate. Put on the untried yoke.
CASS. Apollo! Apollo!
CHOR. Why do you cry like this upon Apollo?
        He is not the kind of god that calls for dirges.
CASS. Apollo! Apollo!
CHOR. Once more her funereal cries invoke the god
        Who has no place at the scene of lamentation.
CASS. Apollo! Apollo!
        God of the Ways! My destroyer!   690
        Destroyed again—and this time utterly!
CHOR. She seems about to predict her own misfortunes.
        The gift of the god endures, even in a slave's mind.
CASS. Apollo! Apollo!
        God of the Ways! My destroyer!
        Where? To what house? Where, where have you brought me?
CHOR. To the house of the sons of Atreus. If you do not know it,
        I will tell you so. You will not find it false.
CASS. No, no, but to a god-hated, but to an accomplice
        In much kin-killing, murdering nooses,   700
        Man-shambles, a floor asperged with blood.
CHOR. The stranger seems like a hound with a keen scent,
        Is picking up a trail that leads to murder.
CASS. Clues! I have clues! Look! They are these.
        These wailing, these children, butchery of children;
        Roasted flesh, a father sitting to dinner.
CHOR. Of your prophetic fame we have heard before
        But in this matter prophets are not required.

CASS. What is she doing? What is she planning? 710
What is this new great sorrow?
Great crime . . . within here . . . planning
Unendurable to his folk, impossible
Ever to be cured. For help
Stands far distant.

CHOR. This reference I cannot catch. But the children
I recognized; that refrain is hackneyed.

CASS. Damned, damned, bringing this work to completion—
Your husband who shared your bed
To bathe him, to cleanse him, and then—
How shall I tell of the end? 720
Soon, very soon, it will fall.
The end comes hand over hand
Grasping in greed.

CHOR. Not yet do I understand. After her former riddles
Now I am baffled by these dim pronouncements.

CASS. Ah God, the vision! God, God, the vision!
A net, is it? Net of Hell!
But herself is the net; shared bed; shares murder.
O let the pack ever-hungering after the family
Howl for the unholy ritual, howl for the victim. 730

CHOR. What black Spirit is this you call upon the house—
To raise aloft her cries? Your speech does not lighten me.
Into my heart runs back the blood
Yellow as when for men by the spear fallen
The blood ebbs out with the rays of the setting life
And death strides quickly.

CASS. Quick! Be on your guard! The bull—
Keep him clear of the cow.
Caught with a trick, the black horn's point,
She strikes. He falls; lies in the water. 740
Murder; a trick in a bath. I tell what I see.

CHOR. I would not claim to be expert in oracles
But these, as I deduce, portend disaster.
Do men ever get a good answer from oracles?

No. It is only through disaster
That their garrulous craft brings home
The meaning of the prophet's panic.

CASS. And for me also, for me, chance ill-destined!
My own now I lament, pour into the cup my own.
Where is this you have brought me in my misery?   750
Unless to die as well. What else is meant?

CHOR. You are mad, mad, carried away by the god,
Raising the dirge, the tuneless
Tune, for yourself. Like the tawny
Unsatisfied singer from her luckless heart
Lamenting "Itys, Itys," the nightingale
Lamenting a life luxuriant with grief.

CASS. Oh the lot of the songful nightingale!
The gods enclosed her in a winged body,
Gave her a sweet and tearless passing.   760
But for me remains the two-edged cutting blade.

CHOR. From whence these rushing and God-inflicted
Profitless pains?
Why shape with your sinister crying
The piercing hymn—fear-piercing?
How can you know the evil-worded landmarks
    On the prophetic path?

CASS. Oh the wedding, the wedding of Paris—death to his people!
O river Scamander, water drunk by my fathers!
When I was young, alas, upon your beaches   770
I was brought up and cared for.
But now it is the River of Wailing and the banks of Hell
    That shall hear my prophecy soon.

CHOR. What is this clear speech, too clear?
A child could understand it.
I am bitten with fangs that draw blood
By the misery of your cries,
Cries harrowing the heart.

CASS. O trouble on trouble of a city lost, lost utterly!
My father's sacrifices before the towers,   780

Much killing of cattle and sheep,
No cure—availed not at all
To prevent the coming of what came to Troy,
And I, my brain on fire, shall soon enter the trap.

CHOR. This speech accords with the former.
What god, malicious, over-heavy, persistently pressing,
Drives you to chant of these lamentable
Griefs with death their burden?
But I cannot see the end.

[CASSANDRA *now steps down from the car.*]

CASS. The oracle now no longer from behind veils   790
Will be peeping forth like a newly-wedded bride;
But I can feel it like a fresh wind swoop
And rush in the face of the dawn and, wave-like, wash
Against the sun a vastly greater grief
Than this one. I shall speak no more conundrums.
And bear me witness, pacing me, that I
Am trailing on the scent of ancient wrongs.
For this house here a choir never deserts,
Chanting together ill. For they mean ill,
And to puff up their arrogance they have drunk   800
Men's blood, this band of revellers that haunts the house,
Hard to be rid of, fiends that attend the family.
Established in its rooms they hymn their hymn
Of that original sin, abhor in turn
The adultery that proved a brother's ruin.
A miss? Or do my arrows hit the mark?
Or am I a quack prophet who knocks at doors, a babbler?
Give me your oath, confess I have the facts,
The ancient history of this house's crimes.   809

LEAD. And how could an oath's assurance, however finely assured,
Turn out a remedy? I wonder, though, that you
Being brought up overseas, of another tongue,
Should hit on the whole tale as if you had been standing by.

CASS. Apollo the prophet set me to prophesy.

LEAD. Was he, although a god, struck by desire?

CASS. Till now I was ashamed to tell that story.

LEAD. Yes. Good fortune keeps us all fastidious.

CASS. He wrestled hard upon me, panting love.

LEAD. And did you come, as they do, to child-getting?

CASS. No. I agreed to him. And I cheated him.   820

LEAD. Were you already possessed by the mystic art?

CASS. Already I was telling the townsmen all their future suffering.

LEAD. Then how did you escape the doom of Apollo's anger?

CASS. I did not escape. No one ever believed me.

LEAD. Yet to us your words seem worthy of belief.

CASS. Oh misery, misery!

 Again comes on me the terrible labour of true
 Prophecy, dizzying prelude; distracts . . .
 Do you see these who sit before the house,
 Children, like the shapes of dreams?   830
 Children who seem to have been killed by their kinsfolk,
 Filling their hands with meat, flesh of themselves,
 Guts and entrails, handfuls of lament—
 Clear what they hold—the same their father tasted.
 For this I declare someone is plotting vengeance—
 A lion? Lion but coward, that lurks in bed,
 Good watchdog truly against the lord's return—
 My lord, for I must bear the yoke of serfdom.
 Leader of the ships, overturner of Troy,
 He does not know what plots the accursed hound   840
 With the licking tongue and the pricked-up ear will plan
 In the manner of a lurking doom, in an evil hour.
 A daring criminal! Female murders male.
 What monster could provide her with a title?
 An amphisbaena or hag of the sea who dwells
 In rocks to ruin sailors—
 A raving mother of death who breathes against her folk
 War to the finish. Listen to her shout of triumph,
 Who shirks no horrors, like men in a rout of battle.
 And yet she poses as glad at their return.   850
 If you distrust my words, what does it matter?

That which will come will come. You too will soon stand here
And admit with pity that I spoke too truly.

LEAD. Thyestes' dinner of his children's meat
    I understood and shuddered, and fear grips me
    To hear the truth, not framed in parables.
    But hearing the rest I am thrown out of my course.

CASS. It is Agamemnon's death I tell you you shall witness.

LEAD. Stop! Provoke no evil. Quiet your mouth!

CASS. The god who gives me words is here no healer.   860

LEAD. Not if this shall be so. But may some chance avert it.

CASS. *You* are praying. But others are busy with murder.

LEAD. What man is he promotes this terrible thing?

CASS. Indeed you have missed my drift by a wide margin!

LEAD. But I do not understand the assassin's method.

CASS. And yet too well I know the speech of Greece!

LEAD. So does Delphi but the replies are hard.

CASS. Ah what a fire it is! It comes upon me.
    Apollo, Wolf-Destroyer, pity, pity . . .
    It is the two-foot lioness who beds   870
    Beside a wolf, the noble lion away,
    It is she will kill me. Brewing a poisoned cup
    She will mix my punishment too in the angry draught
    And boasts, sharpening the dagger for her husband,
    To pay back murder for my bringing here.
    Why then do I wear these mockeries of myself,
    The wand and the prophet's garland round my neck?
    My hour is coming—but you shall perish first.
    Destruction! Scattered thus you give me my revenge;
    Go and enrich some other woman with ruin.   880
    See: Apollo himself is stripping me
    Of my prophetic gear, who has looked on
    When in this dress I have been a laughing-stock
    To friends and foes alike, and to no purpose;
    They called me crazy, like a fortune-teller,
    A poor starved beggar-woman—and I bore it.
    And now the prophet undoing his prophetess

Has brought me to this final darkness.
Instead of my father's altar the executioner's block
Waits me the victim, red with my hot blood.　　　　890
But the gods will not ignore me as I die.
One will come after to avenge my death,
A matricide, a murdered father's champion.
Exile and tramp and outlaw he will come back
To gable the family house of fatal crime;
His father's outstretched corpse shall lead him home.
Why need I then lament so pitifully?
For now that I have seen the town of Troy
Treated as she was treated, while her captors
Come to their reckoning thus by the gods' verdict,　　900
I will go in and have the courage to die.
Look, these gates are the gates of Death. I greet them.
And I pray that I may meet a deft and mortal stroke
So that without a struggle I may close
My eyes and my blood ebb in easy death.

LEAD. Oh woman very unhappy and very wise,
　　　Your speech was long. But if in sober truth
　　　You know your fate, why like an ox that the gods
　　　Drive, do you walk so bravely to the altar?

CASS. There is no escape, strangers. No; not by postponement.　910

LEAD. But the last moment has the privilege of hope.

CASS. The day is here. Little should I gain by flight.

LEAD. This patience of yours comes from a brave soul.

CASS. A happy man is never paid that compliment.

LEAD. But to die with credit graces a mortal man.

CASS. Oh my father! You and your noble sons!

　　　[*She approaches the door, then suddenly recoils.*]

LEAD. What is it? What is the fear that drives you back?

CASS. Faugh.

LEAD. Why faugh? Or is this some hallucination?

CASS. These walls breathe out a death that drips with blood.　920

LEAD. Not so. It is only the smell of the sacrifice.

CASS. It is like a breath out of a charnel-house.

LEAD. You think our palace burns odd incense then!
CASS. But I will go to lament among the dead
My lot and Agamemnon's. Enough of life!
Strangers,
I am not afraid like a bird afraid of a bush
But witness you my words after my death
When a woman dies in return for me a woman
And a man falls for a man with a wicked wife.　　930
I ask this service, being about to die.
LEAD. Alas, I pity you for the death you have foretold.
CASS. One more speech I have; I do not wish to raise
The dirge for my own self. But to the sun I pray
In face of his last light that my avengers
May make my murderers pay for this my death,
Death of a woman slave, an easy victim.

　　　　　　　　　　　　　　　　　[*She enters the palace.*]

LEAD. Ah the fortunes of men! When they go well
A shadow sketch would match them, and in ill-fortune
The dab of a wet sponge destroys the drawing.
It is not myself but the life of man I pity.
CHOR. Prosperity in all men cries
For more prosperity. Even the owner
Of the finger-pointed-at palace never shuts
His door against her, saying "Come no more."
So to our king the blessed gods had granted
To take the town of Priam, and heaven-favoured　　10
He reaches home. But now if for former bloodshed
　He must pay blood
And dying for the dead shall cause
　Other deaths in atonement
What man could boast he was born
　Secure, who heard this story?
AGAM. [*Within*] Oh! I am struck a mortal blow—within!
LEAD. Silence! Listen. Who calls out, wounded with a mortal
　　stroke?

AGAM. Again—the second blow—I am struck again.

LEAD. You heard the king cry out. I think the deed is done.   20
Let us see if we can concert some sound proposal.

2ND OLD MAN. Well, I will tell you my opinion—
Raise an alarm, summon the folk to the palace.

3RD OLD MAN. I say burst in with all speed possible,
Convict them of the deed while still the sword is wet.

4TH OLD MAN. And I am partner to some such suggestion.
I am for taking some course. No time to dawdle.

5TH OLD MAN. The case is plain. This is but the beginning.
They are going to set up dictatorship in the state.

6TH OLD MAN. We are wasting time. The assassins tread to earth   30
The decencies of delay and give their hands no sleep.

7TH OLD MAN. I do not know what plan I could hit on to propose.
The man who acts is in the position to plan.

8TH OLD MAN. So I think, too, for I am at a loss
To raise the dead man up again with words.

9TH OLD MAN. Then to stretch out our life shall we yield thus
To the rule of these profaners of the house?

10TH OLD MAN. It is not to be endured. To die is better.
Death is more comfortable than tyranny.

11TH OLD MAN. And are we on the evidence of groans   40
Going to give oracle that the prince is dead?

12TH OLD MAN. We must know the facts for sure and *then* be angry.
Guesswork is not the same as certain knowledge.

LEAD. Then all of you back me and approve this plan—
To ascertain how it is with Agamemnon.

[*The doors of the palace open, revealing the bodies of* AGAMEM-
NON *and* CASSANDRA. CLYTEMNESTRA *stands above them.*]

CLYT. Much having been said before to fit the moment,
To say the opposite now will not outface me.
How else could one serving hate upon the hated,
Thought to be friends, hang high the nets of doom
To preclude all leaping out?   50
For me I have long been training for this match,
I tried a fall and won—a victory overdue.

I stand here where I struck, above my victims;
So I contrived it—this I will not deny—
That he could neither fly nor ward off death;
Inextricable like a net for fishes
I cast about him a vicious wealth of raiment
And struck him twice and with two groans he loosed
His limbs beneath him, and upon him fallen
I deal him the third blow to the God beneath the earth,   60
To the safe keeper of the dead a votive gift,
And with that he spits his life out where he lies
And smartly spouting blood he sprays me with
The sombre drizzle of bloody dew and I
Rejoice no less than in God's gift of rain
The crops are glad when the ear of corn gives birth.
These things being so, you, elders of Argos,
Rejoice if rejoice you will. Mine is the glory.
And if I could pay this corpse his due libation
I should be right to pour it and more than right;   70
With so many horrors this man mixed and filled
The bowl—and, coming home, has drained the draught him-
    self.

LEAD. Your speech astonishes us. This brazen boast
    Above the man who was your king and husband!
CLYT. You challenge me as a woman without foresight
    But I with unflinching heart to you who know
    Speak. And you, whether you will praise or blame,
    It makes no matter. Here lies Agamemnon,
    My husband, dead, the work of this right hand,
    An honest workman. There you have the facts.   80
CHOR. Woman, what poisoned
    Herb of the earth have you tasted
    Or potion of the flowing sea
    To undertake this killing and the people's curses?
    You threw down, you cut off—The people will cast you out,
    Black abomination to the town.

CLYT. Now your verdict—in my case—is exile
And to have the people's hatred, the public curses,
Though then in no way you opposed this man
Who carelessly, as if it were a head of sheep   90
Out of the abundance of his fleecy flocks,
Sacrificed his own daughter, to me the dearest
Fruit of travail, charm for the Thracian winds.
He was the one to have banished from this land,
Pay off the pollution. But when you hear what I
Have done, you judge severely. But I warn you—
Threaten me on the understanding that I am ready
For two alternatives—Win by force the right
To rule me, but, if God brings about the contrary,
Late in time you will have to learn self-discipline.   100

CHOR. You are high in the thoughts,
You speak extravagant things,
After the soiling murder your crazy heart
Fancies your forehead with a smear of blood.
Unhonoured, unfriended, you must
Pay for a blow with a blow.

CLYT. Listen then to this—the sanction of my oaths:
By the Justice totting up my child's atonement,
By the Avenging Doom and Fiend to whom I killed this man,
For me hope walks not in the rooms of fear   110
So long as my fire is lit upon my hearth
By Aegisthus, loyal to me as he was before.
The man who outraged me lies here,
The darling of each courtesan at Troy,
And here with him is the prisoner clairvoyant,
The fortune-teller that he took to bed,
Who shares his bed as once his bench on shipboard,
A loyal mistress. Both have their deserts.
He lies so; and she who like a swan
Sang her last dying lament   120
Lies his lover, and the sight contributes
An appetiser to my own bed's pleasure.

CHOR. Ah would some quick death come not overpainful,
    Not overlong on the sickbed,
    Establishing in us the ever-
    Lasting unending sleep now that our guardian
    Has fallen, the kindest of men,
    Who suffering much for a woman
    By a woman has lost his life.
      O Helen, insane, being one   130
      One to have destroyed so many
      And many souls under Troy,
      Now is your work complete, blossomed not for oblivion,
      Unfading stain of blood. Here now, if in any home,
      Is Discord, here is a man's deep-rooted ruin.

CLYT. Do not pray for the portion of death
    Weighed down by these things, do not turn
    Your anger on Helen as destroyer of men,
    One woman destroyer of many
    Lives of Greek men,   140
      A hurt that cannot be healed.

CHOR. O Evil Spirit, falling on the family,
    On the two sons of Atreus and using
    Two sisters in heart as your tools,
    A power that bites to the heart—
    See on the body
    Perched like a raven he gloats
    Harshly croaking his hymn.

CLYT. Ah, now you have amended your lips' opinion,
    Calling upon this family's three times gorged   150
    Genius—demon who breeds
    Blood-hankering lust in the belly:
    Before the old sore heals, new pus collects.

CHOR. It is a great spirit—great—
    You tell of, harsh in anger,
    A ghastly tale, alas,
    Of unsatisfied disaster
    Brought by Zeus, by Zeus,

Cause and worker of all.
For without Zeus what comes to pass among us? 160
Which of these things is outside Providence?
> O my king, my king,
> How shall I pay you in tears,
> Speak my affection in words?
> You lie in that spider's web,
> In a desecrating death breathe out your life,
> Lie ignominiously
> Defeated by a crooked death
> And the two-edged cleaver's stroke.

CLYT. You say this is *my* work—mine? 170
Do not cozen yourself that I am Agamemnon's wife.
Masquerading as the wife
Of the corpse there the old sharp-witted Genius
Of Atreus who gave the cruel banquet
Has paid with a grown man's life
The due for children dead.

CHOR. That you are not guilty of
This murder who will attest?
No, but you may have been abetted
By some ancestral Spirit of Revenge. 180
Wading a millrace of the family's blood
The black Manslayer forces a forward path
To make the requital at last
For the eaten children, the blood-clot cold with time.
> O my king, my king,
> How shall I pay you in tears,
> Speak my affection in words?
> You lie in that spider's web,
> In a desecrating death breathe out your life,
> Lie ignominiously 190
> Defeated by a crooked death
> And the two-edged cleaver's stroke.

CLYT. Did he not, too, contrive a crooked
Horror for the house? My child by him,

Shoot that I raised, much-wept-for Iphigeneia,
He treated her like this;
So suffering like this he need not make
Any great brag in Hell having paid with death
Dealt by the sword for work of his own beginning.

CHOR. I am at a loss for thought, I lack 200
All nimble counsel as to where
To turn when the house is falling.
I fear the house-collapsing crashing
Blizzard of blood—of which these drops are earnest.
Now is Destiny sharpening her justice
On other whetstones for a new infliction.
O earth, earth, if only you had received me
Before I saw this man lie here as if in bed
In a bath lined with silver.
Who will bury him? Who will keen him? 210
Will you, having killed your own husband,
Dare now to lament him
And after great wickedness make
Unamending amends to his ghost?
And who above this godlike hero's grave
Pouring praises and tears
Will grieve with a genuine heart?

CLYT. It is not your business to attend to that.
By my hand he fell low, lies low and dead,
And I shall bury him low down in the earth, 220
And his household need not weep him
For Iphigeneia his daughter
Tenderly, as is right,
Will meet her father at the rapid ferry of sorrows,
Put her arms round him and kiss him!

CHOR. Reproach answers reproach,
It is hard to decide,
The catcher is caught, the killer pays for his kill.
But the law abides while Zeus abides enthroned
That the wrongdoer suffers. That is established. 230

Who could expel from the house the seed of the Curse?
The race is soldered in sockets of Doom and Vengeance.

CLYT. In this you say what is right and the will of God.
But for my part I am ready to make a contract
With the Evil Genius of the House of Atreus
To accept what has been till now, hard though it is,
But that for the future he shall leave this house
And wear away some other stock with deaths
Imposed among themselves. Of my possessions
A small part will suffice if only I   240
Can rid these walls of the mad exchange of murder.

      [*Enter* AEGISTHUS, *followed by soldiers.*]

AEG. O welcome light of a justice-dealing day!
From now on I will say that the gods, avenging men,
Look down from above on the crimes of earth,
Seeing as I do in woven robes of the Furies
This man lying here—a sight to warm my heart—
Paying for the crooked violence of his father.
For his father Atreus, when he ruled the country,
Because his power was challenged, hounded out
From state and home his own brother Thyestes.   250
My father—let me be plain—was this Thyestes,
Who later came back home a suppliant,
There, miserable, found so much asylum
As not to die on the spot, stain the ancestral floor.
But to show his hospitality godless Atreus
Gave him an eager if not a loving welcome,
Pretending a day of feasting and rich meats
Served my father with his children's flesh.
The hands and feet, fingers and toes, he hid
At the bottom of the dish. My father sitting apart   260
Took unknowing the unrecognizable portion
And ate of a dish that has proved, as you see, expensive.
But when he knew he had eaten worse than poison
He fell back groaning, vomiting their flesh,
And invoking a hopeless doom on the sons of Pelops

Kicked over the table to confirm his curse—
So may the whole race perish!
Result of this—you see this man lie here.
I stitched this murder together; it was my title.
Me the third son he left, an unweaned infant,   270
To share the bitterness of my father's exile.
But I grew up and Justice brought me back,
I grappled this man while still beyond his door,
Having pieced together the programme of his ruin.
So now would even death be beautiful to me
Having seen Agamemnon in the nets of Justice.

LEAD. Aegisthus. I cannot respect brutality in distress.
  You claim that you deliberately killed this prince
  And that you alone planned this pitiful murder.
  Be sure that in your turn your head shall not escape   280
  The people's volleyed curses mixed with stones.

AEG. Do you speak so who sit at the lower oar
  While those on the upper bench control the ship?
  Old as you are, you will find it is a heavy load
  To go to school when old to learn the lesson of tact.
  For old age, too, gaol and hunger are fine
  Instructors in wisdom, second-sighted doctors.
  You have eyes. Cannot you see?
  Do not kick against the pricks. The blow will hurt you.

LEAD. You woman waiting in the house for those who return
      from battle   290
  While you seduce their wives! Was it you devised
  The death of a master of armies?

AEG. And these words, too, prepare the way for tears.
  Contrast your voice with the voice of Orpheus: he
  Led all things after him bewitched with joy, but you
  Having stung me with your silly yelps shall be
  Led off yourself, to prove more mild when mastered.

LEAD. Indeed! So you are now to be king of Argos,
  You who, when you had plotted the king's death,
  Did not even dare to do that thing yourself!   300

AEG. No. For the trick of it was clearly woman's work.
I was suspect, an enemy of old.
But now I shall try with Agamemnon's wealth
To rule the people. Any who is disobedient
I will harness in a heavy yoke, no tracehorse work for him
Like barley-fed colt, but hateful hunger lodging
Beside him in the dark will see his temper soften.

LEAD. Why with your cowardly soul did you yourself
Not strike this man but left that work to a woman
Whose presence pollutes our country and its gods?   310
But Orestes—does he somewhere see the light
That he may come back here by favour of fortune
And kill this pair and prove the final victor?

AEG. [*Summoning his guards*] Well, if such is your design in deeds
and words, you will quickly learn—
Here my friends, here my guards, there is work for you at
hand.

LEAD. Come then, hands on hilts, be each and all of us prepared.
                    [*The old men and the guards threaten each other.*]

AEG. Very well! I too am ready to meet death with sword in hand.

LEAD. We are glad you speak of dying. We accept your words for
luck.

CLYT. No, my dearest, do not so. Add no more to the train of
wrong.
To reap these many present wrongs is harvest enough of
misery.   320
Enough of misery. Start no more. Our hands are red.
But do you, and you old men, go home and yield to fate in
time,
In time before you suffer. We have acted as we had to act.
If only our afflictions now could prove enough, we should
agree—
We who have been so hardly mauled in the heavy claws of the
evil god.
So stands my word, a woman's, if any man thinks fit to hear.

AEG. But to think that these should thus pluck the blooms of an
   idle tongue

   And should throw out words like these, giving the evil god
   his chance,

   And should miss the path of prudence and insult their master
   so!   329

LEAD. It is not the Argive way to fawn upon a cowardly man.

AEG. Perhaps. But I in later days will take further steps with you.

LEAD. Not if the god who rules the family guides Orestes to his
   home.

AEG. Yes. I know that men in exile feed themselves on barren
   hopes.

LEAD. Go on, grow fat defiling justice . . . while you have your
   hour.

AEG. Do not think you will not pay me a price for your stupidity.

LEAD. Boast on in your self-assurance, like a cock beside his hen.

CLYT. Pay no heed, Aegisthus, to these futile barkings. You and I,
   Masters of this house, from now shall order all things well.

                                        [*They enter the palace.*]

Sophocles

OEDIPUS REX

SOPHOCLES' *Oedipus Rex* is a play of self-discovery. Since the audience knows in advance that Oedipus is the man who has unwittingly killed his father and married his mother, the play on one level is a kind of detective story in which we watch Oedipus discover that he is the criminal. An immediately striking thing about his discovery, however, is that it is made through a series of ironic revelations. For example, the eager attempts of Jocasta and the messenger from Corinth to comfort Oedipus provide unintentionally the very facts that prove his guilt. These recurring ironies make us deeply aware that the play, on another level, is about a discovery which is meaningful to all men who wish to know themselves.

Long before the opening action of the play, Oedipus had come to Thebes and had found that its king, Laius, was dead and that its citizens were being killed by a monster, the Sphinx. She could be conquered only by the person who answered her riddle: What goes on four feet, then on two, and finally on three, yet is weakest when it uses the most feet? When Oedipus gave the correct answer, man, the Sphinx destroyed herself, and Oedipus was awarded the empty throne of Thebes by the grateful citizens. At the beginning, then, Oedipus is the hero who had saved society by his intelligence. The action that follows this opening is our discovery with Oedipus of the limitation of human reason. The limitation is emphasized through the continuing ironic reversals, which suggest that man's efforts to outwit the logic of events will only reveal his inadequacy. Human intelligence thus constantly defeated takes on the appearance of mere shrewdness that outsmarts iself. Oedipus, for example,

becoming rigidly proud of his mental powers, assumes cunningly but wrongly that Creon is motivated by ambition and Jocasta by vanity.

The crucial irony, however, is that Oedipus forces his own exposure. His arrogant treatment of unwilling witnesses and his refusal to let well enough alone suggest an almost obsessive desire to get at the truth. We understand that this man unconsciously intent on his own destruction is also heroically realizing his humanity. Our compassion and admiration, and our knowledge that he has sinned as much through ignorance as through pride or passion, may make us feel that his final ruin is unjust, that the punishment does not fit the crime. This seeming inequity is indeed a central aspect of the theme. Oedipus, in the final analysis, is guilty of being human. His very existence is proof that the nature of things cannot be fundamentally altered. In their desire to control the future and to defeat the prophecy that he would kill his father, his parents had cast away the baby Oedipus to die. But in the warfare between the generations the child is always preserved to usurp his elder's place. From this viewpoint, Oedipus' behavior toward old men like Laius and Teiresias is more than a sign of individual arrogance.

Our feeling that Oedipus' final punishment is excessive may also spring from the modern desire for a psychological solution in which the hero, after various excesses, reaches the happiness of a well adjusted personality. Such a conclusion, however, would certainly be false to the implications of the whole play, which have never promised that man can be self-sufficient. An end in which the proud man of reason puts out his eyes and thus symbolically admits the inadequacy of his unaided intelligence is the necessary one for the play.

The Greek audience, however, would have understood that Oedipus' savage self-punishment was also the first step in his reconciliation with the gods. That reconciliation is presented in *Oedipus at Colonus*, which was probably written in 406 B.C., when Sophocles was eighty-nine, and when Athens was hard pressed after more than twenty-five years of the Peloponnesian War against Sparta. One of the themes, appropriately, is the ideal of enlightened justice for Athens, which Aeschylus had proposed at the end of his *Oresteia*. The action in Sophocles' later play occurs near Athens, in

Colonus, his birthplace, at the grove of the Furies, whose sternness had been harmonized with compassion. This just harmony is represented by the magnanimous Theseus, king of Athens, and it is contrasted with the self-centered disorder of Thebes, where after the banishment of Oedipus, his sons, Eteocles and Polyneices had contended for power with each other and with Creon.

In this later play Oedipus, blind and ragged, enters, led by his daughter Antigone. Before his death, he is visited by Creon and Polyneices. Now that Oedipus is beyond practical good and evil he has become valuable to men of ambition. They have been ordered by the gods to make their peace with him, but to do so sincerely would mean giving up their plots and wars; consequently, they go through the form of things only, professing hypocritically to have come out of concern for Oedipus' welfare. His savage denunciation of them exposes their duplicity and is an index to his hard-won insight into truth. When he has performed the necessary rites, which are now truly symbolic, Oedipus, without a guide, enters the grove and is there taken up by the gods, after first entrusting to Theseus the secret wisdom which transcends reason.

OEDIPUS REX

AN ENGLISH VERSION
BY DUDLEY FITTS AND ROBERT FITZGERALD

Characters

OEDIPUS

A PRIEST

CREON

TEIRESIAS

IOCASTÊ

MESSENGER

SHEPHERD OF LAÏOS

SECOND MESSENGER

CHORUS OF THEBAN ELDERS

THE SCENE—*Before the palace of Oedipus, King of Thebes. A central door and two lateral doors open onto a platform which runs the length of the façade. On the platform, right and left, are altars; and three steps lead down into the "orchestra," or chorus-ground. At the beginning of the action these steps are crowded by suppliants who have brought branches and chaplets of olive leaves and who lie in various attitudes of despair.* OEDIPUS *enters.*

PROLOGUE

OED. My children, generations of the living
   In the line of Kadmos, nursed at his ancient hearth:
   Why have you strewn yourselves before these altars

THE OEDIPUS REX of Sophocles: An English Version. Translated by Dudley Fitts and Robert Fitzgerald, copyright, 1949, by Harcourt, Brace and Company, Inc.

In supplication, with your boughs and garlands?
The breath of incense rises from the city
With a sound of prayer and lamentation.
                                                    Children,
I would not have you speak through messengers,
And therefore I have come myself to hear you—
I, Oedipus, who bear the famous name.

                                        [*To a* PRIEST.]

You, there, since you are eldest in the company,   10
Speak for them all, tell me what preys upon you,
Whether you come in dread, or crave some blessing:
Tell me, and never doubt that I will help you
In every way I can; I should be heartless
Were I not moved to find you suppliant here.
PRIEST. Great Oedipus, O powerful King of Thebes!
You see how all the ages of our people
Cling to your altar steps: here are boys
Who can barely stand alone, and here are priests
By weight of age, as I am a priest of God,   20
And young men chosen from those yet unmarried;
As for the others, all that multitude,
They wait with olive chaplets in the squares,
At the two shrines of Pallas, and where Apollo
Speaks in the glowing embers.
                                        Your own eyes
Must tell you: Thebes is in her extremity
And can not lift her head from the surge of death.
A rust consumes the buds and fruits of the earth;
The herds are sick; children die unborn,
And labor is vain. The god of plague and pyre   30
Raids like detestable lightning through the city,
And all the house of Kadmos is laid waste,
All emptied, and all darkened: Death alone
Battens upon the misery of Thebes.

You are not one of the immortal gods, we know;
Yet we have come to you to make our prayer

As to the man of all men best in adversity
And wisest in the ways of God. You saved us
From the Sphinx, that flinty singer, and the tribute
We paid to her so long; yet you were never   40
Better informed than we, nor could we teach you:
It was some god breathed in you to set us free.

Therefore, O mighty King, we turn to you:
Find us our safety, find us a remedy,
Whether by counsel of the gods or men.
A king of wisdom tested in the past
Can act in a time of troubles, and act well.
Noblest of men, restore
Life to your city! Think how all men call you
Liberator for your triumph long ago;   50
Ah, when your years of kingship are remembered,
Let them not say *We rose, but later fell*—
Keep the State from going down in the storm!
Once, years ago, with happy augury,
You brought us fortune; be the same again!
No man questions your power to rule the land:
But rule over men, not over a dead city!
Ships are only hulls, citadels are nothing,
When no life moves in the empty passageways.

OED. Poor children! You may be sure I know   60
All that you longed for in your coming here.
I know that you are deathly sick; and yet,
Sick as you are, not one is as sick as I.
Each of you suffers in himself alone
His anguish, not another's; but my spirit
Groans for the city, for myself, for you.

I was not sleeping, you are not waking me.
No, I have been in tears for a long while
And in my restless thought walked many ways.
In all my search, I found one helpful course,   70
And that I have taken: I have sent Creon,

Son of Menoikeus, brother of the Queen,
To Delphi, Apollo's place of revelation,
To learn there, if he can,
What act or pledge of mine may save the city.
I have counted the days, and now, this very day,
I am troubled, for he has overstayed his time.
What is he doing? He has been gone too long.
Yet whenever he comes back, I should do ill
To scant whatever hint the god may give.   80

PRIEST. It is a timely promise. At this instant
They tell me Creon is here.

OED.   O Lord Apollo!
May his news be fair as his face is radiant!

PRIEST. It could not be otherwise: he is crowned with bay,
The chaplet is thick with berries.

OED.   We shall soon know;
He is near enough to hear us now.

                              [*Enter* CREON.]

                                        O Prince:
Brother: son of Menoikeus:
What answer do you bring us from the god?

CREON. It is favorable. I can tell you, great afflictions
Will turn out well, if they are taken well.   90

OED. What was the oracle? These vague words
Leave me still hanging between hope and fear.

CREON. Is it your pleasure to hear me with all these
Gathered around us? I am prepared to speak,
But should we not go in?

OED.   Let them all hear it.
It is for them I suffer, more than for myself.

CREON. Then I will tell you what I heard at Delphi.

In plain words
The god commands us to expel from the land of Thebes
An old defilement that it seems we shelter.   100
It is a deathly thing, beyond expiation.
We must not let it feed upon us longer.

OED. What defilement? How shall we rid ourselves of it?

CREON. By exile or death, blood for blood. It was
Murder that brought the plague-wind on the city.

OED. Murder of whom? Surely the god has named him?

CREON. My lord: long ago Laïos was our king,
Before you came to govern us.

OED.   I know;
I learned of him from others; I never saw him.

CREON. He was murdered; and Apollo commands us now   110
To take revenge upon whoever killed him.

OED. Upon whom? Where are they? Where shall we find a clue
To solve that crime, after so many years?

CREON. Here in this land, he said.

                       If we make enquiry,
We may touch things that otherwise escape us.

OED. Tell me: Was Laïos murdered in his house,
Or in the fields, or in some foreign country?

CREON. He said he planned to make a pilgrimage.
He did not come home again.

OED.   And was there no one,
No witness, no companion, to tell what happened?   120

CREON. They were all killed but one, and he got away
So frightened that he could remember one thing only.

OED. What was that one thing? One may be the key
To everything, if we resolve to use it.

CREON. He said that a band of highwaymen attacked them,
Outnumbered them, and overwhelmed the King.

OED. Strange, that a highwayman should be so daring—
Unless some faction here bribed him to do it.

CREON. We thought of that. But after Laïos' death
New troubles arose and we had no avenger.   130

OED. What troubles could prevent your hunting down the killers?

CREON. The riddling Sphinx's song
Made us deaf to all mysteries but her own.

OED. Then once more I must bring what is dark to light.
It is most fitting that Apollo shows,
As you do, this compunction for the dead.

You shall see how I stand by you, as I should,
To avenge the city and the city's god,
And not as though it were for some distant friend,
But for my own sake, to be rid of evil.   140
Whoever killed King Laïos might—who knows?—
Decide at any moment to kill me as well.
By avenging the murdered king I protect myself.

Come, then, my children: leave the altar steps,
Lift up your olive boughs!
                    One of you go
And summon the people of Kadmos to gather here.
I will do all that I can; you may tell them that.

                                        [*Exit a* PAGE.]

So, with the help of God,
We shall be saved—or else indeed we are lost.

PRIEST. Let us rise, children. It was for this we came,   150
And now the King has promised it himself.
Phoibos has sent us an oracle; may he descend
Himself to save us and drive out the plague.

[*Exeunt* OEDIPUS *and* CREON *into the palace by the central door.
The* PRIEST *and the* SUPPLIANTS *disperse R and L. After a
short pause the* CHORUS *enters the orchestra.*]

PÁRODOS

CHOR. What is the god singing in his profound   [STROPHE I.]
Delphi of gold and shadow?
What oracle for Thebes, the sunwhipped city?

Fear unjoints me, the roots of my heart tremble.
Now I remember, O Healer, your power, and wonder:
Will you send doom like a sudden cloud, or weave it
Like nightfall of the past?   160

Ah no: be merciful, issue of holy sound:
Dearest to our expectancy: be tender!

[ANTISTROPHE 1.]

Let me pray to Athenê, the immortal daughter of Zeus,
And to Artemis her sister
Who keeps her famous throne in the market ring,
And to Apollo, bowman at the far butts of heaven—

O gods, descend! Like three streams leap against
The fires of our grief, the fires of darkness;
Be swift to bring us rest!

As in the old time from the brilliant house   170
Of air you stepped to save us, come again!

Now our afflictions have no end,   [STROPHE 2.]
Now all our stricken host lies down
And no man fights off death with his mind;

The noble plowland bears no grain,
And groaning mothers can not bear—

See, how our lives like birds take wing,
Like sparks that fly when a fire soars,
To the shore of the god of evening.

The plague burns on, it is pitiless,   [ANTISTROPHE 2.]   180
Though pallid children laden with death
Lie unwept in the stony ways,

And old gray women by every path
Flock to the strand about the altars

There to strike their breasts and cry
Worship of Zeus in wailing prayers:
Be kind, God's golden child!

There are no swords in this attack by fire,   [STROPHE 3.]
No shields, but we are ringed with cries.

Send the besieger plunging from our homes   190
Into the vast sea-room of the Atlantic
Or into the waves that foam eastward of Thrace—

For the day ravages what the night spares—

Destroy our enemy, lord of the thunder!
Let him be riven by lightning from heaven!

Phoibos Apollo, stretch the sun's bowstring,   [ANTISTROPHE 3.]
That golden cord, until it sing for us,
Flashing arrows in heaven!
                                    Artemis, Huntress,
   Race with flaring lights upon our mountains!

O scarlet god, O golden-banded brow,   200
O Theban Bacchos in a storm of Maenads,
                [*Enter* OEDIPUS, CHORUS.]
Whirl upon Death, that all the Undying hate!
Come with blinding cressets, come in joy!

SCENE I

OED. Is this your prayer? It may be answered. Come,
Listen to me, act as the crisis demands,
And you shall have relief from all these evils.

Until now I was a stranger to this tale,
As I had been a stranger to the crime.
Could I track down the murderer without a clue?
But now, friends,   210
As one who became a citizen after the murder,
I make this proclamation to all Thebans:
If any man knows by whose hand Laïos, son of Labdakos,
Met his death, I direct that man to tell me everything,
No matter what he fears for having so long withheld it.

Let it stand as promised that no further trouble
Will come to him, but he may leave the land in safety.

Moreover: If anyone knows the murderer to be foreign,
Let him not keep silent: he shall have his reward from me.
However, if he does conceal it; if any man   220
Fearing for his friend or for himself disobeys this edict,
Hear what I propose to do:

I solemnly forbid the people of this country,
Where power and throne are mine, ever to receive that man
Or speak to him, no matter who he is, or let him
Join in sacrifice, lustration, or in prayer.
I decree that he be driven from every house,
Being, as he is, corruption itself to us: the Delphic
Voice of Zeus has pronounced this revelation.
Thus I associate myself with the oracle   230
And take the side of the murdered king.

As for the criminal, I pray to God—
Whether it be a lurking thief, or one of a number—
I pray that that man's life be consumed in evil and
       wretchedness.
And as for me, this curse applies no less
If it should turn out that the culprit is my guest here,
Sharing my hearth.
                    You have heard the penalty.
I lay it on you now to attend to this
For my sake, for Apollo's, for the sick
Sterile city that heaven has abandoned.   240
Suppose the oracle had given you no command:
Should this defilement go uncleansed for ever?
You should have found the murderer: your king,
A noble king, had been destroyed!
                              Now I,
Having the power that he held before me,
Having his bed, begetting children there

Upon his wife, as he would have, had he lived—
Their son would have been my children's brother,
If Laïos had had luck in fatherhood!
(But surely ill luck rushed upon his reign)—   250
I say I take the son's part, just as though
I were his son, to press the fight for him
And see it won! I'll find the hand that brought
Death to Labdakos' and Polydoros' child,
Heir of Kadmos' and Agenor's line.
And as for those who fail me,
May the gods deny them the fruit of the earth,
Fruit of the womb, and may they rot utterly!
Let them be wretched as we are wretched, and worse!

For you, for loyal Thebans, and for all   260
Who find my actions right, I pray the favor
Of justice, and of all the immortal gods.
CHOR. Since I am under oath, my lord, I swear
    I did not do the murder, I can not name
    The murderer. Might not the oracle
    That has ordained the search tell where to find him?
OED. An honest question. But no man in the world
    Can make the gods do more than the gods will.
CHOR. There is one last expedient—
OED.   Tell me what it is.
    Though it seem slight, you must not hold it back.   270
CHOR. A lord clairvoyant to the lord Apollo,
    As we all know, is the skilled Teiresias.
    One might learn much about this from him, Oedipus.
OED. I am not wasting time:
    Creon spoke of this, and I have sent for him—
    Twice, in fact; it is strange that he is not here.
CHOR. The other matter—that old report—seems useless.
OED. Tell me. I am interested in all reports.
CHOR. The King was said to have been killed by highwaymen.
OED. I know. But we have no witnesses to that.   280

CHOR. If the killer can feel a particle of dread,
    Your curse will bring him out of hiding!
OED.   No.
    The man who dared that act will fear no curse.
        [*Enter the blind seer* TEIRESIAS, *led by a* PAGE.]
CHOR. But there is one man who may detect the criminal.
    This is Teiresias, this is the holy prophet
    In whom, alone of all men, truth was born.
OED. Teiresias: seer: student of mysteries,
    Of all that's taught and all that no man tells,
    Secrets of Heaven and secrets of the earth:
    Blind though you are, you know the city lies   290
    Sick with plague; and from this plague, my lord,
    We find that you alone can guard or save us.

    Possibly you did not hear the messengers?
    Apollo, when we sent to him,
    Sent us back word that this great pestilence
    Would lift, but only if we established clearly
    The identity of those who murdered Laïos.
    They must be killed or exiled.
                                    Can you use
    Birdflight or any art of divination
    To purify yourself, and Thebes, and me   300
    From this contagion? We are in your hands.
    There is no fairer duty
    Than that of helping others in distress.
TEIR. How dreadful knowledge of the truth can be
    When there's no help in truth! I knew this well,
    But did not act on it: else I should not have come.
OED. What is troubling you? Why are your eyes so cold?
TEIR. Let me go home. Bear your own fate, and I'll
    Bear mine. It is better so: trust what I say.
OED. What you say is ungracious and unhelpful   310
    To your native country. Do not refuse to speak.
TEIR. When it comes to speech, your own is neither temperate
    Nor opportune. I wish to be more prudent.

OED. In God's name, we all beg you—

TEIR.   You are all ignorant.
    No; I will never tell you what I know.
    Now it is my misery; then, it would be yours.

OED. What! You do know something, and will not tell us?
    You would betray us all and wreck the State?

TEIR. I do not intend to torture myself, or you.
    Why persist in asking? You will not persuade me.   320

OED. What a wicked old man you are! You'd try a stone's
    Patience! Out with it! Have you no feeling at all?

TEIR. You call me unfeeling. If you could only see
    The nature of your own feelings . . .

OED.   Why,
    Who would not feel as I do? Who could endure
    Your arrogance toward the city?

TEIR.   What does it matter!
    Whether I speak or not, it is bound to come.

OED. Then, if "it" is bound to come, you are bound to tell me.

TEIR. No, I will not go on. Rage as you please.

OED. Rage? Why not!
                    And I'll tell you what I think: 330
    You planned it, you had it done, you all but
    Killed him with your own hands: if you had eyes,
    I'd say the crime was yours, and yours alone.

TEIR. So? I charge you, then,
    Abide by the proclamation you have made:
    From this day forth
    Never speak again to these men or to me;
    You yourself are the pollution of this country.

OED. You dare say that! Can you possibly think you have
    Some way of going free, after such insolence?   340

TEIR. I have gone free. It is the truth sustains me.

OED. Who taught you shamelessness? It was not your craft.

TEIR. You did. You made me speak. I did not want to.

OED. Speak what? Let me hear it again more clearly.

TEIR. Was it not clear before? Are you tempting me?

OED. I did not understand it. Say it again.

TEIR. I say that you are the murderer whom you seek.

OED. Now twice you have spat out infamy. You'll pay for it!

TEIR. Would you care for more? Do you wish to be really angry?

OED. Say what you will. Whatever you say is worthless.   350

TEIR. I say that you live in hideous love with her
    Who is nearest you in blood. You are blind to the evil.

OED. It seems you can go on mouthing like this for ever.

TEIR. I can, if there is power in truth.

OED.   There is:
    But not for you, not for you,
    You sightless, witless, senseless, mad old man!

TEIR. You are the madman. There is no one here
    Who will not curse you soon, as you curse me.

OED. You child of endless night! You can not hurt me
    Or any other man who sees the sun.   360

TEIR. True: it is not from me your fate will come.
    That lies within Apollo's competence,
    As it is his concern.

OED.   Tell me:
    Are you speaking for Creon, or for yourself?

TEIR. Creon is no threat. You weave your own doom.

OED. Wealth, power, craft of statesmanship!
    Kingly position, everywhere admired!
    What savage envy is stored up against these,
    If Creon, whom I trusted, Creon my friend,
    For this great office which the city once   370
    Put in my hands unsought—if for this power
    Creon desires in secret to destroy me!

    He has bought this decrepit fortune-teller, this
    Collector of dirty pennies, this prophet fraud—
    Why, he is no more clairvoyant than I am!

                                         Tell us:
    Has your mystic mummery ever approached the truth?
    When that hellcat the Sphinx was performing here,
    What help were you to these people?
    Her magic was not for the first man who came along:

It demanded a real exorcist. Your birds— 380
What good were they? or the gods, for the matter of that?
But I came by,
Oedipus, the simple man, who knows nothing—
I thought it out for myself, no birds helped me!
And this is the man you think you can destroy,
That you may be close to Creon when he's king!
Well, you and your friend Creon, it seems to me,
Will suffer most. If you were not an old man,
You would have paid already for your plot.

CHOR. We can not see that his words or yours 390
Have been spoken except in anger, Oedipus,
And of anger we have no need. How can God's will
Be accomplished best? That is what most concerns us.

TEIR. You are a king. But where argument's concerned
I am your man, as much a king as you.
I am not your servant, but Apollo's.
I have no need of Creon to speak for me.

Listen to me. You mock my blindness, do you?
But I say that you, with both your eyes, are blind:
You can not see the wretchedness of your life, 400
Nor in whose house you live, no, nor with whom.
Who are your father and mother? Can you tell me?
You do not even know the blind wrongs
That you have done them, on earth and in the world below.
But the double lash of your parents' curse will whip you
Out of this land some day, with only night
Upon your precious eyes.
Your cries then—where will they not be heard?
What fastness of Kithairon will not echo them?
And that bridal-descant of yours—you'll know it then, 410
The song they sang when you came here to Thebes
And found your misguided berthing.
All this, and more, that you can not guess at now,
Will bring you to yourself among your children.

Be angry, then. Curse Creon. Curse my words.
I tell you, no man that walks upon the earth
Shall be rooted out more horribly than you.

OED. Am I to bear this from him?—Damnation
Take you! Out of this place! Out of my sight!

TEIR. I would not have come at all if you had not asked me.   420

OED. Could I have told that you'd talk nonsense, that
You'd come here to make a fool of yourself, and of me?

TEIR. A fool? Your parents thought me sane enough.

OED. My parents again!—Wait: who were my parents?

TEIR. This day will give you a father, and break your heart.

OED. Your infantile riddles! Your damned abracadabra!

TEIR. You were a great man once at solving riddles.

OED. Mock me with that if you like; you will find it true.

TEIR. It was true enough. It brought about your ruin.

OED. But if it saved this town?

                                                 [To the PAGE.]

TEIR. Boy, give me your hand.   430

OED. Yes, boy; lead him away.

                  —While you are here
We can do nothing. Go; leave us in peace.

TEIR. I will go when I have said what I have to say.
How can you hurt me? And I tell you again:
The man you have been looking for all this time,
The damned man, the murderer of Laïos,
That man is in Thebes. To your mind he is foreign-born,
But it will soon be shown that he is a Theban,
A revelation that will fail to please.

                          A blind man,
Who has his eyes now; a penniless man, who is rich now;   440
And he will go tapping the strange earth with his staff.
To the children with whom he lives now he will be
Brother and father—the very same; to her
Who bore him, son and husband—the very same
Who came to his father's bed, wet with his father's blood.

Enough. Go think that over.
If later you find error in what I have said,
You may say that I have no skill in prophecy.

[*Exit* TEIRESIAS, *led by his* PAGE. OEDIPUS *goes into the palace.*]

ODE I

CHOR. The Delphic stone of prophecies   [STROPHE I.]
   Remembers ancient regicide   450
   And a still bloody hand.
   That killer's hour of flight has come.
   He must be stronger than riderless
   Coursers of untiring wind,
   For the son of Zeus armed with his father's thunder
   Leaps in lightning after him;
   And the Furies follow him, the sad Furies.

   Holy Parnassos' peak of snow   [ANTISTROPHE I.]
   Flashes and blinds that secret man,
   That all shall hunt him down: 460
   Though he may roam the forest shade
   Like a bull gone wild from pasture
   To rage through glooms of stone.
   Doom comes down on him; flight will not avail him;
   For the world's heart calls him desolate,
   And the immortal Furies follow, for ever follow.

   But now a wilder thing is heard   [STROPHE 2.]
   From the old man skilled at hearing Fate in the wingbeat of
      a bird.
   Bewildered as a blown bird, my soul hovers and can not find
   Foothold in this debate, or any reason or rest of mind.   470
   But no man ever brought—none can bring
   Proof of strife between Thebes' royal house,
   Labdakos' line, and the son of Polybos;

And never until now has any man brought word
Of Laïos' dark death staining Oedipus the King.

Divine Zeus and Apollo hold   [ANTISTROPHE 2.]
Perfect intelligence alone of all tales ever told;
And well though this diviner works, he works in his own
     night;
No man can judge that rough unknown or trust in second
     sight,
For wisdom changes hands among the wise.   480
Shall I believe my great lord criminal
At a raging word that a blind old man let fall?
I saw him, when the carrion woman faced him of old,
Prove his heroic mind! These evil words are lies.

SCENE II

CREON. Men of Thebes:
     I am told that heavy accusations
     Have been brought against me by King Oedipus.

     I am not the kind of man to bear this tamely.

     If in these present difficulties
     He holds me accountable for any harm to him   490
     Through anything I have said or done—why, then,
     I do not value life in this dishonor.
     It is not as though this rumor touched upon
     Some private indiscretion. The matter is grave.
     The fact is that I am being called disloyal
     To the State, to my fellow citizens, to my friends.
CHOR. He may have spoken in anger, not from his mind.
CREON. But did you not hear him say I was the one
     Who seduced the old prophet into lying?
CHOR. The thing was said; I do not know how seriously.   500

CREON. But you were watching him! Were his eyes steady?
   Did he look like a man in his right mind?

CHOR.   I do not know.
   I can not judge the behavior of great men.
   But here is the King himself.

                    [*Enter* OEDIPUS.]

OED.   So you dared come back.
   Why? How brazen of you to come to my house,
   You murderer!
                    Do you think I do not know
   That you plotted to kill me, plotted to steal my throne?
   Tell me, in God's name: am I coward, a fool,
   That you should dream you could accomplish this?
   A fool who could not see your slippery game?   510
   A coward, not to fight back when I saw it?
   You are the fool, Creon, are you not? hoping
   Without support or friends to get a throne?
   Thrones may be won or bought: you could do neither.

CREON. Now listen to me. You have talked; let me talk, too.
   You can not judge unless you know the facts.

OED. You speak well: there is one fact; but I find it hard
   To learn from the deadliest enemy I have.

CREON. That above all I must dispute with you.

OED. That above all I will not hear you deny.   520

CREON. If you think there is anything good in being stubborn
   Against all reason, then I say you are wrong.

OED. If you think a man can sin against his own kind
   And not be punished for it, I say you are mad.

CREON. I agree. But tell me: what have I done to you?

OED. You advised me to send for that wizard, did you not?

CREON. I did. I should do it again.

OED.   Very well. Now tell me:
   How long has it been since Laïos—

CREON.   What of Laïos?

OED. Since he vanished in that onset by the road?

CREON. It was long ago, a long time.

OED. And this prophet, 530
    Was he practicing here then?

CREON.   He was; and with honor, as now.

OED. Did he speak of me at that time?

CREON.   He never did;
    At least, not when I was present.

OED.   But . . . the enquiry?
    I suppose you held one?

CREON.   We did, but we learned nothing.

OED. Why did the prophet not speak against me then?

CREON. I do not know; and I am the kind of man
    Who holds his tongue when he has no facts to go on.

OED. There's one fact that you know, and you could tell it.

CREON. What fact is that? If I know it, you shall have it.

OED. If he were not involved with you, he could not say 540
    That it was I who murdered Laïos.

CREON. If he says that, you are the one that knows it!—
    But now it is my turn to question you.

OED. Put your questions. I am no murderer.

CREON. First, then: You married my sister?

OED.   I married your sister.

CREON. And you rule the kingdom equally with her?

OED. Everything that she wants she has from me.

CREON. And I am the third, equal to both of you?

OED. That is why I call you a bad friend.

CREON. No. Reason it out, as I have done. 550
    Think of this first: Would any sane man prefer
    Power, with all a king's anxieties,
    To that same power and the grace of sleep?
    Certainly not I.
    I have never longed for the king's power—only his rights.
    Would any wise man differ from me in this?
    As matters stand, I have my way in everything
    With your consent, and no responsibilities.
    If I were king, I should be a slave to policy.

How could I desire a scepter more   560
Than what is now mine—untroubled influence?
No, I have not gone mad; I need no honors,
Except those with the perquisites I have now.
I am welcome everywhere; every man salutes me,
And those who want your favor seek my ear,
Since I know how to manage what they ask.
Should I exchange this ease for that anxiety?
Besides, no sober mind is treasonable.
I hate anarchy
And never would deal with any man who likes it.   570

Test what I have said. Go to the priestess
At Delphi, ask if I quoted her correctly.
And as for this other thing: if I am found
Guilty of treason with Teiresias,
Then sentence me to death! You have my word
It is a sentence I should cast my vote for—
But not without evidence!
                              You do wrong
When you take good men for bad, bad men for good.
A true friend thrown aside—why, life itself
Is not more precious!
                              In time you will know this well: 580
For time, and time alone, will show the just man,
Though scoundrels are discovered in a day.
CHOR. This is well said, and a prudent man would ponder it.
      Judgments too quickly formed are dangerous.
OED. But is he not quick in his duplicity?
      And shall I not be quick to parry him?
      Would you have me stand still, hold my peace, and let
      This man win everything, through my inaction?
CREON. And you want—what is it, then? To banish me?
OED. No, not exile. It is your death I want,   590
      So that all the world may see what treason means.
CREON. You will persist, then? You will not believe me?
OED. How can I believe you?

CREON.   Then you are a fool.

OED. To save myself?

CREON.   In justice, think of me.

OED. You are evil incarnate.

CREON.   But suppose that you are wrong?

OED. Still I must rule.

CREON.   But not if you rule badly.

OED. O city, city!

CREON.   It is my city, too!

CHOR. Now, my lords, be still. I see the Queen,
    Iocastê, coming from her palace chambers;
    And it is time she came, for the sake of you both.   600
    This dreadful quarrel can be resolved through her.

                 [*Enter* IOCASTÊ.]

IOC. Poor foolish men, what wicked din is this?
    With Thebes sick to death, is it not shameful
    That you should rake some private quarrel up?

                        [*To* OEDIPUS.]
    Come into the house.

               —And you, Creon, go now:
    Let us have no more of this tumult over nothing.

CREON Nothing? No, sister: what your husband plans for me
    Is one of two great evils: exile or death.

OED. He is right.

         Why, woman I have caught him squarely
    Plotting against my life.

CREON.   No! Let me die   610
    Accurst if ever I have wished you harm!

IOC. Ah, believe it, Oedipus!
    In the name of the gods, respect this oath of his
    For my sake, for the sake of these people here!

                       [STROPHE I.]

CHOR. Open your mind to her, my lord. Be ruled by her, I beg you!

OED. What would you have me do?

CHOR. Respect Creon's word. He has never spoken like a fool,
    And now he has sworn an oath.

OED.   You know what you ask?

CHOR.   I do.

OED.   Speak on, then.

CHOR. A friend so sworn should not be baited so,   620
    In blind malice, and without final proof.

OED. You are aware, I hope, that what you say
    Means death for me, or exile at the least.

CHOR. No, I swear by Helios, first in Heaven!   [STROPHE 2.]
        May I die friendless and accurst,
    The worst of deaths, if ever I meant that!
            It is the withering fields
                That hurt my sick heart:
            Must we bear all these ills,
                And now your bad blood as well?   630

OED. Then let him go. And let me die, if I must,
    Or be driven by him in shame from the land of Thebes.
    It is your unhappiness, and not his talk,
    That touches me.

                As for him—
    Wherever he is, I will hate him as long as I live.

CREON. Ugly in yielding, as you were ugly in rage!
    Natures like yours chiefly torment themselves.

OED. Can you not go? Can you not leave me?

CREON.   I can.
    You do not know me; but the city knows me,
    And in its eyes I am just, if not in yours.   640
                                        [*Exit* CREON.]

                                        [ANTISTROPHE I.]
CHOR. Lady Iocastê, did you not ask the King to go to his chambers?

IOC. First tell me what has happened.

CHOR. There was suspicion without evidence; yet it rankled
        As even false charges will.

IOC.   On both sides?

CHOR.   On both.

IOC.   But what was said?

CHOR. Oh let it rest, let it be done with!
    Have we not suffered enough?

OED. You see to what your decency has brought you:
    You have made difficulties where my heart saw none.

[ANTISTROPHE 2.]

CHOR. Oedipus, it is not once only I have told you—   650
    You must know I should count myself unwise
    To the point of madness, should I now forsake you—
        You, under whose hand,
          In the storm of another time,
        Our dear land sailed out free.
        But now stand fast at the helm!

IOC. In God's name, Oedipus, inform your wife as well:
    Why are you so set in this hard anger?

OED. I will tell you, for none of these men deserves
    My confidence as you do. It is Creon's work,   660
    His treachery, his plotting against me.

IOC. Go on, if you can make this clear to me.

OED. He charges me with the murder of Laïos.

IOC. Has he some knowledge? Or does he speak from hearsay?

OED. He would not commit himself to such a charge,
    But he has brought in that damnable soothsayer
    To tell his story.

IOC.   Set your mind at rest.
    If it is a question of soothsayers, I tell you
    That you will find no man whose craft gives knowledge
    Of the unknowable.
               Here is my proof: 670

An oracle was reported to Laïos once
(I will not say from Phoibos himself, but from
His appointed ministers, at any rate)
That his doom would be death at the hands of his own son—
His son, born of his flesh and of mine!

Now, you remember the story: Laïos was killed
By marauding strangers where three highways meet;
But his child had not been three days in this world
Before the King had pierced the baby's ankles
And had him left to die on a lonely mountain.   680

Thus, Apollo never caused that child
To kill his father, and it was not Laïos' fate
To die at the hands of his son, as he had feared.
This is what prophets and prophecies are worth!
Have no dread of them.
                            It is God himself
Who can show us what he wills, in his own way.

OED. How strange a shadowy memory crossed my mind,
    Just now while you were speaking; it chilled my heart.

IOC. What do you mean? What memory do you speak of?

OED. If I understand you, Laïos was killed   690
    At a place where three roads meet.

IOC.   So it was said;
    We have no later story.

OED.   Where did it happen?

IOC. Phokis, it is called: at a place where the Theban Way
    Divides into the roads toward Delphi and Daulia.

OED. When?

IOC.   We had the news not long before you came
    And proved the right to your succession here.

OED. Ah, what net has God been weaving for me?

IOC. Oedipus! Why does this trouble you?

OED.   Do not ask me yet.
    First, tell me how Laïos looked, and tell me
    How old he was.

IOC.   He was tall, his hair just touched   700
    With white; his form was not unlike your own.

OED. I think that I myself may be accurst
    By my own ignorant edict.

IOC.   You speak strangely.
    It makes me tremble to look at you, my King.

OED. I am not sure that the blind man can not see.
But I should know better if you were to tell me—

IOC. Anything—though I dread to hear you ask it.

OED. Was the King lightly escorted, or did he ride
With a large company, as a ruler should?

IOC. There were five men with him in all: one was a herald; 710
And a single chariot, which he was driving.

OED. Alas, that makes it plain enough!

But who—
Who told you how it happened?

IOC. A household servant,
The only one to escape.

OED. And is he still
A servant of ours?

IOC. No; for when he came back at last
And found you enthroned in the place of the dead king,
He came to me, touched my hand with his, and begged
That I would send him away to the frontier district
Where only the shepherds go—
As far away from the city as I could send him. 720
I granted his prayer; for although the man was a slave,
He had earned more than this favor at my hands.

OED. Can he be called back quickly?

IOC. Easily.
But why?

OED. I have taken too much upon myself
Without enquiry; therefore I wish to consult him.

IOC. Then he shall come.

But am I not one also
To whom you might confide these fears of yours?

OED. That is your right; it will not be denied you,
Now least of all; for I have reached a pitch
Of wild foreboding. Is there anyone 730
To whom I should sooner speak?

Polybos of Corinth is my father.
My mother is a Dorian: Meropê.

I grew up chief among the men of Corinth
Until a strange thing happened—
Not worth my passion, it may be, but strange.

At a feast, a drunken man maundering in his cups
Cries out that I am not my father's son!

I contained myself that night, though I felt anger
And a sinking heart. The next day I visited   740
My father and mother, and questioned them. They stormed,
Calling it all the slanderous rant of a fool;
And this relieved me. Yet the suspicion
Remained always aching in my mind;
I knew there was talk; I could not rest;
And finally, saying nothing to my parents,
I went to the shrine at Delphi.

The god dismissed my question without reply;
He spoke of other things.
                        Some were clear,
Full of wretchedness, dreadful, unbearable: 750
As, that I should lie with my own mother, breed
Children from whom all men would turn their eyes;
And that I should be my father's murderer.

I heard all this, and fled. And from that day
Corinth to me was only in the stars
Descending in that quarter of the sky,
As I wandered farther and farther on my way
To a land where I should never see the evil
Sung by the oracle. And I came to this country
Where, so you say, King Laïos was killed.   760

I will tell you all that happened there, my lady.

There were three highways
Coming together at a place I passed;

And there a herald came towards me, and a chariot
Drawn by horses, with a man such as you describe
Seated in it. The groom leading the horses
Forced me off the road at his lord's command;
But as this charioteer lurched over towards me
I struck him in my rage. The old man saw me
And brought his double goad down upon my head   770
As I came abreast.

      He was paid back, and more!
Swinging my club in this right hand I knocked him
Out of his car, and he rolled on the ground.

            I killed him.

I killed them all.
Now if that stranger and Laïos were—kin,
Where is a man more miserable than I?
More hated by the gods? Citizen and alien alike
Must never shelter me or speak to me—
I must be shunned by all.

        And I myself
Pronounced this malediction upon myself!   780

Think of it: I have touched you with these hands,
These hands that killed your husband. What defilement!

Am I all evil, then? It must be so,
Since I must flee from Thebes, yet never again
See my own countrymen, my own country,
For fear of joining my mother in marriage
And killing Polybos, my father.

          Ah,
If I was created so, born to this fate,
Who could deny the savagery of God?

O holy majesty of heavenly powers!   790
May I never see that day! Never!

Rather let me vanish from the race of men
Than know the abomination destined me!

CHOR. We too, my lord, have felt dismay at this.

But there is hope: you have yet to hear the shepherd.

OED. Indeed, I fear no other hope is left me.

IOC. What do you hope from him when he comes?

OED.   This much:

If his account of the murder tallies with yours,
Then I am cleared.

IOC.   What was it that I said
Of such importance?

OED.   Why, "marauders," you said,   800
Killed the King, according to this man's story.
If he maintains that still, if there were several,
Clearly the guilt is not mine: I was alone.
But if he says one man, singlehanded, did it,
Then the evidence all points to me.

IOC. You may be sure that he said there were several;
And can he call back that story now? He cán not.
The whole city heard it as plainly as I.
But suppose he alters some detail of it:
He can not ever show that Laïos' death   810
Fulfilled the oracle: for Apollo said
My child was doomed to kill him; and my child—
Poor baby!—it was my child that died first.

No. From now on, where oracles are concerned,
I would not waste a second thought on any.

OED. You may be right.

                                But come: let someone go
For the shepherd at once. This matter must be settled.

IOC. I will send for him.

I would not wish to cross you in anything,
And surely not in this.—Let us go in.   820

[*Exeunt into the palace.*]

ODE II

CHOR. Let me be reverent in the ways of right,   [STROPHE 1.]
 Lowly the paths I journey on;
 Let all my words and actions keep
 The laws of the pure universe
 From highest Heaven handed down.
 For Heaven is their bright nurse,
 Those generations of the realms of light;
 Ah, never of mortal kind were they begot,
 Nor are they slaves of memory, lost in sleep:
 Their Father is greater than Time, and ages not.   830

 The tyrant is a child of Pride   [ANTISTROPHE 1.]
 Who drinks from his great sickening cup
 Recklessness and vanity,
 Until from his high crest headlong
 He plummets to the dust of hope.
 That strong man is not strong.
 But let no fair ambition be denied;
 May God protect the wrestler for the State
 In government, in comely policy,
 Who will fear God, and on His ordinance wait.   840

 Haughtiness and the high hand of disdain   [STROPHE 2.]
 Tempt and outrage God's holy law;
 And any mortal who dares hold
 No immortal Power in awe
 Will be caught up in a net of pain:
 The price for which his levity is sold.
 Let each man take due earnings, then,
 And keep his hands from holy things,
 And from blasphemy stand apart—
 Else the crackling blast of heaven   850
 Blows on his head, and on his desperate heart;

Though fools will honor impious men,
In their cities no tragic poet sings.

Shall we lose faith in Delphi's obscurities,   [ANTISTROPHE 2.]
We who have heard the world's core
Discredited, and the sacred wood
Of Zeus at Elis praised no more?
The deeds and the strange prophecies
Must make a pattern yet to be understood.
Zeus, if indeed you are lord of all,   860
Throned in light over night and day,
Mirror this in your endless mind:
Our masters call the oracle
Words on the wind, and the Delphic vision blind!
Their hearts no longer know Apollo,
And reverence for the gods has died away.

SCENE III

[*Enter* IOCASTÊ.]

IOC. Princes of Thebes, it has occurred to me
To visit the altars of the gods, bearing
These branches as a suppliant, and this incense.
Our King is not himself: his noble soul   870
Is overwrought with fantasies of dread,
Else he would consider
The new prophecies in the light of the old.
He will listen to any voice that speaks disaster,
And my advice goes for nothing.

[*She approaches the altar, R.*]

     To you, then, Apollo,
Lycean lord, since you are nearest, I turn in prayer.
Receive these offerings, and grant us deliverance
From defilement. Our hearts are heavy with fear

When we see our leader distracted, as helpless sailors
Are terrified by the confusion of their helmsman.   880

[*Enter* MESSENGER.]

MESS. Friends, no doubt you can direct me:
  Where shall I find the house of Oedipus,
  Or, better still, where is the King himself?
CHOR. It is this very place, stranger; he is inside.
  This is his wife and mother of his children.
MESS. I wish her happiness in a happy house,
  Blest in all the fulfillment of her marriage.
IOC. I wish as much for you: your courtesy
  Deserves a like good fortune. But now, tell me:
  Why have you come? What have you to say to us?   890
MESS. Good news, my lady, for your house and your husband.
IOC. What news? Who sent you here?
MESS.   I am from Corinth.
  The news I bring ought to mean joy for you,
  Though it may be you will find some grief in it.
IOC. What is it? How can it touch us in both ways?
MESS. The people of Corinth, they say,
  Intend to call Oedipus to be their king.
IOC. But old Polybos—is he not reigning still?
MESS. No. Death holds him in his sepulchre.
IOC. What are you saying? Polybos is dead?   900
MESS. If I am not telling the truth, may I die myself.

[*To a* MAIDSERVANT.]

IOC. Go in, go quickly; tell this to your master.

  O riddlers of God's will, where are you now!
  This was the man whom Oedipus, long ago,
  Feared so, fled so, in dread of destroying him—
  But it was another fate by which he died.

[*Enter* OEDIPUS, CHORUS.]

OED. Dearest Iocastê, why have you sent for me?
IOC. Listen to what this man says, and then tell me
  What has become of the solemn prophecies.

OED. Who is this man? What is his news for me?   910
IOC. He has come from Corinth to announce your father's death!
OED. Is it true, stranger? Tell me in your own words.
MESS. I can not say it more clearly: the King is dead.
OED. Was it by treason? Or by an attack of illness?
MESS. A little thing brings old men to their rest.
OED. It was sickness, then?
                              Yes, and his many years.
OED. Ah!
     Why should a man respect the Pythian hearth, or
     Give heed to the birds that jangle above his head?
     They prophesied that I should kill Polybos,   920
     Kill my own father; but he is dead and buried,
     And I am here—I never touched him, never,
     Unless he died of grief for my departure,
     And thus, in a sense, through me. No. Polybos
     Has packed the oracles off with him underground.
     They are empty words.
IOC.   Had I not told you so?
OED. You had; it was my faint heart that betrayed me.
IOC. From now on never think of those things again.
OED. And yet—must I not fear my mother's bed?
IOC. Why should anyone in this world be afraid,   930
     Since Fate rules us and nothing can be foreseen?
     A man should live only for the present day.

     Have no more fear of sleeping with your mother:
     How many men, in dreams, have lain with their mothers!
     No reasonable man is troubled by such things.
OED. That is true; only—
     If only my mother were not still alive!
     But she is alive. I can not help my dread.
IOC. Yet this news of your father's death is wonderful.
OED. Wonderful. But I fear the living woman.   940
MESS. Tell me, who is this woman that you fear?
OED. It is Meropê, man; the wife of King Polybos.
MESS. Meropê? Why should you be afraid of her?

OED. An oracle of the gods, a dreadful saying.

MESS. Can you tell me about it or are you sworn to silence?

OED. I can tell you, and I will.

Apollo said through his prophet that I was the man
Who should marry his own mother, shed his father's blood
With his own hands. And so, for all these years
I have kept clear of Corinth, and no harm has come—   950
Though it would have been sweet to see my parents again.

MESS. And is this the fear that drove you out of Corinth?

OED. Would you have me kill my father?

MESS.   As for that

You must be reassured by the news I gave you.

OED. If you could reassure me, I would reward you.

MESS. I had that in mind, I will confess: I thought

I could count on you when you returned to Corinth.

OED. No: I will never go near my parents again.

MESS. Ah, son, you still do not know what you are doing—

OED. What do you mean? In the name of God tell me!   960

MESS. —If these are your reasons for not going home.

OED. I tell you, I fear the oracle may come true.

MESS. And guilt may come upon you through your parents?

OED. That is the dread that is always in my heart.

MESS. Can you not see that all your fears are groundless?

OED. How can you say that? They are my parents, surely?

MESS. Polybos was not your father.

OED.   Not my father?

MESS. No more your father than the man speaking to you.

OED. But you are nothing to me!

MESS.   Neither was he.

OED. Then why did he call me son?

MESS.   I will tell you: 970

Long ago he had you from my hands, as a gift.

OED. Then how could he love me so, if I was not his?

MESS. He had no children, and his heart turned to you.

OED. What of you? Did you buy me? Did you find me by chance?

MESS. I came upon you in the crooked pass of Kithairon.

OED. And what were you doing there?

MESS.   Tending my flocks.

OED. A wandering shepherd?

MESS.   But your savior, son, that day.

OED. From what did you save me?

MESS.   Your ankles should tell you that.

OED. Ah, stranger, why do you speak of that childhood pain?

MESS. I cut the bonds that tied your ankles together.   980

OED. I have had the mark as long as I can remember.

MESS. That was why you were given the name you bear.

OED. God! Was it my father or my mother who did it?
     Tell me!

MESS.   I do not know. The man who gave you to me
     Can tell you better than I.

OED. It was not you that found me, but another?

MESS. It was another shepherd gave you to me.

OED. Who was he? Can you tell me who he was?

MESS. I think he was said to be one of Laïos' people.

OED. You mean the Laïos who was king here years ago?   990

MESS. Yes; King Laïos; and the man was one of his herdsmen.

OED. Is he still alive? Can I see him?

MESS.   These men here
     Know best about such things.

OED.   Does anyone here
     Know this shepherd that he is talking about?
     Have you seen him in the fields, or in the town?
     If you have, tell me. It is time things were made plain.

CHOR. I think the man he means is that same shepherd
     You have already asked to see. Iocastê perhaps
     Could tell you something.

OED.   Do you know anything
     About him, Lady? Is he the man we have summoned?   1000
     Is that the man this shepherd means?

IOC.   Why think of him?
     Forget this herdsman. Forget it all.
     This talk is a waste of time.

OED.   How can you say that,
     When the clues to my true birth are in my hands?

IOC. For God's love, let us have no more questioning!
  Is your life nothing to you?
  My own is pain enough for me to bear.

OED. You need not worry. Suppose my mother a slave,
  And born of slaves: no baseness can touch you.

IOC. Listen to me, I beg you: do not do this thing!   1010

OED. I will not listen; the truth must be made known.

IOC. Everything that I say is for your own good!

OED.   My own good
  Snaps my patience, then; I want none of it.

IOC. You are fatally wrong! May you never learn who you are!

OED. Go, one of you, and bring the shepherd here.
  Let us leave this woman to brag of her royal name.

IOC. Ah, miserable!
  That is the only word I have for you now.
  That is the only word I can ever have.

                                         [*Exit into the palace.*]

CHOR. Why has she left us, Oedipus? Why has she gone   1020
  In such a passion of sorrow? I fear this silence:
  Something dreadful may come of it.

OED.   Let it come!
  However base my birth, I must know about it.
  The Queen, like a woman, is perhaps ashamed
  To think of my low origin. But I
  Am a child of Luck; I cannot be dishonored.
  Luck is my mother; the passing months, my brothers,
  Have seen me rich and poor.
                                         If this is so,
  How could I wish that I were someone else?
  How could I not be glad to know my birth?   1030

ODE III

CHOR. If ever the coming time were known   [STROPHE.]
  To my heart's pondering,
  Kithairon, now by Heaven I see the torches

At the festival of the next full moon,
And see the dance, and hear the choir sing
A grace to your gentle shade:
Mountain where Oedipus was found,
O mountain guard of a noble race!
May the god who heals us lend his aid,
And let that glory come to pass   1040
For our king's cradling-ground.

Of the nymphs that flower beyond the years,   [ANTISTROPHE.]
Who bore you, royal child,
To Pan of the hills or the timberline Apollo,
Cold in delight where the upland clears,
Or Hermês for whom Kyllenê's heights are piled?
Or flushed as evening cloud,
Great Dionysos, roamer of mountains,
He—was it he who found you there,
And caught you up in his own proud   1050
Arms from the sweet god-ravisher
Who laughed by the Muses' fountains?

SCENE IV

OED. Sirs: though I do not know the man,
      I think I see him coming, this shepherd we want:
      He is old, like our friend here, and the men
      Bringing him seem to be servants of my house.
      But you can tell, if you have ever seen him.
            [*Enter* SHEPHERD *escorted by servants.*]
CHOR. I know him, he was Laïos' man. You can trust him.
OED. Tell me first, you from Corinth: is this the shepherd
      We were discussing?
MESS.   This is the very man.   1060
                                    [*To* SHEPHERD.]

OED. Come here. No, look at me. You must answer
Everything I ask.—You belonged to Laïos?

SHEP. Yes: born his slave, brought up in his house.

OED. Tell me: what kind of work did you do for him?

SHEP. I was a shepherd of his, most of my life.

OED. Where mainly did you go for pasturage?

SHEP. Sometimes Kithairon, sometimes the hills near-by.

OED. Do you remember ever seeing this man out there?

SHEP. What would he be doing there? This man?

OED. This man standing here. Have you ever seen him before? 1070

SHEP. No. At least, not to my recollection.

MESS. And that is not strange, my lord. But I'll refresh
His memory: he must remember when we two
Spent three whole seasons together, March to September,
On Kithairon or thereabouts. He had two flocks;
I had one. Each autumn I'd drive mine home
And he would go back with his to Laïos' sheepfold.—
Is this not true, just as I have described it?

SHEP. True, yes; but it was all so long ago.

MESS. Well, then: do you remember, back in those days, 1080
That you gave me a baby boy to bring up as my own?

SHEP. What if I did? What are you trying to say?

MESS. King Oedipus was once that little child.

SHEP. Damn you, hold your tongue!

OED. No more of that!
It is your tongue needs watching, not this man's.

SHEP. My King, my Master, what is it I have done wrong?

OED. You have not answered his question about the boy.

SHEP. He does not know. . . . He is only making trouble. . . .

OED. Come, speak plainly, or it will go hard with you.

SHEP. In God's name, do not torture an old man! 1090

OED. Come here, one of you; bind his arms behind him.

SHEP. Unhappy king! What more do you wish to learn?

OED. Did you give this man the child he speaks of?

SHEP. I did.
And I would to God I had died that very day.

OED. You will die now unless you speak the truth.

SHEP. Yet if I speak the truth, I am worse than dead.

OED. Very well; since you insist upon delaying—

SHEP. No! I have told you already that I gave him the boy.

OED. Where did you get him? From your house? From somewhere else?

SHEP. Not from mine, no. A man gave him to me.   1100

OED. Is that man here? Do you know whose slave he was?

SHEP. For God's love, my King, do not ask me any more!

OED. You are a dead man if I have to ask you again.

SHEP. Then . . . Then the child was from the palace of Laïos.

OED. A slave child? or a child of his own line?

SHEP. Ah, I am on the brink of dreadful speech!

OED. And I of dreadful hearing. Yet I must hear.

SHEP. If you must be told, then . . .

                They said it was Laïos' child;
But it is your wife who can tell you about that.

OED. My wife!—Did she give it to you?

SHEP.   My lord, she did.   1110

OED. Do you know why?

SHEP.   I was told to get rid of it.

OED. An unspeakable mother!

SHEP.   There had been prophecies . . .

OED. Tell me.

SHEP.   It was said that the boy would kill his own father.

OED. Then why did you give him over to this old man?

SHEP. I pitied the baby, my King,
And I thought that this man would take him far away
To his own country.

                He saved him—but for what a fate!
For if you are what this man says you are,
No man living is more wretched than Oedipus.

OED. Ah God!   1120
    It was true!

             All the prophecies!

                —Now,
O Light, may I look on you for the last time!

I, Oedipus,
Oedipus, damned in his birth, in his marriage damned,
Damned in the blood he shed with his own hand!

[*He rushes into the palace.*]

ODE IV

CHOR. Alas for the seed of men. [STROPHE 1.]

What measure shall I give these generations
That breathe on the void and are void
And exist and do not exist?

Who bears more weight of joy 1130
Than mass of sunlight shifting in images,
Or who shall make his thoughts stay on
That down time drifts away?

Your splendor is all fallen.

O naked brow of wrath and tears,
O change of Oedipus!
I who saw your days call no man blest—
Your great days like ghósts góne.

That mind was a strong bow. [ANTISTROPHE 1.]

Deep, how deep you drew it then, hard archer, 1140
At a dim fearful range,
And brought dear glory down!

You overcame the stranger—
The virgin with her hooking lion claws—
And though death sang, stood like a tower
To make pale Thebes take heart.

Fortress against our sorrow!

Divine king, giver of laws,
Majestic Oedipus!
No prince in Thebes had ever such renown,   1150
No prince won such grace of power.

And now of all men ever known   [STROPHE 2.]
Most pitiful is this man's story:
His fortunes are most changed, his state
Fallen to a low slave's
Ground under bitter fate.

O Oedipus, most royal one!
The great door that expelled you to the light
Gave at night—ah, gave night to your glory:
As to the father, to the fathering son.   1160

All understood too late.

How could that queen whom Laïos won,
The garden that he harrowed at his height,
Be silent when that act was done?

But all eyes fail before time's eye,   [ANTISTROPHE 2.]
All actions come to justice there.
Though never willed, though far down the deep past,
Your bed, your dread sirings,
Are brought to book at last.

Child by Laïos doomed to die,   1170
Then doomed to lose that fortunate little death,
Would God you never took breath in this air
That with my wailing lips I take to cry:

For I weep the world's outcast.

Blind I was, and can not tell why;
Asleep, for you had given ease of breath;
A fool, while the false years went by.

ÉXODOS

[*Enter, from the palace,* SECOND MESSENGER.]

2ND MESS. Elders of Thebes, most honored in this land,
What horrors are yours to see and hear, what weight
Of sorrow to be endured, if, true to your birth,   1180
You venerate the line of Labdakos!
I think neither Istros nor Phasis, those great rivers,
Could purify this place of the corruption
It shelters now, or soon must bring to light—
Evil not done unconsciously, but willed.

The greatest griefs are those we cause ourselves.

CHOR. Surely, friend, we have grief enough already;
What new sorrow do you mean?

2ND MESS.   The Queen is dead.

CHOR. Iocastê? Dead? But at whose hand?

2ND MESS.   Her own.
The full horror of what happened you cannot know,   1190
For you did not see it; but I, who did, will tell you
As clearly as I can how she met her death.

When she had left us,
In passionate silence, passing through the court,
She ran to her apartment in the house,
Her hair clutched by the fingers of both hands.
She closed the doors behind her; then, by that bed
Where long ago the fatal son was conceived—
That son who should bring about his father's death—
We heard her call upon Laïos, dead so many years,   1200
And heard her wail for the double fruit of her marriage,
A husband by her husband, children by her child.

Exactly how she died I do not know:
For Oedipus burst in moaning and would not let us
Keep vigil to the end: it was by him
As he stormed about the room that our eyes were caught.
From one to another of us he went, begging a sword,
Cursing the wife who was not his wife, the mother
Whose womb had carried his own children and himself.
I do not know: it was none of us aided him,   1210
But surely one of the gods was in control!
For with a dreadful cry
He hurled his weight, as though wrenched out of himself,
At the twin doors: the bolts gave, and he rushed in.
And there we saw her hanging, her body swaying
From the cruel cord she had noosed about her neck.
A great sob broke from him, heartbreaking to hear,
As he loosed the rope and lowered her to the ground.

I would blot out from my mind what happened next!
For the King ripped from her gown the golden brooches   1220
That were her ornament, and raised them, and plunged them
       down
Straight into his own eyeballs, crying, "No more,
No more shall you look on the misery about me,
The horrors of my own doing! Too long you have known
The faces of those whom I should never have seen,
Too long been blind to those for whom I was searching!
From this hour, go in darkness!" And as he spoke,
He struck at his eyes—not once, but many times;
And the blood spattered his beard,
Bursting from his ruined sockets like red hail.   1230

So from the unhappiness of two this evil has sprung,
A curse on the man and woman alike. The old
Happiness of the house of Labdakos
Was happiness enough: where is it today?
It is all wailing and ruin, disgrace, death—all

The misery of mankind that has a name—
And it is wholly and for ever theirs.
CHOR. Is he in agony still? Is there no rest for him?
2ND MESS. He is calling for someone to lead him to the gates
So that all the children of Kadmos may look upon   1240
His father's murderer, his mother's—no,
I can not say it!
                    And then he will leave Thebes,
Self-exiled, in order that the curse
Which he himself pronounced may depart from the house.
He is weak, and there is none to lead him,
So terrible is his suffering.
                    But you will see:
Look, the doors are opening; in a moment
You will see a thing that would crush a heart of stone.

[*The central door is opened;* OEDIPUS, *blinded, is led in.*]

CHOR. Dreadful indeed for men to see.
Never have my own eyes   1250
Looked on a sight so full of fear.

Oedipus!
What madness came upon you, what daemon
Leaped on your life with heavier
Punishment than a mortal man can bear?
No; I can not even
Look at you, poor ruined one.
And I would speak, question, ponder,
If I were able. No.
You make me shudder.   1260
OED. God.   God.
Is there a sorrow greater?
Where shall I find harbor in this world?
My voice is hurled far on a dark wind.
What has God done to me?
CHOR. Too terrible to think of, or to see.

OED. O cloud of night, [STROPHE I.]
    Never to be turned away: night coming on,
    I can not tell how: night like a shroud!

    My fair winds brought me here.
                                        O God. Again   1270
    The pain of the spikes where I had sight,
    The flooding pain
    Of memory, never to be gouged out.
CHOR. This is not strange.
    You suffer it all twice over, remorse in pain,
    Pain in remorse.

OED. Ah dear friend [ANTISTROPHE I.]
    Are you faithful even yet, you alone?
    Are you still standing near me, will you stay here,
    Patient, to care for the blind?
                                        The blind man!   1280
    Yet even blind I know who it is attends me,
    By the voice's tone—
    Though my new darkness hide the comforter.
CHOR. Oh fearful act!
    What god was it drove you to rake black
    Night across your eyes?

OED. Apollo. Apollo. Dear [STROPHE 2.]
    Children, the god was Apollo.
    He brought my sick, sick fate upon me.
    But the blinding hand was my own!   1290
    How could I bear to see
    When all my sight was horror everywhere?
CHOR. Everywhere; that is true.
OED. And now what is left?
    Images? Love? A greeting even,
    Sweet to the senses? Is there anything?
    Ah, no, friends: lead me away.

Lead me away from Thebes.

                                 Lead the great wreck

And hell of Oedipus, whom the gods hate.

CHOR. Your fate is clear, you are not blind to that. 1300

    Would God you had never found it out!

OED. Death take the man who unbound   [ANTISTROPHE 2.]

    My feet on that hillside

    And delivered me from death to life! What life?

    If only I had died,

    This weight of monstrous doom

    Could not have dragged me and my darlings down.

CHOR. I would have wished the same.

OED. Oh never to have come here

    With my father's blood upon me! Never   1310

    To have been the man they call his mother's husband!

    Oh accurst! Oh child of evil,

    To have entered that wretched bed—

                           the selfsame one!

    More primal than sin itself, this fell to me.

CHOR. I do not know how I can answer you.

    You were better dead than alive and blind.

OED. Do not counsel me any more. This punishment

    That I have laid upon myself is just.

    If I had eyes,

    I do not know how I could bear the sight   1320

    Of my father, when I came to the house of Death,

    Or my mother: for I have sinned against them both

    So vilely that I could not make my peace

    By strangling my own life.

                       Or do you think my children,

Born as they were born, would be sweet to my eyes?

Ah never, never! Nor this town with its high walls,

Nor the holy images of the gods.

                        For I,

Thrice miserable!—Oedipus, noblest of all the line

Of Kadmos, have condemned myself to enjoy

These things no more, by my own malediction   1330
Expelling that man whom the gods declared
To be a defilement in the house of Laïos.
After exposing the rankness of my own guilt,
How could I look men frankly in the eyes?
No, I swear it,
If I could have stifled my hearing at its source,
I would have done it and made all this body
A tight cell of misery, blank to light and sound:
So I should have been safe in a dark agony
Beyond all recollection.

                                    Ah Kithairon!   1340
Why did you shelter me? When I was cast upon you,
Why did I not die? Then I should never
Have shown the world my execrable birth.

Ah Polybos! Corinth, city that I believed
The ancient seat of my ancestors: how fair
I seemed, your child! And all the while this evil
Was cancerous within me!

                                    For I am sick
In my daily life, sick in my origin.

O three roads, dark ravine, woodland and way
Where three roads met: you, drinking my father's blood,   1350
My own blood, spilled by my own hand: can you remember
The unspeakable things I did there, and the things
I went on from there to do?

                                    O marriage, marriage!
The act that engendered me, and again the act
Performed by the son in the same bed—

                                    Ah, the net
Of incest, mingling fathers, brothers, sons,
With brides, wives, mothers: the last evil
That can be known by men: no tongue can say
How evil!

No. For the love of God, conceal me
Somewhere far from Thebes; or kill me; or hurl me   1360
Into the sea, away from men's eyes for ever.

Come, lead me. You need not fear to touch me.
Of all men, I alone can bear this guilt.

[*Enter* CREON.]

CHOR. We are not the ones to decide; but Creon here
    May fitly judge of what you ask. He only
    Is left to protect the city in your place.
OED. Alas, how can I speak to him? What right have I
    To beg his courtesy whom I have deeply wronged?
CREON. I have not come to mock you, Oedipus,
    Or to reproach you, either.

[*To* ATTENDANTS.]
                —You, standing there: 1370
    If you have lost all respect for man's dignity,
    At least respect the flame of Lord Helios:
    Do not allow this pollution to show itself
    Openly here, an affront to the earth
    And Heaven's rain and the light of day. No, take him
    Into the house as quickly as you can.
    For it is proper
    That only the close kindred see his grief.
OED. I pray you in God's name, since your courtesy
    Ignores my dark expectation, visiting   1380
    With mercy this man of all men most execrable:
    Give me what I ask—for your good, not for mine.
CREON. And what is it that you would have me do?
OED. Drive me out of this country as quickly as may be
    To a place where no human voice can ever greet me.
CREON. I should have done that before now—only,
    God's will had not been wholly revealed to me.
OED. But his command is plain: the parricide
    Must be destroyed. I am that evil man.
CREON.—That is the sense of it, yes; but as things are,   1390
    We had best discover clearly what is to be done.

OED. You would learn more about a man like me?

CREON. You are ready now to listen to the god.

OED. I will listen. But it is to you
    That I must turn for help. I beg you, hear me.

The woman in there—
Give her whatever funeral you think proper:
She is your sister.
          —But let me go, Creon!
Let me purge my father's Thebes of the pollution
Of my living here, and go out to the wild hills,   1400
To Kithairon, that has won such fame with me,
The tomb my mother and father appointed for me,
And let me die there, as they willed I should.
And yet I know
Death will not ever come to me through sickness
Or in any natural way: I have been preserved
For some unthinkable fate. But let that be.

As for my sons, you need not care for them.
They are men, they will find some way to live.
But my poor daughters, who have shared my table,   1410
Who never before have been parted from their father—
Take care of them, Creon; do this for me.
And will you let me touch them with my hands
A last time, and let us weep together?
Be kind, my lord,
Great prince, be kind!
                Could I but touch them,
They would be mine again, as when I had my eyes.

      [*Enter* ANTIGONE *and* ISMENE, *attended.*]
Ah, God!
Is it my dearest children I hear weeping?
Has Creon pitied me and sent my daughters?   1420

CREON. Yes, Oedipus: I knew that they were dear to you
    In the old days, and know you must love them still.

OED. May God bless you for this—and be a friendlier
Guardian to you than he has been to me!

Children, where are you?
Come quickly to my hands: they are your brother's—
Hands that have brought your father's once clear eyes
To this way of seeing—

    Ah dearest ones,
I had neither sight nor knowledge then, your father
By the woman who was the source of his own life!   1430
And I weep for you—having no strength to see you—,
I weep for you when I think of the bitterness
That men will visit upon you all your lives.
What homes, what festivals can you attend
Without being forced to depart again in tears?
And when you come to marriageable age,
Where is the man, my daughters, who would dare
Risk the bane that lies on all my children?
Is there any evil wanting? Your father killed
His father; sowed the womb of her who bore him;   1440
Engendered you at the fount of his own existence!

That is what they will say of you.

       Then, whom
Can you ever marry? There are no bridegrooms for you,
And your lives must wither away in sterile dreaming.

O Creon, son of Menoikeus!
You are the only father my daughters have,
Since we, their parents, are both of us gone for ever.
They are your own blood: you will not let them
Fall into beggary and loneliness;
You will keep them from the miseries that are mine!   1450
Take pity on them; see, they are only children,
Friendless except for you. Promise me this,
Great Prince, and give me your hand in token of it.

      [CREON *clasps his right hand.*]

Children:
I could say much, if you could understand me,
But as it is, I have only this prayer for you:
Live where you can, be as happy as you can—
Happier, please God, than God has made your father!

CREON. Enough. You have wept enough. Now go within.

OED. I must; but it is hard.

CREON.   Time eases all things.   1460

OED. But you must promise—

CREON.   Say what you desire.

OED. Send me from Thebes!

CREON.   God grant that I may!

OED. But since God hates me . . .

CREON.   No, he will grant your wish.

OED. You promise?

CREON.   I can not speak beyond my knowledge.

OED. Then lead me in.

CREON.   Come now, and leave your children.

OED. No! Do not take them from me!

CREON.   Think no longer
That you are in command here, but rather think
How, when you were, you served your own destruction.

     [*Exeunt into the house all but the* CHORUS; *the* CHORAGOS
               chants directly to the audience.]

CHOR. Men of Thebes: look upon Oedipus.
This is the king who solved the famous riddle   1470
And towered up, most powerful of men.
No mortal eyes but looked on him with envy,
Yet in the end ruin swept over him.

Let every man in mankind's frailty
Consider his last day; and let none
Presume on his good fortune until he find
Life, at his death, a memory without pain.

Ben Jonson

VOLPONE, OR THE FOX

Jonson's *Volpone* was written during five weeks early in the year 1606; it was performed successfully at the Globe Theater in London and before the Universities of Oxford and Cambridge; and it was published a year later with a dedication in which Jonson strongly defended the serious function of comedy, "to imitate justice and instruct to life." *Volpone* is not only more serious than the farces and other entertainments at which Jonson was glancing; it is also more serious than his own earlier comedies, such as *Everyman in His Humour.*

The Elizabethan term "humour" came from the medieval belief that the body contained four fluids or humours—black bile, blood, bile, and phlegm, corresponding to the four elements of earth, air, fire, and water. In a healthy and normal person the humours were thought to be justly balanced; but when a person was abnormally melancholy, sanguine, choleric, or phlegmatic the matching humour was thought to be excessive. A person was humorous, as Jonson put it, "when some one peculiar quality doth possess [him], that it doth draw all his affects, his spirits, and his powers . . . all to run one way." Humorous characters, then, were type figures who could be easily satirized for their affectations or eccentricities. Sir Politic Would-Be and his lady are "humourous" characters in *Volpone,* as their name and behavior make clear. The greed of the major characters, however, has struck most readers as something more serious than any "humour" that Jonson might have observed, for example, in connection with the growth of trade and finance in London.

The plot of the legacy-hunters through which the greed is exhibited he derived in fact from his reading in the satires of Lucian,

Horace, and Petronius. They had described sardonically the Greek and Roman practice in which legacy-hunters made lavish gifts in order to be named the heirs of the rich man, who in turn commonly lured them on with feigned illness and frequently outlived them. This basic formula Jonson transferred to Renaissance Italy, which many Englishmen (by a habit of nationalism not unfamiliar today) complacently believed to have a monopoly on sensational vices and Machiavellian intrigue. Partly as a result of Jonson's choice of plot and setting, *Volpone* is superior to the usual attack against greed. The conjunction of greed and death, for example, heightens the moral seriousness of the satire; and the diabolical qualities attributed to Italy enlarge the vice of greed into a fundamental perversion of human powers.

This enlargement is perhaps most evident in the characterization of Volpone and Mosca. Instead of being conventionally cautious misers, they are men of extraordinary daring and resourcefulness. They are not so much interested in the acquisition of property as they are in the sheer exercise of skill and unfettered intelligence. It is not merely their particular greed that is being represented, but rather the permanently terrifying picture of what happens when great rational powers are unguided by moral and social obligations. Volpone and Mosca are condemned, of course, by their ultimate failure and by the poetic justice finally meted out to them. Perhaps an even more effective judgment, however, is made continuously by the lurid, confined, and unhealthy atmosphere in which they are set, and by the very intricacy of the plot, which demands an abnormal alertness against fraud and deceit. By these and other means that the reader will discover, there is constantly implied an ideal of justice founded on good faith and self-knowledge; and it was the imitation or envisioning of such an ideal that Jonson believed to be the proper function of comedy.

VOLPONE, OR THE FOX

TO THE MOST NOBLE AND MOST EQUAL SISTERS, THE TWO FAMOUS UNI-
VERSITIES, FOR THEIR LOVE AND ACCEPTANCE SHOWN TO HIS POEM IN
THE PRESENTATION, BEN JONSON, THE GRATEFUL ACKNOWLEDGER, DEDI-
CATES BOTH IT AND HIMSELF.

Characters

VOLPONE, *a magnifico*

MOSCA, *his parasite*

VOLTORE, *an advocate*

CORBACCIO, *an old gentleman*

CORVINO, *a merchant*

BONARIO, *a young gentleman*

POLITIC WOULD-BE, *a knight*

PEREGRINE, *a gentleman traveller*

NANO, *a dwarf*

CASTRONE, *an eunuch*

ANDROGYNO, *a hermaphrodite*

GREGE, *mob*

COMMANDADORI, *officers*

MERCATORI, *three merchants*

AVOCATORI, *four magistrates*

NOTARIO, *the register*

SERVITORE, *a servant*

MADAM WOULD-BE, *the knight's
wife*

CELIA, *Corvino's wife*

WOMEN

SCENE—*Venice.*

THE ARGUMENT

V olpone, childless, rich, feigns sick, despairs,

O ffers his state to hopes of several heirs,

L ies languishing; his parasite receives

P resents of all, assures, deludes; then weaves

O ther cross plots, which ope themselves, are told.

N ew tricks for safety are sought; they thrive: when, bold,

E ach tempts th' other again, and all are sold.

Characters. Mosca: a fly; **Voltore:** vulture; **Corbaccio:** raven; **Corvino:** crow;
Bonario: debonair, good.

PROLOGUE

Now, luck yet send us, and a little wit
   Will serve to make our play hit;
According to the palates of the season,
   Here is rhyme, not empty of reason.
This we were bid to credit from our poet,
   Whose true scope, if you would know it,
In all his poems still hath been this measure,
   To mix profit with your pleasure;
And not as some, whose throats their envy failing,
   Cry hoarsely, "All he writes is railing,"   10
And when his plays come forth, think they can flout them,
   With saying he was a year about them.
To this there needs no lie, but this his creature,
   Which was two months since no feature;
And, though he dares give them five lives to mend it,
   'Tis known, five weeks fully penn'd it,
From his own hand, without a coadjutor,
   Novice, journeyman, or tutor.
Yet thus much I can give you as a token
   Of his play's worth: no eggs are broken,   20
Nor quaking custards with fierce teeth affrighted,
   Wherewith your rout are so delighted;
Nor hales he in a gull, old ends reciting,
   To stop gaps in his loose writing;
With such a deal of monstrous and forc'd action,
   As might make Beth'lem a faction.
Nor made he his play for jests stol'n from each table,
   But makes jests to fit his fable;
And so presents quick comedy refined,
   As best critics have designed;   30

Prologue: 23. gull: a fool. **old ends:** old scraps of poetry. **26. Beth'lem a faction:** Bethlehem (Bedlam, insane asylum) more disorderly.

The laws of time, place, persons he observeth,
  From no needful rule he swerveth.
All gall and copperas from his ink he draineth;
  Only, a little salt remaineth;
Wherewith he'll rub your cheeks, till, red with laughter,
  They shall look fresh a week after.

ACT ONE

SCENE I. *A room in Volpone's house.*

[*Enter* VOLPONE *and* MOSCA.]

VOLP. Good morning to the day; and next, my gold.
Open the shrine, that I may see my saint.—
Hail the world's soul, and mine. More glad than is
The teeming earth to see the long'd-for sun
Peep through the horns of the celestial Ram,
Am I, to view thy splendor darkening his;
That, lying here, amongst my other hoards,
Show'st like a flame by night, or like the day
Struck out of chaos, when all darkness fled
Unto the center. O thou son of Sol,   10
But brighter than thy father, let me kiss,
With adoration, thee, and every relic
Of sacred treasure in this blessed room.
Well did wise poets, by thy glorious name,
Title that age which they would have the best;
Thou being the best of things, and far transcending
All style of joy, in children, parents, friends,
Or any other waking dream on earth.
Thy looks when they to Venus did ascribe,
They should have giv'n her twenty thousand Cupids;   20

3. **copperas:** vitriol.

Such are thy beauties and our loves! Dear saint,
Riches, the dumb god, that giv'st all men tongues,
That canst do nought, and yet mak'st men do all things;
The price of souls; even hell, with thee to boot,
Is made worth Heaven. Thou art virtue, fame,
Honor, and all things else! Who can get thee,
He shall be noble, valiant, honest, wise—

MOS.   And what he will, sir. Riches are in fortune
A greater good than wisdom is in nature.

VOLP.   True, my beloved Mosca. Yet I glory   30
More in the cunning purchase of my wealth
Than in the glad possession, since I gain
No common way; I use no trade, no venture;
I wound no earth with ploughshares, fat no beasts
To feed the shambles; have no mills for iron,
Oil, corn, or men, to grind 'em into powder;
I blow no subtle glass, expose no ships
To threat'nings of the furrow-faced sea;
I turn no monies in the public bank,
No usure private—

MOS.   No, sir, nor devour   40
Soft prodigals. You shall ha' some will swallow
A melting heir as glibly as your Dutch
Will pills of butter, and ne'er purge for 't;
Tear forth the fathers of poor families
Out of their beds, and coffin them alive
In some kind clasping prison, where their bones
May be forthcoming, when the flesh is rotten.
But your sweet nature doth abhor these courses;
You loathe the widow's or the orphan's tears
Should wash your pavements, or their piteous cries   50
Ring in your roofs, and beat the air for vengeance.

VOLP.   Right, Mosca; I do loathe it.—

Act I. Sc. i. **22. dumb god:** silence is golden. **31. purchase:** acquisition. **33.**
venture: investments. **40. usure:** usury, loans at exorbitant rates.

MOS.   And, besides, sir,
You are not like the thresher that doth stand
With a huge flail, watching a heap of corn,
And, hungry, dares not taste the smallest grain,
But feeds on mallows, and such bitter herbs;
Nor like the merchant, who hath fill'd his vaults
With Romagnía, rich and Candian wines,
Yet drinks the lees of Lombard's vinegar.
You will not lie in straw, whilst moths and worms   60
Feed on your sumptuous hangings and soft beds.
You know the use of riches, and dare give now
From that bright heap, to me, your poor observer,
Or to your dwarf, or your hermaphrodite,
Your eunuch, or what other household trifle
Your pleasure allows maintenance.—

VOLP.   Hold thee, Mosca;
Take of my hand; thou strik'st on truth in all,
And they are envious term thee parasite.
Call forth my dwarf, my eunuch, and my fool,
And let 'em make me sport.   [*Exit* MOSCA.]
                          What should I do,   70
But cocker up my genius, and live free
To all delights my fortune calls me to?
I have no wife, no parent, child, ally,
To give my substance to; but whom I make
Must be my heir; and this makes men observe me.
This draws new clients daily to my house,
Women and men of every sex and age,
That bring me presents, send me plate, coin, jewels,
With hope that when I die (which they expect
Each greedy minute) it shall then return   8c
Tenfold upon them; whilst some, covetous
Above the rest, seek to engross me whole,
And counter work the one unto the other,

58. Romagnía: Greek. Candian: Cretan. 63. observer: servant. 71. cocker . . .
genius: cater to my inclination. 82. engross: monopolize.

Contend in gifts, as they would seem in love;
All which I suffer, playing with their hopes,
And am content to coin 'em into profit,
And look upon their kindness, and take more,
And look on that; still bearing them in hand,
Letting the cherry knock against their lips,
And draw it by their mouths, and back again.— 90
How now!

SCENE II

[*Enter* MOSCA *with* NANO, ANDROGYNO, *and* CASTRONE.]

NAN. Now, room for fresh gamesters, who do will you to know
They do bring you neither play nor university show,
And therefore do entreat you that whatsoever they rehearse
May not fare a whit the worse for the false pace of the verse.
If you wonder at this, you will wonder more ere we pass;
For know, here is enclos'd the soul of Pythagoras,
That juggler divine, as hereafter shall follow,
Which soul, fast and loose, sir, came first from Apollo,
And was breath'd into Aethalides, Mercurius his son,
Where it had the gift to remember all that ever was done.   10
From thence it fled forth, and made quick transmigration
To goldy-lock'd Euphorbus, who was kill'd, in good fashion,
At the siege of old Troy, by the cuckold of Sparta.
Hermotimus was next (I find it in my charta);
To whom it did pass, where no sooner it was missing,
But with one Pyrrhus of Delos it learn'd to go a-fishing;
And thence did it enter the sophist of Greece.
From Pythagore, she went into a beautiful piece,
Hight Aspasia, the meretrix; and the next toss of her
Was again of a whore—she became a philosopher,   20

88. bearing . . . hand: leading them on.

Sc. ii. 6. here: i.e., in Androgyno. 9. Aethalides: son of Mercury and herald of the Argonauts. 13. cuckold of Sparta: Menelaus. 19. Hight: named. meretrix: prostitute.

Crates the cynic, as itself doth relate it.
Since, kings, knights, and beggars, knaves, lords, and fools
    gat it,
Besides ox and ass, camel, mule, goat, and brock,
In all which it hath spoke, as in the cobbler's cock.
But I come not here to discourse of that matter,
Or his one, two, or three, or his great oath, "By QUATER!"
His musics, his trigon, his golden thigh,
Or his telling how elements shift; but I
Would ask, how of late thou hast suffered translation,
And shifted thy coat in these days of reformation.   30

AND. Like one of the reformed, a fool, as you see,
    Counting all old doctrine heresy.

NAN. But not on thine own forbid meats hast thou ventur'd?

AND. On fish, when first a Carthusian I enter'd.

NAN. Why, then thy dogmatical silence hath left thee?

AND. Of that an obstreperous lawyer bereft me.

NAN. O wonderful change! When sir lawyer forsook thee,
    For Pythagore's sake, what body then took thee?

AND. A good dull mule.

NAN.   And how! by that means
    Thou wert brought to allow of the eating of beans?   40

AND. Yes.

NAN.   But from the mule into whom didst thou pass?

AND. Into a very strange beast, by some writers call'd an ass;
    By others a precise, pure, illuminate brother
    Of those devour flesh—and sometimes one another;
    And will drop you forth a libel, or a sanctifi'd lie,
    Betwixt every spoonful of a nativity-pie.

NAN. Now quit thee, fore Heaven, of that profane nation;
    And gently report thy next transmigration.

AND. To the same that I am.

---

23. brock: badger. **24. cobbler's cock:** This section on the transmigration of souls is based on Lucian's dialogue of the cobbler and the cock. **43. precise:** puritanical. **44. those:** those who. **46. nativity-pie:** Christmas pie.

NAN.   A creature of delight,
   And, what is more than a fool, an hermaphrodite!   50
   Now, pray thee, sweet soul, in all thy variation,
   Which body wouldst thou choose to take up thy station?
AND. Troth, this I am in; even here would I tarry.
NAN. 'Cause here the delight of each sex thou canst vary?
AND. Alas, those pleasures be stale and forsaken;
   No, 'tis your fool wherewith I am so taken,
   The only one creature that I can call blessed;
   For all other forms I have prov'd most distressed.
NAN. Spoke true, as thou wert in Pythagoras still.
   This learned opinion we celebrate will,   60
   Fellow eunuch, as behoves us, with all our wit and art,
   To dignify that whereof ourselves are so great and special a
      part.
VOLP. Now, very, very pretty. Mosca, this
   Was thy invention?
MOS.   If it please my patron,
   Not else.
VOLP.   It doth, good Mosca.
MOS.   Then it was, sir.   *[Sings.]*

   Fools they are the only nation
   Worth men's envy or admiration;
   Free from care or sorrow taking,
   Selves and others merry making:
   All they speak or do is sterling.   70
   Your fool he is your great man's dearling,
   And your ladies' sport and pleasure;
   Tongue and bauble are his treasure.
   E'en his face begetteth laughter,
   And he speaks truth free from slaughter;
   He's the grace of every feast,
   And sometimes the chiefest guest;

75. slaughter: punishment.

Hath his trencher and his stool,
When wit waits upon the fool.
   O, who would not be   80
He, he, he?

                                       [One knocks without.]

VOLP. Who's that? Away! Look, Mosca.
MOS.   Fool, begone!

               [Exeunt NANO, CASTRONE, *and* ANDROGYNO.]
'Tis Signior Voltore, the advocate;
I know him by his knock.

VOLP.   Fetch me my gown,
My furs, and nightcaps; say my couch is changing,
And let him entertain himself awhile
Without, i' th' gallery. *[Exit* MOSCA.] Now, now my clients
Begin their visitation! Vulture, kite,
Raven, and gorcrow, all my birds of prey,
That think me turning carcase, now they come;   90
I am not for 'em yet.

          [Re-enter MOSCA, *with the gown, etc.]*
                 How now! the news?

MOS. A piece of plate, sir.
VOLP.   Of what bigness?
MOS.   Huge,
Massy, and antique, with your name inscrib'd,
And arms engraven.

VOLP.   Good! and not a fox
Stretch'd on the earth, with fine delusive sleights,
Mocking a gaping crow? ha, Mosca?
MOS.   Sharp, sir.
VOLP. Give me my furs.—Why dost thou laugh so, man?
MOS. I cannot choose, sir, when I apprehend
What thoughts he has without now, as he walks:
That this might be the last gift he should give,   100
That this would fetch you; if you died today,

89. **gorcrow:** scavenger crow.

And gave him all, what he should be tomorrow;
What large return would come of all his ventures;
How he should worshipp'd be, and reverenc'd;
Ride with his furs and footcloths, waited on
By herds of fools and clients; have clear way
Made for his mule, as letter'd as himself;
Be call'd the great and learned advocate!
And then concludes there's nought impossible.

VOLP. Yes, to be learned, Mosca.

MOS.   O, no! rich   110
Implies it. Hood an ass with reverend purple,
So you can hide his two ambitious ears,
And he shall pass for a cathedral doctor.

VOLP. My caps, my caps, good Mosca. Fetch him in.

MOS. Stay, sir; your ointment for your eyes.

VOLP.   That's true;
Dispatch, dispatch; I long to have possession
Of my new present.

MOS.   That, and thousands more,
I hope to see you lord of.

VOLP.   Thanks, kind Mosca.

MOS. And that, when I am lost in blended dust,
And hundred such as I am, in succession—   120

VOLP. Nay, that were too much, Mosca.

MOS.   You shall live
Still to delude these harpies.

VOLP.   Loving Mosca!
'Tis well; my pillow now, and let him enter.   [*Exit* MOSCA.]
Now, my feign'd cough, my phthisic, and my gout,
My apoplexy, palsy, and catarrhs,
Help, with your forced functions this my posture,
Wherein, this three year, I have milk'd their hopes.
He comes; I hear him— Uh, uh, uh, uh!—Oh!

124. phthisic: consumption. 126. posture: deception.

SCENE III

[Enter MOSCA *with* VOLTORE.*]*

MOS. You still are what you were, sir. Only you,
Of all the rest, are he commands his love,
And you do wisely to preserve it thus,
With early visitation and kind notes
Of your good meaning to him, which, I know,
Cannot but come most grateful. Patron! sir!
Here's Signior Voltore is come—

VOLP.   What say you?

MOS. Sir, Signior Voltore is come this morning
    To visit you.

VOLP.   I thank him.

MOS.   And hath brought
    A piece of antique plate, bought of St. Mark,   10
    With which he here presents you.

VOLP.   He is welcome.
    Pray him to come more often.

MOS.   Yes.

VOLT.   What says he?

MOS. He thanks you, and desires you see him often.

VOLP. Mosca.

MOS.   My patron!

VOLP.   Bring him near. Where is he?
    I long to feel his hand.

MOS.   The plate is here, sir.

VOLT. How fare you, sir?

VOLP.   I thank you, Signior Voltore.
    Where is the plate? mine eyes are bad.

VOLT.   I'm sorry
    To see you still thus weak.

MOS. *[Aside]*   That he is not weaker.

Sc. iii. 10. St. Mark: goldsmith in St. Mark's Square.

VOLP. You are too munificent.

VOLT.   No, sir; would to Heaven
    I could as well give health to you, as that plate.   **20**

VOLP. You give, sir, what you can. I thank you. Your love
    Hath taste in this, and shall not be unanswer'd.
    I pray you see me often.

VOLT.   Yes, I shall, sir.

VOLP. Be not far from me.

MOS.   Do you observe that, sir?

VOLP. Hearken unto me still; it will concern you.

MOS. You are a happy man, sir; know your good.

VOLP. I cannot now last long—

MOS. [*Aside*]   You are his heir, sir.

VOLT. [*Aside*] Am I?

VOLP. I feel me going—uh, uh, uh, uh!—
    I'm sailing to my port—uh, uh, uh, uh!—
    And I am glad I am so near my haven.   **30**

MOS. Alas, kind gentleman; well, we must all go—

VOLT. But, Mosca—

MOS.   Age will conquer.

VOLT.   'Pray thee, hear me.
    Am I inscrib'd his heir, for certain?

MOS.   Are you!
    I do beseech you, sir, you will vouchsafe
    To write me i' your family. All my hopes
    Depend upon your Worship. I am lost
    Except the rising sun do shine on me.

VOLT. It shall both shine, and warm thee, Mosca.

MOS.   Sir,
    I am a man that hath not done your love
    All the worst offices: here I wear your keys,   **40**
    See all your coffers and your caskets lock'd,
    Keep the poor inventory of your jewels,
    Your plate, and monies; am your steward, sir,
    Husband your goods here.

35. write . . . family: enroll me among your servants.

VOLT.   But am I sole heir?

MOS. Without a partner, sir; confirm'd this morning;
    The wax is warm yet, and the ink scarce dry
    Upon the parchment.

VOLT.   Happy, happy me!
    By what good chance, sweet Mosca?

MOS.   Your desert, sir;
    I know no second cause.

VOLT.   Thy modesty
    Is loth to know it; well, we shall requite it.   50

MOS. He ever lik'd your course, sir; that first took him.
    I oft have heard him say how he admir'd
    Men of your large profession, that could speak
    To every cause, and things mere contraries,
    Till they were hoarse again, yet all be law;
    That, with most quick agility, could turn,
    And return; make knots, and undo them;
    Give forked counsel; take provoking gold
    On either hand, and put it up; these men,
    He knew, would thrive with their humility.   60
    And, for his part, he thought he should be blest
    To have his heir of such a suffering spirit,
    So wise, so grave, of so perplex'd a tongue,
    And loud withal, that would not wag, nor scarce
    Lie still, without a fee; when every word
    Your Worship but lets fall, is a *cecchine!*

                              [*Another knocks.*]

    Who's that? One knocks; I would not have you seen, sir.
    And yet—pretend you came and went in haste;
    I'll fashion an excuse. And, gentle sir,
    When you do come to swim in golden lard,   70
    Up to the arms in honey, that your chin

59. **put it up:** pocket it.   63. **perplex'd:** clever.   66. **cecchine:** a Venetian gold
coin.

Is borne up stiff with fatness of the flood,
Think on your vassal; but remember me:
I ha' not been your worst of clients.

VOLT.   Mosca—

MOS. When will you have your inventory brought, sir?
Or see a copy of the will?—Anon.—
I'll bring 'em to you, sir. Away, begone,
Put business i' your face.   [*Exit* VOLTORE.]

VOLP.   Excellent Mosca!
Come hither, let me kiss thee.

MOS.   Keep you still, sir.
Here is Corbaccio.

VOLP.   Set the plate away.   80
The vulture's gone, and the old raven's come.

SCENE IV

[MOSCA *and* VOLPONE *remain.*]

MOS. Betake you to your silence, and your sleep.—
    [*To the plate*] Stand there and multiply.—[*Aside*] Now shall
        we see
    A wretch who is indeed more impotent
    Than this can feign to be; yet hopes to hop
    Over his grave.—
                        [*He admits* CORBACCIO.]
                        Signior Corbaccio!
    You're very welcome, sir.

CORB.   How does your patron?

MOS. Troth, as he did, sir; no amends.

CORB.   What? mends he?

MOS. No, sir: he is rather worse.

CORB.   That's well. Where is he?

MOS. Upon his couch, sir, newly fall'n asleep.

Sc. iv. 4. this: i.e., Volpone.

CORB. Does he sleep well?

MOS.   No wink, sir, all this night,   10
    Nor yesterday; but slumbers.

CORB.   Good! he should take
    Some counsel of physicians. I have brought him
    An opiate here, from mine own doctor—

MOS. He will not hear of drugs.

CORB.   Why? I myself
    Stood by while 'twas made, saw all th' ingredients,
    And know it cannot but most gently work.
    My life for his, 'tis but to make him sleep.

VOLP. [*Aside*] Ay, his last sleep, if he would take it.

MOS.   Sir,
    He has no faith in physic.

CORB.   Say you? say you?

MOS. He has no faith in physic; he does think   20
    Most of your doctors are the greater danger,
    And worse disease, t' escape. I often have
    Heard him protest that your physician
    Should never be his heir.

CORB.   Not I his heir?

MOS. Not your physician, sir.

CORB.   O, no, no, no;
    I do not mean it.

MOS.   No, sir, nor their fees
    He cannot brook; he says they flay a man
    Before they kill him.

CORB.   Right, I do conceive you.

MOS. And then they do it by experiment;
    For which the law not only doth absolve 'em,   30
    But gives them great reward; and he is loth
    To hire his death so.

CORB.   It is true, they kill
    With as much licence as a judge.

11. slumbers: dozes.

MOS.   Nay, more;
 For he but kills, sir, where the law condemns,
 And these can kill him too.

CORB.   Ay, or me,
 Or any man. How does his apoplex?
 Is that strong on him still?

MOS.   Most violent.
 His speech is broken, and his eyes are set,
 His face drawn longer than 'twas wont—

CORB.   How? how?
 Stronger than he was wont?

MOS.   No, sir; his face   40
 Drawn longer than 'twas wont.

CORB.   O, good.

MOS.   His mouth
 Is ever gaping, and his eyelids hang.

CORB.   Good.

MOS. A freezing numbness stiffens all his joints,
 And makes the color of his flesh like lead.

CORB.   'Tis good.

MOS. His pulse beats slow, and dull.

CORB.   Good symptoms still.

MOS. And from his brain—

CORB.   Ha? How? Not from his brain?

MOS. Yes, sir, and from his brain—

CORB.   I conceive you; good.

MOS. Flows a cold sweat, with a continual rheum,
 Forth the resolved corners of his eyes.

CORB. Is 't possible? Yet I am better, ha!   50
 How does he with the swimming of his head?

MOS. O, sir, 'tis past the scotomy; he now
 Hath lost his feeling, and hath left to snort;
 You hardly can perceive him, that he breathes.

___

49. resolved: rotting. **52. scotomy:** dizziness. **53. left to snort:** stopped
snoring.

CORB. Excellent, excellent; sure I shall outlast him;
    This makes me young again, a score of years.
MOS. I was a-coming for you, sir.
CORB.   Has he made his will?
    What has he giv'n me?
MOS.   No, sir.
CORB.   Nothing? ha?
MOS. He has not made his will, sir.
CORB.   Oh, oh, oh.
    What then did Voltore, the lawyer, here?   60
MOS. He smelt a carcass, sir, when he but heard
    My master was about his testament;
    As I did urge him to it for your good—
CORB. He came unto him, did he? I thought so.
MOS. Yes, and presented him this piece of plate.
CORB. To be his heir?
MOS.   I do not know, sir.
CORB.   True;
    I know it too.
MOS. [*Aside*] By your own scale, sir.
CORB.   Well,
    I shall prevent him yet. See, Mosca, look,
    Here I have brought a bag of bright *cecchines,*
    Will quite weigh down his plate.
MOS.   Yea, marry, sir.   70
    This is true physic, this your sacred medicine;
    No talk of opiates to this great elixir!
CORB. 'Tis *aurum palpabile,* if not *potabile.*
MOS. It shall be minister'd to him in his bowl!
CORB. Ay, do, do, do.
MOS.   Most blessed cordial!
    This will recover him.
CORB.   Yes, do, do, do.

---

73. aurum . . . potabile: gold that can be touched if not drunk; the latter
elixir was known as the sovereign remedy.

MOS. I think it were not best, sir.

CORB.   What?

MOS.   To recover him.

CORB. O, no, no, no; by no means.

MOS.   Why, sir, this
   Will work some strange effect, if he but feel it.

CORB. 'Tis true; therefore forbear. I'll take my venture;   80
   Give me 't again.

MOS.   At no hand; pardon me,
   You shall not do yourself that wrong, sir. I
   Will so advise you, you shall have it all.

CORB. How?

MOS.   All, sir; 'tis your right, your own; no man
   Can claim a part; 'tis yours without a rival,
   Decreed by destiny.

CORB.   How, how, good Mosca?

MOS. I'll tell you, sir. This fit he shall recover—

CORB. I do conceive you.

MOS.   And, on first advantage
   Of his gain'd sense, will I re-importune him
   Unto the making of his testament,   90
   And show him this.   [*Points to the money.*]

CORB.   Good, good.

MOS.   'Tis better yet,
   If you will hear, sir.

CORB.   Yes, with all my heart.

MOS. Now would I counsel you, make home with speed;
   There, frame a will; whereto you shall inscribe
   My master your sole heir.

CORB.   And disinherit
   My son?

MOS.   O, sir, the better; for that color
   Shall make it much more taking.

CORB.   O, but color?

81. **At no hand:** by no means. **96. color:** pretense.

MOS. This will, sir, you shall send it unto me.
    Now, when I come to enforce, as I will do,
    Your cares, your watchings, and your many prayers,   100
    Your more than many gifts, your this day's present,
    And last, produce your will; where (without thought
    Or least regard unto your proper issue,
    A son so brave, and highly meriting)
    The stream of your diverted love hath thrown you
    Upon my master, and made him your heir;
    He cannot be so stupid or stone-dead,
    But, out of conscience and mere gratitude—
CORB. He must pronounce me his?
MOS.   'Tis true.
CORB.   This plot
    Did I think on before.
MOS.   I do believe it.   110
CORB. Do you not believe it?
MOS.   Yes, sir.
CORB.   Mine own project.
MOS. Which, when he hath done, sir—
CORB.   Publish'd me his heir?
MOS. And you so certain to survive him—
CORB.   Ay.
MOS. Being so lusty a man—
CORB.   'Tis true.
MOS.   Yes, sir—
CORB. I thought on that too. See, how he should be
    The very organ to express my thoughts!
MOS. You have not only done yourself a good—
CORB. But multiplied it on my son!
MOS.   'Tis right, sir.
CORB. Still, my invention.
MOS.   'Las, sir! Heaven knows,
    It hath been all my study, all my care,   120
    (I e'en grow gray withal) how to work things—

103. **proper issue:** own child.

CORB. I do conceive, sweet Mosca.

MOS.   You are he
    For whom I labor here.

CORB.   Ay, do, do, do.
    I'll straight about it.

MOS. [*Aside*]   Rook go with you, raven.

CORB. I know thee honest.

MOS.   You do lie, sir—

CORB.   And—

MOS. Your knowledge is no better than your ears, sir.

CORB. I do not doubt to be a father to thee.

MOS. Nor I to gull my brother of his blessing.

CORB. I may ha' my youth restor'd to me, why not?

MOS. Your Worship is a precious ass—

CORB.   What say'st thou?   130

MOS. I do desire your Worship to make haste, sir.

CORB. 'Tis done, 'tis done; I go.   [*Exit.*]

VOLP. [*Leaping from his couch*] Oh, I shall burst!
    Let out my sides, let out my sides—

MOS.   Contain
    Your flux of laughter, sir; you know this hope
    Is such a bait, it covers any hook.

VOLP. O, but thy working, and thy placing it!
    I cannot hold; good rascal, let me kiss thee;
    I never knew thee in so rare a humor.

MOS. Alas, sir, I but do as I am taught;
    Follow your grave instructions, give 'em words,   140
    Pour oil into their ears, and send them hence.

VOLP. 'Tis true, 'tis true. What a rare punishment
    Is avarice to itself!

MOS.   Ay, with our help, sir.

VOLP. So many cares, so many maladies,
    So many fears attending on old age.
    Yea, death so often call'd on, as no wish

124. **Rook . . . you:** may you be rooked. 128. **gull:** cheat.

Can be more frequent with 'em, their limbs faint,
Their senses dull, their seeing, hearing, going,
All dead before them; yea, their very teeth,
Their instruments of eating, failing them.   150
Yet this is reckon'd life! Nay, here was one,
Is now gone home, that wishes to live longer!
Feels not his gout, nor palsy; feigns himself
Younger by scores of years, flatters his age
With confident belying it, hopes he may
With charms like Aeson have his youth restor'd;
And with these thoughts so battens, as if fate
Would be as easily cheated on as he;
And all turns air! Who's that there, now? a third?

                                        [*Another knocks.*]
MOS. Close; to your couch again; I hear his voice.   160
     It is Corvino, our spruce merchant.
VOLP. [*Lying down*]   Dead.
MOS. Another bout, sir, with your eyes. [*Anointing them*]—Who's
     there?

SCENE V

[*Enter* CORVINO.]
     Signior Corvino! come most wish'd for! Oh,
     How happy were you, if you knew it, now!
CORV. Why? what? wherein?
MOS.   The tardy hour is come, sir.
CORV. He is not dead?
MOS.   Not dead, sir, but as good;
     He knows no man.
CORV.   How shall I do then?
MOS.   Why, sir?
CORV. I have brought him here a pearl.
MOS.   Perhaps he has
     So much remembrance left as to know you, sir.

148. going: motion. 157. battens: feeds and fattens.

He still calls on you; nothing but your name
Is in his mouth. Is your pearl orient, sir?

CORV. Venice was never owner of the like.　　　　　　　　**10**

VOLP. Signior Corvino!

MOS.　　　　　　Hark!

VOLP.　　　　　　　　　Signior Corvino.

MOS. He calls you; step and give it him.—H' is here, sir.
And he has brought you a rich pearl.

CORV.　　　　　　　　　　　　How do you, sir?—
Tell him it doubles the twelfth carat.

MOS.　　　　　　　　　　Sir,
He cannot understand: his hearing's gone;
And yet it comforts him to see you—

CORV.　　　　　　　　　　　　Say
I have a diamond for him, too.

MOS.　　　　　　　　　Best show 't, sir;
Put it into his hand; 'tis only there
He apprehends; he has his feeling yet.
See, how he grasps it!

CORV.　　　　　　　'Las, good gentleman!　　　　**20**
How pitiful the sight is!

MOS.　　　　　　Tut, forget, sir.
The weeping of an heir should still be laughter
Under a visor.

CORV.　　　　Why, am I his heir?

MOS. Sir, I am sworn, I may not show the will
Till he be dead. But here has been Corbaccio,
Here has been Voltore, here were others too—
I cannot number 'em, they were so many—
All gaping here for legacies; but I,
Taking the vantage of his naming you,
"Signior Corvino, Signior Corvino," took　　　　　**30**
Paper, and pen, and ink, and there I ask'd him
Whom he would have his heir! "Corvino." Who

Sc. v. 9. orient: of high quality. 23. visor: mask.

Should be executor? "Corvino." And
To any question he was silent to,
I still interpreted the nods he made,
Through weakness, for consent; and sent home th' others,
Nothing bequeath'd them, but to cry and curse.

CORV. Oh, my dear Mosca. [*They embrace.*] Does he not perceive
    us?

MOS. No more than a blind harper. He knows no man,
No face of friend, nor name of any servant,   40
Who 'twas that fed him last, or gave him drink;
Not those he hath begotten, or brought up,
Can he remember.

CORV.   Has he children?

MOS.   Bastards,
Some dozen, or more, that he begot on beggars,
Gypsies, and Jews, and black-moors, when he was drunk.
Knew you not that, sir? 'Tis the common fable.
The dwarf, the fool, the eunuch, are all his;
H' is the true father of his family,
In all save me. But he has giv'n 'em nothing.

CORV. That's well, that's well. Art sure he does not hear us?   50

MOS. Sure, sir! Why, look you, credit your own sense. [*Shouts in*
     VOLPONE'S *ear.*]
The pox approach, and add to your diseases,
If it would send you hence the sooner, sir;
For your incontinence it hath deserv'd it
Throughly and throughly, and the plague to boot!—
You may come near, sir.—Would you would once close
Those filthy eyes of yours, that flow with slime
Like two frog-pits; and those same hanging cheeks,
Cover'd with hide instead of skin—Nay, help, sir—
That look like frozen dishclouts set on end.   60

CORV. Or like an old smok'd wall, on which the rain
Ran down in streaks.

MOS.   Excellent, sir! speak out;

46. fable: gossip. **52. pox:** venereal disease.

You may be louder yet; a culverin
Discharged in his ear would hardly bore it.

CORV. His nose is like a common sewer, still running.

MOS. 'Tis good! And what his mouth?

CORV.   A very draught.

MOS. O, stop it up—

CORV.   By no means.

MOS.   Pray you, let me;
Faith, I could stifle him rarely with a pillow
As well as any woman that should keep him.

CORV. Do as you will; but I'll be gone.

MOS.   Be so;   70
It is your presence makes him last so long.

CORV. I pray you use no violence.

MOS.   No, sir? why?
Why should you be thus scrupulous, 'pray you, sir?

CORV. Nay, at your discretion.

MOS.   Well, good sir, begone.

CORV. I will not trouble him now to take my pearl?

MOS. Pooh, nor your diamond. What a needless care
Is this afflicts you? Is not all here yours?
Am not I here, whom you have made, your creature,
That owe my being to you?

CORV.   Grateful Mosca!
Thou art my friend, my fellow, my companion,   80
My partner, and shalt share in all my fortunes.

MOS. Excepting one.

CORV.   What's that?

MOS.   Your gallant wife, sir.

[*Exit* CORVINO.]

Now is he gone; we had no other means
To shoot him hence but this.

VOLP.   My divine Mosca!
Thou hast today outgone thyself. Who's there?

[*Another knocks.*]

63. culverin: cannon. 68. rarely: quickly.

I will be troubled with no more. Prepare
Me music, dances, banquets, all delights;
The Turk is not more sensual in his pleasures
Than will Volpone. [*Exit* MOSCA.] Let me see; a pearl!
A diamond! plate! *cecchines!* Good morning's purchase.   90
Why, this is better than rob churches, yet;
Or fat, by eating, once a month, a man—
                    [*Re-enter* MOSCA.]
Who is 't?

MOS.   The beauteous Lady Would-be, sir,
Wife to the English knight, Sir Politic Would-be—
This is the style, sir, is directed me—
Hath sent to know how you have slept tonight,
And if you would be visited.

VOLP.   Not now.
Some three hours hence—

MOS.   I told the squire so much.

VOLP. When I am high with mirth and wine; then, then.
'Fore Heaven, I wonder at the desperate valor   100
Of the bold English, that they dare let loose
Their wives to all encounters!

MOS.   Sir, this knight
Had not his name for nothing: he is politic,
And knows, howe'er his wife affect strange airs,
She hath not yet the face to be dishonest.
But had she Signior Corvino's wife's face—

VOLP. Hath she so rare a face?

MOS.   O, sir, the wonder,
The blazing star of Italy! a wench
Of the first year! a beauty ripe as harvest!
Whose skin is whiter than a swan, all over!   110
Than silver, snow, or lilies! a soft lip,
Would tempt you to eternity of kissing!

90. purchase: loot. 98. squire: servant. 105. dishonest: unfaithful.

And flesh that melteth in the touch to blood!
Bright as your gold! and lovely as your gold!

VOLP. Why had not I known this before?

MOS.   Alas, sir,
Myself but yesterday discover'd it.

VOLP. How might I see her?

MOS.   Oh, not possible;
She's kept as warily as is your gold;
Never does come abroad, never takes air
But at a windore. All her looks are sweet,   120
As the first grapes or cherries, and are watch'd
As near as they are.

VOLP.   I must see her—

MOS.   Sir,
There is a guard of ten spies thick upon her,
All his whole household; each of which is set
Upon his fellow, and have all their charge,
When he goes out, when he comes in, examin'd.

VOLP. I will go see her, though but at her windore.

MOS. In some disguise then.

VOLP.   That is true; I must
Maintain mine own shape still the same; we'll think.

                                              [*Exeunt.*]

ACT TWO

SCENE I. Before Corvino's house in St. Mark's Square.

[*Enter* SIR POLITIC WOULD-BE, *and* PEREGRINE.]

POL. Sir, to a wise man, all the world's his soil:
It is not Italy, nor France, nor Europe,
That must bound me, if my fates call me forth.
Yet I protest, it is no salt desire

113. blood: passion. 120. windore: window.

Act II. Sc. i. 4. salt: intense.

Of seeing countries, shifting a religion,
Nor any disaffection to the state
Where I was bred, and unto which I owe
My dearest plots, hath brought me out; much less
That idle, antic, stale, grey-headed project
Of knowing men's minds and manners, with Ulysses!   10
But a peculiar humor of my wife's
Laid for this height of Venice, to observe,
To quote, to learn the language, and so forth—
I hope you travel, sir, with license?

PER.   Yes.

POL. I dare the safelier converse.—How long, sir,
Since you left England?

PER.   Seven weeks.

POL.   So lately!
You ha' not been with my Lord Ambassador?

PER.   Not yet, sir.

POL. Pray you, what news, sir, vents our climate?
I heard last night a most strange thing reported
By some of my Lord's followers, and I long   20
To hear how 'twill be seconded!

PER.   What was 't, sir?

POL. Marry, sir, of a raven that should build
In a ship royal of the king's.

PER. [*Aside*]   This fellow,
Does he gull me, trow? or is gull'd?—Your name, sir?

POL. My name is Politic Would-be.

PER. [*Aside*]   O, that speaks him.—
A knight, sir?

POL.   A poor knight, sir.

PER.   Your lady
Lies here in Venice, for intelligence
Of tires and fashions and behavior,
Among the courtesans? The fine Lady Would-be?

12. Laid . . . Venice: directed toward Venice. 13. quote: note. 14. license:
government permission—required of nobility. 18. vents our climate: comes
from England. 28. tires: styles.

POL. Yes, sir; the spider and the bee ofttimes   30
    Suck from one flower.

PER.   Good Sir Politic!
    I cry you mercy; I have heard much of you.
    'Tis true, sir, of your raven.

POL.   On your knowledge?

PER. Yes, and your lion's whelping in the Tower.

POL. Another whelp!

PER.   Another, sir.

POL.   Now Heaven!
    What prodigies be these? The fires at Berwick!
    And the new star! These things concurring, strange!
    And full of omen! Saw you those meteors?

PER. I did, sir.

POL.   Fearful! Pray you, sir, confirm me,
    Were there three porpoises seen, above the Bridge,   40
    As they give out?

PER.   Six, and a sturgeon, sir.

POL. I am astonish'd!

PER.   Nay, sir, be not so;
    I'll tell you a greater prodigy then these—

POL. What should these things portend?

PER.   The very day,
    Let me be sure, that I put forth from London,
    There was a whale discover'd in the river,
    As high as Woolwich, that had waited there,
    Few know how many months, for the subversion
    Of the Stode fleet.

POL.   Is 't possible? Believe it,
    'Twas either sent from Spain, or the Archduke's!   50
    Spinola's whale, upon my life, my credit!

34. **Tower**: of London, where a lion was born August 5, 1604, and another on February 26, 1606. 36. **fires**: meteors. 48-9. **subversion . . . fleet**: to destroy the fleet from Stode, near Hamburg. 51. **Spinola**: Spanish general who captured Ostend in 1604 and used novel weapons.

Will they not leave these projects? Worthy sir,
Some other news.

PER.   Faith, Stone, the fool, is dead,
And they do lack a tavern fool extremely.

POL. Is Mas' Stone dead?

PER.   He's dead, sir; why, I hope
You thought him not immortal?—[*Aside*] Oh, this knight,
Were he well known, would be a precious thing
To fit our English stage. He that should write
But such a fellow, should be thought to feign
Extremely, if not maliciously.

POL.   Stone dead!   60

PER. Dead.—Lord! how deeply, sir, you apprehend it!
He was no kinsman to you?

POL.   That I know of.
Well! that same fellow was an unknown fool.

PER. And yet you knew him, it seems?

POL.   I did so. Sir,
I knew him one of the most dangerous heads
Living within the state, and so I held him.

PER. Indeed, sir?

POL.   While he liv'd, in action,
He has receiv'd weekly intelligence,
Upon my knowledge, out of the Low Countries,
For all parts of the world, in cabbages;   70
And those dispens'd again to ambassadors,
In oranges, muskmelons, apricots,
Lemons, pome-citrons, and such like; sometimes
In Colchester oysters, and your Selsey cockles.

PER. You make me wonder!

POL.   Sir, upon my knowledge.
Nay, I have observ'd him, at your public ordinary,
Take his advertisement from a traveller
(A conceal'd statesman) in a trencher of meat;

---

62. **That:** not that. 63. **unknown:** pretended. 76. **ordinary:** tavern. 77. **advertisement:** information.

And instantly, before the meal was done,
Convey an answer in a toothpick.

PER.   Strange!   80
How could this be, sir?

POL.   Why, the meat was cut
So like his character, and so laid as he
Must easily read the cipher.

PER.   I have heard
He could not read, sir.

POL.   So 'twas given out,
In polity, by those that did employ him;
But he could read, and had your languages,
And to 't, as sound a noddle—

PER.   I have heard, sir,
That your baboons were spies, and that they were
A kind of subtle nation near to China.

POL. Ay, ay, your Mamaluchi. Faith, they had   90
Their hand in a French plot or two; but they
Were so extremely given to women, as
They made discovery of all: yet I
Had my advices here, on Wednesday last,
From one of their own coat, they were return'd,
Made their relations, as the fashion is,
And now stand fair for fresh employment.

PER. [*Aside*]   Heart!
This Sir Pol will be ignorant of nothing.—
It seems, sir, you know all.

POL.   Not all, sir. But
I have some general notions. I do love   100
To note and to observe. Though I live out,
Free from the active torrent, yet I'd mark
The currents and the passages of things

82. **character:** writing. 85. **In polity:** cunningly. 87. **And to' t:** in addition.
90. **Mamaluchi:** actually Mamelukes, or white slaves converted to Islamism
and powerful in Egypt from the 13th century. 92. **as:** that. 95. **coat:** party.
96. **relations:** reports.

For mine own private use; and know the ebbs
And flows of state.

PER.   Believe it, sir, I hold
Myself in no small tie unto my fortunes,
For casting me thus luckily upon you,
Whose knowledge, if your bounty equal it,
May do me great assistance, in instruction
For my behavior, and my bearing, which   110
Is yet so rude and raw—

POL.   Why? came you forth
Empty of rules for travel?

PER.   Faith, I had
Some common ones, from out that vulgar grammar,
Which he that cri'd Italian to me, taught me.

POL. Why, this it is that spoils all our brave bloods,
Trusting our hopeful gentry unto pedants,
Fellows of outside, and mere bark. You seem
To be a gentleman of ingenuous race.—
I not profess it, but my fate hath been   120
To be where I have been consulted with,
In this high kind, touching some great men's sons,
Persons of blood and honor.—

PER.   Who be these, sir?

SCENE II

[*Enter* MOSCA *and* NANO *disguised, with workmen who erect a stage.*]

MOS. Under that windore, there 't must be. The same.

POL. Fellows to mount a bank! Did your instructor
In the dear tongues never discourse to you
Of the Italian mountebanks?

PER.   Yes, sir.

106. **tie:** obligation. 114. **cri'd:** taught.
Sc. ii. 2. **bank:** platform.

POL.   Why,
  Here shall you see one.
PER.   They are quacksalvers,
  Fellows that live by venting oils and drugs!
POL. Was that the character he gave you of them?
PER. As I remember.
POL.   Pity his ignorance.
  They are the only knowing men of Europe!
  Great general scholars, excellent physicians,   10
  Most admir'd statesmen, profess'd favorites
  And cabinet counsellors to the greatest princes!
  The only languag'd men of all the world!
PER. And, I have heard, they are most lewd impostors;
  Made all of terms and shreds; no less beliers
  Of great men's favors, than their own vile med'cines;
  Which they will utter upon monstrous oaths;
  Selling that drug for twopence, ere they part,
  Which they have valu'd at twelve crowns before.
POL. Sir, calumnies are answer'd best with silence.   20
  Yourself shall judge.—Who is it mounts, my friends?
MOS. Scoto of Mantua, sir.
POL.   Is 't he? Nay, then
  I'll proudly promise, sir, you shall behold
  Another man than has been phant'sied to you.
  I wonder yet, that he should mount his bank
  Here in this nook, that has been wont t' appear
  In face of the Piazza! Here he comes.
    [*Enter* VOLPONE, *disguised as a mountebank doctor, and followed
                    by a crowd of people.*]
VOLP. [*To* NANO] Mount, zany.
GRE.   Follow, follow, follow, follow, follow.
POL. See how the people follow him! he's a man
  May write ten thousand crowns in bank here. Note,   30

6. **venting:** selling. **14. lewd:** ignorant. **17. utter:** sell; **oaths:** testimonials.
22. Scoto of Mantua: an Italian juggler, then in England. **24. phant'sied:**
imaginatively described.

Mark but his gesture— I do use to observe
The state he keeps in getting up!

PER.   'Tis worth it, sir.

VOLP. Most noble gentlemen, and my worthy patrons, it may seem
strange that I, your Scoto Mantuano, who was ever wont to
fix my bank in the face of the public Piazza, near the shelter
of the portico to the Procuratia, should now, after eight months'
absence from this illustrious city of Venice, humbly retire myself into an obscure nook of the Piazza.

POL. Did not I now object the same?

PER.   Peace, sir.   39

VOLP. Let me tell you: I am not, as your Lombard proverb saith,
cold on my feet; or content to part with my commodities at a
cheaper rate than I accustomed—look not for it. Nor that the
calumnious reports of that impudent detractor, and shame to our
profession (Alessandro Buttone, I mean), who gave out, in
public, I was condemn'd *a' sforzato* to the galleys, for poisoning the Cardinal Bembo's cook, hath at all attached, much
less dejected me. No, no, worthy gentlemen; to tell you true,
I cannot endure to see the rabble of these ground *ciarlitani* that
spread their cloaks on the pavement, as if they meant to do
feats of activity, and then come in lamely, with their mouldy
tales out of Boccaccio, like stale Tabarin, the fabulist; some of
them discoursing their travels, and of their tedious captivity in
the Turk's galleys, when, indeed, were the truth known, they
were the Christian's galleys, where very temperately they ate
bread, and drunk water, as a wholesome penance, enjoin'd
them by their confessors, for base pilferies.   56

POL. Note but his bearing, and contempt of these.

VOLP. These turdy-facy-nasty-paty-lousy-fartical rogues, with one
poor groat's-worth of unprepar'd antimony, finely wrapp'd up
in several *scartoccios,* are able, very well, to kill their twenty a
week, and play; yet these meagre, starv'd spirits, who have half

---

45. a' sforzato: at forced labor. **48. ciarlitani:** smalltime charlatans. **51. fabulist:**
storyteller. **60. scartoccios:** papers.

stopp'd the organs of their minds with earthy oppilations, want
not their favorers among your shrivell'd salad-eating artisans,
who are overjoy'd that they may have their half-pe'rth of
physic; though it purge 'em into another world, 't makes no
matter.   66

POL. Excellent! ha' you heard better language, sir?

VOLP. Well, let 'em go. And, gentlemen, honorable gentlemen,
know that for this time our bank, being thus remov'd from the
clamours of the *canaglia,* shall be the scene of pleasure and
delight; for I have nothing to sell, little or nothing to sell.

POL. I told you, sir, his end.

PER.   You did so, sir.   72

VOLP. I protest I and my six servants are not able to make of this
precious liquor so fast as it is fetch'd away from my lodging by
gentlemen of your city, strangers of the terra-firma, worshipful
merchants, ay, and senators, too, who, ever since my arrival,
have detained me to their uses, by their splendidous liberali-
ties. And worthily. For what avails your rich man to have his
magazines stuff'd with *moscadelli,* or of the purest grape,
when his physicians prescribe him, on pain of death, to drink
nothing but water cocted with aniseeds? O health! health! the
blessing of the rich! the riches of the poor! who can buy thee
at too dear a rate, since there is no enjoying this world without thee? Be not then so sparing of your purses, honorable
gentlemen, as to abridge the natural course of life—   85

PER. You see his end.

POL.   Ay, is 't not good?

VOLP. For, when a humid flux, or catarrh, by the mutability of
air, falls from your head into an arm or shoulder, or any other
part, take you a ducat, or your *cecchine* of gold, and apply to
the place affected; see what good effect it can work. No, no;
'tis this blessed *unguento,* this rare extraction, that hath only

62. oppilations: obstructions of the vital spirits. 70. canaglia: canaille, rabble.
75. terra-firma: mainland. 79. magazines: storage places; moscadelli: muscatel
wine. 81. cocted: boiled.

power to disperse all malignant humors that proceed either of
hot, cold, moist, or windy causes—   93
PER. I would he had put in dry too.
POL.   'Pray you, observe.
VOLP. To fortify the most indigest and crude stomach, ay, were it
of one that, through extreme weakness, vomited blood, applying only a warm napkin to the place, after the unction and
fricace;—for the *vertigine* in the head, putting but a drop into
your nostrils, likewise behind the ears, a most sovereign and
approv'd remedy; the *mal caduco,* cramps, convulsions, paral-
yses, epilepsies, *tremor cordia,* retir'd nerves, ill vapors of the
spleen, stoppings of the liver, the stone, the strangury, *hernia
ventosa, iliaca passio;* stops a *dysenteria* immediately; easeth the
torsion of the small guts; and cures *melancholia hypochondriaca,*
being taken and applied according to my printed receipt.
[*Pointing to his bill and his glass*] For this is the physician,
this the medicine; this counsels, this cures; this gives direction,
this works the effect; and, in sum, both together may be
term'd an abstract of the theoric and practic in the Aescu-
lapian art. 'Twill cost you eight crowns.—And, Zan Fritada,
pray thee sing a verse, extempore, in honor of it.   III
POL. How do you like him, sir?
PER.   Most strangely, I!
POL. Is not his language rare?
PER.   But alchemy,
I never heard the like, or Broughton's books.
NANO. [*Sings*]
        Had old Hippocrates, or Galen,
        That to their books put med'cines all in,
        But known this secret, they had never
        (Of which they will be guilty ever)
        Been murderers of so much paper,
        Or wasted many a hurtless taper;

98. fricace: rubbing; vertigine: dizziness. 100. mal caduco: epilepsy. 101.
tremor cordia: heart trouble; retir'd: shrunken. 103. iliaca passio: colic.
113. But: except for. 114. Broughton: an eccentric preacher.

No Indian drug had e'er been famed,   121
Tobacco, sassafras, not named;
Ne yet of guacum one small stick, sir,
Nor Raymund Lully's great elixir.
Ne had been known the Danish Gonswart,   .
Or Paracelsus, with his long-sword.

PER. All this, yet, will not do; eight crowns is high.   127
VOLP. No more.—Gentlemen, if I had but time to discourse to you
the miraculous effects of this my oil, surnamed *oglio del Scoto,*
with the countless catalogue of those I have cured of th' afore-
said, and many more diseases; the patents and privileges of
all the princes and commonwealths of Christendom; or but the
depositions of those that appear'd on my part, before the
signiory of the Sanitâ and most learned College of Physicians;
where I was authorized, upon notice taken of the admirable
virtues of my medicaments, and mine own excellency in matter
of rare and unknown secrets, not only to disperse them publicly in this famous city, but in all the territories that happily
joy under the government of the most pious and magnificent
states of Italy. But may some other gallant fellow say, "Oh,
there be divers that make profession to have as good, and as
experimented receipts as yours." Indeed, very many have as-
say'd, like apes, in imitation of that which is really and essentially in me, to make of this oil; bestow'd great cost in fur-
naces, stills, alembics, continual fires, and preparation of the
ingredients (as indeed there goes to it six hundred several
simples, besides some quantity of human fat, for the congluti-
nation, which we buy of the anatomists); but when these
practitioners come to the last decoction—blow, blow, puff, puff,
and all flies in fumo. Ha, ha, ha! Poor wretches! I rather pity
their folly and indiscretion, than their loss of time and money;
for those may be recovered by industry; but to be a fool born,
is a disease incurable. For myself, I always from my youth
have endeavor'd to get the rarest secrets, and book them,

134. signiory . . . Sanitâ: directors of the hospital.

either in exchange or for money; I spared nor cost nor labor where anything was worthy to be learned. And, gentlemen, honorable gentlemen, I will undertake, by virtue of chemical art, out of the honorable hat that covers your head, to extract the four elements; that is to say, the fire, air, water, and earth, and return you your felt without burn or stain. For, whilst others have been at the *balloo* I have been at my book; and am now past the craggy paths of study, and come to the flow'ry plains of honor and reputation.   163

POL. I do assure you, sir, that is his aim.

VOLP. But, to our price.

PER.   And that withal, Sir Pol.

VOLP. You all know, honorable gentlemen, I never valu'd this *ampulla,* or vial, at less than eight crowns; but for this time, I am content to be depriv'd of it for six; six crowns is the price, and less in courtesy I know you cannot offer me; take it or leave it, howsoever, both it and I am at your service. I ask you not as the value of the thing, for then I should demand of you a thousand crowns; so the Cardinals Montalto, Fernese, the great Duke of Tuscany, my gossip, with divers other princes, have given me; but I despise money. Only to show my affection to you, honorable gentlemen, and your illustrious state here, I have neglected the messages of these princes, mine own offices, fram'd my journey hither, only to present you with the fruits of my travels.—Tune your voices once more to the touch of your instruments, and give the honorable assembly some delightful recreation.   180

PER. What monstrous and most painful circumstance
Is here, to get some three or four gazets,
Some threepence i' the whole! for that 'twill come to.

NANO. [*Sings*]
        You that would last long, list to my song;
        Make no more coil, but buy of this oil.

---

161. balloo: ball game. **173. gossip:** intimate friend. **182. gazets:** small coins. **185. coil:** fuss.

> Would you be ever fair, and young?
> Stout of teeth, and strong of tongue?
> Tart of palate? quick of ear?
> Sharp of sight? of nostril clear?
> Moist of hand? and light of foot?   190
> Or (I will come nearer to 't)
> Would you live free from all diseases?
> Do the act your mistress pleases,
> Yet fright all aches from your bones?
> Here's a med'cine for the nones.

VOLP. Well, I am in a humor, at this time, to make a present of the small quantity my coffer contains; to the rich in courtesy, and to the poor for God's sake. Wherefore now mark: I ask'd you six crowns; and six crowns, at other times, you have paid me; you shall not give me six crowns, nor five, nor four, nor three, nor two, nor one; nor half a ducat; no, nor a *moccinigo.* Sixpence it will cost you, or six hundred pound—expect no lower price, for, by the banner of my front, I will not bate a bagatine,—that I will have, only, a pledge of your loves, to carry something from amongst you, to show I am not contemn'd by you. Therefore, now, toss your handkerchiefs, cheerfully, cheerfully; and be advertised, that the first heroic spirit that deigns to grace me with a handkerchief, I will give it a little remembrance of something beside, shall please it better than if I had presented it with a double pistolet.   210

PER. Will you be that heroic spark, Sir Pol?

     [CELIA, *at the window, throws down her handkerchief.*]
O, see! the windore has prevented you.

VOLP. Lady, I kiss your bounty; and, for this timely grace you have done your poor Scoto of Mantua, I will return you, over and above my oil, a secret of that high and inestimable nature, shall make you for ever enamor'd on that minute wherein your eye first descended on so mean, yet not altogether to be

195. **nones:** purpose. 212. **prevented:** anticipated.

despis'd, an object. Here is a powder conceal'd in this paper, of which, if I should speak to the worth, nine thousand volumes were but as one page, that page as a line, that line as a word; so short is this pilgrimage of man, which some call life, to the expressing of it. Would I reflect on the price? Why, the whole world is but as an empire, that empire as a province, that province as a bank, that bank as a private purse, to the purchase of it. I will only tell you: it is the powder that made Venus a goddess, given her by Apollo, that kept her perpetually young, clear'd her wrinkles, firm'd her gums, fill'd her skin, color'd her hair; from her deriv'd to Helen, and at the sack of Troy unfortunately lost; till now, in this our age, it was as happily recover'd, by a studious antiquary, out of some ruins of Asia, who sent a moiety of it to the court of France (but much sophisticated), wherewith the ladies there now color their hair. The rest, at this present, remains with me, extracted to a quintessence; so that, wherever it but touches, in youth it perpetually preserves, in age restores the complexion; seats your teeth, did they dance like virginal jacks, firm as a wall; makes them white as ivory, that were black as—   237

SCENE III

[*Enter* CORVINO.]

COR. Spite o' the devil, and my shame! Come down here;
Come down!—No house but mine to make your scene?
Signior Flaminio, will you down, sir? down?
What, is my wife your Franciscina, sir?
No windores on the whole piazza, here,
To make your properties, but mine? but mine?
              [*He beats away the mountebank, etc.*]
Heart! ere tomorrow I shall be new christen'd,

236. virginal jacks: musical keys.

Sc. iii. 4. Franciscina: stock servant girl stage character.

And called the *Pantalone di Bisognosi;*
About the town.

PER.   What should this mean, Sir Pol?

POL. Some trick of state, believe it; I will home.   10

PER. It may be some design on you.

POL.   I know not.
I'll stand upon my guard.

PER.   It is your best, sir.

POL. This three weeks, all my advices, all my letters,
They have been intercepted.

PER.   Indeed, sir?
Best have a care.

POL.   Nay, so I will.

PER. [*Aside*]   This knight,
I may not lose him, for my mirth, till night.   [*Exeunt.*]

SCENE IV. *A room in Volpone's house.*

[*Enter* VOLPONE *and* MOSCA.]

VOLP. O, I am wounded.

MOS.   Where, sir?

VOLP.   Not without;
Those blows were nothing; I could bear them ever.
But angry Cupid, bolting from her eyes,
Hath shot himself into me like a flame;
Where now he flings about his burning heat,
As in a furnace some ambitious fire
Whose vent is stopp'd. The fight is all within me.
I cannot live, except thou help me, Mosca;
My liver melts, and I, without the hope
Of some soft air from her refreshing breath,   10
Am but a heap of cinders.

MOS.   'Las, good sir,
Would you had never seen her.

Sc. iii. 8. **Pantalone di Bisognosi:** fool of the beggars.

VOLP.   Nay, would thou
   Hadst never told me of her.

MOS.   Sir, 'tis true;
   I do confess I was unfortunate,
   And you unhappy; but I am bound in conscience,
   No less than duty, to effect my best
   To your release of torment, and I will, sir.

VOLP. Dear Mosca, shall I hope?

MOS.   Sir, more than dear,
   I will not bid you to despair of aught
   Within a human compass.

VOLP.   O, there spoke   20
   My better angel. Mosca, take my keys,
   Gold, plate, and jewels, all 's at thy devotion;
   Employ them how thou wilt—nay, coin me too—
   So thou in this but crown my longings, Mosca!

MOS. Use but your patience.

VOLP.   So I have.

MOS.   I doubt not
   To bring success to your desires.

VOLP.   Nay, then,
   I not repent me of my late disguise.

MOS. If you can horn him, sir, you need not.

VOLP.   True.
   Besides, I never meant him for my heir.
   Is not the color o' my beard and eyebrows   30
   To make me known?

MOS.   No jot.

VOLP.   I did it well.

MOS. So well, would I could follow you in mine,
   With half the happiness; and yet I would
   Escape your epilogue.

VOLP.   But were they gull'd
   With a belief that I was Scoto?

Sc. iv. 28. **horn**: two-time.

MOS.   Sir,
Scoto himself could hardly have distinguish'd!
I have not time to flatter you now; we'll part,
And as I prosper, so applaud my art.   [*Exeunt.*]

SCENE V. A room in Corvino's house.

[*Enter* CORVINO, *with his sword in his hand, dragging in* CELIA.]
CORV. Death of mine honor, with the city's fool!
A juggling, tooth-drawing, prating mountebank!
And at a public windore! where, whilst he,
With his strain'd action, and his dole of faces,
To his drug-lecture draws your itching ears,
A crew of old, unmarried, noted lechers,
Stood leering up like satyrs; and you smile
Most graciously! and fan your favors forth,
To give your hot spectators satisfaction!
What, was your mountebank their call? their whistle?   10
Or were you enamor'd on his copper rings,
His saffron jewel, with the toad-stone in 't,
Or his embroid'red suit, with the cope-stitch,
Made of a hearse cloth, or his old tilt-feather,
Or his starch'd beard? Well! you shall have him, yes.
He shall come home, and minister unto you
The fricace for the mother. Or, let me see,
I think you'd rather mount! Would you not mount?
Why, if you'll mount, you may; yes, truly, you may.
And so you may be seen, down to th' foot.   20
Get you a cittern, Lady Vanity,
And be a dealer with the virtuous man;
Make one. I'll but protest myself a cuckold,
And save your dowry. I am a Dutchman, I!

Sc. v. 4. dole of faces: horrible expressions. 17. fricace . . . mother: massage
for hysteria. 18. mount: go on the stage. 21. cittern: guitar.

For if you thought me an Italian,
You would be damn'd ere you did this, you whore.
Thou 'dst tremble to imagine that the murder
Of father, mother, brother, all thy race,
Should follow, as the subject of my justice!

CEL. Good sir, have patience!

CORV.   What couldst thou propose   30
Less to thyself, than in this heat of wrath,
And stung with my dishonor, I should strike
This steel into thee, with as many stabs
As thou wert gaz'd upon with goatish eyes?

CEL. Alas, sir, be appeas'd! I could not think
My being at the windore should more now
Move your impatience than at other times.

CORV. No? not to seek and entertain a parley
With a known knave? before a multitude?
You were an actor with your handkerchief!   40
Which he most sweetly kiss'd in the receipt,
And might, no doubt, return it with a letter
And 'point the place where you might meet; your sister's,
Your mother's, or your aunt's might serve the turn.

CEL. Why, dear sir, when do I make these excuses,
Or ever stir abroad, but to the church?
And that so seldom—

CORV.   Well, it shall be less;
And thy restraint before was liberty,
To what I now decree; and therefore mark me.
First, I will have this bawdy light damn'd up;   50
And till 't be done, some two or three yards off
I'll chalk a line; o'er which if thou but chance
To set thy desp'rate foot, more hell, more horror,
More wild remorseless rage shall seize on thee
Than on a conjuror that had heedless left
His circle's safety ere his devil was laid.
Then here's a lock which I will hang upon thee,

50. light: window.

And, now I think on 't, I will keep thee backwards;
Thy lodging shall be backwards, thy walks backwards,
Thy prospect—all be backwards, and no pleasure,   60
That thou shalt know but backwards. Nay, since you force
My honest nature, know it is your own
Being too open, makes me use you thus.
Since you will not contain your subtle nostrils
In a sweet room, but they must snuff the air
Of rank and sweaty passengers—[*Knock within*] one knocks.
Away, and be not seen, pain of thy life;
Nor look toward the windore; if thou dost—
Nay, stay, hear this—let me not prosper, whore,
But I will make thee an anatomy,   70
Dissect thee mine own self, and read a lecture
Upon thee to the city, and in public.
Away!—   [*Exit* CELIA.]
                        [*Enter* SERVITORE.]
          Who's there?

SER.   'Tis Signior Mosca, sir.

SCENE VI

                [CORVINO *and* SERVITORE *remain.*]

CORV. Let him come in. [*Exit* SERVITORE.]—His master's dead!
    There's yet
    Some good to help the bad.—[*Enter* MOSCA.] My Mosca, wel-
    come;
    I guess your news.

MOS.   I fear you cannot, sir.

CORV. Is 't not his death?

MOS.   Rather the contrary.

CORV. Not his recovery?

MOS.   Yes, sir.

66. **passengers:** passers-by.

CORV.   I am curs'd;
    I am bewitch'd; my crosses meet to vex me.
    How? how? how? how?
MOS.   Why, sir, with Scoto's oil!
    Corbaccio and Voltore brought of it,
    Whilst I was busy in an inner room—
CORV. Death! that damn'd mountebank! but for the law,   10
    Now, I could kill the rascal. 'T cannot be
    His oil should have that virtue. Ha' not I
    Known him a common rogue, come fiddling in
    To th' *osteria,* with a tumbling whore,
    And, when he has done all his forc'd tricks, been glad
    Of a poor spoonful of dead wine, with flies in 't?
    It cannot be. All his ingredients
    Are a sheep's gall, a roasted bitch's marrow,
    Some few sod earwigs, pounded caterpillars,
    A little capon's grease, and fasting spittle: 20
    I know 'em to a dram.
MOS.   I know not, sir;
    But some on 't, there, they pour'd into his ears,
    Some in his nostrils, and recover'd him;
    Applying but the fricace.
CORV.   Pox o' that fricace.
MOS. And, since, to seem the more officious
    And flatt'ring of his health, there, they have had,
    At extreme fees, the college of physicians
    Consulting on him, how they might restore him;
    Where one would have a cataplasm of spices,
    Another a flay'd ape clapp'd to his breast,   30
    A third would ha' it a dog, a fourth an oil,
    With wildcats' skins. At last, they all resolv'd
    That, to preserve him, was no other means
    But some young woman must be straight sought out,
    Lusty, and full of juice, to sleep by him;

Sc. vi. 14. osteria: inn; **tumbling whore:** female acrobat. **19. sod:** boiled
29. cataplasm: poultice.

And to this service most unhappily,
And most unwillingly, am I now employ'd,
Which here I thought to pre-acquaint you with,
For your advice, since it concerns you most;
Because I would not do that thing might cross   40
Your ends, on whom I have my whole dependence, sir.
Yet, if I do not they may delate
My slackness to my patron, work me out
Of his opinion; and there all your hopes,
Ventures, or whatsoever, are all frustrate.
I do but tell you, sir. Besides, they are all
Now striving who shall first present him. Therefore—
I could entreat you, briefly, conclude somewhat:
Prevent 'em if you can.

CORV.   Death to my hopes!
This is my villainous fortune! Best to hire   50
Some common courtesan!

MOS.   Ay, I thought on that, sir;
But they are all so subtle, full of art—
And age again doting and flexible,
So as—I cannot tell—we may, perchance,
Light on a quean may cheat us all.

CORV.   'Tis true.

MOS. No, no; it must be one that has no tricks, sir,
Some simple thing, a creature made unto it;
Some wench you may command. Ha' you no kinswoman?
Gods so—Think, think, think, think, think, think, think,
    sir.
One o' the doctors offer'd there his daughter.   60

CORV. How!

MOS.   Yes, Signior Lupo, the physician.

CORV. His daughter!

MOS.   And a virgin, sir. Why, alas,
He knows the state of 's body, what it is:

42. delate: blame. 57. made unto: coached for.

That naught can warm his blood, sir, but a fever,
Nor any incantation raise his spirit;
A long forgetfulness hath seiz'd that part.
Besides, sir, who shall know it? Someone or two—

CORV. I pray thee give me leave.—[*Stepping aside*] If any man
But I had had this luck—The thing in 't self,
I know, is nothing.—Wherefore should not I   70
As well command my blood and my affections
As this dull doctor? In the point of honor,
The cases are all one of wife and daughter.

MOS. [*Aside*] I hear him coming.

CORV. [*Aside*] She shall do 't; 'tis done.
'Slight! if this doctor, who is not engag'd,
Unless 't be for his counsel, which is nothing,
Offer his daughter, what should I, that am
So deeply in? I will prevent him. Wretch!
Covetous wretch!—Mosca, I have determin'd.

MOS. How, sir?

CORV.   We'll make all sure. The party you wot of   80
Shall be mine own wife, Mosca.

MOS.   Sir, the thing,
But that I would not seem to counsel you,
I should have motion'd to you, at the first;
And make your count, you have cut all their throats.
Why! 'tis directly taking a possession!
And in his next fit, we may let him go.
'Tis but to pull the pillow from his head,
And he is throttled; it had been done before
But for your scrupulous doubts.

CORV.   Ay, a plague on 't;
My conscience fools my wit! Well, I'll be brief,   90
And so be thou, lest they should be before us.
Go home; prepare him; tell him with what zeal
And willingness I do it. Swear it was

83. **motion'd**: proposed.

On the first hearing, as thou mayst do, truly,
Mine own free motion.

MOS.   Sir, I warrant you,
I'll so possess him with it, that the rest
Of his starv'd clients shall be banish'd all;
And only you receiv'd. But come not, sir,
Until I send, for I have something else
To ripen for your good—you must not know 't.   100

CORV. But do not you forget to send, now.

MOS.   Fear not.   [*Exit.*]

SCENE VII

[CORVINO *remains.*]

CORV. Where are you, wife? My Celia! Wife!

[*Enter* CELIA.]

                                —What, blubbering?
Come, dry those tears. I think thou thought'st me in earnest;
Ha? By this light I talk'd so but to try thee.
Methinks, the lightness of the occasion
Should ha' confirm'd thee. Come, I am not jealous.

CEL. No?

CORV.   Faith I am not, I, nor never was;
It is a poor, unprofitable humor.
Do not I know, if women have a will,
They'll do 'gainst all the watches o' the world,
And that the fiercest spies are tam'd with gold?   10
Tut, I am confident in thee, thou shalt see 't;
And see I'll give thee cause, too, to believe it.
Come, kiss me.—Go, and make thee ready straight,
In all thy best attire, thy choicest jewels,
Put 'em all on, and, with 'em, thy best looks:
We are invited to a solemn feast,
At old Volpone's, where it shall appear
How far I am free from jealousy or fear.   [*Exeunt.*]

ACT THREE

SCENE I. *A street.*

[*Enter* MOSCA.]

MOS. I fear I shall begin to grow in love
    With my dear self and my most prosp'rous parts;
    They do so spring and burgeon. I can feel
    A whimsy i' my blood—I know not how—
    Success hath made me wanton. I could skip
    Out of my skin now, like a subtle snake,
    I am so limber. Oh! your parasite
    Is a most precious thing, dropp'd from above,
    Not bred 'mongst clods and clotpolls, here on earth.
    I muse the mystery was not made a science,   10
    It is so liberally profess'd! Almost
    All the wise world is little else, in nature,
    But parasites or sub-parasites. And yet
    I mean not those that have your bare town-art,
    To know who's fit to feed 'em; have no house,
    No family, no care, and therefore mold
    Tales for men's ears, to bait that sense; or get
    Kitchen-invention, and some stale receipts
    To please the belly, and the groin; nor those,
    With their court dog-tricks, that can fawn and fleer,   20
    Make their revenue out of legs and faces,
    Echo my Lord, and lick away a mote:
    But your fine, elegant rascal, that can rise
    And stoop, almost together, like an arrow;
    Shoot through the air as nimbly as a star;
    Turn short as doth a swallow; and be here,
    And there, and here, and yonder, all at once;
    Present to any humor, all occasion;

Act III. Sc. i. 10. mystery: profession. **17. bait:** feed **21. legs:** bows.

And change a visor swifter than a thought!
This is the creature had the art born with him;   30
Toils not to learn it, but doth practise it
Out of most excellent nature; and such sparks
Are the true parasites, others but their zanies.

SCENE II

[*Enter* BONARIO.]

MOS. Who's this? Bonario, old Corbaccio's son?
　　　The person I was bound to seek. Fair sir,
　　　You are happ'ly met.
BON. 　　　　　　　　　That cannot be by thee.
MOS. Why, sir?
BON. 　　　　　Nay, 'pray thee know thy way, and leave me.
　　　I would be loth to interchange discourse
　　　With such a mate as thou art.
MOS. 　　　　　　　　　　　Courteous sir,
　　　Scorn not my poverty.
BON. 　　　　　　　　Not I, by Heaven;
　　　But thou shalt give me leave to hate thy baseness.
MOS. Baseness!
BON. 　　　　　Ay; answer me, is not thy sloth
　　　Sufficient argument? thy flattery?   10
　　　Thy means of feeding?
MOS. 　　　　　　　　　Heaven be good to me.
　　　These imputations are too common, sir,
　　　And eas'ly stuck on virtue, when she's poor.
　　　You are unequal to me, and howe'er
　　　Your sentence may be righteous, yet you are not,
　　　That, ere you know me, thus proceed in censure.
　　　St. Mark bear witness 'gainst you, 'tis inhuman.   [*Weeps.*]

29. visor: expression, put on like a mask.

Sc. ii. 14. unequal: unjust.

BON. [*Aside*] What! does he weep? the sign is soft and good!
 I do repent me that I was so harsh.

MOS. 'Tis true, that, sway'd by strong necessity,   20
 I am enforc'd to eat my careful bread
 With too much obsequy; 'tis true, beside,
 That I am fain to spin mine own poor raiment
 Out of my mere observance, being not born
 To a free fortune; but that I have done
 Base offices, in rending friends asunder,
 Dividing families, betraying counsels,
 Whispering false lies, or mining men with praises,
 Train'd their credulity with perjuries,
 Corrupted chastity, or am in love   30
 With mine own tender ease, but would not rather
 Prove the most rugged and laborious course,
 That might redeem my present estimation,
 Let me here perish, in all hope of goodness.

BON. [*Aside*] This cannot be a personated passion!—
 I was to blame, so to mistake thy nature;
 'Pray thee forgive me; and speak out thy bus'ness.

MOS. Sir, it concerns you; and though I may seem
 At first to make a main offence in manners,
 And in my gratitude unto my master,   40
 Yet for the pure love which I bear all right,
 And hatred of the wrong, I must reveal it.
 This very hour your father is in purpose
 To disinherit you—

BON.   How!

MOS.   And thrust you forth,
 As a mere stranger to his blood; 'tis true, sir.
 The work no way engageth me, but as
 I claim an interest in the general state
 Of goodness and true virtue, which I hear

22. **obsequy:** obsequiousness. 24. **observance:** service. 29. **Train'd:** led on.

T' abound in you; and for which mere respect,
Without a second aim, sir, I have done it.   50
BON. This tale hath lost thee much of the late trust
    Thou hadst with me; it is impossible.
    I know not how to lend it any thought
    My father should be so unnatural.
MOS. It is a confidence that well becomes
    Your piety; and form'd, no doubt, it is
    From your own simple innocence; which makes
    Your wrong more monstrous and abhorr'd. But, sir,
    I now will tell you more. This very minute,
    It is, or will be doing; and if you   60
    Shall be but pleas'd to go with me, I'll bring you,
    I dare not say where you shall see, but where
    Your ear shall be a witness of the deed;
    Hear yourself written bastard, and profess'd
    The common issue of the earth.
BON.   I'm maz'd!
MOS. Sir, if I do it not, draw your just sword,
    And score your vengeance on my front and face;
    Mark me your villain. You have too much wrong,
    And I do suffer for you, sir. My heart   69
    Weeps blood in anguish—
BON.   Lead. I follow thee.   [*Exeunt.*]

SCENE III. *A room in Volpone's house.*

[*Enter* VOLPONE, NANO, ANDROGYNO, *and* CASTRONE.]
VOLP. Mosca stays long, methinks.—Bring forth your sports,
    And help to make the wretched time more sweet.
NAN. Dwarf, fool, and eunuch, well met here we be.
    A question it were now, whether of us three,
    Being all the known delicates of a rich man,
    In pleasing him, claim the precedency can?

CAS. I claim for myself.

AND.   And so doth the fool.

NAN. 'Tis foolish indeed; let me set you both to school.
     First for your dwarf, he's little and witty,
     And everything, as it is little, is pretty;   10
     Else why do men say to a creature of my shape,
     So soon as they see him, "It's a pretty little ape"?
     And why a pretty ape, but for pleasing imitation
     Of greater men's action, in a ridiculous fashion?
     Beside, this feat body of mine doth not crave
     Half the meat, drink, and cloth, one of your bulks will have.
     Admit your fool's face be the mother of laughter,
     Yet, for his brain, it must always come after;
     And though that do feed him, it's a pitiful case,
     His body is beholding to such a bad face.   20

                         [*One knocks.*]

VOLP. Who's there? My couch; away! Look, Nano, see.—

                    [*Exeunt* ANDROGYNO *and* CASTRONE.]

     Give me my caps first—go, inquire. [*Exit* NANO.] Now, Cupid
     Send it be Mosca, and with fair return.

                    [*Re-enter* NANO.]

NAN. It is the beauteous Madam—

VOLP.   Would-be—is it?

NAN. The same.

VOLP.   Now torment on me! Squire her in;
     For she will enter, or dwell here for ever.
     Nay, quickly. [*Exit* NANO; VOLPONE *retires to his couch*.]—That
        my fit were past! I fear
     A second hell too, that my loathing this
     Will quite expel my appetite to the other.
     Would she were taking now her tedious leave.   30
     Lord, how it threats me what I am to suffer!

Sc. iii. 15. feat: dainty.

SCENE IV

[*Enter* NANO *and* LADY POLITIC WOULD-BE.]

LADY. I thank you, good sir. Pray you signify
  Unto your patron I am here.—This band
  Shows not my neck enough.—I trouble you, sir;
  Let me request you bid one of my women
  Come hither to me. [*Exit* NANO.]—In good faith, I am dress'd
  Most favorably today; it is no matter;
  'Tis well enough.
          [*Re-enter* NANO *with a* WAITING WOMAN.]
              Look, see, these petulant things!
  How they have done this!
VOLP. [*Aside*]   I do feel the fever
  Ent'ring in at mine ears; oh, for a charm
  To fright it hence.
LADY.   Come nearer. Is this curl   10
  In his right place? or this? Why is this higher
  Than all the rest? You ha' not wash'd your eyes yet?
  Or do they not stand even i' your head?
  Where's your fellow? call her.   [*Exit* WOMAN.]
NAN. [*Aside*]   Now, St. Mark
  Deliver us! anon she'll beat her women,
  Because her nose is red.
          [*Re-enter* WOMAN *with another.*]
LADY.   I pray you view
  This tire, forsooth. Are all things apt, or no?
WOM. One hair a little here sticks out, forsooth.
LADY. Does 't so, forsooth! and where was your dear sight,
  When it did so, forsooth? What now! bird-ey'd?   20
  And you, too? 'Pray you, both approach and mend it.
  Now, by that light I muse you're not asham'd!

Sc. iv. 17. tire: headdress.

I, that have preach'd these things so oft unto you,
Read you the principles, argu'd all the grounds,
Disputed every fitness, every grace,
Call'd you to counsel of so frequent dressings—

NAN. [*Aside*] More carefully than of your fame or honor.

LADY. Made you acquainted what an ample dowry
The knowledge of these things would be unto you,
Able alone to get you noble husbands   30
At your return; and you thus to neglect it!
Besides, you seeing what a curious nation
Th' Italians are, what will they say of me?
"The English lady cannot dress herself."
Here's a fine imputation to our country!
Well, go your ways, and stay i' the next room.
This fucus was too coarse too; it's no matter.—
Good sir, you'll give 'em entertainment?

[*Exeunt* NANO *and* WAITING WOMEN.]

VOLP. [*Aside*] The storm comes toward me.

LADY. [*Going to the couch*]   How does my Volpone?

VOLP. Troubled with noise; I cannot sleep. I dreamt   40
That a strange Fury ent'red now my house,
And, with the dreadful tempest of her breath,
Did cleave my roof asunder.

LADY.   Believe me, and I
Had the most fearful dream, could I remember 't—

VOLP. [*Aside*] Out on my fate! I ha' giv'n her the occasion
How to torment me: she will tell me hers.

LADY. Methought the golden mediocrity,
Polite, and delicate—

VOLP.   O, if you do love me,
No more; I sweat, and suffer, at the mention
Of any dream. Feel how I tremble yet.   50

LADY. Alas, good soul! the passion of the heart.
Seed-pearl were good now, boil'd with syrup of apples,

32. curious: fastidious. 37. fucus: rouge.

Tincture of gold, and coral, citron-pills,
Your elecampane root, myrobalans—
VOLP. Ay me, I have ta'en a grasshopper by the wing!
LADY. Burnt silk and amber. You have muscadel
    Good i' the house—
VOLP.   You will not drink, and part?
LADY. No, fear not that. I doubt we shall not get
    Some English saffron—half a dram would serve;
    Your sixteen cloves, a little musk, dried mints,   60
    Bugloss, and barley meal—
VOLP. [*Aside*]   She's in again;
    Before I feign'd diseases—now I have one.
LADY. And these appli'd with a right scarlet cloth—
VOLP. [*Aside*] Another flood of words! a very torrent!
LADY. Shall I, sir, make you a poultice?
VOLP.   No, no, no.
    I am very well; you need prescribe no more.
LADY. I have a little studied physic; but now
    I'm all for music, save i' the forenoons,
    An hour or two for painting. I would have
    A lady, indeed, t' have all letters and arts,   70
    Be able to discourse, to write, to paint;
    But principal, as Plato holds, your music
    (And so does wise Pythagoras, I take it)
    Is your true rapture, when there is concent
    In face, in voice, and clothes, and is, indeed,
    Our sex's chiefest ornament.
VOLP.   The poet
    As old in time as Plato, and as knowing,
    Says that your highest female grace is silence.
LADY. Which o' your poets? Petrarch, or Tasso, or Dante?
    Guarini? Ariosto? Aretine?   80
    Cieco di Hadria? I have read them all.

---

54. myrobalans: dried fruit containing tannin, and regarded as a cure for melancholy like the preceding items. **55. grasshopper:** cicada. **74. concent:** harmony.

VOLP. [*Aside*] Is everything a cause to my destruction?

LADY. I think I ha' two or three of 'em about me.

VOLP. [*Aside*] The sun, the sea, will sooner both stand still
    Than her eternal tongue! Nothing can 'scape it.

LADY. Here's *Pastor Fido*—

VOLP. [*Aside*]   Profess obstinate silence;
    That's now my safest.

LADY.   All our English writers,
    I mean such as are happy in th' Italian,
    Will deign to steal out of this author, mainly;
    Almost as much as from Montagnié: 90
    He has so modern and facile a vein,
    Fitting the time, and catching the court-ear.
    Your Petrarch is more passionate, yet he,
    In days of sonneting, trusted 'em with much.
    Dante is hard, and few can understand him.
    But for a desperate wit, there's Aretine!
    Only, his pictures are a little obscene—
    You mark me not!

VOLP.   Alas, my mind's perturb'd.

LADY. Why, in such cases, we must cure ourselves,
    Make use of our philosophy—

VOLP.   Oh, ay me!   100

LADY. And as we find our passions do rebel,
    Encounter 'em with reason, or divert 'em,
    By giving scope unto some other humor
    Of lesser danger; as, in politic bodies,
    There's nothing more doth overwhelm the judgment,
    And clouds the understanding, than too much
    Settling and fixing, and, as 'twere, subsiding
    Upon one object. For the incorporating
    Of these same outward things into that part
    Which we call mental, leaves some certain faeces   110

86. Pastor Fido: *The Faithful Shepherd,* a pastoral drama by Guarini. **94.
trusted:** provided.

That stop the organs, and, as Plato says,
Assassinates our knowledge.

VOLP. [*Aside*]   Now, the spirit
Of patience help me.

LADY.   Come, in faith, I must
Visit you more, a'days, and make you well—
Laugh and be lusty.

VOLP. [*Aside*]   My good angel save me!

LADY. There was but one sole man in all the world
With whom I e'er could sympathise; and he
Would lie you, often, three, four hours together
To hear me speak; and be sometime so rapt,
As he would answer me quite from the purpose,   120
Like you, and you are like him, just. I'll discourse,
An 't be but only, sir, to bring you asleep,
How we did spend our time and loves together,
For some six years.

VOLP.   Oh, oh, oh, oh, oh, oh!

LADY. For we were coaetanei, and brought up—

VOLP. [*Aside*] Some power, some fate, some fortune rescue me!

SCENE V

[*Enter* MOSCA.]

MOS. God save you, madam.

LADY.   Good sir.

VOLP.   Mosca! welcome—
[*Aside*] Welcome to my redemption.

MOS. [*Aside*]   Why, sir?

VOLP. [*Aside*]   Oh,
Rid me of this my torture, quickly, there;
My madam with the everlasting voice.
The bells, in time of pestilence, ne'er made

125. coaetanei: of the same age.

Like noise, or were in that perpetual motion—
The cockpit comes not near it. All my house,
But now, steam'd like a bath with her thick breath,
A lawyer could not have been heard; nor scarce
Another woman, such a hail of words   10
She has let fall. For hell's sake, rid her hence.

MOS. Has she presented?

VOLP.   Oh, I do not care:
I'll take her absence upon any price,
With any loss.

MOS.   Madam—

LADY.   I ha' brought your patron
A toy, a cap here, of mine own work—

MOS.   'Tis well.
I had forgot to tell you I saw your knight
Where you'd little think it—

LADY.   Where?

MOS.   Marry,
Where yet, if you make haste, you may apprehend him,
Rowing upon the water in a gondola,
With the most cunning courtesan of Venice.   20

LADY. Is 't true?

MOS.   Pursue 'em, and believe your eyes;
Leave me to make your gift. [*Exit* LADY.]—I knew 'twould
        take;
For, lightly, they that use themselves most licence,
Are still most jealous.

VOLP.   Mosca, hearty thanks
For thy quick fiction, and delivery of me.
Now to my hopes, what say'st thou?
                        [*Re-enter* LADY.]

LADY.   But do you hear, sir?—

VOLP. [*Aside*] Again! I fear a paroxysm.

LADY.   Which way
Row'd they together?

Sc. v. 12. presented: given you a present. 23. lightly: generally.

MOS.   Toward the Rialto.

LADY. I pray you lend me your dwarf.

MOS.   I pray you take him.

                                    [*Exit* LADY.]

    Your hopes, sir, are like happy blossoms, fair,   30
    And promise timely fruit, if you will stay
    But the maturing. Keep you at your couch;
    Corbaccio will arrive straight, with the will;
    When he is gone, I'll tell you more.   [*Exit.*]

VOLP.   My blood,
    My spirits are return'd; I am alive;
    And, like your wanton gamester at primero,
    Whose thought had whisper'd to him, not go less,
    Methinks I lie, and draw—for an encounter.

SCENE VI

[*Enter* MOSCA *and* BONARIO.]

MOS. Sir, here conceal'd [*Opening a door*] you may hear all. But,
    pray you,
    Have patience, sir; [*One knocks.*] the same 's your father
    knocks.
    I am compell'd to leave you.   [*Exit.*]

BON.   Do so.—Yet
    Cannot my thought imagine this a truth. [*Goes in.*]

SCENE VII

[*Enter* MOSCA, CORVINO, *and* CELIA.]

MOS. Death on me! You are come too soon. What meant you?
    Did not I say I would send?

---

36. primero: a card game. **37. go:** bet. **38. draw, encounter:** terms in primero,
used punningly as Volpone draws the curtain.

CORV.   Yes, but I fear'd
  You might forget it, and then they prevent us.
MOS. Prevent!—[*Aside*] Did e'er man haste so for his horns?
  A courtier would not ply it so for a place.—
  Well, now there is no helping it, stay here;
  I'll presently return.   [*Exit.*]
CORV.   Where are you, Celia?
  You know not wherefore I have brought you hither?
CEL. Not well, except you told me.
CORV.   Now I will.
  Hark hither.   [*They retire to one side.*]
                        [*Re-enter* MOSCA.]
MOS. [*To* BONARIO] Sir, your father hath sent word   10
  It will be half an hour ere he come;
  And therefore, if you please to walk the while
  Into that gallery—at the upper end,
  There are some books to entertain the time;
  And I'll take care no man shall come unto you, sir.
BON. Yes, I will stay there.—[*Aside*] I do doubt this fellow. [*Exit.*]
MOS. [*Looking after him*] There; he is far enough; he can hear
      nothing.
  And for his father, I can keep him off.
CORV. [*Advancing with* CELIA] Nay, now, there is no starting back,
      and therefore,
  Resolve upon it; I have so decreed.   20
  It must be done. Nor would I move 't afore,
  Because I would avoid all shifts and tricks,
  That might deny me.
CEL.   Sir, let me beseech you,
  Affect not these strange trials; if you doubt
  My chastity, why, lock me up for ever;
  Make me the heir of darkness. Let me live
  Where I may please your fears, if not your trust.
CORV. Believe it, I have no such humor, I.
  All that I speak I mean; yet I am not mad;

Sc. vii. 9. except . . . me: unless you tell me. 21. move 't: suggest it.

Not horn-mad, see you? Go to, show yourself   30
Obedient, and a wife.

CEL.   O Heaven!

CORV.   I say it,
  Do so.

CEL.   Was this the train?

CORV.   I have told you reasons;
  What the physicians have set down; how much
  It may concern me; what my engagements are;
  My means, and the necessity of those means
  For my recovery. Wherefore, if you be
  Loyal, and mine, be won; respect my venture.

CEL. Before your honor?

CORV.   Honor! tut, a breath.
  There's no such thing in nature; a mere term
  Invented to awe fools. What is my gold   40
  The worse for touching, clothes for being look'd on?
  Why, this 's no more. An old decrepit wretch,
  That has no sense, no sinew; takes his meat
  With others' fingers; only knows to gape
  When you do scald his gums; a voice, a shadow;
  And what can this man hurt you?

CEL. [*Aside*]   Lord! what spirit
  Is this hath ent'red him?

CORV.   And for your fame,
  That's such a jig; as if I would go tell it,
  Cry it on the Piazza! Who shall know it
  But he that cannot speak it, and this fellow,   50
  Whose lips are i' my pocket? Save yourself—
  If you'll proclaim 't, you may,—I know no other
  Should come to know it.

CEL.   Are Heaven and saints then nothing?
  Will they be blind or stupid?

CORV.   How?

30. **horn-mad:** madly jealous. 32. **train:** plot. 48. **jig:** joke.

CEL. Good sir,
  Be jealous still, emulate them; and think
  What hate they burn with toward every sin.

CORV. I grant you; if I thought it were a sin
  I would not urge you. Should I offer this
  To some young Frenchman, or hot Tuscan blood
  That had read Aretine, conn'd all his prints,   60
  Knew every quirk within lust's labyrinth,
  And were profess'd critic in lechery;
  And I would look upon him, and applaud him;
  This were a sin: but here, 'tis contrary,
  A pious work, mere charity, for physic,
  And honest polity, to assure mine own.

CEL. O Heaven! canst thou suffer such a change?

VOLP. [*Aside*] Thou art mine honor, Mosca, and my pride,
  My joy, my tickling, my delight! Go bring 'em.

MOS. Please you draw near, sir.

CORV. Come on, what—   70
  You will not be rebellious? By that light—

MOS. Sir, Signior Corvino, here, is come to see you.

VOLP. Oh.

MOS. And hearing of the consultation had,
  So lately, for your health, is come to offer,
  Or rather, sir, to prostitute—

CORV. Thanks, sweet Mosca.

MOS. Freely, unask'd, or unentreated—

CORV. Well.

MOS. As the true fervent instance of his love,
  His own most fair and proper wife, the beauty
  Only of price in Venice—

CORV. 'Tis well urg'd.

MOS. To be your comfortress, and to preserve you.   80

VOLP. Alas, I am past, already! 'Pray you, thank him
  For his good care and promptness; but for that,

78. **proper**: very own. 79. **only of price**: most precious.

'Tis a vain labor e'en to fight 'gainst Heaven;
Applying fire to a stone—uh, uh, uh, uh!—
Making a dead leaf grow again. I take
His wishes gently, though; and you may tell him
What I have done for him; marry, my state is hopeless!
Will him to pray for me; and t' use his fortune
With reverence when he comes to 't.

MOS.   Do you hear, sir?

Go to him with your wife.

CORV.   Heart of my father!   90
Wilt thou persist thus? Come, I pray thee, come.
Thou seest 'tis nothing, Celia. By this hand,
I shall grow violent. Come, do 't, I say.

CEL. Sir, kill me, rather. I will take down poison,
Eat burning coals, do anything—

CORV.   Be damn'd!
Heart, I will drag thee hence home by the hair;
Cry thee a strumpet through the streets; rip up
Thy mouth unto thine ears; and slit thy nose,
Like a raw rochet—Do not tempt me, come;
Yield; I am loth—Death! I will buy some slave   100
Whom I will kill, and bind thee to him alive,
And at my windore hang you forth, devising
Some monstrous crime, which I, in capital letters,
Will eat into thy flesh with aqua fortis,
And burning cor'sives, on this stubborn breast.
Now, by the blood thou hast incens'd, I'll do it!

CEL. Sir, what you please, you may; I am your martyr.

CORV. Be not thus obstinate; I ha' not deserv'd it.
Think who it is entreats you. 'Pray thee, sweet;
Good faith, thou shalt have jewels, gowns, attires,   110
What thou wilt think, and ask. Do but go kiss him.
Or touch him but. For my sake. At my suit.

99. rochet: a red, large-headed fish. 104. aqua fortis: nitric acid.

This once. No? not? I shall remember this.
Will you disgrace me thus? Do you thirst my undoing?
MOS. Nay, gentle lady, be advis'd.
CORV.   No, no.
She has watch'd her time. God's precious, this is scurvy,
'Tis very scurvy; and you are—
MOS.   Nay, good sir.
CORV. An errant locust—by heaven, a locust!—Whore,
Crocodile, that hast thy tears prepar'd,
Expecting how thou'lt bid 'em flow.
MOS.   Nay, 'pray you, sir!   120
She will consider.
CEL.   Would my life would serve
To satisfy—
CORV.   'Sdeath! if she would but speak to him,
And save my reputation, 'twere somewhat;
But spitefully to affect my utter ruin!
MOS. [*Aside to* CORVINO] Ay, now you have put your fortune in her
      hands.
Why, i' faith, it is her modesty, I must quit her.
If you were absent, she would be more coming;
I know it, and dare undertake for her.
What woman can before her husband? 'Pray you,
Let us depart and leave her here.
CORV.   Sweet Celia,   130
Thou mayst redeem all yet; I'll say no more.
If not, esteem yourself as lost.—Nay, stay there.
                                [*Exit with* MOSCA.]
CEL. O God, and his good angels! whither, whither,
Is shame fled human breasts? that with such ease,
Men dare put off your honors, and their own?
Is that which ever was a cause of life
Now plac'd beneath the basest circumstance,
And modesty an exile made, for money?

118. errant: out-and-out. 126. quit: defend. 128. undertake: vouch. 136. cause
of life: marriage.

VOLP. Ay, in Corvino, and such earth-fed minds,
                                    [*He leaps off from his couch.*]
    That never tasted the true heav'n of love.   140
    Assure thee, Celia, he that would sell thee,
    Only for hope of gain, and that uncertain,
    He would have sold his part of Paradise
    For ready money, had he met a copeman.
    Why art thou maz'd to see me thus reviv'd?
    Rather applaud thy beauty's miracle;
    'Tis thy great work, that hath, not now alone,
    But sundry times, rais'd me, in several shapes,
    And, but this morning, like a mountebank,
    To see thee at thy windore; ay, before   150
    I would have left my practice for thy love,
    In varying figures I would have contended
    With the blue Proteus, or the horned flood.
    Now art thou welcome.

CEL.   Sir!

VOLP.   Nay, fly me not,
    Nor let thy false imagination
    That I was bedrid, make thee think I am so—
    Thou shalt not find it. I am now as fresh,
    As hot, as high, and in as jovial plight
    As when, in that so celebrated scene,
    At recitation of our comedy,   160
    For entertainment of the great Valois,
    I acted young Antinoüs, and attracted
    The eyes and ears of all the ladies present,
    T' admire each graceful gesture, note, and footing.   [*Sings.*]

        Come, my Celia, let us prove,
        While we can, the sports of love.
        Time will not be ours for ever,
        He, at length, our good will sever.

---

144. copeman: buyer. **151. practice:** plotting. **153. horned flood:** Oceanus.
161. Valois: Henry III of France at Venice in 1574. **165. prove:** try.

Spend not then his gifts in vain.
Suns that set may rise again;   170
But if once we lose this light,
'Tis with us perpetual night.
Why should we defer our joys?
Fame and rumor are but toys.
Cannot we delude the eyes
Of a few poor household spies?
Or his easier ears beguile,
Thus removed by our wile?
'Tis no sin love's fruits to steal,
But the sweet thefts to reveal;   180
To be taken, to be seen,
These have crimes accounted been.

CEL. Some serene blast me, or dire lightning strike
    This my offending face.
VOLP.   Why droops my Celia?
Thou hast, in place of a base husband, found
A worthy lover; use thy fortune well,
With secrecy and pleasure. See, behold,
What thou art queen of; not in expectation,
As I feed others, but possess'd and crown'd.
See, here, a rope of pearl; and each more orient   190
Than that the brave Egyptian queen carous'd.
Dissolve and drink 'em. See, a carbuncle,
May put out both the eyes of our St. Mark;
A diamond would have bought Lollia Paulina,
When she came in like starlight, hid with jewels
That were the spoils of provinces; take these,
And wear and lose 'em; yet remains an earring
To purchase them again, and this whole state.
A gem but worth a private patrimony

183. serene: poisonous evening fog. **192. carbuncle:** ruby. **194. Lollia Paulina:** wife of the emperor Caligula.

Is nothing; we will eat such at a meal.   200
The heads of parrots, tongues of nightingales,
The brains of peacocks and of estriches,
Shall be our food; and, could we get the phoenix,
Though nature lost her kind, she were our dish.

CEL. Good sir, these things might move a mind affected
With such delights; but I, whose innocence
Is all I can think wealthy, or worth th' enjoying,
And which, once lost, I have naught to lose beyond it,
Cannot be taken with these sensual baits.
If you have conscience—

VOLP.   'Tis the beggar's virtue;   210
If thou hast wisdom, hear me, Celia.
Thy baths shall be the juice of July flowers,
Spirit of roses and of violets,
The milk of unicorns, and panthers' breath
Gather'd in bags and mix'd with Cretan wines.
Our drink shall be prepared gold and amber,
Which we will take until my roof whirl round
With the vertigo; and my dwarf shall dance,
My eunuch sing, my fool make up the antic,
Whilst we, in changed shapes, act Ovid's tales: 220
Thou like Europa now, and I like Jove;
Then I like Mars, and thou like Erycine;
So of the rest, till we have quite run through
And wearied all the fables of the gods.
Then will I have thee in more modern forms,
Attired like some sprightly dame of France,
Brave Tuscan lady, or proud Spanish beauty;
Sometimes unto the Persian sophy's wife,
Or the Grand Signior's mistress; and, for change,
To one of our most artful courtesans,   230
Or some quick Negro, or cold Russian;
And I will meet thee in as many shapes,

204. kind: unique species. 222. Erycine: Venus.

Where we may so transfuse our wand'ring souls
Out at our lips, and score up sums of pleasures,

> That the curious shall not know
> How to tell them as they flow;
> And the envious, when they find
> What their number is, be pin'd.

CEL. If you have ears that will be pierc'd—or eyes
That can be open'd—a heart, may be touch'd—   240
Or any part that yet sounds man about you—
If you have touch of holy saints, or Heaven,
Do me the grace to let me 'scape. If not,
Be bountiful and kill me. You do know
I am a creature hither ill betray'd
By one whose shame I would forget it were;
If you will deign me neither of these graces,
Yet feed your wrath, sir, rather than your lust,
(It is a vice comes nearer manliness)
And punish that unhappy crime of nature,   250
Which you miscall my beauty; flay my face,
Or poison it with ointments for seducing
Your blood to this rebellion. Rub these hands
With what may cause an eating leprosy,
E'en to my bones and marrow, anything
That may disfavor me, save in my honor.
And I will kneel to you, pray for you, pay down
A thousand hourly vows, sir, for your health;
Report, and think you virtuous—
VOLP.   Think me cold,
Frozen, and impotent, and so report me!   260
That I had Nestor's hernia, thou wouldst think.
I do degenerate, and abuse my nation,
To play with opportunity thus long;
I should have done the act, and then have parley'd.
Yield, or I'll force thee.

CEL.   O! just God!

VOLP.   In vain—

BON. [*Leaps out from where* MOSCA *had plac'd him*] Forbear, foul
      ravisher, libidinous swine;
    Free the forc'd lady, or thou di'st, impostor.
    But that I am loth to snatch thy punishment
    Out of the hand of justice, thou shouldst yet
    Be made the timely sacrifice of vengeance,   270
    Before this altar and this dross, thy idol.—
    Lady, let's quit the place; it is the den
    Of villainy; fear naught: you have a guard;
    And he ere long shall meet his just reward.

                                    [*Exeunt* BONARIO *and* CELIA.]

VOLP. Fall on me, roof, and bury me in ruin;
    Become my grave, that wert my shelter. Oh!
    I am unmask'd, unspirited, undone,
    Betray'd to beggary, to infamy—

SCENE VIII

[*Enter* MOSCA.]

MOS. Where shall I run, most wretched shame of men,
    To beat out my unlucky brains?

VOLP.   Here, here.
    What! dost thou bleed?

MOS.   O, that his well-driv'n sword
    Had been so courteous to have cleft me down
    Unto the navel, ere I liv'd to see
    My life, my hopes, my spirits, my patron, all
    Thus desperately engaged, by my error.

VOLP. Woe on thy fortune.

MOS.   And my follies, sir.

VOLP. Th' hast made me miserable.

MOS.   And myself, sir.
    Who would have thought he would have hearken'd so?   10

VOLP. What shall we do?

MOS.   I know not; if my heart
Could expiate the mischance, I'd pluck it out.
Will you be pleas'd to hang me, or cut my throat?
And I'll requite you, sir. Let's die like Romans,
Since we have liv'd like Grecians.   [*They knock without.*]

VOLP.   Hark! who's there?
I hear some footing; officers, the saffi,
Come to apprehend us! I do feel the brand
Hissing already at my forehead; now
Mine ears are boring.

MOS.   To your couch, sir, you;
Make that place good, however. [VOLPONE *lies down as before.*]
    —[*Aside*] Guilty men   20
Suspect what they deserve still.—Signior Corbaccio!

SCENE IX

[*Enter* CORBACCIO.]

CORB. Why, how now, Mosca?

MOS.   O, undone, amaz'd, sir.
Your son, I know not by what accident,
Acquainted with your purpose to my patron,
Touching your will and making him your heir,
Ent'red our house with violence, his sword drawn,
Sought for you, call'd you wretch, unnatural,
Vow'd he would kill you.

CORB.   Me?

MOS.   Yes, and my patron.

CORB. This act shall disinherit him indeed.
Here is the will.

MOS.   'Tis well, sir.

c. viii. **14. Romans:** by suicide. **15. Grecians:** luxuriously. **16. saffi:** bailiffs.
1. **still:** always.

CORB.   Right and well:
  Be you as careful now for me.
                [*Enter* VOLTORE *behind.*]
MOS.   My life, sir,   10
  Is not more tender'd; I am only yours.
CORB. How does he? Will he die shortly, think'st thou?
MOS.   I fear
  He'll outlast May.
CORB.   Today?
MOS.   No, last out May, sir.
CORB. Couldst thou not gi' him a dram?
MOS.   Oh, by no means, sir.
CORB. Nay, I'll not bid you.
VOLT. [*Coming forward*]   This is a knave, I see.
MOS. [*Aside*] How! Signior Voltore! did he hear me?
VOLT.   Parasite!
MOS. Who's that?—Oh, sir, most timely welcome—
VOLT.   Scarce,
  To the discovery of your tricks, I fear.
  You are his, only? and mine also, are you not?
MOS. Who? I, sir!
VOLT.   You, sir. What device is this   20
  About a will?
MOS.   A plot for you, sir.
VOLT.   Come,
  Put not your foists upon me; I shall scent 'em.
MOS. Did you not hear it?
VOLT.   Yes, I hear Corbaccio
  Hath made your patron there his heir.
MOS.   'Tis true,
  By my device, drawn to it by my plot,
  With hope—
VOLT.   Your patron should reciprocate?
  And you have promis'd?

Sc. ix. 11. tender'd: cared for. **22. foists:** tricks.

MOS.   For your good I did, sir.
Nay, more, I told his son, brought, hid him here,
Where he might hear his father pass the deed;
Being persuaded to it by this thought, sir,   30
That the unnaturalness, first, of the act,
And then his father's oft disclaiming in him
(Which I did mean t' help on), would sure enrage him
To do some violence upon his parent,
On which the law should take sufficient hold,
And you be stated in a double hope.
Truth be my comfort, and my conscience,
My only aim was to dig you a fortune
Out of these two rotten sepulchres—

VOLT. I cry thee mercy, Mosca.

MOS.   Worth your patience,   40
And your great merit, sir. And see the change!

VOLT. Why, what success?

MOS.   Most hapless! You must help, sir.
Whilst we expected th' old raven, in comes
Corvino's wife, sent hither by her husband—

VOLT. What, with a present?

MOS.   No, sir, on visitation
(I'll tell you how anon); and, staying long,
The youth he grows impatient, rushes forth,
Seizeth the lady, wounds me, makes her swear
(Or he would murder her—that was his vow)
T' affirm my patron to have done her rape;   50
Which how unlike it is, you see! and hence,
With that pretext he's gone, t' accuse his father,
Defame my patron, defeat you—

VOLT.   Where's her husband?
Let him be sent for straight.

MOS.   Sir, I'll go fetch him.

VOLT. Bring him to the Scrutineo.

55. **Scrutineo**: Senate House.

MOS.   Sir, I will.

VOLT. This must be stopp'd.

MOS.   Oh, you do nobly, sir.
    Alas, 'twas labor'd all, sir, for your good;
    Nor was there want of counsel in the plot.
    But Fortune can, at any time, o'erthrow
    The projects of a hundred learned clerks, sir.   60

CORB. [*Listening*] What's that?

VOLT.   Wilt please you, sir, to go along?
                          [*Exit* CORBACCIO, *followed by* VOLTORE.]

MOS. Patron, go in, and pray for our success.

VOLP. Need makes devotion; Heaven your labor bless!   [*Exeunt.*]

ACT FOUR

SCENE I. A street.

[*Enter* SIR POLITIC WOULD-BE *and* PEREGRINE.]

POL. I told you, sir, it was a plot; you see
    What observation is. You mention'd me
    For some instructions; I will tell you, sir,
    (Since we are met here in this height of Venice)
    Some few particulars I have set down,
    Only for this meridian, fit to be known
    Of your crude traveller; and they are these.
    I will not touch, sir, at your phrase, or clothes,
    For they are old.

PER.   Sir, I have better.

POL.   Pardon,
    I meant, as they are themes.

PER.   Oh, sir, proceed;   10
    I'll slander you no more of wit, good sir.

60. clerks: scholars.

Act IV. Sc. i. 2. mention'd: call on.

POL. First, for your garb, it must be grave and serious,
    Very reserv'd and lock'd; not tell a secret
    On any terms, not to your father; scarce
    A fable, but with caution; make sure choice
    Both of your company and discourse; beware
    You never speak a truth—

PER.   How!

POL.   Not to strangers,
    For those be they you must converse with most;
    Others I would not know, sir, but at distance
    So as I still might be a saver in 'em—   20
    You shall have tricks else pass'd upon you, hourly.
    And then, for your religion, profess none,
    But wonder at the diversity of all;
    And, for your part, protest, were there no other
    But simply the laws o' th' land, you could content you.
    Nic. Machiavel and Monsieur Bodin, both
    Were of this mind. Then must you learn the use
    And handling of your silver fork at meals,
    The metal of your glass (these are main matters
    With your Italian); and to know the hour   30
    When you must eat your melons and your figs.

PER. Is that a point of state too?

POL.   Here, it is;
    For your Venetian, if he see a man
    Preposterous in the least, he has him straight;
    He has; he strips him. I'll acquaint you, sir,
    I now have liv'd here, 'tis some fourteen months.
    Within the first week of my landing here,
    All took me for a citizen of Venice,
    I knew the forms so well—

PER. *[Aside]*   And nothing else.

---

12. garb: conduct. **26. Bodin:** Jean Bodin, 16th century French political
philosopher, whose advanced views were much discussed at the time.

POL. I had read Contarene, took me a house,   40
  Dealt with my Jews to furnish it with movables—
  Well, if I could but find one man, one man,
  To mine own heart, whom I durst trust, I would—
PER. What? what, sir?
POL.   Make him rich; make him a fortune:
  He should not think again. I would command it.
PER. As how?
POL.   With certain projects that I have,
  Which I may not discover.
PER. [*Aside*]   If I had
  But one to wager with, I would lay odds now,
  He tells me instantly.
POL.   One is (and that
  I care not greatly who knows) to serve the state   50
  Of Venice with red herrings for three years,
  And at a certain rate, from Rotterdam,
  Where I have correspondence. There's a letter,
  Sent me from one o' th' states, and to that purpose;
  He cannot write his name, but that's his mark.
PER. He is a chandler?
POL.   No, a cheesemonger.
  There are some other too with whom I treat
  About the same negotiation;
  And I will undertake it; for 'tis thus:
  I'll do 't with ease; I have cast it all. Your hoy   60
  Carries but three men in her, and a boy;
  And she shall make me three returns a year:
  So if there come but one of three, I save;
  If two, I can defalk. But this is now,
  If my main project fail.

40. Contarene: Cardinal Contarini, author of *Commonwealth and Government of Venice,* which appeared in London in 1599. **54. states:** nobles. **56. chandler:** candle merchant (suggested by a grease mark on the paper). **60. cast:** calculated; **hoy:** small ship. **64. defalk:** make a reduction.

PER.   Then you have others?

POL. I should be loth to draw the subtle air
　　Of such a place without my thousand aims.
　　I'll not dissemble, sir: where'er I come,
　　I love to be considerative; and 'tis true,
　　I have at my free hours thought upon   70
　　Some certain goods unto the state of Venice,
　　Which I do call my cautions; and, sir, which
　　I mean, in hope of pension, to propound
　　To the Great Council, then unto the Forty,
　　So to the Ten. My means are made already—

PER. By whom?

POL.   Sir, one that though his place b' obscure,
　　Yet he can sway, and they will hear him. He's
　　A *commandadore*.

PER.   What, a common serjeant?

POL. Sir, such as they are, put it in their mouths,
　　What they should say, sometimes; as well as greater.   80
　　I think I have my notes to show you— [*Searching his pockets.*]

PER.   Good sir.

POL. But you shall swear unto me, on your gentry,
　　Not to anticipate—

PER.   I, sir?

POL.   Nor reveal
　　A circumstance—my paper is not with me.

PER. O, but you can remember, sir.

POL.   My first is
　　Concerning tinder boxes. You must know,
　　No family is here without its box.
　　Now, sir, it being so portable a thing,
　　Put case that you or I were ill affected
　　Unto the state, sir; with it in our pockets,   90
　　Might not I go into the Arsenal,
　　Or you come out again, and none the wiser?

89. Put case: assume.

PER. Except yourself, sir.

POL.   Go to, then. I therefore
    Advertise to the state, how fit it were
    That none but such as were known patriots,
    Sound lovers of their country, should be suffer'd
    T' enjoy them in their houses; and even those
    Seal'd at some office, and at such a bigness
    As might not lurk in pockets.

PER.   Admirable!

POL. My next is, how t' inquire, and be resolv'd   100
    By present demonstration, whether a ship,
    Newly arriv'd from Syria, or from
    Any suspected part of all the Levant,
    Be guilty of the plague; and where they use
    To lie out forty, fifty days, sometimes,
    About the Lazaretto, for their trial,
    I'll save that charge and loss unto the merchant,
    And in an hour clear the doubt.

PER.   Indeed, sir?

POL. Or—I will lose my labor.

PER.   'My faith, that's much.

POL. Nay, sir, conceive me. 'Twill cost me in onions,   110
    Some thirty livres—

PER.   Which is one pound sterling.

POL. Beside my waterworks. For this I do, sir:
    First, I bring in your ship 'twixt two brick walls—
    But those the state shall venture. On the one
    I strain me a fair tarpaulin, and in that
    I stick my onions, cut in halves; the other
    Is full of loopholes, out at which I thrust
    The noses of my bellows; and those bellows
    I keep, with waterworks, in perpetual motion
    (Which is the easi'st matter of a hundred).   120
    Now, sir, your onion, which doth naturally

106. **Lazaretto:** quarantine.

Attract th' infection, and your bellows blowing
The air upon him, will show, instantly,
By his chang'd color, if there be contagion;
Or else remain as fair as at the first.
Now 'tis known, 'tis nothing.

PER.   You are right, sir.

POL. I would I had my note.

PER.   'Faith, so would I;
But you ha' done well for once, sir.

POL.   Were I false,
Or would be made so, I could show you reasons
How I could sell this state now to the Turk,   130
Spite of their galleys, or their—   [*Examining his papers.*]

PER.   Pray you, Sir Pol.

POL. I have 'em not about me.

PER.   That I fear'd.
They are there, sir?

POL.   No, this is my diary,
Wherein I note my actions of the day.

PER. Pray you let's see, sir.—What is here? "*Notandum,*
A rat had gnawn my spur-leathers; notwithstanding,
I put on new, and did go forth; but first
I threw three beans over the threshold. *Item,*
I went and bought two toothpicks, whereof one
I burst immediately, in a discourse   14ᵛ
With a Dutch merchant, 'bout *ragion' del stato.*
From him I went and paid a *moccinigo*
For piecing my silk stockings; by the way
I cheapen'd sprats; and at St. Mark's I urin'd."—
'Faith these are politic notes!

POL.   Sir, I do slip
No action of my life, thus but I quote it.

PER. Believe me, it is wise!

POL.   Nay, sir, read forth.

---

141. **ragion' del stato**: politics. 144. **cheapen'd**: priced.

SCENE II

[*Enter, at a distance,* LADY POLITIC WOULD-BE, NANO, *and the two*
                    WAITING WOMEN.]

LADY. Where should this loose knight be, trow? Sure h' is hous'd.

NAN. Why, then he's fast.

LADY.   Ay, he plays both with me.
  I pray you stay. This heat will do more harm
  To my complexion than his heart is worth.
  (I do not care to hinder, but to take him.)
  How it comes off!   [*Rubs her cheeks.*]

WOM.   My master's yonder.

LADY.   Where?

WOM. With a young gentleman.

LADY.   That same's the party!
  In man's apparel.—Pray you, sir, jog my knight.
  I will be tender to his reputation,
  However he demerit.

POL.   My lady!

PER.   Where?   10

POL. 'Tis she indeed, sir; you shall know her. She is,
  Were she not mine, a lady of that merit,
  For fashion and behavior, and for beauty,
  I durst compare—

PER.   It seems you are not jealous,
  That dare commend her.

POL.   Nay, and for discourse—

PER. Being your wife, she cannot miss that.

POL.   Madam,
  Here is a gentleman, 'pray you use him fairly;
  He seems a youth, but he is—

LADY.   None?

Sc. ii. 2. **both:** fast and loose.

POL.   Yes, one
    Has put his face as soon into the world—
LADY. You mean, as early? But today?
POL.   How's this!   2⁹
LADY. Why, in this habit, sir; you apprehend me.
    Well, Master Would-be, this doth not become you;
    I had thought the odor, sir, of your good name
    Had been more precious to you; that you would not
    Have done this dire massacre on your honor;
    One of your gravity, and rank besides!
    But knights, I see, care little for the oath
    They make to ladies—chiefly their own ladies.
POL. Now, by my spurs, the symbol of my knighthood—
PER. [*Aside*] Lord, how his brain is humbled for an oath.   30
POL. I reach you not.
LADY.   Right, sir: your polity
    May bear it through thus.—[*To* PEREGRINE] Sir, a word with
      you.
    I would be loth to contest publicly
    With any gentlewoman, or to seem
    Froward, or violent, as the courtier says;
    It comes too near rusticity in a lady,
    Which I would shun by all means; and however
    I may deserve from Master Would-be, yet
    'T have one fair gentlewoman thus be made
    Th' unkind instrument to wrong another,   40
    And one she knows not, ay, and to persever,
    In my poor judgment, is not warranted
    From being a solecism in our sex,
    If not in manners.
PER.   How is this!

30. humbled . . . oath: made cheap, because the order of knighthood had been cheapened by the wholesale creation of knights under King James. **43. From . . . sex:** because it would be a breach of etiquette toward the female sex.

POL.   Sweet madam,
    Come nearer to your aim.

LADY.   Marry, and will, sir.
    Since you provoke me with your impudence,
    And laughter of your light land-siren here,
    Your Sporus, your hermaphrodite—

PER.   What's here?
    Poetic fury and historic storms!

POL. The gentleman, believe it, is of worth   50
    And of our nation.

LADY.   Ay, your Whitefriars nation?
    Come, I blush for you, Master Would-be, I;
    And am asham'd you should ha' no more forehead
    Than thus to be the patron, or St. George,
    To a lewd harlot, a base fricatrice,
    A female devil, in a male outside.

POL.   Nay,
    An you be such a one! I must bid adieu
    To your delights. The case appears too liquid.   [*Exit.*]

LADY. Ay, you may carry 't clear, with your state-face!—
    But for your carnival concupiscence,   60
    Who here is fled for liberty of conscience,
    From furious persecution of the marshal,
    Her will I disc'ple.

PER.   This is fine, i' faith!
    And do you use this often? Is this part
    Of your wit's exercise, 'gainst you have occasion?
    Madam—

LADY.   Go to, sir.

PER.   Do you hear me, lady?
    Why, if your knight have set you to beg shirts,
    Or to invite me home, you might have done it
    A nearer way by far.

---

48. Sporus: Nero's eunuch. **51. Whitefriars:** a section of London where criminals and perverts were safe from the law. **53. forehead:** sense of shame. **55. fricatrice:** prostitute. **58. liquid:** clear. **63. disc'ple:** discipline.

LADY.   This cannot work you
    Out of my snare.

PER.   Why, am I in it, then?   70
    Indeed your husband told me you were fair,
    And so you are; only your nose inclines,
    That side that's next the sun, to the queen-apple.

LADY. This cannot be endur'd by any patience.

SCENE III

[Enter MOSCA.*]*

MOS. What's the matter, madam?

LADY.   If the Senate
    Right not my quest in this, I will protest 'em
    To all the world no aristocracy.

MOS. What is the injury, lady?

LADY.   Why, the callet
    You told me of, here I have ta'en disguis'd.

MOS. Who? this? what means your Ladyship? The creature
    I mention'd to you is apprehended now,
    Before the Senate; you shall see her—

LADY.   Where?

MOS. I'll bring you to her. This young gentleman,
    I saw him land this morning at the port.   10

LADY. Is 't possible? How has my judgment wander'd!
    Sir, I must, blushing, say to you, I have err'd;
    And plead your pardon.

PER.   What! more changes yet?

LADY. I hope you've not the malice to remember
    A gentlewoman's passion. If you stay
    In Venice here, please you to use me, sir—

MOS. Will you go, madam?

73. **queen-apple:** which is red on the sunward side.

Sc. iii. 4. **callet:** prostitute.

LADY.   'Pray you, sir, use me; in faith,
   The more you see me the more I shall conceive
   You have forgot our quarrel.
   [*Exeunt* LADY WOULD-BE, MOSCA, NANO, *and* WAITING WOMEN.]
PER.   This is rare!
   Sir Politic Would-be? No, Sir Politic Bawd!   20
   To bring me thus acquainted with his wife!
   Well, wise Sir Pol, since you have practis'd thus
   Upon my freshmanship, I'll try your salthead,
   What proof it is against a counterplot.   [*Exit.*]

SCENE IV. *The Senate House.*

   [*Enter* VOLTORE, CORBACCIO, CORVINO, *and* MOSCA.]
VOLT. Well, now you know the carriage of the business,
   Your constancy is all that is requir'd
   Unto the safety of it.   [*He stands aside.*]
MOS.   Is the lie
   Safely convey'd amongst us? Is that sure?
   Knows every man his burden?
CORV.   Yes.
MOS.   Then shrink not.
CORV. But knows the advocate the truth?
MOS.   Oh, sir,
   By no means; I devis'd a formal tale,
   That salv'd your reputation. But be valiant, sir.
CORV. I fear no one but him, that this his pleading
   Should make him stand for a co-heir—
MOS.   Co-halter!   10
   Hang him; we will but use his tongue, his noise,
   As we do croaker's here.
CORV.   Ay, what shall he do?

23. salthead: opposite of freshman.

Sc. iv. 4. convey'd: arranged. **12. croaker's:** Corbaccio's.

MOS. When we ha' done, you mean?

CORV. Yes.

MOS. Why, we'll think;
Sell him for mummia: he's half dust already.—
[*To* VOLTORE] Do you not smile, to see this buffalo,
How he doth sport it with his head?—[*Aside*] I should,
If all were well and past.—[*To* CORBACCIO] Sir, only you
Are he that shall enjoy the crop of all,
And these not know for whom they toil.

CORB. Ay, peace.

MOS. [*To* CORVINO] But you shall eat it.—[*Aside*] Much!—[*Then to*
VOLTORE *again*] Worshipful sir,   20
Mercury sit upon your thund'ring tongue,
Or the French Hercules, and make your language
As conquering as his club, to beat along,
As with a tempest, flat, our adversaries;
But much more yours, sir.

VOLT. Here they come; ha' done.

MOS. I have another witness, if you need, sir,
I can produce.

VOLT. Who is it?

MOS. Sir, I have her.

SCENE V

[*Enter four* AVOCATORI, BONARIO, CELIA, NOTARIO, COMMANDADORI,
SAFFI, *and other* OFFICERS OF JUSTICE.]

1 AVOC. The like of this the Senate never heard of.

2 AVOC. 'Twill come most strange to them when we report it.

4 AVOC. The gentlewoman has been ever held
Of unreproved name.

3 AVOC. So, the young man.

14. mummia: drug made from mummies. 15. buffalo: cuckold. 22. French
Hercules: Ogmius, symbol of eloquence.

4 AVOC. The more unnatural part that of his father.

2 AVOC. More of the husband.

1 AVOC.   I not know to give
    His act a name, it is so monstrous!

4 AVOC. But the impostor, he is a thing created
    T' exceed example!

1 AVOC.   And all after-times!

2 AVOC. I never heard a true voluptuary   10
    Describ'd but him.

3 AVOC.   Appear yet those were cited?

NOT. All but the old magnifico, Volpone.

1 AVOC. Why is not he here?

MOS.   Please your Fatherhoods.
    Here is his advocate. Himself's so weak,
    So feeble—

4 AVOC.   What are you?

BON.   His parasite,
    His knave, his pander. I beseech the court
    He may be forc'd to come, that your grave eyes
    May bear strong witness of his strange impostures.

VOLT. Upon my faith and credit with your Virtues,
    He is not able to endure the air.   20

2 AVOC. Bring him, however.

3 AVOC.   We will see him.

4 AVOC.   Fetch him.

VOLT. Your Fatherhoods' fit pleasures be obey'd;

                     [*Exeunt* OFFICERS.]

    But sure, the sight will rather move your pities
    Than indignation. May it please the court,
    In the meantime, he may be heard in me.
    I know this place most void of prejudice,
    And therefore crave it, since we have no reason
    To fear our truth should hurt our cause.

3 AVOC.   Speak free.

VOLT. Then know, most honor'd fathers, I must now
    Discover to your strangely abused ears,   30

The most prodigious and most frontless piece
Of solid impudence and treachery
That ever vicious nature yet brought forth
To shame the state of Venice. This lewd woman,
That wants no artificial looks or tears
To help the visor she has now put on,
Hath long been known a close adulteress
To that lascivious youth there; not suspected,
I say, but known, and taken in the act
With him; and by this man, the easy husband,   40
Pardon'd; whose timeless bounty makes him now
Stand here, the most unhappy, innocent person
That ever man's own goodness made accus'd.
For these, not knowing how to owe a gift
Of that dear grace, but with their shame, being plac'd
So above all powers of their gratitude,
Began to hate the benefit, and, in place
Of thanks, devise t' extirp the memory
Of such an act. Wherein I pray your Fatherhoods
To observe the malice, yea, the rage of creatures   50
Discover'd in their evils; and what heart
Such take, ev'n from their crimes. But that anon
Will more appear. This gentleman, the father,
Hearing of this foul fact, with many others,
Which daily struck at his too tender ears,
And griev'd in nothing more than that he could not
Preserve himself a parent (his son's ills
Growing to that strange flood), at last decreed
To disinherit him.

1 AVOC.   These be strange turns!
2 AVOC. The young man's fame was ever fair and honest.   60
VOLT. So much more full of danger is his vice,
    That can beguile so, under shade of virtue.

Sc. v. **31. frontless:** shameless. **37. close:** secret. **41. timeless bounty:** untimely
mercy. **44. owe:** value.

But, as I said, my honor'd sires, his father
Having this settled purpose, by what means
To him betray'd, we know not, and this day
Appointed for the deed; that parricide
I cannot style him better, by confederacy
Preparing this his paramour to be there,
Ent'red Volpone's house (who was the man,
Your Fatherhoods must understand, design'd   70
For the inheritance), there sought his father:—
But with what purpose sought he him, my Lords?
I tremble to pronounce it, that a son
Unto a father, and to such a father,
Should have so foul, felonious intent—
It was to murder him; when, being prevented
By his more happy absence, what then did he?
Not check his wicked thoughts; no, now new deeds
(Mischief doth ever end where it begins)—
An act of horror, fathers! He dragg'd forth   80
The aged gentleman that had there lain bedrid
Three years and more, out off his innocent couch,
Naked upon the floor; there left him; wounded
His servant in the face; and with this strumpet,
The stale to his forg'd practice, who was glad
To be so active,—I shall here desire
Your Fatherhoods to note but my collections,
As most remarkable,—thought at once to stop
His father's ends, discredit his free choice
In the old gentleman, redeem themselves,   90
By laying infamy upon this man,
To whom, with blushing, they should owe their lives.

I AVOC. What proofs have you of this?
BON.   Most honor'd fathers,
I humbly crave there be no credit given
To this man's mercenary tongue.

---

85. stale . . . practice: front to his fabricated plot. 87. collections: evidence.

2 AVOC.   Forbear.

BON. His soul moves in his fee.

3 AVOC.   O, sir.

BON.   This fellow,
   For six sols more would plead against his Maker.

1 AVOC. You do forget yourself.

VOLT.   Nay, nay, grave fathers,
   Let him have scope! Can any man imagine
   That he will spare his accuser, that would not   100
   Have spar'd his parent?

1 AVOC.   Well, produce your proofs.

CEL. I would I could forget I were a creature.

VOLT. Signior Corbaccio.

4 AVOC.   What is he?

VOLT.   The father.

2 AVOC. Has he had an oath?

NOT.   Yes.

CORB.   What must I do now?

NOT. Your testimony's crav'd.

CORB.   Speak to the knave?
   I'll ha' my mouth first stopp'd with earth; my heart
   Abhors his knowledge: I disclaim in him.

1 AVOC. But for what cause?

CORB.   The mere portent of nature.
   He is an utter stranger to my loins.

BON. Have they made you to this!

CORB.   I will not hear thee,   110
   Monster of men, swine, goat, wolf, parricide;
   Speak not, thou viper.

BON.   Sir, I will sit down,
   And rather wish my innocence should suffer
   Than I resist the authority of a father.

VOLT. Signior Corvino.

107. disclaim in: disown. **110. made:** coached.

2 AVOC.   This is strange!

1 AVOC.   Who's this?

NOT. The husband.

4 AVOC.   Is he sworn?

NOT.   He is.

3 AVOC.   Speak then.

CORV. This woman, please your Fatherhoods, is a whore,
       Of most hot exercise, more than a partridge,
       Upon record—

1 AVOC.   No more.

CORV.   Neighs like a jennet.

NOT. Preserve the honor of the court.

CORV.   I shall,   120
       And modesty of your most reverend ears.
       And yet I hope that I may say these eyes
       Have seen her glu'd unto that piece of cedar,
       That fine well-timber'd gallant; and that here
       The letters may be read, thorough the horn,
       That make the story perfect.

MOS. [*Aside to* CORVINO]   Excellent, sir!

CORV. [*Aside to* MOSCA] There is no shame in this now, is there?

MOS. [*Aside to* CORVINO]   None.

CORV. Or if I said, I hop'd that she were onward
       To her damnation, if there be a hell
       Greater than whore and woman, a good Catholic   130
       May make the doubt.

3 AVOC.   His grief hath made him frantic.

1 AVOC. Remove him hence.

2 AVOC.   Look to the woman.   [*She swoons.*]

CORV.   Rare!
       Prettily feign'd! again!

4 AVOC.   Stand from about her.

1 AVOC. Give her the air.

3 AVOC. [*To* MOSCA]   What can you say?

125. **horn:** of a hornbook (primer) and a cuckold.

MOS.   My wound,
  May 't please your Wisdoms, speaks for me, receiv'd
  In aid of my good patron, when he miss'd
  His sought-for father, when that well-taught dame
  Had her cue giv'n her to cry out, "A rape!"
BON. O most laid impudence! Fathers—
3 AVOC.   Sir, be silent;
  You had your hearing free, so must they theirs.   140
2 AVOC. I do begin to doubt th' imposture here.
4 AVOC. This woman has too many moods.
VOLT.   Grave fathers,
  She is a creature of a most profess'd
  And prostituted lewdness.
CORV.   Most impetuous!
  Unsatisfied, grave fathers!
VOLT.   May her feignings
  Not take your wisdoms. But this day she baited
  A stranger, a grave knight, with her loose eyes
  And more lascivious kisses. This man saw 'em
  Together on the water, in a gondola.
MOS. Here is the lady herself, that saw 'em too,   150
  Without; who then had in the open streets
  Pursu'd them, but for saving her knight's honor.
1 AVOC. Produce that lady.
2 AVOC.   Let her come.   [*Exit* MOSCA.]
4 AVOC.   These things,
  They strike with wonder!
3 AVOC.   I am turn'd a stone!

SCENE VI

[*Re-enter* MOSCA *with* LADY WOULD-BE.]
MOS. Be resolute, madam.
LADY.   Ay, this same is she.—

139. laid: contrived.

Out, thou chameleon harlot! now thine eyes
Vie tears with the hyena. Dar'st thou look
Upon my wronged face?—I cry your pardons.
I fear I have forgettingly transgress'd
Against the dignity of the court—

2 AVOC.   No, madam.

LADY. And been exorbitant—

2 AVOC.   You have not, lady.

4 AVOC. These proofs are strong.

LADY.   Surely, I had no purpose
To scandalize your honors, or my sex's.

3 AVOC. We do believe it.

LADY.   Surely you may believe it.   10

2 AVOC. Madam, we do.

LADY.   Indeed you may; my breeding
Is not so coarse—

4 AVOC.   We know it.

LADY.   To offend
With pertinacy—

3 AVOC.   Lady—

LADY.   Such a presence;
No, surely.

1 AVOC.   We will think it.

LADY.   You may think it.

1 AVOC. Let her o'ercome.—What witnesses have you,
To make good your report?

BON.   Our consciences.

CEL. And Heaven, that never fails the innocent.

1 AVOC. These are no testimonies.

BON.   Not in your courts,
Where multitude and clamor overcomes.

1 AVOC. Nay, then you do wax insolent.

          [VOLPONE *is brought in, as impotent.*]

VOLT.   Here, here,   20
The testimony comes that will convince,
And put to utter dumbness their bold tongues.

See here, grave fathers, here's the ravisher,
The rider on men's wives, the great impostor,
The grand voluptuary! Do you not think
These limbs should affect venery? or these eyes
Covet a concubine? Pray you mark these hands.
Are they not fit to stroke a lady's breasts?
Perhaps he doth dissemble!

BON.   So he does.

VOLT. Would you ha' him tortur'd?

BON.   I would have him prov'd. 30

VOLT. Best try him then with goads, or burning irons;
   Put him to the strappado; I have heard
   The rack hath cur'd the gout; faith, give it him,
   And help him of a malady; be courteous.
   I'll undertake, before these honor'd fathers,
   He shall have yet as many left diseases,
   As she has known adulterers, or thou strumpets.
   O, my most equal hearers, if these deeds,
   Acts of this bold and most exorbitant strain,
   May pass with sufferance, what one citizen   40
   But owes the forfeit of his life, yea, fame,
   To him that dares traduce him? Which of you
   Are safe, my honor'd fathers? I would ask,
   With leave of your grave Fatherhoods, if their plot
   Have any face or color like to truth?
   Or if, unto the dullest nostril here,
   It smell not rank, and most abhorred slander?
   I crave your care of this good gentleman,
   Whose life is much endanger'd by their fable;
   And as for them, I will conclude with this: 50
   That vicious persons, when they are hot, and flesh'd
   In impious acts, their constancy abounds:
   Damn'd deeds are done with greatest confidence.

Sc. vi. 38. equal: just.

1 AVOC. Take 'em to custody, and sever them.

2 AVOC. 'Tis pity two such prodigies should live.

1 AVOC. Let the old gentleman be return'd with care.

                       [Exeunt OFFICERS *with* VOLPONE.]

    I am sorry our credulity wrong'd him.

4 AVOC. These are two creatures!

3 AVOC.   I have an earthquake in me!

2 AVOC. Their shame, even in their cradles, fled their faces.

4 AVOC. You have done a worthy service to the state, sir,   60

    In their discovery.

1 AVOC.   You shall hear, ere night,

    What punishment the court decrees upon 'em.

    [Exeunt AVOCATORI, NOTARIO, *and* OFFICERS *with* BONARIO *and*

                                      CELIA.]

VOLT. We thank your Fatherhoods.—How like you it?

MOS.   Rare.

    I'd ha' your tongue, sir, tipp'd with gold for this;

    I'd ha' you be the heir to the whole city;

    The earth I'd have want men ere you want living:

    They are bound to erect your statue in St. Mark's.—

    Signior Corvino, I would have you go

    And show yourself that you have conquer'd.

CORV.   Yes.

MOS. It was much better that you should profess   70

    Yourself a cuckold thus, than that the other

    Should have been prov'd.

CORV.   Nay, I consider'd that;

    Now it is her fault.

MOS.   Then, it had been yours.

CORV. True.—*[Aside to* MOSCA*]* I do doubt this advocate still.

MOS. *[Aside]*   I' faith,

    You need not; I dare ease you of that care.

CORV. *[Aside]* I trust thee, Mosca.

MOS. *[Aside]*   As your own soul, sir.

                          [Exit CORVINO.]

CORB.   Mosca!

MOS. Now for your business, sir.

CORB.   How? ha' you business?

MOS. Yes, yours, sir.

CORB.   O, none else?

MOS.   None else, not I.

CORB. Be careful then.

MOS.   Rest you with both your eyes, sir.

CORB. Dispatch it.

MOS.   Instantly.

CORB.   And look that all,   80
     Whatever, be put in, jewels, plate, monies,
     Household stuff, bedding, curtains.

MOS.   Curtain-rings, sir;
     Only, the advocate's fee must be deducted.

CORB. I'll pay him now; you'll be too prodigal.

MOS. Sir, I must tender it.

CORB.   Two *cecchines* is well.

MOS. No, six, sir.

CORB.   'Tis too much.

MOS.   He talk'd a great while;
     You must consider that, sir.

CORB.   Well, there's three—

MOS. I'll give it him.

CORB.   Do so, and there's for thee.   [*Exit.*]

MOS. [*Aside*] Bountiful bones! What horrid strange offence
     Did he commit 'gainst nature, in his youth,   90
     Worthy this age?—[*Aside to* VOLTORE] You see, sir, how I work
     Unto your ends; take you no notice.

VOLT.   No,
     I'll leave you.

MOS. [*Aside*]   All is yours, the devil and all,
     Good advocate.—Madam, I'll bring you home.

LADY. No, I'll go see your patron.

79. Rest . . . eyes: leave it to me.

MOS.   That you shall not;
    I'll tell you why. My purpose is to urge
    My patron to reform his will, and for
    The zeal you have shown today, whereas before
    You were but third or fourth, you shall be now
    Put in the first; which would appear as begg'd   100
    If you were present. Therefore—

LADY.   You shall sway me.
                                               [Exeunt.]

ACT FIVE

SCENE I. A room in Volpone's house.

[*Enter* VOLPONE.]

VOLP. Well, I am here, and all this brunt is past.
    I ne'er was in dislike with my disguise
    Till this fled moment: here 'twas good, in private;
    But in your public,—*cave,* whilst I breathe.
    'Fore God, my left leg 'gan to have the cramp.
    And I apprehended straight some power had struck me
    With a dead palsy. Well, I must be merry,
    And shake it off. A many of these fears
    Would put me into some villainous disease,
    Should they come thick upon me. I'll prevent 'em.   10
    Give me a bowl of lusty wine, to fright
    This humor from my heart.—[*He drinks.*] Hum, hum, hum!—
    'Tis almost gone already; I shall conquer.
    Any device now of rare ingenious knavery,
    That would possess me with a violent laughter,
    Would make me up again!—[*Drinks again.*] So, so, so, so!—
    This heat is life; 'tis blood by this time.—Mosca!

97. reform: revise.

Act V. Sc. i. 4. cave: beware.

SCENE II

[Enter MOSCA.]

MOS. How now, sir? Does the day look clear again?
　　Are we recover'd, and wrought out of error,
　　Into our way, to see our path before us?
　　Is our trade free once more?
VOLP.　　　　　　　　　　Exquisite Mosca!
MOS. Was it not carri'd learnedly?
VOLP.　　　　　　　　　　And stoutly:
　　Good wits are greatest in extremities.
MOS. It were folly beyond thought to trust
　　Any grand act unto a cowardly spirit.
　　You are not taken with it enough, methinks.
VOLP. Oh, more than if I had enjoy'd the wench;　　　　10
　　The pleasure of all womankind's not like it.
MOS. Why, now you speak, sir. We must here be fix'd;
　　Here we must rest; this is our masterpiece;
　　We cannot think to go beyond this.
VOLP.　　　　　　　　　　True,
　　Thou hast play'd thy prize, my precious Mosca.
MOS.　　　　　　　　　　Nay, sir,
　　To gull the court—
VOLP.　　　　　And quite divert the torrent
　　Upon the innocent.
MOS.　　　　　Yes, and to make
　　So rare a music out of discords—
VOLP.　　　　　　　　　　Right.
　　That yet to me's the strangest! how th' hast borne it!
　　That these, being so divided 'mongst themselves,　　　　20
　　Should not scent somewhat, or in me or thee,
　　Or doubt their own side.
MOS.　　　　　True, they will not see 't.
　　Too much light blinds 'em, I think. Each of 'em

Is so possess'd and stuff'd with his own hopes
That anything unto the contrary,
Never so true, or never so apparent,
Never so palpable, they will resist it—
VOLP. Like a temptation of the Devil.
MOS.   Right, sir.
Merchants may talk of trade, and your great signiors
Of land that yields well; but if Italy   30
Have any glebe more fruitful than these fellows,
I am deceiv'd. Did not your advocate rare?
VOLP. Oh—"My most honor'd fathers, my grave fathers,
Under correction of your Fatherhoods,
What face of truth is here? If these strange deeds
May pass, most honor'd fathers"—I had much ado
To forbear laughing.
MOS.   'T seem'd to me you sweat, sir.
VOLP. In troth, I did a little.
MOS.   But confess, sir,
Were you not daunted?
VOLP.   In good faith, I was
A little in a mist, but not dejected;   40
Never, but still myself.
MOS.   I think it, sir.
Now, so truth help me, I must needs say this, sir,
And out of conscience for your advocate,
He has taken pains, in faith, sir, and deserv'd,
In my poor judgment, I speak it under favor,
Not to contrary you, sir, very richly—
Well—to be cozen'd.
VOLP.   Troth, and I think so too,
By that I heard him in the latter end.
MOS. O, but before, sir: had you heard him first
Draw it to certain heads, then aggravate,   50
Then use his vehement figures—I look'd still

Sc. ii. 47. **cozen'd:** tricked. 50. **aggravate:** emphasize.

When he would shift a shirt; and doing this
Out of pure love, no hope of gain—

VOLP.   'Tis right.
I cannot answer him, Mosca, as I would,
Not yet; but for thy sake, at thy entreaty,
I will begin, ev'n now—to vex 'em all,
This very instant.

MOS.   Good sir.

VOLP.   Call the dwarf
And eunuch forth.

MOS.   Castrone, Nano!

[*Enter* CASTRONE *and* NANO.]

NANO.   Here.

VOLP. Shall we have a jig now?

MOS.   What you please, sir.

VOLP.   Go,
Straight give out about the streets, you two,   60
That I am dead; do it with constancy,
Sadly, do you hear? Impute it to the grief
Of this late slander.   [*Exeunt* CASTRONE *and* NANO.]

MOS.   What do you mean, sir?

VOLP.   Oh,
I shall have instantly my Vulture, Crow,
Raven, come flying hither, on the news,
To peck for carrion, my she-wolf, and all,
Greedy, and full of expectation—

MOS. And then to have it ravish'd from their mouths?

VOLP. 'Tis true. I will ha' thee put on a gown,
And take upon thee, as thou wert mine heir;   70
Show 'em a will. Open that chest, and reach
Forth one of those that has the blanks. I'll straight
Put in thy name.

MOS.   It will be rare, sir.

VOLP.   Ay,
When they e'en gape, and find themselves deluded—

62. Sadly: seriously.

MOS. Yes.

VOLP.   And thou use them scurvily. Dispatch;
  Get on thy gown.

MOS.   But what, sir, if they ask
  After the body?

VOLP.   Say, it was corrupted.

MOS. I'll say it stunk, sir; and was fain t' have it
  Coffin'd up instantly, and sent away.

VOLP. Anything; what thou wilt.—Hold, here's my will.   80
  Get thee a cap, a count-book, pen and ink,
  Papers afore thee; sit as thou wert taking
  An inventory of parcels. I'll get up
  Behind the curtain, on a stool, and hearken;
  Sometime peep over, see how they do look,
  With what degrees their blood doth leave their faces!
  O, 'twill afford me a rare meal of laughter.

MOS. Your advocate will turn stark dull upon it.

VOLP. It will take off his oratory's edge.

MOS. But your clarissimo, old roundback, he   90
  Will crump you like a hog-louse, with the touch.

VOLP. And what Corvino?

MOS.   O, sir, look for him,
  Tomorrow morning, with a rope and a dagger,
  To visit all the streets; he must run mad.
  My Lady too, that came into the court,
  To bear false witness for your Worship—

VOLP.   Yes.
  And kiss'd me 'fore the fathers, when my face
  Flow'd all with oils—

MOS.   And sweat, sir. Why, your gold
  Is such another med'cine, it dries up
  All those offensive savors. It transforms   100
  The most deformed, and restores 'em lovely,
  As 'twere the strange poetical girdle. Jove

90. clarissimo: Corbaccio. 91. crump you: curl up. 102. girdle: of Venus.

Could not invent t' himself a shroud more subtle
To pass Acrisius' guards. It is the thing
Makes all the world her grace, her youth, her beauty.

VOLP. I think she loves me.

MOS.   Who? the lady, sir?
    She's jealous of you.

VOLP.   Dost thou say so?   [*Knocking within.*]

MOS.   Hark.
    There's some already.

VOLP.   Look.

MOS.   It is the Vulture;
    He has the quickest scent.

VOLP.   I'll to my place,
    Thou to thy posture.   [*Goes behind the curtain.*]

MOS.   I am set.

VOLP.   But, Mosca,   110
    Play the artificer now: torture 'em rarely.

SCENE III

[*Enter* VOLTORE.]

VOLT. How now, my Mosca?

MOS. [*Writing*]   Turkey carpets, nine—

VOLT. Taking an inventory! that is well.

MOS. Two suits of bedding, tissue—

VOLT.   Where's the will?
    Let me read that the while.

            [*Enter* SERVANTS *with* CORBACCIO *in a chair.*]

CORB.   So, set me down,
    And get you home.   [*Exeunt* SERVANTS.]

VOLT.   Is he come now, to trouble us?

MOS. Of cloth of gold, two more—

CORB.   Is it done, Mosca?

104. **Acrisius':** father of Danae, to whom amorous Jove descended as a shower of gold.

MOS. Of several velvets, eight—

VOLT.   I like his care.

CORB. Dost thou not hear?

[*Enter* CORVINO.]

CORV.   Ha! is the hour come, Mosca?

VOLP. [*Aside*] Ay, now they muster.

[*Peeps from behind a traverse.*]

CORV.   What does the advocate here?

    Or this Corbaccio?

CORB.   What do these here?

[*Enter* LADY WOULD-BE.]

LADY.   Mosca!   10

    Is his thread spun?

MOS.   Eight chests of linen—

VOLP. [*Aside*]   Oh,

    My fine Dame Would-be, too!

CORV.   Mosca, the will,

    That I may show it these, and rid 'em hence.

MOS. Six chests of diaper, four of damask—there. [*Gives the will.*]

CORB. Is that the will?

MOS. [*Writing*]   Down-beds, and bolsters—

VOLP. [*Aside*]   Rare!

    Be busy still. Now they begin to flutter;

    They never think of me. Look, see, see, see!

    How their swift eyes run over the long deed,

    Unto the name, and to the legacies,

    What is bequeath'd them there—

MOS.   Ten suits of hangings—   20

VOLP. [*Aside*] Ay, in their garters, Mosca. Now their hopes

    Are at the gasp.

VOLT.   Mosca the heir!

CORB.   What's that?

VOLP. [*Aside*] My advocate is dumb; look to my merchant—

    He has heard of some strange storm; a ship is lost—

Sc. iii. 14. diaper: kind of damask.

He faints. My Lady will swoon. Old glazen-eyes,
He hath not reach'd his despair yet.

CORB.   All these
Are out of hope; I am, sure, the man.   [*Takes the will.*]

CORV.   But, Mosca—

MOS. Two cabinets—

CORV.   Is this in earnest?

MOS.   One
Of ebony—

CORV.   Or do you but delude me?

MOS. The other, mother-of-pearl—I am very busy.   30
Good faith, it is a fortune thrown upon me—
Item, one salt of agate—not my seeking.

LADY. Do you hear, sir?

MOS.   A perfum'd box—'pray you forbear;
You see I am troubled—made of an onyx—

LADY.   How!

MOS. Tomorrow or next day, I shall be at leisure
To talk with you all.

CORV.   Is this my large hope's issue?

LADY. Sir, I must have a fairer answer.

MOS.   Madam!
Marry, and shall: 'pray you, fairly quit my house.
Nay, raise no tempest with your looks; but hark you,
Remember what your Ladyship off'red me   40
To put you in an heir; go to; think on it.
And what you said e'en your best madams did
For maintenance, and why not you? Enough.
Go home, and use the poor Sir Pol, your knight, well,
For fear I tell some riddles; go, be melancholic.

          [*Exit* LADY WOULD-BE.]

VOLP. [*Aside*] Oh, my fine devil!

CORV.   Mosca, pray you a word.

MOS. Lord! will not you take your dispatch hence yet?
Methinks, of all, you should have been th' example.

32. **salt**: saltcellar.

Why should you stay here? with what thought, what promise?
Hear you; do not you know, I know you an ass,   50
And that you would most fain have been a wittol
If fortune would have let you? that you are
A declar'd cuckold, on good terms? This pearl,
You'll say, was yours? right; this diamond?
I'll not deny 't, but thank you. Much here else?
It may be so. Why, think that these good works
May help to hide your bad. I'll not betray you;
Although you be but extraordinary,
And have it only in title, it sufficeth: 59
Go home; be melancholic too, or mad.   [*Exit* CORVINO.]

VOLP. [*Aside*] Rare Mosca! how his villainy becomes him!
VOLT. [*Aside*] Certain he doth delude all these for me.
CORB. Mosca the heir?
VOLP. [*Aside*]   O, his four eyes have found it!
CORB. I am cozen'd, cheated, by a parasite-slave;
    Harlot, th' hast gull'd me.
MOS.   Yes, sir. Stop your mouth,
    Or I shall draw the only tooth is left.
    Are not you he, that filthy covetous wretch,
    With the three legs, that here, in hope of prey,
    Have, any time this three year, snuff'd about,
    With your most grov'ling nose, and would have hir'd   70
    Me to the pois'ning of my patron, sir?
    Are not you he that have today in court
    Profess'd the disinheriting of your son?
    Perjur'd yourself? Go home, and die, and stink;
    If you but croak a syllable, all comes out:
    Away, and call your porters! [*Exit* CORBACCIO.] Go, go, stink.
VOLP. [*Aside*] Excellent varlet!
VOLT.   Now, my faithful Mosca,
    I find thy constancy—
MOS.   Sir!

51. wittol: willing cuckold.

VOLT.   Sincere.

MOS. [*Writing*]   A table

Of porphyry—I mar'l you'll be thus troublesome.

VOLT. Nay, leave off now, they are gone.

MOS.   Why, who are you?   80

What! who did send for you? Oh, cry you mercy,

Reverend sir! Good faith, I am griev'd for you,

That any chance of mine should thus defeat

Your (I must needs say) most deserving travails;

But I protest, sir, it was cast upon me,

And I could almost wish to be without it,

But that the will o' th' dead must be observ'd.

Marry, my joy is that you need it not;

You have a gift, sir, (thank your education)

Will never let you want, while there are men,   90

And malice, to breed causes. Would I had

But half the like, for all my fortune, sir.

If I have any suits, as I do hope,

Things being so easy and direct, I shall not,

I will make bold with your obstreperous aid;

Conceive me—for your fee, sir. In meantime,

You that have so much law, I know ha' the conscience

Not to be covetous of what is mine.

Good sir, I thank you for my plate; 'twill help

To set up a young man. Good faith, you look   100

As you were costive; best go home and purge, sir.

[*Exit* VOLTORE.]

VOLP. [*Coming from behind the curtain*] Bid him eat lettuce well.

My witty mischief,

Let me embrace thee. O that I could now

Transform thee to a Venus!—Mosca, go,

Straight take my habit of clarissimo,

And walk the streets; be seen, torment 'em more;

91. causes: lawsuits. 95. obstreperous: leather-lunged. 101. costive: consti-
pated. 105. habit of clarissimo: grandee's suit.

We must pursue, as well as plot. Who would
Have lost this feast?

MOS.   I doubt it will lose them.

VOLP. O, my recovery shall recover all.

That I could now but think on some disguise   110
To meet 'em in, and ask 'em questions.

How I would vex 'em still at every turn!

MOS. Sir, I can fit you.

VOLP.   Canst thou?

MOS.   Yes, I know

One o' the commandadori, sir; so like you,
Him will I straight make drunk, and bring you his habit.

VOLP. A rare disguise, and answering thy brain!

O, I will be a sharp disease unto 'em.

MOS. Sir, you must look for curses—

VOLP.   Till they burst;

The Fox fares ever best when he is curs'd.   *[Exeunt.]*

SCENE IV. A hall in Sir Politic's house.

[*Enter* PEREGRINE *disguised and three* MERCATORI.]

PER. Am I enough disguis'd?

1 MER.   I warrant you.

PER. All my ambition is to fright him only.

2 MER. If you could ship him away, 'twere excellent.

3 MER. To Zant, or to Aleppo!

PER.   Yes, and ha' his

Adventures put i' th' Book of Voyages,
And his gull'd story regist'red for truth!
Well, gentlemen, when I am in awhile,
And that you think us warm in our discourse,
Know your approaches.

Sc. iv. 4. **Zant:** a Greek island. **5. Book of Voyages:** Hakluyt's *Principall Navigations, Voiages, and Discoveries of the English Nation,* which had just appeared in a second edition.

1 MER.   Trust it to our care.

[*Exeunt* MERCATORI.]

[*Enter* WAITING WOMAN.]

PER. Save you, fair lady! Is Sir Pol within?   10
WOM. I do not know, sir.
PER.   'Pray you say unto him
   Here is a merchant, upon earnest business,
   Desires to speak with him.
WOM.   I will see, sir.   [*Exit.*]
PER.   'Pray you.
   I see the family is all female here.

[*Re-enter* WAITING WOMAN.]

WOM. He says, sir, he has weighty affairs of state,
   That now require him whole; some other time
   You may possess him.
PER.   'Pray you say again,
   If those require him whole, these will exact him,
   Whereof I bring him tidings. [*Exit* WOMAN.] What might be
   His grave affair of state now! How to make   20
   Bolognian sausages here in Venice, sparing
   One o' th' ingredients?

[*Re-enter* WAITING WOMAN.]

WOM.   Sir, he says he knows
   By your word "tidings," that you are no statesman,
   And therefore wills you stay.
PER.   Sweet, 'pray you return him
   I have not read so many proclamations,
   And studied them for words, as he has done—
   But—here he deigns to come.   [*Exit* WOMAN.]

[*Enter* SIR POLITIC.]

POL.   Sir, I must crave
   Your courteous pardon. There hath chanc'd today
   Unkind disaster 'twixt my lady and me;
   And I was penning my apology,   30
   To give her satisfaction, as you came now.

PER. Sir, I am griev'd I bring you worse disaster.
The gentleman you met at th' port today,
That told you he was newly arriv'd—

POL.   Ay, was
A fugitive punk?

PER.   No, sir, a spy set on you;
And he has made relation to the Senate,
That you profess'd to him to have a plot
To sell the state of Venice to the Turk.

POL. O me!

PER.   For which warrants are sign'd by this time,
To apprehend you, and to search your study   40
For papers—

POL.   Alas, sir, I have none, but notes
Drawn out of play-books—

PER.   All the better, sir.

POL. And some essays. What shall I do?

PER.   Sir, best
Convey yourself into a sugar-chest;
Or, if you could lie round, a frail were rare;
And I could send you aboard.

POL.   Sir, I but talk'd so.
For discourse sake merely.   [*They knock without.*]

PER.   Hark! they are there.

POL. I am a wretch, a wretch!

PER.   What will you do, sir?
Have you ne'er a currant-butt to leap into?
They'll put you to the rack; you must be sudden.   50

POL. Sir, I have an engine—

3 MER. [*Within*]   Sir Politic Would-be!

2 MER. [*Within*] Where is he?

POL.   That I've thought upon, before time.

PER. What is it?

---

45. frail were rare: basket would be perfect. **49. currant-butt:** wine cask.
51. engine: contraption.

POL. I shall ne'er endure the torture.—
Marry, it is, sir, of a tortoise shell,
Fitted for these extremities; 'pray you, sir, help me.
Here I have a place, sir, to put back my legs,
Please you to lay it on, sir, [*Lies down while* PEREGRINE *places
the shell upon him.*] with this cap,
And my black gloves. I'll lie, sir, like a tortoise,
Till they are gone.

PER. And call you this an engine?

POL. Mine own device.—Good sir, bid my wife's women   60
To burn my papers. [*Exit* PEREGRINE.]

[*The three* MERCATORI *rush in.*]

1 MER. Where's he hid?

3 MER. We must,
And will, sure, find him.

2 MER. Which is his study?

[*Re-enter* PEREGRINE.]

1 MER. What
Are you, sir?

PER. I am a merchant, that came here
To look upon this tortoise.

3 MER. How?

1 MER. St. Mark!
What beast is this?

PER. It is a fish.

2 MER. Come out here!

PER. Nay, you may strike him, sir, and tread upon him;
He'll bear a cart.

1 MER. What, to run over him?

PER. Yes, sir.

3 MER. Let's jump upon him.

2 MER. Can he not go?

PER. He creeps, sir.

1 MER. Let's see him creep.

PER. No, good sir, you will hurt him.

2 MER. Heart, I'll see him creep, or prick his guts.   70

3 MER. Come out here.

PER.   Pray you, sir!—[*Aside to* SIR POLITIC] Creep a little.

1 MER.   Forth.

2 MER. Yet further.

PER.   Good sir!—[*Aside*] Creep!

2 MER.   We'll see his legs.
          [*They pull off the shell and discover him.*]

3 MER. Gods so, he has garters!

1 MER.   Ay, and gloves!

2 MER.   Is this
     Your fearful tortoise?

PER. [*Discovering himself*] Now, Sir Pol, we are even;
     For your next project I shall be prepar'd;
     I am sorry for the funeral of your notes, sir.

1 MER. 'Twere a rare motion to be seen in Fleet Street.

2 MER. Ay, i' the term.

1 MER.   Or Smithfield, in the fair.

3 MER. Methinks 'tis but a melancholic sight!

PER. Farewell, most politic tortoise.

                              [*Exeunt* PEREGRINE *and* MERCATORI.]
                              [*Re-enter* WAITING WOMAN.]

POL.   Where's my Lady?   80
     Knows she of this?

WOM.   I know not, sir.

POL.   Inquire.—
     Oh, I shall be the fable of all feasts,
     The freight of the gazetti, ship-boys' tale;
     And, which is worst, even talk for ordinaries.

WOM. My Lady's come most melancholic home,
     And says, sir, she will straight to sea, for physic.

POL. And I, to shun this place and clime for ever,
     Creeping with house on back, and think it well
     To shrink my poor head in my politic shell.   [*Exeunt.*]

---

77. motion: sight. **78. term:** during the season, when courts are in session.
83. freight . . . gazetti: content of the newspapers. **84. ordinaries:** taverns.

SCENE V. *A room in Volpone's house.*

[*Enter* VOLPONE *and* MOSCA, *the first in the habit of a commandadore, the other of a clarissimo.*]

VOLP. Am I then like him?

MOS.   O, sir, you are he;
    No man can sever you.

VOLP.   Good.

MOS.   But what am I?

VOLP. 'Fore Heav'n, a brave clarissimo; thou becom'st it!
    Pity thou wert not born one.

MOS.   If I hold
    My made one, 'twill be well.

VOLP.   I'll go and see
    What news first at the court.   [*Exit.*]

MOS.   Do so.—My Fox
    Is out on his hole, and ere he shall re-enter,
    I'll make him languish in his borrow'd case,
    Except he come to composition with me.—
    Androgyno, Castrone, Nano!

            [*Enter* ANDROGYNO, CASTRONE, *and* NANO.]

ALL.   Here.   10

MOS. Go, recreate yourselves abroad; go, sport.—

                    [*Exeunt all but* MOSCA.]
    So, now I have the keys, and am possess'd.
    Since he will needs be dead afore his time,
    I'll bury him, or gain by him. I am his heir,
    And so will keep me, till he share, at least.
    To cozen him of all, were but a cheat
    Well plac'd; no man would construe it a sin;
    Let his sport pay for 't. This is call'd the Fox-trap.   [*Exit.*]

Sc. v. **2. sever:** tell you apart. **8. case:** skin. **9. composition:** terms.

SCENE VI. *A Street.*

[*Enter* CORBACCIO *and* CORVINO.]

CORB. They say the court is set.

CORV.   We must maintain
Our first tale good, for both our reputations.

CORB. Why, mine's no tale; my son would there have kill'd me.

CORV. That's true; I had forgot;—[*Aside*] mine is, I am sure.—
But for your will, sir.

CORB.   Ay, I'll come upon him
For that hereafter, now his patron's dead.

[*Enter* VOLPONE *disguised.*]

VOLP. Signior Corvino! and Corbaccio! sir,
Much joy unto you.

CORV.   Of what?

VOLP.   The sudden good
Dropp'd down upon you—

CORB.   Where?

VOLP.   And none knows how—
From old Volpone, sir.

CORB.   Out, errant knave!   10

VOLP. Let not your too much wealth, sir, make you furious.

CORB. Away, thou varlet.

VOLP.   Why, sir?

CORB.   Dost thou mock me?

VOLP. You mock the world, sir; did you not change wills?

CORB. Out, harlot.

VOLP.   O! belike you are the man,
Signior Corvino? Faith, you carry it well;
You grow not mad withal; I love your spirit.
You are not overleaven'd with your fortune.
You should ha' some would swell now like a wine-fat,
With such an autumn.—Did he gi' you all, sir?

Sc. vi. 17. overleaven'd: puffed up. 18. fat: vat. 19. autumn: harvest.

CORV. Avoid, you rascal.

VOLP.   Troth, your wife has shown   20
  Herself a very woman; but you are well,
  You need not care, you have a good estate,
  To bear it out, sir, better by this chance—
  Except Corbaccio have a share.

CORB.   Hence, varlet.

VOLP. You will not be acknown, sir; why, 'tis wise.
  Thus do all gamesters, at all games, dissemble:
  No man will seem to win. [*Exeunt* CORVINO *and* CORBACCIO.]
      Here comes my vulture,
  Heaving his beak up i' the air, and snuffing.

SCENE VII

[*Enter* VOLTORE.]

VOLT. Outstripp'd thus, by a parasite! a slave!
  Would run on errands, and make legs for crumbs!
  Well, what I'll do—

VOLP.   The court stays for your Worship.
  I e'en rejoice, sir, at your Worship's happiness,
  And that it fell into so learned hands,
  That understand the fingering—

VOLT.   What do you mean?

VOLP. I mean to be a suitor to your Worship,
  For the small tenement, out of reparations,
  That at the end of your long row of houses,
  By the Piscaria; it was, in Volpone's time,   10
  Your predecessor, ere he grew diseas'd,
  A handsome, pretty, custom'd bawdyhouse
  As any was in Venice, none disprais'd;

20. **Avoid:** get out. 25. **be acknown:** admit it.

Sc. vii. 8. **reparations:** repair. 12. **custom'd:** popular.

But fell with him: his body and that house
Decay'd together.

VOLT.   Come, sir, leave your prating.

VOLP. Why, if your Worship give me but your hand
That I may ha' the refusal, I have done.
'Tis a mere toy to you, sir, candle-rents;
As your learn'd Worship knows—

VOLT.   What do I know?

VOLP. Marry, no end of your wealth, sir; God decrease it!   20

VOLT. Mistaking knave! what, mock'st thou my misfortune?
                                                        [*Exit.*]

VOLP. His blessing on your heart, sir; would 'twere more!—
Now to my first again, at the next corner.   [*Exit.*]

SCENE VIII. Another corner of the street.

[*Enter* CORBACCIO *and* CORVINO, MOSCA *passant.*]

CORB. See, in our habit! see the impudent varlet!

CORV. That I could shoot mine eyes at him, like gun-stones.

[*Enter* VOLPONE.]

VOLP. But is this true, sir, of the parasite?

CORB. Again, t' afflict us? monster!

VOLP.   In good faith, sir,
I am heartily griev'd, a beard of your grave length
Should be so overreach'd. I never brook'd
That parasite's hair; methought his nose should cozen:
There still was somewhat in his look, did promise
The bane of a clarissimo.

CORB.   Knave—

VOLP.   Methinks
Yet you, that are so traded i' the world,   10
A witty merchant, the fine bird, Corvino,
That have such moral emblems on your name,

Sc. viii. Stage direction. passant: passing by. 1. habit: dress. 6. brook'd: could
endure.

Should not have sung your shame, and dropp'd your cheese,
  To let the Fox laugh at your emptiness.
CORV. Sirrah, you think the privilege of the place,
  And your red saucy cap, that seems to me
  Nail'd to your jolt-head with those two *cecchines,*
  Can warrant your abuses; come you hither;
  You shall perceive, sir, I dare beat you; approach.
VOLP. No haste, sir, I do not know your valor well,   20
  Since you durst publish what you are, sir.
CORV.   Tarry,
  I'd speak with you.
VOLP.   Sir, sir, another time—
CORV. Nay, now.
VOLP.   O God, sir! I were a wise man,
  Would stand the fury of a distracted cuckold.

                                        [MOSCA *walks by 'em.*]
CORB. What, come again!
VOLP.   Upon 'em, Mosca; save me.
CORB. The air's infected where he breathes.
CORV.   Let's fly him.
                    [*Exeunt* CORVINO *and* CORBACCIO.]
VOLP. Excellent basilisk! turn upon the Vulture.

SCENE IX

[*Enter* VOLTORE.]
VOLT. Well, flesh-fly, it is summer with you now;
  Your winter will come on.
MOS.   Good advocate,
  'Pray thee not rail, nor threaten out of place thus;
  Thou 'lt make a solecism, as Madam says.
  Get you a biggin more; your brain breaks loose.   [*Exit.*]

17. **cecchines:** i.e., gilt buttons. 27. **basilisk:** mythical beast that killed with a look.

Sc. ix. 5. **biggin more:** larger lawyer's cap.

VOLT. Well sir.

VOLP.   Would you ha' me beat the insolent slave?
Throw dirt upon his first good clothes?

VOLT.   This same
Is doubtless some familiar!

VOLP.   Sir, the court,
In troth, stays for you. I am mad, a mule
That never read Justinian should get up   10
And ride an advocate. Had you no quirk
To avoid gullage, sir, by such a creature?
I hope you do but jest; he has not done 't;
This 's but confederacy to blind the rest.
You are the heir?

VOLT.   A strange, officious,
Troublesome knave! Thou dost torment me.

VOLP.   I know—
It cannot be, sir, that you should be cozen'd;
'Tis not within the wit of man to do it;
You are so wise, so prudent; and 'tis fit
That wealth and wisdom still should go together.   20

                                        [*Exeunt.*]

SCENE X. *The Senate House.*

[*Enter four* AVOCATORI, NOTARIO, BONARIO, CELIA, CORBACCIO, CORVINO,
COMMANDADORI, SAFFI, *etc.*]

1 AVOC. Are all the parties here?

NOT.   All but the advocate.

2 AVOC. And here he comes.

               [*Enter* VOLTORE *and* VOLPONE.]

1 AVOC.   Then bring 'em forth to sentence

VOLT. O, my most honor'd fathers, let your mercy
Once win upon your justice, to forgive—
I am distracted—

Sc. ix. **8. familiar:** attendant demon. **12. gullage:** being tricked.

VOLP. [*Aside*]   What will he do now?

VOLT.   Oh,
    I know not which t' address myself to first;
    Whether your Fatherhoods, or these innocents—

CORV. [*Aside*] Will he betray himself?

VOLT.   Whom equally
    I have abus'd, out of most covetous ends—

CORV. The man is mad!

CORB.   What's that?

CORV.   He is possess'd.   10

VOLT. For which, now struck in conscience, here I prostrate
    Myself at your offended feet, for pardon.

1, 2 AVOC. Arise.

CEL.   O Heav'n, how just thou art!

VOLP.   I am caught
    I' mine own noose—

CORV. [*To* CORBACCIO]   Be constant, sir; naught now
    Can help but impudence.

1 AVOC.   Speak forward.

COM.   Silence!

VOLT. It is not passion in me, reverend fathers,
    But only conscience, conscience, my good sires,
    That makes me now tell truth. That parasite,
    That knave, hath been the instrument of all.

1 AVOC. Where is that knave? Fetch him.

VOLP.   I go.   [*Exit.*]

CORV.   Grave fathers,   20
    This man's distracted; he confess'd it now:
    For, hoping to be old Volpone's heir,
    Who now is dead—

3 AVOC.   How?

2 AVOC.   Is Volpone dead?

CORV. Dead since, grave fathers.

BON.   O sure vengeance!

Sc. x. 24. since: since the trial.

1 AVOC.   **Stay;**

Then he was no deceiver?

VOLT.   Oh, no, none.

This parasite, grave fathers—

CORV.   He does speak

Out of mere envy, 'cause the servant's made

The thing he gap'd for. Please your Fatherhoods,

This is the truth, though I'll not justify

The other, but he may be somedeal faulty.   30

VOLT. Ay, to your hopes, as well as mine, Corvino;

But I'll use modesty. Pleaseth your Wisdoms

To view these certain notes, and but confer them;

As I hope favor, they shall speak clear truth.

CORV. The Devil has ent'red him!

BON.   Or bides in you.

4 AVOC. We have done ill, by a public officer

To send for him, if he be heir.

2 AVOC.   For whom?

4 AVOC. Him that they call the parasite.

3 AVOC.   'Tis true,

He is a man of great estate, now left.

4 AVOC. Go you, and learn his name, and say the court   40

Entreats his presence here, but to the clearing

Of some few doubts.   [*Exit* NOTARIO.]

2 AVOC.   This same's a labyrinth!

1 AVOC. Stand you unto your first report?

CORV.   My state,

My life, my fame—

BON.   Where is 't?

CORV.   Are at the stake.

1 AVOC. Is yours so too?

CORB.   The advocate's a knave,

And has a forked tongue—

2 AVOC.   Speak to the point.

32. **modesty:** moderation. 33. **confer:** compare.

CORB. So is the parasite too.

1 AVOC.   This is confusion.

VOLT. I do beseech your Fatherhoods, read but those—

                                        [*Giving them papers.*]

CORV. And credit nothing the false spirit hath writ:

It cannot be but he's possess'd, grave fathers.   50

                                        [*The scene closes.*]

SCENE XI. *A street.*

[*Enter* VOLPONE.]

VOLP. To make a snare for mine own neck, and run

My head into it, wilfully! with laughter!

When I had newly 'scap'd, was free and clear!

Out of mere wantonness! Oh, the dull devil

Was in this brain of mine when I devis'd it,

And Mosca gave it second; he must now

Help to sear up this vein, or we bleed dead.

          [*Enter* NANO, ANDROGYNO, *and* CASTRONE.]

How now! Who let you loose? Whither go you now?

What, to buy gingerbread, or to drown kitlings?

NAN. Sir, Master Mosca call'd us out of doors,   10

And bid us all go play, and took the keys.

AND. Yes.

VOLP.   Did Master Mosca take the keys? Why, so!

I'm farther in. These are my fine conceits!

I must be merry, with a mischief to me!

What a vile wretch was I, that could not bear

My fortune soberly? I must ha' my crochets,

And my conundrums!—Well, go you, and seek him;

His meaning may be truer than my fear.

Bid him he straight come to me to the court;

Thither will I, and, if 't be possible,   20

Sc. xi. 13. conceits: ideas. 16. crochets: eccentric whims.

Unscrew my advocate, upon new hopes.
When I provok'd him, then I lost myself.   [*Exeunt.*]

SCENE XII. *The Senate House.*

[AVOCATORI, *etc., are discovered, as before.*]

1 AVOC. These things can ne'er be reconcil'd. He here
                                                  [*Shows the papers.*]
    Professeth that the gentleman was wrong'd,
    And that the gentlewoman was brought thither,
    Forc'd by her husband, and there left.

VOLT.   Most true.

CEL. How ready is Heav'n to those that pray!

1 AVOC.   But that
    Volpone would have ravish'd her, he holds
    Utterly false, knowing his impotence.

CORV. Grave fathers, he is possess'd; again, I say,
    Possess'd; nay, if there be possession,
    And obsession, he has both.

3 AVOC.   Here comes our officer.   10

[*Enter* VOLPONE.]

VOLP. The parasite will straight be here, grave fathers.

4 AVOC. You might invent some other name, Sir Varlet.

3 AVOC. Did not the notary meet him?

VOLP.   Not that I know.

4 AVOC. His coming will clear all.

2 AVOC.   Yet it is misty.

VOLT. May 't please your Fatherhoods—

VOLP. [*Whispers the* ADVOCATE]   Sir, the parasite
    Will'd me to tell you that his master lives;
    That you are still the man; your hopes the same;
    And this was only a jest—

VOLT.   How?

VOLP.   Sir, to try
    If you were firm, and how you stood affected.

VOLT. Art sure he lives?

VOLP.   Do I live, sir?

VOLT.   O me!   20
  I was too violent.

VOLP.   Sir, you may redeem it.
  They said you were possess'd; fall down, and seem so:
  I'll help to make it good. [VOLTORE *falls.*] God bless the man!—
  [*Aside to* VOLTORE] Stop your wind hard, and swell.—See, see,
      see, see!
  He vomits crooked pins! His eyes are set,
  Like a dead hare's hung in a poulter's shop!
  His mouth's running away! Do you see, signior?
  Now it is in his belly.

CORV.   Ay, the devil!

VOLP. Now in his throat.

CORV.   Ay, I perceive it plain.

VOLP. 'Twill out, 'twill out! stand clear. See where it flies!   30
  In shape of a blue toad, with a bat's wings!
  Do not you see it, sir?

CORB.   What? I think I do.

CORV. 'Tis too manifest.

VOLP.   Look! he comes t' himself!

VOLT. Where am I?

VOLP.   Take good heart, the worst is past, sir.
  You're dispossess'd.

1 AVOC.   What accident is this?

2 AVOC. Sudden and full of wonder!

3 AVOC.   If he were
  Possess'd, as it appears, all this is nothing.

CORV. He has been often subject to these fits.

1 AVOC. Show him that writing:—do you know it, sir?

VOLP. [*Aside to* VOLTORE] Deny it, sir, forswear it; know it not.   40

VOLT. Yes, I do know it well: it is my hand;
  But all that it contains is false.

BON.   O practice!

Sc. xii. 42. **practice**: trickery.

2 AVOC. What maze is this!

1 AVOC.   Is he not guilty then,
     Whom you there name the parasite?

VOLT.   Grave fathers,
     No more than his good patron, old Volpone.

4 AVOC. Why, he is dead.

VOLT.   O no, my honor'd fathers.
     He lives—

1 AVOC.   How! lives?

VOLT.   Lives.

2 AVOC.   This is subtler yet!

3 AVOC. You said he was dead!

VOLT.   Never.

3 AVOC.   You said so!

CORV.   I heard so.

4 AVOC. Here comes the gentleman; make him way.
                              [*Enter* MOSCA.]

3 AVOC.   A stool.

4 AVOC. [*Aside*] A proper man! and, were Volpone dead,   50
     A fit match for my daughter.

3 AVOC.   Give him way.

VOLP. [*Aside to* MOSCA] Mosca, I was a'most lost: the advocate
     Had betray'd all; but now it is recover'd;
     All's on the hinge again—say I am living.

MOS. What busy knave is this?—Most reverend fathers,
     I sooner had attended your grave pleasures,
     But that my order for the funeral
     Of my dear patron did require me—

VOLP. [*Aside*]   Mosca!

MOS. Whom I intend to bury like a gentleman.

VOLP. [*Aside*] Ay, quick, and cozen me of all.

2 AVOC.   Still stranger!   60
     More intricate!

1 AVOC.   And come about again!

4 AVOC. [*Aside*] It is a match; my daughter is bestow'd.

60. quick: alive.

MOS. [*Aside to* VOLPONE] Will you gi' me half?

VOLP. [*Aside*]   First I'll be hang'd.

MOS. [*Aside*]   I know
  Your voice is good; cry not so loud.

I AVOC.   Demand
  The advocate.—Sir, did not you affirm
  Volpone was alive?

VOLP.   Yes, and he is;
  This gent'man told me so.—[*Aside to* MOSCA] Thou shalt have
    half.

MOS. Whose drunkard is this same? Speak, some that know him;
  I never saw his face.—[*Aside to* VOLPONE] I cannot now
  Afford it you so cheap.

VOLP. [*Aside*]   No?

I AVOC.   What say you?   70

VOLT. The officer told me.

VOLP.   I did, grave fathers,
  And will maintain he lives, with mine own life,
  And that this creature [*Pointing to* MOSCA] told me.—[*Aside*]
    I was born
  With all good stars my enemies.

MOS.   Most grave fathers,
  If such an insolence as this must pass
  Upon me, I am silent; 'twas not this
  For which you sent, I hope.

2 AVOC.   Take him away.

VOLP. Mosca!

3 AVOC.   Let him be whipp'd.

VOLP. [*Aside to* MOSCA] Wilt thou betray me? Cozen me?

3 AVOC.   And taught to bear himself
  Toward a person of his rank.

4 AVOC.   Away.   80

MOS. I humbly thank your Fatherhoods.

VOLP.   Soft, soft;—[*Aside*] whipp'd!
  And lose all that I have! If I confess,
  It cannot be much more.

4 AVOC.   Sir, are you married?

VOLP. They'll be alli'd anon; I must be resolute;
   The Fox shall here uncase.   [*He puts off his disguise.*]

MOS. [*Aside*]   Patron!

VOLP.   Nay, now
   My ruins shall not come alone; your match
   I'll hinder sure; my substance shall not glue you,
   Nor screw you into a family.

MOS. [*Aside*]   Why, patron!

VOLP. I am Volpone, and this [*Pointing to* MOSCA] is my knave;
   This [*To* VOLTORE], his own knave; this [*To* CORBACCIO], ava-
      rice's fool;   90
   This [*To* CORVINO], a chimaera of wittol, fool, and knave:
   And, reverend fathers, since we all can hope
   Naught but a sentence, let's not now despair it.
   You hear me brief.

CORV.   May it please your Fatherhoods—

COM.   Silence.

1 AVOC. The knot is now undone, by miracle!

2 AVOC. Nothing can be more clear.

3 AVOC.   Or can more prove
   These innocent.

1 AVOC.   Give 'em their liberty.

BON. Heaven could not long let such gross crimes be hid.

2 AVOC. If this be held the highway to get riches,
   May I be poor.

3 AVOC. This 's not the gain, but torment.   100

1 AVOC. These possess wealth, as sick men possess fevers,
   Which trulier may be said to possess them.

2 AVOC. Disrobe that parasite.

CORV. and MOS.   Most honor'd fathers—

1 AVOC. Can you plead aught to stay the course of justice?
   If you can, speak.

CORV. and VOLT.   We beg favor.

CEL.   And mercy.

1 AVOC. You hurt your innocence, suing for the guilty.
    Stand forth; and, first, the parasite. You appear
    T' have been the chiefest minister, if not plotter,
    In all these lewd impostures, and now, lastly,
    Have with your impudence abus'd the court,
    And habit of a gentleman of Venice,   110
    Being a fellow of no birth or blood;
    For which our sentence is, first, thou be whipp'd;
    Then live perpetual prisoner in our galleys.
VOLP. I thank you for him.
MOS.   Bane to thy wolfish nature!
1 AVOC. Deliver him to the saffi.—Thou, Volpone,
    By blood and rank a gentleman, canst not fall
    Under like censure; but our judgment on thee
    Is that thy substance all be straight confiscate
    To the hospital of the Incurabili.   120
    And since the most was gotten by imposture,
    By feigning lame, gout, palsy, and such diseases,
    Thou art to lie in prison, cramp'd with irons,
    Till thou be'st sick and lame indeed.—Remove him.
VOLP. This is called mortifying of a Fox.
1 AVOC. Thou, Voltore, to take away the scandal
    Thou hast giv'n all worthy men of thy profession,
    Art banish'd from their fellowship, and our state.—
    Corbaccio!—Bring him near.—We here possess
    Thy son of all thy state, and confine thee   130
    To the monastery of San' Spirito;
    Where, since thou knew'st not how to live well here,
    Thou shalt be learn'd to die well.
CORB.   Ha! what said he?
COM. You shall know anon, sir.
1 AVOC.   Thou, Corvino, shalt
    Be straight embark'd from thine own house, and row'd
    Round about Venice, through the Grand Canal,
    Wearing a cap, with fair long ass's ears,

Instead of horns; and so to mount, a paper
Pinn'd on thy breast, to the Berlina.

CORV.   Yes,
And have mine eyes beat out with stinking fish,   140
Bruis'd fruit, and rotten eggs—'tis well. I am glad
I shall not see my shame yet.

1 AVOC.   And to expiate
Thy wrongs done to thy wife, thou art to send her
Home to her father, with her dowry trebled;
And these are all your judgments.

ALL.   Honor'd fathers—

1 AVOC. Which may not be revok'd. Now you begin,
When crimes are done and past, and to be punish'd,
To think what your crimes are.—Away with them!
Let all that see these vices thus rewarded,
Take heart, and love to study 'em. Mischiefs feed   150
Like beasts, till they be fat, and then they bleed.   [*Exeunt.*]

VOLPONE

The seasoning of a play is the applause.
Now, though the Fox be punish'd by the laws,
He yet doth hope, there is no suff'ring due,
For any fact which he hath done 'gainst you;
If there be, censure him; here he doubtful stands.
If not, fare jovially, and clap your hands.   [*Exit.*]

139. Berlina: pillory.

Moliere

THE WOULD-BE INVALID

IN 1658 Molière (Jean Baptiste Poquelin) returned to Paris at the age of thirty-six, an experienced and expert man of the theater after twelve years of touring the provinces as actor, manager, and playwright. His first production won the approval of Louis XIV, who installed him in the Théâtre du Palais Royale. Here, from 1661 until his death in 1673, he wrote and produced a remarkable series of comedies. Most of them derided the affectations and pretenses of social types. Medical quacks were exposed in *The Doctor in Spite of Himself* (1666); *Tartuffe* (1669) caricatured the religious impostor; *The Misanthrope* (1666), *The Miser* (1668), *The Would-Be Gentleman* (1670), and *The Learned Women* (1672) were directed at the targets suggested by their titles. *The Would-Be Invalid* was Molière's last play; he suffered a hemorrhage of the lungs while playing the part of Argan and died February 17, 1673.

Argan, a hypochondriac, is a "humorous" character in Ben Jonson's sense, but *Volpone* and *The Would-Be Invalid* are different kinds of comedy. *Volpone,* with its depiction and final judgment of unfettered human pride, leans toward tragedy; *The Would-Be Invalid* leans toward masque and farce. It is related in this respect to Latin comedy and to the *commedia dell'arte,* a form developed by professional Italian actors during the latter half of the sixteenth century. The Italian companies, made up of eight or nine men and three or four women, improvised lines and farcical stage business on the basis of an outline plot and stereotyped characters, including a pedant, a domineering father, a pair of young lovers, and a clever servant.

The first act of *The Would-Be Invalid* presents such characters in a typical situation. The father, Argan, suffers from the delusion

that he is an invalid. This monomania puts him at the mercy of his hypocritical doctors and his young and greedy second wife, and leads him to try to thwart the love of his daughter, Angélique, for Cléante. He attempts to force on her a stupid and pedantic young physician so that he will have as a son-in-law a doctor to care for his imaginary illness. Opposed to the rigid and sterile influence of Argan, to the stepmother who would disinherit Angélique by forcing her into a nunnery, and to the leechlike doctors are the clever maidservant, Toinette, and Argan's reasonable brother, Béralde. Their exuberance and common sense free the young lovers in the course of the play from the bonds of the "humorous" father and lead to the carnival energy and flexibility of the concluding marriage and comic ballet.

The movement of the play from restriction and inflexibility to festive release is marked by a rich use of farcical pantomime, burlesque tableaux and costumes, and comic incongruities. The doctors, whose devotion to laxatives and enemas was painfully close to fact in Molière's time, are caricatured and burlesqued at the very moments they think themselves most impressive. The sight of a solemn bigwig with an enormous stage syringe advancing slowly and menacingly toward the crouching Argan puts doctor and patient into healthful perspective. The only kind of language permitted the doctors is transparent double talk or set speeches. Like all one-dimensional experts, they have lost their human flexibility and the sense of social appropriateness. The young doctor courts Angélique carrying a huge thesis, and for romantic entertainment he invites her to watch a dissection. Argan's attitude toward these fake experts has become one of neurotic superstition, and as a result his language and actions are comically repetitive and predictable. The spontaneous Toinette, flowing easily from role to role, makes fun of him, pummels him with pillows, shows him the truth about himself and his situation, and finally helps us all to unbend and join the dance which ends the play.

THE WOULD-BE INVALID

(Le Malade imaginaire)

TRANSLATED AND EDITED BY MORRIS BISHOP

Characters

[*The specifications of costume are taken mostly from seventeenth-century editions of the play.*]

ARGAN, *a prosperous bourgeois. He wears a nightcap with lace crown, a neckerchief carelessly knotted, a red dressing-jacket with lace or braid, tight knee-breeches, heavy stockings, slippers.*

BÉLINE, *Argan's second wife, considerably younger than he. Good-looking elegant dress of the period.*

ANGÉLIQUE, *Argan's daughter by his first marriage. Attractive young-girl costume of the period.*

LOUISON. *Argan's daughter by his first marriage. She is about six.*

BÉRALDE, *Argan's brother. Sober gentleman's costume.*

CLÉANTE, *in love with Angélique. Costumed as fine young gentle-man of the period. He wears a curled, flowing wig.*

MONSIEUR DIAFOIRUS, *physician. He wears formal dress of seventeenth-century physician: a long, flowing black robe, a large wig, and a toque, or brimless cylindrical hat about 8 inches high, encircled with varicolored rings of bright velvet.*

THOMAS DIAFOIRUS, *his son. Same costume as his father, but with plain broad white collar. Instead of a wig, he wears his own hair, plastered to his skull.*

MONSIEUR PURGON, *physician. Dressed like Monsieur Diafoirus.*

MONSIEUR FLEURANT, *apothecary. Dressed in black or gray-brown gown, and wig. No hat.*

MONSIEUR DE BONNEFOI, *notary. Dressed in formal black.*

TOINETTE, *maidservant. Dainty, sprightly, but not elaborate house dress.*

PROLOGUE

[*At the first production, in February, 1673, the performance opened with an allegorical ballet, celebrating the recent military triumphs of Louis XIV in Holland. The text is omitted here.*]

ACT I

[*All the action takes place in* ARGAN'S *bedroom. The most conspicuous feature of the setting is an enormous four-poster bed, on the spectator's right. It stands on a platform, raised one step above the stage level. On the spectator's left is* ARGAN'S *easy chair. Near at hand is a table, loaded with medicines. Also a small portable table, and chairs. At rear of stage, three steps leading up to a small platform, with a curtain masking the rear entrance. This is the entrance for visitors from outside the house. The actors coming from other rooms in the house, or going to them, enter and exit at either side. Practicable doors are unnecessary; the exits may be masked by curtains.*

As the curtain rises, ARGAN *is found sitting in his easy chair, wearing a dressing-jacket. He is a ruddy, vigorous-looking man, capable of quick and excited action, with which his exaggerated airs of illness make a humorous contrast. On the small table before him are a large ledger, an inkwell, a quill pen, a glass of water, two bowls.*

He is reading a druggist's bill. As he completes each addition he takes the proper number of counters from a bowl and drops them in the second bowl. He reads the items of the druggist's bill in a rapid, chanting monotone.]

ARGAN. Three and two is five and five is ten and ten is twenty. Three and two is five. [*He drops a handful of counters in the second bowl, utters a sound of relief, takes a drink of water, gargles long and loud, spits into a bowl beside him on the floor. Reads from the druggist's bill.*] "Item, on the twenty-fourth, a little enema, insinuating, emollient, alleviating, [*he enjoys the phrases*] to mollify, humidify, and refresh the intestinal tract of the gentleman." What I like about the bills from Monsieur Fleurant the apothecary is that they are always so respectful. "The intestinal tract of the gentleman, thirty sous." [*He realizes after a moment* [10 *the high price.*] Yes, but Monsieur Fleurant, it is not enough to be respectful, you must also be reasonable and not swindle the sick. Thirty sous for an enema! I am your very humble servant, but I won't pay it. In your other bills you put them down at twenty sous, and when a druggist says twenty sous, he really means ten sous. Here they are, ten sous. [*Drops counters in bowl. Reads*] "Plus, on the same day, a good detergent enema, composed of double catholicon, rhubarb, honey, et cetera, according to prescription, to cleanse, purify, and expurgate the intestinal tract of the gentleman, thirty sous." With your kind permission, ten sous. "Plus, on the [20 same day, in the evening, an hepatic julep, soporific and somniferous, compounded to induce sleep in the gentleman, thirty-five sous." I don't complain of that, for it did put me to sleep. Ten, fifteen, sixteen, seventeen sous, six farthings. "Plus, on the twenty-fifth, a fine purgative tonic, compounded of fresh cassia with levantine senna and other drugs, according to the prescription of Doctor Purgon, to expel and evacuate the bile of the gentleman, four francs." [*With incredulous fury*] Yes, but Monsieur Fleurant, you are going too far, your patients have got to live, haven't they? Doctor Purgon didn't order you to put down four francs. Three [30 francs, put down three francs, if you please. And a half of that is thirty sous. [*Drops counters in bowl.*] "Plus, on the same day, an

anodine astringent potion, to relax the gentleman, thirty sous."
Good; fifteen sous. "Plus, on the twenty-sixth, a carminative enema,
to reduce the gentleman's gas, thirty sous." Let's say ten sous, Monsieur Fleurant. "Plus the gentleman's enema repeated in the evening, as above, thirty sous." My dear Monsieur Fleurant, ten
sous. "Plus, on the twenty-seventh, a good medicine designed to
hasten elimination, and to banish the gentleman's humors, three
francs." A half of that is thirty sous. [*His anger has dwindled; he* [40
pauses, wipes his brow, resumes his reckoning with real gusto.]
I am glad you're more reasonable. "Plus, on the twenty-eighth, a
compound of whey, clarified and sweetened, to dulcify, mollify,
temper and refresh the gentleman's blood, twenty sous." Good, ten
sous. "Plus a cordial and preservative potion, composed of twelve
grains of bezoar-stone, syrup of lemon and pomegranate, and other
ingredients according to prescription, five francs." Ah, Monsieur
Fleurant, wait a minute, please. If you treat people that way, who's
going to get sick? Content yourself with four francs. Twenty, forty
sous. Three and two is five and five is ten and ten is twenty. [50
Sixty-three francs four sous six farthings. So this month I have taken
one, two, three, four, five, six, seven, eight purges, and one, two,
three, four, five, six, seven, eight, nine, ten, eleven, twelve enemas.
And last month, there were twelve purges and twenty enemas. No
wonder I'm not so well this month as I was last month. I'll tell that
to Doctor Purgon, he'll fix it. . . . Come now, take all this stuff
away. [*He shuts his ledger and waits for someone to execute his
order. Silence. He looks in both directions.*] Nobody here! There's
no use my talking, they always go and leave me alone. There's no
way to keep them around. [*He rings the small bell on his table.*] [60
They don't hear anything, and my bell doesn't make enough noise.
[*He rings bell and shouts at the same time, getting steadily more
angry.*] Jingle, jingle, jingle, jingle! No use. Jingle, jingle, jingle,
jingle! They're deaf! Toinette! Jingle, jingle, jingle! I might just as
well not be ringing at all. Shameless hussy! Jingle, jingle, jingle!
You'll drive me crazy! [*He throws bell on the floor, in a fury.*]
Jingle, jingle, jingle, the devil take you, you slut! Is it possible that
they can leave a poor invalid alone like that? Jingle, jingle, jingle;
it's really sad. Jingle, jingle, jingle! Good heavens, they're going to

leave me here alone to die! [*Feebly, as a last appeal for help*] Jingle,
jingle, jingle!   71
[*Enter* TOINETTE. *She is the soubrette, the pert parlor-maid, who has
a secure place in the household.*]

TOINETTE. All right, here I am.

ARGAN. [*Collapsing, fanning his face with handkerchief*] Oh, you
slut! Oh, you hussy!

TOINETTE. [*Comes downstage, beside* ARGAN's *chair. Recognizes
she is about to be scolded, and takes her defensive measures*] The
deuce take your impatience! You made me rush so I gave my head
a terrible bang on a shutter.   80

ARGAN. [*Feebly*] You scoundrel—

TOINETTE. [*Interrupting*] Oh—oh—

ARGAN. It's been already—

TOINETTE. Oh—oh—

ARGAN. It's been an hour already—

TOINETTE. Oh—oh—

ARGAN. You left me alone—

TOINETTE. Oh—oh—

ARGAN. [*Shouting above* TOINETTE's *wails*] Shut up, you hag, and
let me give you a good going over.   90

TOINETTE. Yes, that's a nice idea, after the way I hurt myself.

ARGAN. [*Feebly*] You made me yell myself hoarse, you rascal.

TOINETTE. And you made me bump my head, so we're even.
We'll call it off, if you like.

ARGAN. What, you hussy?

TOINETTE. Oh—oh—

ARGAN. You little devil! You would—

TOINETTE. Oh—oh—

ARGAN. [*Surrendering*] What! I won't even have the pleasure of
scolding her!   100

TOINETTE. [*Turning suddenly sweet*] Scold all you like; I don't
mind.

ARGAN. [*Furiously*] You don't let me, you devil, by interrupting
me all the time.

TOINETTE. [*Reasonably*] If you have the pleasure of scolding me,
I certainly ought to have the pleasure of crying. That's fair, isn't

it? [ARGAN *prepares to protest;* TOINETTE *begins to howl.*] Oh—oh—
[ARGAN *gives up, and puts his hands over his ears.*]

ARGAN. All right, all right; let it go. Take all this stuff away, you
rapscallion; take it away. [TOINETTE *picks up the small table and
starts off.* ARGAN *seizes her by the arm.*] Did my enema today come
out well? 112

TOINETTE. Your enema?

ARGAN. Yes. Was there much bile?

TOINETTE. Goodness, I don't worry about those things. That's up
to Monsieur Fleurant, since he gets his money out of it.
[*She sets the table down.*]

ARGAN. [*Offended*] Anyway, be sure and get some hot water
ready for the enema I'll have to take soon.

TOINETTE. [*Comes back beside* ARGAN's *chair*] That Monsieur
Fleurant and that Doctor Purgon, they're making a fool out of you
and that nasty old body of yours. They're milking you like a cow.
I'd like to ask them what's wrong with you really, to make you take
so much medicine and things. 124
[*She picks up the bowl from the floor and puts it under the medicine table.*]

ARGAN. Shut up, stupid. It isn't your business to criticize the conclusions of medical science. Send in my daughter Angélique.
There's something I want to tell her.

TOINETTE. [*Moving to the rear, sees* ANGÉLIQUE, *offstage*] She's
coming of her own accord. She guessed what you were thinking.
[*Enter* ANGÉLIQUE. *She comes downstage.*] 132

ARGAN. Come here, Angélique. I am glad you came in; I wanted
to talk to you.

ANGÉLIQUE. I am glad to hear what you have to say.
[*She stands beside his chair.*]

ARGAN. [*Contorts himself violently*] No. Wait a minute. Give me
my stick. I'll be right back.
[TOINETTE *comes from behind his chair, helps him to rise, gives
him his stick, takes him under the arm, and helps him out, at
a hobbling run. She returns alone.*] 141

TOINETTE. Hurry up, sir, hurry. Monsieur Fleurant gives us plenty
to do. [*She goes to bed, begins to make it up.*]

ANGÉLIQUE. [*Confidentially, in fear that her father may return*] Toinette!

TOINETTE. What?

ANGÉLIQUE. Look at me a minute.

[*She looks shyly at audience.* TOINETTE *straightens up, stares at* ANGÉLIQUE.]

TOINETTE. All right. I'm looking at you.

ANGÉLIQUE. [*Sighs*] Toinette!　　　　　　　　　　　　　150

TOINETTE. What do you mean, "Toinette"?

ANGÉLIQUE. Don't you guess what I want to talk about?

TOINETTE. I can guess all right. About our young lover. [*She resumes her bedmaking.*] He's been our only subject of conversation for a week, and if you don't talk about him all the time, I know something's wrong.

ANGÉLIQUE. [*Turning to* TOINETTE] Since you know that, why don't you bring the subject up of your own accord?

TOINETTE. [*Stops her work*] You never give me time. I never can get ahead of you.　　　　　　　　　　　　　161

ANGÉLIQUE. I admit that I never seem to tire of talking about him, and it makes my heart happy to confide in you. [TOINETTE *goes back to work.* ANGÉLIQUE *joins her on the far side of the bed.* TOINETTE *tucks in the bedclothes. After each speech, she pushes* ANGÉLIQUE *along, as she tucks in the bed.* ANGÉLIQUE, *in a glassy-eyed trance, makes no objection.*] But tell me, Toinette, do you condemn the feeling that I have for him?

TOINETTE. Far from it.

ANGÉLIQUE. Am I wrong in abandoning myself to these sweet emotions?　　　　　　　　　　　　　171

TOINETTE. I don't say that at all.

ANGÉLIQUE. Would you expect me to be absolutely insensible to all the tender protestations of ardent passion he makes to me?

TOINETTE. [*Finishes tucking in the far side of the bed, passes in front of* ANGÉLIQUE, *begins tucking in the near side*] Heavens, no.

ANGÉLIQUE. [*Joins* TOINETTE. *Same business.*] Just tell me, don't you think there is something fateful, something almost super-natural, in the extraordinary way we met?

TOINETTE. Yes.　　　　　　　　　　　　　180

ANGÉLIQUE. Don't you think that the way he came to my defense without knowing me marks him as a really gallant gentleman?

TOINETTE. Yes.

ANGÉLIQUE. And that no one could have acted in a more honorable way?

TOINETTE. I agree entirely.

ANGÉLIQUE. That there was something very polished about his manners?

TOINETTE. Oh, yes, yes.

[*She goes to head of bed, arranges pillows.*]   190

ANGÉLIQUE. [*Turns shyly away, toward audience*] Toinette, don't you think he is really unusually good-looking?

TOINETTE. Most assuredly.

ANGÉLIQUE. That there's something sort of distinguished about him?

TOINETTE. I certainly do.

ANGÉLIQUE. That there's something noble in his language, just as there is in his actions?

TOINETTE. Oh, absolutely.

ANGÉLIQUE. That there's a really sincere emotion in everything he says to me?   201

TOINETTE. That's true, too.

ANGÉLIQUE. [*Turns impulsively to* TOINETTE] And that there's nothing more dreadful than the way they keep me shut up, so that there can be no proper expression for the mutual ardor which heaven inspires in us?

TOINETTE. [*In a soothing tone*] You are absolutely right.

[*She goes to the medicine table.*]

ANGÉLIQUE. [*Following* TOINETTE] But dear Toinette, do you think he loves me as much as he says?   210

TOINETTE. Hé hé! Those matters are sometimes a little open to doubt. The imitations of love look a lot like the real thing, and I have seen some people who were wonderful actors in that line.

ANGÉLIQUE. [*Taking* TOINETTE's *banter seriously*] Oh, Toinette, what do you mean? [TOINETTE *signals to her to talk less loud*.] Oh dear, the way he talks to me, would it be possible he weren't telling the truth?

TOINETTE. [*Embraces* ANGÉLIQUE] Anyway, you'll soon know the answer. Since he wrote to you yesterday that he was going to ask for your hand in marriage, you should soon find out whether he is sincere towards you or not. That will be the real proof.   221

ANGÉLIQUE. Oh, Toinette, if he is deceiving me, I will never believe in any man as long as I live.

TOINETTE. Here's your father coming back.

[*She takes her stand by the armchair and awaits him. Enter* ARGAN, *looking cheerful.* TOINETTE *inquires, in dumbshow:* "*Was it all right?*" ARGAN *nods.* TOINETTE *takes his stick, hangs it on the back of the chair, helps him to sit down.*]

ARGAN. Well, Daughter, I am going to give you a bit of news which will perhaps surprise you. Your hand has been requested in marriage. [ANGÉLIQUE *laughs.*] How's that? You laugh? Yes, mar- [231 riage, that's a funny word. Nothing seems more laughable to girls, eh? Ah, nature, nature, human nature! As nearly as I can see, my dear, there's no use my asking you whether you want to get married.

ANGÉLIQUE. Father, it is my duty to do everything it may please you to order.   [*Curtseys.*]

ARGAN. I am very happy to have such an obedient daughter. So the matter is settled. I have promised your hand.

ANGÉLIQUE. It is only proper, Father, that I should blindly obey all your dispositions.   [*Curtseys.*]   240

ARGAN. [*Pulls out his handkerchief*] Your stepmother wanted me to make you a nun, and so did your little sister Louison. That has been your stepmother's idea right along.

[*Blows his nose ceremoniously.*]

TOINETTE. [*Aside*] The old witch has her reasons.

ARGAN. She didn't want to consent to this marriage; but I won out, and my word has been given.

ANGÉLIQUE. Oh, Father, how grateful I am to you for all your kindness!   [*She kisses his hand.*]

TOINETTE. [*Moves to side of* ARGAN's *chair*] In fact, I am grateful to you too, and this is the most sensible thing you have done in your life.

                                                          252

[ARGAN *looks at her angrily.* TOINETTE *mimics:* "*Oh, I beg your pardon!*" *goes to the medicine table, and listens to the conversation.*]

ARGAN. I haven't yet seen the young man in question; but they tell me that I will be very well pleased with him, and you too.

ANGÉLIQUE. Oh, certainly, Father.

ARGAN. What do you mean? Have you seen him?

[ANGÉLIQUE *recognizes her blunder, appeals mutely for help to* TOINETTE. TOINETTE *signals that she should admit everything.* ARGAN *looks suspiciously at* TOINETTE, *who fusses with medicines.*] 263

ANGÉLIQUE. [*Kneels beside her father, takes his hand*] Since your consent makes it possible for me to tell you my heart's secrets, I won't conceal from you that we met quite by chance, only six days ago, and that the request for marriage you have received is the result of the liking we conceived for each other, at very first sight.

ARGAN. They didn't tell me that, but I'm glad of it, and it's a good thing that's the way it was. They say he's a tall, handsome young man.

ANGÉLIQUE. Yes, Father.

ARGAN. Well built.   273

ANGÉLIQUE. Oh, certainly.

ARGAN. Nice manners.

ANGÉLIQUE. Yes indeed.

ARGAN. Good looking.

ANGÉLIQUE. Very good looking.

ARGAN. Well behaved; good family.

ANGÉLIQUE. Absolutely.

ARGAN. A decent young man.

ANGÉLIQUE. Oh, as decent as can be.

ARGAN. Speaks Latin and Greek well.   283

ANGÉLIQUE. I don't know about that.

ARGAN. He will become a doctor in three days.

ANGÉLIQUE. Will he, Father?

ARGAN. Yes. Didn't he tell you?

ANGÉLIQUE. No, he didn't. Who told *you?*

ARGAN. Doctor Purgon.

ANGÉLIQUE. Does Doctor Purgon know him?

ARGAN. What a question! Of course he knows him, since he's Doctor Purgon's nephew.

292

ANGÉLIQUE. Cléante is Doctor Purgon's nephew?

ARGAN. What Cléante? We're talking about the young man who has asked your hand in marriage.

ANGÉLIQUE. Yes, exactly.

ARGAN. Well, it's Doctor Purgon's nephew, who is the son of his brother-in-law, Doctor Diafoirus; and that son's name is Thomas Diafoirus, and not Cléante. [TOINETTE *claps her hand over her mouth.*] And we concluded that marriage this morning, Doctor Purgon, Monsieur Fleurant, and I. And tomorrow this new son-in-law of ours is to be brought in by his father. What's the matter? You look like a duck in a fit.

303

ANGÉLIQUE. The fact is, Father, I know now you were talking about one person, and I thought you meant another.

[*She rises, and turns away from her father.*]

TOINETTE. [*Comes downstage, beside* ARGAN's *chair*] What, sir! You have actually done this silly thing? With all your money, you would think of marrying your daughter to a mere doctor?

ARGAN. Yes. What business is it of yours, you brazen hussy?

TOINETTE. Calm down; no bad language. Can't we have a reasonable argument without your getting angry? [ARGAN *moves to protest.*] There, there, let's be calm and cool. What, may I ask, is your reason for such a marriage?

314

ARGAN. My reason is that, sick and infirm as I am [*he forces a cough, and speaks in a whining tone*], I want to have a son-in-law and other alliances in the medical world, so that I can be assured of proper aid against illness, and so that I can have access to the necessary remedies in my own family and get full profit from consultations and prescriptions.

TOINETTE. [*Soothingly*] Well, that certainly is a reason, and it is really a pleasure to be able to discuss things soberly and calmly. But sir, put your hand on your conscience. Are you really sick?

323

ARGAN. [*Overcome; feebly*] What do you mean, hussy, am I really sick? [*Furious; bellowing.*] Am I really sick, hussy?

TOINETTE. All right, all right; you're sick. Let's not dispute about that. Yes, you are very sick; I agree. Sicker than you think. [ARGAN *is startled*.] That's all settled. But your daughter is to marry a husband for herself, and as she isn't sick, it isn't necessary to give her a doctor.

ARGAN. [*Naïvely*] It's for me I'm giving her a doctor. [*He looks at* ANGÉLIQUE.] A proper daughter ought to be happy to marry someone who is useful to her father's health. 333

TOINETTE. Look here, sir, would you like me to give you a bit of friendly advice?

ARGAN. [*Wearily*] What is this friendly advice?

TOINETTE. Just give up this marriage.

ARGAN. And the reason is?

TOINETTE. The reason is that your daughter won't consent to it.

ARGAN. She won't consent to it?

TOINETTE. No.

ARGAN. My daughter? 342

TOINETTE. Your daughter. She will tell you that she has no concern with Dr. Diafoirus, nor with his son Thomas Diafoirus, nor with all the Diafoiruses in the world.

ARGAN. [*Shouting*] I have concern with them, I have plenty. Not to mention the fact that this is a better match than you think. Dr. Diafoirus has just that one son, who is his only heir. And besides, Dr. Purgon, who hasn't any wife or children, will leave him all his property in view of this marriage; and Dr. Purgon is a man who has a good eight thousand francs a year income.

TOINETTE. He must have killed a lot of people to get so rich. 352

ARGAN. Eight thousand francs a year is something, not to mention the father's property.

TOINETTE. That's all very fine, sir; but I come back to my point just the same. I advise you, between ourselves, to choose some other husband for her; she isn't made to be Madame Diafoirus.

ARGAN. [*Calmly*] It is my desire that this should be the case.

TOINETTE. Tut tut, don't say that.

ARGAN. What do you mean, don't say that?

TOINETTE. By no means.

ARGAN. And why shouldn't I say it? 362

TOINETTE. People will say that you don't know what you're talking about.

ARGAN. They can say what they please, but I have given my word, and I expect her to carry it out.

TOINETTE. No, I am sure she won't do it.

ARGAN. I'll make her do it.

TOINETTE. She won't do it, I tell you.

ARGAN. She will do it, or I'll put her in a convent.

TOINETTE. You?

ARGAN. Me.

TOINETTE. Good. 372

ARGAN. What do you mean, good?

TOINETTE. You won't put her in a convent.

ARGAN. I won't put her in a convent?

TOINETTE. No.

ARGAN. No?

TOINETTE. [*Shouts in* ARGAN's *face*] No.

ARGAN. [*Shouts in* TOINETTE's *face*] Well, well, that's very nice! I won't put my daughter in a convent if I want to?

TOINETTE. No, I tell you.

ARGAN. Who will stop me? 382

TOINETTE. You will yourself.

ARGAN. [*Amazed*] I will myself?

TOINETTE. Yes. You won't have the heart to do it.

ARGAN. Yes I will.

TOINETTE. You're being silly.

ARGAN. I am not being silly.

TOINETTE. Your fatherly affection will get the better of you.

ARGAN. It won't get the better of me. 391

TOINETTE. [*Passes behind his chair*] She'll cry a little, throw her arms around your neck [*she throws her arms around* ARGAN's *neck from behind; he struggles*] and she'll say tenderly: "Oh my dear little papa," and that will be enough to move you.

ARGAN. [*Shakes her off*] It won't move me a bit.

TOINETTE. Yes it will!

[*She pats the top of* ARGAN's *head; he slaps at her hand.*]

ARGAN. I tell you I won't change my mind.

TOINETTE. [*Beside* ARGAN's *chair*] Nonsense.   400

ARGAN. Don't say nonsense.

TOINETTE. Goodness, I know you. You're naturally kind.

[*She starts to walk away.*]

ARGAN. [*Rises, furious, walks toward* TOINETTE, *his arm uplifted to strike her*] I am not kind. I can be ugly when I want to.

TOINETTE. [*Protecting herself with her arm*] Careful, sir. You're forgetting you're sick.

[ARGAN *stops; he totters, turns, runs to collapse in his chair. The two women rush to his side.* TOINETTE *fetches a glass of water from medicine-table;* ARGAN *drinks greedily. The two women rise up, relieved.*] 411

ARGAN. [*Feebly*] I command her absolutely to get ready to marry the husband I choose for her.

TOINETTE. [*Imitating him*] And I absolutely forbid her to do anything of the sort.

ARGAN. [*Shouts and waves the glass dangerously*] What are we coming to! What kind of insolence is this, for a rascally servant to talk that way in front of her master?

TOINETTE. [*Saves the glass from* ARGAN's *hand, reprovingly; puts it on medicine table*] When a master doesn't know what he's doing, it's the duty of a sensible servant to put him in the right way.   421

[*She has her back to* ARGAN.]

ARGAN. [*Rises, goes behind chair, takes his cane*] You insolent scoundrel, I'll have to teach you a lesson.

TOINETTE. [*Turns, sees* ARGAN, *utters a cry, runs to opposite side of chair from him. Provokingly*] It is my duty to prevent you from doing something which would dishonor you.

ARGAN. [*Moves around chair to reach her*] Come here, come here; I'll teach you how to talk.

TOINETTE. [*Circles around chair*] I am naturally interested in keeping you from doing something silly.   431

ARGAN. [*Pursues* TOINETTE *around chair, waving his stick*] Slut!

TOINETTE. [*Circles chair, runs behind bed*] No, I will never consent to this marriage.

ARGAN. [*Following her*] You she-devil!

TOINETTE. [*Circles bed, with* ARGAN *on opposite side*] I don't wish her to marry your Thomas Diafoirus.

ARGAN. [*Tries to hit* TOINETTE *across bed; falls flat on it*] Wench!

TOINETTE. [*Comes downstage behind* ANGÉLIQUE, *who has remained petrified in center*] She will obey me instead of you. 440

ARGAN. [*Stands up on bed*] Angélique, won't you stop that rascal there?

ANGÉLIQUE. Oh, Father, don't make yourself ill again!

ARGAN. If you don't stop her, I will put my parental curse on you.

TOINETTE. And as for me, I will disinherit her if she obeys you.

[*Enter* BÉLINE. *She stops in surprise.* TOINETTE *and* ANGÉLIQUE *turn toward her, curtsey to her, and exit, one on each side.* ARGAN *collapses on bed and slides to floor.*]

ARGAN. Oh, oh, oh, I'm done for. This will kill me. . . . Oh, oh, come here, darling. 450

BÉLINE. [*Going to him; in cajoling tone*] What's the matter, my poor dear?

ARGAN. Come here and help me.

BÉLINE. [*Picks him up and helps him to sit on the platform at foot of bed*] What's the matter, my little boy?

ARGAN. My darling!

BÉLINE. My baby!

ARGAN. They've been making me angry, precious.

BÉLINE. Oh, my poor little lambie! How did they do that, my sweet? 460

ARGAN. Your slut of a Toinette has become more insolent than ever.

BÉLINE. Now don't get excited, my little pet.

ARGAN. She put me in a rage, darling.

BÉLINE. Calm down, baby; there, there.

ARGAN. She went on for an hour interfering with the things I want to do.

BÉLINE. There, there, just take things easy.

ARGAN. And she had the impudence to tell me I am not sick. [*He begins to cough;* BÉLINE *draws back, with an involuntary quiver of disgust.*] 470

BÉLINE. She's an impertinent hussy.

ARGAN. You know, darling, that's not so. [*He coughs until he is out of breath.*]

BÉLINE. Yes, dearest, she's quite wrong.

ARGAN. [*Continuing to cough*] Sweetheart, that wench will be the death of me.

BÉLINE. [*Pats* ARGAN's *back*] There, there; there, there.

ARGAN. [*Draws a long whistling breath, stops coughing. He pats his stomach.*] She is the cause of all the bile I'm producing.

BÉLINE. Don't get so excited, baby. 480

ARGAN. And I've been telling you for I don't know how long to get rid of her.

BÉLINE. [*Becoming annoyed*] After all, darling, all servants have something wrong with them. You have to put up with their bad qualities on account of their good ones. Toinette knows her business and she's a good worker; and most of all she's trustworthy. And you know that nowadays you have to be very careful about the kind of people you take into your home. [ARGAN *mumbles, unconvinced.* BÉLINE *calls, turning her back on* ARGAN.] Oh, Toinette!

[*Enter* TOINETTE, *wearing the sweetest of expressions.*] 490

TOINETTE. Yes, ma'am?

BÉLINE. Tell me, why did you make my husband angry?

TOINETTE. Me, ma'am? Oh dear, I don't know what you mean. I always do my best to make him happy in every way.

ARGAN. [*Bounding in his chair*] Oh, the scamp!

[BÉLINE *soothes him.*]

TOINETTE. He told us that he wanted to marry Angélique to the son of Dr. Diafoirus. I only said that I thought it would be a very good match for her, but I thought he would do better to put her in a convent. 500

BÉLINE. [*Turning to* ARGAN] There's nothing so bad about that. I rather think she is right.

ARGAN. What, darling, you believe her? She's a villain; she was just as impudent as could be.

BÉLINE. Of course, dearie, of course. There, there, calm down. [*Turns toward* TOINETTE.] Listen, Toinette. If you ever make my husband angry, I will discharge you. [TOINETTE *is about to protest.* BÉLINE *signals to her:* "Hush, it's just to satisfy him." TOINETTE

smiles broadly.] There, give me his fur-lined gown. [*She rouses* ARGAN. TOINETTE *goes to the bed, takes gown, brings it back and* [510 *puts it around* ARGAN's *shoulders.*] And some pillows. [TOINETTE *makes a pile of six pillows.* BÉLINE *helps* ARGAN *to his chair.*] I'll fix him up nicely in his little chair. You're all every which way, darling. [ARGAN *sits down, and sneezes.*] Pull down your little night-cap over your precious ears. The best way to catch a cold is through the ears.

ARGAN. Oh, sweetheart, how grateful I am to you for all the good care you take of me! 518

[*During this speech,* TOINETTE *has come up with the pile of pillows.* BÉLINE *tries to take the top one, which is out of her reach.* TOINETTE *bends over, and rises up every time* BÉLINE *takes a pillow.*]

BÉLINE. Get up a second, let me put this under you. Let's put this one here for you to rest your arm on . . . and this one on the other side. [*She passes around chair.*] And we'll put this one behind your back . . . and this one to support your sweet head. 526

TOINETTE. And this one to protect you from the bad air!
[*She slaps the last pillow on his face, and runs out.* BÉLINE *restrains her impulse to laugh.*]

ARGAN. Oh, you rapscallion, you want to smother me to death!
[*He rises, furious, throws the last pillow into the wings, after* TOINETTE. *He takes the pillow from under his right arm and throws it savagely at the bed platform.*]

BÉLINE. There, there; there, there! [*She goes to pick up the second pillow.* ARGAN *takes the pillow from under his left arm, throws it wildly—but it hits* BÉLINE's *back as she is bending over to pick up the second pillow.*] What's the matter with you anyway? 537
[*She picks up the third pillow.*]

ARGAN. [*To avoid a scolding, sinks back in his chair*] Oh, dear, oh dear, I'm all in!
[*Feeling a troublesome pillow beneath him, he pulls it out and throws it into the wings. He collapses in the chair.*]

BÉLINE. [*Returns to him, disposes around him the two pillows she is carrying*] Why do you get so angry? She thought she was being nice to you. 545

ARGAN. Darling, you don't know how sly that little devil is. Oh, oh, she has put me in a terrible state. I'll need more than eight purges and a dozen enemas to make up for all this.

BÉLINE. [*Arranging* ARGAN's *nightcap*] There, there, my sweet, just calm down.

ARGAN. My dearest, you are all my consolation in this world.

BÉLINE. My poor baby!

ARGAN. [*Takes* BÉLINE's *hands, places them affectionately around his neck*] And just to show that I appreciate all your love for me, dearest, I want to make my will, as I've already told you.   555

BÉLINE. [*Coming beside chair*] Oh, darling, let's not talk about that sort of thing, I beg you. I just can't bear such a thought, and if you merely mention the word "will," it makes me shudder all over.

ARGAN. But didn't I tell you to speak to your notary about that?

BÉLINE. [*Pointing to rear*] I did bring him; he's right outside.

ARGAN. Bring him in, my love.

BÉLINE. Oh dear, my darling, when a girl loves her husband so much, she's in no condition to think about things like that.   563

[*She kisses* ARGAN *lightly on the brow, goes to rear steps. Music. The curtains open, disclosing the notary, bowing almost double. He straightens up, descends the steps, and bows again to the ground as music ceases.*]

ARGAN. Come here, Monsieur de Bonnefoi, come here. [*The notary makes a third bow to* ARGAN.] Take a chair, won't you? [*The notary does so.*] My dear sir, my wife has told me that you are a very trustworthy man, and an excellent friend of hers. So I told her to speak to you about a will I am thinking of making.   572

BÉLINE. [*Goes beside* ARGAN. *He takes her hand.*] Oh, dear, I just can't talk about things like that.

BONNEFOI. [*Sharp and business-like*] Monsieur, she has explained to me your intentions and the purposes you have with regard to her. And I must tell you on that score that you cannot give anything to your wife by will.

ARGAN. And why not?   579

BONNEFOI. [*Emphatic; categorical*] Common law forbids it. If we were in a region of statute law, it would be possible. But in Paris and in the areas of common law, or at least in most of them, that is

not permitted, and such a disposition would be null and void. The only special provision that a man and woman conjoined by marriage can make one for the other is a mutual gift or donation *inter vivos,* while they are both alive. And even in that case it is stipulated that there must be no children, whether of the two conjoined, or of one separately, at the time of the decease of the first to so decede.

589

ARGAN. That's a very unreasonable common law, it seems to me, if a husband can't leave anything to a wife who loves him tenderly and who takes such good care of him! [*Glances at* BÉLINE.] I would like to consult my lawyer to see if I can't do anything.

BONNEFOI. [*Reflecting whether something mightn't be done*] I shouldn't consult any lawyers on the subject, for they are ordinarily very particular about this sort of thing, and they think it's a great crime to make any dispositions which might get around the law. They're people who do nothing but make difficulties, and they pay no attention to the special cases and requirements of a man's conscience. But there are other people you can consult who are much [600 more accommodating, who know the expedients for getting around the law and justifying what is not permitted in theory, and who can smooth out the difficulties of certain cases and find ways of slipping through the common law for some particular advantage. If it weren't for that, where would we all be? There has to be a certain facility in things; otherwise nothing would ever be accomplished, and our business wouldn't be worth a penny.

ARGAN. In fact, my wife had told me, sir, that you were a very clever notary [BONNEFOI *bows*] and a very honest man. [BONNEFOI *bows again.*] Tell me, please, how I can give her my property and keep it out of the hands of my children? 611

BONNEFOI. How you can do that? [*He rises, and, holding the chair to his seat, moves close to* ARGAN's *chair. Conspiratorially*] You can just pick out some close friend of your wife's, and duly give him in your will all that you can; and then this friend will give everything back to her. [*He looks at* BÉLINE; *she signals "No" with her finger.*] Or again, you can make out a large number of notes, all open and above-board, toward certain creditors, and they will make these over to your wife, and put a signed statement in her

hands that their procedure has been entirely for her convenience and pleasure. [*Same business with* BÉLINE.] Or again, you can put actual cash in her hands while you are still alive [*he glances at* BÉLINE, *who nods assent*] or notes which you will make payable to bearer. 624

BÉLINE. Oh, dear, you mustn't worry your head about things like that. If you should ever go away and leave us, my darling, I don't want to live another day.

ARGAN. My sweet!

BÉLINE. Yes, dearest, if I should be so unhappy as to lose you—

ARGAN. My own dear wife!

BÉLINE. Life won't mean a thing to me.

ARGAN. My love!

BÉLINE. And I will follow you to the other world, just to show how much I love you. [*She throws herself into* ARGAN's *arms. Both weep.*] 635

ARGAN. Darling, you're breaking my heart. Cheer up, please; cheer up.

BONNEFOI. [*Sniffling with sympathy*] There is no reason for tears. Things haven't got to that point yet.

BÉLINE. [*Rising*] My dear sir, you don't know what it is to have a husband you love with all your heart.

ARGAN. If I die, darling, I have only one regret; it is that I haven't got a child by you. But Dr. Purgon told me that he would arrange it. 644

BONNEFOI. Oh well, that may happen any time.

ARGAN. [*Shakes his head despondently, then decides to get down to business*] I must make my will, darling, as this gentleman has suggested. But just as a precaution I am going to put in your hands twenty thousand francs in gold which I have hidden behind the panelling, and two notes payable to bearer which are due, one from Monsieur Damon, the other from Monsieur Géronte.

BÉLINE. [*With a gesture of refusal*] No, I don't want any of it at all. [*She returns toward him.*] How much did you say there is behind the panelling? 654

ARGAN. Twenty thousand francs, my love.

BÉLINE. [*Shuddering*] Don't talk about money, please. . . . How much are the two notes for?

ARGAN. Darling, one is for four thousand francs, the other for six.

BÉLINE. Sweetheart, all the money in the world is nothing to me in comparison with you.

[*She throws herself into his arms.* BONNEFOI *turns aside politely, and coughs to indicate his presence.*]

BONNEFOI. Would you like to draft the will immediately? 663

ARGAN. Yes, indeed, but we will be more comfortable in my study. [*He rises without aid, and suddenly remembers his illness.*] Darling, help me out, please.

BÉLINE. Come, my poor little baby.

[*She takes his arm, and leads him toward exit. She gets* ARGAN *in front of her, takes a purse from her corsage and holds it out to* BONNEFOI. *He receives it, bowing deeply. Exit* ARGAN, BÉLINE, BONNEFOI.

[*Enter* TOINETTE *rapidly from opposite side. She crosses stage to exit where the three have gone out. She listens; runs back and fetches* ANGÉLIQUE, *pulling her onstage by the hand.*] 674

TOINETTE. They are in there with the notary, and I heard them talking about a will. Your stepmother has all her wits about her. I'll bet she is getting your father into some kind of plot against your interests.

ANGÉLIQUE. Let him dispose of his property as he pleases, provided he does not dispose of my heart. Toinette, you can see how they are leading him around by the nose. Don't abandon me, dear, in this awful situation. 682

TOINETTE. Would I abandon you? I'd rather die. It's no use if your stepmother does play up to me and try to get me tangled up in her plans, I never could stand her, and I've always been on your side. Just leave it to me; I'll do everything to help you out. But if I'm really going to help you out, I'd better not come into the open. I'd better pretend to agree with your father and your stepmother.

ANGÉLIQUE. Only try to let Cléante know about the marriage that has been arranged.

BÉLINE. [*Offstage*] Toinette!

TOINETTE. She's calling me. Good-bye. [*She goes to exit; turns back to* ANGÉLIQUE.] Trust in me!   [*Exit.* ANGÉLIQUE *sighs.*]

CURTAIN

FIRST ENTR'ACTE

[*This interlude, a carnival scene with dance and song, has nothing to do with the plot of the play, and is therefore omitted.*]

ACT II

[*The scene is unchanged. Musical overture. The curtain rises on an empty stage. Musical theme for* CLÉANTE. *Curtains at rear open, disclosing* CLÉANTE *motionless, facing audience. He descends steps, advances downstage, surveys room with interest. Enter* TOINETTE. *She does not recognize him; shows surprise.*]

TOINETTE. What do you want here, sir?

CLÉANTE. [*Turns toward her*] What do I want?

TOINETTE. Aha, it's you! What a surprise! But what are you doing here?   [*Both talk hastily and confidentially, in fear of surprise.*]

CLÉANTE. I have come to learn my fate, to speak to my lovely Angélique, to discover the state of her feelings, and to ask her what she plans to do about that appalling engagement which has been reported to me.

TOINETTE. Yes, but you won't have a chance to talk things over openly with Angélique. You know how carefully they watch over [10 her; they won't let her go out or talk to anyone; and the only reason we were allowed to go to the play where your little romance began was because her old aunt was so crazy to see the show. And naturally we have been very careful not to talk about that adventure.

CLÉANTE. I know. And that's why I have not come here today as her suitor Cléante. I have come as a friend of her music teacher. He has given me permission to say that I'm replacing him.

TOINETTE. Here's her father. You go out for a minute, and let me tell him you're here.   19

[*She pulls him offstage, and exits after him. Enter* ARGAN. *He is about to take a walk for exercise. He halts, his leg and cane in mid-air.*]

ARGAN. Dr. Purgon told me to walk twelve times across my room in the morning, but I forgot to ask him whether he meant the long way or the short way.

[*He makes up his mind, starts again. Enter* TOINETTE *hurriedly.*]

TOINETTE. Monsieur, there's a man here . . .

ARGAN. Don't talk so loud, you slut! You get my brains all rattled, and you never seem to realize that you mustn't talk so loud to invalids.   30

TOINETTE. I just wanted to tell you, sir . . .

ARGAN. [*Walking with concentration*] Don't talk so loud, I tell you.   [*He walks to side of stage, turns, obviously keeping count.*]

TOINETTE. [*Joins him as he walks, speaks confidentially into his ear*] Monsieur . . .

ARGAN. [*Stops, center, cranes his head toward her*] What's that?

TOINETTE. I'm trying to tell you . . .

ARGAN. What are you saying?

TOINETTE. [*Shouting in his ear*] I'm saying there's a man here who wants to speak to you.   40

ARGAN. [*Putting his hand over his ears*] Tell him to come in.

[*He resumes his walk, counting his trips.* TOINETTE *signals to* CLÉANTE *to enter.* ARGAN *continues his walk to the wings, turns, and makes the return trip solemnly. Enter* CLÉANTE.]

CLÉANTE. [*Loudly, with determination*] Sir . . . [ARGAN *halts.*]

TOINETTE. [*Runs to* CLÉANTE's *side, her finger on lips*] Don't talk so loud, or you'll make his brains rattle.

[CLÉANTE *is bewildered.* ARGAN *resumes his promenade.*]

CLÉANTE. [*Ingratiatingly*] Sir, I am delighted to find that you are up and to see that your health is better.   [ARGAN *stops, annoyed.*]

TOINETTE. What do you mean, his health is better? That's not true. Monsieur is always sick.   52

[ARGAN *smiles, resumes his promenade.*]

CLÉANTE. [*Uncomprehending*] I had heard that Monsieur was better, and I think he is looking very well.

TOINETTE. What do you mean, he's looking very well? He's looking very badly, and anyone who says he's looking better is crazy. He's never been so sick.

ARGAN. She's quite right.

TOINETTE. He walks, sleeps, eats and drinks like anybody else. But that doesn't keep him from being very sick. 61

ARGAN. That's very true.

CLÉANTE. [*Getting the idea, and joining* ARGAN *on his trips to and fro*] Sir, I am shocked indeed to hear it. I have been sent by your daughter's singing teacher. He has had to go to the country for a few days, and since I'm his good friend, he sent me in his place to continue her lessons, so that she won't have to interrupt them and forget everything she has learned.

ARGAN. Very well. Call Angélique.

TOINETTE. [*Joining* ARGAN] I think, sir, it would be better to take this gentleman to her room. 71

ARGAN. No, bring her here.

TOINETTE. [*After exchange of glances with* CLÉANTE] He won't be able to give her a proper lesson unless they're alone.

ARGAN. Yes he will, yes he will.

TOINETTE. [*Planting herself before* ARGAN *and checking his promenade*] Monsieur, that will just upset you, and the slightest thing is enough to distress you in your present state, and rattle your brains.

ARGAN. No, no, not at all; I like music, and I would be very glad to . . . [*Enter* ANGÉLIQUE. CLÉANTE *turns his back to her. Seeing a* [80 *stranger, she stops.*] Ah, here she is. [*To* TOINETTE.] You go and see if my wife is dressed yet. [*Exit* TOINETTE. ARGAN *goes to* ANGÉLIQUE, *takes her hand, leads her downstage.* CLÉANTE *turns to her and bows deeply, so that she sees only his peruke.*] Come, my dear; your music teacher has gone to the country, and here's a person he has sent in his place to give you your lesson.

[*He drops her hand and prepares to resume his constitutional. He has his back to the pair.* CLÉANTE *stands upright.*]

ANGÉLIQUE. Good heavens!

ARGAN. [*Turning around*] What's the matter? Why are you surprised? 91

ANGÉLIQUE. It's . . .

ARGAN. What? What upsets you so?

ANGÉLIQUE. Father, this is really a surprising thing.

ARGAN. What do you mean?

ANGÉLIQUE. I dreamt last night that I was in some dreadful trouble, and a man who looked just like this gentleman here presented himself [ARGAN *looks suspiciously at* CLÉANTE] and I asked him for help, and he rescued me from all the trouble I was in. So I was much surprised to see here unexpectedly just what I had the idea of last night. 101

CLÉANTE. One must regard himself as fortunate who can occupy your thoughts, whether you are asleep or awake. Certainly I should be very happy if you should be in some trouble from which you would judge me worthy of rescuing you; and there is nothing I would not do to . . .

[*Enter* TOINETTE, *running and talking. She takes* ARGAN's *arm. During her speech, she and* ARGAN *survey his clothing, to make sure he is presentable. Meanwhile* CLÉANTE *seizes the occasion to kiss* ANGÉLIQUE's *hands.*] 110

TOINETTE. To tell you the truth, sir, now I'm on your side, and I take back everything I said yesterday. Here is Dr. Diafoirus the father and Dr. Diafoirus the son; they've come to pay you a visit. What a son-in-law you are going to have! You are going to see the finest-looking young fellow on earth, and so bright! He only said two words, but those were so well said! Your daughter is going to be charmed with him.

ARGAN. [*Turns around;* CLÉANTE *springs away from* ANGÉLIQUE. *To* CLÉANTE, *thinking* CLÉANTE *is taking his leave*] Don't go away, Monsieur. The fact is, I am having my daughter married, and now they are bringing her future husband here, whom she hasn't yet seen. 122

CLÉANTE. You honor me very much, sir, to wish me to be a witness of such a delightful interview.

ARGAN. He's the son of a very good doctor, and the marriage will take place in four days.

CLÉANTE. Very fine.

ARGAN. You let her music teacher know about it, and tell him to come to the wedding.

CLÉANTE. I won't fail to.

ARGAN. You come too.

CLÉANTE. You do me too much honor. 132

TOINETTE. Now everybody get ready. Here they are.

[*Music. The curtains, rear, are opened, revealing the* DIAFOI-RUSES, *father and son, posing.* THOMAS *has an enormous roll of parchment, his thesis, under his arm. Accompanied by his musical motif,* DR. DIAFOIRUS *advances majestically. To his motif,* THOMAS *trots forward to join him. They bow in unison, as music ceases. Curtains at rear remain open.*]

ARGAN. [*Bows*] Sir, Dr. Purgon has forbidden me to bare my head. You, as a member of the profession, know what the consequences would be. 142

DIAFOIRUS. Sir, it is our constant concern to bring aid to the ill, and never to jeopardize their health.

ARGAN. I accept, sir . . .

DIAFOIRUS. We have come here, sir . . .

ARGAN. With much joy . . .

DIAFOIRUS. My son Thomas and I . . .

ARGAN. The honor you do me . . .

DIAFOIRUS. To testify to you, sir . . .

ARGAN. And I would have dearly liked . . .

DIAFOIRUS. The pleasure which is ours . . . 152

ARGAN. To be able to call at your home . . .

DIAFOIRUS. At the honor you do us . . .

ARGAN. To assure you of my pleasure . . .

DIAFOIRUS. In receiving us so honorably . . .

ARGAN. But you know, sir . . .

DIAFOIRUS. Into the honor, sir . . .

ARGAN. What a poor invalid is . . .

DIAFOIRUS. Of an alliance with you . . .

ARGAN. Who can do nothing else . . .

DIAFOIRUS. And to assure you . . . 162

ARGAN. Than to tell you now . . .

DIAFOIRUS. That in every matter relating to our profession . . .

ARGAN. That I will seek every occasion . . .

DIAFOIRUS. As in every other matter . . .

ARGAN. To make evident to you . . .

DIAFOIRUS. We shall always be ready, sir . . .

ARGAN. That I am entirely at your service. . . .

DIAFOIRUS. To testify to you our zeal and good will.   170

[*In the stage version, these speeches may be otherwise grouped, to make them intelligible to the audience. The two begin ceremoniously, then talk louder and more impatiently. The last three pairs of speeches are made simultaneously, each speaker shouting at the top of his lungs.*]

DIAFOIRUS. [*Out of breath*] Come here, Thomas. Pay your compliments.

THOMAS. [*Steps forward, hesitates, turns back to his father. In a high, bleating voice*] Don't I begin with the father?

DIAFOIRUS. Yes.   180

THOMAS. [*Takes his stand before* ARGAN, *throws his head back, shuts his eyes, and recites a painfully memorized speech*] Sir, I come to salute recognize cherish and revere in you a second father but a second father to whom if I may say so I am more deeply indebted than to my first father. The first father gave me birth but you have freely chosen me. He received me through necessity but you have accepted me through your good grace. What I have from him is a work of the body but what I have from you is a work of the will, and just as much as the spiritual faculties are superior to the corporeal so much the more am I indebted to you and so much the more do I hold precious this future filial relationship for which I come to you today to render you in advance my most humble and most respectful homage.   193

[*He smiles with great satisfaction at his father.* DIAFOIRUS, *who has been muttering the same speech with his lips, smiles broadly in return.*]

TOINETTE. Hurrah for the colleges which produce such brilliant men!

THOMAS. [*Confidentially*] Was it all right, Father?

DIAFOIRUS. *Optime.*

ARGAN [*To* ANGÉLIQUE] Come, salute the young gentleman.

[ANGÉLIQUE *drops a deep curtsey.*]

THOMAS. [*Replies with an awkward bob of the knees. To his father*] Do I kiss?   204

DIAFOIRUS. Yes, yes.

THOMAS. [*Happily approaches* ANGÉLIQUE, *to kiss her forehead. She avoids the kiss by making another curtsey, and nearly upsets* THOMAS. ARGAN *intervenes between the two.*] Madame, it is with justice that heaven has bestowed upon you the title of stepmother, since . . .   [TOINETTE *bursts out laughing.*]

ARGAN. That isn't my wife, it's my daughter you're talking to.

THOMAS. Where is your wife?

ARGAN. She is coming.   213

THOMAS [*Returns to his father*] Do I wait for her to come?

DIAFOIRUS. [*Annoyed at his son's error*] Go ahead and make Mademoiselle's compliment.

THOMAS [*Takes ceremonious stand before* ANGÉLIQUE. *His speech is almost a chant, without emphasis.* DR. DIAFOIRUS *accompanies his speech with movements of the lips.*] Mademoiselle, just as the statue of Memnon rendered forth a harmonious sound when it was first lit by the rays of the sun so do I feel myself animated by sweet transport at the appearance of the sun of your beauty. And as naturalists have observed that the flower called heliotrope turns incessantly toward that orb of day so will my heart hencefore turn [224 always toward the resplendent orbs of your adorable eyes as towards its only pole. [*His memory fails him; he repeats "only pole" desperately. His father prompts him: "Permit me." THOMAS smiles gratefully and resumes.*] Permit me therefore mademoiselle to hang upon the altar of your charms the offering of this heart [*gesture toward heart*] which breathes and aspires to no other glory than to be all its life mademoiselle your most humble most obedient and most faithful servant and husband.

[*He returns to his father's side and is congratulated in dumbshow.*]

TOINETTE. That's what education does; you learn to say such beautiful things.   235

ARGAN. [*To* CLÉANTE] Well! What do you say to that?

CLÉANTE. I should say that the gentleman does marvellously well. If he's as good a doctor as he is a public speaker, it would be a pleasure to be one of his patients.

TOINETTE. Yes indeed. It will be wonderful, if he cures as well as he talks.

ARGAN. Come now, quick, my chair, and seats for everybody.

[TOINETTE *disposes the chairs. She pushes forward* ARGAN'S *easy chair; he posts himself in front of it. She puts a stool beside it;* DIAFOIRUS *takes his place before it.* ARGAN *was preparing to sit; he straightens up and mimics to* DIAFOIRUS: "*After you.*" DIAFOIRUS *starts to sit, then straightens, gesturing to* ARGAN: "*After you.*" *After some byplay, the two succeed in sitting* [248 *down together. Meanwhile,* TOINETTE *has placed a stool for* THOMAS. *As he is about to sit,* TOINETTE *utters a little scream. He starts up, frightened.*]

ARGAN. You sit down there, my dear daughter. [*He points to* THOMAS' *stool.* ANGÉLIQUE *crosses, prepares to sit.* THOMAS *looks for a place to sit.* ARGAN *signals to* TOINETTE *to fetch him a chair. She exits, as* CLÉANTE *takes his seat. To* DIAFOIRUS] You see, sir, that everyone admires your son, and I am very happy to find him such a fine fellow.

257

[TOINETTE *returns with a child's high chair and places it beside* ANGÉLIQUE'S *stool.* THOMAS *struggles to insert himself in it, finally succeeds.*]

DIAFOIRUS. [*Speaks when everyone is seated. During his speech* ARGAN *dozes,* THOMAS *attempts to cajole* ANGÉLIQUE, CLÉANTE *watches with an angry air.*] Sir, if I may attempt to speak without paternal prejudice, I may say that I have every reason to be well satisfied with him. All who know him agree that there is not an ounce of wickedness in him. He has never had a very lively imagination, nor that fiery nature which is so common, but for that very reason I have always augured well of his judgment, the quality most requisite for the exercise of our art. When he was small, he was [269 never mischievous and troublesome. He was always quiet and well behaved, he never said a word, and he never played at those games known as juvenile. We had all sorts of trouble teaching him to read, and when he was nine years old he didn't yet know his letters.

"Good," I said to myself, "slow-growing trees are the ones which produce the best fruit. It is harder to engrave upon marble than upon sand, but what is inscribed thereon lasts much longer; and this slowness of comprehension, this heaviness of imagination, is the mark of a good judgment to come." When I sent him to school, he had indeed some trouble; but he reacted against all the difficulties, and his teachers reported most favorably on his persistence and his industry. Finally, by everlastingly sticking to it, he suc- [281 ceeded in getting his degrees most creditably; and I may say without vanity that during the last two years, when he has been working for the final degree, no candidate has made more noise than he in all the school discussions. He has become really formidable; whenever any proposition is brought up he will argue to the bitter end for the opposite side. He is firm in dispute, obstinate as a mule on his principles, he never alters his opinion, and he follows a line of reasoning to the last confines of logic. But above all what I like in him is that, following my own example, he accepts without question the opinions of the great Ancients, and he has always refused to listen for a moment to the arguments and experiments concerning the alleged discoveries of our own time with regard to the circulation of the blood and similar nonsense.   294

THOMAS. [*Extricating himself from his chair*] I have written a thesis against the believers in the circulation of the blood, and if Monsieur Argan will permit me, I may venture to present it to Mademoiselle as a fitting homage of the first-fruits of my achievement.   [*He proudly lays the great roll on her knees.*]

ANGÉLIQUE. Sir, I really don't know what to do with it; I am no judge of such matters.

TOINETTE. Give it to me; maybe there's a picture in it; we could put it on the wall.   [*She takes the roll and throws it on the bed.*]

THOMAS. If Monsieur Argan will permit, I should like to invite you, for your entertainment, to come and see the dissection of a woman, which I am to demonstrate.   306

TOINETTE. That will be a delightful entertainment. Some suitors put on a play for their fiancées, but to put on a dissection would be much more genteel.

DIAFOIRUS. [*Beckons* ARGAN *to him; confidentially*] Besides, as for the qualities requisite for marriage and propagation, I may assure you that, according to the rules of medicine, he is all that could be wished. He possesses the prolific virtue to a laudable degree, and he is of the proper temperament to engender and procreate well-conditioned children.   315

[*Mutual gesture of understanding.* THOMAS, *who has overheard, coughs complacently.*]

ARGAN. [*In an offhand manner, disguising his real concern*] Is it not your intention, sir, to push him at court and to establish him as a court physician?

DIAFOIRUS. To speak frankly, I have never cared for the practice of our profession among the nobles; I have always thought that we do much better to practice with the general public. The public treats you properly. You don't have to justify your actions to anyone; if you merely follow the rules of our art, you have no trouble about anything that may happen. But the annoying thing about dealing with the nobles is that when they fall ill they absolutely demand that their doctors cure them.   328

TOINETTE. How absurd! They are certainly unreasonable to expect that you gentlemen should *cure* them! That's not what you're there for. Your job is to prescribe the remedies, for your fees; it's up to them to get well, if they can.

DIAFOIRUS. Quite right. We are required only to treat patients according to the proper forms.

[THOMAS *laughs a giggling laugh.* DIAFOIRUS *reproves him with a glance. An awkward moment.*]

ARGAN. [*To* CLÉANTE, *to clear the air*] Sir, won't you have my daughter sing something to the company?   338

CLÉANTE. [*Rises and advances*] I was expecting such an order, sir, and it occurred to me that I might divert the company by singing with mademoiselle a scene from an opera which has just appeared. [*Bows to* ANGÉLIQUE.] Here is your part.

[*Offers her a sheet of music.*]

ANGÉLIQUE. Me?   [*She rises and takes the music.*]

CLÉANTE. [*Takes* ANGÉLIQUE *by the hand, leads her to the bed-platform, stations her on it, while making an aside to her.*] Don't

refuse, please, and let me tell you what the scene is that we're going to sing. [*To the assembled group.*] I really haven't a singing voice, but it's enough if I carry the meaning, and you will be kind enough to excuse me, so that you may hear mademoiselle sing.   350

ARGAN. It's poetry?

CLÉANTE. It's really a little impromptu opera, and you will hear only prose in cadence, or a sort of free verse, such as emotion and the circumstances may inspire in people who are saying things naturally and are speaking without preparation.

ARGAN. All right. Let's hear it.

CLÉANTE. [*After a moment's hesitation*] Here is the subject of the scene. A shepherd was watching some performance which was beginning, when he was distracted by a noise near him. He turns around, and he sees a brutal fellow insulting a shepherdess with [360 insolent words. He comes to her rescue; and after giving the brute a proper punishment, he goes to the shepherdess whose tears— beautiful tears—[*he turns toward* ANGÉLIQUE] were falling from the most beautiful eyes he had ever seen. [*He turns back to the family.*] "Alas!" he says to himself, "how can anyone outrage so lovely a person? What human being, nay what barbarian, would not be moved by such distress?" He does his best to dry those tears which he finds so beautiful; and the lovely shepherdess tries to thank him for the slight service he has rendered her, but in such a charming manner, so tender, so heartfelt [*he turns toward* ANGÉLIQUE] that [370 the shepherd cannot resist, and every word, every glance, is a flaming shaft which seems to pierce his heart. [*He is forgetting his public; he comes to himself and turns toward them.*] He says to himself: "Is there anything which can merit such delightful thanks? What wouldn't one do, what dangers would one not gladly risk, to gain for a moment the touching effusions of this grateful heart?" So the spectacle they were watching continues, but he pays no attention to it. He complains only that it is too short, because when it is over he must separate from his adorable shepherdess. And from this first sight, this first moment, he is smitten by a love so [380 intense that it seems the product of years of devotion. He feels all the sufferings of absence; he is tortured because he sees her no more. He tries his best to have access to her [*he turns toward* AN-

GÉLIQUE], but she is so closely guarded that he finds no means. He resolves to ask the hand in marriage of this adorable creature without whom he can no longer live, and he asks her permission to pay his suit, in a letter which he gets into her hands; and she grants her permission. [ARGAN *nods approvingly*.] But at the same time he is warned that the father of this lovely girl has arranged her marriage with another, and that they are preparing to proceed with [390 the ceremony. You may imagine how the unhappy shepherd suffers. He cannot bear the appalling thought of seeing his beloved in another's arms, and his desperate love discovers a way to get into the house of his shepherdess [*he turns toward* ANGÉLIQUE] to learn the state of her feelings and to find from her the fate to which he must resign himself. [*Turns back to the group; addresses* THOMAS.] He finds there all in preparation for what he most fears; he sees there the unworthy rival whom the caprice of a father is opposing to the tenderness of his love. He sees this ridiculous rival triumphant, in the presence of the lovely shepherdess, as if she were an [400 assured conquest, and this sight fills him with anger which he can hardly control. [*He turns to* ANGÉLIQUE.] He looks with grief on his adored one, but the presence of her father, and respect for him, prevent him from speaking, except with his eyes. [*He turns toward the two fathers.*] But finally he overcomes all his constraint, and the transport of his love obliges him to speak to her, thus [*He leaps on the bed-platform, beside* ANGÉLIQUE, *who unrolls her music. Sings*]:

> Fair Phyllis, I've suffered, I've suffered too long;
> An end to your silence, and answer my song!
> And tell me what fate, what fortune have I: 410
>   To live or to die?

ANGÉLIQUE. You see me, Tircis, sorrowful, despairing,
>   Watching the wedding others are preparing.
> I look to Heaven, and look at you, and sigh;
>   What other course have I?

ARGAN. [*Much pleased, to* DIAFOIRUS] Well, well! I didn't know my daughter could sing so well at sight without hesitating.

CLÉANTE.   Alas, fair Phyllis,
>   Can it be true that ardent Tircis

May have a share of rapture for his part   420
And hold a little place within your heart?

ANGÉLIQUE. What can I say in midst of my distress?
Tircis, I love you, I confess.

CLÉANTE.   Oh what a glorious revelation!
Could I have made a misinterpretation?
Dear Phyllis, make again your declaration!

ANGÉLIQUE. Yes, Tircis, I love you.

CLÉANTE. Again, again!

ANGÉLIQUE. I love you.

CLÉANTE. Begin again a hundred times, and never weary of it.

ANGÉLIQUE. I love you, I love you.   431
Yes, Tircis I love you.

CLÉANTE. [*Facing the family group*]:
Oh gods, oh kings, who see the world beneath your feet,
Can you compare your happiness to mine?
But Phyllis, there's a thought that comes to me
To trouble all my joy—
A rival, a rival . . .

ANGÉLIQUE. [*To the family group*]:
Oh, I hate him worse than death;   440
Even his presence tortures me
E'en as it tortures you.

CLÉANTE.   What of the father's cruel commands?
He bids you to comply.

ANGÉLIQUE. [*To* CLÉANTE]:
Ah no, I'd rather die!
I never will comply!
I'd rather, rather die, I'd rather die!

ARGAN. And what does the father say to all this?

CLÉANTE. [*In his rapture, takes a moment to understand* ARGAN's
question] He doesn't say anything.   451
[*Impatiently, he turns again toward* ANGÉLIQUE, *prepares to sing.*]

ARGAN. That father is a fool, to let such nonsense go on without
saying a thing.

CLÉANTE. [*Has paid no attention to* ARGAN. *He gives* ARGAN *a hasty, polite smile, turns to* ANGÉLIQUE. *Sings*] Ah, my love . . .

ARGAN. No, no, that's enough of that. That play gives a very bad example. That shepherd Tircis is a very impudent fellow, and the shepherdess Phyllis is impertinent to talk that way in front of her father. Show me that paper. [ANGÉLIQUE *reluctantly hands the music to* ARGAN. *He turns it over, up and down.*] Aha! Where are the words you sang? There's nothing written here but the music!   462

CLÉANTE. [*Comes downstage, faces* ARGAN] Didn't you know, sir, that we now have a way of writing the words with the notes themselves?

ARGAN. All right. Very good. I am at your service, sir. And goodbye. [*He hands the music to* CLÉANTE. CLÉANTE *picks up his hat from his chair, bows to the assembly, and starts for rear exit.*] We could have well done without your idiotic opera.

CLÉANTE. [*Turning around*] I thought it would amuse you, sir.

ARGAN. Nonsense is not amusing. [CLÉANTE *bows profoundly, exits rear, with dignity. The curtains are drawn after him. A chilly moment.* ARGAN *sees* BÉLINE *entering. This is a relief.*] Ah, here's my wife.   474

[*Enter* BÉLINE. *All rise, except* THOMAS, *who has enjoyed* CLÉANTE's *song, and is still following him with his eyes.* ARGAN *goes to meet* BÉLINE, *brings her back by the hand.* DIAFOIRUS *bows,* BÉLINE *curtseys.* ANGÉLIQUE *withdraws to side of stage.*]

ARGAN. My love, here is the son of Dr. Diafoirus.

[DIAFOIRUS *turns toward* THOMAS, *still seated, looking backward, absorbed; gives him a sharp blow on the shins with his cane.* THOMAS *turns his body, falls out of high chair, takes his stand before* BÉLINE, *makes a hasty bow, begins his singsong compliment.*]   484

THOMAS. Madame, it is with justice that Heaven has bestowed upon you the title of stepmother, since it has taken steps . . .

BÉLINE. Monsieur, I am delighted to have come here in time to have the honor to see you.

THOMAS. Since it has taken steps . . . [DIAFOIRUS *prompts him, but he does not hear.*] Since it has taken steps . . . Madame, you

interrupted me in the middle of my speech, and that has upset my memory.

DIAFOIRUS. Thomas, save that for another time.   493

[THOMAS, *crestfallen, joins his father, who scolds him in dumbshow.*]

ARGAN. [*To dissipate the chill; to* BÉLINE] My dear, I wish you had been here earlier.

TOINETTE. Oh madame, you certainly missed it, about the second father, the statue of Memnon, and the flower called heliotrope.

[*She brings* ANGÉLIQUE'S *chair cross-stage to* BÉLINE. DIAFOIRUS *is mollified by her compliments.* BÉLINE *sits, as do* ARGAN *and* DIAFOIRUS. *A moment's pause.*]   501

ARGAN. [*To* ANGÉLIQUE] Come, my dear, take the young gentleman's hand and pledge him as your husband.

[THOMAS, *beaming, holds out his hand to* ANGÉLIQUE.]

ANGÉLIQUE. [*Hesitates, makes up her mind. Protesting*] Father!

ARGAN. [*Surprised and offended*] What's that, "Father"? What do you mean by that?

ANGÉLIQUE. Father, please, don't hurry things. Give us at least time to get acquainted with each other, so that we can develop that natural inclination which is necessary for a perfect union.   510

THOMAS. As for me, Mademoiselle, it has already developed in me, and I don't need to wait any longer.

ANGÉLIQUE. [*As politely as possible*] If you are so quick, sir, it isn't the same with me, and I admit to you that your merits have not yet made a sufficient impression on my spirit.

ARGAN. [*Somewhat reassured*] Oh well, if that's all! Your inclination will have plenty of time to develop when you're married. [*He laughs, to make the unpleasantness pass off.* DIAFOIRUS *responds with a laugh.*]   519

ANGÉLIQUE. [*Protesting*] Look, Father—give me time, I beg of you. [*Catches herself, becomes amiable.*] Marriage is a bond to which a heart should never be submitted by force. [*Pleading, to* THOMAS.] And if Monsieur is a gentleman, he should be unwilling to accept a person who is given to him under constraint.

THOMAS. [*Taking a chair and placing it in front of him, as if he were in a pulpit*] *Nego consequentiam,* I deny the consequence,

Mademoiselle, and I can be a gentleman and still be willing to accept you from the hands of your honored father.

ANGÉLIQUE. It's a poor way to gain someone's love, by persecuting her.   530

THOMAS. [*Climbs on bottom rung of chair, raises his forefinger. Oratorically*] We read in the ancients, Mademoiselle, that it was their custom to carry off marriageable girls by force from their fathers' homes, so that it would appear that it was not by their own consent that they were received into a husband's arms.

ANGÉLIQUE. [*Sharply*] The ancients, sir, were ancients, and we are people of today. Such affectations are not necessary in our time, and when a marriage is pleasing to us, we are perfectly able to go to it without being dragged. [*Tries to be cajoling.*] Just be patient; if you love me, sir, you should wish everything that I wish.   540

THOMAS. Yes, Mademoiselle, but up to and exclusive of the interests of my love.

ANGÉLIQUE. But the great mark of love is that one submits oneself to the wishes of the person one loves.

THOMAS. [*Climbs on second rung of chair*] *Distinguo,* Mademoiselle; in all that does not concern the possession of the loved one, *concedo,* I grant it. But in what does regard the possession, *nego,* I deny it.

[*As* ANGÉLIQUE *is about to reply sharply,* TOINETTE *intervenes, to indicate a wiser course.* THOMAS *descends carefully from his perch.*]   551

TOINETTE. [*To* ANGÉLIQUE] Theres' no use your arguing. The young gentleman is fresh out of college, and he'll always come out ahead of you. Why do you resist so much and refuse the glory of being associated with the noble Faculty of Medicine?

BÉLINE. [*Who has been facing the audience, with an air of disgust, speaks sharply, without turning her head*] Perhaps she has some other little fancy in mind.

ANGÉLIQUE. [*Exploding*] If I did have, Madame, it would be an entirely reasonable and proper one.   560

ARGAN. [*More annoyed than angry*] Phoo! This certainly puts me in a nice position.

BÉLINE. [*Calming him*] If I were you, my darling, I wouldn't force her to marry. I know very well what I would do.

ANGÉLIQUE. [*To* BÉLINE] I know what you mean, Madame, and I know all your kindness toward me. But perhaps your excellent advice will not be put into execution.

BÉLINE. The fact is that nice, well brought up girls like you care nothing about obeying their father's wills and wishes. It was different in the old days.   570

ANGÉLIQUE. The duty of a daughter has its limits, Madame; and according to both reason and the law her duty doesn't include everything.

BÉLINE. That must mean that you're thinking about marriage, but you want to pick a husband according to your own fancy.

ANGÉLIQUE. [*Angrily, losing control of her prudence*] If my father won't give me a husband I like, at least I will beg him not to force me to marry one I can't love.

[*General shock*. THOMAS *is revolted. After a stupefied moment,* DIAFOIRUS *rises, full of dignity, joins* THOMAS. *The two start toward rear exit.*]

ARGAN. [*Rises, joins the* DIAFOIRUSES *at foot of rear steps, to restrain them*] Gentlemen, I beg your pardon for all this.   583

ANGÉLIQUE. [*A little overawed by events, looks to* TOINETTE *for help, and encounters the hard glance of* BÉLINE] Everyone has his own purposes in getting married. As for me, I want a husband I can truly love, to whom I can give all my affection for life, and I want to take proper precautions. There are some girls who take a husband only to escape from the repression of their parents, in order to be free to do what they want. There are others, Madame, who make of marriage a mere matter of self-interest; they only marry to get marriage-settlements, to get rich by the death of their husbands, and they run without scruple from husband to husband in order to get hold of their legacies. [BÉLINE *turns sharply to* ANGÉLIQUE *to answer, but* ANGÉLIQUE *continues.*] Those persons, truly enough, are not at all particular, and they are little concerned about the individual they marry.   597

BÉLINE. [*Rises in anger;* ANGÉLIQUE *remains calm*] You seem to be full of ideas today. I would like to know what you mean by all that.

ANGÉLIQUE. [*Innocently*] I, Madame? What could I mean, except what I say?

BÉLINE. You're so stupid, my dear, that you're really unendurable. [*Shrugs her shoulders and turns away, toward audience.*]

ANGÉLIQUE. I know, Madame, you'd like to get me to say something out of order; but I warn you, you won't have that advantage.

BÉLINE. [*To* ANGÉLIQUE] I never heard such insolence.   606

ANGÉLIQUE. It's no use, Madame.

BÉLINE. And you have such a ridiculous pride, such an absurd presumption, that everybody washes his hands of you. [*Turns back toward audience.* THOMAS *shrugs his shoulders sympathetically.*]

ANGÉLIQUE. Madame, all this won't help you at all; you can't make me lose my temper. And to deprive you of all hope of succeeding in your purposes, I shall remove myself from your presence. [*She curtsies to* BÉLINE, *comes downstage, and, with her back to the audience, drops a deep curtsey to the* DIAFOIRUSES, *who reply with a short nod. She starts for side exit.*] 617

ARGAN. [*Joins* ANGÉLIQUE *near exit*] Look, you've got to make up your mind one way or the other. Either you marry the young gentleman within four days or—into a convent. [ANGÉLIQUE, *stony-faced, exits. To* BÉLINE, *in soothing tone*] Don't you worry, my dear. I'll bring her round.

BÉLINE. [*Unnerved*] I am sorry to leave you, darling, but I have an important errand in town. I will be back soon.

ARGAN. [*Confidentially*] That's all right, my love. And stop in at your notary's and tell him to send on that little—you know. 626 [*Kisses her hand.* BÉLINE *moves toward side exit, curtseying to the* DIAFOIRUSES. *They bow deeply.*]

BÉLINE [*Turning toward* ARGAN] Good-bye, my sweet.

ARGAN. [*Springs to* BÉLINE, *kisses her hands lingeringly*] Good-bye, my beautiful. [*Exit* BÉLINE. ARGAN *stares after her, blows her a kiss, turns back to the* DIAFOIRUSES.] There's a woman who loves me so—well, you can hardly believe it.

DIAFOIRUS. Sir, we must now take leave of you.

ARGAN. First, sir, I beg you just to tell me how I look to you. [*Sits in his easy chair.*] 636

DIAFOIRUS. [*Goes to his side, pulls out his watch, takes* ARGAN's *pulse, beckons to* THOMAS] Come, Thomas, take the gentleman's other wrist, to see if you can make a proper judgment about his pulse. [THOMAS *comes to other side of chair, pulls out watch, imitates his father's actions;* ARGAN's *two arms are held aloft.*] *Quid dicis?*

THOMAS. *Dico* that the gentleman's pulse is the pulse of a man who is not well.

DIAFOIRUS. Good.

THOMAS. It is a little bit hardish; one might even say hard.   646

DIAFOIRUS. Excellent.

THOMAS. Throbbing.

DIAFOIRUS. *Bene.*

THOMAS. Even a little fluttering.

DIAFOIRUS. *Optime.*

THOMAS. Which indicates a disorder in the splenic parenchyma, which is to say the spleen.

DIAFOIRUS. Very good.

ARGAN. [*Pulls away his arms and crosses them defensively on his chest*] No; Dr. Purgon says it's my liver that's out of order.   656

DIAFOIRUS. [*Returning his watch to his pocket, as does* THOMAS] Oh well, when you say parenchyma you mean both, because of their close relationship, by means of the *vas breve,* the *pylorus,* and often the *choledochic meatuses.* No doubt he orders you to eat a lot of roast meat.

ARGAN. No, nothing but boiled meat.

DIAFOIRUS. Oh well, roast meat, boiled meat, all the same. He is prescribing very well for you; you couldn't be in better hands.

    [*He bows, moves toward rear entrance. Curtains open.*   THOMAS, *following his father, notices* TOINETTE, *is much taken*   *by her. She holds out her hand; he feels her pulse.*]   667

ARGAN. [*Rises to reconduct* DIAFOIRUS, *stopping the latter as he is mounting the steps*] Doctor, how many grains of salt should I put on an egg?

DIAFOIRUS. [*Turns toward* ARGAN; *majestically*] Six, eight, or ten; always according to the even numbers; as medicines are administered according to the odd numbers.

ARGAN. [*Bows*] Good day, sir.

DIAFOIRUS. [*Bows; notices* THOMAS *and* TOINETTE. *Sharply*]
Thomas! 676

[*Points to exit.* THOMAS, *in a panic, runs up steps, under his
father's outstretched arm.* THOMAS *stops, faces audience.* DIA-
FOIRUS *joins him, faces audience. Music. The* DIAFOIRUSES *about
face, exit in cadence. Curtains are drawn. Exit* TOINETTE. ARGAN
goes to his chair, counting on his fingers. Enter BÉLINE, *hurriedly.*]

BÉLINE. My darling, I had to stop on my way out to tell you something terrible! I was just going past Angélique's door, and I saw a
man with her, a young man! As soon as he saw me he ran away.

ARGAN. A young man with my daughter! 686

BÉLINE. Yes. Your daughter Louison was with them, and she can
tell you something.

ARGAN. Send her here, my love, send her here. [*Exit* BÉLINE. ARGAN
*takes a switch from the medicine table, hides it behind his back,
sits in his chair.*] Oh, the brazen creature! Now I understand why
she resisted.

[*Enter* LOUISON, *carrying a doll in her arms. She stops in mid-stage,
occupying herself with doll.*]

LOUISON. What do you want, Papa dear? Stepmother said you
were looking for me. 696

ARGAN. [*With feigned kindliness*] Yes. Come here. [*She advances
two steps.*] Farther. [*She takes two more steps.*] Turn around. [*She
faces him.*] Raise your head. [*She obeys.*] Look at me. [*She does
so. Suddenly and sharply*] Hey?

LOUISON. What is it, Papa?

ARGAN. Well?

LOUISON. What?

ARGAN. Haven't you something to tell me? 704

LOUISON. I'll tell you about Red Riding Hood, if you want to hear
a nice story. Or I can recite the poem about the Fox and the Crow.

ARGAN. That's not what I'm asking you.

LOUISON. What is it then?

ARGAN. Oh, you sly little thing, you know very well what I mean.

LOUISON. Oh no, I beg your pardon, Papa.

ARGAN. [*Severely*] Is that the way you obey me?

LOUISON. What way?

ARGAN. Didn't I tell you to come and tell me right away anything you saw? 714

LOUISON. Yes, Papa.

ARGAN. And did you do it?

LOUISON. Yes, Papa. I came and told you everything I saw.

ARGAN. And didn't you see anything today?

LOUISON. No, Papa.

ARGAN. No?

LOUISON. No, Papa.

ARGAN. You're sure?

LOUISON. Oh yes, I'm sure, Papa.

ARGAN. Well now, I'm going to show *you* something. 724
[*Pulls out the switch.*]

LOUISON. Oh, Papa!

ARGAN. [*Rising, approaching* LOUISON] Aha, you bad little girl, you wouldn't tell me that you saw a man in your sister's room?

LOUISON. Papa!

ARGAN. [*Takes her by the wrist; doll falls to floor. He flourishes switch*] Here's something which will teach you to lie!

LOUISON. [*Falling on her knees*] Oh Papa, I ask your pardon. You see, sister told me not to tell you, but I'll tell you everything. 733

ARGAN. First you must be whipped for lying. Then afterwards, we'll see.

LOUISON. Forgive me, Papa.

ARGAN. No, no.

LOUISON. Dear Papa, don't whip me.

ARGAN. Yes I will.

LOUISON. Papa, Papa, please don't whip me.

ARGAN. That's enough. [*He whips her twice.*]

LOUISON. Oh, Papa, you hurt me! Oh, you've killed me, I think.
[*She collapses on floor and lies motionless.*] 743

ARGAN. What's this, what's this? Louison! Louison! Oh my God! Louison! [*He kneels behind her, facing audience. Shakes her.*] Heaven help me, she's really dead! Oh misery, what have I done? Curses on the switch! The devil take the switch! [*He throws it*

away, and crouches over LOUISON.] Oh, my poor darling, my poor little Louison!

LOUISON. [*Sits up*] There, there, Papa, don't cry so much; I'm not quite dead.

ARGAN. Well! What a sly little creature! [*He rises, picks her up.*] Oh, all right; I'll pardon you this time, on condition that you tell me everything straight.   754

LOUISON. Oh yes, Papa.

ARGAN. [*Leads her to the bed-platform, sits on bed, seats* LOUISON *on his knee.*] Now at least be very careful, for there's my little finger, which knows everything, and it will tell me if you lie.

LOUISON. But Papa, don't tell sister I told you.

ARGAN. Oh no.

LOUISON. Well then, Papa, a man came into sister's room when I was there.

ARGAN. Well then?   763

LOUISON. I asked him what he wanted, and he said he was her singing teacher.

ARGAN. Oho! So that's it! Well then?

LOUISON. She said to him: "Get out, get out! Dear God, get out! You'll drive me mad!"

ARGAN. Well then?

LOUISON. He didn't want to get out.

ARGAN. What did he say to her?

LOUISON. He said—oh, a lot of things.

ARGAN. And what else?   773

LOUISON. He said all this and all that, he loved her a lot, and she was the prettiest girl in the world.

ARGAN. Then what?

LOUISON. Then he got down on his knees in front of her.

ARGAN. And then what?

LOUISON. And then he kissed her hands.

ARGAN. [*Very apprehensive*] And then what?   780

LOUISON. Then stepmother came to the door, and he ran away.

ARGAN. [*Much relieved*] There wasn't anything else?

LOUISON. No, Papa.

ARGAN. Still, there's my little finger mumbling something. Wait a minute. [*Puts little finger in his ear.*] What? Aha! Yes? Oho! There's my little finger telling me you saw something and you haven't told me.

LOUISON. Oh Papa, your little finger is a story-teller.

ARGAN. Look out! 789

LOUISON. No, Papa, don't believe him; he's telling fibs, I know.

ARGAN. Oh, all right; we'll see about that. Now run along. And keep your eyes open. [*Puts her down.*] Run away. [LOUISON *picks up doll, curtseys to* ARGAN, *and runs out.*] Oh, there aren't any children any more. [*Rises stiffly, steps down from platform.*] Oh, what a lot of trouble! [*His eye catches the medicine table. He runs to it.*] I don't even have time to think about my illness. [*Pours some medicine into a glass and sips it.*] Really, I can't stand it much longer. [*Leans on table.*]

[*Enter* BÉRALDE, *side entrance.*] 799

BÉRALDE. How d'ye do, brother Argan? How are you today?

ARGAN. Ah, brother, I'm pretty bad. [*Puts down glass.*]

BÉRALDE. What do you mean, pretty bad?

ARGAN. [*Goes to his chair, leans on it*] Yes, I'm so weak you can hardly believe it.

BÉRALDE. [*Lightly*] That's too bad.

ARGAN. I am hardly able to speak.

BÉRALDE. [*Discounting* ARGAN's *complaints*] Brother Argan, I've come to propose to you a match for my niece Angélique.

ARGAN. [*Furious, shouting*] Brother, don't mention that good-for-nothing to me! She's an impudent, impertinent rapscallion, and I'll put her in a convent before two days are up. 811

BÉRALDE. Why, all right, all right. I am glad your strength is coming back; my visit is doing you good. [ARGAN *shrugs his shoulders, collapses in chair.*] Now, now, we'll talk of business later. I've brought along some performers; they will cheer you up and put you in a better state of mind for our discussion. They are some gypsies dressed up as Moors; they will dance and sing for you, and I think they'll do you more good than one of Dr. Purgon's prescriptions. All right—

END OF ACT II

SECOND ENTR'ACTE

[*Enter* TOINETTE, *who moves the chairs to the side of the stage. Musical overture. Enter a troupe of gypsies, who sing songs in praise of love, and perform various dances, in one of which their pet monkeys participate. The text of the songs is here omitted.*]

ACT III

[*The rear curtains have been closed during the entr'acte. At its end,* TOINETTE, *supporting* ARGAN, *leads him to his chair in its old position.* BÉRALDE *follows.*]

BÉRALDE. Well, brother, what do you say to that? Isn't that as good as a dose of castor oil?

TOINETTE. Hmm; good castor oil is good.

[*She establishes* ARGAN *in his chair.*]

BÉRALDE. Now look, wouldn't you like to have a little talk?

ARGAN. [*Seized by pangs*] Be patient a minute, brother, I'll be right back.   [*He rises and moves rapidly toward exit.*]

TOINETTE. Wait a minute, sir, you've forgotten that you can't walk without your stick.   12

[*She hands stick to* ARGAN, *takes him by the shoulders and pushes him toward exit.*]

ARGAN. You're right.   [*Exit.*]

TOINETTE. [*Confidentially, to* BÉRALDE] Please, you're going to help your niece out, aren't you?

BÉRALDE. I will do everything I can to obtain for her what she desires.

TOINETTE. We must absolutely prevent this fantastic marriage he's got into his head, and I thought it would be a good idea if I could bring in here a doctor of our own, to disgust him with his Dr. Purgon and his way of handling the case. But as we haven't got anybody on hand for that, I'd thought of playing a little trick.   24

BÉRALDE. What do you mean?

TOINETTE. Well, it's kind of crazy. But perhaps it will turn out better than if it was sensible. You just let me alone; and you do what you can. Here he is now.

[*The two separate and assume an innocent expression. Enter* ARGAN *sulkily. "Any luck?" inquires* TOINETTE *in dumbshow. "None at all,"* ARGAN *indicates.* TOINETTE *mimics her grieved sympathy. She takes his cane, hangs it on back of easy chair, helps him to sit. She puts a wash-basin on floor before him, pours water in it from a jug, which she places beside chair. Exit* TOINETTE. ARGAN *removes slippers, places one on each side of basin, removes stockings.*] 36

BÉRALDE. [*After watching* ARGAN *commiseratingly, takes up his subject in a soothing voice*] My dear brother, I should like to ask you especially not to let yourself get excited.

ARGAN. That's all right.

[*He throws a stocking back over his shoulder.*]

BÉRALDE. And not to show any ill humor at anything I may say.

ARGAN. Yes.

BÉRALDE. And to deal with the matters under discussion with a calm mind, without any emotion. 45

ARGAN. Good God, yes. [*Throws second stocking over his shoulder.* BÉRALDE *fetches a chair for himself.*] My, what an introduction. [*He dips his toe cautiously in the water. It is too hot; he lifts his foot high.*]

BÉRALDE. [*Places his chair beside* ARGAN's *and sits down*] How does it happen, my dear brother, that with all your money, and with only one daughter, for I'm not counting the little one, how does it happen, I say, that you talk of putting her into a convent? 53

ARGAN. How does it happen, my dear brother, that I am master in my own house to do whatever seems best to me?

BÉRALDE. Your wife is always advising you to get rid of your two daughters in this way, and I have no doubt that out of pure charity she would be delighted to see them both holy nuns.

ARGAN. Oh, now we're coming to it! [*Incautiously dips his foot in the water; he lifts it, in pain and anger.*] My poor wife is mixed up in it now. She's the one who makes all the trouble, and everybody has it in for her. 62

BÉRALDE. No, no, brother. We'll leave her out of it. She's a woman who has the best intentions in the world for your family; there's nothing selfish about her; she has a remarkable love for you, and she shows your children an affection and kindness which are hardly conceivable; that's certain. Let's not talk of her, but come back to your daughter. What is your idea in marrying her to a doctor's son?

ARGAN. [*Putting his feet, one after the other, in the water, with the utmost precaution*] My idea, my dear brother, is to get the right sort of son-in-law.

BÉRALDE. Yes, but brother, that isn't quite the thing for your daughter, and there's a match proposed which is much more suitable for her.   74

ARGAN. Yes, but brother, this match is more suitable for me.

BÉRALDE. But should her future husband be for her or for you?

ARGAN. He should be, my dear brother, both for her and for me, and I want to get into my family the people I need.

BÉRALDE. According to that reasoning, if your little Louison were grown up, you would give her an apothecary for a husband.

ARGAN. [*Innocently*] Why not?

BÉRALDE. [*Disgusted, rises and paces stage*] Is it possible that you will always be so infatuated with your apothecaries and physicians, and that you insist on being sick in spite of everybody and in spite of nature?   85

ARGAN. What do you mean by that, my dear brother?

BÉRALDE. [*Sharply; irritated*] I mean that I've never seen anyone who is less sick than you are, and I couldn't ask for a better constitution than yours. [ARGAN *shrugs his shoulders.* BÉRALDE *masters his anger, comes to* ARGAN's *side. Bantering*] A very good sign that you are well, and that you have a strong and vigorous body, is that with all the medical care you've had, you haven't yet succeeded in ruining your system, and you haven't died of all the medicines they've made you take.   94

ARGAN. [*Tragically*] But don't you know that that's what keeps me going, and that Dr. Purgon says I would pass away if he shouldn't be able to take care of me for even three days?

BÉRALDE. If you don't look out, he will take such good care of you that he will send you to the other world.

ARGAN. [*Has finally got both feet solidly in the water. He sits back.* BÉRALDE *sits. As discussion proceeds,* ARGAN *becomes more and more excited, shouts louder and louder.*] But just let's talk this over for a moment. So you don't believe in medicine?   103

BÉRALDE. No, brother, and for health's sake I don't see that it is necessary to believe in it.

ARGAN. What! you don't accept as true a thing which has been agreed upon by everybody, and which has been revered by all past time?

BÉRALDE. Far from accepting it as true, I find it, between you and me, one of the greatest follies of mankind; and if I look at it from a philosophical point of view, I've never seen a sillier lot of humbuggery. I don't think there is anything more ridiculous than that one man should undertake to cure another.   113

ARGAN. And why, pray, shouldn't one man be able to cure another?

BÉRALDE. For this reason: that the functioning of man's machine has been a mystery, up to the present, and man has hardly been able to understand anything of it. Nature has put before our eyes some veils too thick for us to be able to penetrate them.

ARGAN. So doctors don't know anything, according to you?

BÉRALDE. Oh yes they do. Most of them have had a very good education, they know how to talk very good Latin, and how to name all the diseases in Greek, and define them and classify them; but as for curing them, that's what they don't know at all.   124

ARGAN. But you must still admit that on this subject the doctors know more than other people.

BÉRALDE. My dear brother, they know just what I have told you, which isn't very much. All the excellence of their art consists in a pompous jargon, in a fine high-sounding lingo, which gives you words for reasons and promises for results.

ARGAN. But after all, there are people as sensible as you are; and we see that in time of sickness everybody calls in the doctors.   132

BÉRALDE. That's an indication of human weakness, not of the genuineness of their art.

ARGAN. But the doctors must certainly think their art is genuine, since they use it on themselves.

BÉRALDE. The fact is that there are some among them who accept the popular delusion, by which they profit, and others who profit by it without accepting the delusion. Your Dr. Purgon, for instance, doesn't know any better; he is a man who is all doctor, from head to foot, a man who believes in his rules more than in all the demonstrations of mathematics, who would think it a crime to venture to examine his rules. He doesn't see anything obscure in medicine, or anything doubtful or difficult. With his impetuous [144 prejudice, his rigid self-confidence, his brutality in applying what he thinks is reasonable, he gives his purgings and his bleedings, come what come may, and he never pauses to consider anything. You shouldn't hold any grudge against him for anything he may do to you; it's with the best faith in the world that he will finish you off, and in killing you he will do just what he has done to his wife and children, and what, if the occasion should arise, he will do to himself. 152

ARGAN. The fact is, brother, you just never have liked him. [*Pours more hot water from jug into basin. Resigned gesture by* BÉRALDE.] But anyway, let's come to the point. What should you do when you're sick?

BÉRALDE. Nothing, my dear brother.

ARGAN. [*Amazed*] Nothing?

BÉRALDE. Nothing. Just stay quiet. When we let nature alone, she recovers by herself from the disorder she's fallen into. It's our disquiet, our impatience which upsets everything; and most men die of their remedies, and not of their illnesses. 162

ARGAN. But you must agree that we can aid that nature in certain ways.

BÉRALDE. [*Becoming excited*] Dear heaven, those are mere ideas that we like to befool ourselves with. Men have always been full of fine fancies which we come to believe because they flatter us, and because it would be very nice if they were true. When a doctor talks to you about aiding, supporting, relieving nature, about taking from nature what interferes with her and supplying her what she lacks, about restoring nature and making her function properly; [171 when he talks to you about rectifying the blood, tempering the vital organs and the brain, readjusting the lungs, repairing the liver and

fortifying the heart, about his having secrets to make you live years longer, he is telling you medicine's fairy tale. But when you come down to truth and experience, you find nothing of all that; it's like one of those lovely dreams which leave you, when you wake up, only the distress of having believed them.

ARGAN. [*Angrily*] That is to say that all the knowledge in the world is shut up in your head, and you think you know more than all the great medical men of our time.   181

BÉRALDE. In speech and action, your great medical men are two different sorts of people. To hear them talk, they're the most skillful people on earth; but in action, they're the most ignorant men alive.

ARGAN. Yeah! You're a great doctor, I can see that. I wish that one of those gentlemen were here to answer your arguments and make you sing small for a change.

BÉRALDE. [*Yielding, out of policy*] Why, brother, I don't take it on myself to fight medicine. Everybody, at his own risk and peril, can believe what he likes. What I am saying is just between us two. I would have liked to save you from some of your mistakes; and to cheer you up, I would have liked to take you to see a comedy of Molière.   193

ARGAN. [*Annoyed*] He's an impudent fellow, that Molière of yours; and that's a fine business, for him to make fun of honest men like doctors.

BÉRALDE. It isn't the doctors he makes fun of, but the absurdities of doctoring.

ARGAN. And what business is it of his to criticize doctoring? He's a stupid, impertinent fool, to make fun of consultations and prescriptions, to attack the honorable corps of physicians, and to go and put on his stage distinguished people like those gentlemen.   202

BÉRALDE. What should he put on his stage, if not the various professions of men? Every day you can see princes and kings on the stage, and they certainly stand as high as doctors do.

ARGAN. Oh, the devil! If I were the doctors, I'd get back at him for his insolence; and when he gets sick, I'd let him die without giving him any help. Let him say and do what he likes, I wouldn't prescribe the slightest little bleeding, the smallest little enema; and

I'd say to him: "Croak! Croak! That will teach you next time to make fun of the Faculty of Medicine!" 211

BÉRALDE. He certainly makes you angry.

ARGAN. Yes, he's a trouble-making fool, and if the doctors have any sense, they will do what I say.

BÉRALDE. He will have more sense than your doctors, for he won't ask them for any help.

ARGAN. All the worse for him, if he won't seek the benefit of their remedies.

BÉRALDE. He has his reasons not to want any, and he maintains that that is only permissible for vigorous, robust people who have strength and to spare to bear the remedies with the disease; but as for him, he has only strength enough to bear his illness. 222

ARGAN. What a lot of rubbish! Look, let's not talk about that man any more; that rouses my bile, and you'd be likely to give me his sickness. [*Pours more hot water in his basin and settles back.*]

BÉRALDE. All right, brother; and to change the subject I will tell you that just because your daughter objects to your plans you shouldn't make so violent a decision as to put her in a convent. And I'll say that in choosing a son-in-law, you shouldn't follow blindly this passion which possesses you, and that in these circumstances you should accommodate yourself a little to your daughter's inclinations, since it's for all her life, and all the happiness of a marriage is at stake. 233

[*Music. Rear curtains open, revealing* MONSIEUR FLEURANT, *a fussy, dapper, choleric apothecary, bearing an enormous syringe. To music, he comes downstage, steps on bed-platform, beckons to* ARGAN *to approach, and prepares to give enema.*]

ARGAN. [*Putting on slippers*] Oh brother, if you will permit me—

BÉRALDE. How's that? What do you want to do?

ARGAN. To take this little enema. It will be just a moment.

[*He rises.*]

BÉRALDE. Don't be foolish. [*Thrusts* ARGAN *back in his chair.*] Can't you be a moment without an enema or a purge? Put it off till some other time, and stay quiet a while. 244

ARGAN [*overawed*] Monsieur Fleurant, we'll leave it till this evening or tomorrow morning.

FLEURANT. [*Advances on* BÉRALDE *threateningly*] What business is it of yours to oppose the prescriptions of medicine and to prevent this gentleman from taking my enema? I'm amazed at your effrontery.

BÉRALDE. [*Advances toward* FLEURANT] Come, sir, come; it's clear that you aren't used to talking to people's faces.   252

FLEURANT. [*Screaming with rage*] You have no right to make light of medicine and make me lose my time. [BÉRALDE *takes him by the arm and pushes him backward.*] I came here by doctor's orders with a proper prescription, and I'll tell Dr. Purgon [BÉRALDE *again thrusts him backward*] how I have been prevented from executing his orders and doing my duty. [*Goes to rear, up two steps, and turns back to* BÉRALDE.] You will see! [*Moves toward exit, turns back again.*] You will see!   [*Exit. Rear curtains are drawn.*]

ARGAN. Brother, I'm afraid you're going to be the cause of some dreadful misfortune.   262

BÉRALDE. [*Returning downstage*] What a misfortune it is, not to take an enema Dr. Purgon has ordered! Once more, brother, is it possible there is no way to cure you of the disease of doctors? Do you want to spend your whole life tortured by their remedies?

ARGAN. Good heavens, you talk about it like a well man; but if you were in my place, you would change your tune quick enough. It's easy to talk against medicine when you're in good health.

BÉRALDE. But just what is your illness anyway?

ARGAN. You'll drive me crazy! I wish that you had my illness; we'd see if you'd talk so much.   272

[*Roll of drums. Rear curtains open, revealing* DR. PURGON, *standing majestically, forefinger upraised.* FLEURANT *is beside him, happily foreseeing* ARGAN's *punishment. Enter* TOINETTE *from side.*]

ARGAN. Aha! Here's Dr. Purgon!

[PURGON *advances impressively, to music.* FLEURANT *remains on rear platform.* ARGAN *is terrified.*]

PURGON. [*Slowly, ominously*] I have just heard, here at your door, a pretty piece of news, that my prescriptions are being trifled with, that there has been a refusal to take the remedy which I had prescribed.   283

ARGAN. Doctor, it isn't . . .

PURGON. That is very great audacity, and a very strange rebellion of a patient against his physician.

TOINETTE. How appalling!

PURGON. [*Turning toward* TOINETTE] An enema which I had taken pleasure in composing myself.

ARGAN. It wasn't me!

PURGON. [*Turning toward* ARGAN] Invented and drawn up according to all the rules of the art.   292

TOINETTE. He was quite wrong.

PURGON. [*Turning toward* TOINETTE] And which was destined to have in the intestinal tract a most marvellous effect.

ARGAN. It was my brother . . .

PURGON. [*Facing audience*] To reject it with scorn!

ARGAN. He was the one . . .

PURGON. [*Taking step toward* ARGAN] It was an unimaginable action.

TOINETTE. That's right.

PURGON. [*Taking another step toward* ARGAN] A monstrous crime against Medicine.   303

ARGAN. He was responsible . . .

PURGON. [*Another step toward* ARGAN] A crime of contempt of Faculty which cannot be sufficiently punished.

TOINETTE. Absolutely right.

PURGON. [*Beside* ARGAN's *chair. He draws himself up imposingly*] I declare to you that I break off all relations with you.

ARGAN. It was my brother . . .

PURGON. That I no longer wish to have any family alliance with you.

TOINETTE. Quite right too.   313

PURGON. And in order to put an end to all our dealings, here is the settlement I was making on my nephew in favor of his marriage. [*He tears up the settlement, throws pieces on floor, stamps on them. He proceeds upstage.*]

ARGAN. It was my brother who made all the trouble.

PURGON. [*At foot of steps, turns sharply on* ARGAN] To scorn my enema!

ARGAN. Bring it here, I'll take it right away!

[*He rises from his chair, runs to bed, climbs on it, crouches on it, his back to audience.*]   323

PURGON. [*Advancing step by step toward bed*] I would have cured you in no time at all.

TOINETTE. He doesn't deserve it.

PURGON. I was going to cleanse your whole body and evacuate entirely the evil humors.

ARGAN. [*Collapses on bed in sitting position*] Oh, my brother!

PURGON. And I only needed a dozen medications to clean up the whole business.

TOINETTE. He is unworthy to be treated by you.   332

PURGON. [*Jumps on bed-platform.* ARGAN, *in terror, leans backward, supporting himself on his elbows.* PURGON *bends over him savagely.*] But since you wouldn't be cured through my ministrations . . .

ARGAN. It isn't my fault.

PURGON. Since you have departed from the obedience which one owes to one's physician . . .

TOINETTE. He's got to pay for it.

PURGON. Since you have declared yourself a rebel against the remedies which I prescribed for you . . .   342

ARGAN. Oh, not at all.

PURGON. I have only to tell you that I abandon you to your bad constitution, to the disorder of your intestinal tract, to the corruption of your blood, to the bitterness of your bile, and to the turbidity of your humors.

[*He moves rapidly to the rear, and begins to mount steps.*]

TOINETTE. And a very good thing too.

ARGAN. [*Falls flat on bed, his face in his hands*] My God!

PURGON. [*Turns on step, raises right forefinger, thunders at* ARGAN] And I hope that within four days you will fall into an incurable state.   353

ARGAN. [*Falls out of bed, scrambles to foot of steps, holds up clasped hands to* PURGON] Mercy!

PURGON. And that you may fall into the clutch of gastritis . . .

[*Points his forefinger at* ARGAN.]

ARGAN. [*Falls on his knees*] Dr. Purgon!

PURGON. [*Raising forefinger*] And from gastritis into colitis . . .
[*Points forefinger. The same business is repeated during following
speeches.*]

ARGAN. Dr. Purgon!   362

PURGON. And from colitis into enteritis . . .

ARGAN. Dr. Purgon!

PURGON. And from enteritis into hepatitis . . .

ARGAN. Dr. Purgon!

PURGON. And from hepatitis into appendicitis . . .

ARGAN. Dr. Purgon!

PURGON. And from appendicitis into peritonitis . . .

ARGAN. Dr. Purgon!

PURGON. And from peritonitis to the extinction of life, which
will be the final result of your folly.   372

[*Turns and goes rapidly out rear exit.* FLEURANT *laughs dia-
bolically. Curtains are drawn.* TOINETTE *exits at side, laughing.*
ARGAN *lies flat on floor.*]

ARGAN. Dear God, I'm a dead man. Brother, you have killed me.

BÉRALDE. What? What's the matter?

ARGAN. I'm done for. I can feel already that Medicine is taking
its revenge on me.

BÉRALDE. Dear brother, you're crazy. [*Picks up* ARGAN *from floor,
helps him impatiently to his chair, settles him in it.*] For a good
deal I wouldn't like people to see you acting this way. Just examine
yourself a little. Get hold of yourself, and don't give in so much to
your imagination.   384

ARGAN. [*Groaning, with chattering teeth*] You heard the terrible
diseases he threatened me with.

BÉRALDE. Really, how simple you are.

ARGAN. He said I would become incurable in less than four days.

BÉRALDE. Yes, but what he says has nothing to do with the facts.
Was that an oracle that spoke? To hear you, it would seem that
Dr. Purgon holds the thread of your life in his hands, and by some
mighty authority he extends it and shortens it as he pleases. Just
reflect that the principles of your life are within yourself, and that

Dr. Purgon's anger can't make you die any more than his remedies can make you live. [*Pause.* BÉRALDE *recalls* TOINETTE's *proposal, at* [395 *beginning of act.*] This episode ought to bring you to the point of getting free of all doctors; or if you're born to be a man who can't do without them, it's easy to get another, with whom you may run a little less risk.

ARGAN. Oh brother, he knows my whole constitution and the way I should take care of it.

BÉRALDE. I must say you're a man of fixed ideas; you certainly see things from a strange point of view.   403

[*Enter* TOINETTE, *busy and bustling. She picks up* ARGAN's *basin, puts it under medicine table.*]

TOINETTE. Monsieur, there's a doctor here who wants to see you.

ARGAN. What doctor?

TOINETTE. [*Puts jug beside basin*] A medical doctor.

ARGAN. I'm asking you who he is.

TOINETTE. [*Between* ARGAN *and* BÉRALDE] I don't know him; but he looks a lot like me [*she winks at* BÉRALDE], and if I weren't sure that my mother was an honest woman, I would say he is probably some little brother she's given me after my father's death.   413

ARGAN. Bring him in. [*Exit* TOINETTE, *quickly.*]

BÉRALDE. That's a bit of good luck. One doctor leaves you, and another shows up.

ARGAN. I am very much afraid that you will be the cause of some terrible misfortune.

BÉRALDE. What, again? You keep coming back to that.

ARGAN. You see, I'm oppressed by all those diseases I don't know about, those . . .

[*Music. Rear curtains open.* TOINETTE, *in doctor's gown, wig, and toque, is revealed. Large spectacles. She comes downstage, to music. She imitates the manner of* DR. DIAFOIRUS.]   424

TOINETTE. Monsieur, permit me to pay you my respects and to offer to you my best services for all the bleedings and purges you may need.   [*Bows deeply.*]

ARGAN. [*Bowing*] Sir, I am deeply obliged to you. [*To* BÉRALDE] My faith, he looks just like Toinette.

TOINETTE. Sir, I beg you to excuse me a moment. I forgot to give an order to my servant. I will be right back.

[*Exits, rear, with a combination of haste and dignity*]

ARGAN. Eh, wouldn't you say it really is Toinette? 433

BÉRALDE. It's true there is a very great resemblance; but it isn't the first time that has happened. There are innumerable cases of these tricks of nature.

ARGAN. As for me, I am much surprised, and . . .

[*Enter* TOINETTE, *side, in her ordinary costume. She is very matter-of-fact.*]

TOINETTE. What did you want, sir?

ARGAN. What?

TOINETTE. Didn't you call me?

ARGAN. Me? No. 443

TOINETTE. My ears must have been burning.   [*She starts to go.*]

ARGAN. Wait here a minute and see how much the doctor looks like you.

TOINETTE. Yes, indeed! I'm busy downstairs. I've seen him plenty already.   [*Exit, side.*]

ARGAN. [*Watches her go*] If I hadn't seen them both, I would have thought it was the same person.

BÉRALDE. I have read some very surprising examples of such resemblances as this; there have been some cases in our own times which have fooled everybody. 453

ARGAN. As for me, I would have been fooled by this case; I would have sworn it's the same person.

[*Enter* TOINETTE, *in doctor's costume, rear. She is unhurried.*]

TOINETTE. Sir, I most earnestly beg your pardon.   [*Bows.*]

ARGAN. [*To* BÉRALDE] It is really extraordinary.

TOINETTE. I trust that you will not take amiss the curiosity I have felt to see so distinguished an invalid as you are; and your reputation, which has extended far, may excuse the liberty I have taken.

ARGAN. Sir, I am at your service. 462

TOINETTE. I see, sir, that you are looking at me very attentively. How old do you think I am?

ARGAN. I think that at the most you may be twenty-six or twenty-seven.

TOINETTE. Ha, ha, ha! I am ninety.

ARGAN. Ninety?

TOINETTE. Yes. You see the results of the secrets of my art, which keep me thus fresh and vigorous.   [*She executes a pirouette.*]

ARGAN. My word, there's a fine young old gentleman for ninety.

TOINETTE. I am a roving doctor. I go from city to city, from province to province, from country to country, in order to study [473 matters worthy of my attention and invalids worthy of my interest, who may be fit subjects for the great secrets I have discovered in medical science. I scorn to waste my time on all the trifling everyday illnesses, trivial rheumatisms and catarrhs, wretched little fevers, vapors and migraines. What I want is important diseases, good long fevers with delirium, fine high fevers with purple eruptions, good old plagues, nice well-formed dropsies, splendid plueirisies with inflammation of the lungs. That's what I like, that's where I triumph. [*Bends over* ARGAN, *pointing her finger at him.*] And I should be delighted, sir, if you had all the diseases I have just named, and if you were given up by all the doctors, in desperation, in your last agony [*straightens up, smiling, and bows*] just so I could show you the excellence of my cures, and my earnest desire to render you service.   487

ARGAN. [*Disconsolately*] I am much obliged to you, sir, for all your kindness to me.

TOINETTE. Give me your pulse. [*He extends his arm apprehensively. A pause; she shakes his arm.*] Come on, beat properly. Oh, I'll make you behave. [*Shakes his arm violently.*] Oho! This pulse is trying to cut up; I see it doesn't know me yet. [*Flings* ARGAN'S *arm from her; it hits the chair-arm; he grimaces. In a scornful tone*] Who is your doctor?

ARGAN. Dr. Purgon.   496

TOINETTE. Purgon? That name is not on my list of the great doctors. What does he say is your illness?

ARGAN. He says it's the liver. [TOINETTE *indicates amazement.*] But others say it's the spleen.

TOINETTE. [*Rolls up her sleeves, taps* ARGAN'S *chest smartly; goes behind his chair, bends his head back, inspects his eyes, opens his mouth.* ARGAN *sticks out his tongue; she feels it with her finger.*

She closes his mouth by clapping him under the chin; ARGAN *bites his tongue. She returns to face him.*] They are all blockheads. It's the lungs that are causing the trouble.   506

ARGAN. The lungs?

TOINETTE. [*Facing audience, with air of knowing all the answers, and seeking only supporting evidence*] Yes. How do you feel?

ARGAN. Sometimes I feel pains in my head.

TOINETTE. Exactly. The lungs.

ARGAN. It seems to me sometimes I have a cloud in front of my eyes.   513

TOINETTE. The lungs.

ARGAN. Sometimes I have pains in my heart.

TOINETTE. The lungs.

ARGAN. And occasionally I feel a general weakness in all my limbs.

TOINETTE. Lungs.

ARGAN. And sometimes I have pains in my stomach, as if it were colic.

TOINETTE. Lungs. Do you have much appetite for what you eat?

ARGAN. [*Smiling*] Yes, Doctor.   522

TOINETTE. [*Pokes him suddenly in the breast*] Lungs. [ARGAN *shrinks back.*] You like to drink a little wine?

ARGAN. Yes, Doctor.

TOINETTE. Lungs. You feel sleepy after your meals, and you're glad to take a little nap?

ARGAN. Yes, Doctor.

TOINETTE. Lungs, lungs, I tell you. What does your doctor order for your diet?

ARGAN. He orders soup.

TOINETTE. Blockhead!   532

ARGAN. And fowl.

TOINETTE. Blockhead!

ARGAN. Veal.

TOINETTE. Blockhead!

ARGAN. Bouillons.

TOINETTE. Blockhead!

ARGAN. Fresh eggs.

TOINETTE. [*Horrified*] Blockhead!

ARGAN. And in the evening, prunes to relax the bowels.

TOINETTE. [*With a scornful laugh*] Blockhead!   542

ARGAN. And especially, to take my wine with a lot of water.

TOINETTE. Ignorantus, ignoranta, ignorantum! You must drink your wine straight, and to thicken your blood, which is too dilute, you must eat good rich beef, good rich pork, good Holland cheese, grits and rice, chestnuts and cakes, in order to solidify and conglutinate the system. Your doctor is a fool. I am going to send you a competent one, and I will come and see you from time to time, as long as I am in the city.

ARGAN. [*With a gesture of gratitude with his left arm*] You will oblige me very much.   552

TOINETTE. [*Grabbing his arm*] What the devil are you doing with that arm?

ARGAN. [*Terrified*] What?

TOINETTE. There's an arm I would have cut off immediately, if I were you.

ARGAN. Why?

TOINETTE. Don't you realize that it draws all the nourishment to itself, and it prevents that whole side from profiting by it?

ARGAN. [*Pulls back his arm, protects it with his right arm*] Yes, but I need my arm.   562

TOINETTE. [*Points at his right eye.* ARGAN *protects it with his hand*] You've got a right eye there that I would get rid of, if I were in your place.

ARGAN. Get rid of an eye?

TOINETTE. Don't you see that it incapacitates the other eye and deprives it of its proper nourishment? Believe me, you should get rid of it as soon as possible, and you will see much better with the left eye.

ARGAN. There's no hurry.   571

TOINETTE. [*With gesture of resignation*] Well, good-bye. I am sorry to leave you so soon, but I have to be at an important conference at the bedside of a man who died yesterday.

[*Moves toward rear.*]

ARGAN. [*Bewildered*] A man who died yesterday?

TOINETTE. [*On rear steps*] Yes, to consult about what ought to have been done to cure him. Good-bye.   [*Bows deeply.*]

ARGAN. You know that patients cannot see you to the door.

[TOINETTE *bows again, exits with dignity. The curtains are drawn.*]

BÉRALDE. [*Suppressing a desire to laugh*] There is a doctor who seems to know his business.   582

ARGAN. Yes, but he goes a little too quick.

BÉRALDE. All great physicians are like that.

ARGAN. Cut off my arm, put out my eye, so that the others will do better! I'd a good deal rather they didn't do so well. That's a fine operation, to make me one-eyed and one-armed!

[*Enter* TOINETTE, *from side.*]

TOINETTE. [*Speaking into wings*] All right, all right, excuse me, please. I'm in no mood for fun.

ARGAN. What's all this?   591

TOINETTE. Why, it's your doctor, who wanted to feel my pulse.

[*She goes to the bed and rearranges bedclothes.*]

ARGAN. Well, think of that, at the age of ninety.

BÉRALDE. Look here, since you've broken off with Dr. Purgon, don't you want me to say something about the offer that has been made for your daughter's hand?

ARGAN. [*Ill-humored again*] No, brother; I want to put her in a convent, since she has opposed my wishes. I can see very well there's some love-affair at the bottom of all this, and I've discovered a certain secret interview that they don't know I've discovered.   601

BÉRALDE. Well, even if there were some small inclination, would that be so criminal, and can a trifle offend you, when it all leads to an honorable end like marriage?

ARGAN. However that may be, brother, she will be a nun; that's settled.

BÉRALDE. You want to do pleasure to someone.

ARGAN. I understand you. You always come back to that; you have my poor wife on the brain.

BÉRALDE. [*Getting angry*] Well, yes, since I must speak frankly, it's your wife I mean; and just as I can't bear your obsession with medicine, I can't bear your obsession with her; and I hate to see you running headlong into all the traps she lays for you.   613

TOINETTE. [*Descends from platform, joins the pair*] Oh, sir, don't speak of Madame; she's a woman you can't say anything against, all frank and above-board, and how she loves Monsieur Argan, oh, how she loves him! There aren't any words for it.

ARGAN. [*To* BÉRALDE] Just ask her how she coddles me.

TOINETTE. That's right.

ARGAN. And how worried she is about my illness.

TOINETTE. Absolutely.

ARGAN. And all the trouble and care she takes for me. 622

TOINETTE. That's certain. [*To* BÉRALDE] Do you want me to convince you and show you in a minute how Madame loves Monsieur? [*To* ARGAN] Monsieur, let me show him how simple he is, and prove he's mistaken.

ARGAN. How do you mean?

TOINETTE. Madame is just coming in. You stretch out there [*indicates bed*] and pretend to be dead. You will see how she grieves when I tell her the news.

ARGAN. [*Reflects a moment*] I'm willing. 631
　　　　　　　　　　　　　　　　　[*Rises, goes toward bed.*]

TOINETTE. [*Accompanying* ARGAN] Yes, but don't leave her in despair very long, for she might die of it.

ARGAN. Leave it to me. [*Lies down on bed.*]

TOINETTE. [*Returns to* BÉRALDE, *hides him behind curtain at side*] Now you hide yourself in this corner.

ARGAN. [*Sitting up suddenly*] Isn't there some danger in pretending to be dead?

TOINETTE. [*Returning to* ARGAN, *making him lie down*] No, no. What danger could there be? Just lie down. [*Confidentially*] It will be a pleasure to show up your brother. [*Glances at door.*] Here is Madame now. You stay still. [*Sits on bed-platform, her back to bed.*] Oh, dear God! Oh, dear, oh, dear! Oh, what a frightful accident! 645

BÉLINE. [*Entering at side*] What's the matter, Toinette?

TOINETTE. Oh, Madame!

BÉLINE. What is it?

TOINETTE. Your husband is dead!

BÉLINE. My husband is dead?

TOINETTE. Oh, dear, yes. The dear departed has deceased.

BÉLINE. You're quite sure?

TOINETTE. Quite sure. No one knows anything about it yet; I was here all by myself. He just passed away in my arms. Look, there he is all stretched out on his bed. 655

BÉLINE. [*Hesitates a moment, goes to bedside, leans over* ARGAN. *She straightens up.*] Well, heaven be praised! I've got rid of a terrible burden. [TOINETTE *sobs.* BÉLINE *takes some steps toward her.*] You're a fool, Toinette, to distress yourself about his death.

TOINETTE. Madame, I thought I ought to cry.

BÉLINE. Come, come; it isn't worth the trouble. It isn't much of a loss; what good was he on earth? [*Moves back toward head of bed, relieving her long pent-up rancor.*] A man who was always troublesome to everyone, dirty, disgusting, always with an enema or a purge in him, always blowing his nose, coughing, spitting; stupid, tiresome, sulky, wearing everybody out, scolding the servants all day and all night. 667

TOINETTE. There's a fine funeral oration.

BÉLINE. [*Descends from bed-platform, leads* TOINETTE *to center*] Toinette, you must help me to carry out my plan, and you may be sure that you'll get a good reward for helping me. Fortunately no one has been informed yet, so let's say nothing until I have done my little job. There are some papers and some money I'd like to get hold of, and it isn't right that I should have spent the best years of my life with him without some return. [*Starts toward door.*] Come on, Toinette. [*She has a new idea.*] But first let's take his [676 keys. [*Goes on tiptoe to foot of bed, kneels down to pull out the strong-box under the bed. She opens the box and looks for keys. Meanwhile* ARGAN *sits up cautiously, moves on all fours to foot of bed, so that his face is above* BÉLINE.]

ARGAN. [*Gently*] Take it easy.

BÉLINE. [*Springs to her feet and recoils to center of stage*] Oh!

ARGAN. [*Stands up on bed*] Yes, my dear wife! So that's how you love me! 684

TOINETTE. [*Collapses, laughing, in* ARGAN's *easy chair*] Ha, ha, ha! The deceased isn't dead!

ARGAN. [*To* BÉLINE] I am very happy to observe your love for me and to hear the fine tribute you made to me. [BÉLINE, *who has been staring entranced at* ARGAN, *turns and runs out, with a scream which continues after she is in the wings.*] There is a word to the wise which will come in handy in the future, and which will keep me from doing a lot of things. 692

BÉRALDE. [*Has emerged from his hiding-place when* BÉLINE *screamed*] Well, brother, you see.

TOINETTE. [*Glances offstage*] My word, I never would have believed it. [*Rises; goes to* ARGAN.] But I hear your daughter outside; get back the way you were, and we'll see how she will take the news of your death. [*Tries to persuade* ARGAN *to lie down; he resists.*] Well, there's no harm in trying it out; and now that you've got started, you can learn this way the feelings that your whole family has for you. 701

[ARGAN *sees* ANGÉLIQUE *offstage, throws himself down and lies motionless.* TOINETTE *hides* BÉRALDE *again, returns to bed-platform, turns her back to* ANGÉLIQUE *and sobs quietly.*]

TOINETTE. Oh, heaven! Oh, how terrible! Oh, unlucky day!

ANGÉLIQUE. [*Enters, stops a moment in surprise, advances to center*] What's the matter, Toinette? Why are you crying?

TOINETTE [*Going toward* ANGÉLIQUE] Oh dear, I've some sad news to give you.

ANGÉLIQUE. What is it?

TOINETTE. Your father is dead.

ANGÉLIQUE. My father is dead, Toinette? 712

TOINETTE. Yes; you see him there. He died just a moment ago in a sudden spell of weakness.

ANGÉLIQUE. [*Remains motionless a moment, starts toward bed. But her courage fails her; she turns and falls, weeping, into* TOINETTE's *arms*] Oh, dear heaven! What a misfortune! What a cruel blow this is! Oh dear, must I lose my father, all that's left to me in the world, and what's even more dreadful, must I lose him at a time when he was angry with me? What will happen to me now in my trouble, and what consolation can I ever find for losing my father? 722

[*Enter* CLÉANTE, *cheerily and impetuously. On seeing* AN-GÉLIQUE *in tears, he stops, then moves slowly toward* ANGÉLIQUE *and* TOINETTE.]

CLÉANTE. What is the matter, my lovely Angélique? What are you crying for?

ANGÉLIQUE. Oh dear! I'm crying because I've lost the dearest and most precious thing in my life. I am crying for the death of my father.

CLÉANTE. Good heavens, how dreadful! And how sudden! And to think—I had just asked your uncle to make a proposal for me, and I was on my way to see your father and try to move him to accept my offer.   734

ANGÉLIQUE. Oh, Cléante, let's say no more about all that. Let's drop all our thoughts of marriage. After losing my father, I never want to lead a family life; I give it up forever. [*Steps on bed-platform.*] Yes, Father, if I have resisted your desires in the past, I now want to follow at least one of your intentions, and make amends for all the grief I know I have given you. [*Kneels.*] Father, permit me to give you my word that I will enter a convent, and let me kiss you to prove my gratitude for all you have done for me. [*Takes* ARGAN's *hand to kiss it.*]   743

ARGAN. [*Sitting up, much moved*] Ah, my dear daughter!

ANGÉLIQUE. [*Springs from bedside into* TOINETTE's *arms*] Oh!

[TOINETTE *laughs.* BÉRALDE *emerges from hiding-place.* ARGAN *rises, steps off foot of bed to platform.*]

ARGAN. Come my dear, don't be afraid. I'm not dead. [ANGÉLIQUE *flings herself into father's arms. He embraces her warmly.*] Come, come; you're my own true daughter, and I am delighted to see your real nature.   751

ANGÉLIQUE. Oh, what a wonderful surprise, Father! And now that heaven has given you back to us, to our great joy, let me kneel before you to beg just one thing of you. [*Kneels;* ARGAN *turns his head away.*] If you don't agree to the choice of my own heart, if you refuse to grant me Cléante for a husband, I beg you at least not to force me to marry anyone else. And that is the only indulgence I ask of you.

CLÉANTE. [*Kneels on other side of* ARGAN, *who looks aloft*] Oh, sir, let yourself be moved by her prayers and by mine, and do not oppose the honorable love we share.   761

BÉRALDE. [*Stepping forward*] Brother, can you hold out against them?

TOINETTE. [*Kneeling*] Sir, can you be insensible to so much love?

ARGAN. [*To* BÉRALDE] Let him become a doctor, and I'll consent to the marriage. [*To* CLÉANTE] Yes, become a doctor, and I give you my daughter.

CLÉANTE. [*Springs to his feet.* TOINETTE *rises*] I'll be very glad to. If that's all I need to be your son-in-law, I'll become a doctor, and an apothecary too, if you like. [*Raises* ANGÉLIQUE *to her feet and walks with her to side of stage.*] That's no trouble, and I would do a great deal more to obtain my beautiful Angélique.   772

BÉRALDE. But brother, I have an idea. Become a doctor yourself. It would be much more convenient to have everything you need in your own person.

TOINETTE. [*To* BÉRALDE] That's right. That's the real way to get well quick; there's no disease that's so bold as to trifle with the person of a doctor.

ARGAN. Brother, I think you're making fun of me. Am I of an age to start in studying?

BÉRALDE. Studying? Nonsense. You know enough already. There are plenty of them who don't know as much as you do.   782

ARGAN. But you have to know how to talk Latin, and know all the diseases and the remedies for them.

BÉRALDE. When you receive the cap and gown of the doctor, you will learn all that, and afterwards you will know more than you want to.

ARGAN. What! You know how to talk about diseases when you have that costume on?

BÉRALDE. Certainly. You just have to talk. When you have a cap and gown on, any gibberish becomes wisdom, and all nonsense becomes sound reason.   792

TOINETTE. Look sir, if it were only for your beard, that's a lot already; the beard makes more than half the doctor.

CLÉANTE. In any case, I'm ready for anything.

BÉRALDE. Would you like to have the matter arranged immediately?

ARGAN. What do you mean, immediately?

BÉRALDE. Yes, right here in your house.

ARGAN. In my house?

BÉRALDE. Yes. I have some friends on the Faculty who will come immediately to perform the ceremony in your room. It won't cost you anything. 803

ARGAN. But as for me, what do I say? What do I answer?

BÉRALDE. They will tell you in just a few words, and they'll give you in writing what you have to read. Now you go and get decently dressed, and I'll send for them.

ARGAN. All right, come on, let's do it.

[*He descends from bed-platform and exits, with* TOINETTE *accompanying him to exit.*]

CLÉANTE. [*Comes downstage with* ANGÉLIQUE] But what are you up to, and what do you mean by these friends on the Faculty? 812

TOINETTE. [*Returning to* ANGÉLIQUE's *side*] What's going on anyway?

BÉRALDE. We're going to have a little fun. There's a troupe of actors who have made a skit on the conferring of a doctor's degree, with music and dances. I want to have them put on their act for us, with my brother taking the part of the principal character.

ANGÉLIQUE. But Uncle, it seems to me that you're treating my father rather too lightly.

BÉRALDE. Well, my dear niece, we aren't so much treating him lightly as accommodating ourselves to his fancies. All this is just in the family. We can each of us take part, and thus put on a show for our own amusement. That's all right in carnival time. So come and get things ready. 825

CLÉANTE. [*To* ANGÉLIQUE] Do you agree?

ANGÉLIQUE. Well, all right, since Uncle is taking the responsibility.

[CLÉANTE *and* BÉRALDE *place the arm-chair on the bed-platform;* TOINETTE *arranges the stools, pushes back the medicine-table.* *Exeunt all.*]

END OF ACT III

FINALE

[NOTE: *This finale is a burlesque, with music and ballet, of the solemn ceremony of the examination and reception of a Doctor of Medicine by the Faculty of the University. As the examinations were conducted in Latin, Molière's text is written in very bad Latin, with intrusions of French and Italian. He could assume that his audience had a sufficient smattering of Latin to enjoy his burlesque. The translator has kept Molière's Latin, but has freely substituted Englishisms for Molière's lapses into French or Italian. Anyone with the slightest tincture of Latin can get the idea, by reading the text fast, without pausing for analysis.*]

[*Music. Rear curtains open. Enter eight syringe-bearers, six apothecaries, with mortars and pestles, twenty-two doctors. Then* ARGAN *with a large roll of paper. Then eight dancing surgeons, two singing surgeons. Then* BÉRALDE *with* LOUISON, ANGÉLIQUE *with* CLÉANTE, TOINETTE. *The presiding officer mounts a portable pulpit. All take their places in a semi-circle around* ARGAN.]

PRESIDING OFFICER.   Savantissimi doctores
     Medicinae professores,
     Qui hic assemblati estis,
     Et vos, altri Messiores,
     Sententiarum Facultatis
     Fideles executores,
    Chirurgiani et apothecari,
    Atque tota compania also,
     Salus, honor et argentum
     Atque bonum appetitum.   10
     [*Orchestra plays a ritornelle, or interlude.*]

     Non possum, docti confreri,
     Myselfus satis admirari
     Qualis bona inventio
     Est medici professio,

Quam bella thinga est, et bene trovata,
Medicina illa benedicta,
  Quae suo nomine solo,
  Surprisingo miraculo,
Since so longo tempore   20
Facit life of Riley-o
Such a lot of populo.
                   [*Ritornelle is repeated.*]

  Per totam terram videmus
  Grandam vogam ubi sumus;
  Vere dico, bene cautus
  Omnes sunt so mad about us.
Totus mundus, currens ad nostros remedios,
  Nos regardat sicut Deos;
  Et nostris prescriptionibus   30
Principes et reges submissos videtis.
                   [*A second ritornelle.*]

Well then, est nostrae sapientiae,
Boni sensus atque prudentiae
  Earnestemente laborare
  A nos bene conservare
In tali credito, voga, et honore,
Et takum care a non recevere
  In nostro docto corpore
  Quam personas capabiles,   40
  Et totas dignas providere
  Has plazas honorabiles.
              [*Second ritornelle is repeated.*]

That's why nunc convocati estis;
  Et credo quod findabitis
  Dignam materiam medici
  In savanti homine here you see,
  And him, in thingis omnibus
  Dono ad interrogandum,

Et thoroughly examinandum   50
Vostris capacitatibus.
[*He sits down. A third and longer ritornelle.*]

FIRST DOCTOR.   Si mihi dat licentiam Dominus Praeses,
Et tanti docti Doctores,
Et also-presentes illustres,
Most savanti Bacheliero
Quem estimo et honoro,
Demandabo causam et rationem quare
Opium facit dormire.   59

[*He sits down.* BÉRALDE *signals to* ARGAN, *the* BACHELIERUS. *He rises.*
BÉRALDE *prompts him.*]

ARGAN.   Mihi a docto Doctore
Demandatur causam et rationem quare
Opium facit dormire.
And to that respondeo
Quia est in eo
Virtus dormitiva
Cujus est natura
Sensus tranquillizare.

CHORUS.   Bene, bene, bene, bene respondere!   70
Dignus, dignus est entrare
In nostro docto corpore.

SECOND DOCTOR.   Cum permissione Domini Praesidis,
Doctissimae Facultatis,
Et totius his nostris actis
Companiae presentis,
Demandabo tibi, docte Bacheliere,
Quae sunt remedia
Quae in maladia
Called hydropisia   80
Convenit facere.

ARGAN.   Give 'emam enemam,
'N'enemam bleedemam,
'N'enemam purgemam.

CHORUS.   Bene, bene, bene, bene respondere!
                 Dignus, dignus est entrare
                 In nostro docto corpore.

THIRD DOCTOR. Si paret OK by Domine Praesidi,
                 Doctissimae Facultati,
                 Et companiae presenti,   90
               Demandabo tibi, docte Bacheliere,
                 Quae remedia eticis
                 Pulmonicis, atque asmaticis
                 You finda fittinga facere.

ARGAN.   Give 'emam enemam,
                 'N'enemam bleedemam,
                 'N'enemam purgemam.

CHORUS.   Bene, bene, bene, bene respondere!
                 Dignus, dignus est entrare
                 In nostro docto corpore.   100

FOURTH DOCTOR. Super illas maladias
               Doctus Bachelierus dixit marvelias;
               But si non annoyo Dominum Praesidem,
                 Doctissimam Facultatem
                 Et totam honorabilem
                 Companiam listeninginam,
               Faciam illi unam quaestionem.
                 Yesterdayo maladus unus
                 Landedavit in meas manus;
               Habet grandam fievram cum redoublamentis,
                 Grandem dolorem capitis,   111
                 Et grandem malum in the sidis,
                 Cum granda difficultate
                 Et troubla de respirare.
                   Be so goodo mihi dire,
                   Docte Bacheliere,
                   Quid illi facere?

ARGAN.   Give 'emam enemam,
                 'N'enemam bleedemam,
                 'N'enemam purgemam.   120

FIFTH DOCTOR. But if maladia
Obstinativa
Non vult get wella
Quid illi facere?

ARGAN. Give 'emam enemam,
'N'enemam bleedemam,
'N'enemam purgemam;
'N'enemam bleedemam purgemam againemam.

CHORUS. Bene, bene, bene, bene respondere!
Dignus, dignus est entrare   130
In nostro docto corpore.

PRESIDING OFFICER. [*Rises solemnly; other doctors rise also*]
Juras guardare statuta
Per Facultatem praescripta
Cum sensu et jugeamento?

ARGAN. [*Extending right hand*] Juro

PRESIDING OFFICER. Essere in omnibus
Consultationibus
Ancieni opinione,
Aut bono   140
Aut baddo?

ARGAN. Juro.

PRESIDING OFFICER. Et never make uso
Of remediis anyis
Exceptus those doctae Facultatis,
Though maladus should croakere
Et mori de suo malo?

ARGAN. Juro.

PRESIDING OFFICER. Ego, cum isto boneto
Venerabili et docto,   150
Dono tibi et concedo
Virtutem et puissanciam
Medicandi,
Purgandi,
Bleedandi,

Pierçandi,
Cuttandi,
Slashandi,
Et murderandi
Impune per totam terram.   160

[PRESIDING OFFICER *and companions seat themselves. First apothecary invests* ARGAN *with his gown, to music. The second puts on his wig, the third his toque. Ballet. All the surgeons and apothecaries salute* ARGAN. *He opens roll of paper and reads.*]

ARGAN.   Grandes doctores doctrinae
                          Of rhubarb et senna,
                      In me it would be ridiculosissimum,
                          Absurdum, ineptum,
                          If I undertookum   170
                          To give vobis gloriam.
                          I'd superimposo
                          Lux to the sunno,
                          Stellas to caelo,
                          Undas Oceano,
                          Rosas to summero.
                          Kindly recipito
                          My gratitudo,
                      Molto obbligato corpori docto.
                          Vobis, vobis debeo   180
                      More than to nature and patri meo.
                          Natura et pater meus
                          Hominem me habent factum;
                          But vos me, what's a lot more,
                          Habetis factum medicum;
                          Honor, favor, et gratia
                          Qui in hoc corde right here
                          Imprintant gratitudinem
                          Qui endurerit in saecula.   189

[*He bows. The doctors rise; all join in chorus.*]

CHORUS.
    Vivat, vivat, vivat, vivat, a hundred times vivat
    Novus Doctor, qui tam bene parlat!
    Mille, mille annis et eatet et drinket
    Et bleedet et killet!

[*Music. The doctors salute* ARGAN *and exit. The surgeons and apothecaries dance and sing, to the accompaniment of hand-clapping and the clinking of apothecaries' mortars.*]

SURGEON.
    May he see doctas
    Suas prescriptiones
    Omnium chirurgorum   200
    Et apothicarum
    Fill up the shoppos!

CHORUS.
    Vivat, vivat, vivat, vivat, a hundred times vivat
    Novus Doctor, qui tam bene parlat!
    Mille, mille annis et eatet et drinket
    Et bleedet et killet!

SURGEON.
    May toti anni
    Be to him boni
    Et favorabiles;
    Et may he have plenty   210
    Of pestas and poxas,
    Fievras, pleuresias,
    Hemorrhagias, et dysenterias!

CHORUS.
    Vivat, vivat, vivat, vivat, a hundred times vivat
    Novus Doctor, qui tam bene parlat!
    Mille, mille annis et eatet et drinket
    Et bleedet et killet!

[*Dancers exit according to their rank. The members of the family salute* ARGAN, *who salutes the public.*]

CURTAIN

William Congreve

THE WAY OF THE WORLD

THE LAST of five plays by William Congreve, *The Way of the World* (1700) is a comedy that reflects and criticizes the fashionable society which grew up around Charles II after his restoration to the English throne in 1660. The reader enters the play's representation of that society through a chocolate-house, an important gathering place for gallants, and he is at once in the midst of witty repartee and of knowing references to intrigue and complicated personal relationships. The effect is rather confusing. A resumé of the plot might help the reader, but perhaps better still is some foreknowledge of the play's themes and structure—the kind of general preparation that presumably would have been brought to the play by an experienced spectator of Restoration comedies.

The basic organization of the play is not that of a straightforward narrative. True, the various lines of intrigue are complicated and resolved, but the plot is not so much an end in itself as it is a device for describing the social world and for setting the characters in a variety of revealing relationships. As an implied description of society, the tangled intrigues suggest endless maneuvering and posturing. Since they are largely directed toward superficial ends, their resolution does not provide the fruitful stability for which their animation arouses a desire. The reader hopes that a true resolution will be provided by the marriage of Mirabell and Millamant. The play, then, is organized around a problem or question: How can true love be reconciled with the ways of the world?

Congreve never cheats in reaching that reconciliation. The world of intrigue, with all its cynicism and pretense, is the only one acknowledged by the play. The two lovers cannot escape to the coun-

try, for the country is brought to the court in the person of blunt Sir Wilfull, and is shown to be boorish. The ideal country of shepherds and shepherdesses is also laughed out of existence through Lady Wishfort's determination to retire to it. On every side are extremes of behavior, and as they are presented dramatically they define by exclusion the relationship which Mirabell and Millamant must try to achieve. This relationship must avoid the superficiality of the Witwouds and the gracelessness of the Wilfulls; it must catch the sexual vitality which coquettish Lady Wishfort only wishes for; it must hold its own in the game of wits with Fainal and the others, but not make that game an end in itself, with the consequent cost in bitterness and loss of individuality.

When the reader is attentive to these and other contrasts, the initial confusion is clarified, the play takes form, and the climactic betrothal or bargaining scene is put in its proper setting. Act IV, in which this scene occurs, is particularly rich, one will notice, in actions that balance and interpret each other and contribute to the definition of love. There are other parallels to be found, for example, besides the major one between Mirabell and Millamant and "Sir Rowland's" proposal to Lady Wishfort.

The success of the bargaining scene is the result, of course, not only of the context in which it is so carefully placed, but also of its own style and content. The language of the two lovers is still the witty banter of the fashionable world rather than anything awkwardly emotional, yet it is possible to distinguish between their true wittiness and the would-be wit of lesser characters. The wittiness and the superficially legal form of the bargaining, for example, may suggest the self-discipline of the two lovers, their superiority to the social world on its own terms, their success in uniting intelligence and emotion, and their ability to give more to each other by keeping a proper pride in their separate personalities. These overtones of meaning help to lift the play from its particular social setting and make it perennially significant.

THE WAY OF THE WORLD

Characters

MEN

FAINALL, *in love with Mrs. Marwood*

EDWARD MIRABELL, *in love with Mrs. Millamant*

ANTHONY WITWOUD ⎱ *followers of Mrs. Millamant*
PETULANT ⎰

SIR WILFULL WITWOUD, *half-brother to Witwoud, nephew to Lady Wishfort*

WAITWELL, *servant to Mirabell*

WOMEN

LADY WISHFORT, *enemy to Mirabell, for having falsely pretended love to her*

MRS. MILLAMANT, *a fine lady, niece to Lady Wishfort, and loves Mirabell*

MRS. MARWOOD, *friend to Mr. Fainall, and likes Mirabell*

MRS. ARABELLA FAINALL, *daughter to Lady Wishfort, and wife to Fainall, formerly friend to Mirabell*

FOIBLE, *woman to Lady Wishfort*

MINCING, *woman to Mrs. Millamant*

BETTY, *servant in a chocolate-house*

PEG, *servant to Lady Wishfort*

DANCERS, FOOTMEN, *and* ATTENDANTS

SCENE—*London. The time equal to that of the presentation.*

Characters. Mrs.: used for all women and girls, whether married or not.

ACT ONE

SCENE. *A chocolate-house.*

[MIRABELL *and* FAINALL, *rising from cards.* BETTY *waiting.*]

MIRA. You are a fortunate man, Mr. Fainall.

FAIN. Have we done?

MIRA. What you please. I'll play on to entertain you.

FAIN. No, I'll give you your revenge another time, when you are not so indifferent; you are thinking of something else now, and play too negligently; the coldness of a losing gamester lessens the pleasure of the winner. I'd no more play with a man that slighted his ill fortune, than I'd make love to a woman who undervalued the loss of her reputation.

MIRA. You have a taste extremely delicate, and are for refining on your pleasures.   11

FAIN. Prithee, why so reserved? Something has put you out of humour.

MIRA. Not at all: I happen to be grave today; and you are gay; that's all.

FAIN. Confess, Millamant and you quarrelled last night, after I left you; my fair cousin has some humours that would tempt the patience of a Stoic. What! some coxcomb came in, and was well received by her, while you were by.

MIRA. Witwoud and Petulant; and what was worse, her aunt, your wife's mother, my evil genius; or to sum up all in her own name, my old Lady Wishfort came in—   22

FAIN. Oh, there it is then—she has a lasting passion for you, and with reason.—What! then my wife was there?

MIRA. Yes, and Mrs. Marwood and three or four more, whom I never saw before; seeing me, they all put on their grave faces, whispered one another, then complained aloud of the vapours, and after fell into a profound silence.

Act. I. 27. vapours: the blues, genteel indisposition.

FAIN. They had a mind to be rid of you. 29

MIRA. For which reason I resolved not to stir. At last the good old lady broke through her painful taciturnity, with an invective against long visits. I would not have understood her, but Millamant joining in the argument, I rose and with a constrained smile told her I thought nothing was so easy as to know when a visit began to be troublesome; she reddened and I withdrew, without expecting her reply.

FAIN. You were to blame to resent what she spoke only in compliance with her aunt.

MIRA. She is more mistress of herself than to be under the necessity of such a resignation. 40

FAIN. What? though half her fortune depends upon her marrying with my lady's approbation?

MIRA. I was then in such a humour, that I should have been better pleased if she had been less discreet.

FAIN. Now I remember, I wonder not they were weary of you; last night was one of their cabal-nights; they have 'em three times a week, and meet by turns, at one another's apartments, where they come together like the coroner's inquest, to sit upon the murdered reputations of the week. You and I are excluded; and it was once proposed that all the male sex should be excepted; but somebody moved that to avoid scandal there might be one man of the community; upon which motion Witwoud and Petulant were enrolled members. 53

MIRA. And who may have been the foundress of this sect? My Lady Wishfort, I warrant, who publishes her detestation of mankind; and full of the vigour of fifty-five, declares for a friend and ratafia; and let posterity shift for itself, she'll breed no more.

FAIN. The discovery of your sham addresses to her, to conceal your love to her niece, has provoked this separation: had you dissembled better, things might have continued in the state of nature.

MIRA. I did as much as man could, with any reasonable conscience; I proceeded to the very last act of flattery with her, and

35. expecting: waiting for. **57. ratafia:** a liqueur.

was guilty of a song in her commendation. . . . But for the discovery of this amour, I am indebted to your friend, or your wife's friend, Mrs. Marwood. 65

FAIN. What should provoke her to be your enemy, unless she has made you advances, which you have slighted? Women do not easily forgive omissions of that nature.

MIRA. She was always civil to me, till of late. I confess I am not one of those coxcombs who are apt to interpret a woman's good manners to her prejudice; and think that she who does not refuse 'em everything, can refuse 'em nothing.

FAIN. You are a gallant man, Mirabell; and though you may have cruelty enough not to satisfy a lady's longing, you have too much generosity not to be tender of her honour. Yet you speak with an indifference which seems to be affected, and confesses you are conscious of a negligence. 77

MIRA. You pursue the argument with a distrust that seems to be unaffected, and confesses you are conscious of a concern for which the lady is more indebted to you than your wife.

FAIN. Fie, fie, friend, if you grow censorious I must leave you. I'll look upon the gamesters in the next room.

MIRA. Who are they?

FAIN. Petulant and Witwoud. [*To* BETTY] Bring me some chocolate. [*Exit.*]

MIRA. Betty, what says your clock? 86

BET. Turned of the last canonical hour, sir.

MIRA. How pertinently the jade answers me! Ha! almost one o'clock! [*Looking on his watch*] Oh, y'are come—
[*Enter a* SERVANT.]

MIRA. Well, is the grand affair over? You have been something tedious.

SERV. Sir, there's such coupling at Pancras that they stand behind one another, as 'twere in a country dance. Ours was the last couple to lead up; and no hopes appearing of dispatch, besides, the parson growing hoarse, we were afraid his lungs would have failed

92. **Pancras:** St. Pancras church, notorious for hasty marriages.

before it came to our turn; so we drove round to Duke's Place; and
there they were rivetted in a trice.   97

MIRA. So, so, you are sure they are married.

SERV. Married and bedded, sir: I am witness.

MIRA. Have you the certificate?

SERV. Here it is, sir.

MIRA. Has the tailor brought Waitwell's clothes home, and the
new liveries?

SERV. Yes, sir.

MIRA. That's well. Do you go home again, d'ye hear, and ad-
journ the consummation till farther order; bid Waitwell shake his
ears, and Dame Partlet rustle up her feathers, and meet me at one
o'clock by Rosamond's Pond; that I may see her before she returns
to her lady: and as you tender your ears, be secret.   [*Exit* SERVANT.]
                                    [*Re-enter* FAINALL.]

FAIN. Joy of your success, Mirabell; you look pleased.   110

MIRA. Ay; I have been engaged in a matter of some sort of
mirth, which is not yet ripe for discovery. I am glad this is not a
cabal-night. I wonder, Fainall, that you who are married, and of
consequence should be discreet, will suffer your wife to be of such
a party.

FAIN. Faith, I am not jealous. Besides, most who are engaged
are women and relations; and for the men, they are of a kind too
contemptible to give scandal.   118

MIRA. I am of another opinion. The greater the coxcomb, always
the more the scandal: for a woman who is not a fool can have but
one reason for associating with a man who is one.

FAIN. Are you jealous as often as you see Witwoud entertained
by Millamant?

MIRA. Of her understanding I am, if not of her person.

FAIN. You do her wrong; for to give her her due, she has wit.

MIRA. She has beauty enough to make any man think so; and
complaisance enough not to contradict him who shall tell her so.

FAIN. For a passionate lover, methinks you are a man somewhat
too discerning in the failings of your mistress.   129

MIRA. And for a discerning man, somewhat too passionate a lover; for I like her with all her faults; nay, like her for her faults. Her follies are so natural, or so artful, that they become her; and those affectations which in another woman would be odious, serve but to make her more agreeable. I'll tell thee, Fainall, she once used me with that insolence, that in revenge I took her to pieces; sifted her, and separated her failings; I studied 'em, and got 'em by rote. The catalogue was so large, that I was not without hopes, one day or other, to hate her heartily: to which end I so used myself [138 to think of 'em, that at length, contrary to my design and expectation, they gave me every hour less and less disturbance; till in a few days it became habitual to me to remember 'em without being displeased. They are now grown as familiar to me as my own frailties; and in all probability in a little time longer I shall like 'em as well.

FAIN. Marry her, marry her; be half as well acquainted with her charms as you are with her defects, and my life on't, you are your own man again. 146

MIRA. Say you so?

FAIN. Ay, ay; I have experience: I have a wife, and so forth.

[*Enter* MESSENGER.]

MESS. Is one Squire Witwoud here?

BET. Yes; what's your business?

MESS. I have a letter for him, from his brother, Sir Wilfull, which I am charged to deliver into his own hands.

BET. He's in the next room, friend—that way. [*Exit* MESSENGER.]

MIRA. What, is the chief of that noble family in town, Sir Wilfull Witwoud?

FAIN. He is expected today. Do you know him?

MIRA. I have seen him; he promises to be an extraordinary person; I think you have the honour to be related to him. 158

FAIN. Yes; he is half-brother to this Witwoud by a former wife, who was sister to my Lady Wishfort, my wife's mother. If you marry Millamant, you must call cousins too.

MIRA. I had rather be his relation than his acquaintance.

FAIN. He comes to town in order to equip himself for travel.

MIRA. For travel! Why the man that I mean is above forty.

FAIN. No matter for that; 'tis for the honour of England that all Europe should know we have blockheads of all ages.

MIRA. I wonder there is not an act of Parliament to save the credit of the nation, and prohibit the exportation of fools.   168

FAIN. By no means, 'tis better as 'tis; 'tis better to trade with a little loss than to be quite eaten up, with being overstocked.

MIRA. Pray, are the follies of this knight-errant, and those of the squire his brother, anything related?

FAIN. Not at all; Witwoud grows by the knight, like a medlar grafted on a crab. One will melt in your mouth, and t'other set your teeth on edge; one is all pulp, and the other all core.

MIRA. So one will be rotten before he be ripe, and the other will be rotten without ever being ripe at all.   177

FAIN. Sir Wilfull is an odd mixture of bashfulness and obstinacy. —But when he's drunk, he's as loving as the monster in *The Tempest,* and much after the same manner. To give t'other his due, he has something of good nature, and does not always want wit.

MIRA. Not always; but as often as his memory fails him, and his commonplace of comparisons. He is a fool with a good memory, and some few scraps of other folks' wit. He is one whose conversation can never be approved, yet it is now and then to be endured. He has indeed one good quality, he is not exceptious; for he so passionately affects the reputation of understanding raillery, that he will construe an affront into a jest; and call downright rudeness and ill language, satire and fire.   190

FAIN. If you have a mind to finish his picture, you have an opportunity to do it at full length. Behold the original.

[*Enter* WITWOUD.]

WIT. Afford me your compassion, my dears; pity me, Fainall, Mirabell, pity me.

MIRA. I do from my soul.

FAIN. Why, what's the matter?

WIT. No letters for me, Betty?   197

BET. Did not the messenger bring you one but now, sir?

WIT. Ay, but no other?

BET. No, sir.

WIT. That's hard, that's very hard;—a messenger, a mule, a beast of burden: he has brought me a letter from the fool my brother, as heavy as a panegyric in a funeral sermon, or a copy of commendatory verses from one poet to another. And what's worse, 'tis as sure a forerunner of the author as an epistle dedicatory.

MIRA. A fool, and your brother, Witwoud!

WIT. Ay, ay, my half-brother. My half-brother he is, no nearer upon honour.   208

MIRA. Then 'tis possible he may be but half a fool.

WIT. Good, good, Mirabell, *le drôle!* Good, good!—hang him, don't let's talk of him.—Fainall, how does your lady? Gad, I say anything in the world to get this fellow out of my head. I beg pardon that I should ask a man of pleasure, and the town, a question at once so foreign and domestic. But I talk like an old maid at a marriage, I don't know what I say; but she's the best woman in the world.

FAIN. 'Tis well you don't know what you say, or else your commendation would go near to make me either vain or jealous.

WIT. No man in town lives well with a wife but Fainall. Your judgment, Mirabell.   220

MIRA. You had better step and ask his wife if you would be credibly informed.

WIT. Mirabell.

MIRA. Ay.

WIT. My dear, I ask ten thousand pardons.—Gad, I have forgot what I was going to say to you.

MIRA. I thank you heartily, heartily.

WIT. No, but prithee excuse me—my memory is such a memory.

MIRA. Have a care of such apologies, Witwoud; for I never knew a fool but he affected to complain, either of the spleen or his memory.

FAIN. What have you done with Petulant?   232

WIT. He's reckoning his money—my money it was; I have no luck today.

FAIN. You may allow him to win of you at play, for you are sure to be too hard for him at repartee: since you monopolize the wit that is between you, the fortune must be his, of course.

MIRA. I don't find that Petulant confesses the superiority of wit to be your talent, Witwoud. 239

WIT. Come, come, you are malicious now, and would breed debates. Petulant's my friend, and a very honest fellow, and a very pretty fellow, and has a smattering—faith and troth, a pretty deal of an odd sort of a small wit. Nay, I'll do him justice. I'm his friend, I won't wrong him, neither. And if he had but any judgment in the world, he would not be altogether contemptible. Come, come, don't detract from the merits of my friend.

FAIN. You don't take your friend to be over-nicely bred. 247

WIT. No, no, hang him, the rogue has no manners at all, that I must own—no more breeding than a bum-baily, that I grant you. 'Tis pity, faith; the fellow has fire and life.

MIRA. What, courage?

WIT. Hum, faith, I don't know as to that—I can't say as to that. Yes, faith, in a controversy he'll contradict anybody.

MIRA. Though 'twere a man whom he feared, or a woman whom he loved. 255

WIT. Well, well, he does not always think before he speaks. We have all our failings; you're too hard upon him, you are, faith. Let me excuse him—I can defend most of his faults, except one or two; one he has, that's the truth on't, if he were my brother, I could not acquit him. That, indeed, I could wish were otherwise.

MIRA. Ay, marry, what's that, Witwoud?

WIT. Oh, pardon me! Expose the infirmities of my friend? No, my dear, excuse me there.

FAIN. What! I warrant he's unsincere, or 'tis some such trifle.

WIT. No, no, what if he be? 'Tis no matter for that, his wit will excuse that: a wit should no more be sincere than a woman constant; one argues a decay of parts, as t'other of beauty. 267

MIRA. Maybe you think him too positive?

249. bum-baily: policeman, flatfoot.

WIT. No, no, his being positive is an incentive to argument, and keeps up conversation.

FAIN. Too illiterate.

WIT. That! that's his happiness. His want of learning gives him the more opportunities to show his natural parts.

MIRA. He wants words.

WIT. Ay; but I like him for that now; for his want of words gives me the pleasure very often to explain his meaning.

FAIN. He's impudent.   277

WIT. No, that's not it.

MIRA. Vain.

WIT. No.

MIRA. What, he speaks unseasonable truths sometimes, because he has not wit enough to invent an evasion!

WIT. Truths! Ha, ha, ha! No, no, since you will have it—I mean, he never speaks truth at all—that's all. He will lie like a chambermaid, or a woman of quality's porter. Now that is a fault.

[*Enter* COACHMAN.]

COACH. Is Master Petulant here, mistress?   286

BET. Yes.

COACH. Three gentlewomen in a coach would speak with him.

FAIN. O brave Petulant, three!

BET. I'll tell him.

COACH. You must bring two dishes of chocolate and a glass of cinnamon-water.   [*Exeunt* BETTY *and* COACHMAN.]

WIT. That should be for two fasting strumpets, and a bawd troubled with wind. Now you may know what the three are.

MIRA. You are very free with your friend's acquaintance.   295

WIT. Ay, ay, friendship without freedom is as dull as love without enjoyment, or wine without toasting; but to tell you a secret, these are trulls whom he allows coach-hire, and something more by the week, to call on him once a day at public places.

MIRA. How!

WIT. You shall see he won't go to 'em because there's no more company here to take notice of him—Why, this is nothing to what

he used to do;—before he found out this way, I have known him call for himself—

FAIN. Call for himself? What dost thou mean?   305

WIT. Mean? why he would slip you out of this chocolate-house, just when you had been talking to him—as soon as your back was turned—whip he was gone;—then trip to his lodging, clap on a hood and scarf, and a mask, slap into a hackney-coach, and drive hither to the door again in a trice; where he would send in fcr himself, that I mean, call for himself, wait for himself, nay and what's more, not finding himself, sometimes leave a letter for himself.

MIRA. I confess this is something extraordinary—I believe he waits for himself now, he is so long a coming. Oh, I ask his pardon.

[*Enter* PETULANT *and* BETTY.]

BET. Sir, the coach stays.   [*Exit.*]   316

PET. Well, well; I come.—'Sbud, a man had as good be a professed midwife as a professed whoremaster, at this rate; to be knocked up and raised at all hours, and in all places! Pox on 'em, I won't come.—D'ee hear, tell 'em I won't come. Let 'em snivel and cry their hearts out.

FAIN. You are very cruel, Petulant.

PET. All's one, let it pass—I have a humour to be cruel.

MIRA. I hope they are not persons of condition that you use at this rate.   325

PET. Condition! condition's a dried fig, if I am not in humour. By this hand, if they were your—a—a—your what-d'ee-call-'ems themselves, they must wait or rub off, if I want appetite.

MIRA. What-d'ee-call-'ems! What are they, Witwoud?

WIT. Empresses, my dear—by your what-d'ee-call-'ems he means sultana queens.

PET. Ay, Roxolanas.

MIRA. Cry you mercy.

FAIN. Witwoud says they are—

PET. What does he say th' are?   335

WIT. I—fine ladies, I say.

PET. Pass on, Witwoud.—Hark 'ee, by this light, his relations—two co-heiresses his cousins, and an old aunt, that loves cater-wauling better than a conventicle.

WIT. Ha, ha, ha! I had a mind to see how the rogue would come off. Ha, ha, ha! Gad, I can't be angry with him, if he said they were my mother and my sisters.

MIRA. No!

WIT. No, the rogue's wit and readiness of invention charm me: dear Petulant!   345

[Re-enter BETTY.]

BET. They are gone, sir, in great anger.

PET. Enough, let 'em trundle. Anger helps complexion, saves paint.

FAIN. This continence is all dissembled; this is in order to have something to brag of the next time he makes court to Millamant, and swears he has abandoned the whole sex for her sake.

MIRA. Have you not left off your impudent pretensions there yet? I shall cut your throat, sometime or other, Petulant, about that business.   354

PET. Ay, ay, let that pass—there are other throats to be cut.

MIRA. Meaning mine, sir?

PET. Not I—I mean nobody—I know nothing.—But there are uncles and nephews in the world—and they may be rivals. What then? All's one for that—

MIRA. How! Harkee, Petulant, come hither. Explain, or I shall call your interpreter.

PET. Explain! I know nothing.—Why, you have an uncle, have you not, lately come to town, and lodges by my Lady Wishfort's?

MIRA. True.   364

PET. Why, that's enough—you and he are not friends; and if he should marry and have a child, you may be disinherited, ha?

MIRA. Where hast thou stumbled upon all this truth?

PET. All's one for that; why, then say I know something.

MIRA. Come, thou art an honest fellow, Petulant, and shalt make

339. conventicle: church.

love to my mistress, thou shalt, faith. What has thou heard of my uncle?

PET. I? nothing I. If throats are to be cut, let swords clash; snug's the word, I shrug and am silent.

373

MIRA. Oh, raillery, raillery. Come, I know thou art in the women's secrets.—What, you're a cabalist, I know you stayed at Millamant's last night, after I went. Was there any mention made of my uncle or me? Tell me; if thou hadst but good nature equal to thy wit, Petulant, Tony Witwoud, who is now thy competitor in fame, would show as dim by thee as a dead whiting's eye by a pearl of Orient; he would no more be seen by thee than Mercury is by the sun: Come, I'm sure thou wo't tell me.

PET. If I do, will you grant me common sense then, for the future?

383

MIRA. Faith, I'll do what I can for thee, and I'll pray that Heaven may grant it thee in the meantime.

PET. Well, hark'ee. [*They converse aside.*]

FAIN. Petulant and you both will find Mirabell as warm a rival as a lover.

WIT. Pshaw, pshaw, that she laughs at Petulant is plain. And for my part—but that it is almost a fashion to admire her, I should—hark'ee—to tell you a secret, but let it go no further—between friends, I shall never break my heart for her.

FAIN. How!

393

WIT. She's handsome; but she's a sort of an uncertain woman.

FAIN. I thought you had died for her.

WIT. Umh—no—

FAIN. She has wit.

WIT. 'Tis what she will hardly allow anybody else. Now, demme, I should hate that, if she were as handsome as Cleopatra. Mirabell is not so sure of her as he thinks for.

FAIN. Why do you think so?

401

WIT. We stayed pretty late there last night; and heard something of an uncle to Mirabell, who is lately come to town—and is between him and the best part of his estate. Mirabell and he are at some distance, as my Lady Wishfort has been told; and you know she

hates Mirabell, worse than a Quaker hates a parrot, or than a fish-
monger hates a hard frost. Whether this uncle has seen Mrs. Millamant or not, I cannot say; but there were items of such a treaty
being in embryo; and if it should come to life, poor Mirabell would
be in some sort unfortunately fobbed, i'faith.   410

FAIN. 'Tis impossible Millamant should hearken to it.

WIT. Faith, my dear, I can't tell; she's a woman and a kind of a
humourist.

MIRA. [*Conversing apart with* PETULANT] And this is the sum of
what you could collect last night.

PET. The quintessence. Maybe Witwoud knows more, he stayed
longer.—Besides, they never mind him; they say anything before
him.

MIRA. I thought you had been the greatest favourite.   419

PET. Ay, *tête-à-tête;* but not in public, because I make remarks.

MIRA. You do?

PET. Ay, ay, pox, I'm malicious, man. Now he's soft, you know,
they are not in awe of him—the fellow's well bred, he's what you
call a—what-d'ee-call-'em. A fine gentleman, but he's silly withal.

MIRA. I thank you, I know as much as my curiosity requires.
Fainall, are you for the Mall?

FAIN. Ay, I'll take a turn before dinner.

WIT. Ay, we'll all walk in the Park, the ladies talked of being
there.   429

MIRA. I thought you were obliged to watch for your brother Sir
Wilfull's arrival.

WIT. No, no, he comes to his aunt's, my Lady Wishfort; pox on
him, I shall be troubled with him too; what shall I do with the
fool?

PET. Beg him for his estate; that I may beg you afterwards; and
so have but one trouble with you both.

WIT. O rare Petulant! thou art as quick as fire in a frosty morning; thou shalt to the Mall with us; and we'll be very severe.

PET. Enough! I'm in a humour to be severe.   439

410. fobbed: put off by a trick.

MIRA. Are you? Pray then walk by yourselves,—let not us be accessory to your putting the ladies out of countenance, with your senseless ribaldry, which you roar out aloud as often as they pass by you; and when you have made a handsome woman blush, then you think you have been severe.

PET. What, what? Then let 'em either show their innocence by not understanding what they hear, or else show their discretion by not hearing what they would not be thought to understand.

MIRA. But hast not thou then sense enough to know that thou ought'st to be most ashamed of thyself, when thou hast put another out of countenance? 450

PET. Not I, by this hand—I always take blushing either for a sign of guilt, or ill breeding.

MIRA. I confess you ought to think so. You are in the right, that you may plead the error of your judgment in defence of your practice.

> Where modesty's ill manners, 'tis but fit
> That impudence and malice pass for wit.   [*Exeunt.*]

ACT TWO

SCENE. *St. James's Park.*

[*Enter* MRS. FAINALL *and* MRS. MARWOOD.]

MRS. FAIN. Ay, ay, dear Marwood, if we will be happy, we must find the means in ourselves, and among ourselves. Men are ever in extremes, either doting or averse. While they are lovers, if they have fire and sense, their jealousies are insupportable; and when they cease to love (we ought to think at least) they loathe; they look upon us with horror and distaste; they meet us like the ghosts of what we were, and as from such, fly from us. 7

MRS. MAR. True, 'tis an unhappy circumstance of life, that love should ever die before us; and that the man so often should outlive the lover. But say what you will, 'tis better to be left than never

to have been loved. To pass our youth in dull indifference, to refuse
the sweets of life because they once must leave us, is as preposterous
as to wish to have been born old, because we one day must be old.
For my part, my youth may wear and waste, but it shall never rust
in my possession.   15

MRS. FAIN. Then it seems you dissemble an aversion to mankind
only in compliance to my mother's humour.

MRS. MAR. Certainly. To be free; I have no taste of those insipid dry
discourses, with which our sex of force must entertain themselves,
apart from men. We may affect endearments to each other, profess
eternal friendships, and seem to dote like lovers; but 'tis not in our
natures long to persevere. Love will resume his empire in our
breasts, and every heart, or soon or late, receive and readmit him as
its lawful tyrant.

MRS. FAIN. Bless me, how have I been deceived! Why, you profess a libertine.   26

MRS. MAR. You see my friendship by my freedom. Come, be as
sincere, acknowledge that your sentiments agree with mine.

MRS. FAIN. Never.

MRS. MAR. You hate mankind?

MRS. FAIN. Heartily, inveterately.

MRS. MAR. Your husband?

MRS. FAIN. Most transcendently; ay, though I say it, meritoriously.

MRS. MAR. Give me your hand upon it.

MRS. FAIN. There.   35

MRS. MAR. I join with you; what I have said has been to try you.

MRS. FAIN. Is it possible? Dost thou hate those vipers, men?

MRS. MAR. I have done hating 'em, and am now come to despise
'em; the next thing I have to do, is eternally to forget 'em.

MRS. FAIN. There spoke the spirit of an Amazon, a Penthesilea.

MRS. MAR. And yet I am thinking sometimes to carry my aversion
further.

MRS. FAIN. How?

MRS. MAR. Faith, by marrying; if I could but find one that loved
me very well, and would be thoroughly sensible of ill usage, I think
I should do myself the violence of undergoing the ceremony.   46

MRS. FAIN. You would not make him a cuckold?

MRS. MAR. No; but I'd make him believe I did, and that's as bad.

MRS. FAIN. Why had not you as good do it?

MRS. MAR. Oh, if he should ever discover it, he would then know the worst, and be out of his pain; but I would have him ever to continue upon the rack of fear and jealousy.

MRS. FAIN. Ingenious mischief! Would thou wert married to Mirabell.

MRS. MAR. Would I were!   55

MRS. FAIN. You change colour.

MRS. MAR. Because I hate him.

MRS. FAIN. So do I; but I can hear him named. But what reason have you to hate him in particular?

MRS. MAR. I never loved him; he is, and always was, insufferably proud.

MRS. FAIN. By the reason you give for your aversion, one would think it dissembled; for you have laid a fault to his charge of which his enemies must acquit him.   64

MRS. MAR. Oh, then it seems you are one of his favourable enemies. Methinks you look a little pale, and now you flush again.

MRS. FAIN. Do I? I think I am a little sick o' the sudden.

MRS. MAR. What ails you?

MRS. FAIN. My husband. Don't you see him? He turned short upon me unawares, and has almost overcome me.

[*Enter* FAINALL *and* MIRABELL.]

MRS. MAR. Ha, ha, ha! he comes opportunely for you.

MRS. FAIN. For you, for he has brought Mirabell with him.

FAIN. My dear.

MRS. FAIN. My soul.

FAIN. You don't look well today, child.   75

MRS. FAIN. D'ee think so?

MIRA. He is the only man that does, madam.

MRS. FAIN. The only man that would tell me so, at least; and the only man from whom I could hear it without mortification.

FAIN. O my dear, I am satisfied of your tenderness; I know you

cannot resent anything from me; especially what is an effect of my concern.

MRS. FAIN. Mr. Mirabell, my mother interrupted you in a pleasant relation last night: I would fain hear it out.   84

MIRA. The persons concerned in that affair have yet a tolerable reputation.—I am afraid Mr. Fainall will be censorious.

MRS. FAIN. He has a humour more prevailing than his curiosity, and will willingly dispense with the hearing of one scandalous story, to avoid giving an occasion to make another by being seen to walk with his wife. This way, Mr. Mirabell, and I dare promise you will oblige us both.   [*Exeunt* MRS. FAINALL *and* MIRABELL.]

FAIN. Excellent creature! Well, sure if I should live to be rid of my wife, I should be a miserable man.

MRS. MAR. Ay!   94

FAIN. For having only that one hope, the accomplishment of it, of consequence, must put an end to all my hopes; and what a wretch is he who must survive his hopes! Nothing remains when that day comes, but to sit down and weep like Alexander, when he wanted other worlds to conquer.

MRS. MAR. Will you not follow 'em?

FAIN. I think not.

MRS. MAR. Pray let us; I have a reason.

FAIN. You are not jealous?

MRS. MAR. Of whom?

FAIN. Of Mirabell.   105

MRS. MAR. If I am, is it inconsistent with my love to you that I am tender of your honour?

FAIN. You would intimate, then, as if there were a fellow-feeling between my wife and him.

MRS. MAR. I think she does not hate him to that degree she would be thought.

FAIN. But he, I fear, is too insensible.

MRS. MAR. It may be you are deceived.

FAIN. It may be so. I do now begin to apprehend it.

MRS. MAR. What?   115

FAIN. That I have been deceived, madam, and you are false.

MRS. MAR. That I am false? What mean you?

FAIN. To let you know I see through all your little arts. Come, you both love him; and both have equally dissembled your aversion. Your mutual jealousies of one another have made you clash till you have both struck fire. I have seen the warm confession reddening on your cheeks, and sparkling from your eyes.

MRS. MAR. You do me wrong.   123

FAIN. I do not—'twas for my ease to oversee and wilfully neglect the gross advances made him by my wife; that by permitting her to be engaged, I might continue unsuspected in my pleasures; and take you oftener to my arms in full security. But could you think, because the nodding husband would not wake, that e'er the watchful lover slept?

MRS. MAR. And wherewithal can you reproach me?

FAIN. With infidelity, with loving another, with love of Mirabell.

MRS. MAR. 'Tis false. I challenge you to show an instance that can confirm your groundless accusation. I hate him.   133

FAIN. And wherefore do you hate him? He is insensible, and your resentment follows his neglect. An instance? The injuries you have done him are a proof: your interposing in his love. What cause had you to make discoveries of his pretended passion? To undeceive the credulous aunt, and be the officious obstacle of his match with Millamant?

MRS. MAR. My obligations to my lady urged me: I had professed a friendship to her, and could not see her easy nature so abused by that dissembler.

FAIN. What, was it conscience, then? Professed a friendship! Oh, the pious friendships of the female sex!   144

MRS. MAR. More tender, more sincere, and more enduring than all the vain and empty vows of men, whether professing love to us, or mutual faith to one another.

FAIN. Ha, ha, ha! you are my wife's friend too.

MRS. MAR. Shame and ingratitude! Do you reproach me? You, you upbraid me! Have I been false to her, through strict fidelity to you, and sacrificed my friendship to keep my love inviolate? And have you the baseness to charge me with the guilt, unmindful of

the merit! To you it should be meritorious, that I have been vicious.
And do you reflect that guilt upon me which should lie buried in
your bosom?   155

FAIN. You misinterpret my reproof. I meant but to remind you
of the slight account you once could make of strictest ties, when
set in competition with your love to me.

MRS. MAR. 'Tis false, you urged it with deliberate malice—'twas
spoke in scorn, and I never will forgive it.

FAIN. Your guilt, not your resentment, begets your rage. If yet
you loved, you could forgive a jealousy; but you are stung to find
you are discovered.   163

MRS. MAR. It shall be all discovered. You too shall be discovered;
be sure you shall. I can but be exposed—if I do it myself I shall
prevent your baseness.

FAIN. Why, what will you do?

MRS. MAR. Disclose it to your wife; own what has passed between
us.

FAIN. Frenzy!   170

MRS. MAR. By all my wrongs I'll do't—I'll publish to the world
the injuries you have done me, both in my fame and fortune. With
both I trusted you, you bankrupt in honour, as indigent of wealth.

FAIN. Your fame I have preserved. Your fortune has been bestowed as the prodigality of your love would have it, in pleasures
which we both have shared. Yet, had not you been false, I had ere
this repaid it. 'Tis true—had you permitted Mirabell with Millamant to have stolen their marriage, my lady had been incensed beyond all means of reconcilement; Millamant had forfeited the
moiety of her fortune, which then would have descended to my
wife. And wherefore did I marry, but to make lawful prize of a
rich widow's wealth, and squander it on love and you?   182

MRS. MAR. Deceit and frivolous pretence!

FAIN. Death, am I not married? What's pretence? Am I not im-
prisoned, fettered? Have I not a wife? Nay, a wife that was a
widow, a young widow, a handsome widow; and would be again
a widow, but that I have a heart of proof, and something of a

166. **prevent:** anticipate.

constitution to bustle through the ways of wedlock and this world. Will you yet be reconciled to truth and me? 189

MRS. MAR. Impossible. Truth and you are inconsistent—I hate you, and shall for ever.

FAIN. For loving you?

MRS. MAR. I loathe the name of love after such usage; and next to the guilt with which you would asperse me, I scorn you most. Farewell.

FAIN. Nay, we must not part thus.

MRS. MAR. Let me go.

FAIN. Come, I'm sorry.

MRS. MAR. I care not—let me go—break my hands, do—I'd leave 'em to get loose. 200

FAIN. I would not hurt you for the world. Have I no other hold to keep you here?

MRS. MAR. Well, I have deserved it all.

FAIN. You know I love you.

MRS. MAR. Poor dissembling!—Oh, that—well, it is not yet—

FAIN. What? What is it not? What is it not yet? It is not yet too late—

MRS. MAR. No, it is not yet too late—I have that comfort.

FAIN. It is, to love another. 209

MRS. MAR. But not to loathe, detest, abhor mankind, myself, and the whole treacherous world.

FAIN. Nay, this is extravagance.—Come, I ask your pardon—no tears—I was to blame, I could not love you and be easy in my doubts. Pray forbear—I believe you; I'm convinced I've done you wrong; and any way, every way will make amends;—I'll hate my wife yet more, damn her, I'll part with her, rob her of all she's worth, and we'll retire somewhere, anywhere, to another world. I'll marry thee—be pacified.—'Sdeath, they come, hide your face, your tears. You have a mask, wear it a moment. This way, this way, be persuaded. *[Exeunt.]* 220

[Enter MIRABELL *and* MRS. FAINALL.]

MRS. FAIN. They are here yet.

MIRA. They are turning into the other walk.

MRS. FAIN. While I only hated my husband, I could bear to see him; but since I have despised him, he's too offensive.

MIRA. Oh, you should hate with prudence.

MRS. FAIN. Yes, for I have loved with indiscretion.

MIRA. You should have just so much disgust for your husband as may be sufficient to make you relish your lover. 228

MRS. FAIN. You have been the cause that I have loved without bounds, and would you set limits to that aversion, of which you have been the occasion? Why did you make me marry this man?

MIRA. Why do we daily commit disagreeable and dangerous actions? To save that idol, reputation. If the familiarities of our loves had produced that consequence of which you were apprehensive, where could you have fixed a father's name with credit, but on a husband? I knew Fainall to be a man lavish of his morals, an interested and professing friend, a false and a designing lover; yet one whose wit and outward fair behaviour have gained a reputation with the town, enough to make that woman stand excused who has suffered herself to be won by his addresses. A better man ought not to have been sacrificed to the occasion; a worse had not answered to the purpose. When you are weary of him, you know your remedy. 243

MRS. FAIN. I ought to stand in some degree of credit with you, Mirabell.

MIRA. In justice to you, I have made you privy to my whole design, and put it in your power to ruin or advance my fortune.

MRS. FAIN. Whom have you instructed to represent your pretended uncle?

MIRA. Waitwell, my servant.

MRS. FAIN. He is an humble servant to Foible, my mother's woman, and may win her to your interest. 252

MIRA. Care is taken for that—she is won and worn by this time. They were married this morning.

MRS. FAIN. Who?

MIRA. Waitwell and Foible. I would not tempt my servant to betray me by trusting him too far. If your mother, in hopes to ruin

me, should consent to marry my pretended uncle, he might, like Mosca in *The Fox,* stand upon terms; so I made him sure beforehand.

MRS. FAIN. So, if my poor mother is caught in a contract, you will discover the imposture betimes; and release her by producing a certificate of her gallant's former marriage.   263

MIRA. Yes, upon condition that she consent to my marriage with her niece, and surrender the moiety of her fortune in her possession.

MRS. FAIN. She talked last night of endeavouring at a match between Millamant and your uncle.

MIRA. That was by Foible's direction, and my instruction, that she might seem to carry it more privately.

MRS. FAIN. Well, I have an opinion of your success; for I believe my lady will do anything to get an husband; and when she has this, which you have provided for her, I suppose she will submit to anything to get rid of him.   274

MIRA. Yes, I think the good lady would marry anything that resembled a man, though 'twere no more than what a butler could pinch out of a napkin.

MRS. FAIN. Female frailty! We must all come to it, if we live to be old, and feel the craving of a false appetite when the true is decayed.

MIRA. An old woman's appetite is depraved like that of a girl— 'tis the green-sickness of a second childhood; and like the faint offer of a latter spring, serves but to usher in the fall, and withers in an affected bloom.   284

MRS. FAIN. Here's your mistress.

[*Enter* MRS. MILLAMANT, WITWOUD, *and* MINCING.]

MIRA. Here she comes, i'faith, full sail, with her fan spread and streamers out, and a shoal of fools for tenders. Ha, no, I cry her mercy!

MRS. FAIN. I see but one poor empty sculler; and he tows her woman after him.

MIRA. You seem to be unattended, madam—you used to have the

beau-monde throng after you; and a flock of gay fine perukes hovering round you.   293

WIT. Like moths about a candle.—I had like to have lost my comparison for want of breath.

MILLA. Oh, I have denied myself airs today. I have walked as fast through the crowd—

WIT. As a favourite just disgraced, and with as few followers.

MILLA. Dear Mr. Witwoud, truce with your similitudes; for I am as sick of 'em—

WIT. As a physician of a good air.—I cannot help it, madam, though 'tis against myself.   302

MILLA. Yet again! Mincing, stand between me and his wit.

WIT. Do, Mrs. Mincing, like a screen before a great fire. I confess I do blaze today, I am too bright.

MRS. FAIN. But, dear Millamant, why were you so long?

MILLA. Long! Lord, have I not made violent haste? I have asked every living thing I met for you; I have enquired after you, as after a new fashion.

WIT. Madam, truce with your similitudes.—No, you met her husband, and did not ask him for her.

MIRA. By your leave, Witwoud, that were like enquiring after an old fashion, to ask a husband for his wife.   313

WIT. Hum, a hit, a hit, a palpable hit, I confess it.

MRS. FAIN. You were dressed before I came abroad.

MILLA. Ay, that's true—Oh, but then I had—Mincing, what had I? Why was I so long?

MINC. O mem, your la'ship stayed to peruse a pecquet of letters.

MILLA. Oh ay, letters—I had letters—I am persecuted with letters —I hate letters—nobody knows how to write letters; and yet one has 'em, one does not know why.—They serve one to pin up one's hair.   322

WIT. Is that the way? Pray, madam, do you pin up your hair with all your letters? I find I must keep copies.

MILLA. Only with those in verse, Mr. Witwoud. I never pin up my hair with prose. I think I tried once, Mincing.

MINC. O mem, I shall never forget it.

MILLA. Ay, poor Mincing tift and tift all the morning.

MINC. 'Til I had the cremp in my fingers, I'll vow, mem. And all to no purpose. But when your la'ship pins it up with poetry, it sits so pleasant the next day as anything, and is so pure and so crips.

WIT. Indeed, so crips?   332

MINC. You're such a critic, Mr. Witwoud.

MILLA. Mirabell, did not you take exceptions last night? Oh ay, and went away.—Now I think on't I'm angry—no, now I think on't I'm pleased—for I believe I gave you some pain.

MIRA. Does that please you?

MILLA. Infinitely; I love to give pain.

MIRA. You would affect a cruelty which is not in your nature; your true vanity is in the power of pleasing.

MILLA. Oh, I ask your pardon for that—one's cruelty is one's power, and when one parts with one's cruelty, one parts with one's power; and when one has parted with that, I fancy one's old and ugly.   344

MIRA. Ay, ay, suffer your cruelty to ruin the object of your power, to destroy your lover—and then how vain, how lost a thing you'll be! Nay, 'tis true: you are no longer handsome when you've lost your lover; your beauty dies upon the instant. For beauty is the lover's gift; 'tis he bestows your charms—your glass is all a cheat. The ugly and the old, whom the looking-glass mortifies, yet after commendation can be flattered by it, and discover beauties in it; for that reflects our praises, rather than your face.   352

MILLA. Oh, the vanity of these men! Fainall, d'ee hear him? If they did not commend us, we were not handsome! Now you must know they could not commend one, if one was not handsome. Beauty the lover's gift—Lord, what is a lover, that it can give? Why, one makes lovers as fast as one pleases, and they live as long as one pleases, and they die as soon as one pleases; and then if one pleases, one makes more.

WIT. Very pretty. Why you make no more of making of lovers, madam, than of making so many card-matches.   361

MILLA. One no more owes one's beauty to a lover than one's wit to an echo; they can but reflect what we look and say, vain empty things if we are silent or unseen, and want a being.

MIRA. Yet, to those two vain empty things, you owe two the greatest pleasures of your life.

MILLA. How so?

MIRA. To your lover you owe the pleasure of hearing yourselves praised, and to an echo the pleasure of hearing yourselves talk.

WIT. But I know a lady that loves talking so incessantly, she won't give an echo fair play; she has that everlasting rotation of tongue, that an echo must wait till she dies before it can catch her last words.   373

MILLA. Oh, fiction! Fainall, let us leave these men.

MIRA. [*Aside to* MRS. FAINALL] Draw off Witwoud.

MRS. FAIN. [*Aside*] Immediately.—I have a word or two for Mr. Witwoud.

MIRA. I would beg a little private audience too. [*Exeunt* WITWOUD *and* MRS. FAINALL.] You had the tyranny to deny me last night; though you knew I came to impart a secret to you that concerned my love.

MILLA. You saw I was engaged.   382

MIRA. Unkind. You had the leisure to entertain a herd of fools, things who visit you from their excessive idleness, bestowing on your easiness that time which is the incumbrance of their lives. How can you find delight in such society? It is impossible they should admire you, they are not capable; or if they were, it should be to you as a mortification, for sure to please a fool is some degree of folly.

MILLA. I please myself—besides, sometimes to converse with fools is for my health.

MIRA. Your health! Is there a worse disease than the conversation of fools?   393

MILLA. Yes, the vapours; fools are physic for it, next to asafetida.

MIRA. You are not in a course of fools?

395. course: sequence of remedies.

MILLA. Mirabell, if you persist in this offensive freedom, you'll displease me. I think I must resolve, after all, not to have you—we shan't agree.

MIRA. Not in our physic, it may be.

MILLA. And yet our distemper in all likelihood will be the same; for we shall be sick of one another. I shan't endure to be reprimanded, nor instructed; 'tis so dull to act always by advice, and so tedious to be told of one's faults—I can't bear it. Well, I won't have you, Mirabell—I'm resolved—I think—you may go—ha, ha, ha! What would you give, that you could help loving me?

MIRA. I would give something that you did not know I could not help it. 407

MILLA. Come, don't look grave, then. Well, what do you say to me?

MIRA. I say that a man may as soon make a friend by his wit, or a fortune by his honesty, as win a woman with plain dealing and sincerity.

MILLA. Sententious Mirabell! Prithee don't look with that violent and inflexible wise face, like Solomon at the dividing of the child in an old tapestry hanging.

MIRA. You are merry, madam, but I would persuade you for a moment to be serious. 417

MILLA. What, with that face? No, if you keep your countenance, 'tis impossible I should hold mine. Well, after all, there is something very moving in a lovesick face. Ha, ha, ha!—Well I won't laugh, don't be peevish.—Heigho! Now I'll be melancholy, as melancholy as a watch-light. Well, Mirabell, if ever you will win me, woo me now.—Nay, if you are so tedious, fare you well—I see they are walking away. 424

MIRA. Can you not find in the variety of your disposition one moment—

MILLA. To hear you tell me Foible's married, and your plot like to speed?—No.

MIRA. But how you came to know it—

MILLA. Without the help of the devil, you can't imagine; unless

she should tell me herself. Which of the two it may have been, I will leave you to consider; and when you have done thinking of that, think of me. [*Exit.*] 433

MIRA. I have something more—Gone!—Think of you! To think of a whirlwind, though 'twere in a whirlwind, were a case of more steady contemplation; a very tranquillity of mind and mansion. A fellow that lives in a windmill has not a more whimsical dwelling than the heart of a man that is lodged in a woman. There is no point of the compass to which they cannot turn, and by which they are not turned; and by one as well as another, for motion, not method, is their occupation. To know this, and yet continue to be in love, is to be made wise from the dictates of reason, and yet persevere to play the fool by the force of instinct.—Oh, here come my pair of turtles.—What, billing so sweetly! Is not Valentine's Day over with you yet? 445

[*Enter* WAITWELL *and* FOIBLE.]

MIRA. Sirrah, Waitwell, why sure you think you were married for your own recreation, and not for my conveniency.

WAIT. Your pardon, sir. With submission, we have indeed been solacing in lawful delights; but still with an eye to business, sir. I have instructed her as well as I could. If she can take your directions as readily as my instructions, sir, your affairs are in a prosperous way.

MIRA. Give you joy, Mrs. Foible.

FOIB. Oh 'las, sir, I'm so ashamed—I'm afraid my lady has been in a thousand inquietudes for me. But I protest, sir, I made as much haste as I could. 456

WAIT. That she did indeed, sir. It was my fault that she did not make more.

MIRA. That I believe.

FOIB. But I told my lady as you instructed me, sir. That I had a prospect of seeing Sir Rowland your uncle; and that I would put her ladyship's picture in my pocket to show him; which I'll be sure

444. turtles: turtledoves.

to say has made him so enamoured of her beauty that he burns with impatience to lie at her ladyship's feet and worship the original.

MIRA. Excellent Foible! Matrimony has made you eloquent in love.   466

WAIT. I think she has profited, sir. I think so.

FOIB. You have seen Madam Millamant, sir?

MIRA. Yes.

FOIB. I told her, sir, because I did not know that you might find an opportunity; she had so much company last night.

MIRA. Your diligence will merit more.—In the meantime—[*Gives money*.]

FOIB. O dear sir, your humble servant.

WAIT. Spouse!   475

MIRA. Stand off, sir, not a penny.—Go on and prosper, Foible—the lease shall be made good and the farm stocked, if we succeed.

FOIB. I don't question your generosity, sir; and you need not doubt of success. If you have no more commands, sir, I'll be gone; I'm sure my lady is at her toilet, and can't dress till I come.—Oh dear, I'm sure that [*Looking out*] was Mrs. Marwood that went by in a mask; if she has seen me with you I'm sure she'll tell my lady. I'll make haste home and prevent her. Your servant, sir. B'w'y, Waitwell.   [*Exit* FOIBLE.]

WAIT. Sir Rowland, if you please. The jade's so pert upon her preferment she forgets herself.   486

MIRA. Come, sir, will you endeavour to forget yourself—and transform into Sir Rowland.

WAIT. Why, sir, it will be impossible I should remember myself—married, knighted, and attended all in one day! 'Tis enough to make any man forget himself. The difficulty will be how to recover my acquaintance and familiarity with my former self, and fall from my transformation to a reformation into Waitwell. Nay, I shan't be quite the same Waitwell neither—for now I remember me, I'm married, and can't be my own man again.

> Ay there's my grief; that's the sad change of life;
> To lose my title, and yet keep my wife.   [*Exeunt*.]

ACT THREE

SCENE. A room in LADY WISHFORT'S *house.*

[LADY WISHFORT *at her toilet,* PEG *waiting.*]

LADY W. Merciful, no news of Foible yet?

PEG. No, madam.

LADY W. I have no more patience. If I have not fretted myself till I am pale again, there's no veracity in me. Fetch me the red—the red, do you hear, sweetheart? An arrant ash colour, as I'm a person. Look you how this wench stirs! Didst thou not hear me, mopus?

PEG. The red ratafia, does your ladyship mean, or the cherry brandy?   9

LADY W. Ratafia, fool! No, fool. Not the ratafia, fool—grant me patience! I mean the Spanish paper, idiot—complexion, darling. Paint, paint, paint, dost thou understand that, changeling, dangling thy hands like bobbins before thee? Why dost thou not stir, puppet? —thou wooden thing upon wires!

PEG. Lord, madam, your ladyship is so impatient. I cannot come at the paint, madam; Mrs. Foible has locked it up, and carried the key with her.

LADY W. A pox take you both! Fetch me the cherry brandy, then. [*Exit* PEG.] I'm as pale and as faint, I look like Mrs. Qualmsick the curate's wife, that's always breeding.—Wench, come, come, wench, what art thou doing, sipping? tasting? Save thee, dost thou not know the bottle?   22

[*Enter* PEG *with a bottle and china cup.*]

PEG. Madam, I was looking for a cup.

LADY W. A cup, save thee, and what a cup hast thou brought! Dost thou take me for a fairy, to drink out of an acorn? Why didst thou not bring thy thimble? Hast thou ne'er a brass thimble clinking in thy pocket with a bit of nutmeg? I warrant thee. Come, fill, fill.—So—again. [*One knocks.*] See who that is.—Set down the

bottle first. Here, here, under the table. What, wouldst thou go with the bottle in thy hand like a tapster? [*Exit* PEG.] As I'm a person, this wench has lived in an inn upon the road, before she came to me, like Maritornes the Asturian in *Don Quixote*. [*Re-enter* PEG.] No Foible yet?

33

PEG. No, madam—Mrs. Marwood.

LADY W. Oh, Marwood! let her come in. Come in, good Marwood.

[*Enter* MRS. MARWOOD.]

MRS. MAR. I'm surprised to find your ladyship in dishabille at this time of day.

LADY W. Foible's a lost thing; has been abroad since morning, and never heard of since.

40

MRS. MAR. I saw her but now, as I came masked through the Park, in conference with Mirabell.

LADY W. With Mirabell! You call my blood into my face, with mentioning that traitor. She durst not have the confidence. I sent her to negotiate an affair, in which if I'm detected I'm undone. If that wheedling villain has wrought upon Foible to detect me, I'm ruined. Oh, my dear friend, I'm a wretch of wretches if I'm detected.

48

MRS. MAR. O madam, you cannot suspect Mrs. Foible's integrity.

LADY W. Oh, he carries poison in his tongue that would corrupt integrity itself. If she has given him an opportunity, she has as good as put her integrity into his hands. Ah, dear Marwood, what's integrity to an opportunity?—Hark! I hear her.—Dear friend, retire into my closet, that I may examine her with more freedom.—You'll pardon me, dear friend, I can make bold with you.—There are books over the chimney—Quarles and Prynne, and the *Short View of the Stage,* with Bunyan's works to entertain you. [*To* PEG] Go, you thing, and send her in.   [*Exeunt* MARWOOD *and* PEG.]   58

[*Enter* FOIBLE.]

56-57. **Quarles . . . Stage:** Francis Quarles (1592-1644), a religious poet; William Prynne (1600-1699), Puritan author of *Histrio-Mastix, or The Players' Scourge; A Short View of the Immorality and Profaneness of the English Stage* (1698) by Jeremy Collier.

LADY W. O Foible, where hast thou been? what hast thou been doing?

FOIB. Madam, I have seen the party.

LADY W. But what hast thou done?

FOIB. Nay, 'tis your ladyship has done, and are to do; I have only promised. But a man so enamoured—so transported! Well, if worshipping of pictures be a sin—poor Sir Rowland, I say.

LADY W. The miniature has been counted like—but hast thou not betrayed me, Foible? Hast thou not detected me to that faithless Mirabell? What hadst thou to do with him in the Park? Answer me, has he got nothing out of thee?   69

FOIB. [*Aside*] So, the devil has been beforehand with me; what shall I say?—Alas, madam, could I help it, if I met that confident thing? Was I in fault? If you had heard how he used me, and all upon your ladyship's account, I'm sure you would not suspect my fidelity. Nay, if that had been the worst, I could have borne: but he had a fling at your ladyship, too; and then I could not hold, but, i' faith, I gave him his own.

LADY W. Me? What did the filthy fellow say?   77

FOIB. O madam, 'tis a shame to say what he said—with his taunts and his fleers, tossing up his nose. "Humph!" says he, "what, you are a hatching some plot," says he, "you are so early abroad, or catering," says he, "ferreting for some disbanded officer, I warrant—half pay is but thin subsistence," says he. "Well, what pension does your lady propose? Let me see," says he; "what, she must come down pretty deep now: she's superannuated," says he, "and—"

LADY W. Ods my life, I'll have him—I'll have him murdered. I'll have him poisoned. Where does he eat? I'll marry a drawer to have him poisoned in his wine. I'll send for Robin from Locket's immediately.   88

FOIB. Poison him? Poisoning's too good for him. Starve him, madam, starve him; marry Sir Rowland and get him disinherited. Oh, you would bless yourself, to hear what he said.

LADY W. A villain! "superannuated!"

86. **drawer**: tavern waiter.

FOIB. "Humph!" says he, "I hear you are laying designs against me, too," says he, "and Mrs. Millamant is to marry my uncle,"—(he does not suspect a word of your ladyship)—"but," says he, "I'll fit you for that, I warrant you," says he, "I'll hamper you for that," says he, "you and your old frippery, too," says he, "I'll handle you—" 98

LADY W. Audacious villain! handle me! would he durst! "Frippery? old frippery!" Was there ever such a foul-mouthed fellow? I'll be married tomorrow, I'll be contracted tonight.

FOIB. The sooner the better, madam.

LADY W. Will Sir Rowland be here, say'st thou? When, Foible?

FOIB. Incontinently, madam. No new sheriff's wife expects the return of her husband after knighthood with that impatience in which Sir Rowland burns for the dear hour of kissing your ladyship's hands after dinner. 107

LADY W. "Frippery? superannuated frippery!" I'll frippery the villain; I'll reduce him to frippery and rags. A tatterdemalion!—I hope to see him hung with tatters, like a Long Lane pent-house, or a gibbet-thief. A slander-mouthed railer. I warrant the spendthrift prodigal's in debt as much as the million lottery, or the whole court upon a birthday. I'll spoil his credit with his tailor. Yes, he shall have my niece with her fortune, he shall.

FOIB. He! I hope to see him lodge in Ludgate first, and angle into Blackfriars for brass farthings, with an old mitten. 116

LADY W. Ay, dear Foible; thank thee for that, dear Foible. He has put me out of all patience. I shall never recompose my features to receive Sir Rowland with any economy of face. This wretch has fretted me that I am absolutely decayed. Look, Foible.

FOIB. Your ladyship has frowned a little too rashly, indeed, madam. There are some cracks discernible in the white varnish.

LADY W. Let me see the glass—Cracks, say'st thou? Why, I am arrantly flayed. I look like an old peeled wall. Thou must repair me, Foible, before Sir Rowland comes, or I shall never keep up to my picture. 126

110. Long Lane pent-house: secondhand store. **115. Ludgate:** debtors' prison.

FOIB. I warrant you, madam; a little art once made your picture like you, and now a little of the same art must make you like your picture. Your picture must sit for you, madam.

LADY W. But art thou sure Sir Rowland will not fail to come? Or will a' not fail when he does come? Will he be importunate, Foible, and push? For if he should not be importunate— I shall never break decorums—I shall die with confusion, if I am forced to advance—Oh no, I can never advance—I shall swoon if he should expect advances. No, I hope Sir Rowland is better bred than to put a lady to the necessity of breaking her forms. I won't be too coy neither.—I won't give him despair—but a little disdain is not amiss; a little scorn is alluring.   138

FOIB. A little scorn becomes your ladyship.

LADY W. Yes, but tenderness becomes me best—a sort of a dyingness.—You see that picture has a sort of a—ha, Foible? A swimmingness in the eyes.—Yes, I'll look so—my niece affects it, but she wants features. Is Sir Rowland handsome? Let my toilet be removed—I'll dress above. I'll receive Sir Rowland here. Is he handsome? Don't answer me. I won't know; I'll be surprised. I'll be taken by surprise.

FOIB. By storm, madam. Sir Rowland's a brisk man.   147

LADY W. Is he! Oh, then he'll importune, if he's a brisk man. I shall save decorums if Sir Rowland importunes. I have a mortal terror at the apprehension of offending against decorums. Oh, I'm glad he's a brisk man. Let my things be removed, good Foible.

[Exit.]

[Enter MRS. FAINALL.*]*

MRS. FAIN. O Foible, I have been in a fright, lest I should come too late. That devil, Marwood, saw you in the Park with Mirabell, and I'm afraid will discover it to my lady.

FOIB. Discover what, madam?   155

MRS. FAIN. Nay, nay, put not on that strange face. I am privy to the whole design, and know that Waitwell, to whom thou wert this morning married, is to personate Mirabell's uncle, and as such, winning my lady, to involve her in those difficulties from which

Mirabell only must release her, by his making his conditions to have my cousin and her fortune left to her own disposal.

FOIB. O dear madam, I beg your pardon. It was not my confidence in your ladyship that was deficient; but I thought the former good correspondence between your ladyship and Mr. Mirabell might have hindered his communicating this secret.

MRS. FAIN. Dear Foible, forget that. 166

FOIB. O dear madam, Mr. Mirabell is such a sweet winning gentleman!—But your ladyship is the pattern of generosity.—Sweet lady, to be so good! Mr. Mirabell cannot choose but be grateful. I find your ladyship has his heart still. Now, madam, I can safely tell your ladyship our success. Mrs. Marwood had told my lady, but I warrant I managed myself. I turned it all for the better. I told my lady that Mr. Mirabell railed at her. I laid horrid things to his charge, I'll vow; and my lady is so incensed, that she'll be contracted to Sir Rowland tonight, she says.—I warrant I worked her up, that he may have her for asking for, as they say of a Welsh maidenhead. 177

MRS. FAIN. O rare Foible!

FOIB. Madam, I beg your ladyship to acquaint Mr. Mirabell of his success. I would be seen as little as possible to speak to him—besides, I believe Madam Marwood watches me.—She has a month's mind; but I know Mr. Mirabell can't abide her.—[*Calls.*] John—remove my lady's toilet. Madam, your servant. My lady is so impatient, I fear she'll come for me if I stay.

MRS. FAIN. I'll go with you up the back stairs, lest I should meet her. [*Exeunt.*] 186
[*Enter* MRS. MARWOOD.]

MRS. MAR. Indeed, Mrs. Engine, is it thus with you? Are you become a go-between of this importance? Yes, I shall watch you. Why this wench is the *passe-partout,* a very master-key to everybody's strongbox. My friend Fainall, have you carried it so swimmingly? I thought there was something in it; but it seems it's over with you. Your loathing is not from a want of appetite, then, but

187. Engine: plotter.

from a surfeit. Else you could never be so cool to fall from a principal to be an assistant; to procure for him! A pattern of generosity, that I confess. Well, Mr. Fainall, you have met with your match.—O man, man! Woman, woman! The devil's an ass: if I were a [196 painter, I would draw him like an idiot, a driveler with a bib and bells. Man should have his head and horns, and woman the rest of him. Poor simple fiend! "Madam Marwood has a month's mind, but he can't abide her."—'Twere better for him you had not been his confessor in that affair, without you could have kept his counsel closer. I shall not prove another pattern of generosity—he has not obliged me to that with those excesses of himself; and now I'll have none of him. Here comes the good lady, panting ripe; with a heart full of hope, and a head full of care, like any chemist upon the day of projection. 206

[*Enter* LADY WISHFORT.]

LADY W. O dear Marwood, what shall I say for this rude forgetfulness?—but my dear friend is all goodness.

MRS. MAR. No apologies, dear madam. I have been very well entertained.

LADY W. As I'm a person I am in a very chaos to think I should so forget myself—but I have such an olio of affairs really I know not what to do.—[*Calls.*]—Foible!—I expect my nephew Sir Wilfull every moment too.—Why, Foible!—He means to travel for improvement. 215

MRS. MAR. Methinks Sir Wilfull should rather think of marrying than travelling at his years. I hear he is turned of forty.

LADY W. Oh, he's in less danger of being spoiled by his travels.—I am against my nephew's marrying too young. It will be time enough when he comes back, and has acquired discretion to choose for himself.

MRS. MAR. Methinks Mrs. Millamant and he would make a very fit match. He may travel afterwards. 'Tis a thing very usual with young gentlemen. 224

205-06. chemist . . . projection: alchemist on the day of his attempt to turn base metal into gold. 212. olio: hodgepodge.

LADY W. I promise you I have thought on't—and since 'tis your judgment, I'll think on't again. I assure you I will; I value your judgment extremely. On my word I'll propose it. [*Enter* FOIBLE.] Come, come, Foible—I had forgot my nephew will be here before dinner—I must make haste.

FOIB. Mr. Witwoud and Mr. Petulant are come to dine with your ladyship.

LADY W. Oh, dear, I can't appear till I am dressed. Dear Marwood, shall I be free with you again, and beg you to entertain 'em? I'll make all imaginable haste. Dear friend, excuse me.   234

                        [*Exeunt* LADY WISHFORT *and* FOIBLE.]

               [*Enter* MRS. MILLAMANT *and* MINCING.]

MILLA. Sure never anything was so unbred as that odious man.— Marwood, your servant.

MRS. MAR. You have a colour, what's the matter?

MILLA. That horrid fellow Petulant has provoked me into a flame —I have broke my fan.—Mincing, lend me yours.—Is not all the powder out of my hair?

MRS. MAR. No. What has he done?   241

MILLA. Nay, he has done nothing; he has only talked.—Nay, he has said nothing neither, but he has contradicted everything that has been said. For my part, I thought Witwoud and he would have quarrelled.

MINC. I vow, mem, I thought once they would have fit.

MILLA. Well, 'tis a lamentable thing I swear, that one has not the liberty of choosing one's acquaintance as one does one's clothes.

MRS. MAR. If we had that liberty, we should be as weary of one set of acquaintance, though never so good, as we are of one suit, though never so fine. A fool and a doily stuff would now and then find days of grace, and be worn for variety.   252

MILLA. I could consent to wear 'em, if they would wear alike; but fools never wear out—they are such *drap-de-Berry* things! Without one could give 'em to one's chambermaid after a day or two.

MRS. MAR. 'Twere better so indeed. Or what think you of the play-house? A fine gay glossy fool should be given there, like a new

251. doily: cheap material. **254. drap-de-Berry:** heavy material.

masking habit, after the masquerade is over, and we have done with the disguise. For a fool's visit is always a disguise, and never admitted by a woman of wit but to blind her affair with a lover of sense. If you would but appear bare-faced now, and own Mirabell, you might as easily put off Petulant and Witwoud as your hood and scarf. And indeed 'tis time, for the town has found it: the secret is grown too big for the pretence: 'tis like Mrs. Primly's great belly; she may lace it down before, but it burnishes on her hips. Indeed, Millamant, you can no more conceal it than my Lady Strammel can her face, that goodly face, which in defiance of her Rhenish-wine tea, will not be comprehended in a mask.   268

MILLA. I'll take my death, Marwood, you are more censorious than a decayed beauty, or a discarded toast. Mincing, tell the men they may come up. My aunt is not dressing here; their folly is less provoking than your malice. [*Exit* MINCING.] "The town has found it." What has it found? That Mirabell loves me is no more a secret than it is a secret that you discovered it to my aunt, or than the reason why you discovered it is a secret.

MRS. MAR. You are nettled.

MILLA. You're mistaken. Ridiculous!   277

MRS. MAR. Indeed, my dear, you'll tear another fan if you don't mitigate those violent airs.

MILLA. O silly! Ha, ha, ha! I could laugh immoderately. Poor Mirabell! His constancy to me has quite destroyed his complaisance for all the world beside. I swear, I never enjoined it him, to be so coy. If I had the vanity to think he would obey me, I would command him to show more gallantry—'tis hardly well bred to be so particular on one hand, and so insensible on the other. But I despair to prevail, and so let him follow his own way. Ha, ha, ha! Pardon me, dear creature, I must laugh, ha, ha, ha! though I grant you 'tis a little barbarous, ha, ha, ha!   288

MRS. MAR. What pity 'tis, so much fine raillery, and delivered with so significant gesture, should be so unhappily directed to miscarry.

MILLA. Heh? Dear creature, I ask your pardon—I swear I did not mind you.

MRS. MAR. Mr. Mirabell and you both may think it a thing impossible, when I shall tell him by telling you—

MILLA. Oh, dear, what? for it is the same thing if I hear it—ha, ha, ha!   297

MRS. MAR. That I detest him, hate him, madam.

MILLA. O madam, why so do I—and yet the creature loves me, ha, ha, ha! How can one forbear laughing to think of it—I am a sibyl if I am not amazed to think what he can see in me. I'll take my death, I think you are handsomer—and within a year or two as young. If you could but stay for me, I should overtake you— but that cannot be. Well, that thought makes me melancholic—now I'll be sad.

MRS. MAR. Your merry note may be changed sooner than you think.   307

MILLA. D'ee say so? Then I'm resolved I'll have a song to keep up my spirits.

[*Enter* MINCING.]

MINC. The gentlemen stay but to comb, madam, and will wait on you.

MILLA. Desire Mrs. —— that is in the next room to sing the song I would have learnt yesterday. You shall hear it, madam.—Not that there's any great matter in it—but 'tis agreeable to my humour.

SONG

Set by Mr. John Eccles, and sung by Mrs. Hodgson

I

Love's but the frailty of the mind,
When 'tis not with ambition joined;
A sickly flame, which if not fed expires;
And feeding, wastes in self-consuming fires.

2

'Tis not to wound a wanton boy
Or amorous youth, that gives the joy;   322
But 'tis the glory to have pierced a swain,
For whom inferior beauties sighed in vain.

3

Then I alone the conquest prize,
When I insult a rival's eyes:
If there's delight in love, 'tis when I see
That heart which others bleed for, bleed for me.

[*Enter* PETULANT *and* WITWOUD.]

MILLA. Is your animosity composed, gentlemen?

WIT. Raillery, raillery, madam; we have no animosity—we hit off a little wit now and then, but no animosity. The falling out of wits is like the falling out of lovers. We agree in the main, like treble and bass. Ha, Petulant?   333

PET. Ay, in the main—but when I have a humour to contradict—

WIT. Ay, when he has a humour to contradict, then I contradict too. What, I know my cue. Then we contradict one another like two battledores; for contradictions beget one another like Jews.

PET. If he says black's black—if I have a humour to say 'tis blue—let that pass—all's one for that. If I have a humour to prove it, it must be granted.

WIT. Not positively must—but it may—it may.   341

PET. Yes, it positively must, upon proof positive.

WIT. Ay, upon proof positive it must; but upon proof presumptive it only may. That's a logical distinction now, madam.

MRS. MAR. I perceive your debates are of importance, and very learnedly handled.

PET. Importance is one thing, and learning's another; but a debate's a debate, that I assert.

WIT. Petulant's an enemy to learning; he relies altogether on his parts.

PET. No, I'm no enemy to learning; it hurts not me.   351

MRS. MAR. That's a sign indeed it's no enemy to you.

PET. No, no, it's no enemy to anybody, but them that have it.

MILLA. Well, an illiterate man's my aversion. I wonder at the impudence of any illiterate man, to offer to make love.

WIT. That I confess I wonder at too.

MILLA. Ah! to marry an ignorant! that can hardly read or write.

PET. Why should a man be any further from being married though he can't read, than he is from being hanged? The ordinary's paid for setting the psalm, and the parish-priest for reading the ceremony. And for the rest which is to follow in both cases, a man may do it without book—so all's one for that.   362

MILLA. D'ee hear the creature? Lord, here's company, I'll be gone.

[*Exeunt* MILLAMANT *and* MINCING.]

WIT. In the name of Bartlemew and his fair, what have we here?

MRS. MAR. 'Tis your brother, I fancy. Don't you know him?

WIT. Not I—yes, I think it is he—I've almost forgot him; I have not seen him since the Revolution.

[*Enter* SIR WILFULL WITWOUD *in a country riding habit, and* SERVANT *to* LADY WISHFORT.]

SERV. Sir, my lady's dressing. Here's company, if you please to walk in, in the meantime.   369

SIR WIL. Dressing! What, it's but morning here, I warrant, with you in London; we should count it towards afternoon in our parts, down in Shropshire. Why then belike my aunt han't dined yet—ha, friend?

SERV. Your aunt, sir?

SIR WIL. My aunt, sir, yes, my aunt, sir, and your lady, sir; your lady is my aunt, sir.—Why, what, dost thou not know me, friend? Why, then send somebody hither that does. How long hast thou lived with thy lady, fellow, ha?   378

SERV. A week, sir; longer than anybody in the house, except my lady's woman.

SIR WIL. Why, then belike thou dost not know thy lady, if thou see'st her, ha, friend?

SERV. Why truly, sir, I cannot safely swear to her face in a morning, before she is dressed. 'Tis like I may give a shrewd guess at her by this time.

SIR WIL. Well, prithee try what thou canst do; if thou canst not guess, enquire her out, dost hear, fellow? And tell her, her nephew, Sir Wilfull Witwoud, is in the house.   388

359-60. ordinary's . . . psalm: before a hanging, the ordinary or chaplain read a psalm.

serv. I shall, sir.

sir wil. Hold ye, hear me, friend; a word with you in your ear, prithee who are these gallants?

serv. Really, sir, I can't tell; here come so many here, 'tis hard to know 'em all.   [*Exit* servant.]

sir wil. Oons, this fellow knows less than a starling; I don't think a' knows his own name.

mrs. mar. Mr. Witwoud, your brother is not behindhand in for- getfulness—I fancy he has forgot you too.   397

wit. I hope so—the devil take him that remembers first, I say.

sir wil. Save you, gentlemen and lady.

mrs. mar. For shame, Mr. Witwoud; why won't you speak to him?—And you, sir.

wit. Petulant, speak.

pet. And you, sir.

sir wil. No offence, I hope. [*Salutes* marwood.]

mrs. mar. No, sure, sir.

wit. This is a vile dog, I see that already. No offence! Ha, ha, ha! To him; to him, Petulant, smoke him.   407

pet. It seems as if you had come a journey, sir; hem, hem. [*Sur- veying him round.*]

sir wil. Very likely, sir, that it may seem so.

pet. No offence, I hope, sir.

wit. Smoke the boots, the boots; Petulant, the boots; ha, ha, ha!

sir wil. Maybe not, sir; thereafter as 'tis meant, sir.

pet. Sir, I presume upon the information of your boots.

sir wil. Why, 'tis like you may, sir. If you are not satisfied with the information of my boots, sir, if you will step to the stable, you may enquire further of my horse, sir.

pet. Your horse, sir! Your horse is an ass, sir!   418

sir wil. Do you speak by way of offence, sir?

mrs. mar. The gentleman's merry, that's all, sir. [*Aside*]—S'life, we shall have a quarrel betwixt an horse and an ass, before they find one another out. [*Aloud*] You must not take anything amiss from your friends, sir. You are among your friends here, though it

may be you don't know it.—If I am not mistaken, you are Sir Wilfull Witwoud.

SIR WIL. Right, lady; I am Sir Wilfull Witwoud, so I write myself; no offence to anybody, I hope; and nephew to the Lady Wishfort of this mansion.   428

MRS. MAR. Don't you know this gentleman, sir?

SIR WIL. Hum! What, sure 'tis not—Yea, by'r Lady, but 'tis— 'Sheart, I know not whether 'tis or no.—Yea, but 'tis, by the Wrekin. Brother Antony! What, Tony, i' faith! What, dost thou not know me? By'r Lady, nor I thee, thou art so becravated, and so beperriwigged—'Sheart, why dost not speak? Art thou o'erjoyed?

WIT. Odso, brother, is it you? Your servant, brother.

SIR WIL. Your servant! Why, yours, sir. Your servant again.— 'Sheart, and your friend and servant to that—and a—[Puff] and a flap-dragon for your service, sir: and a hare's foot, and a hare's scut for your service, sir; an you be so cold and so courtly!   439

WIT. No offence, I hope, brother.

SIR WIL. 'Sheart, sir, but there is, and much offence.—A pox, is this your Inns o' Court breeding, not to know your friends and your relations, your elders, and your betters?

WIT. Why, brother Wilfull of Salop, you may be as short as a Shrewsbury cake, if you please. But I tell you 'tis not modish to know relations in town. You think you're in the country, where great lubberly brothers slabber and kiss one another when they meet, like a call of serjeants.—'Tis not the fashion here; 'tis not indeed, dear brother.   449

SIR WIL. The fashion's a fool; and you're a fop, dear brother. 'Sheart, I've suspected this.—By'r Lady, I conjectured you were a fop, since you began to change the style of your letters, and write in a scrap of paper gilt round the edges, no bigger than a subpoena. I might expect this when you left off, "Honoured Brother," and "hoping you are in good health," and so forth—to begin with a "Rat me, knight, I'm so sick of a last night's debauch."—'Odsheart, and then tell a familiar tale of a cock and a bull, and a whore and

442. **Inns o' Court:** law school.

a bottle, and so conclude.—You could write news before you were out of your time, when you lived with honest Pumple-Nose, the attorney of Furnival's Inn.—You could intreat to be remembered then to your friends round the Wrekin. We could have gazettes then, and Dawks's Letter, and the weekly bill, 'til of late days.

PET. 'Slife, Witwoud, were you ever an attorney's clerk? of the family of the Furnivals? Ha, ha, ha!   464

WIT. Ay, ay, but that was for a while. Not long, not long. Pshaw! I was not in my own power then. An orphan, and this fellow was my guardian; ay, ay, I was glad to consent to that man to come to London. He had the disposal of me then. If I had not agreed to that, I might have been bound prentice to a felt maker in Shrewsbury; this fellow would have bound me to a maker of felts.

SIR WIL. 'Sheart, and better than to be bound to a maker of fops; where, I suppose, you have served your time, and now you may set up for yourself.   473

MRS. MAR. You intend to travel, sir, as I'm informed.

SIR WIL. Belike I may, madam. I may chance to sail upon the salt seas, if my mind hold.

PET. And the wind serve.

SIR WIL. Serve or not serve, I shan't ask licence of you, sir, nor the weather-cock your companion. I direct my discourse to the lady, sir. 'Tis like my aunt may have told you, madam—yes, I have settled my concerns, I may say now, and am minded to see foreign parts. If an' how that the peace holds, whereby, that is, taxes abate.

MRS. MAR. I thought you had designed for France at all adventures.   484

SIR WIL. I can't tell that; 'tis like I may, and 'tis like I may not. I am somewhat dainty in making a resolution,—because when I make it I keep it. I don't stand shill I, shall I, then; if I say't, I'll do't: but I have thoughts to tarry a small matter in town, to learn somewhat of your lingo first, before I cross the seas. I'd gladly have a spice of your French, as they say, whereby to hold discourse in foreign countries.

462. **Dawks's Letter:** weekly digest of news. **bill:** obituaries.

MRS. MAR. Here is an academy in town for that use.

SIR WIL. There is? 'Tis like there may.

MRS. MAR. No doubt you will return very much improved.

WIT. Yes, refined, like a Dutch skipper from a whale-fishing.

[*Enter* LADY WISHFORT *and* FAINALL.]

LADY W. Nephew, you are welcome.

SIR WIL. Aunt, your servant.

FAIN. Sir Wilfull, your most faithful servant.

SIR WIL. Cousin Fainall, give me your hand.

LADY W. Cousin Witwoud, your servant; Mr. Petulant, your servant—nephew, you are welcome again. Will you drink anything
after your journey, nephew, before you eat? Dinner's almost ready.

SIR WIL. I'm very well, I thank you, aunt—however, I thank you
for your courteous offer. 'Sheart, I was afraid you would have been
in the fashion too, and have remembered to have forgot your relations. Here's your Cousin Tony, belike, I mayn't call him brother
for fear of offence.

LADY W. Oh, he's a rallier, nephew—my cousin's a wit; and your
great wits always rally their best friends to choose. When you have
been abroad, nephew, you'll understand raillery better.

[FAINALL *and* MRS. MARWOOD *talk apart.*]

SIR WIL. Why then, let him hold his tongue in the meantime,
and rail when that day comes.

[*Enter* MINCING.]

MINC. Mem, I come to acquaint your la'ship that dinner is impatient.

SIR WIL. Impatient? Why then belike it won't stay till I pull off
my boots. Sweetheart, can you help me to a pair of slippers? My
man's with his horses, I warrant.

LADY W. Fie, fie, nephew, you would not pull off your boots here.
Go down into the hall—dinner shall stay for you.—My nephew's
a little unbred, you'll pardon him, madam. Gentlemen, will you
walk? Marwood—

MRS. MAR. I'll follow you, madam, before Sir Wilfull is ready.

[*Exeunt.*]

[MRS. MARWOOD *and* FAINALL *remain.*]

FAIN. Why then Foible's a bawd, an arrant, rank, match-making bawd. And I, it seems, am a husband, a rank husband; and my wife a very arrant, rank wife—all in the way of the world. 'Sdeath, to be a cuckold by anticipation, a cuckold in embryo? Sure I was born with budding antlers like a young satyr, or a citizen's child. 'Sdeath, to be outwitted, to be out-jilted—out-matrimonied!—If I had kept my speed like a stag, 'twere somewhat—but to crawl after, with my horns like a snail, and be outstripped by my wife—'tis scurvy wedlock.   531

MRS. MAR. Then shake it off, you have often wished for an opportunity to part—and now you have it. But first prevent their plot—the half of Millamant's fortune is too considerable to be parted with, to a foe, to Mirabell.

FAIN. Damn him, that had been mine, had you not made that fond discovery—that had been forfeited, had they been married. My wife had added lustre to my horns, by that increase of fortune. I could have worn 'em tipt with gold, though my forehead had been furnished like a deputy-lieutenant's hall.   540

MRS. MAR. They may prove a cap of maintenance to you still, if you can away with your wife. And she's no worse than when you had her—I dare swear she had given up her game, before she was married.

FAIN. Hum! That may be—

MRS. MAR. You married her to keep you; and if you can contrive to have her keep you better than you expected, why should you not keep her longer than you intended?   548

FAIN. The means, the means!

MRS. MAR. Discover to my lady your wife's conduct; threaten to part with her—my lady loves her, and will come to any composition to save her reputation. Take the opportunity of breaking it, just upon the discovery of this imposture. My lady will be enraged beyond bounds, and sacrifice niece, and fortune, and all at that conjuncture. And let me alone to keep her warm; if she should flag in her part, I will not fail to prompt her.

FAIN. Faith, this has an appearance.

MRS. MAR. I'm sorry I hinted to my lady to endeavour a match between Millamant and Sir Wilfull; that may be an obstacle.

FAIN. Oh, for that matter leave me to manage him; I'll disable him for that, he will drink like a Dane—after dinner, I'll set his hand in.

562

MRS. MAR. Well, how do you stand affected towards your lady?

FAIN. Why, faith I'm thinking of it.—Let me see—I am married already; so that's over.—My wife has played the jade with me—well, that's over too—I never loved her, or if I had, why that would have been over too by this time.—Jealous of her I cannot be, for I am certain; so there's an end of jealousy. Weary of her, I am and shall be.—No, there's no end of that; no, no, that were too much to hope. Thus far concerning my repose. Now for my reputation.—As to my own, I married not for it; so that's out of the question.—And as to my part in my wife's—why, she had parted with hers before; so bringing none to me, she can take none from me; 'tis against all rule of play that I should lose to one who has not wherewithal to stake.

575

MRS. MAR. Besides, you forget, marriage is honourable.

FAIN. Hum! Faith, and that's well thought on; marriage is honourable, as you say; and if so, wherefore should cuckoldom be a discredit, being derived from so honourable a root?

MRS. MAR. Nay, I know not; if the root be honourable, why not the branches?

FAIN. So, so, why this point's clear.—Well, how do we proceed?

MRS. MAR. I will contrive a letter which shall be delivered to my lady at the time when that rascal who is to act Sir Rowland is with her. It shall come as from an unknown hand—for the less I appear to know of the truth, the better I can play the incendiary. Besides, I would not have Foible provoked if I could help it—because you know she knows some passages—nay, I expect all will come out—but let the mine be sprung first, and then I care not if I am discovered.

590

FAIN. If the worst come to the worst, I'll turn my wife out to grass—I have already a deed of settlement of the best part of her

estate, which I wheedled out of her; and that you shall partake at least.

MRS. MAR. I hope you are convinced that I hate Mirabell now: you'll be no more jealous?

FAIN. Jealous, no,—by this kiss—let husbands be jealous; but let the lover still believe; or if he doubt, let it be only to endear his pleasure, and prepare the joy that follows, when he proves his mistress true. But let husbands' doubts convert to endless jealousy; or if they have belief, let it corrupt to superstition, and blind credulity. I am single, and will herd no more with 'em. True, I wear the badge, but I'll disown the order. And since I take my leave of 'em, I care not if I leave 'em a common motto to their common crest.

> All husbands must, or pain, or shame, endure;
> The wise too jealous are, fools too secure.   [*Exeunt.*]

ACT FOUR

SCENE. *Scene continues.*

[LADY WISHFORT *and* FOIBLE.]

LADY W. Is Sir Rowland coming, say'st thou, Foible? and are things in order?

FOIB. Yes, madam. I have put wax-lights in the sconces; and placed the footmen in a row in the hall, in their best liveries, with the coachman and postilion to fill up the equipage.

LADY W. Have you pulvilled the coachman and postilion, that they may not stink of the stable when Sir Rowland comes by?

FOIB. Yes, madam.   8

LADY W. And are the dancers and the music ready, that he may be entertained in all points with correspondence to his passion?

FOIB. All is ready, madam.

LADY W. And—well—and how do I look, Foible?

FOIB. Most killing well, madam.   13

Act IV. 6. pulvilled: powdered.

LADY W. Well, and how shall I receive him? In what figure shall I give his heart the first impression? There is a great deal in the first impression. Shall I sit?—No, I won't sit—I'll walk—ay, I'll walk from the door upon his entrance; and then turn full upon him.—No, that will be too sudden. I'll lie—ay, I'll lie down—I'll receive him in my little dressing-room, there's a couch—yes, yes, I'll give the first impression on a couch—I won't lie neither, but loll and lean upon one elbow, with one foot a little dangling off, jogging in a thoughtful way—yes—and then as soon as he appears, start, ay, start and be surprised, and rise to meet him in a pretty disorder—yes—oh, nothing is more alluring than a levee from a couch in some confusion—it shows the foot to advantage, and furnishes with blushes, and re-composing airs beyond comparison. Hark! There's a coach.

27

FOIB. 'Tis he, madam.

LADY W. Oh, dear, has my nephew made his addresses to Millamant? I ordered him.

FOIB. Sir Wilfull is set in to drinking, madam, in the parlour.

LADY W. Ods my life, I'll send him to her. Call her down, Foible; bring her hither. I'll send him as I go.—When they are together, then come to me, Foible, that I may not be too long alone with Sir Rowland. [Exit.]

35

[Enter MRS. MILLAMANT and MRS. FAINALL.]

FOIB. Madam, I stayed here, to tell your ladyship that Mr. Mirabell has waited this half-hour for an opportunity to talk with you. Though my lady's orders were to leave you and Sir Wilfull together. Shall I tell Mr. Mirabell that you are at leisure?

MILLA. No—what would the dear man have? I am thoughtful, and would amuse myself—bid him come another time.

> There never yet was woman made,
> Nor shall, but to be cursed.

[Repeating and walking about] That's hard!

MRS. FAIN. You are very fond of Sir John Suckling today, Millamant, and the poets.

46

MILLA. Heh? Ay, and filthy verses—so I am.

FOIB. Sir Wilfull is coming, madam. Shall I send Mr. Mirabell away?

MILLA. Ay, if you please, Foible, send him away—or send him hither—just as you will, dear Foible.—I think I'll see him.—Shall I? Ay, let the wretch come. [*Repeating*]

Thyrsis, a youth of the inspirèd train.

Dear Fainall, entertain Sir Wilfull—thou hast philosophy to undergo a fool, thou art married and hast patience—I would confer with my own thoughts.   56

MRS. FAIN. I am obliged to you, that you would make me your proxy in this affair; but I have business of my own.

[*Enter* SIR WILFULL.]

MRS. FAIN. Oh, Sir Wilfull; you are come at the critical instant. There's your mistress up to the ears in love and contemplation; pursue your point, now or never.

SIR WIL. Yes, my aunt will have it so—I would gladly have been encouraged with a bottle or two, because I'm somewhat wary at first, before I am acquainted—[*This while* MILLAMANT *walks about repeating to herself.*] But I hope, after a time, I shall break my mind—that is upon further acquaintance.—So for the present, cousin, I'll take my leave—if so be you'll be so kind to make my excuse. I'll return to my company—   68

MRS. FAIN. Oh, fie, Sir Wilfull! What, you must not be daunted.

SIR WIL. Daunted! no, that's not it, it is not so much for that—for if so be that I set on't, I'll do't. But only for the present, 'tis sufficient 'til further acquaintance, that's all—your servant.

MRS. FAIN. Nay, I'll swear you shall never lose so favourable an opportunity, if I can help it. I'll leave you together, and lock the door.   [*Exit.*]

SIR WIL. Nay, nay, cousin,—I have forgot my gloves.—What d'ee do? 'Sheart, a' has locked the door indeed, I think.—Nay, Cousin Fainall, open the door.—Pshaw, what a vixen trick is this?—Nay, now a' has seen me too—cousin, I made bold to pass through as it were—I think this door's enchanted—   80

MILLA. [*Repeating*]

> I prithee spare me, gentle boy,
> Press me no more for that slight toy—

SIR WIL. Anan? Cousin, your servant.

MILLA.

> That foolish trifle of a heart—

Sir Wilfull!

SIR WIL. Yes—your servant. No offence, I hope, cousin.

MILLA. [*Repeating*]

> I swear it will not do its part,   89
> Though thou dost thine, employ'st thy power and art.

Natural, easy Suckling!

SIR WIL. Anan? Suckling? No such suckling neither, cousin, nor stripling. I thank Heaven, I'm no minor.

MILLA. Ah, rustic, ruder than Gothic.

SIR WIL. Well, well, I shall understand your lingo one of these days, cousin; in the meanwhile I must answer in plain English.

MILLA. Have you any business with me, Sir Wilfull?

SIR WIL. Not at present, cousin.—Yes, I made bold to see, to come and know if that how you were disposed to fetch a walk this evening; if so be that I might not be troublesome, I would have sought a walk with you.   101

MILLA. A walk? What then?

SIR WIL. Nay, nothing—only for the walk's sake, that's all—

MILLA. I nauseate walking; 'tis a country diversion, I loathe the country and everything that relates to it.

SIR WIL. Indeed! Hah! Look ye, look ye, you do? Nay, 'tis like you may.—Here are choice of pastimes here in town, as plays and the like, that must be confessed indeed—

MILLA. *Ah, l'étourdie!* I hate the town too.   109

SIR WIL. Dear heart, that's much—Hah! that you should hate 'em both! Hah! 'tis like you may; there are some can't relish the town,

109. l'étourdie: the whirl.

and others can't away with the country—'tis like you may be one of those, cousin.

MILLA. Ha, ha, ha! Yes, 'tis like I may.—You have nothing further to say to me?

SIR WIL. Not at present, cousin.—'Tis like when I have an opportunity to be more private, I may break my mind in some measure—I conjecture you partly guess.—However, that's as time shall try—but spare to speak and spare to speed, as they say.   119

MILLA. If it is of no great importance, Sir Wilfull, you will oblige me to leave me. I have just now a little business—

SIR WIL. Enough, enough, cousin; yes, yes, all a case—when you're disposed, when you're disposed. Now's as well as another time; and another time as well as now. All's one for that.—Yes, yes, if your concerns call you, there's no haste; it will keep cold, as they say.—Cousin, your servant.—I think this door's locked.

MILLA. You may go this way, sir.

SIR WIL. Your servant! then with your leave I'll return to my company.   129

MILLA. Ay, ay; ha, ha, ha!

Like Phoebus sung the no less amorous boy.

[*Enter* MIRABELL.]

MIRA.   Like Daphne she, as lovely and as coy.

Do you lock yourself up from me, to make my search more curious? Or is this pretty artifice contrived to signify that here the chase must end, and my pursuit be crowned, for you can fly no further?

MILLA. Vanity! No—I'll fly and be followed to the last moment; though I am upon the very verge of matrimony. I expect you should solicit me as much as if I were wavering at the grate of a monastery, with one foot over the threshold. I'll be solicited to the very last, nay, and afterwards.   140

MIRA. What, after the last?

MILLA. Oh, I should think I was poor and had nothing to bestow, if I were reduced to an inglorious ease, and freed from the agreeable fatigues of solicitation.

MIRA. But do not you know, that when favours are conferred upon instant and tedious solicitation, that they diminish in their value, and that both the giver loses the grace, and the receiver lessens his pleasure? 148

MILLA. It may be in things of common application, but never sure in love. Oh, I hate a lover that can dare to think he draws a moment's air, independent on the bounty of his mistress. There is not so impudent a thing in nature as the saucy look of an assured man, confident of success. The pedantic arrogance of a very husband has not so pragmatical an air. Ah! I'll never marry, unless I am first made sure of my will and pleasure.

MIRA. Would you have 'em both before marriage? Or will you be contented with the first now, and stay for the other till after grace? 158

MILLA. Ah, don't be impertinent.—My dear liberty, shall I leave thee? My faithful solitude, my darling contemplation, must I bid you then adieu? Ay-h, adieu—my morning thoughts, agreeable wakings, indolent slumbers, all ye *douceurs,* ye *sommeils du matin,* adieu—I can't do't, 'tis more than impossible.—Positively, Mirabell, I'll lie abed in a morning as long as I please.

MIRA. Then I'll get up in a morning as early as I please.

MILLA. Ah! Idle creature, get up when you will.—And d'ee hear, I won't be called names after I'm married; positively I won't be called names. 168

MIRA. Names!

MILLA. Ay, as wife, spouse, my dear, joy, jewel, love, sweetheart, and the rest of that nauseous cant, in which men and their wives are so fulsomely familiar—I shall never bear that.—Good Mirabell, don't let us be familiar or fond, nor kiss before folks, like my Lady Fadler and Sir Francis; nor go to Hyde Park together the first Sunday in a new chariot, to provoke eyes and whispers; and then never be seen there together again, as if we were proud of one another the first week, and ashamed of one another ever after. Let us never visit together, nor go to a play together, but let us be very strange and well bred: let us be as strange as if we had been mar-

179. strange: indifferent.

ried a great while, and as well bred as if we were not married
at all.   181

MIRA. Have you any more conditions to offer? Hitherto your demands are pretty reasonable.

MILLA. Trifles—as liberty to pay and receive visits to and from
whom I please; to write and receive letters, without interrogatories
or wry faces on your part; to wear what I please; and choose conversation with regard only to my own taste; to have no obligation
upon me to converse with wits that I don't like, because they are
your acquaintance; or to be intimate with fools because they may
be your relations. Come to dinner when I please, dine in my dressing-room when I'm out of humour, without giving a reason. To
have my closet inviolate; to be sole empress of my tea-table, which
you must never presume to approach without first asking leave. [193
And lastly, wherever I am, you shall always knock at the door before you come in. These articles subscribed, if I continue to endure
you a little longer, I may by degrees dwindle into a wife.

MIRA. Your bill of fare is something advanced in this latter account. Well, have I liberty to offer conditions—that when you are
dwindled into a wife, I may not be beyond measure enlarged into a
husband?

MILLA. You have free leave, propose your utmost, speak and
spare not.   202

MIRA. I thank you. *Imprimis* then, I covenant that your acquaintance be general; that you admit no sworn confident, or intimate of your own sex; no she-friend to screen her affairs under
your countenance, and tempt you to make trial of a mutual secrecy.
No decoy-duck to wheedle you a fop-scrambling to the play in a
mask—then bring you home in a pretended fright, when you think
you shall be found out—and rail at me for missing the play, and disappointing the frolic which you had, to pick me up and prove my
constancy.

MILLA. Detestable *imprimis!* I go to the play in a mask!   212

MIRA. *Item,* I article, that you continue to like your own face as
long as I shall: and while it passes current with me, that you endeavour not to new-coin it. To which end, together with all vizards

for the day, I prohibit all masks for the night, made of oiled-skins and I know not what—hog's bones, hare's gall, pig-water, and the marrow of a roasted cat. In short, I forbid all commerce with the gentlewoman in what-d'ee-call-it Court. *Item,* I shut my doors against all bawds with baskets, and pennyworths of muslin, china, fans, atlases, etc.—*Item,* when you shall be breeding—

MILLA. Ah! name it not. 222

MIRA. Which may be presumed, with a blessing on our endeavours—

MILA. Odious endeavours!

MIRA. I denounce against all strait lacing, squeezing for a shape, till you mould my boy's head like a sugar-loaf; and instead of a man-child, make me father to a crooked billet. Lastly, to the dominion of the tea-table I submit.—But with proviso, that you exceed not in your province, but restrain yourself to native and simple tea-table drinks, as tea, chocolate, and coffee. As likewise to genuine and authorised tea-table talk—such as mending of fashions, spoiling reputations, railing at absent friends, and so forth—but that on no account you encroach upon the men's prerogative, and presume to drink healths, or toast fellows; for prevention of which, I banish all foreign forces, all auxiliaries to the tea-table, as orange-brandy, all aniseed, cinnamon, citron and Barbadoes waters, together with [237 ratafia and the most noble spirit of clary. But for cowslip-wine, poppy-water, and all dormitives, those I allow.—These provisos admitted, in other things I may prove a tractable and complying husband.

MILLA. O horrid provisos! filthy strong waters! I toast fellows, odious men! I hate your odious provisos.

MIRA. Then we're agreed. Shall I kiss your hand upon the contract? and here comes one to be a witness to the scaling of the deed.

[*Enter* MRS. FAINALL.]

MILLA. Fainall, what shall I do? Shall I have him? I think I must have him. 248

221. atlases: silks. 239. dormitives: sedatives.

MRS. FAIN. Ay, ay, take him, take him, what should you do?

MILLA. Well then—I'll take my death I'm in a horrid fright.—Fainall, I shall never say it—well—I think—I'll endure you.

MRS. FAIN. Fie, fie! have him, have him, and tell him so in plain terms; for I am sure you have a mind to him.

MILLA. Are you? I think I have—and the horrid man looks as if he thought so too.—Well, you ridiculous thing you, I'll have you—I won't be kissed, nor I won't be thanked.—Here, kiss my hand though—so, hold your tongue now, don't say a word.   257

MRS. FAIN. Mirabell, there's a necessity for your obedience;—you have neither time to talk nor stay. My mother is coming; and in my conscience, if she should see you, would fall into fits, and maybe not recover time enough to return to Sir Rowland, who, as Foible tells me, is in a fair way to succeed. Therefore spare your ecstasies for another occasion, and slip down the back stairs, where Foible waits to consult you.

MILLA. Ay, go, go! In the meantime I suppose you have said something to please me.

MIRA. I am all obedience.   [*Exit* MIRABELL.]   267

MRS. FAIN. Yonder Sir Wilfull's drunk; and so noisy that my mother has been forced to leave Sir Rowland to appease him; but he answers her only with singing and drinking.—What they may have done by this time I know not, but Petulant and he were upon quarrelling as I came by.

MILLA. Well, if Mirabell should not make a good husband, I am a lost thing; for I find I love him violently.

MRS. FAIN. So it seems; for you mind not what's said to you.—If you doubt him, you had best take up with Sir Wilfull.   276

MILLA. How can you name that superannuated lubber? foh!

      [*Enter* WITWOUD *from drinking.*]

MRS. FAIN. So, is the fray made up, that you have left 'em?

WIT. Left 'em? I could stay no longer—I have laughed like ten christ'nings—I am tipsy with laughing—if I had stayed any longer I should have burst—I must have been let out and pieced in the sides like an unsized camlet.—Yes, yes, the fray is composed; my lady came in like a *nolle prosequi,* and stopped the proceedings.

MILLA. What was the dispute?

WIT. That's the jest; there was no dispute. They could neither of
'em speak for rage, and so fell a sputtering at one another like two
roasting apples. . . .   287

[*Enter* LADY WISHFORT, *and* SIR WILFULL, *drunk.*]

LADY W. Out upon't, out upon't, at years of discretion, and com-
port yourself at this rantipole rate.

SIR WIL. No offence, aunt.

LADY W. Offence? As I'm a person, I'm ashamed of you.—Fogh!
how you stink of wine! D'ye think my niece will ever endure such
a *borachio!* you're an absolute *borachio.*

SIR WIL. *Borachio!*   294

LADY W. At a time when you should commence an amour, and
put your best foot foremost—

SIR WIL. 'Sheart, an you grutch me your liquor, make a bill—
give me more drink, and take my purse. [*Sings.*]

> Prithee fill me the glass
> 'Til it laugh in my face.
> With ale that is potent and mellow;
> He that whines for a lass
> Is an ignorant ass,
> For a bumper has not its fellow.   304

But if you would have me marry my cousin, say the word, and I'll
do't—Wilfull will do't, that's the word—Wilfull will do't, that's
my crest—my motto I have forgot.

LADY W. My nephew's a little overtaken, cousin—but 'tis with
drinking your health.—O' my word you are obliged to him—

SIR WIL. *In vino veritas,* aunt:—If I drunk your health today,
cousin, I am a *borachio.* But if you have a mind to be married
say the word, and send for the piper—Wilfull will do't. If not,
dust it away, and let's have t'other round—Tony, 'odsheart, where's
Tony?—Tony's an honest fellow, but he spits after a bumper, and
that's a fault. [*Sings.*]   315

293. borachio: wine skin.

> We'll drink and we'll never ha' done, boys,
>> Put the glass then around with the sun, boys,
> Let Apollo's example invite us;
>> For he's drunk every night,
>> And that makes him so bright,
> That he's able next morning to light us.

The sun's a good pimple, an honest soaker, he has a cellar at your Antipodes. If I travel, aunt, I touch at your Antipodes—your Antipodes are a good rascally sort of topsy-turvy fellows—if I had a bumper I'd stand upon my head and drink a health to 'em.—A match or no match, cousin, with the hard name—aunt, Wilfull will do't. . . . 327

MILLA. Your pardon, madam, I can stay no longer—Sir Wilfull grows very powerful. Egh! how he smells! I shall be overcome if I stay. Come, cousin. [*Exeunt* MILLAMANT *and* MRS. FAINALL.]

LADY W. Smells! he would poison a tallow-chandler and his family. Beastly creature, I know not what to do with him.—Travel, quoth a; ay, travel, travel, get thee gone, get thee but far enough, to the Saracens, or the Tartars, or the Turks—for thou art not fit to live in a Christian commonwealth, thou beastly pagan. 335

SIR WIL. Turks, no; no Turks, aunt: your Turks are infidels, and believe not in the grape. Your Mahometan, your Mussulman, is a dry stinkard—no offence, aunt. My map says that your Turk is not so honest a man as your Christian—I cannot find by the map that your Mufti is orthodox—whereby it is a plain case, that orthodox is a hard word, aunt, and [*Hiccup*] Greek for claret. [*Sings.*]

> To drink is a Christian diversion,
> Unknown to the Turk and the Persian:
>> Let Mahometan fools
>> Live by heathenish rules, 345
> And be damned over tea-cups and coffee.
>> But let British lads sing,
>> Crown a health to the king,
> And a fig for your sultan and sophy.

Ah, Tony!

[*Enter* FOIBLE *and whispers* LADY WISHFORT.]

LADY W. Sir Rowland impatient? Good lack! what shall I do with this beastly tumbril?—Go lie down and sleep, you sot—or as I'm a person, I'll have you bastinadoed with broomsticks. Call up the wenches.   [*Exit* FOIBLE.]   354

SIR WIL. Ahey! Wenches, where are the wenches?

LADY W. Dear Cousin Witwoud, get him away, and you will bind me to you inviolably. I have an affair of moment that invades me with some precipitation.—You will oblige me to all futurity.

WIT. Come, knight.—Pox on him, I don't know what to say to him.—Will you go to a cock-match?

SIR WIL. With a wench, Tony? Is she a shake-bag, sirrah? Let me bite your cheek for that.

WIT. Horrible! He has a breath like a bagpipe.—Ay, ay; come, will you march, my Salopian?   364

SIR WIL. Lead on, little Tony—I'll follow thee, my Antony, my Tantony. Sirrah, thou sha't be my Tantony; and I'll be thy pig.

—And a fig for your sultan and sophy.

[*Exit singing with* WITWOUD.]

LADY W. This will never do. It will never make a match.—At least before he has been abroad. [*Enter* WAITWELL, *disguised as for Sir Rowland.*] Dear Sir Rowland, I am confounded with confusion at the retrospection of my own rudeness—I have more pardons to ask than the pope distributes in the year of jubilee. But I hope where there is likely to be so near an alliance, we may unbend the severity of decorum, and dispense with a little ceremony.

WAIT. My impatience, madam, is the effect of my transport;—and till I have the possession of your adorable person, I am tantalised on the rack; and do but hang, madam, on the tenter of expectation.   378

LADY W. You have excess of gallantry, Sir Rowland, and press things to a conclusion, with a most prevailing vehemence.—But a day or two for decency of marriage—

WAIT. For decency of funeral, madam. The delay will break my

366. Tantony: St. Antony, patron of swineherds.

heart—or if that should fail, I shall be poisoned. My nephew will get an inkling of my designs, and poison me—and I would willingly starve him before I die—I would gladly go out of the world with that satisfaction.—That would be some comfort to me, if I could but live so long as to be revenged on that unnatural viper. [387

LADY W. Is he so unnatural, say you? Truly I would contribute much both to the saving of your life, and the accomplishment of your revenge—not that I respect myself, though he has been a perfidious wretch to me.

WAIT. Perfidious to you!

LADY W. O Sir Rowland, the hours that he has died away at my feet, the tears that he has shed, the oaths that he has sworn, the palpitations that he has felt, the trances and the tremblings, the ardours and the ecstasies, the kneelings and the risings, the heart-heavings and the hand-grippings, the pangs and the pathetic regards of his protesting eyes! Oh, no memory can register.   398

WAIT. What, my rival! Is the rebel my rival? a' dies.

LADY W. No, don't kill him at once, Sir Rowland, starve him gradually inch by inch.

WAIT. I'll do't. In three weeks he shall be barefoot; in a month out at knees with begging an alms—he shall starve upward and upward, till he has nothing living but his head, and then go out in a stink like a candle's end upon a save-all.

LADY W. Well, Sir Rowland, you have the way—you are no novice in the labyrinth of love—you have the clue.—But as I am a person, Sir Rowland, you must not attribute my yielding to any sinister appetite, or indigestion of widowhood; nor impute my complacency to any lethargy of continence.—I hope you do not think me prone to any iteration of nuptials—   411

WAIT. Far be it from me—

LADY W. If you do, I protest I must recede—or think that I have made a prostitution of decorums, but in the vehemence of compassion, and to save the life of a person of so much importance—

WAIT. I esteem it so—

LADY W. Or else you wrong my condescension—

WAIT. I do not, I do not—

LADY W. Indeed you do.

WAIT. I do not, fair shrine of virtue.

LADY W. If you think the least scruple of carnality was an ingredient—

WAIT. Dear madam, no. You are all camphire and frankincense, all chastity and odour. 424

LADY W. Or that—

[*Enter* FOIBLE.]

FOIB. Madam, the dancers are ready, and there's one with a letter, who must deliver it into your own hands.

LADY W. Sir Rowland, will you give me leave? Think favourably, judge candidly, and conclude you have found a person who would suffer racks in honour's cause, dear Sir Rowland, and will wait on you incessantly. [*Exit.*]

WAIT. Fie, fie!—What a slavery have I undergone; spouse, hast thou any cordial?—I want spirits. 433

FOIB. What a washy rogue art thou, to pant thus for a quarter of an hour's lying and swearing to a fine lady?

WAIT. Oh, she is the antidote to desire. Spouse, thou wilt fare the worse for't—I shall have no appetite to iteration of nuptials this eight and forty hours.—By this hand, I'd rather be a chairman in the dog-days, than act Sir Rowland 'til this time tomorrow.

[*Enter* LADY WISHFORT *with a letter.*]

LADY W. Call in the dancers;—Sir Rowland, we'll sit, if you please, and see the entertainment. 441

[*Dance.*]

Now with your permission, Sir Rowland, I will peruse my letter— I would open it in your presence, because I would not make you uneasy. If it should make you uneasy I would burn it—speak if it does—but you may see, the superscription is like a woman's hand.

FOIB. [*To him*] By heaven! Mrs. Marwood's, I know it—my heart aches—get it from her—

WAIT. A woman's hand? No, madam, that's no woman's hand, I see that already. That's somebody whose throat must be cut.

LADY W. Nay, Sir Rowland, since you give me a proof of your passion by your jealousy, I promise you I'll make a return, by a

frank communication.—You shall see it—we'll open it together—
look you here. [*Reads.*]   453

"Madam, though unknown to you,"—Look you there, 'tis from
nobody that I know—"I have that honour for your character, that
I think myself obliged to let you know you are abused. He who
pretends to be Sir Rowland is a cheat and a rascal—" Oh heavens!
what's this?

FOIB. [*Aside*] Unfortunate, all's ruined.

WAIT. How, how, let me see, let me see! [*Reading*] "A rascal
and disguised, and suborned for that imposture."—Oh, villainy!
Oh, villainy!—"by the contrivance of—"

LADY W. I shall faint, I shall die, oh!

FOIB. [*To him*] Say 'tis your nephew's hand.—Quickly, his plot,
swear, swear it.   465

WAIT. Here's a villain! Madam, don't you perceive it, don't you
see it?

LADY W. Too well, too well. I have seen too much.

WAIT. I told you at first I knew the hand.—A woman's hand?
The rascal writes a sort of a large hand; your Roman hand—I saw
there was a throat to be cut presently. If he were my son, as he is
my nephew, I'd pistol him—

FOIB. Oh, treachery! But are you sure, Sir Rowland, it is his
writing?   474

WAIT. Sure? Am I here? do I live? do I love this pearl of India?
I have twenty letters in my pocket from him, in the same character.

LADY W. How!

FOIB. Oh, what luck it is, Sir Rowland, that you were present
at this juncture! This was the business that brought Mr. Mirabell
disguised to Madam Millamant this afternoon. I thought something
was contriving, when he stole by me and would have hid his face.

LADY W. How, how!—I heard the villain was in the house indeed; and now I remember, my niece went away abruptly, when
Sir Wilfull was to have made his addresses.   484

FOIB. Then, then, madam, Mr. Mirabell waited for her in her
chamber: but I would not tell your ladyship to discompose you
when you were to receive Sir Rowland.

WAIT. Enough, his date is short.

FOIB. No, good Sir Rowland, don't incur the law.

WAIT. Law! I care not for law. I can but die, and 'tis in a good cause—my lady shall be satisfied of my truth and innocence, though it cost me my life.

LADY W. No, dear Sir Rowland, don't fight; if you should be killed I must never show my face; or hanged—oh, consider my reputation, Sir Rowland.—No, you shan't fight.—I'll go in and examine my niece; I'll make her confess. I conjure you, Sir Rowland, by all your love, not to fight. 497

WAIT. I am charmed, madam, I obey. But some proof you must let me give you.—I'll go for a black box, which contains the writings of my whole estate, and deliver that into your hands.

LADY W. Ay, dear Sir Rowland, that will be some comfort, bring the black box.

WAIT. And may I presume to bring a contract to be signed this night? May I hope so far?

LADY W. Bring what you will; but come alive, pray come alive. Oh, this is a happy discovery.

WAIT. Dead or alive I'll come—and married we will be in spite of treachery; ay, and get an heir that shall defeat the last remaining glimpse of hope in my abandoned nephew. Come, my buxom widow: 510

E'er long you shall substantial proof receive
That I'm an arrant knight—

FOIB. [*Aside*] Or arrant knave.

ACT FIVE

SCENE. *Scene continues.*

[LADY WISHFORT *and* FOIBLE.]

LADY W. Out of my house, out of my house, thou viper, thou serpent, that I have fostered! thou bosom traitress, that I raised

from nothing!—begone, begone, begone, go, go!—that I took from washing of old gauze and weaving of dead hair, with a bleak blue nose, over a chafing-dish of starved embers, and dining behind a traverse rag, in a shop no bigger than a bird-cage,—go, go, starve again, do, do!

FOIB. Dear madam, I'll beg pardon on my knees. 8

LADY W. Away, out, out, go set up for yourself again!—do, drive a trade, do, with your three-penny-worth of small ware, flaunting upon a pack-thread, under a brandy-seller's bulk, or against a dead wall by a ballad-monger. Go, hang out an old Frisoneer gorget with a yard of yellow colberteen again! do! an old gnawed mask, two rows of pins and a child's fiddle; a glass necklace with the beads broken, and a quilted nightcap with one ear. Go, go, drive a trade! —These were your commodities, you treacherous trull, this was the merchandise you dealt in, when I took you into my house, placed you next myself, and made you governante of my whole family. You have forgot this, have you, now you have feathered your nest? 20

FOIB. No, no, dear madam. Do but hear me, have but a moment's patience—I'll confess all. Mr. Mirabell seduced me; I am not the first that he has wheedled with his dissembling tongue; your ladyship's own wisdom has been deluded by him, then how should I, a poor ignorant, defend myself? O madam, if you knew but what he promised me, and how he assured me your ladyship should come to no damage—or else the wealth of the Indies should not have bribed me to conspire against so good, so sweet, so kind a lady as you have been to me. 29

LADY W. No damage? What, to betray me, to marry me to a cast-serving-man; to make me a receptacle, an hospital for a decayed pimp? No damage? O thou frontless impudence, more than a big-bellied actress.

FOIB. Pray do but hear me, madam, he could not marry your ladyship, madam, no indeed, his marriage was to have been void in law; for he was married to me first, to secure your ladyship.

Act V. 32. frontless: shameless.

. . . Yes indeed, I enquired of the law in that case before I would meddle or make. 38

LADY W. What, then I have been your property, have I? I have been convenient to you, it seems,—while you were catering for Mirabell; I have been broker for you? What, have you made a passive bawd of me?—This exceeds all precedent; I am brought to fine uses, to become a botcher of second-hand marriages between Abigails and Andrews! I'll couple you. Yes, I'll baste you together, you and your Philander. I'll Duke's Place you, as I'm a person. Your turtle is in custody already; you shall coo in the same cage, if there be constable of warrant in the parish.   [*Exit.*]

FOIB. Oh, that ever I was born! Oh, that I was ever married!— a bride, ay, I shall be a Bridewell-bride. Oh! 49

[*Enter* MRS. FAINALL.]

MRS. FAIN. Poor Foible, what's the matter?

FOIB. O madam, my lady's gone for a constable; I shall be had to a justice, and put to Bridewell to beat hemp; poor Waitwell's gone to prison already.

MRS. FAIN. Have a good heart, Foible, Mirabell's gone to give security for him. This is all Marwood's and my husband's doing.

FOIB. Yes, yes, I know it, madam; she was in my lady's closet, and overheard all that you said to me before dinner. She sent the letter to my lady; and that missing effect, Mr. Fainall laid this plot to arrest Waitwell, when he pretended to go for the papers; and in the meantime Mrs. Marwood declared all to my lady. [60

MRS. FAIN. Was there no mention made of me in the letter?— My mother does not suspect my being in the confederacy? I fancy Marwood has not told her, though she has told my husband.

FOIB. Yes, madam; but my lady did not see that part. We stifled the letter before she read so far. Has that mischievous devil told Mr. Fainall of your ladyship, then?

MRS. FAIN. Ay, all's out, my affair with Mirabell, everything discovered. This is the last day of our living together, that's my comfort. 69

44. Abigails and Andrews: typical names of servants. **49. Bridewell:** prison.

FOIB. Indeed, madam, and so 'tis a comfort if you knew all—he has been even with your ladyship; which I could have told you long enough since, but I love to keep peace and quietness by my good will. I had rather bring friends together than set 'em at distance. But Mrs. Marwood and he are nearer related than ever their parents thought for.

MRS. FAIN. Say'st thou so, Foible? Canst thou prove this?

FOIB. I can take my oath of it, madam, so can Mrs. Mincing; we have had many a fair word from Madam Marwood, to conceal something that passed in our chamber one evening when you were at Hyde Park—and we were thought to have gone a walking; but we went up unawares—though we were sworn to secrecy too. Madam Marwood took a book and swore us upon it: but it was but a book of poems—so long as it was not a Bible-oath, we may break it with a safe conscience.   84

MRS. FAIN. This discovery is the most opportune thing I could wish. Now, Mincing?

[*Enter* MINCING.]

MINC. My lady would speak with Mrs. Foible, mem. Mr. Mirabell is with her; he has set your spouse at liberty, Mrs. Foible, and would have you hide yourself in my lady's closet, till my old lady's anger is abated. Oh, my old lady is in a perilous passion at something Mr. Fainall has said; he swears, and my old lady cries. There's a fearful hurricane, I vow. He says, mem, how that he'll have my lady's fortune made over to him, or he'll be divorced.

MRS. FAIN. Does your lady or Mirabell know that?   94

MINC. Yes, mem, they have sent me to see if Sir Wilfull be sober, and to bring him to them. My lady is resolved to have him, I think, rather than lose such a vast sum as six thousand pound. Oh, come, Mrs. Foible, I hear my old lady.

MRS. FAIN. Foible, you must tell Mincing that she must prepare to vouch when I call her.

FOIB. Yes, yes, madam.

MINC. Oh yes, mem, I'll vouch anything for your ladyship's service, be what it will.   [*Exeunt* MINCING *and* FOIBLE.]   103

[*Enter* LADY WISHFORT *and* MRS. MARWOOD.]

LADY W. O my dear friend, how can I enumerate the benefits that I have received from your goodness? To you I owe the timely discovery of the false vows of Mirabell; to you I owe the detection of the impostor Sir Rowland. And now you are become an intercessor with my son-in-law, to save the honour of my house, and compound for the frailties of my daughter. Well, friend, you are enough to reconcile me to the bad world, or else I would retire to deserts and solitudes; and feed harmless sheep by groves and purling streams. Dear Marwood, let us leave the world, and retire by ourselves and be shepherdesses. 113

MRS. MAR. Let us first dispatch the affair in hand, madam. We shall have leisure to think of retirement afterwards. Here is one who is concerned in the treaty.

LADY W. O daughter, daughter, is it possible thou shouldst be my child, bone of my bone, and flesh of my flesh, and as I may say, another me, and yet transgress the most minute particle of severe virtue? Is it possible you should lean aside to iniquity, who have been cast in the direct mould of virtue? I have not only been a mould but a pattern for you, and a model for you, after you were brought into the world. 123

MRS. FAIN. I don't understand your ladyship.

LADY W. Not understand? Why, have you not been naught? Have you not been sophisticated? Not understand? Here I am ruined to compound for your caprices and your cuckoldoms. I must pawn my plate and my jewels, and ruin my niece, and all little enough—

MRS. FAIN. I am wronged and abused, and so are you. 'Tis a false accusation, as false as hell, as false as your friend there, ay, or your friend's friend, my false husband. 132

MRS. MAR. My friend, Mrs. Fainall? Your husband my friend, what do you mean?

MRS. FAIN. I know what I mean, madam, and so do you; and so shall the world at a time convenient.

MRS. MAR. I am sorry to see you so passionate, madam. More temper would look more like innocence. But I have done. I am

125. naught: immoral.

sorry my zeal to serve your ladyship and family should admit of misconstruction, or make me liable to affronts. You will pardon me, madam, if I meddle no more with an affair in which I am not personally concerned.   142

LADY W. O dear friend, I am so ashamed that you should meet with such returns. [*To* MRS. FAINALL] You ought to ask pardon on your knees, ungrateful creature; she deserves more from you, than all your life can accomplish. [*To* MRS. MARWOOD] Oh, don't leave me destitute in this perplexity—no, stick to me, my good genius.

MRS. FAIN. I tell you, madam, you're abused.—Stick to you? ay, like a leech, to suck your best blood—she'll drop off when she's full. Madam, you shan't pawn a bodkin, nor part with a brass counter, in composition for me. I defy 'em all. Let 'em prove their aspersions: I know my own innocence, and dare stand a [153 trial.   [*Exit.*]

LADY W. Why, if she should be innocent, if she should be wronged after all, ha? I don't know what to think—and I promise you, her education has been unexceptionable—I may say it; for I chiefly made it my own care to initiate her very infancy in the rudiments of virtue, and to impress upon her tender years a young odium and aversion to the very sight of men—ay, friend, she would ha' shrieked if she had but seen a man, till she was in her teens. As I'm a person 'tis true.—She was never suffered to play with a male-child, though but in coats; nay, her very babies were of the feminine gender.—Oh, she never looked a man in the face but her own father, or the chaplain, and him we made a shift to put upon her for a woman, by the help of his long garments, and his sleek face; till she was going in her fifteen.   167

MRS. MAR. 'Twas much she should be deceived so long.

LADY W. I warrant you, or she would never have borne to have been catechised by him; and have heard his long lectures against singing and dancing, and such debaucheries; and going to filthy plays; and profane music-meetings, where the lewd trebles squeak nothing but bawdy, and the basses roar blasphemy. Oh, she would

163. babies: dolls.

have swooned at the sight or name of an obscene play-book—and can I think after all this, that my daughter can be naught? What, a whore? And thought it excommunication to set her foot within the door of a play-house. O dear friend, I can't believe it, no, no; as she says, let him prove it, let him prove it.   178

MRS. MAR. Prove it, madam? What, and have your name prostituted in a public court; yours and your daughter's reputation worried at the bar by a pack of bawling lawyers? To be ushered in with an "Oyez" of scandal; and have your case opened by an old fumbling lecher in a quoif like a man midwife, to bring your daughter's infamy to light; to be a theme for legal punsters, and quibblers by the statute; and become a jest, against a rule of court, where there is no precedent for a jest in any record; not even in Doomsday Book: to discompose the gravity of the bench, and [187 provoke naughty interrogatories in more naughty law Latin; while the good judge, tickled with the proceeding, simpers under a grey beard, and fidges off and on his cushion as if he had swallowed cantharides, or sat upon cowitch.

LADY W. Oh, 'tis very hard!

MRS. MAR. And then to have my young revellers of the Temple take notes, like prentices at a conventicle; and after talk it over again in Commons, or before drawers in an eating-house.

LADY W. Worse and worse.   196

MRS. MAR. Nay, this is nothing; if it would end here 'twere well. But it must after this be consigned by the shorthand writers to the public press; and from thence be transferred to the hands, nay, into the throats and lungs of hawkers, with voices more licentious than the loud flounder-man's: and this you must hear 'til you are stunned; nay, you must hear nothing else for some days.

LADY W. Oh, 'tis insupportable. No, no, dear friend, make it up, make it up; ay, ay, I'll compound. I'll give up all, myself and my all, my niece and her all—anything, everything for composition.

MRS. MAR. Nay, madam, I advise nothing, I only lay before you, as a friend, the inconveniencies which perhaps you have overseen. Here comes Mr. Fainall. if he will be satisfied to huddle up all in

silence, I shall be glad. You must think I would rather congratulate than condole with you.   210

[*Enter* FAINALL.]

LADY W. Ay, ay, I do not doubt it, dear Marwood; no, no, I do
not doubt it.

FAIN. Well, madam, I have suffered myself to be overcome by
the importunity of this lady, your friend; and am content you shall
enjoy your own proper estate during life—on condition you oblige
yourself never to marry, under such penalty as I think convenient.

LADY W. Never to marry?   217

FAIN. No more Sir Rowlands—the next imposture may not be so
timely detected.

MRS. MAR. That condition, I dare answer, my lady will consent
to, without difficulty; she has already but too much experienced
the perfidiousness of men. Besides, madam, when we retire to our
pastoral solitude we shall bid adieu to all other thoughts.

LADY W. Ay, that's true; but in case of necessity; as of health,
or some such emergency—

FAIN. Oh, if you are prescribed marriage, you shall be considered;
I will only reserve to myself the power to choose for you. If your
physic be wholesome, it matters not who is your apothecary. Next,
my wife shall settle on me the remainder of her fortune, not made
over already, and for her maintenance depend entirely on my
discretion.   231

LADY W. This is most inhumanly savage, exceeding the barbarity
of a Muscovite husband.

FAIN. I learned it from his czarish majesty's retinue, in a winter
evening's conference over brandy and pepper, amongst other secrets
of matrimony and policy, as they are at present practised in the
northern hemisphere. But this must be agreed unto, and that positively. Lastly, I will be endowed, in right of my wife, with that six
thousand pound, which is the moiety of Mrs. Millamant's fortune
in your possession, and which she has forfeited (as will appear by
the last will and testament of your deceased husband, Sir Jonathan
Wishfort) by her disobedience in contracting herself against your
consent or knowledge, and by refusing the offered match with Sir

Wilfull Witwoud, which you, like a careful aunt, had provided for her. 245

LADY W. My nephew was *non compos;* and could not make his addresses.

FAIN. I come to make demands—I'll hear no objections.

LADY W. You will grant me time to consider?

FAIN. Yes, while the instrument is drawing, to which you must set your hand till more sufficient deeds can be perfected, which I will take care shall be done with all possible speed. In the meanwhile I will go for the said instrument, and till my return you may balance this matter in your own discretion. [*Exit* FAINALL.]

LADY W. This insolence is beyond all precedent, all parallel; must I be subject to this merciless villain? 256

MRS. MAR. 'Tis severe indeed, madam, that you should smart for your daughter's wantonness.

LADY W. 'Twas against my consent that she married this barbarian, but she would have him, though her year was not out.— Ah! her first husband, my son Languish, would not have carried it thus. Well, that was my choice, this is hers; she is matched now with a witness.—I shall be mad, dear friend; is there no comfort for me? Must I live to be confiscated at this rebel-rate?—Here come two more of my Egyptian plagues, too.

[*Enter* MILLAMANT *and* SIR WILFULL.]

SIR WIL. Aunt, your servant. 266

LADY W. Out, caterpillar, call not me aunt; I know thee not.

SIR WIL. I confess I have been a little in disguise, as they say— 'Sheart! and I'm sorry for't. What would you have? I hope I committed no offence, aunt—and if I did I am willing to make satisfaction; and what can a man say fairer? If I have broke anything I'll pay for't, an it cost a pound. And so let that content for what's past, and make no more words. For what's to come, to pleasure you I'm willing to marry my cousin. So pray let's all be friends; she and I are agreed upon the matter before a witness.

LADY W. How's this, dear niece? Have I any comfort? Can this be true? 277

MILLA. I am content to be a sacrifice to your repose, madam; and to convince you that I had no hand in the plot, as you were mis-informed, I have laid my commands on Mirabell to come in per-son, and be a witness that I give my hand to this flower of knight-hood; and for the contract that passed between Mirabell and me, I have obliged him to make a resignation of it in your ladyship's presence—he is without, and waits your leave for admittance.

LADY W. Well, I'll swear I am something revived at this testi-mony of your obedience; but I cannot admit that traitor.—I fear I cannot fortify myself to support his appearance. He is as terrible to me as a Gorgon; if I see him I fear I shall turn to stone, petrify incessantly. 289

MILLA. If you disoblige him he may resent your refusal, and insist upon the contract still. Then, 'tis the last time he will be offensive to you.

LADY W. Are you sure it will be the last time?—If I were sure of that—shall I never see him again?

MILLA. Sir Wilfull, you and he are to travel together, are you not?

SIR WIL. 'Sheart, the gentleman's a civil gentleman, aunt, let him come in; why, we are sworn brothers and fellow-travellers.—We are to be Pylades and Orestes, he and I—he is to be my inter-preter in foreign parts. He has been overseas once already; and with proviso that I marry my cousin, will cross 'em once again, only to bear me company.—'Sheart, I'll call him in—an I set on't once, he shall come in, and see who'll hinder him. [*Exit.*] 302

MRS. MAR. [*Aside*] This is precious fooling, if it would pass; but I'll know the bottom of it.

LADY W. O dear Marwood, you are not going?

MAR. Not far, madam; I'll return immediately. [*Exit.*]

[*Re-enter* SIR WILFULL *and* MIRABELL.]

SIR WIL. Look up, man, I'll stand by you, 'sbud, an she do frown, she can't kill you.—Besides—hark'ee, she dare not frown desper-ately, because her face is none of her own; 'sheart, an she should, her forehead would wrinkle like the coat of a cream-cheese; but mum for that, fellow-traveller. 311

MIRA. If a deep sense of the many injuries I have offered to so good a lady, with a sincere remorse, and a hearty contrition, can but obtain the least glance of compassion, I am too happy.—Ah, madam, there was a time—but let it be forgotten—I confess I have deservedly forfeited the high place I once held, of sighing at your feet; nay, kill me not, by turning from me in disdain—I come not to plead for favour—nay, not for pardon; I am a suppliant only for pity—I am going where I never shall behold you more—

SIR WIL. How, fellow-traveller!—You shall go by yourself then.

MIRA. Let me be pitied first; and afterwards forgotten—I ask no more. 322

SIR WIL. By'r Lady, a very reasonable request, and will cost you nothing, aunt.—Come, come, forgive and forget, aunt, why, you must an you are a Christian.

MIRA. Consider, madam, in reality, you could not receive much prejudice; it was an innocent device; though I confess it had a face of guiltiness, it was at most an artifice which love contrived—and errors which love produces have ever been accounted venial. At least think it is punishment enough that I have lost what in my heart I hold most dear, that to your cruel indignation I have offered up this beauty, and with her my peace and quiet; nay, all my hopes of future comfort. 333

SIR WIL. An he does not move me, would I may never be o' the quorum—an it were not as good a deed as to drink, to give her to him again, I would I might never take shipping!—Aunt, if you don't forgive quickly, I shall melt, I can tell you that. My contract went no farther than a little mouth-glue, and that's hardly dry—one doleful sigh more from my fellow-traveller and 'tis dissolved.

LADY W. Well, nephew, upon your account.—Ah, he has a false insinuating tongue!—Well, sir, I will stifle my just resentment at my nephew's request.—I will endeavour what I can to forget—but on proviso that you resign the contract with my niece immediately.

MIRA. It is in writing and with papers of concern; but I have sent my servant for it, and will deliver it to you, with all acknowledgments for your transcendent goodness. 346

LADY W. [*Apart*] Oh, he has witchcraft in his eyes and tongue!—
When I did not see him I could have bribed a villain to his assas-
sination; but his appearance rakes the embers which have so long
lain smothered in my breast.—

[*Enter* FAINALL *and* MRS. MARWOOD.]

FAIN. Your date of deliberation, madam, is expired. Here is the
instrument; are you prepared to sign?

LADY W. If I were prepared, I am not impowered. My niece ex-
erts a lawful claim, having matched herself by my direction to Sir
Wilfull.

FAIN. That sham is too gross to pass on me—though 'tis imposed
on you, madam.

MILLA. Sir, I have given my consent.   358

MIRA. And, sir, I have resigned my pretensions.

SIR WIL. And, sir, I assert my right; and will maintain it in defiance of you, sir, and of your instrument. 'Sheart, an you talk of
an instrument, sir, I have an old fox by my thigh shall hack your
instrument of ram vellum to shreds, sir. It shall not be sufficient
for a mittimus or a tailor's measure; therefore withdraw your instrument, sir, or by'r Lady I shall draw mine.

LADY W. Hold, nephew, hold.

MILLA. Good Sir Wilfull, respite your valour.   367

FAIN. Indeed? Are you provided of your guard, with your single
beef-eater there? But I'm prepared for you, and insist upon my
first proposal. You shall submit your own estate to my manage-
ment, and absolutely make over my wife's to my sole use, as pur-
suant to the purport and tenor of this other covenant.—I suppose,
madam, your consent is not requisite in this case; nor, Mr. Mirabell,
your resignation; nor, Sir Wilfull, your right—you may draw your
fox if you please, sir, and make a bear-garden flourish somewhere
else, for here it will not avail. This, my Lady Wishfort, must be
subscribed, or your darling daughter's turned adrift, like a leaky
hulk to sink or swim, as she and the current of this lewd town
can agree.   379

362. fox: sword. **364. mittimus:** warrant for arrest.

LADY W. Is there no means, no remedy, to stop my ruin? Ungrateful wretch! dost thou not owe thy being, thy subsistence, to my daughter's fortune?

FAIN. I'll answer you when I have the rest of it in my possession.

MIRA. But that you would not accept of a remedy from my hands —I own I have not deserved you should owe any obligation to me; or else perhaps I could advise—

LADY W. Oh, what? what? to save me and my child from ruin, from want, I'll forgive all that's past; nay, I'll consent to anything to come, to be delivered from this tyranny.   389

MIRA. Ay, madam; but that is too late, my reward is intercepted. You have disposed of her, who only could have made me a compensation for all my services—but be it as it may, I am resolved I'll serve you, you shall not be wronged in this savage manner.

LADY W. How! Dear Mr. Mirabell, can you be so generous at last! But it is not possible. Hark'ee, I'll break my nephew's match, you shall have my niece yet, and all her fortune, if you can but save me from this imminent danger.

MIRA. Will you? I take you at your word. I ask no more. I must have leave for two criminals to appear.   399

LADY W. Ay, ay, anybody, anybody!

MIRA. Foible is one, and a penitent.

[*Enter* MRS. FAINALL, FOIBLE, *and* MINCING.]

MRS. MAR. [*To* FAINALL] Oh, my shame! these corrupt things are brought hither to expose me.

FAIN. If it must all come out, why let 'em know it, 'tis but *the way of the world*. That shall not urge me to relinquish or abate one title of my terms, no; I will insist the more.

FOIB. Yes indeed, madam, I'll take my Bible-oath of it.   407

MINC. And so will I, mem.

LADY W. O Marwood, Marwood, art thou false? my friend deceive me? Hast thou been a wicked accomplice with that profligate man?

MRS. MAR. Have you so much ingratitude and injustice, to give credit against your friend, to the aspersions of two such mercenary trulls?

MINC. Mercenary, mem? I scorn your words. 'Tis true we found you and Mr. Fainall in the blue garret; by the same token, you swore us to secrecy upon Messalinas's poems. Mercenary? No, if we would have been mercenary, we should have held our tongues; you would have bribed us sufficiently.   419

FAIN. Go, you are an insignificant thing!—Well, what are you the better for this! Is this Mr. Mirabell's expedient? I'll be put off no longer.—You, thing, that was a wife, shall smart for this. I will not leave thee wherewithal to hide thy shame; your body shall be naked as your reputation.

MRS. FAIN. I despise you, and defy your malice—you have aspersed me wrongfully—I have proved your falsehood—go you and your treacherous—I will not name it, but starve together—perish!

FAIN. Not while you are worth a groat, indeed, my dear. Madam, I'll be fooled no longer.   429

LADY W. Ah, Mr. Mirabell, this is small comfort, the detection of this affair.

MIRA. Oh, in good time.—Your leave for the other offender and penitent to appear, madam.

[*Enter* WAITWELL *with a box of writings.*]

LADY W. O Sir Rowland!—Well, rascal!

WAIT. What your ladyship pleases.—I have brought the black box at last, madam.

MIRA. Give it me. Madam, you remember your promise.

LADY W. Ay, dear sir.   438

MIRA. Where are the gentlemen?

WAIT. At hand, sir, rubbing their eyes—just risen from sleep.

FAIN. 'Sdeath, what's this to me? I'll not wait your private concerns.

[*Enter* PETULANT *and* WITWOUD.]

PET. How now? what's the matter? whose hand's out?

WIT. Heyday! what, are you all got together, like players at the end of the last act?

MIRA. You may remember, gentlemen, I once requested your hands as witnesses to a certain parchment.   447

WIT. Ay, I do, my hand I remember—Petulant set his mark.

MIRA. You wrong him, his name is fairly written, as shall appear.—You do not remember, gentlemen, anything of what that parchment contained? [*Undoing the box.*]

WIT. No.

PET. Not I. I writ, I read nothing.

MIRA. Very well, now you shall know.—Madam, your promise.

LADY W. Ay, ay, sir, upon my honour.

MIRA. Mr. Fainall, it is now time that you should know that your lady, while she was at her own disposal, and before you had by your insinuations wheedled her out of a pretended settlement of the greatest part of her fortune—

FAIN. Sir! pretended!   460

MIRA. Yes, sir. I say that this lady while a widow, having, it seems, received some cautions respecting your inconstancy and tyranny of temper, which from her own partial opinion and fondness of you she could never have suspected—she did, I say, by the wholesome advice of friends and of sages learned in the laws of this land, deliver this same as her act and deed to me in trust, and to the uses within mentioned. You may read if you please—[*Holding out the parchment*] though perhaps what is written on the back may serve your occasions.   469

FAIN. Very likely, sir. What's here? Damnation! [*Reads.*] "A deed of conveyance of the whole estate real of Arabella Languish, widow, in trust to Edward Mirabell."—Confusion!

MIRA. Even so, sir, 'tis *the way of the world,* sir; of the widows of the world. I suppose this deed may bear an elder date than what you have obtained from your lady.

FAIN. Perfidious fiend! then thus I'll be revenged.—[*Offers to run at* MRS. FAINALL.]

SIR WIL. Hold, sir, now you may make your bear-garden flourish somewhere else, sir.   479

FAIN. Mirabell, you shall hear of this, sir, be sure you shall.—Let me pass, oaf.   [*Exit.*]

MRS. FAIN. Madam, you seem to stifle your resentment: you had better give it vent.

MRS. MAR. Yes, it shall have vent—and to your confusion, or I'll perish in the attempt. [*Exit.*]

LADY W. O daughter, daughter, 'tis plain thou hast inherited thy mother's prudence.

MRS. FAIN. Thank Mr. Mirabell, a cautious friend, to whose advice all is owing. 489

LADY W. Well, Mr. Mirabell, you have kept your promise—and I must perform mine.—First, I pardon for your sake Sir Rowland there and Foible—the next thing is to break the matter to my nephew—and how to do that—

MIRA. For that, madam, give yourself no trouble,—let me have your consent.—Sir Wilfull is my friend; he has had compassion upon lovers, and generously engaged a volunteer in this action, for our service; and now designs to prosecute his travels.

SIR WIL. 'Sheart, aunt, I have no mind to marry. My cousin's a fine lady, and the gentleman loves her, and she loves him, and they deserve one another; my resolution is to see foreign parts—I have set on't—and when I'm set on't, I must do't. And if these two gentlemen would travel too, I think they may be spared. 502

PET. For my part, I say little—I think things are best off or on.

WIT. I gad, I understand nothing of the matter—I'm in a maze yet, like a dog in a dancing-school.

LADY W. Well, sir, take her, and with her all the joy I can give you.

MILLA. Why does not the man take me? Would you have me give myself to you over again?

MIRA. Ay, and over and over again. [*Kisses her hand.*] I would have you as often as possibly I can. Well, Heaven grant I love you not too well, that's all my fear. 512

SIR WIL. 'Sheart, you'll have time enough to toy after you're married; or if you will toy now, let us have a dance in the meantime, that we who are not lovers may have some other employment, besides looking on.

MIRA. With all my heart, dear Sir Wilfull. What shall we do for music?

FOIB. O sir, some that were provided for Sir Rowland's entertainment are yet within call.

[*A dance.*]

LADY W. As I am a person, I can hold out no longer—I have wasted my spirits so today already, that I am ready to sink under the fatigue; and I cannot but have some fears upon me yet, that my son Fainall will pursue some desperate course.

524

MIRA. Madam, disquiet not yourself on that account; to my knowledge his circumstances are such, he must of force comply. For my part, I will contribute all that in me lies to a reunion; in the meantime, madam [*To* MRS. FAINALL], let me before these witnesses restore to you this deed of trust; it may be a means, well managed, to make you live easily together.

> From hence let those be warned, who mean to wed;
> Lest mutual falsehood stain the bridal-bed:
> For each deceiver to his cost may find,
> That marriage frauds too oft are paid in kind.

[*Exeunt.*]

Henrik Ibsen

AN ENEMY OF THE PEOPLE

IBSEN's life gave him first-hand knowledge of both the appearance and the inner flaws of modern materialistic culture. He was born March 20, 1828, in the small Norwegian town of Skien. For seven years his family belonged to the prosperous merchant class; then, losing their money, they were forced to move to a small farmhouse on the edge of town. From 1844 to 1849 Ibsen was a druggist's assistant in the provincial community of Grimstad. He left in 1850 to study medicine at the university in Christiana, but turned at once to drama. During the next sixteen years he worked doggedly as playwright and manager until his fame was established by *Brand* in 1866 and *Peer Gynt* in 1867. Then came the problem plays for which Ibsen is best known, and which scandalized Europe. They reflect his wide acquaintance with middle-class types and his awareness of the moral tensions and hypocrisies in late nineteenth-century society. Leading up to *An Enemy of the People* (1882) were the satiric *Pillars of Society* (1877), *A Doll's House* (1879), which reflected the growing feminist movement, and *Ghosts* (1881), which dared to discuss hereditary syphilis.

In *The Quintessence of Ibsenism* (1891, 1913), George Bernard Shaw, who was strongly influenced by Ibsen, defined Ibsen's contribution to drama as the application of forensic techniques to realistic material so that the theater becomes a platform for the dramatic discussion of social problems. The central situation in *An Enemy of the People* was clearly chosen to present a great many controversial problems. Dr. Stockmann, a high-minded public health officer, discovers that sewage from mills upstream is contaminating the medicinal baths which are the chief industry of the town, but when he tries to bring this crucial information to his community

he is denounced rather than acclaimed. This central paradox of the public benefactor as public enemy is approached through a series of events designed to compel our attention and dramatize the issues of the play. Our emotions first are enlisted for Dr. Stockmann's generous idealism and devotion to truth, and then with him we are subjected to the disillusioning discovery that the contaminated water reflects the community's moral pollution of economic self-interest. At the same time Ibsen is busy managing his material to show us another view of Dr. Stockmann; his idealism is gradually seen to be naive, and his public-spiritedness difficult to distinguish from pugnacity and conceit. This complexity is continued throughout the play. Self-centered, impractical, and obstreperous, Dr. Stockmann is still to the end felt to be a figure of quixotic energy, uncontained and unused by the mean society around him. *An Enemy of the People* fulfills its purpose by uncovering and sharpening social and ethical conflicts ordinarily submerged or reduced to a convenient black and white.

AN ENEMY OF THE PEOPLE

Characters

DR. THOMAS STOCKMANN, *Medical Officer of the Municipal Baths.*

MRS. STOCKMANN, *his wife.*

PETRA, *their daughter, a teacher.*

EJLIF ⎫ *their sons (aged 13 and 10 respectively).*
MORTEN ⎭

PETER STOCKMANN, *the Doctor's elder brother; Mayor of the Town and Chief Constable, Chairman of the Baths' Committee, etc., etc.*

MORTEN KIIL, *a tanner* (MRS. STOCKMANN's *adoptive father*).

HOVSTAD, *editor of the "People's Messenger."*

BILLING, *sub-editor.*

CAPTAIN HORSTER.

ASLAKSEN, *a printer.*

MEN *of various conditions and occupations, some few women, and a troop of schoolboys—the audience at a public meeting.*

The action takes place in a coast town in southern Norway.

ACT ONE

SCENE—DR. STOCKMANN's *sitting-room. It is evening. The room is plainly but neatly appointed and furnished. In the right-hand wall are two doors; the farther leads out to the hall, the nearer to the doctor's study. In the left-hand wall, opposite the door leading to the hall, is a door leading to the other rooms occupied by the family. In the middle of the same wall stands the stove, and, further forward, a couch with a looking-glass hanging over it and an oval table in front*

of it. On the table, a lighted lamp, with a lamp shade. At the back of the room, an open door leads to the dining-room. BILLING *is seen sitting at the dining table, on which a lamp is burning. He has a napkin tucked under his chin, and* MRS. STOCKMANN *is standing by the table handing him a large plate-full of roast beef. The other places at the table are empty, and the table somewhat in disorder, a meal having evidently recently been finished.*

MRS. STOCKMANN. You see, if you come an hour late, Mr. Billing, you have to put up with cold meat.

BILLING. [*As he eats*] It is uncommonly good, thank you—remarkably good.

MRS. STOCKMANN. My husband makes such a point of having his meals punctually, you know—

BILLING. That doesn't affect me a bit. Indeed, I almost think I enjoy a meal all the better when I can sit down and eat all by myself and undisturbed.

9

MRS. STOCKMANN. Oh well, as long as you are enjoying it— [*Turns to the hall door, listening.*] I expect that is Mr. Hovstad coming too.

BILLING. Very likely.

[PETER STOCKMANN *comes in. He wears an overcoat and his official hat, and carries a stick.*]

PETER STOCKMANN. Good evening, Katherine.

MRS. STOCKMANN. [*Coming forward into the sitting-room*] Ah, good evening—is it you? How good of you to come up and see us!

PETER STOCKMANN. I happened to be passing, and so— [*Looks into the dining-room*] But you have company with you, I see.

MRS. STOCKMANN. [*A little embarrassed*] Oh, no—it was quite by chance he came in. [*Hurriedly*] Won't you come in and have something, too?

22

PETER STOCKMANN. I! No, thank you. Good gracious—hot meat at night! Not with my digestion.

MRS. STOCKMANN. Oh, but just once in a way—

PETER STOCKMANN. No, no, my dear lady; I stick to my tea and bread and butter. It is much more wholesome in the long run—and a little more economical, too.

MRS. STOCKMANN. [*Smiling*] Now you mustn't think that Thomas and I are spendthrifts.

PETER STOCKMANN. Not you, my dear; I would never think that of you. [*Points to the* DOCTOR's *study.*] Is he not at home?   32

MRS. STOCKMANN. No, he went out for a little turn after supper—he and the boys.

PETER STOCKMANN. I doubt if that is a wise thing to do. [*Listens.*] I fancy I hear him coming now.

MRS. STOCKMANN. No, I don't think it is he. [*A knock is heard at the door.*] Come in! [HOVSTAD *comes in from the hall.*] Oh, it is you, Mr. Hovstad!

HOVSTAD. Yes, I hope you will forgive me, but I was delayed at the printer's. Good evening, Mr. Mayor.

PETER STOCKMANN. [*Bowing a little distantly*] Good evening. You have come on business, no doubt.   43

HOVSTAD. Partly. It's about an article for the paper.

PETER STOCKMANN. So I imagined. I hear my brother has become a prolific contributor to the "People's Messenger."

HOVSTAD. Yes, he is good enough to write in the "People's Messenger" when he has any home truths to tell.

MRS. STOCKMANN. [*To* HOVSTAD] But won't you—?

                                        [*Points to the dining-room.*]

PETER STOCKMANN. Quite so, quite so. I don't blame him in the least, as a writer, for addressing himself to the quarters where he will find the readiest sympathy. And, besides that, I personally have no reason to bear any ill will to your paper, Mr. Hovstad.   54

HOVSTAD. I quite agree with you.

PETER STOCKMANN. Taking one thing with another, there is an excellent spirit of toleration in the town—an admirable municipal spirit. And it all springs from the fact of our having a great common interest to unite us—an interest that is in an equally high degree the concern of every right-minded citizen—

HOVSTAD. The Baths, yes.

PETER STOCKMANN. Exactly—our fine, new, handsome Baths. Mark my words, Mr. Hovstad—the Baths will become the focus of our municipal life! Not a doubt of it!   64

MRS. STOCKMANN. That is just what Thomas says.

PETER STOCKMANN. Think how extraordinarily the place has developed within the last year or two! Money has been flowing in, and there is some life and some business doing in the town. Houses and landed property are rising in value every day.

HOVSTAD. And unemployment is diminishing.

PETER STOCKMANN. Yes, that is another thing. The burden of the poor-rates has been lightened, to the great relief of the propertied classes; and that relief will be even greater if only we get a really good summer this year, and lots of visitors—plenty of invalids, who will make the Baths talked about. 75

HOVSTAD. And there is a good prospect of that, I hear.

PETER STOCKMANN. It looks very promising. Enquiries about apartments and that sort of thing are reaching us every day.

HOVSTAD. Well, the doctor's article will come in very suitably.

PETER STOCKMANN. Has he been writing something just lately?

HOVSTAD. This is something he wrote in the winter, a recommendation of the Baths—an account of the excellent sanitary conditions here. But I held the article over, temporarily. 83

PETER STOCKMANN. Ah,—some little difficulty about it, I suppose?

HOVSTAD. No, not at all; I thought it would be better to wait till the spring, because it is just at this time that people begin to think seriously about their summer quarters.

PETER STOCKMANN. Quite right; you were perfectly right, Mr Hovstad.

MRS. STOCKMANN. Yes, Thomas is really indefatigable when it is a question of the Baths.

PETER STOCKMANN. Well—remember, he is the Medical Officer to the Baths. 93

HOVSTAD. Yes, and what is more, they owe their existence to him.

PETER STOCKMANN. To him? Indeed! It is true I have heard from time to time that some people are of that opinion. And at the same time I must say I imagined that I took a modest part in the enterprise.

MRS. STOCKMANN. Yes, that is what Thomas is always saying.

HOVSTAD. But who denies it, Mr. Stockmann? You set the thing going and made a practical concern of it; we all know that. I only meant that the idea of it came first from the doctor. 102

PETER STOCKMANN. Oh, ideas—yes! My brother has had plenty of them in his time—unfortunately. But when it is a question of putting an idea into practical shape, you have to apply to a man of different mettle, Mr. Hovstad. And I certainly should have thought that in this house at least—

MRS. STOCKMANN. My dear Peter—

HOVSTAD. How can you think that—?

MRS. STOCKMANN. Won't you go in and have something, Mr. Hovstad? My husband is sure to be back directly.

HOVSTAD. Thank you, perhaps just a morsel. 112

[*Goes into the dining-room.*]

PETER STOCKMANN. [*Lowering his voice a little*] It is a curious thing that these farmers' sons never seem to lose their want of tact.

MRS. STOCKMANN. Surely it is not worth bothering about! Cannot you and Thomas share the credit as brothers?

PETER STOCKMANN. I should have thought so; but apparently some people are not satisfied with a share.

MRS. STOCKMANN. What nonsense! You and Thomas get on so capitally together. [*Listens.*] There he is at last, I think. 121

[*Goes out and opens the door leading to the hall.*]

DR. STOCKMANN. [*Laughing and talking outside*] Look here—here is another guest for you, Katherine. Isn't that jolly? Come in, Captain Horster; hang your coat up on this peg. Ah, you don't wear an overcoat. Just think, Katherine; I met him in the street and could hardly persuade him to come up! [CAPTAIN HORSTER *comes into the room and greets* MRS. STOCKMANN. *He is followed by* DR. STOCKMANN.] Come along in, boys. They are ravenously hungry again, you know. Come along, Captain Horster; you must have a slice of beef. [*Pushes* HORSTER *into the dining-room.* EJLIF *and* MORTEN *go in after them.*] 132

MRS. STOCKMANN. But, Thomas, don't you see—?

DR. STOCKMANN. [*Turning in the doorway*] Oh, is it you, Peter? [*Shakes hands with him.*] Now that is very delightful.

PETER STOCKMANN. Unfortunately I must go in a moment—

DR. STOCKMANN. Rubbish! There is some toddy just coming in. You haven't forgotten the toddy, Katherine?

MRS. STOCKMANN. Of course not; the water is boiling now.
[*Goes into the dining-room.*]

PETER STOCKMANN. Toddy too!

DR. STOCKMANN. Yes, sit down and we will have it comfortably.

PETER STOCKMANN. Thanks, I never care about an evening's drinking. 144

DR. STOCKMANN. But this isn't an evening's drinking.

PETER STOCKMANN. It seems to me— [*Looks towards the dining-room.*] It is extraordinary how they can put away all that food.

DR. STOCKMANN. [*Rubbing his hands*] Yes, isn't it splendid to see young people eat? They have always got an appetite, you know! That's as it should be. Lots of food—to build up their strength! They are the people who are going to stir up the fermenting forces of the future, Peter. 152

PETER STOCKMANN. May I ask what they will find here to "stir up," as you put it?

DR. STOCKMANN. Ah, you must ask the young people that—when the time comes. We shan't be able to see it, of course. That stands to reason—two old fogies, like us—

PETER STOCKMANN. Really, really! I must say that is an extremely odd expression to—

DR. STOCKMANN. Oh, you mustn't take me too literally, Peter. I am so heartily happy and contented, you know. I think it is such an extraordinary piece of good fortune to be in the middle of all this growing, germinating life. It is a splendid time to live in! It is as if a whole new world were being created around one. 164

PETER STOCKMANN. Do you really think so?

DR. STOCKMANN. Ah, naturally you can't appreciate it as keenly as I. You have lived all your life in these surroundings, and your impressions have got blunted. But I, who have been buried all these years in my little corner up north, almost without ever seeing a stranger who might bring new ideas with him—well, in my case it has just the same effect as if I had been transported into the middle of a crowded city.

PETER STOCKMANN. Oh, a city—! 173

DR. STOCKMANN. I know, I know; it is all cramped enough here, compared with many other places. But there is life here—there is

promise—there are innumerable things to work for and fight for; and that is the main thing. [*Calls.*] Katherine, hasn't the postman been here?

MRS. STOCKMANN. [*From the dining-room*] No.

DR. STOCKMANN. And then to be comfortably off, Peter! That is something one learns to value, when one has been on the brink of starvation, as we have.

PETER STECKMANN. Oh, surely— 183

DR. STOCKMANN. Indeed I can assure you we have often been very hard put to it, up there. And now to be able to live like a lord! Today, for instance, we had roast beef for dinner—and, what is more, for supper too. Won't you come and have a little bit? Or let me show it to you, at any rate? Come here—

PETER STOCKMANN. No, no—not for worlds!

DR. STOCKMANN. Well, but just come here then. Do you see, we have got a table-cover?

PETER STOCKMANN. Yes, I noticed it. 192

DR. STOCKMANN. And we have got a lamp shade too. Do you see? All out of Katherine's savings! It makes the room so cosy. Don't you think so? Just stand here for a moment—no, no, not there— just here, that's it! Look now, when you get the light on it alto- gether—I really think it looks very nice, doesn't it?

PETER STOCKMANN. Oh, if you can afford luxuries of this kind—

DR. STOCKMANN. Yes, I can afford it now. Katherine tells me I earn almost as much as we spend.

PETER STOCKMANN. Almost—yes!

DR. STOCKMANN. And we have got a lamp shade too. Do you see? style. I am quite sure an ordinary civil servant spends more in a year than I do. 204

PETER STOCKMANN. I daresay. A civil servant—a man in a well-paid position—

DR. STOCKMANN. Well, any ordinary merchant, then! A man in that position spends two or three times as much as—

PETER STOCKMANN. It just depends on circumstances.

DR. STOCKMANN. At all events I assure you I don't waste money unprofitably. But I can't find it in my heart to deny myself the pleasure of entertaining my friends. I need that sort of thing, you

know. I have lived for so long shut out of it all that it is a necessity of life to me to mix with young, eager, ambitious men, men of liberal and active minds; and that describes every one of those fellows who are enjoying their supper in there. I wish you knew more of Hovstad— 217

PETER STOCKMANN. By the way, Hovstad was telling me he was going to print another article of yours.

DR. STOCKMANN. An article of mine?

PETER STOCKMANN. Yes, about the Baths. An article you wrote in the winter.

DR. STOCKMANN. Oh, that one! No, I don't intend that to appear just for the present.

PETER STOCKMANN. Why not? It seems to me that this would be the most opportune moment. 226

DR. STOCKMANN. Yes, very likely—under normal conditions.

[*Crosses the room.*]

PETER STOCKMAN. [*Following him with his eyes*] Is there anything abnormal about the present conditions?

DR. STOCKMANN. [*Standing still*] To tell you the truth, Peter, I can't say just at this moment—at all events not tonight. There may be much that is very abnormal about the present conditions—and it is possible there may be nothing abnormal about them at all. It is quite possible it may be merely my imagination. 235

PETER STOCKMANN. I must say it all sounds most mysterious. Is there something going on that I am to be kept in ignorance of? I should have imagined that I, as Chairman of the governing body of the Baths—

DR. STOCKMANN. And I should have imagined that I— Oh, come, don't let us fly out at one another, Peter.

PETER STOCKMANN. Heaven forbid! I am not in the habit of flying out at people, as you call it. But I am entitled to request most emphatically that all arrangements shall be made in a business-like manner, through the proper channels, and shall be dealt with by the legally constituted authorities. I can allow no going behind our backs by any roundabout means. 247

DR. STOCKMAN. Have I ever at any time tried to go behind your backs?

PETER STOCKMANN. You have an ingrained tendency to take your own way, at all events; and that is almost equally inadmissible in a well-ordered community. The individual ought undoubtedly to acquiesce in subordinating himself to the community—or, to speak more accurately, to the authorities who have the care of the community's welfare.

DR. STOCKMAN. Very likely. But what the deuce has all this got to do with me? 257

PETER STOCKMANN. That is exactly what you never appear to be willing to learn, my dear Thomas. But, mark my words, some day you will have to suffer for it—sooner or later. Now I have told you. Good-bye.

DR. STOCKMANN. Have you taken leave of your senses? You are on the wrong scent altogether.

PETER STOCKMANN. I am not usually that. You must excuse me now if I— [*Calls into the dining-room.*] Good night, Katherine. Good night, gentlemen. [*Goes out.*]

MRS. STOCKMANN. [*Coming from the dining-room*] Has he gone?

DR. STOCKMANN. Yes, and in such a bad temper. 268

MRS. STOCKMANN. But, dear Thomas, what have you been doing to him again?

DR. STOCKMAN. Nothing at all. And, anyhow, he can't oblige me to make my report before the proper time.

MRS. STOCKMANN. What have you got to make a report to him about?

DR. STOCKMANN. Hm! Leave that to me, Katherine.—It is an extraordinary thing that the postman doesn't come.

[HOVSTAD, BILLING, *and* HORSTER *have got up from the table and come into the sitting-room.* EJLIF *and* MORTEN *come in after them.*] 278

BILLING. [*Stretching himself*] Ah!—one feels a new man after a meal like that.

HOVSTAD. The mayor wasn't in a very sweet temper tonight, then.

DR. STOCKMANN. It is his stomach; he has a wretched digestion.

HOVSTAD. I rather think it was us two of the "People's Messenger" that he couldn't digest.

MRS. STOCKMANN. I thought you came out of it pretty well with him.

HOVSTAD. Oh yes; but it isn't anything more than a sort of truce.

BILLING. That is just what it is! That word sums up the situation.

DR. STOCKMANN. We must remember that Peter is a lonely man, poor chap. He has no home comforts of any kind; nothing but [290 everlasting business. And all that infernal weak tea wash that he pours into himself! Now then, my boys, bring chairs up to the table. Aren't we going to have that toddy, Katherine?

MRS. STOCKMANN. [*Going into the dining-room*] I am just getting it.

DR. STOCKMAN. Sit down here on the couch beside me, Captain Horster. We so seldom see you— Please sit down, my friends. [*They sit down at the table.* MRS. STOCKMANN *brings a tray, with a spirit-lamp, glasses, bottles, etc., upon it.*]

MRS. STOCKMANN. There you are! This is arrack, and this is rum, and this one is the brandy. Now every one must help himself.   301

DR. STOCKMANN. [*Taking a glass*] We will. [*They all mix themselves some toddy.*] And let us have the cigars. Ejlif, you know where the box is. And you, Morten, can fetch my pipe. [*The two boys go into the room on the right.*] I have a suspicion that Ejlif pockets a cigar now and then!—but I take no notice of it. [*Calls out.*] And my smoking-cap too, Morten. Katherine, you can tell him where I left it. Ah, he has got it. [*The boys bring the various things.*] Now, my friends. I stick to my pipe, you know. This one has seen plenty of bad weather with me up north. [*Touches glasses with them.*] Your good health! Ah! it is good to be sitting snug and warm here.   312

MRS. STOCKMANN. [*Who sits knitting*] Do you sail soon, Captain Horster?

HORSTER. I expect to be ready to sail next week.

MRS. STOCKMANN. I suppose you are going to America?

HORSTER. Yes, that is the plan.

MRS. STOCKMANN. Then you won't be able to take part in the coming election.

HORSTER. Is there going to be an election?

BILLING. Didn't you know?

HORSTER. No, I don't mix myself up with those things.   322

BILLING. But do you not take an interest in public affairs?

HORSTER. No, I don't know anything about politics.

BILLING. All the same, one ought to vote, at any rate.

HORSTER. Even if one doesn't know anything about what is going on?

BILLING. Doesn't know! What do you mean by that? A community is like a ship; everyone ought to be prepared to take the helm.

HORSTER. Maybe that is all very well on shore, but on board ship it wouldn't work.

HOVSTAD. It is astonishing how little most sailors care about what goes on on shore. 333

BILLING. Very extraordinary.

DR. STOCKMANN. Sailors are like birds of passage; they feel equally at home in any latitude. And that is only an additional reason for our being all the more keen, Hovstad. Is there to be anything of public interest in tomorrow's "Messenger"?

HOVSTAD. Nothing about municipal affairs. But the day after tomorrow I was thinking of printing your article—

DR. STOCKMANN. Ah, devil take it—my article! Look here, that must wait a bit. 342

HOVSTAD. Really? We had just got convenient space for it, and I thought it was just the opportune moment—

DR. STOCKMANN. Yes, yes, very likely you are right; but it must wait all the same. I will explain to you later.

[PETRA *comes in from the hall, in hat and cloak and with a bundle of exercise books under her arm.*]

PETRA. Good evening.

DR. STOCKMANN. Good evening, Petra; come along.

[*Mutual greetings;* PETRA *takes off her things and puts them down on a chair by the door.*] 352

PETRA. And you have all been sitting here enjoying yourselves, while I have been out slaving!

DR. STOCKMANN. Well, come and enjoy yourself too!

BILLING. May I mix a glass for you?

PETRA. [*Coming to the table*] Thanks, I would rather do it; you always mix it too strong. But I forgot, father—I have a letter for you.
[*Goes to the chair where she has laid her things.*]

DR. STOCKMANN. A letter? From whom?

PETRA. [*Looking in her coat pocket*] The postman gave it to me just as I was going out—   362

DR. STOCKMANN. [*Getting up and going to her*] And you only give it to me now!

PETRA. I really had not time to run up again. There it is!

DR. STOCKMANN. [*Seizing the letter*] Let's see, let's see, child! [*Looks at the address.*] Yes, that's all right!

MRS. STOCKMANN. Is it the one you have been expecting so anxiously, Thomas?

DR. STOCKMANN. Yes, it is. I must go to my room now and— Where shall I get a light, Katherine? Is there no lamp in my room again?   372

MRS. STOCKMANN. Yes, your lamp is all ready lit on your desk.

DR. STOCKMANN. Good, good. Excuse me for a moment—

[*Goes into his study.*]

PETRA. What do you suppose it is, mother?

MRS. STOCKMANN. I don't know; for the last day or two he has always been asking if the postman has not been.

BILLING. Probably some country patient.

PETRA. Poor old dad!—he will overwork himself soon. [*Mixes a glass for herself.*] There, that will taste good!

HOVSTAD. Have you been teaching in the evening school again today?   383

PETRA. [*Sipping from her glass*] Two hours.

BILLING. And four hours of school in the morning—

PETRA. Five hours.

MRS. STOCKMANN. And you have still got exercises to correct, I see.

PETRA. A whole heap, yes.

HORSTER. You are pretty full up with work too, it seems to me.

PETRA. Yes—but that is good. One is so delightfully tired after it.

BILLING. Do you like that?

PETRA. Yes, because one sleeps so well then.

MORTEN. You must be dreadfully wicked, Petra.   393

PETRA. Wicked?

MORTEN. Yes, because you work so much. Mr. Rörlund says work is a punishment for our sins.

EJLIF. Pooh, what a duffer you are, to believe a thing like that!

MRS. STOCKMANN. Come, come, Ejlif!

BILLING. [*Laughing*] That's capital!

HOVSTAD. Don't you want to work as hard as that, Morten?

MORTEN. No, indeed I don't.

HOVSTAD. What do you want to be, then?

MORTEN. I should like best to be a Viking. 403

EJLIF. You would have to be a pagan then.

MORTEN. Well, I could become a pagan, couldn't I?

BILLING. I agree with you, Morten! My sentiments, exactly.

MRS. STOCKMANN. [*Signalling to him*] I am sure that is not true, Mr. Billing.

BILLING. Yes, I swear it is! I am a pagan, and I am proud of it. Believe me, before long we shall all be pagans.

MORTEN. And then shall be allowed to do anything we like?

BILLING. Well, you see, Morten— 412

MRS. STOCKMANN. You must go to your room now, boys; I am sure you have some lessons to learn for tomorrow.

EJLIF. I should like so much to stay a little longer—

MRS. STOCKMANN. No, no; away you go, both of you.

[*The boys say good-night and go into the room on the left.*]

HOVSTAD. Do you really think it can do the boys any harm to hear such things?

MRS. STOCKMANN. I don't know, but I don't like it.

PETRA. But you know, mother, I think you really are wrong about it. 422

MRS. STOCKMANN. Maybe, but I don't like it—not in our own home.

PETRA. There is so much falsehood both at home and at school. At home one must not speak, and at school we have to stand and tell lies to the children.

HORSTER. Tell lies?

PETRA. Yes, don't you suppose we have to teach them all sorts of things that we don't believe?

BILLING. That is perfectly true.

PETRA. If only I had the means I would start a school of my own, and it would be conducted on very different lines. 432

BILLING. Oh, bother the means—!

HORSTER. Well if you are thinking of that, Miss Stockmann, I shall be delighted to provide you with a school-room. The great big old house my father left me is standing almost empty; there is an immense dining-room downstairs—

PETRA. [*Laughing*] Thank you very much; but I am afraid nothing will come of it.

HOVSTAD. No, Miss Petra is much more likely to take to journalism, I expect. By the way, have you had time to do anything with that English story you promised to translate for us?   442

PETRA. No, not yet; but you shall have it in good time.

[DR. STOCKMANN *comes in from his room with an open letter in his hand.*]

DR. STOCKMANN. [*Waving the letter*] Well, now the town will have something new to talk about, I can tell you!

BILLING. Something new?

MRS. STOCKMANN. What is this?

DR. STOCKMANN. A great discovery, Katherine.

HOVSTAD. Really?

MRS. STOCKMANN. A discovery of yours?   452

DR. STOCKMANN. A discovery of mine. [*Walks up and down.*] Just let them come saying, as usual, that it is all fancy and a crazy man's imagination! But they will be careful what they say this time, I can tell you!

PETRA. But, father, tell us what it is.

DR. STOCKMANN. Yes, yes—only give me time, and you shall know all about it. If only I had Peter here now! It just shows how we men can go about forming our judgments, when in reality we are as blind as any moles—

HOVSTAD. What are you driving at, Doctor?   462

DR. STOCKMANN. [*Standing still by the table*] Isn't it the universal opinion that our town is a healthy spot?

HOVSTAD. Certainly.

DR. STOCKMANN. Quite an unusually healthy spot, in fact—a place that deserves to be recommended in the warmest possible manner either for invalids or for people who are well—

MRS. STOCKMANN. Yes, but my dear Thomas—

DR. STOCKMANN. And we have been recommending it and praising it—I have written and written, both in the "Messenger" and in pamphlets—   472

HOVSTAD. Well, what then?

DR. STOCKMANN. And the Baths—we have called them the "main artery of the town's life-blood," the "nerve-centre of our town," and the devil knows what else—

BILLING. "The town's pulsating heart" was the expression I once used on an important occasion—

DR. STOCKMANN. Quite so. Well, do you know what they really are, these great, splendid, much praised Baths, that have cost so much money—do you know what they are?

HOVSTAD. No, what are they?   482

MRS. STOCKMANN. Yes, what are they?

DR. STOCKMANN. The whole place is a pesthouse!

PETRA. The Baths, father?

MRS. STOCKMANN. [*At the same time*]. Our Baths!

HOVSTAD. But, Doctor—

BILLING. Absolutely incredible!

DR. STOCKMANN. The whole Bath establishment is a whited, poisoned sepulchre, I tell you—the gravest possible danger to the public health! All the nastiness up at Mölledal, all that stinking filth, is infecting the water in the conduit-pipes leading to the reservoir; and the same cursed, filthy poison oozes out on the shore too—   493

HORSTER. Where the bathing-place is?

DR. STOCKMANN. Just there.

HOVSTAD. How do you come to be so certain of all this, Doctor?

DR. STOCKMANN. I have investigated the matter most conscientiously. For a long time past I have suspected something of the kind. Last year we had some very strange cases of illness among the visitors—typhoid cases, and cases of gastric fever—

MRS. STOCKMANN. Yes, that is quite true.

DR. STOCKMANN. At the time, we supposed the visitors had been infected before they came; but later on, in the winter, I began to have a different opinion; and so I set myself to examine the water, as well as I could.   505

MRS. STOCKMANN. Then that is what you have been so busy with?

DR. STOCKMANN. Indeed I have been busy, Katherine. But here I had none of the necessary scientific apparatus, so I sent samples, both of the drinking-water and of the sea-water, up to the University, to have an accurate analysis made by a chemist.

HOVSTAD. And have you got that?

DR. STOCKMANN. [*Showing him the letter.*] Here it is! It proves the presence of decomposing organic matter in the water—it is full of infusoria. The water is absolutely dangerous to use, either internally or externally.   515

MRS. STOCKMANN. What a mercy you discovered it in time.

DR. STOCKMANN. You may well say so.

HOVSTAD. And what do you propose to do now, Doctor?

DR. STOCKMANN. To see the matter put right—naturally.

HOVSTAD. Can that be done?

DR. STOCKMANN. It must be done. Otherwise the Baths will be absolutely useless and wasted. But we need not anticipate that; I have a very clear idea what we shall have to do.

MRS. STOCKMANN. But why have you kept this all so secret, dear?

DR. STOCKMANN. Do you suppose I was going to run about the town gossiping about it, before I had absolute proof? No, thank you. I am not such a fool.   527

PETRA. Still, you might have told us—

DR. STOCKMANN. Not a living soul. But tomorrow you may run round to the old Badger—

MRS. STOCKMANN. Oh, Thomas! Thomas!

DR. STOCKMANN. Well, to your grandfather, then. The old boy will have something to be astonished at! I know he thinks I am cracked —and there are lots of other people think so too, I have noticed. But now these good folks shall see—they shall just see—! [*Walks about, rubbing his hands.*] There will be a nice upset in the town, Katherine; you can't imagine what it will be. All the conduit-pipes will have to be relaid.   538

HOVSTAD. [*Getting up*] All the conduit-pipes—?

DR. STOCKMANN. Yes, of course. The intake is too low down; it will have to be lifted to a position much higher up.

PETRA. Then you were right after all.

DR. STOCKMANN. Ah, you remember, Petra—I wrote opposing the plans before the work was begun. But at that time no one would listen to me. Well, I am going to let them have it, now! Of course I have prepared a report for the Baths Committee; I have had it ready for a week, and was only waiting for this to come. [*Shows the letter.*] Now it shall go off at once. [*Goes into his room and comes back with some papers.*] Look at that! Four closely written [549 sheets!—and the letter shall go with them. Give me a bit of paper, Katherine—something to wrap them up in. That will do! Now give it to—to— [*Stamps his foot.*]—what the deuce is her name?—give it to the maid, and tell her to take it at once to the Mayor.

[MRS. STOCKMANN *takes the packet and goes out through the dining-room.*]

PETRA. What do you think uncle Peter will say, father?   556

DR. STOCKMANN. What is there for him to say? I should think he would be very glad that such an important truth has been brought to light.

HOVSTAD. Will you let me print a short note about your discovery in the "Messenger"?

DR. STOCKMANN. I shall be very much obliged if you will.

HOVSTAD. It is very desirable that the public should be informed of it without delay.   564

DR. STOCKMANN. Certainly.

MRS. STOCKMANN. [*Coming back*] She has just gone with it.

BILLING. Upon my soul, Doctor, you are going to be the foremost man in the town!

DR. STOCKMANN. [*Walking about happily*] Nonsense! As a matter of fact I have done nothing more than my duty. I have only made a lucky find—that's all. Still, all the same—

BILLING. Hovstad, don't you think the town ought to give Dr. Stockmann some sort of testimonial?

HOVSTAD. I will suggest it, anyway.   574

BILLING. And I will speak to Aslaksen about it.

DR. STOCKMANN. No, my good friends, don't let us have any of that nonsense. I won't hear of anything of the kind. And if the Baths Committee should think of voting me an increase of salary, I will not accept it. Do you hear, Katherine?—I won't accept it.

MRS. STOCKMANN. You are quite right, Thomas.

PETRA. [*Lifting her glass*] Your health, father!

HOVSTAD *and* BILLING. Your health, Doctor! Good health!

HORSTER. [*Touches glasses with* DR. STOCKMANN] I hope it will bring you nothing but good luck.   584

DR. STOCKMANN. Thank you, thank you, my dear fellows! I feel tremendously happy! It is a splendid thing for a man to be able to feel that he has done a service to his native town and to his fellow citizens. Hurrah, Katherine!

[*He puts his arms round her and whirls her round and round, while she protests with laughing cries. They all laugh, clap their hands and cheer the* DOCTOR. *The boys put their heads in at the door to see what is going on.*]

CURTAIN

ACT TWO

SCENE.—*The same. The door into the dining-room is shut. It is morning.* MRS. STOCKMANN, *with a sealed letter in her hand, comes in from the dining-room, goes to the door of the* DOCTOR'S *study and peeps in.*

MRS. STOCKMANN. Are you in, Thomas?

DR. STOCKMANN. [*From within his room*] Yes, I have just come in. [*Comes into the room.*] What is it?

MRS. STOCKMANN. A letter from your brother.

DR. STOCKMANN. Aha, let us see! [*Opens the letter and reads:*] "I return herewith the manuscript you sent me"— [*Reads on in a low murmur.*] Hm!—

MRS. STOCKMANN. What does he say?

DR. STOCKMANN. [*Putting the papers in his pocket*] Oh, he only writes that he will come up here himself about midday.   10

MRS. STOCKMANN. Well, try and remember to be at home this time.

DR. STOCKMANN. That will be all right; I have got through all my morning visits.

MRS. STOCKMANN. I am extremely curious to know how he takes it.

DR. STOCKMANN. You will see he won't like it's having been I, and not he, that made the discovery.

MRS. STOCKMANN. Aren't you a little nervous about that?

DR. STOCKMANN. Oh, he really will be pleased enough, you know. But, at the same time, Peter is so confoundedly afraid of anyone's doing any service to the town except himself.   20

MRS. STOCKMANN. I will tell you what, Thomas—you should be good-natured, and share the credit of this with him. Couldn't you make out that it was he who set you on the scent of this discovery?

DR. STOCKMANN. I am quite willing. If only I can get the thing set right. I—

[MORTEN KIIL *puts his head in through the door leading from the hall, looks round in an enquiring manner and chuckles.*]

MORTEN KIIL. [*Slyly*] Is it—is it true?

MRS. STOCKMANN. [*Going to the door*] Father!—is it you?

DR. STOCKMANN. Ah, Mr. Kiil—good morning, good morning!

MRS. STOCKMANN. But come along in.   31

MORTEN KIIL. If it is true, I will; if not, I am off.

DR. STOCKMANN. If what is true?

MORTEN KIIL. This tale about the water-supply. Is it true?

DR. STOCKMANN. Certainly it is true. But how did you come to hear it?

MORTEN KIIL. [*Coming in*] Petra ran in on her way to the school—

DR. STOCKMANN. Did she?

MORTEN KIIL. Yes; and she declares that— I thought she was only making a fool of me, but it isn't like Petra to do that.

DR. STOCKMANN. Of course not. How could you imagine such a thing?   42

MORTEN KIIL. Oh well, it is better never to trust anybody; you may find you have been made a fool of before you know where you are. But it is really true, all the same?

DR. STOCKMANN. You can depend upon it that it is true. Won't you sit down? [*Settles him on the couch.*] Isn't it a real bit of luck for the town—

MORTEN KIIL. [*Suppressing his laughter*] A bit of luck for the town?

DR. STOCKMANN. Yes, that I made the discovery in good time.   51

MORTEN KIIL. [*As before*] Yes, yes, yes!—But I should never have thought you the sort of man to pull your own brother's leg like this!

DR. STOCKMANN. Pull his leg!

MRS. STOCKMANN. Really, father dear—

MORTEN KIIL. [*Resting his hands and his chin on the handle of his stick and winking slyly at the* DOCTOR] Let me see, what was the story? Some kind of beast that had got into the water-pipes, wasn't it?

DR. STOCKMANN. Infusoria—yes.

MORTEN KIIL. And a lot of these beasts had got in, according to Petra—a tremendous lot.   62

DR. STOCKMANN. Certainly; hundreds of thousands of them, probably.

MORTEN KIIL. But no one can see them—isn't that so?

DR. STOCKMANN. Yes; you can't see them.

MORTEN KIIL. [*With a quiet chuckle*] Damme—it's the finest story I have ever heard!

DR. STOCKMANN. What do you mean?

MORTEN KIIL. But you will never get the Mayor to believe a thing like that.   71

DR. STOCKMANN. We shall see.

MORTEN KIIL. Do you think he will be fool enough to—?

DR. STOCKMANN. I hope the whole town will be fools enough.

MORTEN KIIL. The whole town! Well, it wouldn't be a bad thing. It would just serve them right, and teach them a lesson. They think themselves so much cleverer than we old fellows. They hounded me out of the council; they did, I tell you—they hounded me out. Now they shall pay for it. You pull their legs too, Thomas!

DR. STOCKMANN. Really, I—   80

MORTEN KIIL. You pull their legs! [*Gets up.*] If you can work it so that the Mayor and his friends all swallow the same bait, I will give ten pounds to a charity—like a shot!

DR. STOCKMANN. That is very kind of you.

MORTEN KIIL. Yes, I haven't got much money to throw away, I can tell you; but if you can work this, I will give five pounds to a charity at Christmas.

[HOVSTAD *comes in by the hall door.*]

HOVSTAD. Good morning! [*Stops.*] Oh, I beg your pardon—

DR. STOCKMANN. Not at all; come in.   90

MORTEN KIIL. [*With another chuckle*] Oho!—is he in this too?

HOVSTAD. What do you mean?

DR. STOCKMANN. Certainly he is.

MORTEN KIIL. I might have known it! It must get into the papers. You know how to do it, Thomas! Set your wits to work. Now I must go.

DR. STOCKMANN. Won't you stay a little while?

MORTEN KIIL. No, I must be off now. You keep up this game for all it is worth; you won't repent it, I'm damned if you will!

[*He goes out;* MRS. STOCKMANN *follows him into the hall.*]

DR. STOCKMANN. [*Laughing*] Just imagine—the old chap doesn't believe a word of all this about the water-supply.   102

HOVSTAD. Oh, that was it, then?

DR. STOCKMANN. Yes, that was what we were talking about. Perhaps it is the same thing that brings you here?

HOVSTAD. Yes, it is. Can you spare me a few minutes, Doctor?

DR. STOCKMANN. As long as you like, my dear fellow.

HOVSTAD. Have you heard from the Mayor yet?

DR. STOCKMANN. Not yet. He is coming here later.

HOVSTAD. I have given the matter a great deal of thought since last night.

DR. STOCKMANN. Well?   112

HOVSTAD. From your point of view, as a doctor and a man of science, this affair of the water-supply is an isolated matter. I mean, you do not realise that it involves a great many other things.

DR. STOCKMANN. How do you mean?—Let us sit down, my dear fellow. No, sit here on the couch. [HOVSTAD *sits down on the couch,* DR. STOCKMANN *on a chair on the other side of the table.*] Now then. You mean that—?

HOVSTAD. You said yesterday that the pollution of the water was due to impurities in the soil.

DR. STOCKMANN. Yes, unquestionably it is due to that poisonous morass up at Mölledal. 123

HOVSTAD. Begging your pardon, doctor, I fancy it is due to quite another morass altogether.

DR. STOCKMANN. What morass?

HOVSTAD. The morass that the whole life of our town is built on and is rotting in.

DR. STOCKMANN. What the deuce are you driving at, Hovstad?

HOVSTAD. The whole of the town's interests have, little by little, got into the hands of a pack of officials.

DR. STOCKMANN. Oh, come!—they are not all officials. 132

HOVSTAD. No, but those that are not officials are at any rate the officials' friends and adherents; it is the wealthy folk, the old families in the town, that have got us entirely in their hands.

DR. STOCKMANN. Yes, but after all they are men of ability and knowledge.

HOVSTAD. Did they show any ability or knowledge when they laid the conduit-pipes where they are now?

DR. STOCKMANN. No, of course that was a great piece of stupidity on their part. But that is going to be set right now.

HOVSTAD. Do you think that will be all such plain sailing? 142

DR. STOCKMANN. Plain sailing or no, it has got to be done, anyway.

HOVSTAD. Yes, provided the press takes up the question.

DR. STOCKMANN. I don't think that will be necessary, my dear fellow; I am certain my brother—

HOVSTAD. Excuse me, doctor; I feel bound to tell you I am inclined to take the matter up.

DR. STOCKMANN. In the paper?

HOVSTAD. Yes. When I took over the "People's Messenger," my idea was to break up this ring of self-opinionated old fossils who had got hold of all the influence. 152

DR. STOCKMANN. But you know you told me yourself what the result had been; you nearly ruined your paper.

HOVSTAD. Yes, at the time we were obliged to climb down, a peg or two, it is quite true, because there was a danger of the whole project of the Baths coming to nothing if they failed us. But now

the scheme has been carried through, and we can dispense with these grand gentlemen.

DR. STOCKMANN. Dispense with them, yes; but we owe them a great debt of gratitude. 161

HOVSTAD. That shall be recognised ungrudgingly. But a journalist of my democratic tendencies cannot let such an opportunity as this slip. The bubble of official infallibility must be pricked. The superstition must be destroyed, like any other.

DR. STOCKMANN. I am whole-heartedly with you in that, Mr. Hovstad; if it is a superstition, away with it!

HOVSTAD. I should be very reluctant to bring the Mayor into it, because he is your brother. But I am sure you will agree with me that truth should be the first consideration.

DR. STOCKMANN. That goes without saying. [*With sudden emphasis.*] Yes, but—but— 172

HOVSTAD. You must not misjudge me. I am neither more self-interested nor more ambitious than most men.

DR. STOCKMANN. My dear fellow—who suggests anything of the kind?

HOVSTAD. I am of humble origin, as you know; and that has given me opportunities of knowing what is the most crying need in the humbler ranks of life. It is that they should be allowed some part in the direction of public affairs, Doctor. That is what will develop their faculties and intelligence and self-respect—

DR. STOCKMANN. I quite appreciate that. 182

HOVSTAD. Yes—and in my opinion a journalist incurs a heavy responsibility if he neglects a favorable opportunity of emancipating the masses—the humble and oppressed. I know well enough that in exalted circles I shall be called an agitator, and all that sort of thing; but they may call what they like. If only my conscience doesn't reproach me, then—

DR. STOCKMANN. Quite right! Quite right, Mr. Hovstad. But all the same—devil take it! [*A knock is heard at the door.*] Come in!

[ASLAKSEN *appears at the door. He is poorly but decently dressed, in black, with a slightly crumpled white neckcloth; he wears gloves and has a felt hat in his hand.*]

ASLAKSEN. [*Bowing*] Excuse my taking the liberty, Doctor— 194

DR. STOCKMANN. [*Getting up*] Ah, it is you, Aslaksen!

ASLAKSEN. Yes, Doctor.

HOVSTAD. [*Standing up*] Is it me you want, Aslaksen?

ASLAKSEN. No; I didn't know I should find you here. No, it was the Doctor I—

DR. STOCKMANN. I am quite at your service. What is it?

ASLAKSEN. Is what I heard from Mr. Billing true, sir—that you mean to improve our water-supply?

DR. STOCKMANN. Yes, for the Baths. 203

ASLAKSEN. Quite so, I understand. Well, I have come to say that I will back that up by every means in my power.

HOVSTAD. [*To the* DOCTOR] You see!

DR. STOCKMANN. I shall be very grateful to you but—

ASLAKSEN. Because it may be no bad thing to have us small tradesmen at your back. We form, as it were, a compact majority in the town—if we choose. And it is always a good thing to have the majority with you, Doctor. 211

DR. STOCKMANN. That is undeniably true; but I confess I don't see why such unusual precautions should be necessary in this case. It seems to me that such a plain, straightforward thing—

ASLAKSEN. Oh, it may be very desirable, all the same. I know our local authorities so well; officials are not generally very ready to act on proposals that come from other people. That is why I think it would not be at all amiss if we made a little demonstration.

HOVSTAD. That's right.

DR. STOCKMANN. Demonstration, did you say? What on earth are you going to make a demonstration about? 221

ASLAKSEN. We shall proceed with the greatest moderation, Doctor. Moderation is always my aim; it is the greatest virtue in a citizen—at least, I think so.

DR. STOCKMANN. It is well known to be a characteristic of yours, Mr. Aslaksen.

ASLAKSEN. Yes, I think I may pride myself on that. And this matter of the water-supply is of the greatest importance to us small tradesmen. The Baths promise to be a regular gold-mine for the town. We shall all make our living out of them, especially those of us who are householders. That is why we will back up the proj-

ect as strongly as possible. And as I am at present Chairman of the Householders' Association— 233

DR. STOCKMANN. Yes—?

ASLAKSEN. And, what is more, local secretary of the Temperance Society—you know, sir, I suppose, that I am a worker in the temperance cause?

DR. STOCKMANN. Of course, of course.

ASLAKSEN. Well, you can understand that I come into contact with a great many people. And as I have the reputation of a temperate and law-abiding citizen—like yourself, Doctor—I have a certain influence in the town, a little bit of power, if I may be allowed to say so. 243

DR STOCKMANN. I know that quite well, Mr. Aslaksen.

ASLAKSEN. So you see it would be an easy matter for me to set on foot some testimonial, if necessary.

DR. STOCKMANN. A testimonial?

ASLAKSEN. Yes, some kind of address of thanks from the townsmen for your share in a matter of such importance to the community. I need scarcely say that it would have to be drawn up with the greatest regard to moderation, so as not to offend the authorities—who, after all, have the reins in their hands. If we pay strict attention to that, no one can take it amiss, I should think! 253

HOVSTAD. Well, and even supposing they didn't like it—

ASLAKSEN. No, no, no; there must be no discourtesy to the authorities, Mr. Hovstad. It is no use falling foul of those upon whom our welfare so closely depends. I have done that in my time, and no good ever comes of it. But no one can take exception to a reasonable and frank expression of a citizen's views.

DR. STOCKMANN. [*Shaking him by the hand*] I can't tell you, dear Mr. Aslaksen, how extremely pleased I am to find such hearty support among my fellow citizens. I am delighted—delighted! Now, you will take a small glass of sherry, eh? 263

ASLAKSEN. No, thank you; I never drink alcohol of that kind.

DR. STOCKMANN. Well, what do you say to a glass of beer, then?

ASLAKSEN. Nor that either, thank you, Doctor. I never drink anything as early as this. I am going into town now to talk this over with one or two householders, and prepare the ground.

DR. STOCKMANN. It is tremendously kind of you, Mr. Aslaksen; but I really cannot understand the necessity for all these precautions. It seems to me that the thing should go of itself.

ASLAKSEN. The authorities are somewhat slow to move, Doctor. Far be it from me to seem to blame them— 273

HOVSTAD. We are going to stir them up in the paper tomorrow, Aslaksen.

ASLAKSEN. But not violently, I trust, Mr. Hovstad. Proceed with moderation, or you will do nothing with them. You may take my advice; I have gathered my experience in the school of life. Well, I must say good-bye, Doctor. You know now that we small trades-men are at your back at all events, like a solid wall. You have the compact majority on your side, Doctor.

DR. STOCKMANN. I am very much obliged, dear Mr. Aslaksen. [*Shakes hands with him.*] Good-bye, good-bye. 283

ASLAKSEN. Are you going my way, towards the printing-office, Mr. Hovstad?

HOVSTAD. I will come later; I have something to settle up first.

ASLAKSEN. Very well.

[*Bows and goes out;* STOCKMANN *follows him into the hall.*]

HOVSTAD. [*As* STOCKMANN *comes in again*] Well, what do you think of that, Doctor? Don't you think it is high time we stirred a little life into all this slackness and vacillation and cowardice?

DR. STOCKMANN. Are you referring to Aslaksen? 292

HOVSTAD. Yes, I am. He is one of those who are floundering in a bog—decent enough fellow though he may be, otherwise. And most of the people here are in just the same case—seesawing and edging first to one side and then to the other, so overcome with caution and scruple that they never dare to take any decided step.

DR. STOCKMANN. Yes, but Aslaksen seemed to me so thoroughly well-intentioned.

HOVSTAD. There is one thing I esteem higher than that; and that is for a man to be self-reliant and sure of himself.

DR. STOCKMANN. I think you are perfectly right there. 302

HOVSTAD. That is why I want to seize this opportunity, and try if I cannot manage to put a little virility into these well-intentioned people for once. The idol of Authority must be shattered in this

town. This gross and inexcusable blunder about the water-supply must be brought home to the mind of every municipal voter.

DR. STOCKMANN. Very well; if you are of opinion that it is for the good of the community, so be it. But not until I have had a talk with my brother.

HOVSTAD. Anyway, I will get a leading article ready; and if the Mayor refuses to take the matter up—   312

DR. STOCKMANN. How can you suppose such a thing possible?

HOVSTAD. It is conceivable. And in that case—

DR. STOCKMANN. In that case I promise you— Look here, in that case you may print my report—every word of it.

HOVSTAD. May I? Have I your word for it?

DR. STOCKMANN. [*Giving him the MS.*] Here it is; take it with you. It can do no harm for you to read it through, and you can give it back to me later on.

HOVSTAD. Good, good! That is what I will do. And now good-bye, Doctor.   322

DR. STOCKMANN. Good-bye, good-bye. You will see everything will run quite smoothly, Mr. Hovstad—quite smoothly.

HOVSTAD. Hm!—we shall see.   [*Bows and goes out.*]

DR. STOCKMANN. [*Opens the dining-room door and looks in*] Katherine! Oh, are you back, Petra?

PETRA. [*Coming in*] Yes, I have just come from the school.

MRS. STOCKMANN. [*Coming in*] Has he not been here yet?

DR. STOCKMANN. Peter? No. But I have had a long talk with Hovstad. He is quite excited about my discovery. I find it has a much wider bearing than I at first imagined. And he has put his paper at my disposal if necessity should arise.   333

MRS. STOCKMANN. Do you think it will?

DR. STOCKMANN. Not for a moment. But at all events it makes me feel proud to know that I have the liberal-minded independent press on my side. Yes, and—just imagine—I have had a visit from the Chairman of the Householders' Association!

MRS. STOCKMANN. Oh! What did he want?

DR. STOCKMANN. To offer me his support too. They will support me in a body if it should be necessary. Katherine—do you know what I have got behind me?   342

MRS. STOCKMANN. Behind you? No, what have you got behind you?

DR. STOCKMANN. The compact majority.

MRS. STOCKMANN. Really? Is that a good thing for you, Thomas?

DR. STOCKMANN. I should think it was a good thing. [*Walks up and down rubbing his hands.*] By Jove, it's a fine thing to feel this bond of brotherhood between oneself and one's fellow citizens!

PETRA. And to be able to do so much that is good and useful, father!

DR. STOCKMANN. And for one's own native town into the bargain, my child!

352

MRS. STOCKMANN. That was a ring at the bell.

DR. STOCKMANN. It must be he, then. [*A knock is heard at the door.*] Come in!

PETER STOCKMANN. [*Comes in from the hall*] Good morning.

DR. STOCKMANN. Glad to see you, Peter!

MRS. STOCKMANN. Good morning, Peter. How are you?

PETER STOCKMANN. So so, thank you. [*To* DR. STOCKMANN.] I received from you yesterday, after office-hours, a report dealing with the condition of the water at the Baths.

361

DR. STOCKMANN. Yes. Have you read it?

PETER STOCKMANN. Yes, I have.

DR. STOCKMANN. And what have you to say to it?

PETER STOCKMANN. [*With a sidelong glance*] Hm!—

MRS. STOCKMANN. Come along, Petra.

[*She and* PETRA *go into the room on the left.*]

PETER STOCKMANN. [*After a pause*] Was it necessary to make all these investigations behind my back?

DR. STOCKMANN. Yes, because until I was absolutely certain about it—

371

PETER STOCKMANN. Then you mean that you are absolutely certain now?

DR. STOCKMANN. Surely you are convinced of that.

PETER STOCKMANN. Is it your intention to bring this document before the Baths Committee as a sort of official communication?

DR. STOCKMANN. Certainly. Something must be done in the matter —and that quickly.

PETER STOCKMANN. As usual, you employ violent expressions in your report. You say, amongst other things, that what we offer visitors in our Baths is a permanent supply of poison.   381

DR. STOCKMANN. Well, can you describe it any other way, Peter? Just think—water that is poisonous, whether you drink it or bathe in it! And this we offer to the poor sick folk who come to us trustfully and pay us at an exorbitant rate to be made well again!

PETER STOCKMANN. And your reasoning leads you to this conclusion, that we must build a sewer to draw off the alleged impurities from Mölledal and must re-lay the water-conduits.

DR. STOCKMANN. Yes. Do you see any other way out of it? I don't.

PETER STOCKMANN. I made a pretext this morning to go and see the town engineer, and, as if only half seriously, broached the subject of these proposals as a thing we might perhaps have to take under consideration some time later on.   393

DR. STOCKMANN. Some time later on!

PETER STOCKMANN. He smiled at what he considered to be my extravagance, naturally. Have you taken the trouble to consider what your proposed alterations would cost? According to the information I obtained, the expenses would probably mount up to fifteen or twenty thousand pounds.

DR. STOCKMANN. Would it cost so much?

PETER STOCKMANN. Yes; and the worst part of it would be that the work would take at least two years.   402

DR. STOCKMANN. Two years? Two whole years?

PETER STOCKMANN. At least. And what are we to do with the Baths in the meantime? Close them? Indeed we should be obliged to. And do you suppose anyone would come near the place after it had got about that the water was dangerous?

DR. STOCKMANN. Yes, but, Peter, that is what it is.

PETER STOCKMANN. And all this at this juncture—just as the Baths are beginning to be known. There are other towns in the neighborhood with qualifications to attract visitors for bathing purposes. Don't you suppose they would immediately strain every nerve to divert the entire stream of strangers to themselves? Unquestionably they would; and then where should we be? We should probably

have to abandon the whole thing, which has cost us so much money —and then you would have ruined your native town. 416

DR. STOCKMANN. I—should have ruined—!

PETER STOCKMANN. It is simply and solely through the Baths that the town has before it any future worth mentioning. You know that just as well as I.

DR. STOCKMANN. But what do you think ought to be done, then?

PETER STOCKMANN. Your report has not convinced me that the condition of the water at the Baths is as bad as you represent it to be.

DR. STOCKMANN. I tell you it is even worse!—or at all events it will be in summer, when the warm weather comes. 425

PETER STOCKMANN. As I said, I believe you exaggerate the matter considerably. A capable physician ought to know what measures to take—he ought to be capable of preventing injurious influences or of remedying them if they become obviously persistent.

DR. STOCKMANN. Well? What more?

PETER STOCKMANN. The water-supply for the Baths is now an established fact, and in consequence must be treated as such. But probably the Committee, at its discretion, will not be disinclined to consider the question of how far it might be possible to introduce certain improvements consistent with a reasonable expenditure. 435

DR. STOCKMANN. And do you suppose that I will have anything to do with such a piece of trickery as that?

PETER STOCKMANN. Trickery!!

DR. STOCKMANN. Yes, it would be a trick—a fraud, a lie, a downright crime towards the public, towards the whole community!

PETER STOCKMANN. I have not, as I remarked before, been able to convince myself that there is actually any imminent danger.

DR. STOCKMANN. You have not! It is impossible that you should not be convinced. I know I have represented the facts absolutely truthfully and fairly. And you know it very well, Peter, only you won't acknowledge it. It was owing to your action that both the Baths and the water-conduits were built where they are; and that is what you won't acknowledge—that damnable blunder of yours. Pooh!—do you suppose I don't see through you? 449

PETER STOCKMANN. And even if that were true? If I perhaps guard my reputation somewhat anxiously, it is in the interests of the town.

Without moral authority I am powerless to direct public affairs as seems, to my judgment, to be best for the common good. And on that account—and for various other reasons, too—it appears to me to be a matter of importance that your report should not be delivered to the Committee. In the interests of the public, you must withhold it. Then, later on, I will raise the question and we will do our best, privately; but nothing of this unfortunate affair—not a single word of it—must come to the ears of the public.   459

DR. STOCKMANN. I am afraid you will not be able to prevent that now, my dear Peter.

PETER STOCKMANN. It must and shall be prevented.

DR. STOCKMANN. It is no use, I tell you. There are too many people that know about it.

PETER STOCKMANN. That know about it? Who? Surely you don't mean those fellows on the "People's Messenger"?

DR. STOCKMANN. Yes, they know. The liberal-minded independent press is going to see that you do your duty.

PETER STOCKMANN. [*After a short pause*] You are an extraordinarily independent man, Thomas. Have you given no thought to the consequences this may have for yourself?   471

DR. STOCKMANN. Consequences?—for me?

PETER STOCKMANN. For you and yours, yes.

DR. STOCKMANN. What the deuce do you mean?

PETER STOCKMANN. I believe I have always behaved in a brotherly way to you—have always been ready to oblige or to help you?

DR. STOCKMANN. Yes, you have, and I am grateful to you for it.

PETER STOCKMANN. There is no need. Indeed, to some extent I was forced to do so—for my own sake. I always hoped that, if I helped to improve your financial position, I should be able to keep some check on you.   481

DR. STOCKMANN. What!! Then it was only for your own sake—!

PETER STOCKMANN. Up to a certain point, yes. It is painful for a man in an official position to have his nearest relative compromising himself time after time.

DR. STOCKMANN. And do you consider that I do that?

PETER STOCKMANN. Yes, unfortunately, you do, without even being aware of it. You have a restless, pugnacious, rebellious disposition.

And then there is that disastrous propensity of yours to want to write about every sort of possible and impossible thing. The moment an idea comes into your head, you must needs go and write a newspaper article or a whole pamphlet about it. 492

DR. STOCKMANN. Well, but is it not the duty of a citizen to let the public share in any new ideas he may have?

PETER STOCKMANN. Oh, the public doesn't require any new ideas. The public is best served by the good, old-established ideas it already has.

DR. STOCKMANN. And that is your honest opinion?

PETER STOCKMANN. Yes, and for once I must talk frankly to you. Hitherto I have tried to avoid doing so, because I know how irritable you are; but now I must tell you the truth, Thomas. You have no conception what an amount of harm you do yourself by your impetuosity. You complain of the authorities, you even complain of the government—you are always pulling them to pieces; you insist that you have been neglected and persecuted. But what else can such a cantankerous man as you expect? 506

DR. STOCKMANN. What next! Cantankerous, am I?

PETER STOCKMANN. Yes, Thomas, you are an extremely cantankerous man to work with—I know that to my cost. You disregard everything that you ought to have consideration for. You seem completely to forget that it is me you have to thank for your appointment here as medical officer to the Baths—

DR. STOCKMANN. I was entitled to it as a matter of course!—I and nobody else! I was the first person to see that the town could be made into a flourishing watering-place, and I was the only one who saw it at that time. I had to fight single-handed in support of the idea for many years; and I wrote and wrote— 517

PETER STOCKMANN. Undoubtedly. But things were not ripe for the scheme then—though, of course, you could not judge of that in your out-of-the-way corner up north. But as soon as the opportune moment came I—and the others—took the matter into our hands—

DR. STOCKMANN. Yes, and made this mess of all my beautiful plan. It is pretty obvious now what clever fellows you were!

PETER STOCKMANN. To my mind the whole thing only seems to mean that you are seeking another outlet for your combativeness.

You want to pick a quarrel with your superiors—an old habit of yours. You cannot put up with any authority over you. You look [527 askance at anyone who occupies a superior official position; you regard him as a personal enemy, and then any stick is good enough to beat him with. But now I have called your attention to the fact that the town's interests are at stake—and, incidentally, my own too. And therefore I must tell you, Thomas, that you will find me inexorable with regard to what I am about to require you to do.

DR. STOCKMANN. And what is that?   534

PETER STOCKMANN. As you have been so indiscreet as to speak of this delicate matter to outsiders, despite the fact that you ought to have treated it as entirely official and confidential, it is obviously impossible to hush it up now. All sorts of rumors will get about directly, and everybody who has a grudge against us will take care to embellish these rumors. So it will be necessary for you to refute them publicly.

DR. STOCKMANN. I! How? I don't understand.   542

PETER STOCKMANN. What we shall expect is that, after making further investigations, you will come to the conclusion that the matter is not by any means as dangerous or as critical as you imagined in the first instance.

DR. STOCKMANN. Oho!—so that is what you expect!

PETER STOCKMANN. And, what is more, we shall expect you to make public profession of your confidence in the Committee and in their readiness to consider fully and conscientiously what steps may be necessary to remedy any possible defects.   551

DR. STOCKMANN. But you will never be able to do that by patching and tinkering at it—never! Take my word for it, Peter; I mean what I say, as deliberately and emphatically as possible.

PETER STOCKMANN. As an officer under the Committee, you have no right to any individual opinion.

DR. STOCKMANN. [*Amazed*] No right?

PETER STOCKMANN. In your official capacity, no. As a private person, it is quite another matter. But as a subordinate member of the staff of the Baths, you have no right to express any opinion which runs contrary to that of your superiors.   561

DR. STOCKMANN. This is too much! I, a doctor, a man of science, have no right to—!

PETER STOCKMANN. The matter in hand is not simply a scientific one. It is a complicated matter, and has its economic as well as its technical side.

DR. STOCKMANN. I don't care what it is! I intend to be free to express my opinion on any subject under the sun.

PETER STOCKMANN. As you please—but not on any subject concerning the Baths. That we forbid.   570

DR. STOCKMANN. [*Shouting*] You forbid—! You! A pack of—

PETER STOCKMANN. *I* forbid it—I, your chief; and if I forbid it, you have to obey.

DR. STOCKMANN. [*Controlling himself*] Peter—if you were not my brother—

PETRA [*Throwing open the door*] Father, you shan't stand this!

MRS. STOCKMANN. [*Coming in after her*] Petra, Petra!

PETER STOCKMANN. Oh, so you have been eavesdropping.

MRS. STOCKMANN. You were talking so loud, we couldn't help—

PETRA. Yes, I was listening.

PETER STOCKMANN. Well, after all, I am very glad—   581

DR. STOCKMANN. [*Going up to him*] You were saying something about forbidding and obeying?

PETER STOCKMANN. You obliged me to take that tone with you.

DR. STOCKMANN. And so I am to give myself the lie, publicly?

PETER STOCKMANN. We consider it absolutely necessary that you should make some such public statement as I have asked for.

DR. STOCKMANN. And if I do not—obey?

PETER STOCKMANN. Then we shall publish a statement ourselves to reassure the public.   590

DR. STOCKMANN. Very well; but in that case I shall use my pen against you. I stick to what I have said; I will show that I am right and that you are wrong. And what will you do then?

PETER STOCKMANN. Then I shall not be able to prevent your being dismissed.

DR. STOCKMANN. What—?

PETRA. Father—dismissed!

MRS. STOCKMANN. Dismissed!

PETER STOCKMANN. Dismissed from the staff of the Baths. I shall be obliged to propose that you shall immediately be given notice, and shall not be allowed any further participation in the Baths' affairs. 602

DR. STOCKMANN. You would dare to do that!

PETER STOCKMANN. It is you that are playing the daring game.

PETRA. Uncle, that is a shameful way to treat a man like father!

MRS. STOCKMANN. Do hold your tongue, Petra!

PETER STOCKMANN. [*Looking at* PETRA] Oh, so we volunteer our opinions already, do we? Of course. [*To* MRS. STOCKMANN.] Katherine, I imagine you are the most sensible person in this house. Use any influence you may have over your husband, and make him see what this will entail for his family as well as—

DR. STOCKMANN. My family is my own concern and nobody else's!

PETER STOCKMANN. —for his own family, as I was saying, as well as for the town he lives in. 614

DR. STOCKMANN. It is I who have the real good of the town at heart! I want to lay bare the defects that sooner or later must come to the light of day. I will show whether I love my native town.

PETER STOCKMANN. You, who in your blind obstinacy want to cut off the most important source of the town's welfare?

DR. STOCKMANN. The source is poisoned, man! Are you mad? We are making our living by retailing filth and corruption! The whole of our flourishing municipal life derives its sustenance from a lie!

PETER STOCKMANN. All imagination—or something even worse. The man who can throw out such offensive insinuations about his native town must be an enemy of our community. 625

DR. STOCKMANN. [*Going up to him*] Do you dare to—!

MRS. STOCKMANN. [*Throwing herself between them*] Thomas!

PETRA. [*Catching her father by the arm*] Don't lose your temper, father!

PETER STOCKMANN. I will not expose myself to violence. Now you have had a warning; so reflect on what you owe to yourself and your family. Good-bye. [*Goes out.*]

DR. STOCKMANN. [*Walking up and down*] Am I to put up with such treatment as this? In my own house, Katherine! What do you think of that! 635

MRS. STOCKMANN. Indeed it is both shameful and absurd, Thomas—

PETRA. If only I could give uncle a piece of my mind—

DR. STOCKMANN. It is my own fault. I ought to have flown out at him long ago!—shown my teeth!—bitten! To hear him call me an enemy to our community! Me! I shall not take that lying down, upon my soul!

MRS. STOCKMANN. But, dear Thomas, your brother has power on his side—

DR. STOCKMANN. Yes, but I have right on mine, I tell you.

MRS. STOCKMANN. Oh yes, right—right. What is the use of having right on your side if you have not got might? 646

PETRA. Oh, mother!—how can you say such a thing!

DR. STOCKMANN. Do you imagine that in a free country it is no use having right on your side? You are absurd, Katherine. Besides, haven't I got the liberal-minded, independent press to lead the way, and the compact majority behind me? That is might enough, I should think!

MRS. STOCKMANN. But, good heavens, Thomas, you don't mean to—? 654

DR. STOCKMANN. Don't mean to what?

MRS. STOCKMANN. To set yourself up in opposition to your brother.

DR. STOCKMANN. In God's name, what else do you suppose I should do but take my stand on right and truth?

PETRA. Yes, I was just going to say that.

MRS. STOCKMANN. But it won't do you any earthly good. If they won't do it, they won't.

DR. STOCKMANN. Oho, Katherine! Just give me time, and you will see how I will carry the war into their camp.

MRS. STOCKMANN. Yes, you carry the war into their camp, and you get your dismissal—that is what you will do. 665

DR. STOCKMANN. In any case I shall have done my duty towards the public—towards the community. I, who am called its enemy!

MRS. STOCKMANN. But towards your family, Thomas? Towards your own home! Do you think that is doing your duty towards those you have to provide for?

PETRA. Ah, don't think always first of us, mother.

MRS. STOCKMANN. Oh, it is easy for you to talk; you are able to shift for yourself, if need be. But remember the boys, Thomas; and think a little, too, of yourself, and of me—

DR. STOCKMANN. I think you are out of your senses, Katherine! If I were to be such a miserable coward as to go on my knees to Peter and his damned crew, do you suppose I should ever know an hour's peace of mind all my life afterwards? 678

MRS. STOCKMANN. I don't know anything about that; but God preserve us from the peace of mind we shall have, all the same, if you go on defying him! You will find yourself again without the means of subsistence, with no income to count upon. I should think we had had enough of that in the old days. Remember that, Thomas; think what that means.

DR. STOCKMANN. [*Collecting himself with a struggle and clenching his fists*] And this is what this slavery can bring upon a free, honorable man! Isn't it horrible, Katherine? 687

MRS. STOCKMANN. Yes, it is sinful to treat you so, it is perfectly true. But, good heavens, one has to put up with so much injustice in this world.—There are the boys, Thomas! Look at them! What is to become of them? Oh, no, no, you can never have the heart— [EJLIF *and* MORTEN *have come in while she was speaking, with their school books in their hands.*]

DR. STOCKMANN. The boys—! [*Recovers himself suddenly.*] No, even if the whole world goes to pieces, I will never bow my neck to this yoke! [*Goes towards his room.*]

MRS. STOCKMANN. [*Following him*] Thomas—what are you going to do! 698

DR. STOCKMANN. [*At his door*] I mean to have the right to look my sons in the face when they are grown men. [*Goes into his room.*]

MRS. STOCKMANN. [*Bursting into tears*] God help us all!

PETRA. Father is splendid! He will not give in.

[*The boys look on in amazement;* PETRA *signs to them not to speak.*]

CURTAIN

ACT THREE

SCENE—*The editorial office of the "People's Messenger." The entrance door is on the left-hand side of the back wall; on the right-hand side is another door with glass panels through which the printing-room can be seen. Another door in the right-hand wall. In the middle of the room is a large table covered with papers, newspapers, and books. In the foreground on the left a window, before which stand a desk and a high stool. There are a couple of easy chairs by the table, and other chairs standing along the wall. The room is dingy and uncomfortable; the furniture is old, the chairs stained and torn. In the printing-room the compositors are seen at work, and a printer is working a hand-press.* HOVSTAD *is sitting at the desk, writing.* BILLING *comes in from the right with* DR. STOCKMANN's *manuscript in his hand.*

BILLING. Well, I must say!

HOVSTAD. [*Still writing*] Have you read it through?

BILLING. [*Laying the MS. on the desk*] Yes, indeed I have.

HOVSTAD. Don't you think the Doctor hits them pretty hard?

BILLING. Hard? Bless my soul, he's crushing! Every word falls like—how shall I put it?—like the blow of a sledgehammer.

HOVSTAD. Yes, but they are not the people to throw up the sponge at the first blow.

BILLING. That is true; and for that reason we must strike blow upon blow until the whole of this aristocracy tumbles to pieces. As I sat in there reading this, I almost seemed to see a revolution in being.

12

HOVSTAD. [*Turning round*] Hush!—Speak so that Aslaksen cannot hear you.

BILLING. [*Lowering his voice*] Aslaksen is a chicken-hearted chap, a coward; there is nothing of the man in him. But this time you will insist on your own way, won't you? You will put the Doctor's article in?

HOVSTAD. Yes, and if the Mayor doesn't like it—

BILLING. That will be the devil of a nuisance.   20

HOVSTAD. Well, fortunately we can turn the situation to good account, whatever happens. If the Mayor will not fall in with the Doctor's project, he will have all the small tradesmen down on him —the whole of the Householders' Association and the rest of them. And if he does fall in with it, he will fall out with the whole crowd of large shareholders in the Baths, who up to now have been his most valuable supporters—

BILLING. Yes, because they will certainly have to fork out a pretty penny—

HOVSTAD. Yes, you may be sure they will. And in this way the ring will be broken up, you see, and then in every issue of the paper we will enlighten the public on the Mayor's incapability on one point and another, and make it clear that all the positions of trust in the town, the whole control of municipal affairs, ought to be put in the hands of the Liberals.   35

BILLING. That is perfectly true! I see it coming—I see it coming; we are on the threshold of a revolution!

[*A knock is heard at the door.*]

HOVSTAD. Hush! [*Calls out.*] Come in! [DR. STOCKMANN *comes in by the street door.* HOVSTAD *goes to meet him.*] Ah, it is you, Doctor! Well?

DR. STOCKMANN. You may set to work and print it, Mr. Hovstad!

HOVSTAD. Has it come to that, then?

BILLING. Hurrah!   44

DR. STOCKMANN. Yes, print away. Undoubtedly it has come to that. Now they must take what they get. There is going to be a fight in the town, Mr. Billing!

BILLING. War to the knife, I hope! We will get our knives to their throats, Doctor!

DR. STOCKMANN. This article is only a beginning. I have already got four or five more sketched out in my head. Where is Aslaksen?

BILLING. [*Calls into the printing-room*] Aslaksen, just come here for a minute!

HOVSTAD. Four or five more articles, did you say? On the same subject?   55

DR. STOCKMANN. No—far from it, my dear fellow. No, they are about quite another matter. But they all spring from the question of the water-supply and the drainage. One thing leads to another, you know. It is like beginning to pull down an old house, exactly.

BILLING. Upon my soul, it's true; you find you are not done till you have pulled all the old rubbish down.

ASLAKSEN. [*Coming in*] Pulled down? You are not thinking of pulling down the Baths surely, Doctor?

HOVSTAD. Far from it; don't be afraid.

DR. STOCKMANN. No, we meant something quite different. Well, what do you think of my article, Mr. Hovstad? 66

HOVSTAD. I think it is simply a masterpiece—

DR. STOCKMANN. Do you really think so? Well, I am very pleased, very pleased.

HOVSTAD. It is so clear and intelligible. One need have no special knowledge to understand the bearing of it. You will have every enlightened man on your side.

ASLAKSEN. And every prudent man too, I hope?

BILLING. The prudent and the imprudent—almost the whole town.

ASLAKSEN. In that case we may venture to print it. 75

DR. STOCKMANN. I should think so!

HOVSTAD. We will put it in tomorrow morning.

DR. STOCKMANN. Of course—you must not lose a single day. What I wanted to ask you, Mr. Aslaksen, was if you would supervise the printing of it yourself.

ASLAKSEN. With pleasure.

DR. STOCKMANN. Take care of it as if it were a treasure! No misprints—every word is important. I will look in again a little later; perhaps you will be able to let me see a proof. I can't tell you how eager I am to see it in print, and see it burst upon the public—

BILLING. Burst upon them—yes, like a flash of lightning! 86

DR. STOCKMANN. —and to have it submitted to the judgment of my intelligent fellow-townsmen. You cannot imagine what I have gone through today. I have been threatened first with one thing and then with another; they have tried to rob me of my most elementary rights as a man—

BILLING. What! Your rights as a man!

DR. STOCKMANN. —they have tried to degrade me, to make a coward of me, to force me to put personal interests before my most sacred convictions— 95

BILLING. That is too much—I'm damned if it isn't.

HOVSTAD. Oh, you mustn't be surprised at anything from that quarter.

DR. STOCKMANN. Well, they will get the worst of it with me; they may assure themselves of that. I shall consider the "People's Messenger" my sheet-anchor now, and every single day I will bombard them with one article after another, like bomb-shells—

ASLAKSEN. Yes, but—

BILLING. Hurrah!—it is war, it is war! 104

DR. STOCKMANN. I shall smite them to the ground—I shall crush them—I shall break down all their defences, before the eyes of the honest public! That is what I shall do!

ASLAKSEN. Yes, but in moderation, Doctor—proceed with moderation—

BILLING. Not a bit of it, not a bit of it! Don't spare the dynamite!

DR. STOCKMANN. Because it is not merely a question of water-supply and drains now, you know. No—it is the whole of our social life that we have got to purify and disinfect— 113

BILLING. Spoken like a deliverer!

DR. STOCKMANN. All the incapables must be turned out, you understand—and that in every walk of life! Endless vistas have opened themselves to my mind's eye today. I cannot see it all quite clearly yet, but I shall in time. Young and vigorous standard-bearers—those are what we need and must seek, my friends; we must have new men in command at all our outposts.

BILLING. Hear, hear! 121

DR. STOCKMANN. We only need to stand by one another, and it will all be perfectly easy. The revolution will be launched like a ship that runs smoothly off the stocks. Don't you think so?

HOVSTAD. For my part I think we have now a prospect of getting the municipal authority into the hands where it should lie.

ASLAKSEN. And if only we proceed with moderation, I cannot imagine that there will be any risk.

DR. STOCKMANN. Who the devil cares whether there is any risk or not? What I am doing, I am doing in the name of truth and for the sake of my conscience. 131

HOVSTAD. You are a man who deserves to be supported, Doctor.

ASLAKSEN. Yes, there is no denying that the Doctor is a true friend to the town—a real friend to the community, that he is.

BILLING. Take my word for it, Aslaksen, Dr. Stockmann is a friend of the people.

ASLAKSEN. I fancy the Householders' Association will make use of that expression before long. 138

DR. STOCKMANN. [*Affected, grasps their hands*] Thank you, thank you, my dear staunch friends. It is very refreshing to me to hear you say that; my brother called me something quite different. By Jove, he shall have it back, with interest! But now I must be off to see a poor devil— I will come back, as I said. Keep a very careful eye on the manuscript, Aslaksen, and don't for worlds leave out any of my notes of exclamation! Rather put one or two more in! Capital, capital! Well, good-bye for the present—good-bye, good-bye!

[*They show him to the door, and bow him out.*]

HOVSTAD. He may prove an invaluably useful man to us. 148

ASLAKSEN. Yes, so long as he confines himself to this matter of the Baths. But if he goes farther afield, I don't think it would be advisable to follow him.

HOVSTAD. Hm!—that all depends—

BILLING. You are so infernally timid, Aslaksen!

ASLAKSEN. Timid? Yes, when it is a question of the local authorities, I am timid, Mr. Billing; it is a lesson I have learnt in the school of experience, let me tell you. But try me in higher politics, in matters that concern the government itself, and then see if I am timid. 158

BILLING. No, you aren't, I admit. But this is simply contradicting yourself.

ASLAKSEN. I am a man with a conscience, and that is the whole matter. If you attack the government, you don't do the community any harm, anyway; those fellows pay no attention to attacks, you see—they go on just as they are, in spite of them. But *local* authorities are different; they *can* be turned out, and then perhaps you may

get an ignorant lot into office who may do irreparable harm to the householders and everybody else.   167

HOVSTAD. But what of the education of citizens by self-government—don't you attach any importance to that?

ASLAKSEN. When a man has interests of his own to protect, he cannot think of everything, Mr. Hovstad.

HOVSTAD. Then I hope I shall never have interests of my own to protect!

BILLING. Hear, hear!

ASLAKSEN. [*With a smile*] Hm! [*Points to the desk*] Mr. Sheriff Stensgaard was your predecessor at that editorial desk.

BILLING. [*Spitting*] Bah! That turncoat.   177

HOVSTAD. I am not a weathercock—and never will be.

ASLAKSEN. A politician should never be too certain of anything, Mr. Hovstad. And as for you, Mr. Billing, I should think it is time for you to be taking in a reef or two in your sails, seeing that you are applying for the post of secretary to the Bench.

BILLING. I—!

HOVSTAD. Are you, Billing?

BILLING. Well, yes—but you must clearly understand I am doing it only to annoy the bigwigs.   186

ASLAKSEN. Anyhow, it is no business of mine. But if I am to be accused of timidity and of inconsistency in my principles, this is what I want to point out: my political past is an open book. I have never changed, except perhaps to become a little more moderate, you see. My heart is still with the people; but I don't deny that my reason has a certain bias towards the authorities—the local ones, I mean.   [*Goes into the printing-room.*]

BILLING. Oughtn't we to try and get rid of him, Hovstad?

HOVSTAD. Do you know anyone else who will advance the money for our paper and printing bill?

BILLING. It is an infernal nuisance that we don't possess some capital to trade on.   198

HOVSTAD. [*Sitting down at his desk*] Yes, if we only had that, then—

BILLING. Suppose you were to apply to Dr. Stockmann?

HOVSTAD. [*Turning over some papers*] What is the use? He has got nothing.

BILLING. No, but he has got a warm man in the background, old Morten Kiil—"the Badger," as they call him.

HOVSTAD. [*Writing*] Are you so sure *he* has got anything?

BILLING. Good Lord, of course he has! And some of it must come to the Stockmanns. Most probably he will do something for the children, at all events.   209

HOVSTAD. [*Turning half round*] Are you counting on that?

BILLING. Counting on it? Of course I am not counting on anything.

HOVSTAD. That is right. And I should not count on the secretary-ship to the Bench either, if I were you; for I can assure you—you won't get it.

BILLING. Do you think I am not quite aware of that? My object is precisely *not* to get it. A slight of that kind stimulates a man's fighting power—it is like getting a supply of fresh bile—and I am sure one needs that badly enough in a hole-and-corner place like this, where so seldom anything happens to stir one up.   220

HOVSTAD. [*Writing*] Quite so, quite so.

BILLING. Ah, I shall be heard of yet!—Now I shall go and write the appeal to the Householders' Association.

[*Goes into the room on the right.*]

HOVSTAD. [*Sitting at his desk, biting his penholder, says slowly*] Hm!—that's it, is it? [*A knock is heard.*] Come in! [PETRA *comes in by the outer door.* HOVSTAD *gets up.*] What, you!—here?

PETRA. Yes, you must forgive me—

HOVSTAD. [*Pulling a chair forward*] Won't you sit down?

PETRA. No, thank you; I must go again in a moment.   230

HOVSTAD. Have you come with a message from your father, by any chance?

PETRA. No, I have come on my own account. [*Takes a book out of her coat pocket.*] Here is the English story.

HOVSTAD. Why have you brought it back?

PETRA. Because I am not going to translate it.

HOVSTAD. But you promised me faithfully—

PETRA. Yes, but then I had not read it. I don't suppose you have read it either?

HOVSTAD. No, you know quite well I don't understand English; but—   241

PETRA. Quite so. That is why I wanted to tell you that you must find something else. [*Lays the book on the table.*] You can't use this for the "People's Messenger."

HOVSTAD. Why not?

PETRA. Because it conflicts with all your opinions.

HOVSTAD. Oh, for that matter—

PETRA. You don't understand me. The burden of this story is that there is a supernatural power that looks after the so-called good people in this world and makes everything happen for the best in their case—while all the so-called bad people are punished.   251

HOVSTAD. Well, but that is all right. That is just what our readers want.

PETRA. And are you going to be the one to give it to them? For myself, I do not believe a word of it. You know quite well that things do not happen so in reality.

HOVSTAD. You are perfectly right, but an editor cannot always act as he would prefer. He is often obliged to bow to the wishes of the public in unimportant matters. Politics are the most important thing in life—for a newspaper, anyway; and if I want to carry my public with me on the path that leads to liberty and progress, I must not frighten them away. If they find a moral tale of this sort in the serial at the bottom of the page, they will be all the more ready to read what is printed above it; they feel more secure, as it were.   264

PETRA. For shame! You would never go and set a snare like that for your readers; you are not a spider!

HOVSTAD. [*Smiling*] Thank you for having such a good opinion of me. No; as a matter of fact that is Billing's idea and not mine.

PETRA. Billing's!

HOVSTAD. Yes; anyway he propounded that theory here one day. And it is Billing who is so anxious to have that story in the paper; I don't know anything about the book.

PETRA. But how can Billing, with his emancipated views—   273

HOVSTAD. Oh, Billing is a many-sided man. He is applying for the post of secretary to the Bench, too, I hear.

PETRA. I don't believe it, Mr. Hovstad. How could he possibly bring himself to do such a thing?

HOVSTAD. Ah, you must ask him that.

PETRA. I should never have thought it of him.

HOVSTAD. [*Looking more closely at her*] No? Does it really surprise you so much?

PETRA. Yes. Or perhaps not altogether. Really, I don't quite know—

HOVSTAD. We journalists are not worth much, Miss Stockmann.

PETRA. Do you really mean that?

HOVSTAD. I think so sometimes.

PETRA. Yes, in the ordinary affairs of everyday life, perhaps; I can understand that. But now, when you have taken a weighty matter in hand—

HOVSTAD. This matter of your father's, you mean?

PETRA. Exactly. It seems to me that now you must feel you are a man worth more than most.

HOVSTAD. Yes, today I do feel something of that sort.

PETRA. Of course you do, don't you? It is a splendid vocation you have chosen—to smooth the way for the march of unappreciated truths and new and courageous lines of thought. If it were nothing more than because you stand fearlessly in the open and take up the cause of an injured man—

HOVSTAD. Especially when that injured man is—ahem!—I don't rightly know how to—

PETRA. When that man is so upright and so honest, you mean?

HOVSTAD. [*More gently*] Especially when he is your father, I meant.

PETRA. [*Suddenly checked*] That?

HOVSTAD. Yes, Petra—Miss Petra.

PETRA. Is it *that*, that is first and foremost with you? Not the matter itself? Not the truth?—not my father's big generous heart?

HOVSTAD. Certainly—of course—that too.

PETRA. No, thank you; you have betrayed yourself, Mr. Hovstad, and now I shall never trust you again in anything.

HOVSTAD. Can you really take it so amiss in me that it is mostly for your sake—?

PETRA. I am angry with you for not having been honest with my father. You talked to him as if the truth and the good of the community were what lay nearest to your heart. You have made fools of both my father and me. You are not the man you made yourself out to be. And that I shall never forgive you—never!

HOVSTAD. You ought not to speak so bitterly, Miss Petra—least of all now.   317

PETRA. Why not now, especially?

HOVSTAD. Because your father cannot do without my help.

PETRA. [*Looking him up and down*] Are you that sort of man too? For shame!

HOVSTAD. No, no, I am not. This came upon me so unexpectedly—you must believe that.

PETRA. I know what to believe. Good-bye.

ASLAKSEN. [*Coming from the printing-room, hurriedly and with an air of mystery*] Damnation, Hovstad!—[*Sees* PETRA.] Oh, this is awkward—   327

PETRA. There is the book; you must give it to someone else.

[*Goes towards the door.*]

HOVSTAD. [*Following her*] But, Miss Stockmann—

PETRA. Good-bye.   [*Goes out.*]

ASLAKSEN. I say—Mr. Hovstad—

HOVSTAD. Well, well!—what is it?

ASLAKSEN. The Mayor is outside in the printing-room.

HOVSTAD. The Mayor, did you say?

ASLAKSEN. Yes, he wants to speak to you. He came in by the back door—didn't want to be seen, you understand.   337

HOVSTAD. What can he want? Wait a bit—I will go myself. [*Goes to the door of the printing-room, opens it, bows and invites* PETER STOCKMANN *in.*] Just see, Aslaksen, that no one—

ASLAKSEN. Quite so.   [*Goes into the printing-room.*]

PETER STOCKMANN. You did not expect to see me here, Mr. Hovstad?

HOVSTAD. No, I confess I did not.

PETER STOCKMANN. [*Looking round.*] You are very snug in here—very nice indeed.

HOVSTAD. Oh—

PETER STOCKMANN. And here I come, without any notice, to take up your time!

HOVSTAD. By all means, Mr. Mayor. I am at your service. But let me relieve you of your— [*Takes* STOCKMANN's *hat and stick and puts them on a chair.*] Won't you sit down?

PETER STOCKMANN. [*Sitting down by the table*] Thank you. [HOVSTAD *sits down.*] I have had an extremely annoying experience today, Mr. Hovstad.

HOVSTAD. Really? Ah well, I expect with all the various business you have to attend to—

PETER STOCKMANN. The Medical Officer of the Baths is responsible for what happened today.

HOVSTAD. Indeed? The Doctor?

PETER STOCKMANN. He has addressed a kind of report to the Baths Committee on the subject of certain supposed defects in the Baths.

HOVSTAD. Has he indeed?

PETER STOCKMANN. Yes—has he not told you? I thought he said—

HOVSTAD. Ah, yes—it is true he did mention something about—

ASLAKSEN. [*Coming from the printing-room*] I ought to have that copy—

HOVSTAD. [*Angrily*] Ahem!—there it is on the desk.

ASLAKSEN. [*Taking it*] Right.

PETER STOCKMANN. But look there—that is the thing I was speaking of!

ASLAKSEN. Yes, that is the Doctor's article, Mr. Mayor.

HOVSTAD. Oh, is *that* what you were speaking about?

PETER STOCKMANN. Yes, that is it. What do you think of it?

HOVSTAD. Oh, I am only a layman—and I have only taken a very cursory glance at it.

PETER STOCKMANN. But you are going to print it?

HOVSTAD. I cannot very well refuse a distinguished man—

ASLAKSEN. I have nothing to do with editing the paper, Mr. Mayor—

PETER STOCKMANN. I understand.

ASLAKSEN. I merely print what is put into my hands.

PETER STOCKMANN. Quite so.

ASLAKSEN. And so I must—

[*Moves off towards the printing-room.*]

PETER STOCKMANN. No, but wait a moment, Mr. Aslaksen. You will allow me, Mr. Hovstad?   387

HOVSTAD. If you please, Mr. Mayor.

PETER STOCKMANN. You are a discreet and thoughtful man, Mr. Aslaksen.

ASLAKSEN. I am delighted to hear you think so, sir.

PETER STOCKMANN. And a man of very considerable influence.

ASLAKSEN. Chiefly among the small tradesmen, sir.

PETER STOCKMANN. The small taxpayers are the majority—here as everywhere else.

ASLAKSEN. That is true.

PETER STOCKMANN. And I have no doubt you know the general trend of opinion among them, don't you?   398

ASLAKSEN. Yes, I think I may say I do, Mr. Mayor.

PETER STOCKMANN. Yes. Well, since there is such a praiseworthy spirit of self-sacrifice among the less wealthy citizens of our town—

ASLAKSEN. What?

HOVSTAD. Self-sacrifice?

PETER STOCKMANN. It is pleasing evidence of a public-spirited feeling, extremely pleasing evidence. I might almost say I hardly expected it. But you have a closer knowledge of public opinion than I.

ASLAKSEN. But, Mr. Mayor—   407

PETER STOCKMANN. And indeed it is no small sacrifice that the town is going to make.

HOVSTAD. The town?

ASLAKSEN. But I don't understand. Is it the Baths—?

PETER STOCKMANN. At a provisional estimate, the alterations that the Medical Officer asserts are desirable will cost somewhere about twenty thousand pounds.

ASLAKSEN. That is a lot of money, but—

PETER STOCKMANN. Of course it will be necessary to raise a municipal loan.   417

HOVSTAD. [*Getting up*] Surely you never mean that the town must pay—?

ASLAKSEN. Do you mean that it must come out of the municipal funds?—out of the ill-filled pockets of the small tradesmen?

PETER STOCKMANN. Well, my dear Mr. Aslaksen, where else is the money to come from?

ASLAKSEN. The gentlemen who own the Baths ought to provide that.

PETER STOCKMANN. The proprietors of the Baths are not in a position to incur any further expense.

ASLAKSEN. Is that absolutely certain, Mr. Mayor?

PETER STOCKMANN. I have satisfied myself that it is so. If the town wants these very extensive alterations, it will have to pay for them.

ASLAKSEN. But, damn it all—I beg your pardon—this is quite another matter, Mr. Hovstad!

HOVSTAD. It is, indeed.

PETER STOCKMANN. The most fatal part of it is that we shall be obliged to shut the Baths for a couple of years.

HOVSTAD. Shut them? Shut them altogether?

ASLAKSEN. For two years?

PETER STOCKMANN. Yes, the work will take as long as that—at least.

ASLAKSEN. I'm damned if we will stand that, Mr. Mayor! What are we householders to live upon in the meantime?

PETER STOCKMANN. Unfortunately, that is an extremely difficult question to answer, Mr. Aslaksen. But what would you have us do? Do you suppose we shall have a single visitor in the town, if we go about proclaiming that our water is polluted, that we are living over a plague spot, that the entire town—

ASLAKSEN. And the whole thing is merely imagination?

PETER STOCKMANN. With the best will in the world, I have not been able to come to any other conclusion.

ASLAKSEN. Well then, I must say it is absolutely unjustifiable of Dr. Stockmann—I beg your pardon, Mr. Mayor—

PETER STOCKMANN. What you say is lamentably true, Mr. Aslaksen. My brother has, unfortunately, always been a headstrong man.

ASLAKSEN. After this, do you mean to give him your support, Mr. Hovstad?

HOVSTAD. Can you suppose for a moment that I—?

PETER STOCKMANN. I have drawn up a short *résumé* of the situation as it appears from a reasonable man's point of view. In it I have indicated how certain possible defects might suitably be remedied without outrunning the resources of the Baths Committee.

HOVSTAD. Have you got it with you, Mr. Mayor?

PETER STOCKMANN. [*Fumbling in his pocket*] Yes, I brought it with me in case you should—   462

ASLAKSEN. Good Lord, there he is!

PETER STOCKMANN. Who? My brother?

HOVSTAD. Where? Where?

ASLAKSEN. He has just gone through the printing-room.

PETER STOCKMANN. How unlucky! I don't want to meet him here, and I had still several things to speak to you about.

HOVSTAD. [*Pointing to the door on the right*] Go in there for the present.

PETER STOCKMANN. But—?

HOVSTAD. You will only find Billing in there.   472

ASLAKSEN. Quick, quick, Mr. Mayor—he is just coming.

PETER STOCKMANN. Yes, very well; but see that you get rid of him quickly.

[*Goes out through the door on the right, which* ASLAKSEN *opens for him and shuts after him.*]

HOVSTAD. Pretend to be doing something, Aslaksen.

[*Sits down and writes.* ASLAKSEN *begins foraging among a heap of newspapers that are lying on a chair.*]

DR. STOCKMANN. [*Coming in from the printing-room*] Here I am again.   [*Puts down his hat and stick.*]   482

HOVSTAD. [*Writing*] Already, Doctor? Hurry up with what we were speaking about, Aslaksen. We are very pressed for time today.

DR. STOCKMANN. [*To* ASLAKSEN] No proof for me to see yet, I hear.

ASLAKSEN. [*Without turning round*] You couldn't expect it yet, Doctor.

DR. STOCKMANN. No, no; but I am impatient, as you can understand. I shall not know a moment's peace of mind till I see it in print.

HOVSTAD. Hm!—it will take a good while yet, won't it, Aslaksen?

ASLAKSEN. Yes, I am almost afraid it will.   492

DR. STOCKMANN. All right, my dear friends; I will come back. I do not mind coming back twice if necessary. A matter of such great importance—the welfare of the town at stake—it is no time to shirk trouble. [*Is just going, but stops and comes back.*] Look here—there is one thing more I want to speak to you about.

HOVSTAD. Excuse me, but could it not wait till some other time?

DR. STOCKMANN. I can tell you in half a dozen words. It is only this. When my article is read tomorrow and it is realized that I have been quietly working the whole winter for the welfare of the town—

502

HOVSTAD. Yes, but, Doctor—

DR. STOCKMANN. I know what you are going to say. You don't see how on earth it was any more than my duty—my obvious duty as a citizen. Of course it wasn't; I know that as well as you. But my fellow citizens, you know—! Good Lord, think of all the good souls who think so highly of me—!

ASLAKSEN. Yes, our townsfolk have had a very high opinion of you so far, Doctor.

DR. STOCKMANN. Yes, and that is just why I am afraid they— Well, this is the point; when this reaches them, especially the poorer classes, and sounds in their ears like a summons to take the town's affairs into their own hands for the future—

514

HOVSTAD. [*Getting up*] Ahem! Doctor, I won't conceal from you the fact—

DR. STOCKMANN. Ah!—I knew there was something in the wind! But I won't hear a word of it. If anything of that sort is being set on foot—

HOVSTAD. Of what sort?

DR. STOCKMANN. Well, whatever it is—whether it is a demonstration in my honor, or a banquet, or a subscription list for some presentation to me—whatever it is, you must promise me solemnly and faithfully to put a stop to it. You too, Mr. Aslaksen; do you understand?

525

HOVSTAD. You must forgive me, Doctor, but sooner or later we must tell you the plain truth—

[*He is interrupted by the entrance of* MRS. STOCKMANN, *who comes in from the street door.*]

MRS. STOCKMANN. [*Seeing her husband*] Just as I thought!

HOVSTAD. [*Going towards her*] You too, Mrs. Stockmann?

DR. STOCKMANN. What on earth do *you* want here, Katherine?

MRS. STOCKMANN. I should think you know very well what I want.

HOVSTAD. Won't you sit down? Or perhaps—

MRS. STOCKMANN. No, thank you; don't trouble. And you must not be offended at my coming to fetch my husband; I am the mother of three children, you know. 537

DR. STOCKMANN. Nonsense!—we know all about that.

MRS. STOCKMANN. Well, one would not give you credit for much thought for your wife and children today; if you had had that, you would not have gone and dragged us all into misfortune.

DR. STOCKMANN. Are you out of your senses, Katherine? Because a man has a wife and children, is he not to be allowed to proclaim the truth—is he not to be allowed to be an actively useful citizen—is he not to be allowed to do a service to his native town?

MRS. STOCKMANN. Yes, Thomas—in reason.

ASLAKSEN. Just what I say. Moderation is everything. 547

MRS. STOCKMANN. And that is why you wrong us, Mr. Hovstad, in enticing my husband away from his home and making a dupe of him in all this.

HOVSTAD. I certainly am making a dupe of no one—

DR. STOCKMANN. Making a dupe of me! Do you suppose *I* should allow myself to be duped?

MRS. STOCKMANN. It is just what you do. I know quite well you have more brains than anyone in the town, but you are extremely easily duped, Thomas. [*To* HOVSTAD.] Please realize that he loses his post at the Baths if you print what he has written— 557

ASLAKSEN. What!

HOVSTAD. Look here, Doctor—

DR. STOCKMANN. [*Laughing*] Ha—ha!—just let them try! No, no —they will take good care not to. I have got the compact majority behind me, let me tell you!

MRS. STOCKMANN. Yes, that is just the worst of it—your having any such horrid thing behind you.

DR. STOCKMANN. Rubbish, Katherine!—Go home and look after your house and leave me to look after the community. How can

you be so afraid, when I am so confident and happy? [*Walks up and down, rubbing his hands.*] Truth and the People will win the fight, you may be certain! I see the whole of the broad-minded middle class marching like a victorious army—! [*Stops beside a chair.*] What the deuce is that lying there?   571

ASLAKSEN. Good Lord!

HOVSTAD. Ahem!

DR. STOCKMANN. Here we have the topmost pinnacle of authority! [*Takes the* MAYOR'S *official hat carefully between his finger-tips and holds it up in the air.*]

MRS. STOCKMANN. The Mayor's hat!

DR. STOCKMANN. And here is the staff of office too. How in the name of all that's wonderful—?

HOVSTAD. Well, you see—   580

DR. STOCKMANN. Oh, I understand. He has been here trying to talk you over. Ha—ha!—he made rather a mistake there! And as soon as he caught sight of me in the printing-room— [*Bursts out laughing.*] Did he run away, Mr. Aslaksen?

ASLAKSEN. [*Hurriedly*] Yes, he ran away, Doctor.

DR. STOCKMANN. Ran away without his stick or his— Fiddlesticks! Peter doesn't run away and leave his belongings behind him. But what the deuce have you done with him? Ah!—in there, of course. Now you shall see, Katherine.

MRS. STOCKMANN. Thomas—please don't—!

ASLAKSEN. Don't be rash, Doctor.   591

[DR. STOCKMANN *has put on the* MAYOR'S *hat and taken his stick in his hand. He goes up to the door, opens it and stands with his hand to his hat at the salute.* PETER STOCKMANN *comes in, red with anger.* BILLING *follows him.*]

PETER STOCKMANN. What does this tomfoolery mean?

DR. STOCKMANN. Be respectful, my good Peter. I am the chief authority in the town now.   [*Walks up and down.*]

MRS. STOCKMANN. [*Almost in tears*] Really, Thomas!

PETER STOCKMANN. [*Following him about*] Give me my hat and stick.   601

DR. STOCKMANN. [*In the same tone as before*] If you are chief con-

stable, let me tell you that I am the Mayor—I am the master of the whole town, please understand!

PETER STOCKMANN. Take off my hat, I tell you. Remember it is part of an official uniform.

DR. STOCKMANN. Pooh! Do you think the newly awakened lion-hearted people are going to be frightened by an official hat? There is going to be a revolution in the town tomorrow, let me tell you. You thought you could turn me out; but now I shall turn you out—turn you out of all your various offices. Do you think I cannot? Listen to me. I have triumphant social forces behind me. Hovstad and Billing will thunder in the "People's Messenger," and Aslaksen will take the field at the head of the whole Householders' Association— 615

ASLAKSEN. That I won't, Doctor.

DR. STOCKMANN. Of course you will—

PETER STOCKMANN. Ah!—may I ask then if Mr. Hovstad intends to join this agitation?

HOVSTAD. No, Mr. Mayor.

ASLAKSEN. No, Mr. Hovstad is not such a fool as to go and ruin his paper and himself for the sake of an imaginary grievance.

DR. STOCKMANN. [*Looking round him*] What does this mean? 623

HOVSTAD. You have represented your case in a false light, Doctor, and therefore I am unable to give you my support.

BILLING. And after what the Mayor was so kind as to tell me just now, I—

DR. STOCKMANN. A false light! Leave that part of it to me. Only print my article; I am quite capable of defending it.

HOVSTAD. I am not going to print it. I cannot and will not and dare not print it.

DR. STOCKMANN. You dare not? What nonsense!—you are the editor; and an editor controls his paper, I suppose! 633

ASLAKSEN. No, it is the subscribers, Doctor.

PETER STOCKMANN. Fortunately, yes.

ASLAKSEN. It is public opinion—the enlightened public—householders and people of that kind; they control the newspapers.

DR. STOCKMANN. [*Composedly*] And I have all these influences against me?

ASLAKSEN. Yes, you have. It would mean the absolute ruin of the community if your article were to appear.

DR. STOCKMANN. Indeed.

642

PETER STOCKMANN. My hat and stick, if you please. [DR. STOCKMANN *takes off the hat and lays it on the table with the stick*. PETER STOCK-MANN *takes them up*.] Your authority as mayor has come to an untimely end.

DR. STOCKMANN. We have not got to the end yet. [*To* HOVSTAD.] Then it is quite impossible for you to print my article in the "People's Messenger"?

HOVSTAD. Quite impossible—out of regard for your family as well.

MRS. STOCKMANN. You need not concern yourself about his family, thank you, Mr. Hovstad.

652

PETER STOCKMANN. [*Taking a paper from his pocket*] It will be sufficient, for the guidance of the public, if this appears. It is an official statement. May I trouble you?

HOVSTAD. [*Taking the paper*] Certainly; I will see that it is printed.

DR. STOCKMANN. But not mine. Do you imagine that you can silence me and stifle the truth? You will not find it so easy as you suppose. Mr. Aslaksen, kindly take my manuscript at once and print it as a pamphlet—at my expense. I will have four hundred copies—no, five—six hundred.

662

ASLAKSEN. If you offered me its weight in gold, I could not lend my press for any such purpose, Doctor. It would be flying in the face of public opinion. You will not get it printed anywhere in the town.

DR. STOCKMANN. Then give it back to me.

HOVSTAD. [*Giving him the MS.*] Here it is.

DR. STOCKMANN. [*Taking his hat and stick*] It shall be made public all the same. I will read it out at a mass meeting of the townspeople. All my fellow citizens shall hear the voice of truth!

671

PETER STOCKMANN. You will not find any public body in the town that will give you the use of their hall for such a purpose.

ASLAKSEN. Not a single one, I am certain.

BILLING. No, I'm damned if you will find one.

MRS. STOCKMANN. But this is too shameful! Why should everyone turn against you like that?

DR. STOCKMANN. [*Angrily*] I will tell you why. It is because all the men in this town are old women—like you; they all think of nothing but their families, and never of the community.

MRS. STOCKMANN. [*Putting her arm into his*] Then I will show them that an—an old woman can be a man for once. I am going to stand by you, Thomas! 683

DR. STOCKMANN. Bravely said, Katherine! It shall be made public— as I am a living soul! If I can't hire a hall, I shall hire a drum, and parade the town with it and read it at every street corner.

PETER STOCKMANN. You are surely not such an arrant fool as that!

DR. STOCKMANN. Yes, I am.

ASLAKSEN. You won't find a single man in the whole town to go with you.

BILLING. No, I'm damned if you will.

MRS. STOCKMANN. Don't give in, Thomas. I will tell the boys to go with you. 693

DR. STOCKMANN. That is a splendid idea!

MRS. STOCKMANN. Morten will be delighted; and Ejlif will do whatever he does.

DR. STOCKMANN. Yes, and Petra!—and you too, Katherine!

MRS. STOCKMANN. No, I won't do that; but I will stand at the window and watch you, that's what I will do.

DR. STOCKMANN. [*Puts his arms round her and kisses her*] Thank you, my dear! Now you and I are going to try a fall, my fine gentlemen! I am going to see whether a pack of cowards can succeed in gagging a patriot who wants to purify society!

[*He and his wife go out by the street door.*]

PETER STOCKMANN. [*Shaking his head seriously*] Now he has sent *her* out of her senses, too.

CURTAIN

ACT FOUR

SCENE—*A big old-fashioned room in* CAPTAIN HORSTER'S *house. At the back folding-doors, which are standing open, lead to an ante-room. Three windows in the left-hand wall. In the middle of the opposite wall a platform has been erected. On this is a small table with two candles, a water-bottle and glass, and a bell. The room is lit by lamps placed between the windows. In the foreground on the left there is a table with candles and a chair. To the right is a door and some chairs standing near it. The room is nearly filled with a crowd of townspeople of all sorts, a few women and schoolboys being amongst them. People are still streaming in from the back, and the room is soon filled.*

1ST CIT. [*Meeting another*] Hullo, Lamstad! You here too?

2ND CIT. I go to every public meeting, I do.

3RD CIT. Brought your whistle too, I expect!

2ND CIT. I should think so. Haven't you?

3RD CIT. Rather! And old Evensen said he was going to bring a cow-horn, he did.

2ND CIT. Good old Evensen!   [*Laughter among the crowd.*]

4TH CIT. [*Coming up to them*] I say, tell me what is going on here tonight.

2ND CIT. Dr. Stockmann is going to deliver an address attacking the Mayor.   11

4TH CIT. But the Mayor is his brother.

1ST. CIT. That doesn't matter; Dr. Stockmann's not the chap to be afraid.

3RD CIT. But he is in the wrong; it said so in the "People's Messenger."

2ND CIT. Yes, I expect he must be in the wrong this time, because neither the Householders' Association nor the Citizens' Club would lend him their hall for his meeting.

1ST CIT. He couldn't even get the loan of the hall at the Baths.

2ND CIT. No, I should think not.   21

A MAN IN ANOTHER PART OF THE CROWD. I say—who are we to back up in this?

ANOTHER MAN, BESIDE HIM. Watch Aslaksen, and do as he does.

BILLING. [*Pushing his way through the crowd, with a writing-case under his arm*] Excuse me, gentlemen—do you mind letting me through? I am reporting for the "People's Messenger." Thank you very much! [*He sits down at the table on the left.*]

A WORKMAN. Who was that?

2ND WORKMAN. Don't you know him? It's Billing, who writes for Aslaksen's paper. 31

[CAPTAIN HORSTER *brings in* MRS. STOCKMANN *and* PETRA *through the door on the right.* EJLIF *and* MORTEN *follow them in.*]

HORSTER. I thought you might all sit here; you can slip out easily from here, if things get too lively.

MRS. STOCKMANN. Do you think there will be a disturbance?

HORSTER. One can never tell—with such a crowd. But sit down, and don't be uneasy.

MRS. STOCKMANN. [*Sitting down*] It was extremely kind of you to offer my husband the room.

HORSTER. Well, if nobody else would— 41

PETRA. [*Who has sat down beside her mother*] And it was a plucky thing to do, Captain Horster.

HORSTER. Oh, it is not such a great matter as all that.

[HOVSTAD *and* ASLAKSEN *make their way through the crowd.*]

ASLAKSEN. [*Going up to* HORSTER] Has the Doctor not come yet?

HORSTER. He is waiting in the next room.

[*Movement in the crowd by the door at the back.*]

HOVSTAD. Look—here comes the Mayor!

BILLING. Yes, I'm damned if he hasn't come after all! 50

[PETER STOCKMANN *makes his way gradually through the crowd, bows courteously and takes up a position by the wall on the left. Shortly afterwards* DR. STOCKMANN *comes in by the right-hand door. He is dressed in a black frockcoat, with a white tie. There is a little feeble applause, which is hushed down. Silence is obtained.*]

DR. STOCKMANN. [*In an undertone*] How do you feel, Katherine?

MRS. STOCKMANN. All right, thank you. [*Lowering her voice.*] Be
sure not to lose your temper, Thomas.   59

DR. STOCKMANN. Oh, I know how to control myself. [*Looks at his
watch, steps on to the platform and bows.*] It is a quarter past—so
I will begin.   [*Takes his MS. out of his pocket.*]

ASLAKSEN. I think we ought to elect a chairman first.

DR. STOCKMANN. No, it is quite unnecessary.

SOME OF THE CROWD. Yes—yes!

PETER STOCKMANN. I certainly think, too, that we ought to have
a chairman.

DR. STOCKMANN. But I have called this meeting to deliver a lecture,
Peter.

PETER STOCKMANN. Dr. Stockmann's lecture may possibly lead to
a considerable conflict of opinion.   71

VOICES IN THE CROWD. A chairman! A chairman!

HOVSTAD. The general wish of the meeting seems to be that a
chairman shall be elected.

DR. STOCKMANN. [*Restraining himself*] Very well—let the meeting
have its way.

ASLAKSEN. Will the Mayor be good enough to undertake the task?

THREE MEN. [*Clapping their hands*] Bravo! Bravo!

PETER STOCKMANN. For various reasons, which you will easily
understand, I must beg to be excused. But fortunately we have
amongst us a man who I think will be acceptable to you all. I refer
to the President of the Householders' Association, Mr. Aslaksen.

SEVERAL VOICES. Yes—Aslaksen! Bravo, Aslaksen!   83
[DR. STOCKMANN *takes up his MS. and walks up and down the platform.*]

ASLAKSEN. Since my fellow-citizens choose to entrust me with this
duty, I cannot refuse.

                    [*Loud applause.* ASLAKSEN *mounts the platform.*]

BILLING. [*Writing*] "Mr. Aslaksen was elected with enthusiasm."

ASLAKSEN. And now, as I am in this position, I should like to say
a few brief words. I am a quiet and peaceable man, who believes
in discreet moderation, and—and—in moderate discretion. All my
friends can bear witness to that.   93

SEVERAL VOICES. That's right! That's right, Aslaksen!

ASLAKSEN. I have learnt in the school of life and experience that moderation is the most valuable virtue a citizen can possess—

PETER STOCKMANN. Hear, hear!

ASLAKSEN. —And moreover that discretion and moderation are what enable a man to be of most service to the community. I would therefore suggest to our esteemed fellow citizen, who has called this meeting, that he should strive to keep strictly within the bounds of moderation.

A MAN BY THE DOOR. Three cheers for the Moderation Society!

A VOICE. Shame! 104

SEVERAL VOICES. Sh!—Sh!

ASLAKSEN. No interruptions, gentlemen, please! Does anyone wish to make any remarks?

PETER STOCKMANN. Mr. Chairman.

ASLAKSEN. The Mayor will address the meeting.

PETER STOCKMANN. In consideration of the close relationship in which, as you all know, I stand to the present Medical Officer of the Baths, I should have preferred not to speak this evening. But my official position with regard to the Baths and my solicitude for the vital interests of the town compel me to bring forward a motion. I venture to presume that there is not a single one of our citizens present who considers it desirable that unreliable and exaggerated accounts of the sanitary condition of the Baths and the town should be spread abroad. 118

SEVERAL VOICES. No, no! Certainly not! We protest against it!

PETER STOCKMANN. Therefore I should like to propose that the meeting should not permit the Medical Officer either to read or to comment on his proposed lecture.

DR. STOCKMANN. [*Impatiently*] Not permit—! What the devil—!

MRS. STOCKMANN. [*Coughing*] Ahem!—ahem!

DR. STOCKMANN. [*Collecting himself*] Very well. Go ahead!

PETER STOCKMANN. In my communication to the "People's Messenger," I have put the essential facts before the public in such a way that every fair-minded citizen can easily form his own opinion. From it you will see that the main result of the Medical Officer's proposals—apart from their constituting a vote of censure on the

leading men of the town—would be to saddle the taxpayers with an unnecessary expenditure of at least some thousands of pounds.   132

[*Sounds of disapproval among the audience, and some catcalls.*]

ASLAKSEN. [*Ringing his bell*] Silence, please, gentlemen! I beg to support the Mayor's motion. I quite agree with him that there is something behind this agitation started by the Doctor. He talks about the Baths; but it is a revolution he is aiming at—he wants to get the administration of the town put into new hands. No one doubts the honesty of the Doctor's intentions—no one will suggest that there can be any two opinions as to that. I myself am a believer in self-government for the people, provided it does not fall too heavily on the taxpayers. But that would be the case here; and that is why I will see Dr. Stockmann damned—I beg your pardon—before I go with him in the matter. You can pay too dearly for a thing sometimes; that is my opinion.   145

[*Loud applause on all sides.*]

HOVSTAD. I, too, feel called upon to explain my position. Dr. Stockmann's agitation appeared to be gaining a certain amount of sympathy at first, so I supported it as impartially as I could. But presently we had reason to suspect that we had allowed ourselves to be misled by misrepresentation of the state of affairs—

DR. STOCKMANN. Misrepresentation—!

HOVSTAD. Well, let us say a not entirely trustworthy representation. The Mayor's statement has proved that. I hope no one here has any doubt as to my liberal principles; the attitude of the "People's Messenger" towards important political questions is well known to everyone. But the advice of experienced and thoughtful men has convinced me that in purely local matters a newspaper ought to proceed with a certain caution.   159

ASLAKSEN. I entirely agree with the speaker.

HOVSTAD. And, in the matter before us, it is now an undoubted fact that Dr. Stockmann has public opinion against him. Now, what is an editor's first and most obvious duty, gentlemen? Is it not to work in harmony with his readers? Has he not received a sort of tacit mandate to work persistently and assiduously for the welfare of those whose opinions he represents? Or is it possible I am mistaken in that?

VOICES FROM THE CROWD. No, no! You are quite right!   168

HOVSTAD. It has cost me a severe struggle to break with a man in whose house I have been lately a frequent guest—a man who till today has been able to pride himself on the undivided goodwill of his fellow citizens—a man whose only, or at all events whose essential, failing is that he is swayed by his heart rather than his head.

A FEW SCATTERED VOICES. That is true! Bravo, Stockmann!

HOVSTAD. But my duty to the community obliged me to break with him. And there is another consideration that impels me to oppose him, and, as far as possible, to arrest him on the perilous course he has adopted; that is, consideration for his family—   178

DR. STOCKMANN. Please stick to the water-supply and drainage!

HOVSTAD. —consideration, I repeat, for his wife and his children for whom he has made no provision.

MORTEN. Is that us, mother?

MRS. STOCKMANN. Hush!

ASLAKSEN. I will now put the Mayor's proposition to the vote.

DR. STOCKMANN. There is no necessity! Tonight I have no intention of dealing with all that filth down at the Baths. No; I have something quite different to say to you.

PETER STOCKMANN. [*Aside*] What is coming now?   188

A DRUNKEN MAN. [*By the entrance door*] I am a taxpayer! And therefore I have a right to speak too! And my entire—firm—inconceivable opinion is—

A NUMBER OF VOICES. Be quiet at the back there!

OTHERS. He is drunk! Turn him out!   [*They turn him out.*]

DR. STOCKMANN. Am I allowed to speak?

ASLAKSEN. [*Ringing his bell*] Dr. Stockmann will address the meeting.

DR. STOCKMANN. I should like to have seen anyone, a few days ago, dare to attempt to silence me as has been done tonight! I would have defended my sacred rights as a man, like a lion! But now it is all one to me; I have something of even weightier importance to say to you.   201

[*The crowd presses nearer to him,* MORTEN KIIL *conspicuous among them.*]

DR. STOCKMANN. [*Continuing*] I have thought and pondered a great deal, these last few days—pondered over such a variety of things that in the end my head seemed too full to hold them—

PETER STOCKMANN. [*With a cough*] Ahem!

DR. STOCKMANN. —but I got them clear in my mind at last, and then I saw the whole situation lucidly. And that is why I am standing here tonight. I have a great revelation to make to you, my fellow citizens! I will impart to you a discovery of a far wider scope than the trifling matter that our water-supply is poisoned and our medicinal Baths are standing on pestiferous soil.   213

A NUMBER OF VOICES. [*Shouting*] Don't talk about the Baths! We won't hear you! None of that!

DR. STOCKMANN. I have already told you that what I want to speak about is the great discovery I have made lately—the discovery that all the sources of our *moral* life are poisoned and that the whole fabric of our civic community is founded on the pestiferous soil of falsehood.

VOICES OF DISCONCERTED CITIZENS. What is that he says?

PETER STOCKMANN. Such an insinuation—!

ASLAKSEN. [*With his hand on his bell*] I call upon the speaker to moderate his language.   224

DR. STOCKMANN. I have always loved my native town as a man only can love the home of his youthful days. I was not old when I went away from here; and exile, longing, and memories cast, as it were, an additional halo over both the town and its inhabitants. [*Some clapping and applause.*] And there I stayed, for many years, in a horrible hole far away up north. When I came into contact with some of the people that lived scattered about among the rocks, I often thought it would have been more service to the poor half-starved creatures if a veterinary doctor had been sent up there, instead of a man like me.   [*Murmurs among the crowd.*]

BILLING. [*Laying down his pen*] I'm damned if I have ever heard—!   236

HOVSTAD. It is an insult to a respectable population!

DR. STOCKMANN. Wait a bit! I do not think anyone will charge me with having forgotten my native town up there. I was like one of the eider-ducks brooding on its nest, and what I hatched was—

the plans for these Baths. [*Applause and protests.*] And then when fate at last decreed for me the great happiness of coming home again—I assure you, gentlemen, I thought I had nothing more in the world to wish for. Or rather, there was one thing I wished for— eagerly, untiringly, ardently—and that was to be able to be of service to my native town and the good of the community.   246

PETER STOCKMANN. [*Looking at the ceiling*] You chose a strange way of doing it—ahem!

DR. STOCKMANN. And so, with my eyes blinded to the real facts, I revelled in happiness. But yesterday morning—no, to be precise, it was yesterday afternoon—the eyes of my mind were opened wide, and the first thing I realized was the colossal stupidity of the authorities—

[*Uproar, shouts, and laughter.* MRS. STOCKMANN *coughs persistently.*]

PETER STOCKMANN. Mr. Chairman!

ASLAKSEN. [*Ringing his bell*] By virtue of my authority—!   256

DR. STOCKMANN. It is a petty thing to catch me up on a word, Mr. Aslaksen. What I mean is only that I got scent of the unbelievable piggishness our leading men had been responsible for down at the Baths. I can't stand leading men at any price!—I have had enough of such people in my time. They are like billy-goats in a young plantation; they do mischief everywhere. They stand in a free man's way, whichever way he turns, and what I should like best would be to see them exterminated like any other vermin—   [*Uproar.*]

PETER STOCKMANN. Mr. Chairman, can we allow such expressions to pass?   266

ASLAKSEN. [*With his hand on his bell*] Doctor—!

DR. STOCKMANN. I cannot understand how it is that I have only now acquired a clear conception of what these gentry are, when I had almost daily before my eyes in this town such an excellent specimen of them—my brother Peter—slow-witted and hidebound in prejudice—

[*Laughter, uproar, and hisses.* MRS. STOCKMANN *sits coughing assiduously.* ASLAKSEN *rings his bell violently.*]

THE DRUNKEN MAN. [*Who has got in again*] Is it me he is talking about? My name's Petersen, all right—but devil take me if I—

ANGRY VOICES. Turn out that drunken man! Turn him out.   277

[*He is turned out again.*]

PETER STOCKMANN. Who was that person?

1ST CIT. I don't know who he is, Mr. Mayor.

2ND CIT. He doesn't belong here.

3RD CIT. I expect he is a lumberman from over at [*the rest is inaudible*].

ASLAKSEN. He had obviously had too much beer.—Proceed, Doctor; but please strive to be moderate in your language.   285

DR. STOCKMANN. Very well, gentlemen, I will say no more about our leading men. And if anyone imagines, from what I have just said, that my object is to attack these people this evening, he is wrong—absolutely wide of the mark. For I cherish the comforting conviction that these parasites—all these venerable relics of a dying school of thought—are most admirably paving the way for their own extinction; they need no doctor's help to hasten their end. Nor is it folk of that kind who constitute the most pressing danger to the community. It is not they who are most instrumental in poisoning the sources of our moral life and infecting the ground on which we stand. It is not they who are the most dangerous enemies of truth and freedom amongst us.   297

SHOUTS FROM ALL SIDES. Who then? Who is it? Name! Name!

DR. STOCKMANN. You may depend upon it I shall name them! That is precisely the great discovery I made yesterday. [*Raises his voice.*] The most dangerous enemy of truth and freedom amongst us is the compact majority—yes, the damned compact Liberal majority—that is it! Now you know!

[*Tremendous uproar. Most of the crowd are shouting, stamping, and hissing. Some of the older men among them exchange stolen glances and seem to be enjoying themselves.* MRS. STOCKMANN *gets up, looking anxious.* EJLIF *and* MORTEN *advance threateningly upon some schoolboys who are playing pranks.* ASLAKSEN *rings his bell and begs for silence.* HOVSTAD *and* BILLING *both talk at once, but are inaudible. At last quiet is restored.*]   311

ASLAKSEN. As chairman, I call upon the speaker to withdraw the ill-considered expressions he has just used.

DR. STOCKMANN. Never, Mr. Aslaksen! It is the majority in our community that denies me my freedom and seeks to prevent my speaking the truth.

HOVSTAD. The majority always has right on its side.

BILLING. And truth too, by God!

DR. STOCKMANN. The majority *never* has right on its side. Never, I say! That is one of these social lies against which an independent, intelligent man must wage war. Who constitutes the majority of [321 the population in a country? Is it the clever folk or the stupid? I don't imagine you will dispute the fact that at present the stupid people are in an absolutely overwhelming majority all the world over. But, good Lord!—you can never pretend that it is right that the stupid folk should govern the clever ones! [*Uproar and cries.*] Oh, yes— you can shout me down, I know! but you cannot answer me. The majority has *might* on its side—unfortunately; but *right* it has *not*. I am in the right—I and a few other scattered individuals. The minority is always in the right. [*Renewed uproar.*]

HOVSTAD. Aha!—so Dr. Stockmann has become an aristocrat since the day before yesterday! 332

DR. STOCKMANN. I have already said that I don't intend to waste a word on the puny, narrow-chested, short-winded crew whom we are leaving astern. Pulsating life no longer concerns itself with them. I am thinking of the few, the scattered few amongst us, who have absorbed new and vigorous truths. Such men stand, as it were, at the outposts, so far ahead that the compact majority has not yet been able to come up with them; and there they are fighting for truths that are too newly-born into the world of consciousness to have any considerable number of people on their side as yet.

HOVSTAD. So the Doctor is a revolutionary now! 342

DR. STOCKMANN. Good heavens—of course I am, Mr. Hovstad! I propose to raise a revolution against the lie that the majority has the monopoly of the truth. What sort of truths are they that the majority usually supports? They are truths that are of such advanced age that they are beginning to break up. And if a truth is as old as that, it is also in a fair way to become a lie, gentlemen. [*Laughter and mocking cries.*] Yes, believe me or not, as you like; but truths are by no means as long-lived as Methuselah—as some

folk imagine. A normally constituted truth lives, let us say, as a rule seventeen or eighteen, or at most twenty years; seldom longer. But truths as aged as that are always worn frightfully thin, and nevertheless it is only then that the majority recognizes them and recommends them to the community as wholesome moral nourishment. There is no great nutritive value in that sort of fare, I can assure you; and, as a doctor, I ought to know. These "majority truths" are like last year's cured meat—like rancid, tainted ham; and they are the origin of the moral scurvy that is rampant in our communities.

360

ASLAKSEN. It appears to me that the speaker is wandering a long way from his subject.

PETER STOCKMANN. I quite agree with the Chairman.

DR. STOCKMANN. Have you gone clean out of your senses, Peter? I am sticking as closely to my subject as I can; for my subject is precisely this, that it is the masses, the majority—this infernal compact majority—that poisons the sources of our moral life and infects the ground we stand on.

HOVSTAD. And all this because the great, broad-minded majority of the people is prudent enough to show deference only to well-ascertained and well-approved truths?

371

DR. STOCKMANN. Ah, my good Mr. Hovstad, don't talk nonsense about well-ascertained truths! The truths of which the masses now approve are the very truths that the fighters at the outposts held to in the days of our grandfathers. We fighters at the outposts nowadays no longer approve of them; and I do not believe there is any other well-ascertained truth except this, that no community can live a healthy life if it is nourished only on such old marrowless truths.

HOVSTAD. But instead of standing there using vague generalities, it would be interesting if you would tell us what these old marrowless truths are, that we are nourished on.

381

[*Applause from many quarters.*]

DR. STOCKMANN. Oh, I could give you a whole string of such abominations; but to begin with I will confine myself to one wellapproved truth, which at bottom is a foul lie, but upon which nevertheless Mr. Hovstad and the "People's Messenger" and all the "Messenger's" supporters are nourished.

HOVSTAD. And that is—? 388

DR. STOCKMANN. That is, the doctrine you have inherited from your forefathers and proclaim thoughtlessly far and wide—the doctrine that the public, the crowd, the masses are the essential part of the population—that they constitute the People—that the common folk, the ignorant and incomplete element in the community, have the same right to pronounce judgment and to approve, to direct, and to govern, as the isolated, intellectually superior personalities in it. 396

BILLING. Well, damn me if ever I—

HOVSTAD. [*At the same time, shouting out*] Fellow-citizens, take good note of that!

A NUMBER OF VOICES. [*Angrily*] Oho!—we are not the People! Only the superior folks are to govern, are they?

A WORKMAN. Turn the fellow out, for talking such rubbish!

ANOTHER. Out with him!

ANOTHER. [*Calling out*] Blow your horn, Evensen! 404

[*A horn is blown loudly, amidst hisses and an angry uproar.*]

DR. STOCKMANN. [*When the noise has somewhat abated*] Be reasonable! Can't you stand hearing the voice of truth for once? I don't in the least expect you to agree with me all at once; but I must say I did expect Mr. Hovstad to admit I was right, when he had recovered his composure a little. He claims to be a freethinker—

VOICES. [*In murmurs of astonishment*] Freethinker, did he say? Is Hovstad a freethinker?

HOVSTAD. [*Shouting*] Prove it, Dr. Stockmann! When have I said so in print? 414

DR. STOCKMANN. [*Reflecting*] No, confound it, you are right!— you have never had the courage to. Well, I won't put you in a hole, Mr. Hovstad. Let us say it is I that am the freethinker, then. I am going to prove to you, scientifically, that the "People's Messenger" leads you by the nose in a shameful manner when it tells you that you—that the common people, the crowd, the masses are the real essence of the People. That is only a newspaper lie, I tell you! The common people are nothing more than the raw material of which a People is made. [*Groans, laughter and uproar.*] Well, isn't that the case? Isn't there an enormous difference between a well-bred and

an ill-bred strain of animals? Take, for instance, a common [425 barn-door hen. What sort of eating do you get from a shrivelled up old scrag of a fowl like that? Not much, do you? And what sort of eggs does it lay? A fairly good crow or a raven can lay pretty nearly as good an egg. But take a well-bred Spanish or Japanese hen, or a good pheasant or a turkey—then you will see the difference. Or take the case of dogs, with whom we humans are on such intimate terms. Think first of an ordinary common cur—I mean one of the horrible, coarse-haired, low-bred curs that do nothing but run about the streets and befoul the walls of the houses. Compare one of these curs with a poodle whose sires for many generations have been bred in a gentleman's house, where they have had the best of food and had the opportunity of hearing soft voices and music. Do you not think that the poodle's brain is developed to quite a different degree from that of the cur? Of course it is. It is puppies of well-bred poodles like that that showmen train to do incredibly clever tricks— things that a common cur could never learn to do even if it stood on its head.   [*Uproar and mocking cries.*]   442

A CITIZEN. [*Calls out*] Are you going to make out we are dogs, now?

ANOTHER CITIZEN. We are not animals, Doctor!

DR. STOCKMANN. Yes, but, bless my soul, we *are,* my friend! It is true we are the finest animals anyone could wish for; but, even amongst us, exceptionally fine animals are rare. There is a tremendous difference between poodle-men and cur-men. And the amusing part of it is that Mr. Hovstad quite agrees with me as long as it is a question of four-footed animals—   451

HOVSTAD. Yes, it is true enough as far as they are concerned.

DR. STOCKMANN. Very well. But as soon as I extend the principle and apply it to two-legged animals, Mr. Hovstad stops short. He no longer dares to think independently, or to pursue his ideas to their logical conclusion; so he turns the whole theory upside down and proclaims in the "People's Messenger" that it is the barn-door hens and street curs that are the finest specimens in the menagerie. But that is always the way, as long as a man retains the traces of common origin and has not worked his way up to intellectual distinction.   461

HOVSTAD. I lay no claim to any sort of distinction. I am the son of humble countryfolk, and I am proud that the stock I come from is rooted deep among the common people he insults.

VOICES. Bravo, Hovstad! Bravo! Bravo!

DR. STOCKMANN. The kind of common people I mean are not only to be found low down in the social scale; they crawl and swarm all around us—even in the highest social positions. You have only to look at your own fine, distinguished Mayor! My brother Peter is every bit as plebeian as anyone that walks in two shoes—   470

[*Laughter and hisses.*]

PETER STOCKMANN. I protest against personal allusions of this kind.

DR. STOCKMANN. [*Imperturbably*] —and that, not because he is, like myself, descended from some old rascal of a pirate from Pomerania or thereabouts—because that is who we are descended from—

PETER STOCKMANN. An absurd legend. I deny it!

DR. STOCKMANN. —but because he thinks what his superiors think and holds the same opinions as they. People who do that are, intellectually speaking, common people; and that is why my magnificent brother Peter is in reality so very far from any distinction—and consequently also so far from being liberal-minded.   481

PETER STOCKMANN. Mr. Chairman—!

HOVSTAD. So it is only the distinguished men that are liberal-minded in this country? We are learning something quite new!

[*Laughter.*]

DR. STOCKMANN. Yes, that is part of my new discovery too. And another part of it is that broad-mindedness is almost precisely the same thing as morality. That is why I maintain that it is absolutely inexcusable in the "People's Messenger" to proclaim, day in and day out, the false doctrine that the masses, the crowd, the compact majority have the monopoly of broad-mindedness and morality—and that vice and corruption and every kind of intellectual depravity are the result of culture, just as all the filth that is draining into [493 our Baths is the result of the tanneries up at Mölledal! [*Uproar and interruptions.* DR. STOCKMANN *is undisturbed, and goes on, carried away by his ardor, with a smile.*] And yet this same "People's Messenger" can go on preaching that the masses ought to be elevated to higher conditions of life! But, bless my soul, if the "Messenger's"

teaching is to be depended upon, this very raising up the masses would mean nothing more or less than setting them straightway upon the paths of depravity! Happily the theory that culture demoralizes is only an old falsehood that our forefathers believed in and we have inherited. No, it is ignorance, poverty, ugly condi- [503 tions of life that do the devil's work! In a house which does not get aired and swept every day—my wife Katherine maintains that the floor ought to be scrubbed as well, but that is a debatable question— in such a house, let me tell you, people will lose within two or three years the power of thinking or acting in a moral manner. Lack of oxygen weakens the conscience. And there must be a plentiful lack of oxygen in very many houses in this town, I should think, judging from the fact that the whole compact majority can be unconscientious enough to wish to build the town's prosperity on a quagmire of falsehood and deceit. 513

ASLAKSEN. We cannot allow such a grave accusation to be flung at a citizen community.

A CITIZEN. I move that the Chairman direct the speaker to sit down.

VOICES. [*Angrily*] Hear, hear! Quite right! Make him sit down!

DR. STOCKMANN. [*Losing his self-control*] Then I will go and shout the truth at every street corner! I will write it in other town's newspapers! The whole country shall know what is going on here!

HOVSTAD. It almost seems as if Dr. Stockmann's intention were to ruin the town.

DR. STOCKMANN. Yes, my native town is so dear to me that I would rather ruin it than see it flourishing upon a lie. 524

ASLAKSEN. This is really serious.

[*Uproar and catcalls.* MRS. STOCKMANN *coughs, but to no purpose; her husband does not listen to her any longer.*]

HOVSTAD. [*Shouting above the din*] A man must be a public enemy to wish to ruin a whole community!

DR. STOCKMANN. [*With growing fervor*] What does the destruction of a community matter, if it lives on lies! It ought to be razed to the ground, I tell you! All who live by lies ought to be exterminated like vermin! You will end by infecting the whole country; you will bring about such a state of things that the whole country

will deserve to be ruined. And if things come to that pass, I shall say from the bottom of my heart: Let the whole country perish, let all these people be exterminated!   537

VOICES FROM THE CROWD. That is talking like an out-and-out enemy of the people!

BILLING. There sounded the voice of the people, by all that's holy!

THE WHOLE CROWD. [*Shouting*] Yes, yes! He is an enemy of the people! He hates his country! He hates his own people!

ASLAKSEN. Both as a citizen and as an individual, I am profoundly disturbed by what we have had to listen to. Dr. Stockmann has shown himself in a light I should never have dreamed of. I am unhappily obliged to subscribe to the opinion which I have just heard my estimable fellow citizens utter; and I propose that we should give expression to that opinion in a resolution. I propose a resolution as follows: "This meeting declares that it considers Dr. Thomas Stockmann, Medical Officer of the Baths, to be an enemy of the people."   551

[*A storm of cheers and applause. A number of men surround the* DOCTOR *and hiss him.* MRS. STOCKMANN *and* PETRA *have got up from their seats.* MORTEN *and* EJLIF *are fighting the other schoolboys for hissing; some of their elders separate them.*]

DR. STOCKMANN. [*To the men who are hissing him*] Oh, you fools! I tell you that—

ASLAKSEN. [*Ringing his bell*] We cannot hear you now, Doctor. A formal vote is about to be taken; but, out of regard for personal feelings, it shall be by ballot and not verbal. Have you any clean paper, Mr. Billing?   561

BILLING. I have both blue and white here.

ASLAKSEN. [*Going to him*] That will do nicely; we shall get on more quickly that way. Cut it up into small strips—yes, that's it. [*To the meeting*] Blue means no; white means yes. I will come round myself and collect votes.

[PETER STOCKMANN *leaves the hall.* ASLAKSEN *and one or two others go round the room with the slips of paper in their hats.*]

1ST CIT. [*To* HOVSTAD] I say, what has come to the Doctor? What are we to think of it?

HOVSTAD. Oh, you know how headstrong he is. 571

2ND CIT. [*To* BILLING] Billing, you go to their house—have you ever noticed if the fellow drinks?

BILLING. Well, I'm hanged if I know what to say. There are always spirits on the table when you go.

3RD CIT. I rather think he goes quite off his head sometimes.

1ST CIT. I wonder if there is any madness in his family?

BILLING. I shouldn't wonder if there were.

4TH CIT. No, it is nothing more than sheer malice; he wants to get even with somebody for something or other.

BILLING. Well certainly he suggested a rise in his salary on one occasion lately, and did not get it. 582

THE CITIZENS. [*Together*] Ah!—then it is easy to understand how it is!

THE DRUNKEN MAN. [*Who has got amongst the audience again*] I want a blue one, I do! And I want a white one too!

VOICES. It's that drunken chap again! Turn him out!

MORTEN KIIL. [*Going up to* DR. STOCKMANN] Well, Stockmann, do you see what these monkey tricks of yours lead to?

DR. STOCKMANN. I have done my duty.

MORTEN KIIL. What was that you said about the tanneries at Mölledal? 592

DR. STOCKMANN. You heard well enough. I said they were the source of all the filth.

MORTEN KIIL. My tannery too?

DR. STOCKMANN. Unfortunately your tannery is by far the worst.

MORTEN KIIL. Are you going to put that in the papers?

DR. STOCKMANN. I shall conceal nothing.

MORTEN KIIL. That may cost you dear, Stockmann. [*Goes out.*]

A STOUT MAN. [*Going up to* CAPTAIN HORSTER, *without taking any notice of the ladies*] Well, Captain, so you lend your house to enemies of the people? 602

HORSTER. I imagine I can do what I like with my own possessions, Mr. Vik.

THE STOUT MAN. Then you can have no objection to my doing the same with mine.

HORSTER. What do you mean, sir?

THE STOUT MAN. You shall hear from me in the morning.

[*Turns his back on him and moves off.*]

PETRA. Was that not your owner, Captain Horster?

HORSTER. Yes, that was Mr. Vik, the shipowner.   611

ASLAKSEN. [*With the voting-papers in his hands, gets up on to the platform and rings his bell*] Gentlemen, allow me to announce the result. By the votes of everyone here except one person—

A YOUNG MAN. That is the drunk chap!

ASLAKSEN. By the votes of everyone here except a tipsy man, this meeting of citizens declares Dr. Thomas Stockmann to be an enemy of the people. [*Shouts and applause.*] Three cheers for our ancient and honorable citizen community! [*Renewed applause.*] Three cheers for our able and energetic Mayor, who has so loyally suppressed the promptings of family feeling! [*Cheers.*] The meeting is dissolved.   [*Gets down.*]   622

BILLING. Three cheers for the Chairman!

THE WHOLE CROWD. Three cheers for Aslaksen! Hurrah!

DR. STOCKMANN. My hat and coat, Petra! Captain, have you room on your ship for passengers to the New World?

HORSTER. For you and yours we will make room, Doctor.

DR. STOCKMANN. [*As* PETRA *helps him into his coat*] Good. Come, Katherine! Come, boys!

MRS. STOCKMANN. [*In an undertone*] Thomas, dear, let us go out by the back way.   631

DR. STOCKMANN. No back ways for me, Katherine. [*Raising his voice.*] You will hear more of this enemy of the people, before he shakes the dust off his shoes upon you! I am not so forgiving as a certain Person; I do not say: "I forgive you, for ye know not what ye do."

ASLAKSEN. [*Shouting*] That is a blasphemous comparison, Dr. Stockmann!

BILLING. It is, by God! It's dreadful for an earnest man to listen to.

A COARSE VOICE. Threatens us now, does he?

OTHER VOICES. [*Excitedly*] Let's go and break his windows! Duck him in the fjord!   642

ANOTHER VOICE. Blow your horn, Evensen! Pip, pip!

[*Horn-blowing, hisses, and wild cries.* DR. STOCKMANN *goes out through the hall with his family,* HORSTER *elbowing a way for them.*]

THE WHOLE CROWD. [*Howling after them as they go*] Enemy of the People! Enemy of the People!

BILLING. [*As he puts his papers together*] Well, I'm damned if I go and drink toddy with the Stockmanns tonight!

[*The crowd presses towards the exit. The uproar continues outside; shouts of "Enemy of the People!" are heard from without.*]

CURTAIN

ACT FIVE

SCENE—DR. STOCKMANN's *study. Bookcases and cabinets containing specimens line the walls. At the back is a door leading to the hall; in the foreground on the left, a door leading to the sitting-room. In the right-hand wall are two windows, of which all the panes are broken. The* DOCTOR's *desk, littered with books and papers, stands in the middle of the room, which is in disorder. It is morning.* DR. STOCKMANN *in dressing-gown, slippers, and a smoking-cap, is bending down and raking with an umbrella under one of the cabinets. After a little while he rakes out a stone.*

DR. STOCKMANN. [*Calling through the open sitting-room door*] Katherine, I have found another one.

MRS. STOCKMANN. [*From the sitting-room*] Oh, you will find a lot more yet, I expect.

DR. STOCKMANN. [*Adding the stone to a heap of others on the table*] I shall treasure these stones as relics. Ejlif and Morten shall look at them every day, and when they are grown up they shall inherit them as heirlooms. [*Rakes about under a bookcase.*] Hasn't—what the deuce is her name?—the girl, you know—hasn't she been to fetch the glazier yet? 10

MRS. STOCKMANN. [*Coming in*] Yes, but he said he didn't know if he would be able to come today.

DR. STOCKMANN. You will see he won't dare to come.

MRS. STOCKMANN. Well, that is just what Randine thought—that he didn't dare to, on account of the neighbors. [*Calls into the sitting-room.*] What is it you want, Randine? Give it to me. [*Goes in, and comes out again directly.*] Here is a letter for you, Thomas.

DR. STOCKMANN. Let me see it. [*Opens and reads it.*] Ah!—of course.

MRS. STOCKMANN. Who is it from? 20

DR. STOCKMANN. From the landlord. Notice to quit.

MRS. STOCKMANN. Is it possible? Such a nice man—

DR. STOCKMANN. [*Looking at the letter*] Does not dare do otherwise, he says. Doesn't like doing it, but dare not do otherwise—on account of his fellow citizens—out of regard for public opinion. Is in a dependent position—dare not offend certain influential men—

MRS. STOCKMANN. There, you see, Thomas!

DR. STOCKMANN. Yes, yes, I see well enough; the whole lot of them in the town are cowards; not a man among them dares do anything for fear of the others. [*Throws the letter onto the table.*] But it doesn't matter to us, Katherine. We are going to sail away to the New World, and— 32

MRS. STOCKMANN. But, Thomas, are you sure we are well advised to take this step?

DR. STOCKMANN. Are you suggesting that I should stay here, where they have pilloried me as an enemy of the people—branded me—broken my windows! And just look here, Katherine—they have torn a great rent in my black trousers too!

MRS. STOCKMANN. Oh, dear!—and they are the best pair you have got! 40

DR. STOCKMANN. You should never wear your best trousers when you go out to fight for freedom and truth. It is not that I care so much about the trousers, you know; you can always sew them up again for me. But that the common herd should dare to make this attack on me, as if they were my equals—that is what I cannot, for the life of me, swallow!

MRS. STOCKMANN. There is no doubt they have behaved very ill to you, Thomas; but is that sufficient reason for our leaving our native country for good and all? 49

DR. STOCKMANN. If we went to another town, do you suppose we should not find the common people just as insolent as they are here? Depend upon it, there is not much to choose between them. Oh, well, let the curs snap—that is not the worst part of it. The worst is that, from one end of this country to the other, every man is the slave of his Party. Although, as far as that goes, I daresay it is not much better in the free West either; the compact majority, and liberal public opinion, and all that infernal old bag of tricks are probably rampant there too. But there things are done on a larger scale, you see. They may kill you, but they won't put you to death by slow torture. They don't squeeze a free man's soul in a vice, as they do here. And, if need be, one can live in solitude. [*Walks up and down.*] If only I knew where there was a virgin forest or a small South Sea island for sale, cheap— 63

MRS. STOCKMANN. But think of the boys, Thomas.

DR. STOCKMANN. [*Standing still*] What a strange woman you are, Katherine! Would you prefer to have the boys grow up in a society like this? You saw for yourself last night that half the population are out of their minds; and if the other half have not lost their senses, it is because they are mere brutes, with no sense to lose.

MRS. STOCKMANN. But, Thomas dear, the imprudent things you said had something to do with it, you know. 71

DR. STOCKMANN. Well, isn't what I said perfectly true? Don't they turn every idea topsy-turvy? Don't they make a regular hotch-potch of right and wrong? Don't they say that the things I know are true are lies? The craziest part of it all is the fact of these "liberals," men of full age, going about in crowds imagining that they are the broad-minded party! Did you ever hear anything like it, Katherine?

MRS. STOCKMANN. Yes, yes, it's mad enough of them, certainly; but— [PETRA *comes in from the sitting-room.*] Back from school already? 80

PETRA. Yes. I have been given notice of dismissal.

MRS. STOCKMANN. Dismissal?

DR. STOCKMANN. You too?

PETRA. Mrs. Busk gave me my notice; so I thought it was best to go at once.

DR. STOCKMANN. You were perfectly right, too!

MRS. STOCKMANN. Who would have thought Mrs. Busk was a woman like that?

PETRA. Mrs. Busk isn't a bit like that, mother; I saw quite plainly how it hurt her to do it. But she didn't dare do otherwise, she said; and so I got my notice.   91

DR. STOCKMANN. [*Laughing and rubbing his hands*] She didn't dare do otherwise, either! It's delicious!

MRS. STOCKMANN. Well, after the dreadful scenes last night—

PETRA. It was not only that. Just listen to this, father!

DR. STOCKMANN. Well?

PETRA. Mrs. Busk showed me no less than three letters she received this morning—

DR. STOCKMANN. Anonymous, I suppose?

PETRA. Yes.   100

DR. STOCKMANN. Yes, because they didn't dare to risk signing their names, Katherine!

PETRA. And two of them were to the effect that a man, who has been our guest here, was declaring last night at the Club that my views on various subjects are extremely emancipated—

DR. STOCKMANN. You did not deny that, I hope?

PETRA. No, you know I wouldn't. Mrs. Busk's own views are tolerably emancipated, when we are alone together; but now that this report about me is being spread, she dare not keep me on any longer.   110

MRS. STOCKMANN. And someone who had been a guest of ours! That shows you the return you get for your hospitality, Thomas!

DR. STOCKMANN. We won't live in such a disgusting hole any longer. Pack up as quickly as you can, Katherine; the sooner we can get away the better.

MRS. STOCKMANN. Be quiet—I think I hear someone in the hall. See who it is, Petra.

PETRA. [*Opening the door*] Oh, it's you, Captain Horster! Do come in.

HORSTER. [*Coming in*] Good morning. I thought I would just come in and see how you were.   121

DR. STOCKMANN. [*Shaking his hand*] Thanks—that is really kind of you.

MRS. STOCKMANN. And thank you, too, for helping us through the crowd, Captain Horster.

PETRA. How did you manage to get home again?

HORSTER. Oh, somehow or other. I am fairly strong, and there is more sound than fury about these folk.

DR. STOCKMANN. Yes, isn't their swinish cowardice astonishing? Look here, I will show you something! There are all the stones they have thrown through my windows. Just look at them! I'm hanged if there are more than two decently large bits of hardstone in the whole heap; the rest are nothing but gravel—wretched little things. And yet they stood out there bawling and swearing that they would do me some violence; but as for *doing* anything—you don't see much of that in this town. 136

HORSTER. Just as well for you this time, Doctor!

DR. STOCKMANN. True enough. But it makes one angry all the same; because if some day it should be a question of a national fight in real earnest, you will see that public opinion will be in favor of taking to one's heels, and the compact majority will turn tail like a flock of sheep, Captain Horster. That is what is so mournful to think of; it gives me so much concern, that— No, devil take it, it is ridiculous to care about it! They have called me an enemy of the people, so an enemy of the people let me be! 145

MRS. STOCKMANN. You will never be that, Thomas.

DR. STOCKMANN. Don't swear to that, Katherine. To be called an ugly name may have the same effect as a pin scratch in the lung. And that hateful name—I can't get quit of it. It is sticking here in the pit of my stomach, eating into me like a corrosive acid. And no magnesia will remove it.

PETRA. Bah!—you should only laugh at them, father.

HORSTER. They will change their minds some day, Doctor.

MRS. STOCKMANN. Yes, Thomas, as sure as you are standing here.

DR. STOCKMANN. Perhaps, when it is too late. Much good may it do them! They may wallow in their filth then and rue the day when they drove a patriot into exile. When do you sail, Captain Horster? 158

HORSTER. Hm!—that was just what I had come to speak about—

DR. STOCKMANN. Why, has anything gone wrong with the ship?

HORSTER. No; but what has happened is that I am not to sail in it.

PETRA. Do you mean that you have been dismissed from your command?

HORSTER. [*Smiling*] Yes, that's just it.

PETRA. You too.

MRS. STOCKMANN. There, you see, Thomas!

DR. STOCKMANN. And that for the truth's sake! Oh, if I had thought such a thing possible— 168

HORSTER. You mustn't take it to heart; I shall be sure to find a job with some shipowner or other, elsewhere.

DR. STOCKMANN. And that is this man Vik—a wealthy man, independent of everyone and everything—! Shame on him!

HORSTER. He is quite an excellent fellow otherwise; he told me himself he would willingly have kept me on, if only he had dared—

DR. STOCKMANN. But he didn't dare? No, of course not.

HORSTER. It is not such an easy matter, he said, for a party man—

DR. STOCKMANN. The worthy man spoke the truth. A party is like a sausage machine; it mashes up all sorts of heads together into the same mincemeat—fatheads and blockheads, all in one mash! 179

MRS. STOCKMANN. Come, come, Thomas dear!

PETRA. [*To* HORSTER] If only you had not come home with us, things might not have come to this pass.

HORSTER. I do not regret it.

PETRA. [*Holding out her hand to him*] Thank you for that!

HORSTER. [*To* DR. STOCKMANN] And so what I came to say was that if you are determined to go away, I have thought of another plan—

DR. STOCKMANN. That's splendid!—if only we can get away at once. 189

MRS. STOCKMANN. Hush!—wasn't that someone knocking?

PETRA. That is uncle, surely.

DR. STOCKMANN. Aha! [*Calls out.*] Come in!

MRS. STOCKMANN. Dear Thomas, promise me definitely—
　　　　　[PETER STOCKMANN *comes in from the hall.*]

PETER STOCKMANN. Oh, you are engaged. In that case, I will—

DR. STOCKMANN. No, no, come in.

PETER STOCKMANN. But I wanted to speak to you alone.

MRS. STOCKMANN. We will go into the sitting-room in the meanwhile.

HORSTER. And I will look in again later.   200

DR. STOCKMANN. No, go in there with them, Captain Horster; I want to hear more about—

HORSTER. Very well, I will wait, then.

[*He follows* MRS. STOCKMANN *and* PETRA *into the sitting-room.*]

DR. STOCKMANN. I daresay you find it rather draughty here today. Put your hat on.

PETER STOCKMANN. Thank you, if I may. [*Does so.*] I think I caught cold last night; I stood and shivered—

DR. STOCKMANN. Really? I found it warm enough.

PETER STOCKMANN. I regret that it was not in my power to prevent those excesses last night.   211

DR. STOCKMANN. Have you anything particular to say to me besides that?

PETER STOCKMANN. [*Taking a big letter from his pocket*] I have this document for you, from the Baths Committee.

DR. STOCKMANN. My dismissal?

PETER STOCKMANN. Yes, dating from today. [*Lays the letter on the table.*] It gives us pain to do it; but, to speak frankly, we dared not do otherwise on account of public opinion.

DR. STOCKMANN. [*Smiling*] Dared not? I seem to have heard that word before, today.   221

PETER STOCKMANN. I must beg you to understand your position clearly. For the future you must not count on any practice whatever in the town.

DR. STOCKMANN. Devil take the practice! But why are you so sure of that?

PETER STOCKMANN. The Householders' Association is circulating a list from house to house. All right-minded citizens are being called upon to give up employing you; and I can assure you that not a single head of a family will risk refusing his signature. They simply dare not.   231

DR. STOCKMANN. No, no; I don't doubt it. But what then?

PETER STOCKMANN. If I might advise you, it would be best to leave the place for a little while—

DR. STOCKMANN. Yes, the propriety of leaving the place *has* occurred to me.

PETER STOCKMANN. Good. And then, when you have had six months to think things over, if, after mature consideration, you can persuade yourself to write a few words of regret, acknowledging your error—   240

DR. STOCKMANN. I might have my appointment restored to me, do you mean?

PETER STOCKMANN. Perhaps. It is not at all impossible.

DR. STOCKMANN. But what about public opinion, then? Surely you would not dare to do it on account of public feeling.

PETER STOCKMANN. Public opinion is an extremely mutable thing. And, to be quite candid with you, it is a matter of great importance to us to have some admission of that sort from you in writing.

DR. STOCKMANN. Oh, that's what you are after, is it? I will just trouble you to remember what I said to you lately about foxy tricks of that sort!   251

PETER STOCKMANN. Your position was quite different then. At that time you had reason to suppose you had the whole town at your back—

DR. STOCKMANN. Yes, and now I feel I have the whole town *on* my back—[*flaring up*] I would not do it if I had the devil and his dam on my back—! Never—never, I tell you!

PETER STOCKMANN. A man with a family has no right to behave as you do. You have no right to do it, Thomas.

DR. STOCKMANN. I have no right! There is only one single thing in the world a free man has no right to do. Do you know what that is?   262

PETER STOCKMANN. No.

DR. STOCKMANN. Of course you don't, but I will tell you. A free man has no right to soil himself with filth; he has no right to behave in a way that would justify his spitting in his own face.

PETER STOCKMANN. This sort of thing sounds extremely plausible, of course; and if there were no other explanation for your obstinacy— But as it happens there is.

DR. STOCKMANN. What do you mean?   270

PETER STOCKMANN. You understand very well what I mean. But, as your brother and as a man of discretion, I advise you not to build too much upon expectations and prospects that may so very easily fail you.

DR. STOCKMANN. What in the world is all this about?

PETER STOCKMANN. Do you really ask me to believe that you are ignorant of the terms of Mr. Kiil's will?

DR. STOCKMANN. I know that the small amount he possesses is to go to an institution for indigent old work-people. How does that concern me?   280

PETER STOCKMANN. In the first place, it is by no means a small amount that is in question. Mr. Kiil is a fairly wealthy man.

DR. STOCKMANN. I had no notion of that!

PETER STOCKMANN. Hm!—hadn't you really? Then I suppose you had no notion, either, that a considerable portion of his wealth will come to your children, you and your wife having a life income from the capital. Has he never told you so?

DR. STOCKMANN. Never, on my honor! Quite the reverse; he has consistently done nothing but fume at being so unconscionably heavily taxed. But are you perfectly certain of this, Peter?   290

PETER STOCKMANN. I have it from an absolutely reliable source.

DR. STOCKMANN. Then, thank God, Katherine is provided for—and the children too! I must tell her this at once— [*Calls out.*] Katherine, Katherine!

PETER STOCKMANN. [*Restraining him*] Hush, don't say a word yet!

MRS. STOCKMANN. [*Opening the door*] What is the matter?

DR. STOCKMANN. Oh, nothing, nothing; you can go back. [*She shuts the door.* DR. STOCKMANN *walks up and down in his excitement.*] Provided for!—Just think of it, we are all provided for! And for life! What a blessed feeling it is to know one is provided for!

PETER STOCKMANN. Yes, but that is just exactly what you are not. Mr. Kiil can alter his will any day he likes.   302

DR. STOCKMANN. But he won't do that, my dear Peter. The "Badger" is much too delighted at my attack on you and your wise friends.

PETER STOCKMANN. [*Starts and looks intently at him*] Ah, that throws a light on various things.

DR. STOCKMANN. What things?

PETER STOCKMANN. I see that the whole thing was a combined maneuver on your part and his. These violent, reckless attacks that you have made against the leading men of the town, under the pretence that it was in the name of truth—   312

DR. STOCKMANN. What about them?

PETER STOCKMANN. I see that they were nothing else than the stipulated price for that vindictive old man's will.

DR. STOCKMANN. [*Almost speechless*] Peter—you are the most disgusting plebeian I have ever met in all my life.

PETER STOCKMANN. All is over between us. Your dismissal is irrevocable—we have a weapon against you now.   [*Goes out.*]

DR. STOCKMANN. For shame! For shame! [*Calls out.*] Katherine, you must have the floor scrubbed after him! Let—what's her name—devil take it, the girl who has always got soot on her nose—   322

MRS. STOCKMANN. [*In the sitting-room*] Hush, Thomas, be quiet!

PETRA. [*Coming to the door*] Father, grandfather is here, asking if he may speak to you alone.

DR. STOCKMANN. Certainly he may. [*Going to the door.*] Come in, Mr. Kiil. [MORTEN KIIL *comes in.* DR. STOCKMANN *shuts the door after him.*] What can I do for you? Won't you sit down?

MORTEN KIIL. I won't sit. [*Looks around.*] You look very comfortable here today, Thomas.

DR. STOCKMANN. Yes, don't we?   331

MORTEN KIIL. Very comfortable—plenty of fresh air. I should think you have got enough today of that oxygen you were talking about yesterday. Your conscience must be in splendid order today, I should think.

DR. STOCKMANN. It is.

MORTEN KIIL. So I should think. [*Taps his chest.*] Do you know what I have got here?

DR. STOCKMANN. A good conscience, too, I hope.

MORTEN KIIL. Bah!—No, it is something better than that.   340
[*He takes a thick pocket-book from his breast-pocket, opens it, and displays a packet of papers.*]

DR. STOCKMANN. [*Looking at him in astonishment*] Shares in the Baths?

MORTEN KIIL. They were not difficult to get today.

DR. STOCKMANN. And you have been buying—?

MORTEN KIIL. As many as I could pay for.

DR. STOCKMANN. But, my dear Mr. Kiil—consider the state of the Baths' affairs!

MORTEN KIIL. If you behave like a reasonable man, you can soon set the Baths on their feet again. 351

DR. STOCKMANN. Well, you can see for yourself that I have done all I can, but— They are all mad in this town!

MORTEN KIIL. You said yesterday that the worst of this pollution came from my tannery. If that is true, then my grandfather and my father before me, and I myself, for many years past, have been poisoning the town like three destroying angels. Do you think I am going to sit quiet under that reproach?

DR. STOCKMANN. Unfortunately, I am afraid you will have to.

MORTEN KIIL. No, thank you. I am jealous of my name and reputation. They call me "the Badger," I am told. A badger is a kind of pig, I believe; but I am not going to give them the right to call me that. I mean to live and die a clean man. 363

DR. STOCKMANN. And how are you going to set about it?

MORTEN KIIL. You shall cleanse me, Thomas.

DR. STOCKMANN. I!

MORTEN KIIL. Do you know what money I have bought these shares with? No, of course you can't know—but I will tell you. It is the money that Katherine and Petra and the boys will have when I am gone. Because I have been able to save a little bit after all, you know.

DR. STOCKMANN. [*Flaring up*] And you have gone and taken Katherine's money for *this!* 373

MORTEN KIIL. Yes, the whole of the money is invested in the Baths now. And now I just want to see whether you are quite stark, staring mad, Thomas! If you still make out that these animals and other nasty things of that sort come from my tannery, it will be exactly as if you were to flay broad strips of skin from Katherine's body, and Petra's, and the boys'; and no decent man would do that —unless he were mad.

DR. STOCKMANN. [*Walking up and down*] Yes, but I *am* mad; I *am* mad!   382

MORTEN KIIL. You cannot be so absurdly mad as all that, when it is a question of your wife and children.

DR. STOCKMANN. [*Standing still in front of him*] Why couldn't you consult me about it, before you went and bought all that trash?

MORTEN KIIL. What is done cannot be undone.

DR. STOCKMANN. [*Walks about uneasily*] If only I were not so certain about it—! But I am absolutely convinced that I am right.

MORTEN KIIL. [*Weighing the pocket-book in his hand*] If you stick to your mad idea, this won't be worth much, you know. [*Puts the pocket-book in his pocket.*]   392

DR. STOCKMANN. But, hang it all! it might be possible for science to discover some prophylactic, I should think—or some antidote of some kind—

MORTEN KIIL. To kill these animals, do you mean?

DR. STOCKMANN. Yes, or to make them innocuous.

MORTEN KIIL. Couldn't you try some rat's-bane?

DR. STOCKMANN. Don't talk nonsense! They all say it is only imagination, you know. Well, let it go at that! Let them have their own way about it! Haven't the ignorant, narrow-minded curs reviled me as an enemy of the people?—and haven't they been ready to tear the clothes off my back too?   403

MORTEN KIIL. And broken all your windows to pieces!

DR. STOCKMANN. And then there is my duty to my family. I must talk it over with Katherine; she is great on those things.

MORTEN KIIL. That is right; be guided by a reasonable woman's advice.

DR. STOCKMANN. [*Advancing towards him*] To think you could do such a preposterous thing! Risking Katherine's money in this way, and putting me in such a horribly painful dilemma! When I look at you, I think I see the devil himself—   412

MORTEN KIIL. Then I had better go. But I must have an answer from you before two o'clock—yes or no. If it is no, the shares go to a charity, and that this very day.

DR. STOCKMANN. And what does Katherine get?

MORTEN KIIL. Not a halfpenny. [*The door leading to the hall opens, and* HOVSTAD *and* ASLAKSEN *make their appearance.*] Look at those two!

DR. STOCKMANN. [*Staring at them*] What the devil!—have *you* actually the face to come into my house? 421

HOVSTAD. Certainly.

ASLAKSEN. We have something to say to you, you see.

MORTEN KIIL. [*In a whisper*] Yes or no—before two o'clock.

ASLAKSEN. [*Glancing at* HOVSTAD] Aha! [MORTEN KIIL *goes out.*]

DR. STOCKMANN. Well, what do you want with me? Be brief.

HOVSTAD. I can quite understand that you are annoyed with us for our attitude at the meeting yesterday—

DR. STOCKMANN. Attitude, do you call it? Yes, it was a charming attitude! I call it weak, womanish—damnably shameful!

HOVSTAD. Call it what you like; we could not do otherwise.

DR. STOCKMANN. You *dared* not do otherwise—isn't that it? 432

HOVSTAD. Well, if you like to put it that way.

ASLAKSEN. But why did you not let us have word of it before-hand?—just a hint to Mr. Hovstad or to me?

DR. STOCKMANN. A hint? Of what?

ASLAKSEN. Of what was behind it all.

DR. STOCKMANN. I don't understand you in the least.

ASLAKSEN. [*With a confidential nod*] Oh, yes, you do, Dr. Stock-mann.

HOVSTAD. It is no good making a mystery of it any longer. 441

DR. STOCKMANN. [*Looking first at one of them and then at the other*] What the devil do you both mean?

ASLAKSEN. May I ask if your father-in-law is not going round the town buying up all the shares in the Baths?

DR. STOCKMANN. Yes, he has been buying Baths' shares today; but—

ASLAKSEN. It would have been more prudent to get someone else to do it—someone less nearly related to you.

HOVSTAD. And you should not have let your name appear in the affair. There was no need for anyone to know that the attack on the Baths came from you. You ought to have consulted me, Dr. Stockmann. 453

DR. STOCKMANN. [*Looks in front of him; then a light seems to dawn on him and he says in amazement:*] Are such things conceivable? Are such things possible?

ASLAKSEN. [*With a smile*] Evidently they are. But it is better to use a little finesse, you know.

HOVSTAD. And it is much better to have several persons in a thing of that sort, because the responsibility of each individual is lessened, when there are others with him.

DR. STOCKMANN. [*Composedly*] Come to the point, gentlemen. What do you want? 463

ASLAKSEN. Perhaps Mr. Hovstad had better—

HOVSTAD. No, you tell him, Aslaksen.

ASLAKSEN. Well, the fact is that, now we know the bearings of the whole affair, we think we might venture to put the "People's Messenger" at your disposal.

DR. STOCKMANN. Do you dare do that now? What about public opinion? Are you not afraid of a storm breaking upon our heads?

HOVSTAD. We will try to weather it. 471

ASLAKSEN. And you must be ready to go off quickly on a new tack, Doctor. As soon as your invective has done its work—

DR. STOCKMANN. Do you mean, as soon as my father-in-law and I have got hold of the shares at a low figure?

HOVSTAD. Your reasons for wishing to get the control of the Baths are mainly scientific, I take it.

DR. STOCKMANN. Of course; it was for scientific reasons that I persuaded the old "Badger" to stand in with me in the matter. So we will tinker at the conduit-pipes a little, and dig up a little bit of the shore, and it shan't cost the town a sixpence. That will be all right—eh? 482

HOVSTAD. I think so—if you have the "People's Messenger" behind you.

ASLAKSEN. The Press is a power in a free community, Doctor.

DR. STOCKMANN. Quite so. And so is public opinion. And you, Mr. Aslaksen—I suppose you will be answerable for the Householders' Association?

ASLAKSEN. Yes, and for the Temperance Society. You may rely on that.

DR. STOCKMANN. But, gentlemen—I really am ashamed to ask the question—but, what return do you—? 492

HOVSTAD. We should prefer to help you without any return whatever, believe me. But the "People's Messenger" is in rather a shaky condition; it doesn't go really well; and I should be very unwilling to suspend the paper now, when there is so much work to do here in the political way.

DR. STOCKMANN. Quite so; that would be a great trial to such a friend of the people as you are. [*Flares up.*] But I am an enemy of the people, remember! [*Walks about the room.*] Where have I put my stick? Where the devil is my stick? 501

HOVSTAD. What's that?

ASLAKSEN. Surely you never mean—?

DR. STOCKMANN. [*Standing still*] And suppose I don't give you a single penny of all I get out of it? Money is not very easy to get out of us rich folk, please to remember!

HOVSTAD. And you please to remember that this affair of the shares can be represented in two ways!

DR. STOCKMANN. Yes, and you are just the man to do it. If I don't come to the rescue of the "People's Messenger," you will certainly take an evil view of the affair; you will hunt me down, I can well imagine—pursue me—try to throttle me as a dog does a hare.

HOVSTAD. It is a natural law; every animal must fight for its own livelihood. 514

ASLAKSEN. And get its food where it can, you know.

DR. STOCKMANN. [*Walking about the room*] Then you go and look for yours in the gutter, because I am going to show you which is the strongest animal of us three! [*Finds an umbrella and brandishes it above his head.*] Ah, now—!

HOVSTAD. You are surely not going to use violence!

ASLAKSEN. Take care what you are doing with that umbrella.

DR. STOCKMANN. Out of the window with you, Mr. Hovstad!

HOVSTAD. [*Edging to the door*] Are you quite mad? 523

DR. STOCKMANN. Out of the window, Mr. Aslaksen! Jump, I tell you! You will have to do it, sooner or later.

ASLAKSEN. [*Running round the writing-table*] Moderation, Doc-

tor—I am a delicate man—I can stand so little—[*Calls out.*] Help, help!

[MRS. STOCKMANN, PETRA, *and* HORSTER *come in from the sitting-room.*]

MRS. STOCKMANN. Good gracious, Thomas! What is happening?

DR. STOCKMANN. [*Brandishing the umbrella*] Jump out, I tell you! Out into the gutter! 533

HOVSTAD. An assault on an unoffending man! I call you to witness, Captain Horster. [*Hurries out through the hall.*]

ASLAKSEN. [*Irresolutely*] If only I knew the way about here—
[*Steals out through the sitting-room.*]

MRS. STOCKMANN. [*Holding her husband back*] Control yourself, Thomas!

DR. STOCKMANN. [*Throwing down the umbrella*] Upon my soul, they have escaped after all.

MRS. STOCKMANN. What did they want you to do? 542

DR. STOCKMANN. I will tell you later on; I have something else to think about now. [*Goes to the table and writes something on a calling-card.*] Look there, Katherine; what is written there?

MRS. STOCKMANN. Three big No's; what does that mean?

DR. STOCKMANN. I will tell you that too, later on. [*Holds out the card to* PETRA.] There, Petra; tell sooty-face to run over to the "Badger's" with that as quickly as she can. Hurry up!
[PETRA *takes the card and goes out to the hall.*]

DR. STOCKMANN. Well, I think I have had a visit from every one of the devil's messengers today! But now I am going to sharpen my pen till they can feel its point; I shall dip it in venom and gall; I shall hurl my ink-pot at their heads! 554

MRS. STOCKMANN. Yes, but we are going away, you know, Thomas.
[PETRA *comes back.*]

DR. STOCKMANN. Well?

PETRA. She has gone with it.

DR. STOCKMANN. Good.—Going away, did you say? No, I'll be hanged if we are going away! We are going to stay where we are, Katherine! 561

PETRA. Stay here?

MRS. STOCKMANN. Here, in the town?

DR. STOCKMANN. Yes, here. This is the field of battle—this is where the fight will be. This is where I shall triumph! As soon as I have had my trousers sewn up I shall go out and look for another house. We must have a roof over our heads for the winter.

HORSTER. That you shall have in my house.

DR. STOCKMANN. Can I?

HORSTER. Yes, quite well. I have plenty of room, and I am almost never at home.   571

MRS. STOCKMANN. How good of you, Captain Horster!

PETRA. Thank you!

DR. STOCKMANN. [*Grasping his hand*] Thank you, thank you! That is one trouble over! Now I can set to work in earnest at once. There is an endless amount of things to look through here, Katherine! Luckily I shall have all my time at my disposal, because I have been dismissed from the Baths, you know.

MRS. STOCKMANN. [*With a sigh*] Oh, yes, I expected that.   579

DR. STOCKMANN. And they want to take my practice away from me, too. Let them! I have got the poor people to fall back upon, anyway—those that don't pay anything; and, after all, they need me most, too. But, by Jove, they will have to listen to me; I shall preach to them in season and out of season, as it says somewhere.

MRS. STOCKMANN. But, dear Thomas, I should have thought events had showed you what use it is to preach.

DR. STOCKMANN. You are really ridiculous, Katherine. Do you want me to let myself be beaten off the field by public opinion and the compact majority and all that devilry? No, thank you! And what I want to do is so simple and clear and straightforward. I only want [590 to drum into the heads of these curs the fact that the liberals are the most insidious enemies of freedom—that party programs strangle every young and vigorous truth—that considerations of expediency turn morality and justice upside down—and that they will end by making life here unbearable. Don't you think, Captain Horster, that I ought to be able to make people understand that?

HORSTER. Very likely; I don't know much about such things myself.   598

DR. STOCKMANN. Well, look here—I will explain! It is the party leaders that must be exterminated. A party leader is like a wolf,

you see—like a voracious wolf. He requires a certain number of smaller victims to prey upon every year, if he is to live. Just look at Hovstad and Aslaksen! How many smaller victims have they not put an end to—or at any rate maimed and mangled until they are fit for nothing except to be householders or subscribers to the "People's Messenger"! [*Sits down on the edge of the table.*] Come here, Katherine—look how beautifully the sun shines today! And this lovely spring air I am drinking in!

MRS. STOCKMANN. Yes, if only we could live on sunshine and spring air, Thomas. 610

DR. STOCKMANN. Oh, you will have to pinch and save a bit—then we shall get along. That gives me very little concern. What is much worse is that I know of no one who is liberal-minded and high-minded enough to venture to take up my work after me.

PETRA. Don't think about that, father; you have plenty of time before you.—Hullo, here are the boys already!

[EJLIF *and* MORTEN *come in from the sitting-room.*]

MRS. STOCKMANN. Have you got a holiday?

MORTEN. No; but we were fighting with the other boys between lessons— 620

EJLIF. That isn't true; it was the other boys were fighting with us.

MORTEN. Well, and then Mr. Rörlund said we had better stay at home for a day or two.

DR. STOCKMANN. [*Snapping his fingers and getting up from the table*] I have it! I have it, by Jove! You shall never set foot in the school again!

THE BOYS. No more school!

MRS. STOCKMANN. But, Thomas—

DR. STOCKMANN. Never, I say. I will educate you myself; that is to say, you shan't learn a blessed thing— 630

MORTEN. Hooray!

DR. STOCKMANN. —but I will make liberal-minded and high-minded men of you. You must help me with that, Petra.

PETRA. Yes, father, you may be sure I will.

DR. STOCKMANN. And my school shall be in the room where they insulted me and called me an enemy of the people. But we are too few as we are; I must have at least twelve boys to begin with.

An Enemy of the People

493

MRS. STOCKMANN. You will certainly never get them in this town.

DR. STOCKMANN. We shall. [*To the boys.*] Don't you know any street urchins—regular ragamuffins—?

MORTEN. Yes, father, I know lots!

DR. STOCKMANN. That's capital! Bring me some specimens of them. I am going to experiment with curs, just for once; there may be some exceptional heads amongst them.

MORTEN. And what are we going to do, when you have made liberal-minded and high-minded men of us?

DR. STOCKMANN. Then you shall drive all the wolves out of the country, my boys!

[EJLIF *looks rather doubtful about it;* MORTEN *jumps about crying "Hurrah!"*]

MRS. STOCKMANN. Let us hope it won't be the wolves that will drive you out of the country, Thomas.

DR. STOCKMANN. Are you out of your mind, Katherine? Drive me out! Now—when I am the strongest man in the town!

MRS. STOCKMANN. The strongest—now?

DR. STOCKMANN. Yes, and I will go so far as to say that now I am the strongest man in the whole world.

MORTEN. I say!

DR. STOCKMANN. [*Lowering his voice*] Hush! You mustn't say anything about it yet, but I have made a great discovery.

MRS. STOCKMANN. Another one?

DR. STOCKMANN. Yes. [*Gathers them round him, and says confidentially:*] It is this, let me tell you—that the strongest man in the world is he who stands most alone.

MRS. STOCKMANN. [*Smiling and shaking her head*] Oh, Thomas, Thomas!

PETRA. [*Encouragingly, as she grasps her father's hands*] Father!

CURTAIN

Anton Chekhov

THE CHERRY ORCHARD

THE PASSING of the old regime in Russia, which is studied in *The Cherry Orchard,* was a part of Chekhov's personal experience. His grandfather was a former serf who had purchased his freedom in 1841 and who became the supervisor of an aristocratic estate near Taganrog in the Ukraine, where Chekhov was born and spent his boyhood. A few years after winning the Pushkin Prize in 1888 for his short stories, Chekhov bought a six-hundred-acre country estate near Moscow and tried his hand at making practical reforms in rural living. *The Cherry Orchard,* which was produced by the Moscow Art Theater six months before Chekhov's death in 1905, is his last interpretation of a life that clearly contained material for vigorously realistic plays about changing Russian society.

The reader who knows something of Chekhov's life, and who is accustomed to plays that treat social problems satirically or argumentatively may be disturbed at first by the fact that no evils are flatly condemned in *The Cherry Orchard,* and no reforms clearly championed. It is soon clear, in fact, that Chekhov's methods are unusually subtle and symbolic, and that he is interested in something deeper than immediate social problems and their correction.

It will be noticed, for example, that no one character or point of view is allowed to overwhelm the others and to embody a final message of the play. *The Cherry Orchard* might have glorified the peasant's son, Lopakhin, who buys the estate on which his family had been serfs; or it might have been a play of socialistic reform with the progressive intellectual, Trofimoff, as the hero. But Trofimoff only talks about a brave new world, and he spends his

moment at the end of the play looking for his rubbers. Lopakhin is an admirable businessman, but he is also insensitive and envious of the aristocratic traditions and qualities that he cannot really buy and that he may even over-value. The same unheroic balance of virtues and limitations is apparent in the other characters, as the reader will discover.

The observation that the play is not dominated by any one character or point of view implies that its structure is not a straight-line argument or a success story. External actions are begun and completed, it is true—people arrive and leave, the mortgaged estate is sold at auction to Lopakhin, but this was foreseeable, almost in the modern nature of things, and since this aspect is not emphatic, we must look for a more static kind of structure centered around the cherry orchard itself. Since the meaning or value of the orchard is not predicated at the beginning, it can be discovered only through what the characters feel about it. Their feelings, rather than their statements, are apparently what Chekhov is chiefly interested in, and we may infer from his technique that he thought those feelings would be truest and clearest if they were revealed in the midst of casual activities. The irrelevances and the distractions of everyday life that seem to occupy an abnormally large part of the play may be thought of, then, both as a means of muting the possible positive actions or attitudes in the play, and as a kind of proof that the feelings of the characters are true rather than stagy.

It is possible to go farther and to look for the quality that all the feelings about the orchard have in common. In one sense, Lopakhin and Gaieff are opposites. Gaieff is incompetent in the practical world where Lopakhin is a success, but when they are brought into the orbit of the orchard, they may be essentially alike, and like all the other characters. If the orchard, the doomed estate, is the modern world, and if all the characters, finally, have the same feeling or range of feelings about it, then an understanding of those feelings should lead us to the heart of the play. Is their central quality perhaps a preoccupation with self, human separateness in the absence of unifying value, an inability to say and hear important things—and all intensified by the irrelevant busyness of daily life?

THE CHERRY ORCHARD

TRANSLATED BY JENNIE COVAN

Characters

LIUBOFF ANDREIEVNA RANEVSKAYA, *a landowner*

ANYA, *her daughter, aged seventeen*

VARYA, *her adopted daughter, aged twenty-seven*

LEONID ANDREIEVITCH GAIEFF, *Liuboff Andreievna's brother*

YERMOLAI ALEXEIEVITCH LOPAKHIN, *a merchant*

PETER SERGEIEVITCH TROFIMOFF, *a student*

BORIS BORISOVITCH SEMYONOFF-PISHCHIK, *a landowner*

CHARLOTTA IVANOVNA, *a governess*

SEMYON PANTELEIEVITCH YEPIKHODOFF, *a clerk*

DUNYASHA (AVDOTYA FYODOROVNA), *a maidservant*

FIRCE, *an old footman, aged eighty-seven*

YASHA, *a young footman*

A TRAMP

A STATION-MASTER

POST-OFFICE CLERK

GUESTS

A SERVANT

SCENE—*Mme. Ranevskaya's estate.*

ACT ONE

A room still called the nursery. One of the doors leads into Anya's room. It is almost sunrise of a day in May. The cherry-trees are in

THE CHERRY ORCHARD by Anton Chekhov, translated by Jennie Covan. Reprinted by permission of Coward-McCann, Inc. Copyright, 1923, 1933, by Coward-McCann, Inc.

bloom, but the chill of early morning is in the garden. The windows are shut.

[DUNYASHA *enters with a candle, and* LOPAKHIN *with a book in his hand.*]

LOP. The train has arrived, thank God. What's the time?

DUN. It will soon be two. [*Blows out candle.*] It is already light.

LOP. How late was the train? At least two hours. [*Yawns and stretches himself.*] I certainly made a fool of myself! I came here on purpose to meet them at the station, and then overslept myself . . . in my chair. It's a pity. I wish you'd called me.

DUN. I thought you'd gone. [*Listening*] I think I hear them coming.

8

LOP. [*Listens*] No . . . They have to collect their baggage and so on. . . . [*Pause*] Liuboff Andreievna has been living abroad for five years; I don't know what she'll be like now . . . She's a good sort—an easy, simple person. I remember when I was a boy of fifteen, my father, who is dead—he used to keep a shop in the village here—hit me with his fist, and my nose bled . . . We had gone into the yard for something or other, and he was a little drunk. Liuboff Andreievna, as I remember her now, was still young, and very slight, and she took me to the wash-stand here in this very room, the nursery. She said, "Don't cry, my small peasant, all wounds heal at last." [*Pause*] . . . Small peasant! My father was a peasant, true, but here I am in a white vest and brown shoes . . . like a pearl in an oyster shell. I'm rich now, with lots of money, but just think about it and examine me, and you'll find I'm still a peasant to the core. [*Turns over the pages of his book.*] Here I've been reading this book, but I understand nothing. I read and fell asleep. [*Pause*]

DUN. The dogs didn't sleep all night; they feel that their masters are coming.

26

LOP. What's the matter with you, Dunyasha. . . .

DUN. My hands are shaking. I am going to faint.

LOP. You're too sensitive, Dunyasha. You dress just like a lady, and you do your hair like one, too. You shouldn't. You must remember your place in life.

YEP. [*Enters with a bouquet. He wears a short jacket and brilliantly polished boots which squeak audibly. He drops the bouquet as he enters, then picks it up*] The gardener sent these; says they're to go into the dining-room. [*Gives the bouquet to* DUNYASHA.]

LOP. And you'll bring me some kvass. 36

DUN. Yes, sir. [*Exit.*]

YEP. There's a frost this morning—three degrees, and the cherry-trees are all in flower. I can't approve of our climate. [*Sighs.*] I can't. Our climate refuses to favor us even this once. And, Yermolai Alexeievitch, allow me to say to you, in addition, that I bought myself a pair of boots two days ago, and I beg to assure you that they squeak in a perfectly intolerable manner. What shall I put on them?

LOP. Go away. You bore me.

YEP. Some misfortune happens to me every day. But I don't complain; I'm used to it, and I even smile at it. [DUNYASHA *comes in and brings* LOPAKHIN *a glass of kvass.*] I am going. [*Knocks over a chair.*] There. . . . [*Triumphantly*] There, you see, if I may use the word, what circumstances I am in, so to speak. It is simply extraordinary. [*Exit.*] 50

DUN. Let me confess to you, Yermolai Alexeievitch, that Yepikhodoff has proposed to me.

LOP. Ah!

DUN. I don't know what to do about it. He's a nice young man, but every now and then, when he begins talking, you can't understand a word he says. It sounds sincere enough, only I can't understand it. I think I like him. He's madly in love with me. He's an unlucky man; every day something happens to him. We tease him about it. They call him "Two-and-twenty troubles."

LOP. [*Listens*] There they come, I think. 60

DUN. They're coming! What's the matter with me? I'm cold all over.

LOP. There they are, really. Let's go and meet them. Will she know me? We haven't seen each other for five years.

DUN. [*Excited*] I shall faint in a minute. . . . Oh, I'm fainting! [*Two carriages are heard driving up to the house.* LOPAKHIN *and* DUNYASHA *quickly go out. The stage is empty. There are noises in*

the adjoining rooms. FIRCE, *leaning on a stick, walks quickly across the stage; he has just been to meet* LIUBOFF ANDREIEVNA. *He wears an old-fashioned livery and a tall hat. He is saying something to himself, but not a word can be made out. The noise back stage grows louder and louder. A voice is heard: "Let's go in there." Enter* LIUBOFF ANDREIEVNA, ANYA, *and* CHARLOTTA IVANOVNA *leading a little dog on a chain, all dressed in traveling clothes,* VARYA *in a long coat and with a kerchief on her head.* GAIEFF, SEMYONOFF-PISHCHIK, LOPAKHIN, DUNYASHA *with a parcel and an umbrella, and a servant with suitcases—all cross the room.*]

ANYA. Let's go through here. Do you remember this room, mother?

LIUB. [*Joyfully, through her tears*] The nursery!   68

VARYA. How cold it is! My hands are quite numb. [*To* LIUBOFF ANDREIEVNA] Your rooms, the white one and the violet one, are just as they used to be, mother.

LIUB. My dear, beautiful nursery . . . I used to sleep here when I was a baby. [*Kisses her brother, then* VARYA, *then her brother again.*] And Varya is just as she used to be, exactly like a nun. And I recognized Dunyasha. [*Kisses her.*]

GAI. The train was two hours late. There now; how's that for punctuality?

CHAR. [*To* PISHCHIK] My dog eats nuts, too.   78

PISH. [*Astonished*] Just imagine!

[*All leave except* ANYA *and* DUNYASHA.]

DUN. We did have to wait for you! [*Takes off* ANYA's *cloak and hat.*]

ANYA. For four nights on the journey I didn't sleep . . . I'm awfully cold.

DUN. You left during Lent, when it was snowing and frosty, but now? Darling! [*Laughs and kisses her.*] We did have to wait for you, my darling pet! . . . I must tell you at once, I can't wait a minute.   87

ANYA. [*Listlessly*] Something else now . . . ?

DUN. The clerk, Yepikhodoff, proposed to me after Easter.

ANYA. Always the same . . . [*Puts her hair straight.*] I've lost all my hairpins . . . [*She is very tired, and even staggers as she walks.*]

DUN. I don't know what to think about it. He loves me, he loves me so much!

ANYA. [*Looks into her room; in a gentle voice*] My room, my windows, as if I'd never left! I'm at home! Tomorrow morning I'll get up and run out into the garden. . . . Oh, if I could only sleep! I didn't sleep the whole journey, I was so restless.   97

DUN. Peter Sergeievitch came two days ago.

ANYA. [*Joyfully*] Peter!

DUN. He sleeps in the bath-house, he lives there. He said he was afraid he'd be in the way. [*Looks at her watch.*] I should call him, but Varvara Mihkailovna told me not to. "Don't wake him," she said.

[*Enter* VARYA, *a bunch of keys hanging from her belt.*]

VARYA. Dunyasha, coffee, quick. Mother wishes some.

DUN. In a moment.   [*Exit.*]

VARYA. Well, you've come, thank God. Home again. [*Caressing her*] My darling is home again! My pretty one is back at last!

ANYA. I had an awful time, I tell you.   108

VARYA. I can just imagine it!

ANYA. I went away in Holy Week; it was very cold then. Charlotta talked the whole way and would go on performing her tricks. Why did you force her on me?

VARYA. You couldn't go alone, darling, at seventeen!

ANYA. We went to Paris; it's cold there and snowing. I talk French perfectly dreadfully. My mother lives on the fifth floor. I go to her, and find her there with several Frenchmen, women, an old abbé with a book, and everything wreathed in tobacco smoke and the whole place so uninviting. I suddenly became very sorry for mother—so sorry that I took her head in my arms and hugged her and wouldn't let her go. Then mother started hugging me and crying. . . .   121

VARYA. [*Weeping*] Don't say any more, don't say any more . . .

ANYA. She's already sold her villa near Mentone; she has nothing left, nothing. And I haven't a kopeck either; we only just managed

to get here. And mother won't understand! We had dinner at a station; she asked for all the expensive things, and tipped the waiters one ruble each. And Charlotta too. Yasha demands a share, too— It is simply awful. Mother has a footman now, Yasha; we've brought him along.

ANYA. How's business? Has the interest been paid?

VARYA. Not much chance of that.   131

ANYA. Oh God, oh God . . .

VARYA. The place will be sold in August.

ANYA. Oh God . . .

LOP. [*Looks in at the door and moos*] Moo!   [*Exit.*]

VARYA. [*Through her tears*] I'd like to . . . [*Shakes her fist.*]

ANYA. [*Embraces* VARYA, *softly*] Varya, has he proposed to you? [VARYA *shakes her head.*] But he loves you. . . . Why don't you decide? Why do you keep on waiting?

VARYA. I'm afraid it will all come to nothing. He's a busy man. I'm not his sort . . . he pays no attention to me. Bless the man, I don't wish to see him. . . . But everybody talks about our marriage, everybody congratulates me, and there's nothing in it at all, it's all like a dream. [*A different voice*] You have a brooch that looks like a bee.   145

ANYA. [*Wistfully*] Mother bought it. [*Goes into her room, and talks lightly, like a child.*] In Paris I went up in a balloon!

VARYA. My darling has come back, my pretty one is home again! [DUNYASHA *has already returned with the coffee-pot and is making coffee.*] I go about all day, looking after the house, and I think all the time, if only you could marry a rich man, I'd be happy and would go away somewhere by myself, perhaps to Kieff . . . or to Moscow, and so on, from one holy place to another. I'd tramp and tramp. That would be splendid!

ANYA. The birds are singing in the garden. What time is it now?

VARYA. It must be getting on towards three. It's time you went to sleep, darling. [*Goes into* ANYA's *room.*] Splendid!   157

[*Enter* YASHA *with a plaid shawl and a traveling bag.*]

YASHA. [*Crossing the stage; politely*] May I go this way?

DUN. I hardly recognized you, Yasha. You have changed abroad.

YASHA. Hm . . . and who are you?

DUN. When you went away I was only so high. [*Showing with her hand*] I'm Dunyasha, the daughter of Fyodor Kozoyedoff. You don't remember?

YASHA. Oh, you small cucumber! [*Looks round and embraces her. She screams and drops a saucer.* YASHA *goes out quickly.*]

VARYA. [*In the doorway, in an angry voice*] What's that?   166

DUN. [*Through her tears*] I've broken a saucer.

VARYA. It may bring luck.

ANYA. [*Coming out of her room*] We must tell mother that Peter's here.

VARYA. I told them not to call him.

ANYA. [*Thoughtfully*] Father died six years ago, and a month later my brother Grisha was drowned in the river—such a dear little boy of seven! Mother couldn't bear it; she went away, away, without looking round. . . . [*Shudders.*] How I understand her; if only she knew! [*Pause*] And Peter Trofimoff was Grisha's tutor, he might remind her. . . .   177

[*Enter* FIRCE *in a short jacket and white vest. Goes to the coffee-pot.*]

FIRCE. Madame is going to have a bite here. [*He is preoccupied, putting on white gloves.*] Is the coffee ready? [*To* DUNYASHA, *severely*] You!

DUN. Oh, dear me . . . ! [*Leaving hurriedly*]

FIRCE. [*Fussing round the coffee-pot*] Oh, you bungler . . . [*Murmurs to himself.*] Back from Paris . . . the master went to Paris once . . . in a carriage . . . [*Laughs.*]

VARYA. What are you mumbling, Firce?   185

FIRCE. I beg your pardon? [*Joyfully*] The mistress is home again. I've lived to see her! I don't care if I die now . . . [*Weeps with joy.*] [*Enter* LIUBOFF ANDREIEVNA, GAIEFF, LOPAKHIN, *and* SEMYONOFF-PISHCHIK, *the latter in a long jacket of thin cloth and loose trousers.* GAIEFF, *coming in, moves his arms and body about as if he were playing billiards.*]

LIUB. Let me remember now. Red into the corner! Twice into the center!

GAI. Right into the pocket! Once upon a time you and I, sister, both slept in this room, and now I'm fifty-one; it does seem strange.

LOP. Yes, time does fly!

192

GAI. What?

LOP. I said that time does fly.

GAI. It smells of patchouli here.

ANYA. I'm going to bed. Good-night, mother. [*Kisses her.*]

LIUB. My dear little child. [*Kisses her hand.*] Glad to be at home? I can't get over it.

ANYA. Good-night, uncle.

GAI. [*Kisses her face and hands*] God be with you. How you do resemble your mother! [*To his sister*] You were just like her at her age, Liuba.

202

[ANYA *gives her hand to* LOPAKHIN *and* PISHCHIK *and goes out shutting the door behind her.*]

LIUB. She's awfully tired.

PISH. It's a very long journey.

VARYA. [*To* LOPAKHIN *and* PISHCHIK] Well, gentlemen, it's getting on toward three. High time to retire.

LIUB. [*Laughs*] You're just the same as ever, Varya. [*Draws her close and kisses her.*] I'll have some coffee now; then we'll all go. [FIRCE *lays a cushion under her feet.*] Thank you, dear. I'm used to coffee. I drink it day and night. Thank you, dear old man. [*Kisses* FIRCE.]

211

VARYA. I'll go and see whether they've brought in all the luggage.

[*Exit.*]

LIUB. Is it really I who am sitting here? [*Laughs.*] I feel like jumping about and waving my arms. [*Covers her face with her hands.*] But suppose I'm dreaming! God knows I love my own country, I love it dearly; I couldn't look out of the railway carriage, I cried so much. [*Through her tears*] Still, I must have my coffee. Thank you, Firce. Thank you, dear old man. I'm so glad you're still with us.

219

FIRCE. The day before yesterday.

GAI. He doesn't hear well.

LOP. I have to go to Kharkoff by the five o'clock train. I'm awfully sorry! I should like to have a look at you, to gossip a little. You're as fine-looking as ever.

PISH. [*Breathes heavily*] Even finer-looking . . . dressed in Paris fashion . . . confound it all.   226

LOP. Your brother, Leonid Andreievitch, says I'm a snob, a usurer, but that is absolutely nothing to me. Let him talk. Only I do wish you would believe in me as you once did, that your wonderful, touching eyes would look at me as they used to. Merciful God! My father was the serf of your grandfather and your own father, but you—more than anybody else—did so much for me once upon a time that I've forgotten everything and love you as if you were one of my own family . . . and even more.

LIUB. I can't sit still, I can't! [*Jumps up and walks about in great excitement.*] I'll never survive this happiness. . . . You can laugh at me; I'm a silly woman . . . My dear little cupboard. [*Kisses cupboard.*] My little table.   238

GAI. Nurse died during your absence.

LIUB. [*Sits and drinks coffee*] Yes, God rest her soul. I heard by letter.

GAI. And Anastasia died, too. Peter Kosoy has left me and now lives in town with the Commissioner of Police. [*Takes a box of candy out of his pocket and sucks a piece.*]

PISH. My daughter, Dashenka, sends her love.   245

LOP. I wish to say something very pleasant, very delightful, to you. [*Looks at his watch.*] I'm going away at once, I haven't much time . . . but I'll tell you all about it in two or three words. As you already know, your cherry orchard is to be sold to pay your debts, and the sale is arranged for August 22; but you needn't be alarmed, dear madam, you may sleep in peace; there's a way out. Here's my plan. Please listen carefully! Your estate is only thirteen miles from town, the railway runs past it and if the cherry orchard and the land by the river are broken up into building parcels and are then leased as villa sites, you'll have at least twenty-five thousand rubles a year income.   256

GAI. How utterly absurd!

LIUB. I don't understand you at all, Yermolai Alexeievitch.

LOP. You will get twenty-five rubles a year for each dessiatine from the leaseholders at the very least, and if you advertise now, I'm willing to bet that you won't have a vacant parcel left by the autumn; they'll all go. In a word, you're saved. I congratulate you. Only, of course, you'll have to straighten things out carefully . . . For instance, you'll have to pull down all the old buildings, this house, which is of no use to anybody now, and cut down the old cherry orchard. . . .   266

LIUB. Cut it down? My dear man, you must forgive me, but you don't understand anything at all. If there's anything interesting or remarkable in the whole province, it's this cherry orchard of ours.

LOP. The only remarkable thing about the orchard is its great size. It bears fruit only every other year, and even then you don't know what to do with the cherries; nobody buys any.

GAI. This orchard is mentioned in the "Encyclopaedia."

LOP. [*Looks at his watch*] If we can't think of anything and don't make up our minds, then on August 22 both the cherry orchard and the whole estate will be sold at auction. Make up your mind! I swear there's no other way out. You may believe me!

FIRCE. In the old days, forty or fifty years ago, they dried the cherries, soaked them and pickled them, and made jam, and it used to happen that . . .   280

GAI. Be quiet, Firce.

FIRCE. And then we'd send the dried cherries in carts to Moscow and Kharkoff. And money! And the dried cherries were soft, juicy, sweet, and fragrant. They knew the way. . . .

LIUB. How was it done?

FIRCE. They've forgotten. Nobody remembers.

PISH. [*To* LIUBOFF ANDREIEVNA] What about Paris? Eh? Did you eat frogs?   288

LIUB. I ate crocodiles.

PISH. Just imagine!

LOP. Formerly there were only the gentry and the laborers, in the villages, and now the people who live in villas have arrived. All towns now, even small ones, are surrounded by villas. And it's safe

to say that in twenty years' time the villa residents will have increased tremendously. At present they sit on their balconies, and drink tea, but it may well happen that they'll commence to cultivate their patches of land, and then your cherry orchard will be happy, rich, glorious.   298

GAI. [*Angry*] What nonsense!

[*Enter* VARYA *and* YASHA.]

VARYA. There are two telegrams for you, mother dear. [*Picks out a key and noisily unlocks an antique cupboard.*] Here they are.

LIUB. They're from Paris . . . [*Tears them up without reading them.*] I'm through with Paris.

GAI. And do you know, Liuba, how old this cupboard is? A week ago I pulled out the bottom drawer; I looked and saw numbers carved in it. That cupboard was made exactly a hundred years ago. What do you think of that? What? We could celebrate its jubilee. It hasn't a soul of its own, but still, say what you will, it's a fine piece of furniture.   309

PISH. [*Astonished*] A hundred years . . . Just imagine!

GAI. Yes . . . it's a genuine thing. [*Examining it*] My dear and honored cupboard! I congratulate you on your career, which has for more than a hundred years been devoted to the noble ideals of good and justice; your silent call to productive labor has not decreased in the hundred years [*Weeping*] during which you have inspired in our generation virtue and courage and faith for a better future, holding before our eyes lofty ideals and the knowledge of a common consciousness. [*Pause*]   318

LOP. Yes.

LIUB. You're just the same as ever, Leon.

GAI. [*A little confused*] Off the white on the right, into the corner pocket. Red ball goes into the center pocket!

LOP. [*Looks at his watch*] It's time I went.

YASHA. [*Giving* LIUBOFF ANDREIEVNA *her medicine*] Will you take your pills now?

PISH. You shouldn't take medicines, dearest; they do you neither harm nor good . . . Give them to me, dearest. [*Takes the pills,*

turns them out into the palm of his hand, blows on them, puts them into his mouth, and drinks some kvass.] There! 329

LIUB. [*Frightened*] You're mad!

PISH. I've swallowed all the pills.

LOP. You greedy man! [*All laugh.*]

FIRCE. They were here in Easter week and ate half a pailful of cucumbers . . . [*Mumbles.*]

LIUB. What does he mean?

VARYA. He's been mumbling away for three years. We're used to that. 337

YASHA. Senile decay.

[CHARLOTTA IVANOVNA *crosses the stage, dressed in white; she is very thin and tightly laced; she has a lorgnette at her waist.*]

LOP. Excuse me, Charlotta Ivanovna, I haven't bidden you welcome yet. [*Tries to kiss her hand.*]

CHAR. [*Takes her hand away*] If you let people kiss your hand, then they'll want your elbow, then your shoulder, and then . . .

LOP. I'm out of luck today! [*All laugh.*] Show us a trick, Charlotta Ivanovna!

LIUB. Charlotta, do a trick for us! 345

CHAR. It's not necessary. I must go to bed. [*Exit.*]

LOP. We shall see each other in three weeks. [*Kisses* LIUBOFF ANDREIEVNA's *hand.*] Now, good-bye. It's time I went. [*To* GAIEFF] See you again. [*Kisses* PISHCHIK.] Au revoir. [*Gives his hand to* VARYA, *then to* FIRCE *and to* YASHA.] I don't want to go away. [*To* LIUBOFF ANDREIEVNA] If you think about the villas and come to a decision, just let me know, and I'll raise a loan of 50,000 rubles at once. Think about it seriously.

VARYA. [*Angrily*] Do go, now!

LOP. I'm going, I'm going. . . . [*Exit.*] 355

GAI. Snob. Still, I beg pardon . . . Varya's going to marry him, he's Varya's young man.

VARYA. Don't talk too much, uncle.

LIUB. Why not, Varya? I should be glad of it. He's a good man.

PISH. To speak the honest truth . . . he's a worthy man . . . And my Dashenka . . . also says that . . . she says lots of things.

[*Snores, but wakes up again at once.*] But still, dear madam, if you could lend me . . . 240 rubles . . . to pay the interest on my mortgage tomorrow . . .

VARYA. [*Frightened*] We haven't it, we haven't it!   365

LIUB. It's quite true. I've nothing at all.

PISH. You'll manage somehow. [*Laughs.*] I never lose hope. I used to think, "Everything's lost now. I'm a dead man," when, lo and behold, a railway was built across my land . . . and they paid me for it. And something else will happen today or tomorrow. Dashenka may win 20,000 rubles . . . she's got a lottery ticket.

LIUB. The coffee's all gone, we can go to bed.

FIRCE. [*Brushing GAIEFF's trousers; in an insistent tone*] You are wearing the wrong trousers again. What am I to do with you?

VARYA. [*Quietly*] Anya's asleep. [*Opens window quietly.*] The sun has risen already; it isn't cold. Look, mother, dear; what lovely trees! And the air! The starlings are singing!   377

GAI. [*Opens the other window*] The whole garden is white. You haven't forgotten, Liuba? There's that long avenue going straight, straight, like an arrow; it shines on moonlight nights. Do you remember? You haven't forgotten?

LIUB. [*Looks into the garden*] Oh, my childhood, days of my innocence! In this nursery I used to sleep; I used to look out from here into the orchard. Happiness used to wake with me every morning, and then it was just as it is now; nothing has changed. [*Laughs with joy.*] It's all, all white! Oh, my orchard! After the dreary autumns and the cold winters, you're young again, full of happiness, the angels of heaven haven't left you . . . If only I could take this strong burden from my breast and shoulders, if I could forget my past!   390

GAI. Yes, and they'll sell this orchard to pay off the debts. How strange it seems!

LIUB. Look, there's my dead mother walking in the orchard . . . dressed in white! [*Laughs with joy.*] That's she.

GAI. Where?

VARYA. God be with you, mother dear!

LIUB. Nobody is there; I thought I saw somebody. On the right, at the turning by the summer-house, a little white tree bent down, resembling a woman. [*Enter* TROFIMOFF *in a worn student uniform and spectacles*.] What a marvelous garden! White masses of flowers, the blue sky. . . .   401

TROF. Liuboff Andreievna! [*She looks round at him*.] I only wish to pay my respects to you, and I'll go away. [*Kisses her hand warmly*.] I was told to wait till the morning, but I didn't have the patience. [LIUBOFF ANDREIEVNA *looks surprised*.]

VARYA. [*Crying*] It's Peter Trofimoff.

TROF. Peter Trofimoff, once the tutor of your Grisha . . . Have I changed so much? [LIUBOFF ANDREIEVNA *embraces him and cries softly*.]

GAI. [*Confused*] That's enough, that's enough, Liuba.

VARYA. [*Weeps*] But I told you, Peter, to wait till tomorrow.

LIUB. My Grisha . . . my boy . . . Grisha . . . my son.

VARYA. What are we to do, dear mother? It's the will of God.

TROF. [*Softly, through his tears*] It's all right, it's all right.   414

LIUB. [*Still weeping*] My boy's dead; he was drowned. Why? Why, my friend? [*Softly*] Anya's asleep in there. I am speaking so loudly, making so much noise . . . Well, Peter? What's made you look so bad? Why have you grown so old?

TROF. In the train an old woman called me a decayed gentleman.

LIUB. You were quite a boy then, a jolly little student, and now your hair has grown thin and you wear spectacles. Are you really still a student? [*Goes to the door*.]

TROF. I suppose I shall always be a student.

LIUB. [*Kisses her brother, then* VARYA] Well, let's go to bed . . . And you've grown older, Leonid.   425

PISH. [*Follows her*] Yes, we must go to bed . . . Oh, my gout! I'll stay the night here. If only, Liuboff Andreievna, my dear, you could get me 240 rubles tomorrow morning—

GAI. Still the same story.

PISH. Two hundred and forty rubles . . . to pay the interest on the mortgage.

LIUB. I haven't any money, dear man.

PISH. I'll give it back . . . it's a small sum . . .

LIUB. Well then, Leonid will give it to you . . . Let him have it, Leonid.   435

GAI. By all means; hold out your hand.

LIUB. Why not? He wants it; he'll give it back.

[LIUBOFF ANDREIEVNA, TROFIMOFF, PISHCHIK *and* FIRCE *go out.*
GAIEFF, VARYA, *and* YASHA *remain.*]

GAI. My sister hasn't lost the habit of throwing money away. [*To* YASHA] Don't come near me: you smell like a chicken-coop!

YASHA. [*Grins*] You are just the same as ever, Leonid Andreievitch.

GAI. Really? [*To* VARYA] What's he saying?

VARYA. [*To* YASHA] Your mother has come from the village; she's been sitting in the servants' room since yesterday, and wishes to see you . . .   445

YASHA. Bless the woman!

VARYA. Shameless man.

YASHA. A lot of use there is in her coming. She might just as well have come tomorrow.   [*Exit.*]

VARYA. Mother hasn't altered a bit, she's just as she always was. She'd give away everything, if the idea only entered her head.

GAI. Yes . . . [*Pause*] If there's any illness for which people have a remedy of remedies, you may be sure that particular illness is incurable. I work my brains as hard as I can. I've several remedies, very many, and that really means I've none at all. It would be nice to inherit a fortune from somebody, it would be nice to marry off our Anya to a rich man, it would be nice to go to Yaroslavl and try my luck with my aunt the Countess. My aunt is very, very rich.

VARYA. [*Weeps*] If only God would help us.   459

GAI. Don't cry. My aunt's very rich, but she doesn't like us. My sister, in the first place, married a lawyer, not an aristocrat . . . [ANYA *appears in the doorway.*] She not only married a man who was not an aristocrat, but she behaved in a way which cannot be described as proper. She's nice and kind and charming and I'm very fond of her, but say what you will in her favor and you still

have to admit that she's bad; you can feel it in her slightest movements.

VARYA. [*Whispers*] Anya's in the doorway. 468

GAI. Really? [*Pause*] It's curious, something's blown into my right eye . . . I can't see out of it properly. And on Thursday, when I was at the District Court . . .

[*Enter* ANYA.]

VARYA. Why aren't you in bed, Anya?

ANYA. I can't sleep. It's no use.

GAI. My darling. [*Kisses* ANYA's *face and hands.*] My child. [*Crying*] You're not my niece, you're my angel, you're my all . . . Believe in me, believe . . .

ANYA. I do believe you, uncle. Everybody loves and respects you . . . but, uncle dear, you should say nothing, no more than that. What were you saying just now about my mother, about your own sister! Why did you say such things? 480

GAI. Yes, yes. [*Covers his face with her hand.*] Yes, really, it was terrible. Save me, my God! And only just now I made a speech before a cupboard . . . it's so silly! And only when I'd finished I knew how silly it was.

VARYA. Yes, uncle dear, you really should say less. Keep quiet, that's all.

ANYA. You'd be so much happier if you only kept quiet.

GAI. All right, I'll be quiet. [*Kisses their hands.*] I'll be quiet. But let's talk business. On Thursday I was in the District Court, and a lot of us met there and we began to talk of this, that, and the other, and now I think I can arrange a loan to pay the interest to the bank.

VARYA. If only God would help us! 493

GAI. I'll go on Tuesday. I'll talk to you about it again. [*To* VARYA] Don't cry. [*To* ANYA] Your mother will have a talk with Lopakhin; he, of course, won't refuse . . . And when you've rested you'll go to Yaroslavl to the Countess, your grandmother. So you see, we shall have three irons in the fire, and we shall be safe. We'll pay the interest. I'm certain. [*Puts some candy in his mouth.*] I swear on my honor, on anything you wish, that the estate will not be sold!

[*Excitedly*] I swear on my happiness! Here's my hand on it! You may call me a dishonorable sinner if I let it be sold at auction! I swear by all I am!   503

ANYA. [*Calm again and happy*] How good and clever you are, uncle. [*Embraces him.*] I'm happy now! I'm happy! All's well!

[*Enter* FIRCE.]

FIRCE [*Reproachfully*] Leonid Andreievitch, don't you fear God? When are you going to bed?

GAI. Soon, soon. You go away, Firce! I'll undress myself. Well, children, au revoir . . . ! I'll tell you the details tomorrow, but let's go to bed now. [*Kisses* ANYA *and* VARYA.] I'm a man of the eighties . . . People don't praise those years much, but I can still say that I've suffered for my beliefs. The peasants don't love me for nothing, I assure you. We have to learn how to understand the peasants! We should learn how . . .   514

ANYA. You're doing it again, uncle!

VARYA. Be quiet, uncle!

FIRCE. [*Angrily*] Leonid Andreievitch!

GAI. I'm coming, I'm coming . . . Go to bed now. Off two cushions into the center! I turn over a new leaf . . .

[*Exit.* FIRCE *goes out after him.*]

ANYA. I'm more quiet now. I don't wish to go to Yaroslavl, I don't like grandmother; but I'm calm now, thanks to uncle. [*Sits down.*]

VARYA. It's time to go to sleep. I'll go. There have been amazing things happening here during your absence. In the old servants' quarter of the house, as you know, only the old people live—little [524 old Yefim and Polya and Yevstigny, and Karp as well. They commenced letting tramps or the like spend the night there—I said nothing. Then I heard that they were saying I had ordered them to be fed on peas and nothing else; from meanness, you see . . . And it was all Yevstigny's doing. Very well, I thought, if that's what the matter is, just you wait. So I call Yevstigny . . . [*Yawns.*] He comes. "What's this," I say. "Yevstigny, you old fool" . . . [*Looks at* ANYA.] Anya dear! [*Pause*] She's dozed off . . . [*Takes* ANYA's *arm.*] Let's go to bed . . . Come along! . . . [*Leads her.*]

My darling's gone to sleep! Come on . . . [*They go. In the distance, the other side of the orchard, a shepherd plays his pipe.* TROFIMOFF *crosses the stage and stops when he sees* VARYA *and* ANYA.] Sh! She's asleep, asleep. Come on, dear.

537

ANYA. [*Quietly, half-asleep*] I'm so tired . . . I hear bells . . . uncle, dear! Mother and uncle!

VARYA. Come on, dear, come on! [*They go into* ANYA's *room.*]

TROF. [*Deeply moved*] Sunshine! Springtime of my life!

ACT TWO

A field. An old, tumble-down shrine, which has been long abandoned; near it a well and large stones, which apparently are old tombstones, and an old garden seat. The road to Gaieff's estate is seen. On one side dark poplars rise, behind them the cherry orchard begins. In the distance is a row of telegraph poles, and on the far horizon are the indistinct signs of a large town, which can be seen only on the finest and clearest days. It is near sunset.

[CHARLOTTA, YASHA, *and* DUNYASHA *are sitting on a bench.* YEPIKHODOFF *stands nearby playing on a guitar; all seem thoughtful.* CHARLOTTA *wears a man's old peaked cap; she has unslung a rifle from her shoulders and is straightening the strap-buckle.*]

CHAR. [*Thoughtfully*] I haven't a real passport. I don't know how old I am, but I think I'm young. When I was a little girl my father and mother used to travel from fair to fair and give very good performances, and I used to do the somersault and various little things. And when papa and mamma died, a German lady took me to her home and brought me up. I liked it. I grew up and became a governess. And where I came from and who I am, I don't know. . . . Who my parents were—perhaps they weren't married—I don't know. [*Takes a cucumber from her pocket and eats.*] I don't know anything. [*Pause*] I do wish to talk, but I haven't anybody to talk to. . . . I haven't anybody at all.

10

YEP. [*Plays on the guitar and sings*]

> "What do I care for this noisy earth?
> What do I care for friend and foe?"

I like playing on the mandolin!

DUN. That's a guitar, not a mandolin. [*Looks at herself in a little pocket mirror and powders herself.*]

YEP. For a lovelorn lunatic, this constitutes a mandolin. [*Sings.*]

> "Oh would the fire of love
> Warm my pitiful heart!"

[YASHA *sings, too.*]

CHAR. These people sing so badly. . . . Bah! Like jackals.   21

DUN. [*To* YASHA] Still it must be nice to live abroad.

YASHA. Yes, it is. I can't differ from you there. [*Yawns and lights a cigar.*]

YEP. That is perfectly natural. Abroad everything is in such complete harmony.

YASHA. That goes without saying.   27

YEP. I'm an educated man, I read various remarkable books, but I cannot understand where I want to go, myself—whether to keep on living or to shoot myself, as it were. So at any rate, I always carry a revolver about with me. Here it is. [*Shows a revolver.*]

CHAR. I've finished. Now I'll go. [*Slings the rifle over her shoulder.*] You, Yepikhodoff, are a very clever man and very frightful; women must be madly in love with you. Brrr! [*Going*] These wise people are all so stupid. I've nobody to talk to. I'm always alone, alone; I've nobody at all . . . and I don't know who I am or why I live.   [*Exit slowly.*]   37

YEP. As a matter of fact, independently of everything else, I must express my conviction, among other things, that fate has been as merciless in her dealings with me as a storm is to a small ship. Suppose, let us grant, I am wrong; then why did I wake up this morning, for example, and behold an enormous spider on my chest as big as this? [*Shows with both hands.*] And if I do drink kvass, why must I always find in the glass such an unsociable animal as

a cockroach! [*Pause*] Have you read Buckle? [*Pause*] May I have a few words with you, Avdotya Fyodorovna?

DUN. Go on!

YEP. I should prefer to be alone with you. [*Sighs.*]

DUN. [*Shy*] Very well, only please bring me my cloak first. . . . It's by the cupboard. It's a little damp here.   50

YEP. Very well. . . . I'll bring it. . . . Now I know what to do with my revolver.   [*Takes guitar and exit, strumming.*]

YASHA. Two-and-twenty troubles! A foolish man, between you and me and the gatepost. [*Yawns.*]

DUN. [*Pause*] I hope to goodness he won't shoot himself. [*Pause*] I'm so nervous, so worried. I entered service when I was quite a little girl, and now I'm not used to common life, and my hands are as white as a lady's. I'm so tender and so delicate now, respectable and afraid of everything. . . . I'm so frightened. And I don't know what will happen to my nerves if you deceive me, Yasha.   60

YASHA. [*Kisses her*] Tiny cucumber! Of course, every girl must respect herself; there's nothing I dislike more than a badly behaved girl.

DUN. I'm so much in love with you; you're educated, you can talk about everything. [*Pause*]

YASHA. [*Yawns*] Yes, I think that if a girl loves anybody, it means she's immoral. [*Pause*] It's nice to smoke a cigar out in the open air. . . . [*Listens.*] Somebody's coming. It's the mistress, and people with her. [DUNYASHA *embraces him suddenly.*] Go to the house, as if you'd been bathing in the river; go by this path, or they'll run across you and will think I've been meeting you. I can't stand that sort of thing.   72

DUN. [*Coughs quietly*] Your cigar has given me a headache.

[*Exit.* YASHA *remains, sitting by the shrine. Enter* LIUBOFF ANDREI-EVNA, GAIEFF, *and* LOPAKHIN.]

LOP. You must make up your mind definitely—there's no time to waste. The question is perfectly simple. Are you willing to let the land for villas or no? Just one word, yes or no? Just one word!

LIUB. Who's smoking bad cigars here? [*Sits.*]

GAI. They built that railway; that's made this place very convenient. [*Sits.*] Went to town and had lunch . . . red in the center! I'd like to go to the house now and have just one game.   80

LIUB. You'll have time.

LOP. Just one word! [*Imploringly*] Give me an answer!

GAI. [*Yawns*] Really!

LIUB. [*Looks in her purse*] I had a lot of money yesterday, but there's very little left today. My poor Varya feeds everybody on milk soup to save money; in the kitchen the old people get peas only; and I spend recklessly. [*Drops the purse, scattering gold coins.*] There, money all over the place.   88

YASHA. Permit me to pick them up. [*Collects the coins.*]

LIUB. Please do, Yasha. And why did I go and lunch there? . . . A terrible restaurant with a band and tablecloths smelling of soap. . . . Why do you drink so much, Leon? Why do you eat so much? Why do you talk so much? You talked too much again today in the restaurant, and it wasn't at all to the point—about the seventies and about decadents. And to whom? Talking to the waiters about decadents! Imagine!

LOP. Yes.   97

GAI. [*Waves his hand*] I can't be cured, that's obvious. . . . [*Irritably to* YASHA] What's the matter? Why do you always manage to keep in front of me?

YASHA. [*Laughs*] I can't listen to your voice without laughing.

GAI. [*To his sister*] Either he or I . . .

LIUB. Go away, Yasha! Go!

YASHA. [*Gives purse to* LIUBOFF ANDREIEVNA] I'll go at once. [*Hardly able to keep from laughing*] This minute. . . . [*Exit.*]

LOP. That rich man Deriganoff is preparing to buy your estate. They say he'll attend the sale in person.

LIUB. Where did you hear that?   108

LOP. They say so in town.

GAI. Our aunt in Yaroslavl promised to send something, but I don't know when or how much.

LOP. How much will she send? A hundred thousand rubles? Or two, perhaps?

LIUB. I'd be glad if we get ten or fifteen thousand.

LOP. You must excuse my saying so, but I've never met such frivolous people as you before, or anybody so unbusinesslike and peculiar. Here I am telling you in plain language that your estate will be sold, and you don't seem to understand. 118

LIUB. What are we to do? Tell us, what?

LOP. I tell you every day. Every day I say the same thing. Both the cherry orchard and the land must be leased for villas and at once,—the auction is staring you in the face: Understand! Once you definitely make up your minds to the villas, you'll have as much money as you wish and you'll be saved.

LIUB. Villas and villa residents—it's so vulgar, pardon me.

GAI. I agree with you entirely.

LOP. I must cry or yell or faint. I can't! You're too much for me! [*To* GAIEFF] You old woman! 128

GAI. Really!

LOP. Old woman! [*Going out.*]

LIUB. [*Frightened*] No, don't go away, stop; be a dear. Please. Perhaps we'll find some way out!

LOP. There is nothing to think about.

LIUB. Please don't go. It's nicer when you're here. . . . [*Pause*] I keep on waiting for something to happen, as if the house were going to collapse over our heads.

GAI. [*Thinking deeply*] Double in the corner . . . across the center. 138

LIUB. We have been too sinful. . . .

LOP. What sins have you been guilty of?

GAI. [*Puts candy in his mouth*] They say that I've wasted all my money in buying candy. [*Laughs.*]

LIUB. Oh, my sins . . . I've always scattered money about without being able to control myself, like a madwoman, and I married a man who made nothing but debts. My husband died of champagne—he drank terribly—and to my misfortune, I fell in love with another man and went off with him, and just at that time—it was my first punishment, a blow that struck me squarely on the head—here, in the river . . . my boy was drowned, and I went away, [149

abroad, never to return, never to see this river again. . . . I closed
my eyes and ran without thinking, but he ran after me . . . without mercy, without respect. I bought a villa near Mentone because
he fell ill there, and for three years I knew no rest, day or night;
the sick man wore me out, and my soul dried up. And last year,
when they had sold the villa to pay my debts, I went to Paris, and
there he robbed me of all I had and threw me over and went off
with another woman. I tried to poison myself. . . . It was so silly,
so shameful . . . And suddenly I longed to go back to Russia, my
own country, with my little daughter . . . [*Wipes her tears.*] Lord,
Lord be merciful to me, forgive my sins! Punish me no more!
[*Takes a telegram from her pocket.*] I had this today from Paris.
. . . He begs my forgiveness, he implores me to return . . . [*Tears
it up.*] Don't I hear music? [*Listens.*]   163

GAI. That is our famous Jewish band. You remember—four vio-
lins, a flute, and a double-bass.

LIUB. So it still exists? It would be nice if they came some
evening.

LOP. [*Listens*] I can't hear. . . . [*Sings quietly.*] "For money will
the Germans make a Frenchman of a Russian." [*Laughs.*] I saw
such an awfully funny thing at the theatre last night.

LIUB. I'm quite sure there wasn't anything funny at all. You
shouldn't go and see plays, you ought to go and look at yourself.
What a drab life you lead! What a lot of unnecessary things you
say!   174

LOP. It's true. To speak the honest truth, we live a silly life.
[*Pause*] My father was a peasant, an idiot, he understood nothing,
he didn't teach me, he was always drunk, and always beat me. As
a matter of fact, I'm a fool and an idiot, too. I've never learned
anything, my handwriting is bad, I write so that I'm quite ashamed
before people, like a pig!

LIUB. You should marry, my friend.

LOP. Yes . . . that's true.

LIUB. Why not our Varya? She's a nice girl.   183

LOP. Yes.

LIUB. She's a simple, unaffected girl, works all day, and, what matters most, she's in love with you. And you've liked her for a long time.

LOP. Well? I don't mind . . . She's a nice girl. [*Pause*]

GAI. I'm offered a place in a bank. Six thousand rubles a year . . . Did you hear?

LIUB. What's the matter with you! Stay where you are . . .

[*Enter* FIRCE *with an overcoat.*]

FIRCE. [*To* GAIEFF] Please sir, put this on, it's damp. 192

GAI. [*Putting it on*] You're a nuisance, old man.

FIRCE. It's all very well. . . . You went away this morning without telling me. [*Examining* GAIEFF]

LIUB. How old you've grown, Firce!

FIRCE. I beg your pardon?

LOP. She says you've grown very old!

FIRCE. I've lived a long time. They were getting ready to marry me before your father was born . . . [*Laughs.*] And when the Emancipation came I was already first valet. Only I didn't agree with the Emancipation and remained with my masters . . . [*Pause*] I remember everybody was happy, but they didn't know why.

LOP. It was very good for them in the old days. At any rate, they beat them formerly. 205

FIRCE. [*Not hearing*] Rather. The peasants kept their distance from the masters and the masters kept their distance from the peasants, but now everything is in a muddle, and you can't make head or tail of anything.

GAI. Be quiet, Firce. I have to go to town tomorrow. I have the promise of an introduction to a General who may lend me money on a note.

LOP. Nothing will come of it. And you won't pay your interest, don't you worry.

LIUB. He's out of his head. There's no General at all.

[*Enter* TROFIMOFF, ANYA, *and* VARYA.]

GAI. Here, come on, folks! 216

ANYA. Mother's sitting down here.

LIUB. [*Tenderly*] Come, come, my dears . . . [*Embracing* ANYA *and* VARYA] If you two only knew how much I love you. Sit down next to me, like that. [*All sit down.*]

LOP. Our eternal student is always with the ladies.

TROF. That's none of your business.

LOP. He'll soon be fifty, and he's still a student.

TROF. Stop your silly jokes!

LOP. Getting angry, eh, silly?

TROF. Shut up, can't you?   226

LOP. [*Laughs*] I wonder what you think of me?

TROF. I think, Yermolai Alexeievitch, that you're rich, and you'll soon be a millionaire. Just as the wild beast which eats everything it finds is needed to make certain changes in cosmic matter, so you are needed too. [*All laugh.*]

VARYA. Better tell us something about the planets, Peter.

LIUB. No, let's continue yesterday's discussion.

TROF. What was it about?

GAI. About the proud man.   235

TROF. Yesterday we talked for a long time, but we arrived at no conclusion. In your opinion there's something mystic in pride. Perhaps you are right from your point of view, but if you look at the matter sanely, without complicating it, then what pride can there be, what logic in a man who is imperfectly made, physiologically speaking, and who in the vast majority of cases is coarse and stupid and profoundly unhappy? We must stop admiring one another. We must work, nothing more.

GAI. You'll die, all the same.

TROF. Who knows? And what does it mean—you'll die? Perhaps a man has a hundred senses, and when he dies only the five known to us are destroyed and the remaining ninety-five are left alive.

LIUB. How clever of you, Peter!

LOP. [*Ironically*] Oh, awfully!   249

TROF. The human race progresses, perfecting its powers. Everything that is unattainable now will some day be near and intelligible, but we must work, we must help with all our energy, those who seek to know the truth. Meanwhile in Russia only a very few

of us work. The vast majority of those intellectuals whom I know seek for nothing, do nothing, and are at present incapable of hard work. They call themselves intellectuals, but they use "thou" and "thee" to their servants, they treat the peasants like animals, they learn slowly, they read nothing with discernment, they do absolutely nothing, they gabble on about science, about art they understand little. They are all serious, they all have severe faces, they all talk about important things. They philosophize, and at the same time, the vast majority of us, ninety-nine out of a hundred, live like savages, fighting and cursing on the slightest excuse, have filthy table manners, sleep in the dirt, in stuffiness among fleas, stinks, [264 smells, moral stench, and so on. . . . And it's obvious that all our nice talk is only carried on to delude ourselves and others. Tell me, where are those crèches we hear so much of? And where are those reading-rooms? People only write novels about them; they don't really exist. Only dirt, coarseness, and Asiatic barbarism really exist. . . . I'm afraid; and I don't like serious faces at all. I don't like serious conversation. Let's say no more about it.   271

LOP. You know, I get up at five every morning, I work till evening, I am always dealing with money—my own and other people's —and I see what others are like. You have only to start doing anything at all, and you'll find out how few honest, honorable people there are. Sometimes, when I can't sleep, I think: "Oh Lord, you've given us huge forests, infinite fields, and endless horizons, and we, living here, ought really to be giants."

LIUB. You want giants, do you? . . . They're only good in stories, and even there they frighten one. [YEPIKHODOFF *enters at the back of the stage playing his guitar.* LIUBOFF ANDREIEVNA *speaks thoughtfully.*] Yepikhodoff has come.   282

ANYA. [*Thoughtfully*] Yepikhodoff has come.

GAI. The sun's set.

TROF. Yes.

GAI. [*Not loudly, as if declaiming*] Oh, Nature, thou art wonderful, thou shinest with eternal radiance! Oh, beautiful and lofty one, thou whom we call mother, thou containest in thyself life and death, thou livest and destroyest. . . .

Anton Chekhov

VARYA. [*Entreatingly*] Uncle, dear!

ANYA. Uncle, you're doing it again! 291

TROF. You'd better double the yellow into the center.

GAI. I'll be quiet, I'll be quiet.

[*They all sit thoughtfully. It is quiet. Only the mumbling of* FIRCE *is heard. Suddenly a distant sound comes as if from the sky, the sound of a breaking string, which dies away sadly.*]

LIUB. What's that?

LOP. I don't know. Perhaps a bucket fell, down a well somewhere. But it's a long way off.

GAI. Or perhaps it's some bird . . . like a heron.

TROF. Or an owl. 298

LIUB. [*Shudders*] It's unpleasant, somehow. [*A pause*]

FIRCE. Before the catastrophe the same thing happened. An owl screamed and the samovar hummed without stopping.

GAI. Before what catastrophe?

FIRCE. Before the Emancipation. [*A pause*]

LIUB. You know, my friends, let's go in; it's evening now. [*To* ANYA] You've tears in your eyes. . . . What is it, little girl? [*Embraces her.*]

ANYA. It's nothing, mother.

TROF. Some one's coming. 308

[*Enter a* TRAMP *in an old white peaked cap and overcoat. He is slightly drunk.*]

TRAMP. Excuse me, may I go this way straight through to the station?

GAI. You may. Go along this path. . . .

TRAMP. I thank you with all my heart. [*Hiccoughs.*] Lovely weather. . . . [*Declaims.*] My brother, my suffering brother. . . . Come out on the Volga, you whose groans . . . [*To* VARYA] Mademoiselle, please give a hungry Russian thirty kopecks. . . .

[VARYA *screams, frightened.*]

LOP. [*Angrily*] Everybody should have some sort of manners!

LIUB. [*With a start*] Take this . . . here you are . . . [*Feels in her purse.*] There's no silver . . . It doesn't matter, here's gold.

TRAMP. I am very grateful to you!   [*Exit. Laughter*]   319

VARYA. [*Frightened*] I'm going. I'm going. . . . Oh, mother dear, at home there's nothing for the servants to eat, and yet you gave him gold.

LIUB. What is to be done with such a fool as I am! At home, I'll give you everything I have. Yermolai Alexeievitch, lend me some more! . . .

LOP. Very well.

LIUB. Let's go, it's time. And Varya, we've settled your affairs; I congratulate you.

VARYA. [*Crying*] You shouldn't joke about this, mother.

LOP. Ophelia! Get thee to a nunnery.   330

GAI. My hands are trembling; I haven't played billiards for a long time.

LOP. Ophelia! Nymph! Remember me in thine orisons!

LIUB. Come along; it'll soon be suppertime.

VARYA. He frightened me. My heart is beating fast.

LOP. Let me remind you, ladies and gentlemen, on August 22nd, the cherry orchard will be sold. Think of that! . . . Think of that! . . . [*All go out except* TROFIMOFF *and* ANYA.]

ANYA. [*Laughs*] Thanks to the tramp who frightened Varya, we're alone now.   340

TROF. Varya's afraid that we may fall in love with each other and won't leave us alone for days on end. Her narrow mind won't permit her to understand that we are above love. To escape all the petty and deceptive things which prevent our being happy and free, such is the aim and object of our lives. Forward! We go irresistibly on to that bright star which burns there, in the distance! Don't lag behind, friends!

ANYA. [*Clapping her hands*] How beautifully you talk! [*Pause*] It is glorious here today!

TROF. Yes, the weather is wonderful.   350

ANYA. What have you done to me, Peter? I don't love the cherry orchard as I used to. I loved it so tenderly, I thought there was no better place in the world than our orchard.

TROF. All Russia is our orchard. The land is great and beautiful, there are many glorious places in it. [*Pause*] Think, Anya, your grandfather, your great-grandfather, and all your ancestors were serf-owners, they owned human beings; and now, doesn't something human look at you from every cherry in the orchard, every leaf and every branch? Don't you hear voices . . . ? Oh, it's awful, your orchard is frightful; and when in the evening or at night you walk through the orchard, then the old bark on the trees sheds a dim light and the old cherry-trees seem to dream of all that hap- [362 pened a hundred, two hundred years ago, and are burdened with their heavy visions. Still, we've left those two hundred years behind us. So far we've gained nothing at all—we don't yet know what the past will bring us—we only philosophize, we complain that we are dull, or we drink vodka. For it's so clear that to begin to live in the present we must first redeem the past, and that can be done only by suffering, by strenuous, uninterrupted work. Understand that, Anya.   370

ANYA. The house in which we live has long ceased to be our house; I shall go away, I give you my word.

TROF. If you have the keys of the household, throw them down the well and go away. Be as free as the wind.

ANYA. [*Enthusiastically*] How beautifully you said that!

TROF. Believe me, Anya, believe me! I'm not thirty yet, I'm young, I'm still a student, but I have gone through so much already! I'm as hungry as the winter, I'm ill, I'm shaken. I'm as poor as a beggar, and where haven't I been—fate has tossed me everywhere! But my soul is always my own; every minute of the day and the night it is filled with glorious and dim visions. I feel that happiness is coming, Anya, I see it already. . . .   382

ANYA. [*Thoughtful*] The moon is rising.

[YEPIKHODOFF *is heard playing the same sad song on his guitar. The moon rises. Somewhere near the poplars* VARYA *is looking for* ANYA *and calling,* "ANYA, *where are you?"*]

TROF. Yes, the moon has risen. [*Pause*] There is happiness, there it comes; it comes nearer and nearer; I hear its footsteps already.

And if we do not see it, we shall not know it, but what does that matter? Others will see it!

VARYA's VOICE. Anya! Where are you?

TROF. That's Varya again! [*Angry*] Disgraceful!

ANYA. Never mind. Let's go to the river. It's nice there.

TROF. Let's go. [*They leave.*]

VARYA's VOICE. Anya! Anya!

ACT THREE

A reception-room, separated by an arch from a drawing-room. Lighted chandelier. A Jewish band, the one referred to in Act II, is heard playing in another room. Evening. In the drawing-room the cotillion is being danced.

[*Voice of* SEMYONOFF PISHCHIK, "*Promenade à une paire!*" *Dancers come into the reception-room; the first pair are* PISHCHIK *and* CHARLOTTA IVANOVNA; *the second* TROFIMOFF *and* LIUBOFF ANDREI-EVNA; *the third* ANYA *and the* POST OFFICE CLERK; *the fourth* VARYA *and the* STATION-MASTER, *and so on.* VARYA *is crying gently and dries her eyes as she dances.* DUNYASHA *is in the last pair. They go off into the drawing-room, shouting,* "*Grand rond, balancez!*" *and* "*Les cavaliers à genoux et remerciez vos dames!*" FIRCE, *in a dress-coat, carries a tray with seltzer-water across the stage. Enter* PISH-CHIK *and* TROFIMOFF *from the drawing-room.*]

PISH. I'm full-blooded and already I've had two strokes; it's hard for me to dance, but, as they say, if you're in Rome, you must do as the Romans do. I've the constitution of a horse. My late father, who liked a joke, peace to his ashes, used to say, talking of our ancestors, that the ancient stock of the Semyonoff Pishchiks was descended from the identical horse that Caligula appointed senator. . . . [*Sits.*] But the trouble is, I've no money! A hungry dog believes only in meat. [*Drops off to sleep and wakes up again immediately.*] So I . . . believe only in money. . . .

9

TROF. Yes. There is something horsy about your figure.

PISH. Well . . . a horse is a valuable animal . . . you can sell a horse.

[*The sound of billiard playing comes from the next room,* VARYA *appears under the arch.*]

TROF. [*Teasing*] Madame Lopakhin! Madame Lopakhin!

VARYA. [*Angry*] Decayed gentleman!

TROF. Yes, I am a decayed gentleman, and I'm proud of it!

VARYA. [*Bitterly*] We've hired the musicians, but how are they to be paid?   [*Exit.*]   17

TROF. [*To* PISHCHIK] If you would put to better use the energy which you are wasting day by day, in looking for money to pay interest, I believe you'd finally succeed in moving heaven and earth.

PISH. Nietzsche . . . a philosopher . . . a very great and famous man . . . a man of enormous brain, says in his books that you can forge bank-notes.

TROF. And have you read Nietzsche?

PISH. Well . . . Dashenka told me. Now I'm in such a position, I wouldn't mind making counterfeit money . . . I have to pay 310 rubles day after tomorrow . . . I've obtained 130 already . . . [*Feels his pockets, nervously.*] I've lost the money! The money's gone! [*Crying*] Where's the money? [*Joyfully*] Here it is in the lining. . . . Why I was in a cold sweat!   30

[*Enter* LIUBOFF ANDREIEVNA *and* CHARLOTTA IVANOVNA.]

LIUB. [*Humming a Caucasian dance song*] What is keeping Leonid so long? What's he doing in town? [*To* DUNYASHA] Dunyasha, give the musicians some tea.

TROF. The business is off, I suppose.

LIUB. And the musicians needn't have come, and we needn't have arranged this ball. . . . Well, never mind. . . . [*Sits and sings softly.*]

CHAR. [*Gives a pack of cards to* PISHCHIK] Here's a deck of cards, think of any card you like.   39

PISH. I've thought of one.

CHAR. Now shuffle. All right, now. Pass them over, my dear Mr. Pishchik. Eins, zwei, drei! Now look and you'll find it in your hind pocket.

PISH. [*Takes a card out of his hind pocket*] Eight of spades, quite right! [*Surprised*] Just imagine!

CHAR. [*Holds the deck of cards in the palm of her hand. To* TROFIMOFF] Now tell me quickly. What's the top card?

TROF. Well, the queen of spades.   48

CHAR. Right! [*To* PISHCHIK] And now? What card's on top?

PISH. Ace of hearts.

CHAR. Right! [*Clasps her hands, the deck of cards vanishes.*] How lovely the weather is today. [*A mysterious woman's voice answers her, as if from under the floor, "Oh yes, it's lovely weather, Madam."*] You are so beautiful, you are my ideal. [*Voice, "You, Madam, please me very much too."*]

STATION-MASTER. [*Applauds*] Madame the ventriloquist, bravo!

PISH. [*Surprised*] Just imagine! Delightful, Charlotta Ivanovna . . . I'm simply in love. . . .   58

CHAR. In love? [*Shrugging her shoulders*] Can you love? Guter Mensch aber schlechter Musikant.

TROF. [*Slaps* PISHCHIK *on the shoulder*] Oh, you horse!

CHAR. Attention, please, here's another trick. [*Takes a shawl from a chair.*] Here's a very nice plaid shawl. I'm going to sell it. . . . [*Shakes it.*] Won't somebody buy it?

PISH. [*Astonished*] Just imagine!

CHAR. Eins, zwei, drei. [*She quickly lifts up the shawl, which is hanging down.* ANYA *appears behind it; she bows and runs to her mother, hugs her and runs back to the drawing-room amid general applause.*]

LIUB. [*Applauds*] Bravo, bravo!   70

CHAR. Once again! Eins, zwei, drei! [*Lifts the shawl.* VARYA *appears behind it and bows.*]

PISH. [*Astonished*] Just imagine!

CHAR. The end! [*Throws the shawl at* PISHCHIK, *curtseys and runs into the drawing-room.*]

PISH. [*Runs after her*] Little witch! . . . What? Would you?
                                                            [*Exit.*]

LIUB. Leonid hasn't come yet. I don't understand what is keeping him so long in town! Everything must be over by now. The

estate must be sold; or, if the sale never came off, then why does he
stay away so long?   80

VARYA. [*Tries to soothe her*] Uncle has bought it. I'm certain
of it.

TROF. [*Sarcastically*] Oh, yes!

VARYA. Grandmother sent him her authority to buy it in her
name and transfer the debt to her. She's doing it for Anya. And
I'm certain that God will help us and that Uncle will buy it.

LIUB. Grandmother sent fifteen thousand rubles from Yaroslavl
to buy the property in her name—she won't trust us—and that
wasn't even enough to pay the interest. [*Covers her face with her
hands.*] My fate will be settled today, my fate. . . .   90

TROF. [*Teasing* VARYA] Madame Lopakhin!

VARYA. [*Angry*] Eternal student? He's been expelled from the
university, twice already.

LIUB. Why are you growing angry, Varya? He's teasing you about
Lopakhin. Well, what of it? You can marry Lopakhin if you wish.
He's a good, interesting man. . . . You needn't if you don't wish
to; nobody is going to force you against your will, my darling.

VARYA. I look at the matter seriously, mother dear, to be quite
frank. He's a good man, and I like him.   99

LIUB. Then marry him. I don't understand what you're waiting
for.

VARYA. I can't propose to him myself, mother dear. People have
been talking about him to me for two years now, but he either says
nothing, or jokes about it. I understand. He's getting rich, he's
busy, he can't bother about me. If I had some money, even a little,
even only a hundred rubles, I'd throw up everything and go away.
I'd go into a convent.

TROF. What bliss!   108

VARYA. [*To* TROFIMOFF] A student should have common sense!
[*Gently, in tears*] How ugly you are now, Peter, how old you've
grown! [*To* LIUBOFF ANDREIEVNA, *no longer crying*] But I can't go
on without working, mother dear. I'm eager to be doing something
every minute.

[*Enter* YASHA.]

YASHA. [*Nearly laughing*] Yepikhodoff's broken a billiard cue!
[*Exit.*]

VARYA. Why is Yepikhodoff here? Who said he could play billiards? I don't understand these people. [*Exit.*]

LIUB. Don't tease her, Peter, you see that she's unhappy enough without it. 118

TROF. She undertakes too much herself; she is continually interfering in other people's business. The whole summer she gave Anya and me not a moment's peace. She's afraid we'll have a romance all to ourselves. What concern of hers is it? As if I'd ever given her grounds to believe I'd stoop to such vulgarity! We are above love.

LIUB. Then I suppose I must be beneath love. [*In agitation*] Why isn't Leonid here? If I only knew whether the estate is sold or not! The catastrophe seems to me so unbelievable that I don't know what to think, I'm all at sea . . . I may scream . . . or do something foolish. Save me, Peter. Say something, say something. [127

TROF. Isn't it all the same whether the estate is sold today or not? For a long time it's been a foregone conclusion that it would be sold. There's no turning back, the path is obliterated. Be calm, dear, you shouldn't deceive yourself; for once in your life, at any rate, you must look the truth straight in the eyes.

LIUB. What truth? You see where truth is, and where falsehood is, but I seem to have lost my sight and see nothing. You settle all important questions boldly, but tell me, dear, isn't it because you're young, because you have not as yet had time to suffer in settling any one of these questions? You look forward boldly, but isn't it [137 because you neither feel nor expect anything terrible, because so far life has been hidden from your young eyes? You are bolder, more honest, deeper than we are, but only think, be just a little magnanimous, and have pity on me. I was born here, my father and mother lived here, my grandfather, too. I love this house. I couldn't understand my life without that cherry orchard, and if it really must be sold, sell me with it! [*Embraces* TROFIMOFF, *kisses his forehead.*] My son was drowned here . . . [*Weeps.*] Have pity on me, good, kind man.

TROF. You know that I sympathize with all my heart. 147

LIUB. Yes, but it should be said differently. . . . [*Takes another handkerchief, a telegram falls on the floor.*] I'm so sick at heart today, you can't imagine. Here it's so noisy, my soul trembles at every sound. I shake all over, and I can't go away by myself, I'm afraid of the silence. Don't judge me harshly, Peter. . . . I love you, as if you belonged to the family. I'd gladly let Anya marry you, I swear it, only dear, you ought to work to finish your studies. You don't do anything, only fate tosses you about from place to place, it's so strange. . . . Isn't it true? Yes? And you ought to do something to your beard to make it grow better. [*Laughs.*] You are funny! 158

TROF. [*Picking up telegram*] I don't wish to be a Beau Brummell.

LIUB. This telegram's from Paris. I receive one every day. Yesterday and today. That wild man is ill again, he's bad again. . . . He begs for forgiveness, and implores me to come, and I really should go to Paris to be near him. You look severe, Peter, but what can I do, my dear, what can I do? He's ill, he's alone, unhappy, and who's to look after him, who's to keep him out of harm's way, to give him his medicine punctually? And why should I conceal it and say nothing about it? I love him, that's plain, I love him, I love him. . . . That love is a stone round my neck; I shall sink with it to the bottom, but I love that stone and can't live without it. [*Squeezes* TROFIMOFF's *hand.*] Don't think harshly of me, Peter, don't say anything to me, don't say . . . 171

TROF. [*Weeping*] For God's sake forgive my speaking candidly, but that man has robbed you!

LIUB. No, no, you should not say that! [*Stops her ears.*]

TROF. But he's a scoundrel, you alone don't know it! He's a petty thief, a nobody. . . .

LIUB. [*Angry, but restrained*] You're twenty-six or twenty-seven, and still a school-boy of the second grade!

TROF. Why not?

LIUB. You should be a man, at your age you should be able to understand those who love. And you should be in love yourself,

you must fall in love! [*Angry*] Yes, yes! You aren't pure, you're just a freak, a queer fellow, a funny fungus.   183

TROF. [*In horror*] What is she saying?

LIUB. "I'm above love!" You're not above love, you're just what our Firce calls a bungler. Not to have a mistress at your age!

TROF. [*In horror*] This is terrible! What is she saying? [*Goes quickly into the drawing-room, seizing his head with both his hands.*] It's awful . . . I can't stand it, I'll go away. [*Exit, but returns at once.*] All is over between us!   [*Exit.*]

LIUB. [*Shouts after him*] Peter, wait! Silly boy, I was joking! Peter! [*Somebody is heard going out and falling downstairs noisily.* ANYA *and* VARYA *scream; laughter is heard immediately.*] What's that? [ANYA *comes running in, laughing.*]   194

ANYA. Peter's fallen downstairs!   [*Runs out again.*]

LIUB. This Peter's a funny creature!

[*The* STATION-MASTER *stands in the middle of the drawing-room and recites "The Magdalen" by Tolstoy. They listen to him, but he has delivered only a few lines when a waltz is heard from the front room, and the recitation is stopped. Everybody dances.* TROFIMOFF, ANYA, VARYA, *and* LIUBOFF ANDREIEVNA *come in from the front room.*]

LIUB. Well, Peter . . . you pure soul . . . I beg your pardon. . . . Let's dance.   198

[*She dances with* PETER. ANYA *and* VARYA *dance.* FIRCE *enters and leans his stick against a side door.* YASHA *has also come in and watches the dance.*]

YASHA. Well, grandfather?

FIRCE. I'm not well. At our balls some time ago, generals and barons and admirals used to dance, and now we send for post-office clerks and the station-master, and even they come reluctantly. I'm very weak. The dead master, the grandfather, used to give everybody sealing-wax when anything was wrong. I've taken sealing-wax every day for twenty years, and more; possibly that's why I am still alive.   206

YASHA. I'm tired of you, grandfather. [*Yawns.*] If you'd only hurry up and kick the bucket.

FIRCE. [*Muttering*] Oh, you . . . bungler!

[TROFIMOFF *and* LIUBOFF ANDREIEVNA *dance in the reception-room, then into the sitting-room.*]

LIUB. Merci. I'll sit down. [*Sits.*] I'm tired.

[*Enter* ANYA.]

ANYA. [*Excited*] Somebody in the kitchen was saying just now that the cherry orchard was sold today.

LIUB. Sold to whom?

ANYA. He didn't say to whom. He went away. [*Dances out into the reception-room with* TROFIMOFF.] 215

YASHA. Some old man was chattering about it a long time ago. A stranger!

FIRCE. And Leonid Andreievitch isn't here yet, he hasn't come. He's wearing a light autumn overcoat. He'll catch cold. Oh, these young fellows.

LIUB. I'll die of this. Go and find out, Yasha, to whom it's sold.

YASHA. Oh, but he's been gone a long time, the old man. [*Laughs.*]

LIUB. [*Slightly vexed*] Why do you laugh? What are you so happy about? 225

YASHA. Yepikhodoff's too funny. He's a foolish man. Two-and-twenty troubles.

LIUB. Firce, if the estate is sold, where will you go?

FIRCE. I'll go wherever you command me to go.

LIUB. Why do you look like that? Are you ill? I think you should go to bed. . . .

FIRCE. Yes . . . [*With a smile*] I'll go to bed, and who'll hand things round and give orders without me? I've the whole house on my shoulders. 234

YASHA. [*To* LIUBOFF ANDREIEVNA] Liuboff Andreievna! I wish to ask a favor of you, if you'll be so kind! If you go to Paris again, take me along. I beg of you! It's absolutely impossible for me to remain here. [*Looking round; in an undertone*] What's the good of talking about it? You see for yourself that this is an uncivilized country, with an immoral population, and it's so dull. The food in

the kitchen is wretched, and here's this Firce walking about mumbling all kinds of inappropriate things. Take me with you. Please!

[*Enter* PISHCHIK.]

PISH. May I have the pleasure of a little waltz, dear lady . . . ?
[LIUBOFF ANDREIEVNA *goes to him.*] But all the same, you wonderful woman, I must have 180 little rubles from you. . . . I must. . . .
[*They dance.*] 180 little rubles. . . .   246

                    [*They go through into the drawing-room.*]

YASHA. [*Sings softly*]

> "Oh, will you understand
> My soul's deep restlessness?"

[*In the drawing-room a figure in a gray top-hat and in baggy check trousers is waving its hands; and there are cries of "Bravo,* CHARLOTTA IVANOVNA!"]

DUN. [*Stops to powder her face*] The young mistress tells me to dance—there are lots of gentlemen, but few ladies—and my head whirls when I dance, and my heart beats, Firce Nikolaievitch; the Post-office clerk told me something just now that almost took my breath away.   [*The music grows faint.*] 254

FIRCE. What did he tell you?

DUN. He says, "You're like a little flower."

YASHA. [*Yawns*] Impolite. . . .   [*Exit.*]

DUN. Like a little flower. I'm such a delicate girl; I simply love tender words.

FIRCE. You'll lose your head.

                    [*Enter* YEPIKHODOFF.]

YEP. You, Avdotya Fyodorovna, are about as anxious to see me as if I were some insect. [*Sighs.*] Oh, life!

DUN. What do you wish?   263

YEP. Perhaps, doubtless, you may be right. [*Sighs.*] But, certainly, if you consider the matter in that light, then you, if I may say so, and you must excuse my candidness, have absolutely reduced me to the state of mind in which I find myself. I know my fate. Every day something unfortunate happens to me, and I've grown used to

it a long time ago. I never look at my fate with a smile. You gave me your word, and though I. . . .

DUN. Please, we'll talk later on, but leave me alone now. I'm thinking now. [*Fans herself.*]

YEP. Every day something unfortunate happens to me, and I, if I may so express myself, only smile, and even laugh. 274

[VARYA *enters from the drawing-room.*]

VARYA. Haven't you gone yet, Semyon? You really have no respect for anybody. [*To* DUNYASHA] Go away, Dunyasha. [*To* YEPIKHODOFF] You play billiards and break a cue, and stroll about the drawing-room as if you were a visitor!

YEP. You cannot, if I may say so, call me to order.

VARYA. I'm not calling you to order, I'm only telling you. You just walk about from place to place and never do your work. Goodness only knows why we keep a clerk.

YEP. [*Offended*] Whether I work, or walk about, or eat, or play billiards, is only a matter to be settled by people of understanding and my elders. 285

VARYA. You dare talk to me like that! [*Furious*] You dare? You mean to insinuate that I know nothing? Go away! This minute!

YEP. [*Nervous*] I must ask you to express yourself more delicately.

VARYA. [*Beside herself*] Get out this minute. Get out! [*He goes to the door, she follows.*] Two-and-twenty troubles! Not another sign of you here! I don't wish to set eyes on you again! [YEPIKHODOFF *has gone out; his voice can be heard outside: "I'll make a complaint against you."*] What, coming back? [*Snatches up the stick left by* FIRCE *near the door.*] Go . . . go . . . go. I'll show you . . . Are you going? Are you going? Well, then take that. [*She lashes out with the stick as* LOPAKHIN *enters.*]

LOP. Much obliged. 297

VARYA. [*Angry but amused*] I'm sorry.

LOP. Never mind. I thank you for the pleasant reception you gave me!

VARYA. It isn't worthy of thanks. [*Walks away, then looks back and asks gently.*] I didn't hurt you, did I?

LOP. No, not at all. There'll be a huge bump, no more.

VOICES FROM THE DRAWING-ROOM. Lopakhin's returned! Yermolai Alexeievitch!

PISH. Now we'll see what there is to see and hear what there is to hear. . . . [*Kisses* LOPAKHIN.] You smell of brandy, my dashing soul. And we're all enjoying ourselves. 308

[*Enter* LIUBOFF ANDREIEVNA.]

LIUB. Is that you, Yermolai Alexeievitch? Why were you so long? Where's Leonid?

LOP. Leonid Andreievitch returned with me, he's coming. . . .

LIUB. [*Excited*] Well, what? Is it sold? Tell me?

LOP. [*Confused, afraid to show his pleasure*] The sale was over at four o'clock. . . . We missed the train, and had to wait till half-past nine. [*Sighs heavily.*] Ooh! My head's swimming a little.

[*Enter* GAIEFF; *in his right hand he carries things that he has bought, with his left he dries his eyes.*]

LIUB. Leon, what's happened? Leon, well? [*Impatiently, in tears*] Quick, for the love of God. . . . 317

GAI. [*Says nothing to her, only waves his hand; to* FIRCE, *weeping*] Here, take this . . . Here are anchovies, herrings from Kertch. . . . I've had no food today. . . . I have had a time! [*The door from the billiard-room is open; the clicking of the balls is heard, and* YASHA'S *voice, "Seven, eighteen!"* GAIEFF'S *expression changes, he no longer cries.*] I'm awfully tired. Let me change my clothes, Firce. [*Goes out through the drawing-room;* FIRCE *following him.*]

PISH. What happened? Come on, tell us!

LIUB. Is the cherry orchard sold?

LOP. It is sold.

LIUB. Who bought it? 328

LOP. I bought it. [*Pause.* LIUBOFF ANDREIEVNA *is overwhelmed; she would fall if she were not leaning against an armchair and a table.* VARYA *takes her keys off her belt, throws them on the floor into the middle of the room and goes out.*] I bought it! Wait, ladies and gentlemen, please, my head's going round, I can't talk. . . . [*Laughing*] When we reached the sale, Deriganoff was there already. Leonid Andreievitch had only fifteen thousand rubles, and Deriganoff offered thirty thousand on top of the mortgage to begin

with. I saw how matters stood, so I went right after him and bid
forty. He raised his bid to forty-five, I offered fifty-five. That means
he went up by fives and I went up by tens. . . . Well, it came to an
end at last, I bid ninety more than the mortgage; and it stayed [340
with me. The cherry orchard is mine now, mine! [*Roars with
laughter.*] My God, my God, the cherry orchard's mine! Tell me
I'm drunk, or crazy, or dreaming. . . . [*Stamps his feet.*] Don't
laugh at me! If my father and grandfather rose from their graves
and looked at the whole affair, and saw how their Yermolai, their
whipped and illiterate Yermolai, who used to run barefoot in the
winter, how that very Yermolai has bought an estate, the most beautiful spot in the world! I've bought the estate where my grandfather and my father were slaves, where they weren't even allowed
to enter the kitchen. I'm asleep, it's only a dream, an illusion. . . .
It's the fruit of imagination, wrapped in the fog of the unknown.
. . . [*Picks up the keys, gaily smiling.*] She threw down the keys,
she wished to show that she was no longer mistress here. . . . [353
[*Jingles keys.*] Well, it's all one! [*Hears the band tuning up.*] Eh,
musicians, play, I wish to hear you! Come and look at Yermolai
Lopakhin swinging his ax against the cherry orchard, come and
look at the trees falling! We'll build villas here, and our grandsons
and great-grandsons will see a new life here. . . . Play on, music.
[*The band plays.* LIUBOFF ANDREIEVNA *sinks into a chair and weeps
bitterly.* LOPAKHIN *continues reproachfully.*] Why then, why didn't
you take my advice? My poor, dear woman, you can't go back now.
[*Weeps.*] Oh, if only the whole thing were finished, if only our
uneven, unhappy lives were changed!   363
  PISH. [*Takes his arm; in an undertone*] She's crying. Let's go into
the drawing-room and leave her by herself . . . come on . . .
                              [*Takes his arm and leads him out.*]
  LOP. What's that? Bandsmen, play up! Go on, do just as I wish
you to! [*Ironically*] The new owner, the owner of the cherry
orchard is coming! [*He accidentally knocks up against a little table
and nearly upsets the candelabra.*] I can pay for everything now!
                                        [*Exit with* PISHCHIK.]

[*In the reception-room and the drawing-room nobody remains except* LIUBOFF ANDREIEVNA, *who sits huddled up and weeping bitterly. The band plays softly.* ANYA *and* TROFIMOFF *come in quickly.* ANYA *goes up to her mother and kneels in front of her.* TROFIMOFF *stands at the drawing-room entrance.*]

ANYA. Mother! Mother, are you crying? My dear, kind, good mother, my beautiful mother, I love you! Bless you! The cherry orchard is sold. We own it no longer, it's true. But don't cry, mother, you still have your life before you, you've still your beautiful pure soul. . . . Come with me, come, dear, away from here, come! We'll plant a new orchard more beautiful than this, and you'll see it, and you'll understand, and deep soothing joy will enfold your soul, like the evening sun, and you'll smile, mother! Come, dear, let's go!

ACT FOUR

Same as Act I. There are no curtains on the windows, no pictures; only a few pieces of furniture are left piled up in a corner as if for sale. The emptiness is apparent. There are bags and suitcases by the door that leads out of the house and at the back of the stage.

[*The door at the left is open; the voices of* VARYA *and* ANYA *can be heard through it.* LOPAKHIN *stands and waits.* YASHA *holds a tray with little glasses of champagne. Outside,* YEPIKHODOFF *is tying up a box. Voices are heard behind the stage. The peasants have come to say good-bye. The voice of* GAIEFF *is heard; "Thank you, brothers, thank you."*]

YASHA. The peasants have come to say good-bye. I am of the opinion, Yermolai Alexeievitch, that they're good people, but they don't understand very much.

[*The voices die away.* LIUBOFF ANDREIEVNA *and* GAIEFF *enter. She is not crying but is pale, and her face twitches; she can hardly speak.*]

GAI. You gave them your purse, Liuba. You can't go on like that, you can't!

LIUB. I couldn't help myself, I couldn't! [*They go out.*]

5

LOP. [*In the doorway, looking after them*] Please, I ask you most humbly! Just a little glass for farewell. I didn't remember to bring any from town and I found only one bottle at the station. Please, do! [*Pause*] Won't you really have any? [*Goes away from the door.*] If I only knew—I wouldn't have bought any. Well, I shan't drink any, either. [YASHA *carefully puts the tray on a chair.*] You have a drink, Yasha, at any rate.

YASHA. To those departing! And good luck to those who stay behind! [*Drinks.*] I can assure you that this isn't real champagne.

LOP. Eight rubles a bottle. [*Pause*] It's frightfully cold here.

YASHA. We made no fire today, since we're going away. [*Laughs.*]

LOP. What's the matter with you?   18

YASHA. I'm happy—that's all!

LOP. It's October, but it's as sunny and quiet as if it were summer. Good for building. [*Looking at his watch and speaking through the door*] Ladies and gentlemen, please remember that it's only forty-seven minutes till train time! You must leave for the station in twenty minutes. Hurry up.

[TROFIMOFF, *in an overcoat, enters from the outside.*]

TROF. I think it's time we went. The carriages are waiting. Where the devil are my rubbers? They're lost. [*Through the door*] Anya, I can't find my rubbers! I can't!   27

LOP. I have to go to Kharkoff. I'm going on the same train as you. I'm going to spend the whole winter in Kharkoff. I've been hanging around with you people. I am tired of doing nothing. I must have something to do with my hands; they seem to belong to a different person if I don't use them.

TROF. We'll go away now and then you'll start again on your useful occupations!

LOP. Have a glass?

TROF. No—thanks!

LOP. So you're off to Moscow now?   37

TROF. Yes. I'll see them into town and tomorrow I'm going to Moscow.

LOP. Yes . . . I suppose the professors aren't lecturing yet; they're waiting till you turn up!

TROF. That does not concern you.

LOP. How many years have you been going to the university?

TROF. Think of something new! This is old and trite! [*Looking for his rubbers*] You know, we may not meet again, so just let me give you a parting bit of advice: Don't wave your hands about! Get rid of that habit of waving them about. And then, building villas and reckoning on their residents becoming freeholders in time—that's the same thing; it's all a matter of waving your hands . . . I like you in spite of everything . . . You've slender, delicate fingers, like those of an artist, and you've a gentle, refined soul. . . .   51

LOP. [*Embraces him*] Good-bye, dear fellow. Thanks for all you've said. If you need money for the journey, let me give you some.

TROF. What for? I don't need any.

LOP. But you've nothing!

TROF. Yes, I have, thank you; I received some for a translation. Here it is in my pocket. [*Nervously*] But I can't find my rubbers!

VARYA. [*From the other room*] Take your rubbish away! [*Throws a pair of rubbers on stage.*]   60

TROF. Why are you angry, Varya? H'm! These aren't my rubbers!

LOP. In the spring I sowed three thousand acres of poppies, and now I've netted forty thousand rubles profit. Why turn up your nose at it? I'm just a simple peasant. . . . And when my poppies were in bloom, what a picture it was! So, as I was saying, I made forty thousand rubles, and I mean I'd like to lend you some, because I can afford it.   67

TROF. Your father was a peasant, mine was a druggist, and that means nothing at all. [LOPAKHIN *takes out his pocketbook.*] No, no . . . Even if you gave me twenty thousand I should refuse. I'm a free man. And everything that rich and poor alike value so highly carries no more weight with me than thistledown in a wind. I can do without you, I can pass you by. I'm strong and proud. Mankind goes on to the highest possible truths and happiness on earth, and I march in the front ranks!

LOP. Will you reach there?

TROF. I shall! [*Pause*] I'll reach there and show the way to others.
[*Axes cutting the trees are heard in the distance.*]   78

LOP. Well, good-bye, old man. It's time to go. Here we stand pulling one another's noses, but life goes its own way all the while. When I work for a long stretch tirelessly, my thoughts become clearer and it seems to me that I understand the reasons for existence. But think, brother, how many people live in Russia without knowing why—? But all this is beside the point. Leonid Andreievitch, they say, has accepted a post in a bank; he will get six thousand rubles a year . . . But he won't stand it; he's very lazy.

ANYA. [*At the door*] Mother asks if you will stop them cutting down the orchard until she has gone away.   88

TROF. Yes, really, you ought to have enough tact not to do that.
                                                         [*Exit.*]

LOP. All right, all right . . . What funny people!   [*Exit.*]

ANYA. Has Firce been sent to the hospital?

YASHA. I gave the order this morning. I suppose they've sent him.

ANYA. [*To* YEPIKHODOFF, *who crosses the room*] Semyon Panteleievitch, please make inquiries if Firce has been sent to the hospital.

YASHA. [*Offended*] I told Yegor this morning. What's the use of asking ten times?

YEP. That old Firce, in my conclusive opinion, isn't worth mending; he had better join his ancestors. I only envy him. [*Puts a trunk on a hat-box and squashes it.*] Well, of course. I thought so!   99
                                                         [*Exit.*]

YASHA. [*Grinning*] Two-and-twenty troubles.

VARYA. [*Behind the door*] Has Firce been taken away to the hospital?

ANYA. Yes.

VARYA. Why didn't they take the letter to the doctor?

ANYA. It'll have to be sent after him.   [*Exit.*]

VARYA. [*In the next room*] Where's Yasha? Tell him his mother has come and wishes to say good-bye to him.   107

YASHA. [*Waving his hand*] She'll make me lose all patience!
[DUNYASHA *meanwhile has been busying herself with the bags; now that* YASHA *is left alone, she goes to him.*]

DUN. If you would only look at me once, Yasha. You're going away, leaving me behind . . . [*Weeps and hugs him.*]

YASHA. What's the use of crying? [*Drinks champagne.*] In six days I'll be back again in Paris. Tomorrow we get into the express and off we go. I can hardly believe it. Vive la France! It doesn't suit me here, I can't live here . . . it's no good. Well, I've seen the uncivilized world; I have had enough of it. [*Drinks champagne.*] What are you crying for? Behave decently and then you'll have no cause for tears!

DUN. [*Powders herself, looking in the mirror*] Write me from Paris! I loved you so much, Yasha, so much! I am a delicate girl, Yasha.
120

YASHA. Somebody's coming.

[*He bustles around the baggage, singing softly. Enter* LIUBOFF, AN-
DREIEVNA, GAIEFF, ANYA, *and* CHARLOTTA IVANOVNA.]

GAI. We'd better be off. There's no time to lose. [*Looks at* YASHA.] Somebody smells of herring!

LIUB. We needn't get into our carriages for ten minutes. [*Looks round the room.*] Good-bye, dear house, old grandfather. The winter will pass, the spring will come, and then you'll be here no more. You'll be pulled down. How much these walls have seen! [*Passionately kisses her daughter.*] My treasure, you're radiant, your eyes flash like two jewels! Are you happy? Very?

ANYA. Very! A new life is beginning, mother!
130

GAI. [*Gaily*] Yes, really, everything's all right now. Before the cherry orchard was sold we all were excited and worried, and then, when the question was solved once and for all, we all calmed down, and even became cheerful. I'm a bank official now, and a financier . . . red in the center; and you, Liuba, look better for some reason or other, there's no doubt about it.

LIUB. Yes. My nerves are better, it's true. [*She puts on her coat and hat.*] I sleep well. Take my baggage out, Yasha. It's time. [*To* ANYA] My little girl, we'll soon see each other again . . . I'm off to Paris. I'll live there on the money your grandmother from Yaroslavl sent to buy the estate—bless her!—though it won't last long.
142

ANYA. You'll come back soon, soon, mother, won't you? I'll get ready, and pass the examination at the High School, and then I'll work and help you. We'll read all sorts of books together, won't we? [*Kisses her mother's hands.*] We'll read in the autumn evenings; we'll read many books, and a beautiful new world will open up before us . . . [*Thoughtfully*] You'll come, mother. . . .

LIUB. I'll come, my darling. [*Embraces her.*]

[*Enter* LOPAKHIN. CHARLOTTA *is singing to herself.*]

GAI. Charlotta is happy; she's singing!   150

CHAR. [*Takes a bundle, looking like a wrapped-up baby*] My little baby, bye-bye. [*The baby seems to answer, "Oua, oua!"*] Hush, my nice little boy. ["*Oua! Oua!*"] I'm so sorry for you! [*Throws the bundle back.*] So please find me a new place. I can't go on like this.

LOP. We'll find one, Charlotta Ivanovna, don't you be afraid.

GAI. Everybody's leaving us. Varya's going away . . . we've suddenly become unnecessary.

CHAR. I've nowhere to live in town. I must go away. [*Hums.*] Never mind.

[*Enter* PISHCHIK.]

LOP. The miracle of nature!   160

PISH. [*Puffing*] Oh, let me get my breath again. I'm fagged . . . My honorable friends, give me some water . . .

GAI. Come for money did you? I'm your humble servant, and I'm going out of the way of temptation.   [*Exit.*]

PISH. I haven't been here for ever so long . . . dear madam. [*To* LOPAKHIN] You here? Glad to see you . . . man of tremendous brain . . . take this . . . take it . . . [*Gives* LOPAKHIN *money.*] Four hundred rubles . . . that leaves 841—

LOP. [*Shrugs his shoulders in surprise*] It's like a dream. Where did you get this?   170

PISH. Stop . . . it's hot . . . A most unexpected thing happened. A group of Englishmen came along and found some white clay on my land. . . . [*To* LIUBOFF ANDREIEVNA.] And here's four hundred for you . . . beautiful lady . . . [*Gives her money.*] Give you the rest later . . . [*Drinks water.*] Just now a young man in the train was saying that some great philosopher advises us all to jump from

the roofs. "Jump!" he says, and that's all. [*Astonished*] Just imagine! More water!

LOP. Who were these Englishmen? 179

PISH. I've leased the land with the clay to them for twenty-four years . . . Now, excuse me, I've no time. I must hurry or—I'll go to Gnoikoff—to Kardamanoff—I owe everybody—[*Drinks.*] Goodbye—I'll drop in Thursday.

LIUB. We're just starting off to town, and tomorrow I go abroad.

PISH. [*Agitated*] What? Why to town? I see furniture . . . trunks . . . Well, never mind. [*Crying*] Never mind. These Englishmen are men of tremendous intellect . . . Never mind . . . Be happy . . . God will help you . . . Never mind . . . Everything in this world comes to an end . . . [*Kisses* LIUBOFF ANDREIEVNA's [189 *hand.*] And if you should happen to hear that my end has come, just remember this old . . . horse and say: "There used to be a certain fellow called Semyonoff-Pishchik, God bless his soul. . . ." Wonderful weather . . . yes . . . [*Exit deeply moved, but returns at once and says in the door.*] Dashenka sent her love! [*Exit.*]

LIUB. Now we can go. I've two worries, though. The first is poor Firce. [*Looks at her watch.*] We've still five minutes . . .

ANYA. Mother, Firce has already been sent to the hospital. Yasha sent him off this morning. 198

LIUB. The second is Varya. She's used to getting up early and to work, and now she has no work to do, she's like a fish out of water. She's grown thin and pale, and she cries, poor thing. . . . [*Pause*] You know very well, Yermolai Alexeievitch, that I hoped formerly to marry her to you, and I suppose you are going to marry somebody? [*Whispers to* ANYA, *who nods to* CHARLOTTA, *and they both go out.*] She loves you, she's your sort, and I don't understand, I really don't, why you seem to be keeping away from each other. I don't understand! 207

LOP. To tell the truth, I don't understand it myself. It's all so strange. . . . If there's still time, I'll be ready at once. Let's get it over, once and for all; I don't feel as if I could ever propose to her without you.

LIUB. Excellent. It'll take only a minute. I'll call her.

LOP. The champagne comes in very handy. [*Looking at the glass*] They're empty, somebody's drunk them already. [YASHA *coughs.*] I call that licking it up. . . .

LIUB. [*Animated*] Excellent. We'll go out. Yasha, *allez*. I'll call her . . . [*At the door*] Varya, leave that and come here. Come!
[*Exit with* YASHA.]

LOP. [*Looks at his watch*] Yes . . . [*Pause*]   218
[*There is a restrained laugh behind the door, a whisper, then* VARYA *comes in. She examines the luggage at length.*]

VARYA. I can't seem to find it . . .

LOP. What are you looking for?

VARYA. I packed it myself and I don't remember. [*Pause*]

LOP. Where are you going now, Varvara Mikhailovna?

VARYA. I? To the Ragulins . . . I've accepted a position, to look after their household . . . housekeeper or something.

LOP. Is that at Yashnevo? It's about fifty miles. [*Pause*] So life in this house is finished now. . . .   226

VARYA. [*Looking at the baggage*] Where is it? . . . perhaps I've put it away in the trunk . . . Yes, there'll be no more life in this house . . .

LOP. And I'm off to Kharkoff at once . . . by this train. I've a lot of business on hand. I'm leaving Yepikhodoff here . . . I've hired him.

VARYA. Well, well!

LOP. Last year at this time the snow was already falling, if you remember, and now it's nice and sunny. Only it's rather cold . . . There's three degrees of frost.   236

VARYA. I didn't look. [*Pause*] And our thermometer's broken.
. . . [*Pause*]

VOICE AT THE DOOR. Yermolai Alexeievitch!

LOP. [*As if he has long been waiting to be called*] Just a minute. [*Exit quickly.* VARYA, *sitting on the floor, puts her face against a bundle of clothes and weeps gently. The door opens.* LIUBOFF ANDREIEVNA *enters carefully.*]

LIUB. Well? [*Pause*] We must go.

VARYA. [*Not crying now, wipes her eyes*] Yes, it's quite time, dear mother. I'll get to the Ragulins today, if I don't miss the train. . . .

LIUB. [*At the door*] Anya, put on your things. [*Enter* ANYA, *then* GAIEFF, *and* CHARLOTTA IVANOVNA. GAIEFF *wears a warm overcoat with a cape. A servant and drivers come in.* YEPIKHODOFF *bustles around the baggage.*] Now we can go away. 247

ANYA. [*Joyfully*] Away!

GAI. My friends, my dear friends! Can I be silent, in leaving this house forever?—can I restrain myself, in saying farewell, from expressing those feelings which now fill all my soul?

ANYA. [*Imploringly*] Uncle!

VARYA. Uncle, you shouldn't!

GAI. [*Stupidly*] Double the red into the center . . . I'll be quiet.

[*Enter* TROFIMOFF, *then* LOPAKHIN.]

TROF. Well, it's time to go!

LOP. Yepikhodoff, my coat! 256

LIUB. I'll sit here one minute more. It's as if I'd never really noticed what the walls and ceilings of this house were like, and now I look at them greedily, with such tender love. . . .

GAI. I remember, when I was six years old, on Trinity Sunday, I sat at this window and looked and watched my father go to church. . . .

LIUB. Have all the things been taken away? 263

LOP. Yes, all, I think. [*To* YEPIKHODOFF, *putting on his coat*] You see that everything's quite straight, Yepikhodoff.

YEP. [*Hoarsely*] You may depend upon me, Yermolai Alexeievitch!

LOP. What's the matter with your voice?

YEP. I swallowed something just now; I was taking a drink of water.

YASHA. [*Suspiciously*] What manners . . .

LIUB. We go away, and not a soul remains behind.

LOP. Till the spring. 273

VARYA. [*Drags an umbrella out of a bundle, and seems to be waving it about.* LOPAKHIN *appears to be frightened*] What are you doing? . . . I never thought . . .

TROF. Come along, let's take our seats . . . it's time! The train will be in presently.

VARYA. Peter, here they are, your rubbers, by that trunk. [*In tears*] And how old and dirty they are . . .

TROF. [*Putting them on*] Come on!

GAI. [*Deeply moved, nearly crying*] The train . . . the station . . . Cross in the center, a white double in the corner. . . . [283

LIUB. Let's go!

LOP. Are you all here? There's nobody else? [*Locks the side-door on the left.*] There's a lot of things in there. I must lock them up. Come!

ANYA. Good-bye, home! Good-bye, old life!

TROF. Welcome, new life. [*Exit with* ANYA. VARYA *looks round the room and goes out slowly.* YASHA *and* CHARLOTTA, *with her little dog, go out.*]

LOP. Till the spring then! Come on . . . till we meet [292 again! [*Exit.*]

[LIUBOFF ANDREIEVNA *and* GAIEFF *are left alone. They seem to have been waiting for this moment. They fall into each other's arms and sob restrainedly and quietly, fearing that somebody might hear them.*]

GAI. [*In despair*] My sister, my sister . . .

LIUB. My dear, my gentle, beautiful orchard! My life, my youth, my happiness, good-bye! Good-bye!

ANYA'S VOICE. [*Gaily*] Mother!

TROF.'S VOICE. [*Gaily, excited*] Coo-ee!

LIUB. To look at the walls and the windows for the last time . . . My late mother used to like to walk about this room . . .　　299

GAI. My sister, my sister!

ANYA'S VOICE. Mother!

TROF.'S VOICE. [*Gaily, excited*] Coo-ee!

LIUB. We're coming! [*They go out. The stage is empty. The sound of keys turned in the locks is heard, and then the noise of the carriages driving off. It is quiet. Then the sound of an ax against the trees is heard in the silence sadly and staccato. Footsteps are heard.* FIRCE *comes in from the door on the right. He is dressed*

as usual, in a short jacket and white vest, with slippers on his feet.
He is ill. He goes to the door and tries the handle.]
                                                                309

FIRCE. It's locked. They've left. [*Sits on sofa.*] They've forgotten
me. . . . Never mind, I'll sit here . . . And Leonid Andreievitch
has probably gone in a light overcoat instead of putting on his fur
coat . . . [*Sighs anxiously.*] I didn't see. . . . Oh, these young people! [*Mumbles something unintelligible.*] Life's gone on as if I'd
never lived. [*Lying down*] I'll lie down. . . . You've no strength
left in you, nothing left at all. . . . Oh, you . . . bungler! [*He lies*
motionless. The distant sound is heard, as if from the sky, of a string
breaking, dying away morosely. Silence follows it, and only the
sound somewhere in the distance, of the ax falling on the trees, is
audible.]

George Bernard Shaw

PYGMALION

GEORGE BERNARD SHAW, who became famous as a critic of the manners and morals of respectable society, began life, in his own words, as a downstart and an outsider. He was born in 1856, the son of English Protestant parents in Catholic Dublin. His father derided the world in which he was a failure and from which his heavy drinking ostracized the family. After leaving school at fifteen and working for five years as a minor clerk, Shaw joined his mother in London, where she had fled to earn her living as an opera singer and teacher. Between 1876 and 1883 Shaw wrote five satiric and unsuccessful novels, and then joined the new Fabian Society as a speaker and campaigner for its program of gradual social and economic reform. In 1888 he moved closer to the stage by beginning a brilliantly witty and uncompromising career as a music and drama critic. His first play was *Widower's House* (1892), a product of his interest in Ibsen and social reform and his dissatisfaction with the Victorian theater. Taking a conventional romantic plot, he inverted it as a way of shocking the audience into realizing that many "respectable" people live on money from slum housing. *Widower's House* was followed by such well-known plays as *Mrs. Warren's Profession* (1893), *Arms and the Man* (1894), *Candida* (1894), *Caesar and Cleopatra* (1898), and *Major Barbara* (1905). Social and ethical problems absorbed Shaw until his death in 1950, and in dramatizing them he employed the inversions, paradoxes, and other devices typical of satiric comedy.

Pygmalion (1912) belongs in this tradition. Behind it is a story glorifying romantic love. The legendary Pygmalion, revolted by the loose, hard women of his native Cyprus, fashioned an ideally beautiful girl from ivory, and under his caresses she finally came

to life and returned his love. Shaw's Pygmalion is an unromantic, middle-aged bachelor, a professor of phonetics; his heroine, Liza Doolittle, is a flower girl from the slums of London. As Professor Higgins transforms Liza's speech and appearance into those of a duchess, the audience is drawn by the Pygmalion-Cinderella plot in the background to desire a romantic ending, but Shaw arouses and thwarts this desire in order to direct attention to his real subject: the relation between a person's attempt to realize his own individuality and the pressures upon him from social conventions and economic circumstances. This deeper subject is likewise served by Shaw's idea of making his hero a professor of phonetics. In the opening scene of the play Professor Higgins displays his phonetic skill by identifying through their speech the backgrounds of several strangers on a London street corner, but this simple difference of accent is soon enlarged into a major theme and dramatic technique. For example, the first public test of Liza's "improved" speech in Act III is a high moment of the play not simply because it is a climax of the plot but chiefly because of Shaw's skill in creating characters whose "voices" reveal many kinds and layers of reality. How can one find his true voice and be himself? Shaw's witty and compassionate exploration of that question makes *Pygmalion* a perennially interesting comedy.

PYGMALION

A Romance in Five Acts

PREFACE TO PYGMALION—
A PROFESSOR OF PHONETICS

As will be seen later on, Pygmalion needs, not a preface, but a sequel, which I have supplied in its due place. The English have no respect for their language, and will not teach their children to speak it. They spell it so abominably that no man can teach himself what it sounds like. It is impossible for an Englishman to open his mouth without making some other Englishman hate or despise him. German and Spanish are accessible to foreigners; English is not accessible even to Englishmen. The reformer England needs today is an energetic phonetic enthusiast: that is why I have made such a one the hero of a popular play. There have been heroes of that kind crying in the wilderness for many years past. When I became interested in the subject towards the end of the eighteen-seventies, the illustrious Alexander Melville Bell, the inventor of Visible Speech, had emigrated to Canada, where his son invented the telephone; but Alexander J. Ellis was still a London patriarch, with an impressive head always covered by a velvet skull cap, for which he would apologize to public meetings in a very courtly manner. He and Tito Pagliardini, another phonetic veteran, were men whom it was impossible to dislike. Henry Sweet, then a young man, lacked their sweetness of character: he was about as conciliatory to conventional mortals as Ibsen or Samuel Butler. His great ability as a phonetician (he was, I think, the best of them all at his job) would have entitled him to high official recognition, and perhaps enabled

him to popularize his subject, but for his Satanic contempt for all academic dignitaries and persons in general who thought more of Greek than of phonetics. Once, in the days when the Imperial Institute rose in South Kensington, and Joseph Chamberlain was booming the Empire, I induced the editor of a leading monthly review to commission an article from Sweet on the imperial importance of his subject. When it arrived, it contained nothing but a savagely derisive attack on a professor of language and literature whose chair Sweet regarded as proper to a phonetic expert only. The article, being libellous, had to be returned as impossible; and I had to renounce my dream of dragging its author into the limelight. When I met him afterwards, for the first time for many years, I found to my astonishment that he, who had been a quite tolerably presentable young man, had actually managed by sheer scorn to alter his personal appearance until he had become a sort of walking repudiation of Oxford and all its traditions. It must have been largely in his own despite that he was squeezed into something called a Readership of phonetics there. The future of phonetics rests probably with his pupils, who all swore by him; but nothing could bring the man himself into any sort of compliance with the university to which he nevertheless clung by divine right in an intensely Oxonian way. I daresay his papers, if he has left any, include some satires that may be published without too destructive results fifty years hence. He was, I believe, not in the least an illnatured man: very much the opposite, I should say; but he would not suffer fools gladly.

Those who knew him will recognize in my third act the allusion to the patent shorthand in which he used to write postcards, and which may be acquired from a four and sixpenny manual published by the Clarendon Press. The postcards which Mrs. Higgins describes are such as I have received from Sweet. I would decipher a sound which a cockney would represent by *zerr,* and a Frenchman by *seu,* and then write demanding with some heat what on earth it meant. Sweet, with boundless contempt for my stupidity, would reply that it not only meant but obviously was the word Result, as no other word containing that sound, and capable of making sense with the context, existed in any language spoken on earth. That less

expert mortals should require fuller indications was beyond Sweet's patience. Therefore, though the whole point of his Current Shorthand is that it can express every sound in the language perfectly, vowels as well as consonants, and that your hand has to make no stroke except the easy and current ones with which you write m, n, and u, l, p, and q, scribbling them at whatever angle comes easiest to you, his unfortunate determination to make this remarkable and quite legible script serve also as a shorthand reduced it in his own practice to the most inscrutable of cryptograms. His true objective was the provision of a full, accurate, legible script for our noble but ill-dressed language; but he was led past that by his contempt for the popular Pitman system of shorthand, which he called the Pitfall system. The triumph of Pitman was a triumph of business organization: there was a weekly paper to persuade you to learn Pitman: there were cheap textbooks and exercise books and transcripts of speeches for you to copy, and schools where experienced teachers coached you up to the necessary proficiency. Sweet could not organize his market in that fashion. He might as well have been the Sybil who tore up the leaves of prophecy that nobody would attend to. The four and sixpenny manual, mostly in his lithographed handwriting, that was never vulgarly advertized, may perhaps some day be taken up by a syndicate and pushed upon the public as The Times pushed the Encyclopaedia Britannica; but until then it will certainly not prevail against Pitman. I have bought three copies of it during my lifetime; and I am informed by the publishers that its cloistered existence is still a steady and healthy one. I actually learned the system two several times; and yet the shorthand in which I am writing these lines is Pitman's. And the reason is, that my secretary cannot transcribe Sweet, having been perforce taught in the schools of Pitman. Therefore, Sweet railed at Pitman as vainly as Thersites railed at Ajax: his raillery, however it may have eased his soul, gave no popular vogue to Current Shorthand.

Pygmalion Higgins is not a portrait of Sweet, to whom the adventure of Eliza Doolittle would have been impossible; still, as will be seen, there are touches of Sweet in the play. With Higgins's physique and temperament Sweet might have set the Thames on fire. As it was, he impressed himself professionally on Europe to

an extent that made his comparative personal obscurity, and the failure of Oxford to do justice to his eminence, a puzzle to foreign specialists in his subject. I do not blame Oxford, because I think Oxford is quite right in demanding a certain social amenity from its nurslings (heaven knows it is not exorbitant in its requirements!); for although I well know how hard it is for a man of genius with a seriously underrated subject to maintain serene and kindly relations with the men who underrate it, and who keep all the best places for less important subjects which they profess without originality and sometimes without much capacity for them, still, if he overwhelms them with wrath and disdain, he cannot expect them to heap honors on him.

Of the later generations of phoneticians I know little. Among them towers the Poet Laureate, to whom perhaps Higgins may owe his Miltonic sympathies, though here again I must disclaim all portraiture. But if the play makes the public aware that there are such people as phoneticians, and that they are among the most important people in England at present, it will serve its turn.

I wish to boast that Pygmalion has been an extremely successful play all over Europe and North America as well as at home. It is so intensely and deliberately didactic, and its subject is esteemed so dry, that I delight in throwing it at the heads of the wiseacres who repeat the parrot cry that art should never be didactic. It goes to prove my contention that art should never be anything else.

Finally, and for the encouragement of people troubled with accents that cut them off from all high employment, I may add that the change wrought by Professor Higgins in the flower girl is neither impossible nor uncommon. The modern concierge's daughter who fulfils her ambition by playing the Queen of Spain in Ruy Blas at the Théâtre Français is only one of many thousands of men and women who have sloughed off their native dialects and acquired a new tongue. But the thing has to be done scientifically, or the last state of the aspirant may be worse than the first. An honest and natural slum dialect is more tolerable than the attempt of a phonetically untaught person to imitate the vulgar dialect of the golf club; and I am sorry to say that in spite of the efforts of our

Royal Academy of Dramatic Art, there is still too much sham golfing English on our stage, and too little of the noble English of Forbes Robertson.

ACT I

Covent Garden at 11.15 p.m. Torrents of heavy summer rain. Cab whistles blowing frantically in all directions. Pedestrians running for shelter into the market and under the portico of St. Paul's Church, where there are already several people, among them a lady and her daughter in evening dress. They are all peering out gloomily at the rain, except one man with his back turned to the rest, who seems wholly preoccupied with a notebook in which he is writing busily.

The church clock strikes the first quarter.

THE DAUGHTER. [*In the space between the central pillars, close to the one on her left*] I'm getting chilled to the bone. What can Freddy be doing all this time? He's been gone twenty minutes.

THE MOTHER. [*On her daughter's right*] Not so long. But he ought to have got us a cab by this.

A BYSTANDER. [*On the lady's right*] He wont get no cab not until half-past eleven, missus, when they come back after dropping their theatre fares.

THE MOTHER. But we must have a cab. We cant stand here until half-past eleven. It's too bad.   10

THE BYSTANDER. Well, it aint my fault, missus.

THE DAUGHTER. If Freddy had a bit of gumption, he would have got one at the theatre door.

THE MOTHER. What could he have done, poor boy?

THE DAUGHTER. Other people got cabs. Why couldn't he?

[FREDDY *rushes in out of the rain from the Southampton Street side, and comes between them closing a dripping umbrella. He is a young man of twenty, in evening dress, very wet around the ankles.*]

THE DAUGHTER. Well, havnt you got a cab?   20

FREDDY. Theres not one to be had for love or money.

THE MOTHER. Oh, Freddy, there must be one. You cant have tried.

THE DAUGHTER. It's too tiresome. Do you expect us to go and get one ourselves?

FREDDY. I tell you theyre all engaged. The rain was so sudden: nobody was prepared; and everybody had to take a cab. Ive been to Charing Cross one way and nearly to Ludgate Circus the other; and they were all engaged.

THE MOTHER. Did you try Trafalgar Square?

FREDDY. There wasnt one at Trafalgar Square.   30

THE DAUGHTER. Did you try?

FREDDY. I tried as far as Charing Cross Station. Did you expect me to walk to Hammersmith?

THE DAUGHTER. You havnt tried at all.

THE MOTHER. You really are very helpless, Freddy. Go again; and dont come back until you have found a cab.

FREDDY. I shall simply get soaked for nothing.

THE DAUGHTER. And what about us? Are we to stay here all night in this draught, with next to nothing on? You selfish pig—   39

FREDDY. Oh, very well: I'll go, I'll go. [*He opens his umbrella and dashes off Strandwards, but comes into collision with a flower girl, who is hurrying in for shelter, knocking her basket out of her hands. A blinding flash of lightning, followed instantly by a rattling peal of thunder, orchestrates the incident.*]

THE FLOWER GIRL. Nah then, Freddy: look wh' y' gowin, deah.

FREDDY. Sorry. [*He rushes off.*]

THE FLOWER GIRL. [*Picking up her scattered flowers and replacing them in the basket*] Theres menners f' yer! Te-oo banches o voylets trod into the mad. [*She sits down on the plinth of the column, sorting her flowers, on the lady's right. She is not at all an attractive* [50 *person. She is perhaps eighteen, perhaps twenty, hardly older. She wears a little sailor hat of black straw that has long been exposed to the dust and soot of London and has seldom if ever been brushed. Her hair needs washing rather badly: its mousy color can hardly be natural. She wears a shoddy black coat that reaches nearly to her knees and is shaped to her waist. She has a brown skirt with a coarse apron. Her boots are much the worse for wear. She is no doubt as clean as she can afford to be; but compared to the ladies*

she is very dirty. Her features are no worse than theirs; but their condition leaves something to be desired; and she needs the services of a dentist.] 61

THE MOTHER. How do you know that my son's name is Freddy, pray?

THE FLOWER GIRL. Ow, eez ye-ooa san, is e? Wal, fewd dan y' de-ooty bawmz a mather should, eed now bettern to spawl a pore gel's flahrzn than ran awy athaht pyin. Will ye-oo py me f' them? [*Here, with apologies, this desperate attempt to represent her dialect without a phonetic alphabet must be abandoned as unintelligible outside London.*]

THE DAUGHTER. Do nothing of the sort, mother. The idea! 70

THE MOTHER. Please allow me, Clara. Have you any pennies?

THE DAUGHTER. No. Ive nothing smaller than sixpence.

THE FLOWER GIRL. [*Hopefully*] I can give you change for a tanner, kind lady.

THE MOTHER. [*To* CLARA] Give it to me. [CLARA *parts reluctantly.*] Now [*to the girl*] this is for your flowers.

THE FLOWER GIRL. Thank you kindly, lady.

THE DAUGHTER. Make her give you the change. These things are only a penny a bunch.

THE MOTHER. Do hold your tongue, Clara. [*To the girl*] You can keep the change. 81

THE FLOWER GIRL. Oh, thank you, lady.

THE MOTHER. Now tell me how you know that young gentleman's name.

THE FLOWER GIRL. I didnt.

THE MOTHER. I heard you call him by it. Dont try to deceive me.

THE FLOWER GIRL. [*Protesting*] Who's trying to deceive you? I called him Freddy or Charlie same as you might yourself if you was talking to a stranger and wished to be pleasant. [*She sits down beside her basket.*] 90

THE DAUGHTER. Sixpence thrown away! Really, mamma, you might have spared Freddy *that.* [*She retreats in disgust behind the pillar.*]

[*An elderly gentleman of the amiable military type rushes into the shelter, and closes a dripping umbrella. He is in the same*

plight as Freddy, very wet about the ankles. He is in evening dress, with a light overcoat. He takes the place left vacant by the daughter's retirement.]

THE GENTLEMAN. Phew!

THE MOTHER. [*To the gentleman*] Oh, sir, is there any sign of its stopping?

THE GENTLEMAN. I'm afraid not. It started worse than ever about two minutes ago. [*He goes to the plinth beside the flower girl; puts up his foot on it; and stoops to turn down his trouser ends.*]

THE MOTHER. Oh dear! [*She retires sadly and joins her daughter.*]

THE FLOWER GIRL. [*Taking advantage of the military gentleman's proximity to establish friendly relations with him*] If it's worse, it's a sign it's nearly over. So cheer up, Captain; and buy a flower off a poor girl.

THE GENTLEMAN. I'm sorry. I havnt any change.

THE FLOWER GIRL. I can give you change, Captain.

THE GENTLEMAN. For a sovereign? Ive nothing less.

THE FLOWER GIRL. Garn! Oh do buy a flower off me, Captain. I can change half-a-crown. Take this for tuppence.

THE GENTLEMAN. Now dont be troublesome: theres a good girl. [*Trying his pockets.*] I really havnt any change— Stop: heres three hapence, if thats any use to you. [*He retreats to the other pillar.*]

THE FLOWER GIRL. [*Disappointed, but thinking three half-pence better than nothing*] Thank you, sir.

THE BYSTANDER. [*To the girl*] You be careful: give him a flower for it. Theres a bloke here behind taking down every blessed word youre saying. [*All turn to the man who is taking notes.*]

THE FLOWER GIRL. [*Springing up terrified*] I aint done nothing wrong by speaking to the gentleman. Ive a right to sell flowers if I keep off the kerb. [*Hysterically*] I'm a respectable girl: so help me, I never spoke to him except to ask him to buy a flower off me. [*General hubbub, mostly sympathetic to the flower girl, but deprecating her excessive sensibility. Cries of* Dont start hollerin. Who's hurting you? Nobody's going to touch you. Whats the good of fussing? Steady on. Easy easy, etc., *come from the elderly staid spectators, who pat her comfortingly. Less patient ones bid her shut her head, or ask her roughly what is wrong with her. A remoter group, not* [131

knowing what the matter is, crowd in and increase the noise with question and answer: Whats the row? Whatshe do? Where is he? A tec taking her down. What! him? Yes: him over there: Took money off the gentleman, etc. *The flower girl, distraught and mobbed, breaks through them to the gentleman, crying wildly.*] Oh, sir, dont let him charge me. You dunno what it means to me. Theyll take away my character and drive me on the streets for speaking to gentlemen. They—

THE NOTE TAKER. [*Coming forward on her right, the rest crowding after him*] There, there, there, there! who's hurting you, you silly girl? What do you take me for?   142

THE BYSTANDER. It's all right: he's a gentleman: look at his boots. [*Explaining to the note taker.*] She thought you was a copper's nark, sir.

THE NOTE TAKER. [*With quick interest*] Whats a copper's nark?

THE BYSTANDER. [*Inapt at definition*] It's a—well, it's a copper's nark, as you might say. What else would you call it? A sort of informer.

THE FLOWER GIRL. [*Still hysterical*] I take my Bible oath I never said a word—   151

THE NOTE TAKER. [*Overbearing but good-humored*] Oh, shut up, shut up. Do I look like a policeman?

THE FLOWER GIRL. [*Far from reassured*] Then what did you take down my words for? How do I know whether you took me down right? You just shew me what youve wrote about me. [*The note taker opens his book and holds it steadily under her nose, though the pressure of the mob trying to read it over his shoulders would upset a weaker man.*] Whats that? *That* aint proper writing. I cant read that.   160

THE NOTE TAKER. I can. [*Reads, reproducing her pronunciation exactly*] "Cheer ap, Keptin; n' baw ya flahr orf a pore gel."

THE FLOWER GIRL. [*Much distressed*] It's because I called him Captain. I meant no harm. [*To the gentleman*] Oh, sir, don't let him lay a charge agen me for a word like that. You—

THE GENTLEMAN. Charge! I make no charge. [*To the note taker*] Really, sir, if you are a detective, you need not begin protecting me

against molestation by young women until I ask you. Anybody
could see that the girl meant no harm.   169

THE BYSTANDERS GENERALLY. [*Demonstrating against police es-
pionage*] Course they could. What business is it of yours? You
mind your own affairs. He wants promotion, he does. Taking down
people's words! Girl never said a word to him. What harm if she
did? Nice thing a girl cant shelter from the rain without being
insulted, etc., etc., etc. [*She is conducted by the more sympathetic
demonstrators back to her plinth, where she resumes her seat and
struggles with her emotions.*]

THE BYSTANDER. He aint a tec. He's a blooming busybody: thats.
what he is. I tell you, look at his boots.

THE NOTE TAKER. [*Turning on him genially*] And how are all
your people down at Selsey?   181

THE BYSTANDER. [*Suspiciously*] Who told you my people come
from Selsey?

THE NOTE TAKER. Never you mind. They did. [*To the girl*] How
do you come to be up so far east? You were born in Lisson Grove.

THE FLOWER GIRL. [*Appalled*] Oh, what harm is there in my leaving Lisson Grove? It wasnt fit for a pig to live in; and I had to
pay four-and-six a week. [*In tears*] Oh, boo—hoo—oo—

THE NOTE TAKER. Live where you like; but stop that noise.

THE GENTLEMAN. [*To the girl*] Come, come! he cant touch you:
you have a right to live where you please.   191

A SARCASTIC BYSTANDER. [*Thrusting himself between the note taker
and the gentleman*] Park Lane, for instance. I'd like to go into
the Housing Question with you, I would.

THE FLOWER GIRL. [*Subsiding into a brooding melancholy over her
basket, and talking very low-spiritedly to herself*] I'm a good girl,
I am.

THE SARCASTIC BYSTANDER. [*Not attending to her*] Do you know
where I come from?

THE NOTE TAKER. [*Promptly*] Hoxton.   200
[*Titterings. Popular interest in the note taker's performance in-
creases.*]

THE SARCASTIC ONE. [*Amazed*] Well, who said I didnt? Bly me!
You know everything, you do.

THE FLOWER GIRL. [*Still nursing her sense of injury*] Aint no call to meddle with me, he aint.

THE BYSTANDER. [*To her*] Of course he aint. Dont you stand it from him. [*To the note taker*] See here: what call have you to know about people what never offered to meddle with you? Wheres your warrant?   210

SEVERAL BYSTANDERS. [*Encouraged by this seeming point of law*] Yes: wheres your warrant?

THE FLOWER GIRL. Let him say what he likes. I dont want to have no truck with him.

THE BYSTANDER. You take us for dirt under your feet, dont you? Catch you taking liberties with a gentleman!

THE SARCASTIC BYSTANDER. Yes: tell *him* where he come from if you want to go fortune-telling.

THE NOTE TAKER. Cheltenham, Harrow, Cambridge, and India. [219

THE GENTLEMAN. Quite right. [*Great laughter. Reaction in the note taker's favor. Exclamations of* He knows all about it. Told him proper. Hear him tell the toff where he come from? *etc.*] May I ask, sir, do you do this for your living at a music hall?

THE NOTE TAKER. Ive thought of that. Perhaps I shall some day. [*The rain has stopped; and the persons on the outside of the crowd begin to drop off.*]

THE FLOWER GIRL. [*Resenting the reaction*] He's no gentleman, he aint, to interfere with a poor girl.   228

THE DAUGHTER. [*Out of patience, pushing her way rudely to the front and displacing the gentleman, who politely retires to the other side of the pillar*] What on earth is Freddy doing? I shall get pneumonia if I stay in this draught any longer.

THE NOTE TAKER. [*To himself, hastily making a note of her pronunciation of "monia"*] Earlscourt.

THE DAUGHTER. [*Violently*] Will you please keep your impertinent remarks to yourself.

THE NOTE TAKER. Did I say that out loud? I didnt mean to. I beg your pardon. Your mother's Epsom, unmistakably.   238

THE MOTHER. [*Advancing between her daughter and the note taker*] How very curious! I was brought up in Largelady Park, near Epsom.

THE NOTE TAKER. [*Uproariously amused*] Ha! ha! What a devil of a name! Excuse me. [*To the daughter*] You want a cab, do you?

THE DAUGHTER. Dont dare speak to me.

THE MOTHER. Oh please, please, Clara. [*Her daughter repudiates her with an angry shrug and retires haughtily.*] We should be so grateful to you, sir, if you found us a cab. [*The note taker produces a whistle.*] Oh, thank you. [*She joins her daughter.*] 248

[*The note taker blows a piercing blast.*]

THE SARCASTIC BYSTANDER. There! I knowed he was a plainclothes copper.

THE BYSTANDER. That aint a police whistle: thats a sporting whistle.

THE FLOWER GIRL. [*Still preoccupied with her wounded feelings*] He's no right to take away my character. My character is the same to me as any lady's.

THE NOTE TAKER. I dont know whether youve noticed it; but the rain stopped about two minutes ago.

THE BYSTANDER. So it has. Why didn't you say so before? and us losing our time listening to your silliness! [*He walks off towards the Strand.*] 260

THE SARCASTIC BYSTANDER. I can tell where *you* come from. You come from Anwell. Go back there.

THE NOTE TAKER. [*Helpfully*] *H*anwell.

THE SARCASTIC BYSTANDER. [*Affecting great distinction of speech*] Thenk you, teacher. Haw haw! So long. [*He touches his hat with mock respect and strolls off.*]

THE FLOWER GIRL. Frightening people like that! How would he like it himself?

THE MOTHER. It's quite fine now, Clara. We can walk to a motor bus. Come. [*She gathers her skirts above her ankles and hurries off towards the Strand.*] 271

THE DAUGHTER. But the cab— [*Her mother is out of hearing.*] Oh, how tiresome! [*She follows angrily.*]

[*All the rest have gone except the note taker, the gentleman, and the flower girl, who sits arranging her basket and still pitying herself in murmurs.*]

THE FLOWER GIRL. Poor girl! Hard enough for her to live without being worrited and chivied.

THE GENTLEMAN. [*Returning to his former place on the note taker's left*] How do you do it, if I may ask?   280

THE NOTE TAKER. Simply phonetics. The science of speech. Thats my profession: also my hobby. Happy is the man who can make a living by his hobby! You can spot an Irishman or a Yorkshireman by his brogue. *I* can place any man within six miles. I can place him within two miles in London. Sometimes within two streets.

THE FLOWER GIRL. Ought to be ashamed of himself, unmanly coward!

THE GENTLEMAN. But is there a living in that?   288

THE NOTE TAKER. Oh yes. Quite a fat one. This is an age of upstarts. Men begin in Kentish Town with £80 a year, and end in Park Lane with a hundred thousand. They want to drop Kentish Town; but they give themselves away every time they open their mouths. Now I can teach them—

THE FLOWER GIRL. Let him mind his own business and leave a poor girl—

THE NOTE TAKER. [*Explosively*] Woman: cease this detestable boohooing instantly; or else seek the shelter of some other place of worship.   298

THE FLOWER GIRL [*With feeble defiance*] Ive a right to be here if I like, same as you.

THE NOTE TAKER. A woman who utters such depressing and disgusting sounds has no right to be anywhere—no right to live. Remember that you are a human being with a soul and the divine gift of articulate speech: that your native language is the language of Shakespear and Milton and The Bible: and dont sit there crooning like a bilious pigeon.

THE FLOWER GIRL. [*Quite overwhelmed, looking up at him in mingled wonder and deprecation without daring to raise her head*] Ah-ah-ah-ow-ow-ow-oo!   309

THE NOTE TAKER. [*Whipping out his book*] Heavens! what a sound! [*He writes; then holds out the book and reads, reproducing her vowels exactly*] Ah-ah-ah-ow-ow-ow-oo!

THE FLOWER GIRL. [*Tickled by the performance, and laughing in spite of herself*] Garn!

THE NOTE TAKER. You see this creature with her kerbstone English: the English that will keep her in the gutter to the end of her days. Well, sir, in three months I could pass that girl off as a duchess at an ambassador's garden party. I could even get her a place as lady's maid or shop assistant, which requires better English. Thats the sort of thing I do for commercial millionaires. And on the profits of it I do genuine scientific work in phonetics, and a little as a poet on Miltonic lines. 322

THE GENTLEMAN. I am myself a student of Indian dialects; and—

THE NOTE TAKER. [*Eagerly*] Are you? Do you know Colonel Pickering, the author of Spoken Sanscrit?

THE GENTLEMAN. I *am* Colonel Pickering. Who are you?

THE NOTE TAKER. Henry Higgins, author of Higgins's Universal Alphabet.

PICKERING. [*With enthusiasm*] I came from India to meet you.

HIGGINS. I was going to India to meet you. 330

PICKERING. Where do you live?

HIGGINS. 27A Wimpole Street. Come and see me tomorrow.

PICKERING. I'm at the Carlton. Come with me now and lets have a jaw over some supper.

HIGGINS. Right you are.

THE FLOWER GIRL. [*To* PICKERING, *as he passes her*] Buy a flower, kind gentleman. I'm short for my lodging.

PICKERING. I really havnt any change. I'm sorry. [*He goes away.*]

HIGGINS. [*Shocked at the girl's mendacity*] Liar. You said you could change half-a-crown. 340

THE FLOWER GIRL. [*Rising in desperation*] You ought to be stuffed with nails, you ought. [*Flinging her basket at his feet.*] Take the whole blooming basket for sixpence.

[*The church clock strikes the second quarter.*]

HIGGINS. [*Hearing in it the voice of God, rebuking him for his Pharisaic want of charity to the poor girl*] A reminder. [*He raises his hat solemnly; then throws a handful of money into the basket and follows Pickering.*]

THE FLOWER GIRL. [*Picking up a half-crown*] Ah-ow-ooh! [*Picking up a couple of florins*] Aaah-ow-ooh! [*Picking up several coins*]

Aaaaaah-ow-ooh! [*Picking up a half-sovereign*] Aaaaaaaaaaaah-ow-ooh!!!   352

FREDDY. [*Springing out of a taxicab*] Got one at last. Hallo! [*To the girl*] Where are the two ladies that were here?

THE FLOWER GIRL. They walked to the bus when the rain stopped.

FREDDY. And left me with a cab on my hands! Damnation!

THE FLOWER GIRL. [*With grandeur*] Never mind, young man. *I'm* going home in a taxi. [*She sails off to the cab. The driver puts his hand behind him and holds the door firmly shut against her. Quite understanding his mistrust, she shews him her handful of money.*] Eightpence aint no object to me, Charlie. [*He grins and opens the door.*] Angel Court, Drury Lane, round the corner of Micklejohn's oil shop. Lets see how fast you can make her hop it. [*She gets in and pulls the door to with a slam as the taxicab starts.*]

FREDDY. Well, I'm dashed!

ACT II

Next day at 11 a.m. HIGGINS's *laboratory in Wimpole Street. It is a room on the first floor, looking on the street, and was meant for the drawing room. The double doors are in the middle of the back wall; and persons entering find in the corner to their right two tall file cabinets at right angles to one another against the walls. In this corner stands a flat writing-table, on which are a phonograph, a laryngoscope, a row of tiny organ pipes with bellows, a set of lamp chimneys for singing flames with burners attached to a gas plug in the wall by an indiarubber tube, several tuning-forks of different sizes, a life-size image of half a human head, shewing in section the vocal organs, and a box containing a supply of wax cylinders for the phonograph.*

Further down the room, on the same side, is a fireplace, with a comfortable leather-covered easy-chair at the side of the hearth nearest the door, and a coal-scuttle. There is a clock on the mantelpiece. Between the fireplace and the phonograph table is a stand for newspapers.

On the other side of the central door, to the left of the visitor, is a cabinet of shallow drawers. On it is a telephone and the telephone directory. The corner beyond, and most of the side wall, is occupied by a grand piano, with the keyboard at the end furthest from the door, and a bench for the player extending the full length of the keyboard. On the piano is a dessert dish heaped with fruit and sweets, mostly chocolates.

The middle of the room is clear. Besides the easy-chair, the piano bench, and two chairs at the phonograph table, there is one stray chair. It stands near the fireplace. On the walls, engravings: mostly Piranesi and mezzotint portraits. No paintings.

PICKERING *is seated at the table, putting down some cards and a tuning-fork which he has been using.* HIGGINS *is standing up near him, closing two or three file drawers which are hanging out. He appears in the morning light as a robust, vital, appetizing sort of man of forty or thereabouts, dressed in a professional-looking black frock-coat with a white linen collar and black silk tie. He is of the energetic, scientific type, heartily, even violently interested in everything that can be studied as a scientific subject, and careless about himself and other people, including their feelings. He is, in fact, but for his years and size, rather like a very impetuous baby "taking notice" eagerly and loudly, and requiring almost as much watching to keep him out of unintended mischief. His manner varies from genial bullying when he is in a good humor to stormy petulance when anything goes wrong; but he is so entirely frank and void of malice that he remains likeable even in his least reasonable moments.*

HIGGINS. [*As he shuts the last drawer*] Well, I think thats the whole show.

PICKERING. It's really amazing. I havnt taken half of it in, you know.

HIGGINS. Would you like to go over any of it again?

PICKERING. [*Rising and coming to the fireplace, where he plants himself with his back to the fire*] No, thank you; not now. I'm quite done up for this morning.

HIGGINS. [*Following him, and standing beside him on his left*] Tired of listening to sounds?

10

PICKERING. Yes. It's a fearful strain. I rather fancied myself because I can pronounce twenty-four distinct vowel sounds; but your hundred and thirty beat me. I cant hear a bit of difference between most of them.

HIGGINS. [*Chuckling, and going over to the piano to eat sweets*] Oh, that comes with practice. You hear no difference at first; but you keep on listening, and presently you find theyre all as different as A from B. [MRS. PEARCE *looks in: she is* HIGGINS's *housekeeper.*] Whats the matter?

MRS. PEARCE. [*Hesitating, evidently perplexed*] A young woman wants to see you sir.   21

HIGGINS. A young woman! What does she want?

MRS. PEARCE. Well, sir, she says youll be glad to see her when you know what she's come about. She's quite a common girl, sir. Very common indeed. I should have sent her away, only I thought perhaps you wanted her to talk into your machines. I hope Ive not done wrong; but really you see such queer people sometimes—youll excuse me, I'm sure, sir—

HIGGINS. Oh, thats all right, Mrs. Pearce. Has she an interesting accent?   30

MRS. PEARCE. Oh, something dreadful, sir, really. I dont know how you can take an interest in it.

HIGGINS. [*To* PICKERING] Lets have her up. Shew her up, Mrs. Pearce. [*He rushes across to his working table and picks out a cylinder to use on the phonograph.*]

MRS. PEARCE. [*Only half resigned to it*] Very well, sir. It's for you to say. [*She goes downstairs.*]

HIGGINS. This is rather a bit of luck. I'll shew you how I make records. We'll set her talking; and I'll take it down first in Bell's Visible Speech; then in broad Romic; and then we'll get her on the phonograph so that you can turn her on as often as you like with the written transcript before you.

MRS. PEARCE. [*Returning*] This is the young woman, sir.   43
[*The flower girl enters in state. She has a hat with three ostrich feathers, orange, sky-blue, and red. She has a nearly clean apron, and the shoddy coat has been tidied a little. The pathos of this deplorable figure, with its innocent vanity and conse-*]

quential air, touches PICKERING, *who has already straightened himself in the presence of* MRS. PEARCE. *But as to* HIGGINS, *the only distinction he makes between men and women is that when he is neither bullying nor exclaiming to the heavens against some feather-weight cross, he coaxes women as a child coaxes its nurse when it wants to get anything out of her.*]

HIGGINS. [*Brusquely, recognizing her with unconcealed disappointment, and at once, babylike, making an intolerable grievance of it*] Why, this is the girl I jotted down last night. She's no use: Ive got all the records I want of the Lisson Grove lingo; and I'm not going to waste another cylinder on it. [*To the girl*] Be off with you: I dont want you.

THE FLOWER GIRL. Dont you be so saucy. You aint heard what I come for yet. [*To* MRS. PEARCE, *who is waiting at the door for further instructions*] Did you tell him I come in a taxi?

MRS. PEARCE. Nonsense, girl! what do you think a gentleman like Mr. Higgins cares what you came in?

THE FLOWER GIRL. Oh, we are proud! He aint above giving lessons, not him: I heard him say so. Well, I aint come here to ask for any compliment; and if my money's not good enough I can go elsewhere.

HIGGINS. Good enough for what?

THE FLOWER GIRL. Good enough for ye-oo. Now you know, dont you? I'm come to have lessons, I am. And to pay for em too: make no mistake.

HIGGINS. [*Stupent*] Well!!! [*Recovering his breath with a gasp.*] What do you expect me to say to you?

THE FLOWER GIRL. Well, if you was a gentleman, you might ask me to sit down, I think. Dont I tell you I'm bringing you business?

HIGGINS. Pickering: shall we ask this baggage to sit down, or shall we throw her out of the window?

THE FLOWER GIRL. [*Running away in terror to the piano, where she turns at bay*] Ah-ah-oh-ow-ow-ow-oo! [*Wounded and whimpering*] I wont be called a baggage when Ive offered to pay like any lady. [*Motionless, the two men stare at her from the other side of the room, amazed.*]

PICKERING. [*Gently*] What is it you want, my girl?

THE FLOWER GIRL. I want to be a lady in a flower shop stead of selling at the corner of Tottenham Court Road. But they wont take me unless I can talk more genteel. He said he could teach me. Well, here I am ready to pay him—not asking any favor—and he treats me as if I was dirt.

MRS. PEARCE. How can you be such a foolish ignorant girl as to think you could afford to pay Mr. Higgins?   91

THE FLOWER GIRL. Why shouldn't I? I know what lessons cost as well as you do; and I'm ready to pay.

HIGGINS. How much?

THE FLOWER GIRL. [*Coming back to him, triumphant*] Now youre talking! I thought youd come off it when you saw a chance of getting back a bit of what you chucked at me last night. [*Confidentially*] Youd had a drop in, hadnt you?

HIGGINS. [*Peremptorily*] Sit down.   99

THE FLOWER GIRL. Oh, if you're going to make a compliment of it—

HIGGINS. [*Thundering at her*] Sit down.

MRS. PEARCE. [*Severely*] Sit down, girl. Do as youre told. [*She places the stray chair near the hearthrug between* HIGGINS *and* PICKERING, *and stands behind it waiting for the girl to sit down.*]

THE FLOWER GIRL. Ah-ah-ah-ow-ow-oo! [*She stands, half rebellious, half bewildered.*]

PICKERING. [*Very courteous*] Wont you sit down?

THE FLOWER GIRL. [*Coyly*] Dont mind if I do. [*She sits down.* PICKERING *returns to the hearthrug.*]

HIGGINS. What's your name?   110

THE FLOWER GIRL. Liza Doolittle.

HIGGINS. [*Declaiming gravely*]
          Eliza, Elizabeth, Betsy and Bess,
          They went to the woods to get a bird's nes':

PICKERING. They found a nest with four eggs in it:

HIGGINS. They took one apiece, and left three in it.

                    [*They laugh heartily at their own wit.*]

LIZA. Oh, dont be silly.

MRS. PEARCE. You mustnt speak to the gentleman like that.

LIZA. Well, why wont he speak sensible to me? 120

HIGGINS. Come back to business. How much do you propose to pay me for the lessons?

LIZA. Oh, I know whats right. A lady friend of mine gets French lessons for eighteenpence an hour from a real French gentleman. Well, you wouldnt have the face to ask me the same for teaching me my own language as you would for French; so I wont give more than a shilling. Take it or leave it.

HIGGINS. [*Walking up and down the room, rattling his keys and his cash in his pockets*] You know, Pickering, if you consider a shilling, not as a simple shilling, but as a percentage of this girl's income, it works out as fully equivalent to sixty or seventy guineas from a millionaire. 132

PICKERING. How so?

HIGGINS. Figure it out. A millionaire has about £150 a day. She earns about half-a-crown.

LIZA. [*Haughtily*] Who told you I only—

HIGGINS. [*Continuing*] She offers me two-fifths of her day's income for a lesson. Two-fifths of a millionaire's income for a day would be somewhere about £60. It's handsome. By George, it's enormous! it's the biggest offer I ever had. 140

LIZA. [*Rising, terrified*] Sixty pounds! What are you talking about? I never offered you sixty pounds. Where would I get—

HIGGINS. Hold your tongue.

LIZA. [*Weeping*] But I aint got sixty pounds. Oh—

MRS. PEARCE. Dont cry, you silly girl. Sit down. Nobody is going to touch your money.

HIGGINS. Somebody is going to touch you, with a broomstick, if you dont stop snivelling. Sit down.

LIZA. [*Obeying slowly*] Ah-ah-ah-ow-oo-o! One would think you was my father. 150

HIGGINS. If I decide to teach you, I'll be worse than two fathers to you. Here. [*He offers her his silk handkerchief!*]

LIZA. Whats this for?

HIGGINS. To wipe your eyes. To wipe any part of your face that feels moist. Remember: thats your handkerchief; and thats your

sleeve. Dont mistake the one for the other if you wish to become
a lady in a shop.

[LIZA, *utterly bewildered, stares helplessly at him.*]

MRS. PEARCE. It's no use talking to her like that, Mr. Higgins: she
doesn't understand you. Besides, youre quite wrong: she doesn't do
it that way at all. [*She takes the handkerchief.*]   161

LIZA. [*Snatching it*] Here! You give me that handkerchief. He
give it to me, not to you.

PICKERING. [*Laughing*] He did. I think it must be regarded as
her property, Mrs. Pearce.

MRS. PEARCE. [*Resigning herself*] Serve you right, Mr. Higgins.

PICKERING. Higgins: I'm interested. What about the ambassador's
garden party? I'll say youre the greatest teacher alive if you make
that good. I'll bet you all the expenses of the experiment you cant
do it. And I'll pay for the lessons.   170

LIZA. Oh, you are real good. Thank you, Captain.

HIGGINS. [*Tempted, looking at her*] It's almost irresistible. She's
so deliciously low—so horribly dirty—

LIZA. [*Protesting extremely*] Ah-ah-ah-ah-ow-ow-oo-oo!!! I aint
dirty: I washed my face and hands afore I come, I did.

PICKERING. Youre certainly not going to turn her head with flattery, Higgins.

MRS. PEARCE. [*Uneasy*] Oh, dont say that, sir: theres more ways
than one of turning a girl's head; and nobody can do it better than
Mr. Higgins, though he may not always mean it. I do hope, sir,
you wont encourage him to do anything foolish.   181

HIGGINS. [*Becoming excited as the idea grows on him*] What is
life but a series of inspired follies? The difficulty is to find them
to do. Never lose a chance: it doesnt come every day. I shall make
a duchess of this draggletailed guttersnipe.

LIZA. [*Strongly deprecating this view of her*] Ah-ah-ah-ow-ow-oo!

HIGGINS. [*Carried away*] Yes: in six months—in three if she has
a good ear and a quick tongue—I'll take her anywhere and pass
her off as anything. We'll start today: now! this moment! Take
her away and clean her, Mrs. Pearce. Monkey Brand, if it wont
come off any other way. Is there a good fire in the kitchen?

MRS. PEARCE. [*Protesting*] Yes; but—   192

HIGGINS. [*Storming on*] Take all her clothes off and burn them. Ring up Whiteley or somebody for new ones. Wrap her up in brown paper til they come.

LIZA. Youre no gentleman, youre not, to talk of such things. I'm a good girl, I am; and I know what the like of you are, I do.

HIGGINS. We want none of your Lisson Grove prudery here, young woman. Youve got to learn to behave like a duchess. Take her away, Mrs. Pearce. If she gives you any trouble, wallop her.   200

LIZA. [*Springing up and running between* PICKERING *and* MRS. PEARCE *for protection*] No! I'll call the police, I will.

MRS. PEARCE. But Ive no place to put her.

HIGGINS. Put her in the dustbin.

LIZA. Ah-ah-ah-ow-ow-oo!

PICKERING. Oh come, Higgins! be reasonable.

MRS. PEARCE. [*Resolutely*] You *must* be reasonable, Mr. Higgins: really you must. You cant walk over everybody like this.

[HIGGINS, *thus scolded, subsides. The hurricane is succeeded by a zephyr of amiable surprise.*]   210

HIGGINS. [*With professional exquisiteness of modulation*] *I* walk over everybody! My dear Mrs. Pearce, my dear Pickering, I never had the slightest intention of walking over anyone. All I propose is that we should be kind to this poor girl. We must help her to prepare and fit herself for her new station in life. If I did not express myself clearly it was because I did not wish to hurt her delicacy, or yours.

[LIZA, *reassured, steals back to her chair.*]

MRS. PEARCE. [*To* PICKERING] Well, did you ever hear anything like that, sir?   220

PICKERING. [*Laughing heartily*] Never, Mrs. Pearce: never.

HIGGINS. [*Patiently*] Whats the matter?

MRS. PEARCE. Well, the matter is, sir, that you cant take a girl up like that as if you were picking up a pebble on the beach.

HIGGINS. Why not?

MRS. PEARCE. Why not! But you dont know anything about her. What about her parents? She may be married.

LIZA. Garn!

HIGGINS. There! As the girl very properly says, Garn! Married indeed! Dont you know that a woman of that class looks a worn out drudge of fifty a year after she's married?   231

LIZA. Whood marry me?

HIGGINS. [*Suddenly resorting to the most thrillingly beautiful low tones in his best elocutionary style*] By George, Eliza, the streets will be strewn with the bodies of men shooting themselves for your sake before Ive done with you.

MRS. PEARCE. Nonsense, sir. You mustn't talk like that to her.

LIZA. [*Rising and squaring herself determinedly*] I'm going away. He's off his chump, he is. I dont want no balmies teaching me.

HIGGINS [*Wounded in his tenderest point by her insensibility to his elocution*] Oh, indeed! I'm mad, am I? Very well, Mrs. Pearce: you needn't order the new clothes for her. Throw her out.   242

LIZA. [*Whimpering*] Nah-ow. You got no right to touch me.

MRS. PEARCE. You see now what comes of being saucy. [*Indicating the door*] This way, please.

LIZA [*Almost in tears*] I didnt want no clothes. I wouldnt have taken them. [*She throws away the handkerchief*] I can buy my own clothes.

HIGGINS [*Deftly retrieving the handkerchief and intercepting her on her reluctant way to the door*] Youre an ungrateful wicked girl. This is my return for offering to take you out of the gutter and dress you beautifully and make a lady of you.   252

MRS. PEARCE. Stop, Mr. Higgins. I wont allow it. It's you that are wicked. Go home to your parents, girl; and tell them to take better care of you.

LIZA. I aint got no parents. They told me I was big enough to earn my own living and turned me out.

MRS. PEARCE. Wheres your mother?

LIZA. I aint got no mother. Her that turned me out was my sixth stepmother. But I done without them. And I'm a good girl, I am.

HIGGINS. Very well, then, what on earth is all this fuss about? The girl doesnt belong to anybody—is no use to anybody but me. [*He goes to* MRS. PEARCE *and begins coaxing.*] You can adopt her, Mrs. Pearce: I'm sure a daughter would be a great amusement to you. Now dont make any more fuss. Take her downstairs; and—

MRS. PEARCE. But whats to become of her? Is she to be paid anything? Do be sensible, sir.   267

HIGGINS. Oh, pay her whatever is necessary: put it down in the housekeeping book. [*Impatiently*] What on earth will she want with money? She'll have her food and her clothes. She'll only drink if you give her money.

LIZA. [*Turning on him*] Oh you *are* a brute. It's a lie: nobody ever saw the sign of liquor on me. [*She goes back to her chair and plants herself there defiantly.*]

PICKERING. [*In good-humored remonstrance*] Does it occur to you, Higgins, that the girl has some feelings?   276

HIGGINS. [*Looking critically at her*] Oh no, I don't think so. Not any feelings that we need bother about. [*Cheerily*] Have you, Eliza?

LIZA. I got my feelings same as anyone else.

HIGGINS. [*To* PICKERING, *reflectively*] You see the difficulty?

PICKERING. Eh? What difficulty?

HIGGINS. To get her to talk grammar. The mere pronunciation is easy enough.

LIZA. I don't want to talk grammar. I want to talk like a lady.

MRS. PEARCE. Will you please keep to the point, Mr. Higgins? I want to know on what terms the girl is to be here. Is she to have any wages? And what is to become of her when youve finished your teaching? You must look ahead a little.   288

HIGGINS. [*Impatiently*] Whats to become of her if I leave her in the gutter? Tell me that, Mrs. Pearce.

MRS. PEARCE. Thats her own business, not yours, Mr. Higgins.

HIGGINS. Well, when Ive done with her, we can throw her back into the gutter; and then it will be her own business again; so thats all right.

LIZA. Oh, you've no feeling heart in you: you dont care for nothing but yourself. [*She rises and takes the floor resolutely.*] Here! Ive had enough of this. I'm going. [*Making for the door.*] You ought to be ashamed of yourself, you ought.   298

HIGGINS. [*Snatching a chocolate cream from the piano, his eyes suddenly beginning to twinkle with mischief*] Have some chocolates, Eliza.

LIZA. [*Halting, tempted*] How do I know what might be in them? Ive heard of girls being drugged by the like of you.

[HIGGINS *whips out his penknife; cuts a chocolate in two; puts one half into his mouth and bolts it; and offers her the other half.*]

HIGGINS. Pledge of good faith, Eliza. I eat one half: you eat the other. [LIZA *opens her mouth to retort: he pops the half chocolate into it.*] You shall have boxes of them, barrels of them, every day. You shall live on them. Eh? 309

LIZA. [*Who has disposed of the chocolate after being nearly choked by it*] I wouldnt have ate it, only I'm too ladylike to take it out of my mouth.

HIGGINS. Listen, Eliza. I think you said you came in a taxi.

LIZA. Well, what if I did? Ive as good a right to take a taxi as anyone else.

HIGGINS. You have, Eliza; and in future you shall have as many taxis as you want. You shall go up and down and round the town in a taxi every day. Think of that, Eliza.

MRS. PEARCE. Mr. Higgins: youre tempting the girl. It's not right. She should think of the future. 320

HIGGINS. At her age! Nonsense! Time enough to think of the future when you havnt any future to think of. No, Eliza: do as this lady does: think of other people's futures; but never think of your own. Think of chocolates, and taxis, and gold, and diamonds.

LIZA. No: I dont want no gold and no diamonds. I'm a good girl, I am. [*She sits down again, with an attempt at dignity.*]

HIGGINS. You shall remain so, Eliza, under the care of Mrs. Pearce. And you shall marry an officer in the Guards, with a beautiful moustache: the son of a marquis, who will disinherit him for marrying you, but will relent when he sees your beauty and goodness— 331

PICKERING. Excuse me, Higgins; but I really must interfere. Mrs. Pearce is quite right. If this girl is to put herself in your hands for six months for an experiment in teaching, she must understand thoroughly what she's doing.

HIGGINS. How can she? She's incapable of understanding anything. Besides, do any of us understand what we are doing? If we did, would we ever do it?

PICKERING. Very clever, Higgins; but not sound sense. [*To* ELIZA]
Miss Doolittle— 340

LIZA. [*Overwhelmed*] Ah-ah-ow-oo!

HIGGINS. There! Thats all youll get out of Eliza. Ah-ah-ow-oo!
No use explaining. As a military man you ought to know that.
Give her her orders: thats what she wants. Eliza: you are to live
here for the next six months, learning how to speak beautifully,
like a lady in a florist's shop. If youre good and do whatever youre
told, you shall sleep in a proper bedroom, and have lots to eat,
and money to buy chocolates and take rides in taxis. If youre
naughty and idle you will sleep in the back kitchen among the black
beetles, and be walloped by Mrs. Pearce with a broomstick. At the
end of six months you shall go to Buckingham Palace in a carriage,
beautifully dressed. If the King finds out youre not a lady, you will
be taken by the police to the Tower of London, where your head [353
will be cut off as a warning to other presumptuous flower girls. If
you are not found out, you shall have a present of seven-and-six-
pence to start life with as a lady in a shop. If you refuse this offer
you will be a most ungrateful and wicked girl; and the angels will
weep for you. [*To* PICKERING] Now are you satisfied, Pickering?
[*To* MRS. PEARCE] Can I put it more plainly and fairly, Mrs. Pearce?

MRS. PEARCE. [*Patiently*] I think youd better let me speak to the
girl properly in private. I dont know that I can take charge of her
or consent to the arrangement at all. Of course I know you dont
mean her any harm; but when you get what you call interested in
people's accents, you never think or care what may happen to them
or you. Come with me, Eliza. 365

HIGGINS. Thats all right. Thank you, Mrs. Pearce. Bundle her off
to the bathroom.

LIZA. [*Rising reluctantly and suspiciously*] Youre a great bully,
you are. I wont stay here if I don't like. I wont let nobody wallop
me. I never asked to go to Bucknam Palace, I didnt. I was never
in trouble with the police, not me. I'm a good girl—

MRS. PEARCE. Dont answer back, girl. You dont understand the
gentleman. Come with me. [*She leads the way to the door, and
holds it open for* ELIZA.]
374

LIZA. [*As she goes out*] Well, what I say is right. I wont go near the King, not if I'm going to have my head cut off. If I'd known what I was letting myself in for, I wouldnt have come here; I always been a good girl; and I never offered to say a word to him; and I dont owe him nothing; and I dont care; and I wont be put upon; and I have my feelings the same as anyone else—

[MRS. PEARCE *shuts the door; and* ELIZA's *plaints are no longer audible.* PICKERING *comes from the hearth to the chair and sits astride it with his arms on the back.*]

PICKERING. Excuse the straight question, Higgins. Are you a man of good character where women are concerned?   385

HIGGINS. [*Moodily*] Have you ever met a man of good character where women are concerned?

PICKERING. Yes: very frequently.

HIGGINS. [*Dogmatically, lifting himself on his hands to the level of the piano, and sitting on it with a bounce*] Well, I havnt. I find that the moment I let a woman make friends with me, she becomes jealous, exacting, suspicious, and a damned nuisance. I find that the moment I let myself make friends with a woman, I become selfish and tyrannical. Women upset everything. When you let them into your life, you find that the woman is driving at one thing and youre driving at another.   396

PICKERING. At what, for example?

HIGGINS. [*Coming off the piano restlessly*] Oh, Lord knows! I suppose the woman wants to live her own life; and the man wants to live his; and each tries to drag the other on to the wrong track. One wants to go north and the other south; and the result is that both have to go east, though they both hate the east wind. [*He sits down on the bench at the keyboard.*] So here I am, a confirmed old bachelor, and likely to remain so.   404

PICKERING. [*Rising and standing over him gravely*] Come, Higgins. You know what I mean. If I'm to be in this business I shall feel responsible for that girl. I hope it's understood that no advantage is to be taken of her position.

HIGGINS. What! That thing! Sacred, I assure you. [*Rising to explain*] You see, she'll be a pupil; and teaching would be impossible unless pupils were sacred. Ive taught scores of American millionair-

esses how to speak English: the best looking women in the world. I'm seasoned. They might as well be blocks of wood. *I* might as well be a block of wood. It's—   414

[MRS. PEARCE *opens the door. She has* ELIZA'S *hat in her hand.* PICK-ERING *retires to the easy-chair at the hearth and sits down.*]

HIGGINS. [*Eagerly*] Well, Mrs. Pearce: is it all right?

MRS. PEARCE. [*At the door*] I just wish to trouble you with a word, if I may, Mr. Higgins.

HIGGINS. Yes, certainly. Come in. [*She comes forward.*] Dont burn that, Mrs. Pearce. I'll keep it as a curiosity. [*He takes the hat.*]

MRS. PEARCE. Handle it carefully, sir, *please*. I had to promise her not to burn it; but I had better put it in the oven for a while.   423

HIGGINS. [*Putting it down hastily on the piano*] Oh! thank you. Well, what have you to say to me?

PICKERING. Am I in the way?

MRS. PEARCE. Not at all, sir. Mr. Higgins: will you please be very particular what you say before the girl?

HIGGINS. [*Sternly*] Of course. I'm always particular about what I say. Why do you say this to me?   430

MRS. PEARCE. [*Unmoved*] No, sir: youre not at all particular when youve mislaid anything or when you get a little impatient. Now it doesnt matter before me: I'm used to it. But you really must not swear before the girl.

HIGGINS. [*Indignantly*] *I* swear! [*Most emphatically*] I never swear. I detest the habit. What the devil do you mean?

MRS. PEARCE. [*Stolidly*] Thats what I mean, sir. You swear a great deal too much. I dont mind your damning and blasting, and *what* the devil and *where* the devil and *who* the devil—

HIGGINS. Mrs. Pearce: this language from your lips! Really!   440

MRS. PEARCE. [*Not to be put off*] —but there is a certain word I must ask you not to use. The girl has just used it herself because the bath was too hot. It begins with the same letter as bath. She knows no better: she learnt it at her mother's knee. But she must not hear it from *your* lips.

HIGGINS. [*Loftily*] I cannot charge myself with having ever uttered it, Mrs. Pearce. [*She looks at him steadfastly. He adds, hiding an*

uneasy conscience with a judicial air] Except perhaps in a moment
of extreme and justifiable excitement.   449

MRS. PEARCE. Only this morning, sir, you applied it to your boots,
to the butter, and to the brown bread.

HIGGINS. Oh, that! Mere alliteration, Mrs. Pearce, natural to a poet.

MRS. PEARCE. Well, sir, whatever you choose to call it, I beg you
not to let the girl hear you repeat it.

HIGGINS. Oh, very well, very well. Is that all?

MRS. PEARCE. No, sir. We shall have to be very particular with this
girl as to personal cleanliness.

HIGGINS. Certainly. Quite right. Most important.

MRS. PEARCE. I mean not to be slovenly about her dress or untidy
in leaving things about.   460

HIGGINS. [*Going to her solemnly*] Just so. I intended to call your
attention to that. [*He passes on to* PICKERING, *who is enjoying the
conversation immensely.*] It is these little things that matter, Pickering. Take care of the pence and the pounds will take care of themselves is as true of personal habits as of money. [*He comes to anchor
on the hearthrug, with the air of a man in an unassailable position.*]

MRS. PEARCE. Yes, sir. Then might I ask you not to come down to
breakfast in your dressing-gown, or at any rate not to use it as a
napkin to the extent you do, sir. And if you would be so good as
not to eat everything off the same plate, and to remember not to put
the porridge saucepan out of your hand on the clean tablecloth,
it would be a better example to the girl. You know you nearly
choked yourself with a fishbone in the jam only last week.   473

HIGGINS. [*Routed from the hearthrug and drifting back to the
piano*] I may do these things sometimes in absence of mind; but
surely I dont do them habitually. [*Angrily*] By the way: my dressing-gown smells most damnably of benzine.

MRS. PEARCE. No doubt it does, Mr. Higgins. But if you *will* wipe
your fingers—

HIGGINS. [*Yelling*] Oh very well, very well: I'll wipe them in my
hair in future.   481

MRS. PEARCE. I hope youre not offended, Mr. Higgins.

HIGGINS. [*Shocked at finding himself thought capable of an un-*

amiable sentiment] Not at all, not at all. Youre quite right, Mrs. Pearce: I shall be particularly careful before the girl. Is that all?

MRS. PEARCE. No, sir. Might she use some of those Japanese dresses you brought from abroad? I really cant put her back into her old things.

HIGGINS. Certainly. Anything you like. Is *that* all?

MRS. PEARCE. Thank you, sir. Thats all. [*She goes out.*]   490

HIGGINS. You know, Pickering, that woman has the most extraordinary ideas about me. Here I am, a shy, diffident sort of man. Ive never been able to feel really grown-up and tremendous, like other chaps. And yet she's firmly persuaded that I'm an arbitrary overbearing bossing kind of person. I cant account for it.

[MRS. PEARCE *returns.*]

MRS. PEARCE. If you please, sir, the trouble's beginning already. Theres a dustman downstairs, Alfred Doolittle, wants to see you. He says you have his daughter here.

PICKERING. [*Rising*] Phew! I say! [*He retreats to the hearthrug.*]

HIGGINS. [*Promptly*] Send the blackguard up.   501

MRS. PEARCE. Oh, very well. [*She goes out.*]

PICKERING. He may not be a blackguard, Higgins.

HIGGINS. Nonsense. Of course he's a blackguard.

PICKERING. Whether he is or not, I'm afraid we shall have some trouble with him.

HIGGINS. [*Confidently*] Oh no: I think not. If theres any trouble he shall have it with me, not I with him. And we are sure to get something interesting out of him.

PICKERING. About the girl?

HIGGINS. No. I mean his dialect.

PICKERING. Oh!   512

MRS. PEARCE. [*At the door*] Doolittle, sir. [*She admits* DOOLITTLE *and retires.*]

[ALFRED DOOLITTLE *is an elderly but vigorous dustman, clad in the costume of his profession, including a hat with a black brim covering his neck and shoulders. He has well marked and rather interesting features, and seems equally free from fear and conscience. He has a remarkably expressive voice, the re-*

sult of a habit of giving vent to his feelings without reserve. His present pose is that of wounded honor and stern resolution.]

DOOLITTLE. [*At the door, uncertain which of the two gentlemen is his man*] Professor Higgins?   523

HIGGINS. Here. Good morning. Sit down.

DOOLITTLE. Morning, Governor. [*He sits down magisterially.*] I come about a very serious matter, Governor.

HIGGINS. [*To* PICKERING] Brought up in Hounslow. Mother Welsh, I should think. [DOOLITTLE *opens his mouth, amazed.* HIGGINS *continues*] What do you want, Doolittle?

DOOLITTLE. [*Menacingly*] I want my daughter: thats what I want. See?   531

HIGGINS. Of course you do. Youre her father, arnt you? You dont suppose anyone else wants her, do you? I'm glad to see you have some spark of family feeling left. She's upstairs. Take her away at once.

DOOLITTLE. [*Rising, fearfully taken aback*] What!

HIGGINS. Take her away. Do you suppose I'm going to keep your daughter for you?

DOOLITTLE [*Remonstrating*] Now, now, look here, Governor. Is this reasonable? Is it fairity to take advantage of a man like this? The girl belongs to me. You got her. Where do I come in? [*He sits down again.*]   542

HIGGINS. Your daughter had the audacity to come to my house and ask me to teach her how to speak properly so that she could get a place in a flower-shop. This gentleman and my housekeeper have been here all the time. [*Bullying him*] How dare you come here and attempt to blackmail me? You sent her here on purpose.

DOOLITTLE. [*Protesting*] No, Governor.

HIGGINS. You must have. How else could you possibly know that she is here?

DOOLITTLE. Dont take a man up like that, Governor.   551

HIGGINS. The police shall take you up. This is a plant—a plot to extort money by threats. I shall telephone for the police. [*He goes resolutely to the telephone and opens the directory.*]

DOOLITTLE. Have I asked you for a brass farthing? I leave it to the gentleman here: have I said a word about money?

HIGGINS. [*Throwing the book aside and marching down on* DOO-LITTLE *with a poser*] What else did you come for?

DOOLITTLE. [*Sweetly*] Well, what *would* a man come for? Be human, Governor.

HIGGINS. [*Disarmed*] Alfred: did you put her up to it?

DOOLITTLE. So help me, Governor, I never did. I take my Bible oath I aint seen the girl these two months past.   563

HIGGINS. Then how did you know she was here?

DOOLITTLE. [*Most musical, most melancholy*] I'll tell you, Governor, if youll only let me get a word in. I'm willing to tell you. I'm wanting to tell you. I'm waiting to tell you.

HIGGINS. Pickering: this chap has a certain natural gift of rhetoric. Observe the rhythm of his native woodnotes wild. "I'm willing to tell you: I'm wanting to tell you: I'm waiting to tell you." Sentimental rhetoric! thats the Welsh strain in him. It also accounts for his mendacity and dishonesty.   572

PICKERING. Oh, *please,* Higgins: I'm west country myself. [*To* DOOLITTLE] How did you know the girl was here if you didn't send her?

DOOLITTLE. It was like this, Governor. The girl took a boy in the taxi to give him a jaunt. Son of her landlady, he is. He hung about on the chance of her giving him another ride home. Well, she sent him back for her luggage when she heard you was willing for her to stop here. I met the boy at the corner of Long Acre and Endell Street.

HIGGINS. Public house. Yes?   582

DOOLITTLE. The poor man's club, Governor: why shouldn't I?

PICKERING. Do let him tell his story, Higgins.

DOOLITTLE. He told me what was up. And I ask you, what was my feelings and my duty as a father? I says to the boy, "You bring me the luggage," I says—

PICKERING. Why didnt you go for it yourself?

DOOLITTLE. Landlady wouldnt have trusted me with it, Governor. She's that kind of woman: you know. I had to give the boy a penny afore he trusted me with it, the little swine. I brought it to her just to oblige you like, and make myself agreeable. Thats all.   592

HIGGINS. How much luggage?

DOOLITTLE. Musical instrument, Governor. A few pictures, a trifle of jewelry, and a bird-cage. She said she didnt want no clothes. What was I to think from that, Governor? I ask you as a parent what was I to think?

HIGGINS. So you came to rescue her from worse than death, eh?

DOOLITTLE. [*Appreciatively: relieved at being so well understood*] Just so, Governor. Thats right.

PICKERING. But why did you bring her luggage if you intended to take her away? 602

DOOLITTLE. Have I said a word about taking her away? Have I now?

HIGGINS. [*Determinedly*] Youre going to take her away, double quick. [*He crosses to the hearth and rings the bell.*]

DOOLITTLE. [Rising] No, Governor. Dont say that. I'm not the man to stand in my girl's light. Heres a career opening for her, as you might say; and—

[MRS. PEARCE *opens the door and awaits orders.*]

HIGGINS. Mrs. Pearce: this is Eliza's father. He has come to take her away. Give her to him. [*He goes back to the piano, with an air of washing his hands of the whole affair.*] 613

DOOLITTLE. No. This is a misunderstanding. Listen here—

MRS. PEARCE. He cant take her away, Mr. Higgins: how can he? You told me to burn her clothes.

DOOLITTLE. Thats right. I cant carry the girl through the streets like a blooming monkey, can I? I put it to you.

HIGGINS. You have put it to me that you want your daughter. Take your daughter. If she has no clothes go out and buy her some.

DOOLITTLE. [*Desperate*] Wheres the clothes she come in? Did I burn them or did your missus here? 622

MRS. PEARCE. I am the housekeeper, if you please. I have sent for some clothes for your girl. When they come you can take her away. You can wait in the kitchen. This way, please.

[DOOLITTLE, *much troubled, accompanies her to the door; then hesitates; finally turns confidently to* HIGGINS.]

DOOLITTLE. Listen here, Governor. You and me is men of the world, aint we?

HIGGINS. Oh! Men of the world, are we? Youd better go, Mrs. Pearce.

MRS. PEARCE. I think so, indeed, sir. [*She goes, with dignity.*]

PICKERING. The floor is yours, Mr. Doolittle.   633

DOOLITTLE. [*To* PICKERING] I thank you, Governor. [*To* HIGGINS, *who takes refuge on the piano bench, a little overwhelmed by the proximity of his visitor; for* DOOLITTLE *has a professional flavor of dust about him.*] Well, the truth is, Ive taken a sort of fancy to you, Governor; and if you want the girl, I'm not so set on having her back home again but what I might be open to an arrangement. Regarded in the light of a young woman, she's a fine handsome girl. As a daughter she's not worth her keep; and so I tell you straight. All I ask is my rights as a father; and youre the last man alive to expect me to let her go for nothing; for I can see youre one of the straight sort, Governor. Well, whats a five-pound note to you? And whats Eliza to me? [*He returns to his chair and sits down judicially.*]   646

PICKERING. I think you ought to know, Doolittle, that Mr. Higgins's intentions are entirely honorable.

DOOLITTLE. Course they are, Governor. If I thought they wasnt, I'd ask fifty.

HIGGINS [*Revolted*] Do you mean to say, you callous rascal, that you would sell your daughter for £50?

DOOLITTLE. Not in a general way I wouldnt; but to oblige a gentleman like you I'd do a good deal, I do assure you.   654

PICKERING. Have you no morals, man?

DOOLITTLE. [*Unabashed*] Cant afford them, Governor. Neither could you if you was as poor as me. Not that I mean any harm, you know. But if Liza is going to have a bit out of this, why not me too?

HIGGINS. [*Troubled*] I dont know what to do, Pickering. There can be no question that as a matter of morals it's a positive crime to give this chap a farthing. And yet I feel a sort of rough justice in his claim.

DOOLITTLE. Thats it, Governor. Thats all I say. A father's heart, as it were.   664

PICKERING. Well, I know the feeling; but really it seems hardly right—

DOOLITTLE. Dont say that, Governor. Dont look at it that way. What am I, Governors both? I ask you, what am I? I'm one of the undeserving poor: thats what I am. Think of what that means to a man. It means that he's up agen middle class morality all the time. If there's anything going, and I put in for a bit of it, it's always the same story: "Youre undeserving; so you cant have it." But my needs is as great as the most deserving widow's that ever got money out of six different charities in one week for the death of the same husband. I dont need less than a deserving man: I need more. I dont eat less hearty than him; and I drink a lot more. [676 I want a bit of amusement, cause I'm a thinking man. I want cheerfulness and a song and a band when I feel low. Well, they charge me just the same for everything as they charge the deserving. What is middle class morality? Just an excuse for never giving me anything. Therefore, I ask you, as two gentlemen, not to play that game on me. I'm playing straight with you. I aint pretending to be deserving. I'm undeserving; and I mean to go on being undeserving. I like it; and thats the truth. Will you take advantage of a man's nature to do him out of the price of his own daughter what he's brought up and fed and clothed by the sweat of his brow until she's growed big enough to be interesting to you two gentlemen? Is five pounds unreasonable? I put it to you; and I leave it to you.   688

HIGGINS. [*Rising, and going over to* PICKERING] Pickering: if we were to take this man in hand for three months, he could choose between a seat in the Cabinet and a popular pulpit in Wales.

PICKERING. What do you say to that, Doolittle?

DOOLITTLE. Not me, Governor, thank you kindly. I've heard all the preachers and all the prime ministers—for I'm a thinking man and game for politics or religion or social reform same as all the other amusements—and I tell you it's a dog's life any way you look at it. Undeserving poverty is my line. Taking one station in society with another, it's—it's—well, it's the only one that has any ginger in it, to my taste.   699

HIGGINS. I suppose we must give him a fiver.

PICKERING. He'll make a bad use of it, I'm afraid.

DOOLITTLE. Not me, Governor, so help me I wont. Dont you be afraid that I'll save it and spare it and live idle on it. There wont be

a penny of it left by Monday: I'll have to go to work same as if I'd never had it. It wont pauperize me, you bet. Just one good spree for myself and the missus, giving pleasure to ourselves and employment to others, and satisfaction to you to think it's not been throwed away. You couldn't spend it better. 708

HIGGINS. [*Taking out his pocket book and coming between* DOOLITTLE *and the piano.*] This is irresistible. Lets give him ten. [*He offers two notes to the dustman.*]

DOOLITTLE. No, Governor. She wouldn't have the heart to spend ten; and perhaps I shouldn't neither. Ten pounds is a lot of money: it makes a man feel prudent like; and then good-bye to happiness. You give me what I ask you, Governor: not a penny more, and not a penny less.

PICKERING. Why dont you marry that missus of yours? I rather draw the line at encouraging that sort of immorality. 718

DOOLITTLE. Tell her so, Governor: tell her so. I'm willing. It's me that suffers by it. Ive no hold on her. I got to be agreeable to her. I got to give her presents. I got to buy her clothes something sinful. I'm a slave to that woman, Governor, just because I'm not her lawful husband. And she knows it too. Catch her marrying me! Take my advice, Governor: marry Eliza while she's young and dont know no better. If you dont youll be sorry for it after. If you do, *she'll* be sorry for it after; but better her than you, because youre a man, and she's only a woman and dont know how to be happy anyhow. 728

HIGGINS. Pickering: if we listen to this man another minute, we shall have no convictions left. [*To* DOOLITTLE] Five pounds I think you said.

DOOLITTLE. Thank you kindly, Governor.

HIGGINS. Youre sure you wont take ten?

DOOLITTLE. Not now. Another time, Governor.

HIGGINS. [*Handing him a five-pound note*] Here you are.

DOOLITTLE. Thank you, Governor. Good morning. [*He hurries to the door, anxious to get away with his booty. When he opens it he is confronted with a dainty and exquisitely clean young Japanese lady in a simple blue cotton kimono printed cunningly with small*

white jasmine blossoms. MRS. PEARCE *is with her. He gets out of her way deferentially and apologizes.*] Beg pardon, miss.   741

THE JAPANESE LADY. Garn! Dont you know your own daughter?

DOOLITTLE ⎫ [*Exclaiming* ⎧ Bly me! it's Eliza!
HIGGINS   ⎬   *simul-*   ⎨ Whats that! This!
PICKERING ⎭ *taneously*] ⎩ By Jove!

LIZA. Dont I look silly?

HIGGINS. Silly?

MRS. PEARCE. [*At the door*] Now, Mr. Higgins, please dont say anything to make the girl conceited about herself.

HIGGINS. [*Conscientiously*] Oh! Quite right, Mrs. Pearce. [*To* ELIZA] Yes: damned silly.   751

MRS. PEARCE. Please, sir.

HIGGINS. [*Correcting himself*] I mean extremely silly.

LIZA. I should look all right with my hat on. [*She takes up her hat; puts it on; and walks across the room to the fireplace with a fashionable air.*]

HIGGINS. A new fashion, by George! And it ought to look horrible!

DOOLITTLE. [*With fatherly pride*] Well, I never thought she'd clean up as good looking as that, Governor. She's a credit to me, aint she?

LIZA. I tell you, it's easy to clean up here. Hot and cold water on tap, just as much as you like, there is. Woolly towels, there is; and a towel horse so hot, it burns your fingers. Soft brushes to scrub yourself, and a wooden bowl of soap smelling like primroses. Now I know why ladies is so clean. Washing's a treat for them. Wish they saw what it is for the like of me!   765

HIGGINS. I'm glad the bathroom met with your approval.

LIZA. It didnt: not all of it; and I dont care who hears me say it. Mrs. Pearce knows.

HIGGINS. What was wrong, Mrs. Pearce?

MRS. PEARCE. [*Blandly*] Oh, nothing, sir. It doesnt matter.

LIZA. I had a good mind to break it. I didnt know which way to look. But I hung a towel over it, I did.

HIGGINS. Over what?

MRS. PEARCE. Over the looking glass, sir.   774

HIGGINS. Doolittle: you have brought your daughter up too strictly.

DOOLITTLE. Me! I never brought her up at all, except to give her a

lick of a strap now and again. Dont put it on me, Governor. She aint accustomed to it, you see: thats all. But she'll soon pick up your free-and-easy ways.

LIZA. I'm a good girl, I am; and I wont pick up no free-and-easy ways.

HIGGINS. Eliza: if you say again that youre a good girl, your father shall take you home. 783

LIZA. Not him. You dont know my father. All he come here for was to touch you for some money to get drunk on.

DOOLITTLE. Well, what else would I want money for? To put into the plate in church, I suppose. [*She puts out her tongue at him. He is so incensed by this that* PICKERING *presently finds it necessary to step between them.*] Dont you give me none of your lip; and dont let me hear you giving this gentleman any of it neither, or youll hear from me about it. See?

HIGGINS. Have you any further advice to give her before you go, Doolittle? Your blessing, for instance. 793

DOOLITTLE. No, Governor: I aint such a mug as to put up my children to all I know myself. Hard enough to hold them in without that. If you want Eliza's mind improved, Governor, you do it yourself with a strap. So long, gentlemen. [*He turns to go.*]

HIGGINS. [*Impressively*] Stop. Youll come regularly to see your daughter. It's your duty, you know. My brother is a clergyman; and he could help you in your talks with her.

DOOLITTLE. [*Evasively*] Certainly. I'll come, Governor. Not just this week, because I have a job at a distance. But later on you may depend on me. Afternoon, gentlemen. Afternoon, maam. [*He takes off his hat to* MRS. PEARCE, *who disdains the salutation and goes out. He winks at* HIGGINS, *thinking him probably a fellow-sufferer from* MRS. PEARCE's *difficult disposition, and follows her.*] 806

LIZA. Dont you believe the old liar. He'd as soon you set a bull-dog on him as a clergyman. You wont see him again in a hurry.

HIGGINS. I dont want to, Eliza. Do you?

LIZA. Not me. I dont want never to see him again, I dont. He's a disgrace to me, he is, collecting dust, instead of working at his trade.

PICKERING. What is his trade, Eliza? 813

LIZA. Taking money out of other people's pockets into his own. His proper trade's a navvy; and he works at it sometimes too—for exercise—and earns good money at it. Aint you going to call me Miss Doolittle any more?

PICKERING. I beg your pardon, Miss Doolittle. It was a slip of the tongue.

LIZA. Oh, I dont mind; only it sounded so genteel. I *should* just like to take a taxi to the corner of Tottenham Court Road and get out there and tell it to wait for me, just to put the girls in their place a bit. I wouldnt speak to them, you know. 823

PICKERING. Better wait til we get you something really fashionable.

HIGGINS. Besides, you shouldnt cut your old friends now that you have risen in the world. Thats what we call snobbery.

LIZA. You dont call the like of them my friends now, I should hope. Theyve took it out of me often enough with their ridicule when they had the chance; and now I mean to get a bit of my own back. But if I'm to have fashionable clothes, I'll wait. I should like to have some. Mrs. Pearce says youre going to give me some to wear in bed at night different to what I wear in the daytime; but it do seem a waste of money when you could get something to shew. Besides, I never could fancy changing into cold things on a winter night. 835

MRS. PEARCE. [*Coming back*] Now, Eliza. The new things have come for you to try on.

LIZA. Ah-ow-oo-ooh! [*She rushes out.*]

MRS. PEARCE. [*Following her*] Oh, dont rush about like that, girl. [*She shuts the door behind her.*]

HIGGINS. Pickering: we have taken on a stiff job.

PICKERING. [*With conviction*] Higgins: we have.

ACT III

It is MRS. HIGGINS's *at-home day. Nobody has yet arrived. Her drawing room, in a flat on Chelsea Embankment, has three windows looking on the river; and the ceiling is not so lofty as it would be in an older house of the same pretension. The windows are open,*

Pygmalion

giving access to a balcony with flowers in pots. If you stand with your face to the windows, you have the fireplace on your left an the door in the right-hand wall close to the corner nearest the win dows.

MRS. HIGGINS *was brought up on Morris and Burne Jones; and her room, which is very unlike her son's room in Wimpole Street, is not crowded with furniture and little tables and nicknacks. In the middle of the room there is a big ottoman; and this, with the carpet, the Morris wall-papers, and the Morris chintz window curtains and brocade covers of the ottoman and its cushions, supply all the ornament, and are much too handsome to be hidden by odds and ends of useless things. A few good oil-paintings from the exhibitions in the Grosvenor Gallery thirty years ago (the Burne Jones, not the Whistler side of them) are on the walls. The only landscape is a Cecil Lawson on the scale of a Rubens. There is a portrait of* MRS. HIGGINS *as she was when she defied fashion in her youth in one of the beautiful Rosettian costumes which, when caricatured by people who did not understand, led to the absurdities of popular estheticism in the eighteen-seventies.*

In the corner diagonally opposite the door MRS. HIGGINS, *now over sixty and long past taking the trouble to dress out of the fashion, sits writing at an elegantly simple writing-table with a bell button within reach of her hand. There is a Chippendale chair further back in the room between her and the window nearest her side. At the other side of the room, further forward, is an Elizabethan chair roughly carved in the taste of Inigo Jones. On the same side a piano in a decorated case. The corner between the fireplace and the window is occupied by a divan cushioned in Morris chintz.*

It is between four and five in the afternoon.

The door is opened violently; and HIGGINS *enters with his hat on.*

MRS. HIGGINS. [*Dismayed*] Henry [*Scolding him*]! What are you doing here today? It is my at-home day: you promised not to come. [*As he bends to kiss her, she takes his hat off, and presents it to him.*]

HIGGINS. Oh bother! [*He throws the hat down on the table.*]

MRS. HIGGINS. Go home at once.

HIGGINS. [*Kissing her*] I know, mother. I came on purpose.

MRS. HIGGINS. But you mustnt. I'm serious, Henry. You offend all my friends: they stop coming whenever they meet you.

HIGGINS. Nonsense! I know I have no small talk; but people dont mind. [*He sits on the settee.*]   11

MRS. HIGGINS. Oh! dont they? Small talk indeed! What about your large talk? Really, dear, you mustnt stay.

HIGGINS. I must. Ive a job for you. A phonetic job.

MRS. HIGGINS. No use, dear. I'm sorry; but I cant get round your vowels; and though I like to get pretty postcards in your patent shorthand, I always have to read the copies in ordinary writing you so thoughtfully send me.

HIGGINS. Well, this isnt a phonetic job.

MRS. HIGGINS. You said it was.   20

HIGGINS. Not your part of it. Ive picked up a girl.

MRS. HIGGINS. Does that mean that some girl has picked you up?

HIGGINS. Not at all. I dont mean a love affair.

MRS. HIGGINS. What a pity!

HIGGINS. Why?

MRS. HIGGINS. Well, you never fall in love with anyone under forty-five. When will you discover that there are some rather nice-looking young women about?   28

HIGGINS. Oh, I cant be bothered with young women. My idea of a lovable woman is something as like you as possible. I shall never get into the way of seriously liking young women: some habits lie too deep to be changed. [*Rising abruptly and walking about, jingling his money and his keys in his trouser pockets*] Besides, theyre all idiots.

MRS. HIGGINS. Do you know what you would do if you really loved me, Henry?

HIGGINS. Oh bother! What? Marry, I suppose?

MRS. HIGGINS. No. Stop fidgeting and take your hands out of your pockets. [*With a gesture of despair, he obeys and sits down again.*] Thats a good boy. Now tell me about the girl.   40

HIGGINS. She's coming to see you.

MRS. HIGGINS. I dont remember asking her.

HIGGINS. You didnt. *I* asked her. If youd known her you wouldnt have asked her.

MRS. HIGGINS. Indeed! Why?

HIGGINS. Well, it's like this. She's a common flower girl. I picked her off the kerbstone.

MRS. HIGGINS. And invited her to my at-home!

HIGGINS. [*Rising and coming to her to coax her*] Oh, thatll be all right. Ive taught her to speak properly; and she has strict orders as to her behavior. She's to keep to two subjects: the weather and everybody's health—Fine day and How do you do, you know—and not to let herself go on things in general. That will be safe. 53

MRS. HIGGINS. Safe! To talk about our health! about our insides! perhaps about our outsides! How could you be so silly, Henry?

HIGGINS. [*Impatiently*] Well, she must talk about something. [*He controls himself and sits down again.*] Oh, she'll be all right: dont you fuss. Pickering is in it with me. Ive a sort of bet on that I'll pass her off as a duchess in six months. I started on her some months ago; and she's getting on like a house on fire. I shall win my bet. She has a quick ear; and she's been easier to teach than my middle class pupils because she's had to learn a complete new language. She talks English almost as you talk French. 63

MRS. HIGGINS. Thats satisfactory, at all events.

HIGGINS. Well, it is and it isnt.

MRS. HIGGINS. What does that mean?

HIGGINS. You see, Ive got her pronunciation all right; but you have to consider not only *how* a girl pronounces, but *what* she pronounces; and thats where—

[*They are interrupted by the parlor-maid, announcing guests.*]

THE PARLOR-MAID. Mrs. and Miss Eynsford Hill. [*She withdraws.*]

HIGGINS. Oh Lord! [*He rises; snatches his hat from the table; and makes for the door; but before he reaches it his mother introduces him.*] 74

[MRS. *and* MISS EYNSFORD HILL *are the mother and daughter who sheltered from the rain in Covent Garden. The mother is well bred, quiet, and has the habitual anxiety of straitened means. The daughter has acquired a gay air of being very much at home in society: the bravado of genteel poverty.*]

MRS. EYNSFORD HILL. [*To* MRS. HIGGINS] How do you do? [*They shake hands.*]   81

MISS EYNSFORD HILL. How d'you do? [*She shakes.*]

MRS. HIGGINS. [*Introducing*] My son Henry.

MRS. EYNSFORD HILL. Your celebrated son! I have so longed to meet you, Professor Higgins.

HIGGINS. [*Glumly, making no movement in her direction*] Delighted. [*He backs against the piano and bows brusquely.*]

MISS EYNSFORD HILL. [*Going to him with confident familiarity*] How do you do?

HIGGINS. [*Staring at her*] Ive seen you before somewhere. I havnt the ghost of a notion where; but Ive heard your voice. [*Drearily.*] It doesn't matter. Youd better sit down.   92

MRS. HIGGINS. I'm sorry to say that my celebrated son has no manners. You mustn't mind him.

MISS EYNSFORD HILL. [*Gaily*] I dont. [*She sits in the Elizabethan chair.*]

MRS. EYNSFORD HILL. [*A little bewildered*] Not at all. [*She sits on the ottoman between her daughter and* MRS. HIGGINS, *who has turned her chair away from the writing-table.*]

HIGGINS. Oh, have I been rude? I didnt mean to be. [*He goes to the central window, through which, with his back to the company, he contemplates the river and the flowers in Battersea Park on the opposite bank as if they were a frozen desert.*]   103

[*The parlor-maid returns, ushering in* PICKERING.]

THE PARLOR-MAID. Colonel Pickering. [*She withdraws.*]

PICKERING. How do you do, Mrs. Higgins?

MRS. HIGGINS. So glad youve come. Do you know Mrs. Eynsford Hill—Miss Eynsford Hill? [*Exchange of bows. The* COLONEL *brings the Chippendale chair a little forward between* MRS. HILL *and* MRS. HIGGINS, *and sits down.*]

PICKERING. Has Henry told you what weve come for?   III

HIGGINS. [*Over his shoulder*] We were interrupted: damn it!

MRS. HIGGINS. Oh Henry, Henry, really!

MRS. EYNSFORD HILL. [*Half rising*] Are we in the way?

MRS. HIGGINS. [*Rising and making her sit down again*] No, no.

You couldnt have come more fortunately: we want you to meet a friend of ours.

HIGGINS. [*Turning hopefully*] Yes, by George! We want two or three people. Youll do as well as anybody else.

[*The parlor-maid returns, ushering* FREDDY.]

THE PARLOR-MAID. Mr. Eynsford Hill.   121

HIGGINS. [*Almost audibly, past endurance*] God of Heaven! another of them.

FREDDY. [*Shaking hands with* MRS. HIGGINS] Ahdedo?

MRS. HIGGINS. Very good of you to come. [*Introducing*] Colonel Pickering.

FREDDY. [*Bowing*] Ahdedo?

MRS. HIGGINS. I dont think you know my son, Professor Higgins.

FREDDY. [*Going to* HIGGINS] Ahdedo?

HIGGINS. [*Looking at him much as if he were a pickpocket*] I'll take my oath Ive met *you* before somewhere. Where was it?   131

FREDDY. I dont think so.

HIGGINS. [*Resignedly*] It dont matter, anyhow. Sit down. [*He shakes* FREDDY's *hand, and almost slings him on to the ottoman with his face to the windows; then comes round to the other side of it.*]

HIGGINS. Well, here we are, anyhow! [*He sits down on the ottoman next* MRS. EYNSFORD HILL, *on her left.*] And now, what the devil are we going to talk about until Eliza comes?

MRS. HIGGINS. Henry: you are the life and soul of the Royal Society's soirées; but really youre rather trying on more commonplace occasions.   142

HIGGINS. Am I? Very sorry. [*Beaming suddenly*] I suppose I am, you know. [*Uproariously*] Ha, ha!

MISS EYNSFORD HILL. [*Who considers* HIGGINS *quite eligible matrimonially*] I sympathize. *I* havnt any small talk. If people would only be frank and say what they really think!

HIGGINS. [*Relapsing into gloom*] Lord forbid!

MRS. EYNSFORD HILL. [*Taking up her daughter's cue*] But why?

HIGGINS. What they think they ought to think is bad enough, Lord knows; but what they really think would break up the whole

show. Do you suppose it would be really agreeable if I were to come out now with what *I* really think? 153

MISS EYNSFORD HILL. [*Gaily*] Is it so very cynical?

HIGGINS. Cynical! Who the dickens said it was cynical? I mean it wouldnt be decent.

MRS. EYNSFORD HILL. [*Seriously*] Oh! I'm sure you dont mean that, Mr. Higgins.

HIGGINS. You see, we're all savages, more or less. We're supposed to be civilized and cultured—to know all about poetry and philosophy and art and science, and so on; but how many of us know even the meanings of these names? [*To* MISS HILL] What do *you* know of poetry? [*To* MRS. HILL] What do *you* know of science? [*Indicating* FREDDY] What does *he* know of art or science or anything else? What the devil do you imagine I know of philosophy? 165

MRS. HIGGINS. [*Warningly*] Or of manners, Henry?

THE PARLOR-MAID. [*Opening the door*] Miss Doolittle. [*She withdraws.*]

HIGGINS. [*Rising hastily and running to* MRS. HIGGINS] Here she is, mother. [*He stands on tiptoe and makes signs over his mother's head to* ELIZA *to indicate to her which lady is her hostess.*] 171

[ELIZA, *who is exquisitely dressed, produces an impression of such remarkable distinction and beauty as she enters that they all rise, quite fluttered. Guided by* HIGGINS's *signals, she comes to* MRS. HIGGINS *with studied grace.*]

LIZA. [*Speaking with pedantic correctness of pronunciation and great beauty of tone*] How do you do, Mrs. Higgins? [*She gasps slightly in making sure of the H in Higgins, but is quite successful.*] Mr. Higgins told me I might come.

MRS. HIGGINS. [*Cordially*] Quite right: I'm very glad indeed to see you. 181

PICKERING. How do you, Miss Doolittle?

LIZA. [*Shaking hands with him*] Colonel Pickering, is it not?

MRS. EYNSFORD HILL. I feel sure we have met before, Miss Doolittle. I remember your eyes.

LIZA. How do you do? [*She sits down on the ottoman gracefully in the place just left vacant by* HIGGINS.]

MRS. EYNSFORD HILL. [*Introducing*] My daughter Clara.

LIZA. How do you do?

CLARA. [*Impulsively*] How do you do? [*She sits down on the
ottoman beside* ELIZA, *devouring her with her eyes.*]   191

FREDDY. [*Coming to their side of the ottoman*] Ive certainly had
the pleasure.

MRS. EYNSFORD HILL. [*Introducing*] My son Freddy.

LIZA. How do you do?

[FREDDY *bows and sits down in the Elizabethan chair, infatuated.*]

HIGGINS. [*Suddenly*] By George, yes: it all comes back to me!
[*They stare at him.*] Covent Garden! [*Lamentably*] What a
damned thing!

MRS. HIGGINS. Henry, please! [*He is about to sit on the edge of the
table.*] Dont sit on my writing-table: youll break it.   201

HIGGINS. [*Sulkily*] Sorry. [*He goes to the divan, stumbling into
the fender and over the fire-irons on his way; extricating himself
with muttered imprecations; and finishing his disastrous journey
by throwing himself so impatiently on the divan that he almost
breaks it.* MRS. HIGGINS *looks at him, but controls herself and says
nothing. A long and painful pause ensues.*]

MRS. HIGGINS. [*At last, conversationally*] Will it rain, do you think?

LIZA. The shallow depression in the west of these islands is likely
to move slowly in an easterly direction. There are no indications
of any great change in the barometrical situation.   211

FREDDY. Ha! ha! how awfully funny!

LIZA. What is wrong with that, young man? I bet I got it right.

FREDDY. Killing!

MRS. EYNSFORD HILL. I'm sure I hope it wont turn cold. Theres
so much influenza about. It runs right through our whole family
regularly every spring.

LIZA. [*Darkly*] My aunt died of influenza: so they said.

MRS. EYNSFORD HILL. [*Clicks her tongue sympathetically*]!!!

LIZA. [*In the same tragic tone*] But it's my belief they done the
old woman in.   221

MRS. HIGGINS. [*Puzzled*] Done her in?

LIZA. Y-e-e-e-es, Lord love you! Why should *she* die of influenza?

She come through diphtheria right enough the year before. I saw her with my own eyes. Fairly blue with it, she was. They all thought she was dead; but my father he kept ladling gin down her throat til she came to so sudden that she bit the bowl off the spoon.

MRS. EYNSFORD HILL. [*Startled*] Dear me!

LIZA. [*Piling up the indictment*] What call would a woman with that strength in her have to die of influenza? What become of her new straw hat that should have come to me? Somebody pinched it; and what I say is, them as pinched it done her in. 233

MRS. EYNSFORD HILL. What does doing her in mean?

HIGGINS. [*Hastily*] Oh, thats the new small talk. To do a person in means to kill them.

MRS. EYNSFORD HILL. [*To* ELIZA, *horrified*] You surely dont believe that your aunt was killed?

LIZA. Do I not! Them she lived with would have killed her for a hat-pin, let alone a hat.

MRS. EYNSFORD HILL. But it cant have been right for your father to pour spirits down her throat like that. It might have killed her.

LIZA. Not her. Gin was mother's milk to her. Besides, he'd poured so much down his own throat that he knew the good of it. 244

MRS. EYNSFORD HILL. Do you mean that he drank?

LIZA. Drank! My word! Something chronic.

MRS. EYNSFORD HILL. How dreadful for you!

LIZA. Not a bit. It never did him no harm what I could see. But then he did not keep it up regular. [*Cheerfully*] On the burst, as you might say, from time to time. And always more agreeable when he had a drop in. When he was out of work, my mother used to give him fourpence and tell him to go out and not come back until he'd drunk himself cheerful and loving-like. Theres lots of women has to make their husbands drunk to make them fit to live with. [*Now quite at her ease*] You see, it's like this. If a man has a bit of a conscience, it always takes him when he's sober; and then it makes him low-spirited. A drop of booze just takes that off and makes him happy. [*To* FREDDY, *who is in convulsions of suppressed laughter.*] Here! what are you sniggering at? 259

FREDDY. The new small talk. You do it so awfully well.

LIZA. If I was doing it proper, what was you laughing at? [*To* HIGGINS] Have I said anything I oughtnt?

MRS. HIGGINS. [*Interposing*] Not at all, Miss Doolittle.

LIZA. Well, thats a mercy, anyhow. [*Expansively*] What I always say is—

HIGGINS. [*Rising and looking at his watch*] Ahem!

LIZA. [*Looking round at him; taking the hint; and rising*] Well: I must go. [*They all rise.* FREDDY *goes to the door.*] So pleased to have met you. Good-bye. [*She shakes hands with* MRS. HIGGINS.]

MRS. HIGGINS. Good-bye.

LIZA. Good-bye, Colonel Pickering. 271

PICKERING. Good-bye, Miss Doolittle. [*They shake hands.*]

LIZA. [*Nodding to the others*] Good-bye, all.

FREDDY. [*Opening the door for her*] Are you walking across the Park, Miss Doolittle? If so—

LIZA. Walk! Not bloody likely. [*Sensation.*] I am going in a taxi.
[*She goes out.*]

[PICKERING *gasps and sits down.* FREDDY *goes out on the balcony to catch another glimpse of* ELIZA.]

MRS. EYNSFORD HILL. [*Suffering from shock*] Well, I really cant get used to the new ways. 281

CLARA. [*Throwing herself discontentedly into the Elizabethan chair*] Oh, it's all right, mamma, quite right. People will think we never go anywhere or see anybody if you are so old-fashioned.

MRS. EYNSFORD HILL. I daresay I am very old-fashioned; but I do hope you wont begin using that expression, Clara. I have got accustomed to hear you talking about men as rotters, and calling everything filthy and beastly; though I do think it horrible and unladylike. But this last is really too much. Dont you think so, Colonel Pickering? 290

PICKERING. Dont ask me. Ive been away in India for several years; and manners have changed so much that I sometimes dont know whether I'm at a respectable dinner-table or in a ship's forecastle.

CLARA. It's all a matter of habit. Theres no right or wrong in it. Nobody means anything by it. And it's so quaint, and gives such

a smart emphasis to things that are not in themselves very witty. I find the new small talk delightful and quite innocent.

MRS. EYNSFORD HILL. [*Rising*] Well, after that, I think it's time for us to go.

[PICKERING *and* HIGGINS *rise.*]

CLARA. [*Rising*] Oh yes: we have three at-homes to go to still. Good-bye, Mrs. Higgins. Good-bye, Colonel Pickering. Good-bye, Professor Higgins.   303

HIGGINS. [*Coming grimly at her from the divan, and accompanying her to the door*] Good-bye. Be sure you try on that small talk at the three at-homes. Dont be nervous about it. Pitch it in strong.

CLARA. [*All smiles*] I will. Good-bye. Such nonsense, all this early Victorian prudery!

HIGGINS. [*Tempting her*] Such damned nonsense!

CLARA. Such bloody nonsense!

MRS. EYNSFORD HILL. [*Convulsively*] Clara!

CLARA. Ha! ha! [*She goes out radiant, conscious of being thoroughly up to date, and is heard descending the stairs in a stream of silvery laughter.*]   314

FREDDY. [*To the heavens at large*] Well, I ask you— [*He gives it up, and comes to* MRS. HIGGINS.] Good-bye.

MRS HIGGINS. [*Shaking hands*] Good-bye. Would you like to meet Miss Doolittle again?

FREDDY. [*Eagerly*] Yes, I should, most awfully.

MRS. HIGGINS. Well, you know my days.

FREDDY. Yes. Thanks awfully. Good-bye. [*He goes out.*]

MRS. EYNSFORD HILL. Good-bye, Mr. Higgins.   322

HIGGINS. Good-bye. Good-bye.

MRS. EYNSFORD HILL. [*To* PICKERING] It's no use. I shall never be able to bring myself to use that word.

PICKERING. Dont. It's not compulsory, you know. Youll get on quite well without it.

MRS. EYNSFORD HILL. Only, Clara is so down on me if I am not positively reeking with the latest slang. Good-bye.

PICKERING. Good-bye. [*They shake hands.*]

MRS. EYNSFORD HILL. [*To* MRS. HIGGINS] You mustnt mind Clara. [PICKERING, *catching from her lowered tone that this is not meant*

for him to hear, discreetly joins HIGGINS *at the window.*] We're so poor! and she gets so few parties, poor child! She doesn't quite know. [MRS. HIGGINS, *seeing that her eyes are moist, takes her hand sympathetically and goes with her to the door.*] But the boy is nice. Dont you think so?   337

MRS. HIGGINS. Oh, quite nice. I shall always be delighted to see him.

MRS. EYNSFORD HILL. Thank you, dear. Good-bye. [*She goes out.*]

HIGGINS. [*Eagerly*] Well? Is Eliza presentable? [*He swoops on his mother and drags her to the ottoman, where she sits down in* ELIZA's *place with her son on her left.*]

[PICKERING *returns to his chair on her right.*]

MRS. HIGGINS. You silly boy, of course she's not presentable. She's a triumph of your art and of her dressmaker's; but if you suppose for a moment that she doesnt give herself away in every sentence she utters, you must be perfectly cracked about her.   347

PICKERING. But dont you think something might be done? I mean something to eliminate the sanguinary element from her conversation.

MRS. HIGGINS. Not as long as she is in Henry's hands.

HIGGINS. [*Aggrieved*] Do you mean that *my* language is improper?

MRS. HIGGINS. No, dearest: it would be quite proper—say on a canal barge; but it would not be proper for her at a garden party.

HIGGINS. [*Deeply injured*] Well I must say—

PICKERING. [*Interrupting him*] Come, Higgins: you must learn to know yourself. I havnt heard such language as yours since we used to review the volunteers in Hyde Park twenty years ago.   358

HIGGINS. [*Sulkily*] Oh, well, if *you* say so, I suppose I dont always talk like a bishop.

MRS. HIGGINS. [*Quieting* HENRY *with a touch*] Colonel Pickering: will you tell me what is the exact state of things in Wimpole Street?

PICKERING. [*Cheerfully: as if this completely changed the subject*] Well, I have come to live there with Henry. We work together at my Indian Dialects; and we think it more convenient—

MRS. HIGGINS. Quite so. I know all about that: it's an excellent arrangement. But where does this girl live?   367

HIGGINS. With us, of course. Where *should* she live?

MRS. HIGGINS. But on what terms? Is she a servant? If not, what is she?

PICKERING. [*Slowly*] I think I know what you mean, Mrs. Higgins.

HIGGINS. Well, dash me if *I* do! Ive had to work at the girl every day for months to get her to her present pitch. Besides, she's useful. She knows where my things are, and remembers my appointments and so forth.   375

MRS. HIGGINS. How does your housekeeper get on with her?

HIGGINS. Mrs. Pearce? Oh, she's jolly glad to get so much taken off her hands; for before Eliza came, *she* used to have to find things and remind me of my appointments. But she's got some silly bee in her bonnet about Eliza. She keeps saying "You dont *think*, sir": doesnt she, Pick?

PICKERING. Yes: thats the formula. "You dont *think*, sir." Thats the end of every conversation about Eliza.   383

HIGGINS. As if I ever stop thinking about the girl and her confounded vowels and consonants. I'm worn out, thinking about her, and watching her lips and her teeth and her tongue, not to mention her soul, which is the quaintest of the lot.

MRS. HIGGINS. You certainly are a pretty pair of babies, playing with your live doll.   389

HIGGINS. Playing! The hardest job I ever tackled: make no mistake about that, mother. But you have no idea how frightfully interesting it is to take a human being and change her into a quite different human being by creating a new speech for her. It's filling up the deepest gulf that separates class from class and soul from soul.

PICKERING. [*Drawing his chair closer to* MRS. HIGGINS *and bending over to her eagerly*] Yes: it's enormously interesting. I assure you, Mrs. Higgins, we take Eliza very seriously. Every week—every day almost—there is some new change. [*Closer again*] We keep records of every stage—dozens of gramophone disks and photographs—   399

HIGGINS. [*Assailing her at the other ear*] Yes, by George: it's the most absorbing experiment I ever tackled. She regularly fills our lives up: doesnt she, Pick?

PICKERING. We're always talking Eliza.

HIGGINS. Teaching Eliza.

PICKERING. Dressing Eliza.

MRS. HIGGINS. What!

HIGGINS. Inventing new Elizas.

HIGGINS. *[Speaking together]* You know, she has the most extraordinary quickness of ear:

PICKERING. I assure you, my dear Mrs. Higgins, that girl   411

HIGGINS. just like a parrot. Ive tried her with every

PICKERING. is a genius. She can play the piano quite beautifully.

HIGGINS. possible sort of sound that a human being can make—

PICKERING. We have taken her to classical concerts and to music

HIGGINS. Continental dialects, African dialects, Hottentot

PICKERING. halls; and it's all the same to her: she plays everything   422

HIGGINS. clicks, things it took me years to get hold of; and

PICKERING. she hears right off when she comes home, whether it's

HIGGINS. she picks them up like a shot, right away, as if she had

PICKERING. Beethoven and Brahms or Lehar and Lionel Monckton;

HIGGINS. been at it all her life.   431

PICKERING. though six months ago, she'd never as much as touched a piano—

MRS. HIGGINS. *[Putting her fingers in her ears, as they are by this time shouting one another down with an intolerable noise]* Sh-sh-sh —sh! [*They stop.*]

PICKERING. I beg your pardon. [*He draws his chair back apologetically.*]

HIGGINS. Sorry. When Pickering starts shouting nobody can get a word in edgeways.   440

MRS. HIGGINS. Be quiet, Henry. Colonel Pickering: dont you realize that when Eliza walked into Wimpole Street, something walked in with her?

PICKERING. Her father did. But Henry soon got rid of him.

MRS. HIGGINS. It would have been more to the point if her mother had. But as her mother didnt something else did.

PICKERING. But what?

MRS. HIGGINS. [*Unconsciously dating herself by the word*] A problem.

PICKERING. Oh, I see. The problem of how to pass her off as a lady.

HIGGINS. I'll solve that problem. Ive half solved it already.   451

MRS. HIGGINS. No, you two infinitely stupid male creatures: the problem of what is to be done with her afterwards.

HIGGINS. I dont see anything in that. She can go her own way, with all the advantages I have given her.

MRS. HIGGINS. The advantages of that poor woman who was here just now! The manners and habits that disqualify a fine lady from earning her own living without giving her a fine lady's income! Is that what you mean?

PICKERING. [*Indulgently, being rather bored*] Oh, that will be all right, Mrs. Higgins. [*He rises to go.*]   461

HIGGINS. [*Rising also*] We'll find her some light employment.

PICKERING. She's happy enough. Dont you worry about her. Goodbye. [*He shakes hands as if he were consoling a frightened child, and makes for the door.*]

HIGGINS. Anyhow, theres no good bothering now. The thing's done. Good-bye, mother. [*He kisses her, and follows* PICKERING.]

PICKERING. [*Turning for a final consolation*] There are plenty of openings. We'll do whats right. Good-bye.

HIGGINS. [*To* PICKERING *as they go out together*] Let's take her to the Shakespear exhibition at Earls Court.   471

PICKERING. Yes: lets. Her remarks will be delicious.

HIGGINS. She'll mimic all the people for us when we get home.

PICKERING. Ripping. [*Both are heard laughing as they go downstairs.*]

MRS. HIGGINS. [*Rises with an impatient bounce, and returns to her work at the writing-table. She sweeps a litter of disarranged papers*

*out of her way; snatches a sheet of paper from her stationary case;
and tries resolutely to write. At the third line she gives it up; flings
down her pen; grips the table angrily and exclaims]* Oh, men!
men!! men!!!

ACT IV

*The Wimpole Street laboratory. Midnight. Nobody in the room.
The clock on the mantelpiece strikes twelve. The fire is not alight:
it is a summer night.*

Presently HIGGINS *and* PICKERING *are heard on the stairs.*

HIGGINS. *[Calling down to* PICKERING] I say, Pick: lock up, will
you? I shant be going out again.

PICKERING. Right. Can Mrs. Pearce go to bed? We dont want anything more, do we?

HIGGINS. Lord, no

[ELIZA *opens the door and is seen on the lighted landing in
opera cloak, brilliant evening dress, and diamonds, with fan,
flowers, and all accessories. She comes to the hearth, and
switches on the electric lights there. She is tired: her pallor
contrasts strongly with her dark eyes and hair; and her ex-* [10
*pression is almost tragic. She takes off her cloak; puts her fan
and flowers on the piano; and sits down on the bench, brooding and silent.* HIGGINS, *in evening dress, with overcoat and hat,
comes in, carrying a smoking jacket which he has picked up
downstairs. He takes off the hat and overcoat; throws them
carelessly on the newspaper stand; disposes of his coat in the
same way; puts on the smoking jacket; and throws himself
wearily into the easy-chair at the hearth.* PICKERING, *similarly
attired, comes in. He also takes off his hat and overcoat, and
is about to throw them on* HIGGINS's *when he hesitates.]*

PICKERING. I say: Mrs. Pearce will row if we leave these things
lying about in the drawing room.   22

HIGGINS. Oh, chuck them over the bannisters into the hall. She'll
find them there in the morning and put them away all right. She'll
think we were drunk.

PICKERING. We are, slightly. Are there any letters?

HIGGINS. I didnt look. [PICKERING *takes the overcoats and hats and goes downstairs.* HIGGINS *begins half singing half yawning an air from La Fanciulla del Golden West. Suddenly he stops and exclaims*] I wonder where the devil my slippers are!   30

[ELIZA *looks at him darkly; then rises suddenly and leaves the room.* HIGGINS *yawns again, and resumes his song.* PICKERING *returns, with the contents of the letter-box in his hand.*]

PICKERING. Only circulars, and this coroneted billet-doux for you. [*He throws the circulars into the fender, and posts himself on the hearthrug, with his back to the grate.*]

HIGGINS. [*Glancing at the billet-doux*] Money-lender. [*He throws the letter after the circulars.*]

[ELIZA *returns with a pair of large down-at-heel slippers. She places them on the carpet before* HIGGINS, *and sits as before without a word.*]   41

HIGGINS. [*Yawning again*] Oh Lord! What an evening! What a crew! What a silly tomfoolery! [*He raises his shoe to unlace it, and catches sight of the slippers. He stops unlacing and looks at them as if they had appeared there of their own accord.*] Oh! theyre there, are they?

PICKERING. [*Stretching himself*] Well, I feel a bit tired. It's been a long day. The garden party, a dinner party, and the opera! Rather too much of a good thing. But youve won your bet, Higgins. Eliza did the trick, and something to spare, eh?

HIGGINS. [*Fervently*] Thank God it's over!   51

[ELIZA *flinches violently; but they take no notice of her; and she recovers herself and sits stonily as before.*]

PICKERING. Were you nervous at the garden party? *I* was. Eliza didnt seem a bit nervous.

HIGGINS. Oh, *she* wasnt nervous. I knew she'd be all right. No: it's the strain of putting the job through all these months that has told on me. It was interesting enough at first, while we were at the phonetics; but after that I got deadly sick of it. If I hadnt backed myself to do it I should have chucked the whole thing up two months ago. It was a silly notion: the whole thing has been a bore.

PICKERING. Oh come! the garden party was frightfully exciting. My heart began beating like anything. 63

HIGGINS. Yes, for the first three minutes. But when I saw we were going to win hands down, I felt like a bear in a cage, hanging about doing nothing. The dinner was worse: sitting gorging there for over an hour, with nobody but a damned fool of a fashionable woman to talk to! I tell you, Pickering, never again for me. No more artificial duchesses. The whole thing has been simple purgatory.

PICKERING. Youve never been broken in properly to the social routine. [*Strolling over to the piano*] I rather enjoy dipping into it occasionally myself: it makes me feel young again. Anyhow, it was a great success: an immense success. I was quite frightened once or twice because Eliza was doing it so well. You see, lots of the real people cant do it at all: theyre such fools that they think style comes by nature to people in their position; and so they never learn. Theres always something professional about doing a thing superlatively well. 79

HIGGINS. Yes: thats what drives me mad: the silly people dont know their own silly business. [*Rising*] However, it's over and done with; and now I can go to bed at last without dreading tomorrow.

[ELIZA's *beauty becomes murderous.*]

PICKERING. I think I shall turn in too. Still, it's been a great occasion: a triumph for you. Goodnight. [*He goes.*]

HIGGINS. [*Following him*] Goodnight. [*Over his shoulder, at the door*] Put out the lights, Eliza; and tell Mrs. Pearce not to make coffee for me in the morning: I'll take tea. [*He goes out.*] 89

[ELIZA *tries to control herself and feel indifferent as she rises and walks across to the hearth to switch off the lights. By the time she gets there she is on the point of screaming. She sits down in* HIGGINS's *chair and holds on hard to the arms. Finally she gives way and flings herself furiously on the floor, raging.*]

HIGGINS. [*In despairing wrath outside*] What the devil have I done with my slippers? [*He appears at the door.*]

LIZA. [*Snatching up the slippers, and hurling them at him one after the other with all her force*] There are your slippers. And

there. Take your slippers; and may you never have a day's luck
with them!   100

HIGGINS. [*Astounded*] What on earth—! [*He comes to her.*]
Whats the matter? Get up. [*He pulls her up.*] Anything wrong?

LIZA. [*Breathless*] Nothing wrong—with you. Ive won your bet
for you, havnt I? Thats enough for you. *I* dont matter, I suppose.

HIGGINS. *You* won my bet! You! Presumptuous insect! *I* won it.
What did you throw those slippers at me for?

LIZA. Because I wanted to smash your face. I'd like to kill you,
you selfish brute. Why didnt you leave me where you picked me
out of—in the gutter? You thank God it's all over, and that now
you can throw me back again there, do you? [*She crisps her fingers
frantically.*]   111

HIGGINS. [*Looking at her in cool wonder*] The creature is nervous,
after all.

LIZA. [*Gives a suffocated scream of fury, and instinctively darts
her nails at his face*]!!

HIGGINS. [*Catching her wrists*] Ah! would you? Claws in, you cat.
How dare you shew your temper to me? Sit down and be quiet.
[*He throws her roughly into the easy-chair.*]

LIZA. [*Crushed by superior strength and weight*] Whats to become
of me? Whats to become of me?

HIGGINS. How the devil do I know whats to become of you?
What does it matter what becomes of you?   122

LIZA. You dont care. I know you dont care. You wouldnt care if
I was dead. I'm nothing to you—not so much as them slippers.

HIGGINS. [*Thundering*] *Those* slippers.

LIZA. [*With bitter submission*] Those slippers. I didnt think it
made any difference now.

[*A pause.* ELIZA *hopeless and crushed.* HIGGINS *a little uneasy.*]

HIGGINS. [*In his loftiest manner*] Why have you begun going on
like this? May I ask whether you complain of your treatment here?

LIZA. No.   131

HIGGINS. Has anybody behaved badly to you? Colonel Pickering?
Mrs. Pearce? Any of the servants?

LIZA. No.

HIGGINS. I presume you dont pretend that *I* have treated you badly?

LIZA. No.

HIGGINS. I am glad to hear it. [*He moderates his tone.*] Perhaps youre tired after the strain of the day. Will you have a glass of champagne? [*He moves towards the door.*]

LIZA. No. [*Recollecting her manners*] Thank you. 140

HIGGINS. [*Good-humored again*] This has been coming on you for some days. I suppose it was natural for you to be anxious about the garden party. But thats all over now. [*He pats her kindly on the shoulder. She writhes.*] Theres nothing more to worry about.

LIZA. No. Nothing more for *you* to worry about. [*She suddenly rises and gets away from him by going to the piano bench, where she sits and hides her face.*] Oh God! I wish I was dead.

HIGGINS. [*Staring after her in sincere surprise*] Why? In heaven's name, why? [*Reasonably, going to her*] Listen to me, Eliza. All this irritation is purely subjective.

LIZA. I dont understand. I'm too ignorant. 151

HIGGINS. It's only imagination. Low spirits and nothing else. No-body's hurting you. Nothing's wrong. You go to bed like a good girl and sleep it off. Have a little cry and say your prayers: that will make you comfortable.

LIZA. I heard your prayers. "Thank God it's all over!"

HIGGINS. [*Impatiently*] Well, *dont* you thank God it's all over? Now you are free and can do what you like.

LIZA [*Pulling herself together in desperation*] What am I fit for? What have you left me fit for? Where am I to go? What am I to do? Whats to become of me? 161

HIGGINS. [*Enlightened, but not at all impressed*] Oh thats whats worrying you, is it? [*He thrusts his hands into his pockets, and walks about in his usual manner, rattling the contents of his pockets, as if condescending to a trivial subject out of pure kindness.*] I shouldnt bother about it if I were you. I should imagine you wont have much difficulty in settling yourself somewhere or other, though I hadnt quite realized that you were going away. [*She looks quickly at him: he does not look at her, but examines the dessert stand on the piano and decides that he will eat an apple.*] You might marry, you know. [*He bites a large piece out of the apple and munches* [171 *it noisily.*] You see, Eliza, all men are not confirmed old bachelors

like me and the Colonel. Most men are the marrying sort (poor
devils!); and youre not bad-looking: it's quite a pleasure to look
at you sometimes—not now, of course, because youre crying and
looking as ugly as the very devil; but when youre all right and
quite yourself, youre what I should call attractive. That is, to the
people in the marrying line, you understand. You go to bed and
have a good nice rest; and then get up and look at yourself in the
glass; and you wont feel so cheap.   180

> [ELIZA *again looks at him, speechless, and does not stir. The
> look is quite lost on him: he eats his apple with a dreamy ex-
> pression of happiness, as it is quite a good one.*]

HIGGINS. [*A genial afterthought occurring to him*] I daresay my
mother could find some chap or other who would do very well.

LIZA. We were above that at the corner of Tottenham Court Road.

HIGGINS. [*Waking up*] What do you mean?

LIZA. I sold flowers. I didnt sell myself. Now youve made a lady
of me I'm not fit to sell anything else. I wish youd left me where
you found me.   190

HIGGINS. [*Slinging the core of the apple decisively into the grate*]
Tosh, Eliza. Dont you insult human relations by dragging all this
cant about buying and selling into it. You neednt marry the fellow
if you dont like him.

LIZA. What else am I to do?

HIGGINS. Oh, lots of things. What about your old idea of a florist's
shop? Pickering could set you up in one: he's lot of money.
[*Chuckling*] He'll have to pay for all those togs you have been
wearing today; and that, with the hire of the jewellery, will make
a big hole in two hundred pounds. Why, six months ago you would
have thought it the millennium to have a flower shop of your own.
Come! youll be all right. I must clear off to bed: I'm devilish sleepy.
By the way, I came down for something: I forget what it was.

LIZA. Your slippers.   204

HIGGINS. Oh yes, of course. You shied them at me. [*He picks them
up, and is going out when she rises and speaks to him.*]

LIZA. Before you go, sir—

HIGGINS. [*Dropping the slippers in his surprise at her calling him
Sir*] Eh?

LIZA. Do my clothes belong to me or to Colonel Pickering?

HIGGINS. [*Coming back into the room as if her question were the very climax of unreason*] What the devil use would they be to Pickering? 213

LIZA. He might want them for the next girl you pick up to experiment on.

HIGGINS. [*Shocked and hurt*] Is *that* the way you feel towards us?

LIZA. I dont want to hear anything more about that. All I want to know is whether anything belongs to me. My own clothes were burnt.

HIGGINS. But what does it matter? Why need you start bothering about that in the middle of the night? 221

LIZA. I want to know what I may take away with me. I dont want to be accused of stealing.

HIGGINS. [*Now deeply wounded*] Stealing! You shouldnt have said that, Eliza. That shews a want of feeling.

LIZA. I'm sorry. I'm only a common ignorant girl; and in *my* station I have to be careful. There cant be any feelings between the like of you and the like of me. Please will you tell me what belongs to me and what doesnt? 229

HIGGINS. [*Very sulky*] You may take the whole damned houseful if you like. Except the jewels. Theyre hired. Will that satisfy you? [*He turns on his heel and is about to go in extreme dudgeon.*]

LIZA. [*Drinking in his emotion like nectar, and nagging him to provoke a further supply*] Stop, please. [*She takes off her jewels.*] Will you take these to your room and keep them safe? I dont want to run the risk of their being missing.

HIGGINS. [*Furious*] Hand them over. [*She put them into his hands.*] If these belonged to me instead of to the jeweller, I'd ram them down your ungrateful throat. [*He perfunctorily thrusts them into his pockets, unconsciously decorating himself with the protruding ends of the chains.*] 241

LIZA. [*Taking a ring off*] This ring isnt the jeweller's: it's the one you bought me in Brighton. I dont want it now. [HIGGINS *dashes the ring violently into the fireplace, and turns on her so threateningly that she crouches over the piano with her hands over her face, and exclaims*] Dont you hit me.

HIGGINS. Hit you! You infamous creature, how dare you accuse me of such a thing? It is you who have hit me. You have wounded me to the heart.

LIZA. [*Thrilling with hidden joy*] I'm glad. Ive got a little of my own back, anyhow. 251

HIGGINS. [*With dignity, in his finest professional style*] You have caused me to lose my temper: a thing that has hardly ever happened to me before. I prefer to say nothing more tonight. I am going to bed.

LIZA [*Pertly*] Youd better leave a note for Mrs. Pearce about the coffee; for she wont be told by me.

HIGGINS. [*Formally*] Damn Mrs. Pearce; and damn the coffee; and damn you; and damn my own folly in having lavished hardearned knowledge and the treasure of my regard and intimacy on a heartless guttersnipe. [*He goes out with impressive decorum, and spoils it by slamming the door savagely.*]

[*ELIZA smiles for the first time; expresses her feelings by a wild pantomime in which an imitation of HIGGINS's exit is confused with her own triumph; and finally goes down on her knees on the hearthrug to look for the ring.*]

ACT V

MRS. HIGGINS's *drawing room. She is at her writing-table as before. The parlor-maid comes in.*

THE PARLOR-MAID. [*At the door*] Mr. Henry, maam, is downstairs with Colonel Pickering.

MRS. HIGGINS. Well, shew them up.

THE PARLOR-MAID. Theyre using the telephone, maam. Telephoning to the police, I think.

MRS. HIGGINS. What!

THE PARLOR-MAID. [*Coming further in and lowering her voice*] Mr. Henry is in a state, maam. I thought I'd better tell you.

MRS. HIGGINS. If you had told me that Mr. Henry was not in a

state it would have been more surprising. Tell them to come up when theyve finished with the police. I suppose he's lost something.

THE PARLOR-MAID. Yes, maam. [*Going.*]   12

MRS. HIGGINS. Go upstairs and tell Miss Doolittle that Mr. Henry and the Colonel are here. Ask her not to come down til I send for her.

THE PARLOR-MAID. Yes, maam.

[HIGGINS *bursts in. He is, as the parlor-maid has said, in a state.*]

HIGGINS. Look here, mother: heres a confounded thing!

MRS. HIGGINS. Yes, dear. Good morning. [*He checks his impatience and kisses her, whilst the parlor-maid goes out.*] What is it?

HIGGINS. Eliza's bolted.   21

MRS. HIGGINS. [*Calmly continuing her writing*] You must have frightened her.

HIGGINS. Frightened her! nonsense! She was left last night, as usual, to turn out the lights and all that; and instead of going to bed she changed her clothes and went right off: her bed wasnt slept in. She came in a cab for her things before seven this morning; and that fool Mrs. Pearce let her have them without telling me a word about it. What am I to do?

MRS. HIGGINS. Do without, I'm afraid, Henry. The girl has a perfect right to leave if she chooses.   31

HIGGINS. [*Wandering distractedly across the room*] But I cant find anything. I dont know what appointments Ive got. I'm—

[PICKERING *comes in.* MRS. HIGGINS *puts down her pen and turns away from the writing-table.*]

PICKERING. [*Shaking hands*] Good morning, Mrs. Higgins. Has Henry told you? [*He sits down on the ottoman.*]

HIGGINS. What does that ass of an inspector say? Have you offered a reward?

MRS. HIGGINS. [*Rising in indignant amazement*] You dont mean to say you have set the police after Eliza.   41

HIGGINS. Of course. What are the police for? What else could we do? [*He sits in the Elizabethan chair.*]

PICKERING. The inspector made a lot of difficulties. I really think he suspected us of some improper purpose.

MRS. HIGGINS. Well, of course he did. What right have you to go to the police and give the girl's name as if she were a thief, or a lost umbrella, or something? Really! [*She sits down again, deeply vexed.*]

HIGGINS. But we want to find her. 50

PICKERING. We cant let her go like this, you know, Mrs. Higgins. What were we to do?

MRS. HIGGINS. You have no more sense, either of you, than two children. Why—

[*The parlor-maid comes in and breaks off the conversation.*]

THE PARLOR-MAID. Mr. Henry: a gentleman wants to see you very particular. He's been sent on from Wimpole Street.

HIGGINS. Oh, bother! I cant see anyone now. Who is it?

THE PARLOR-MAID. A Mr. Doolittle, sir.

PICKERING. Doolittle! Do you mean the dustman? 60

THE PARLOR-MAID. Dustman! Oh no, sir: a gentleman.

HIGGINS. [*Springing up excitedly*] By George, Pick, it's some relative of hers that she's gone to. Somebody we know nothing about. [*To the parlor-maid*] Send him up, quick.

THE PARLOR-MAID. Yes, sir. [*She goes.*]

HIGGINS. [*Eagerly, going to his mother*] Genteel relatives! now we shall hear something. [*He sits down in the Chippendale chair.*]

MRS. HIGGINS. Do you know any of her people?

PICKERING. Only her father: the fellow we told you about. 69

THE PARLOR-MAID. [*Announcing*] Mr. Doolittle. [*She withdraws.*]

[DOOLITTLE *enters. He is brilliantly dressed in a new fashionable frock-coat, with white waistcoat and grey trousers. A flower in his buttonhole, a dazzling silk hat, and patent leather shoes complete the effect. He is too concerned with the business he has come on to notice* MRS. HIGGINS. *He walks straight to* HIGGINS, *and accosts him with vehement reproach.*]

DOOLITTLE. [*Indicating his own person*] See here! Do you see this? You done this.

HIGGINS. Done what, man?

DOOLITTLE. This, I tell you. Look at it. Look at this hat. Look at this coat. 81

PICKERING. Has Eliza been buying you clothes?

DOOLITTLE. Eliza! not she. Not half. Why would she buy me clothes?

MRS. HIGGINS. Good morning, Mr. Doolittle. Wont you sit down?

DOOLITTLE. [*Taken aback as he becomes conscious that he has forgotten his hostess*] Asking your pardon, maam. [*He approaches her and shakes her proffered hand.*] Thank you. [*He sits down on the ottoman, on* PICKERING's *right.*] I am that full of what has happened to me that I cant think of anything else. 90

HIGGINS. What the dickens *has* happened to you?

DOOLITTLE. I shouldnt mind if it had only happened to me: anything might happen to anybody and nobody to blame but Providence, as you might say. But this is something that you done to me: yes, you, Henry Higgins.

HIGGINS. Have you found Eliza? Thats the point.

DOOLITTLE. Have you lost her?

HIGGINS. Yes.

DOOLITTLE. You have all the luck, you have. I aint found her; but she'll find me quick enough now after what you done to me. 100

MRS. HIGGINS. But what has my son done to you, Mr. Doolittle?

DOOLITTLE. Done to me! Ruined me. Destroyed my happiness. Tied me up and delivered me into the hands of middle class morality.

HIGGINS. [*Rising intolerantly and standing over* DOOLITTLE] Youre raving. Youre drunk. Youre mad. I gave you five pounds. After that I had two conversations with you, at half-a-crown an hour. Ive never seen you since.

DOOLITTLE. Oh! Drunk! am I? Mad? am I? Tell me this. Did you or did you not write a letter to an old blighter in America that was giving five millions to found Moral Reform Societies all over the world, and that wanted you to invent a universal language for him? 113

HIGGINS. What! Ezra D. Wannafeller! He's dead. [*He sits down again carelessly.*]

DOOLITTLE. Yes: he's dead; and I'm done for. Now did you or did you not write a letter to him to say that the most original moralist at present in England, to the best of your knowledge, was Alfred Doolittle, a common dustman.

HIGGINS. Oh, after your last visit I remember making some silly joke of the kind.   121

DOOLITTLE. Ah! you may well call it a silly joke. It put the lid on me right enough. Just give him the chance he wanted to shew that Americans is not like us: that they recognize and respect merit in every class of life, however humble. Them words is in his blooming will, in which, Henry Higgins, thanks to your silly joking, he leaves me a share in his Pre-digested Cheese Trust worth three thousand a year on condition that I lecture for his Wannafeller Moral Reform World League as often as they ask me up to six times a year.

HIGGINS. The devil he does! Whew! [*Brightening suddenly*] What a lark!   131

PICKERING. A safe thing for you, Doolittle. They wont ask you twice.

DOOLITTLE. It aint the lecturing I mind. I'll lecture them blue in the face, I will, and not turn a hair. It's making a gentleman of me that I object to. Who asked him to make a gentleman of me? I was happy. I was free. I touched pretty nigh everybody for money when I wanted it, same as I touched you, Henry Higgins. Now I am worrited; tied neck and heels; and everybody touches me for money. It's a fine thing for you, says my solicitor. Is it? says I. You mean it's a good thing for you, I says. When I was a poor man and had a solicitor once when they found a pram in the dust cart, he got me off, and got shut of me and got me shut of him as quick as he could. Same with the doctors: used to shove me out of the [144 hospital before I could hardly stand on my legs, and nothing to pay. Now they finds out that I'm not a healthy man and cant live unless they looks after me twice a day. In the house I'm not let do a hand's turn for myself: somebody else must do it and touch me for it. A year ago I hadnt a relative in the world except two or three that wouldnt speak to me. Now Ive fifty, and not a decent week's wages among the lot of them. I have to live for others and not for myself: thats middle class morality. You talk of losing Eliza. Dont you be anxious: I bet she's on my doorstep by this: she that could support herself easy by selling flowers if I wasnt respectable. And the next one to touch me will be you, Henry Higgins. I'll have to learn to speak middle class language from you, instead of speaking proper

English. Thats where youll come in; and I daresay thats what you
done it for.   158

MRS. HIGGINS. But, my dear Mr. Doolittle, you need not suffer
all this if you are really in earnest. Nobody can force you to accept
this bequest. You can repudiate it. Isnt that so, Colonel Pickering?

PICKERING. I believe so.

DOOLITTLE. [*Softening his manner in deference to her sex*] Thats
the tragedy of it, maam. It's easy to say chuck it; but I havnt the
nerve. Which of us has? We're all intimidated. Intimidated, maam:
thats what we are. What is there for me if I chuck it but the workhouse in my old age? I have to dye my hair already to keep my job
as a dustman. If I was one of the deserving poor, and had put by
a bit, I could chuck it; but then why should I, acause the deserving
poor might as well be millionaires for all the happiness they ever
has. They dont know what happiness is. But I, as one of the un- [171
deserving poor, have nothing between me and the pauper's uniform
but this here blasted three thousand a year that shoves me into the
middle class. (Excuse the expression, maam: youd use it yourself
if you had my provocation.) Theyve got you every way you turn:
it's a choice between the Skilly of the workhouse and the Char Bydis
of the middle class; and I havnt the nerve for the workhouse. Intimidated: thats what I am. Broke. Brought up. Happier men than
me will call for my dust, and touch me for their tip; and I'll look
on helpless, and envy them. And thats what your son has brought
me to. [*He is overcome by emotion.*]   181

MRS. HIGGINS. Well, I'm very glad youre not going to do anything
foolish, Mr. Doolittle. For this solves the problem of Eliza's future.
You can provide for her now.

DOOLITTLE. [*With melancholy resignation*] Yes, maam: I'm expected to provide for everyone now, out of three thousand a year.

HIGGINS. [*Jumping up*] Nonsense! he cant provide for her. He
shant provide for her. She doesnt belong to him. I paid him five
pounds for her. Doolittle: either youre an honest man or a rogue.

DOOLITTLE. [*Tolerantly*] A little of both, Henry, like the rest of
us: a little of both.   191

HIGGINS. Well, you took that money for the girl; and you have
no right to take her as well.

MRS. HIGGINS. Henry: dont be absurd. If you want to know where Eliza is, she is upstairs.

HIGGINS. [*Amazed*] Upstairs!!! Then I shall jolly soon fetch her downstairs. [*He makes resolutely for the door.*]

MRS. HIGGINS. [*Rising and following him*] Be quiet, Henry. Sit down.

HIGGINS. I— 200

MRS. HIGGINS. Sit down, dear; and listen to me.

HIGGINS. Oh very well, very well, very well. [*He throws himself ungraciously on the ottoman, with his face towards the windows.*] But I think you might have told us this half an hour ago.

MRS. HIGGINS. Eliza came to me this morning. She passed the night partly walking about in a rage, partly trying to throw herself into the river and being afraid to, and partly in the Carlton Hotel. She told me of the brutal way you two treated her.

HIGGINS. [*Bounding up again*] What! 209

PICKERING. [*Rising also*] My dear Mrs. Higgins, she's been telling you stories. We didnt treat her brutally. We hardly said a word to her; and we parted on particularly good terms. [*Turning on HIG-GINS.*] Higgins: did you bully her after I went to bed?

HIGGINS. Just the other way about. She threw my slippers in my face. She behaved in the most outrageous way. I never gave her the slightest provocation. The slippers came bang into my face the moment I entered the room—before I had uttered a word. And used perfectly awful language.

PICKERING. [*Astonished*] But why? What did we do to her? 219

MRS. HIGGINS. I think I know pretty well what you did. The girl is naturally rather affectionate, I think. Isnt she, Mr. Doolittle?

DOOLITTLE. Very tender-hearted, maam. Takes after me.

MRS. HIGGINS. Just so. She had become attached to you both. She worked very hard for you, Henry! I dont think you quite realize what anything in the nature of brain work means to a girl like that. Well, it seems that when the great day of trial came, and she did this wonderful thing for you without making a single mistake, you two sat there and never said a word to her, but talked together of how glad you were that it was all over and how you had been bored with the whole thing. And then you were surprised because she

threw your slippers at you! *I* should have thrown the fire-irons at you.

HIGGINS. We said nothing except that we were tired and wanted to go to bed. Did we, Pick?

PICKERING. [*Shrugging his shoulders*] That was all.

MRS. HIGGINS. [*Ironically*] Quite sure?

PICKERING. Absolutely. Really, that was all.

MRS. HIGGINS. You didn't thank her, or pet her, or admire her, or tell her how splendid she'd been.

HIGGINS. [*Impatiently*] But she knew all about that. We didnt make speeches to her, if thats what you mean.

PICKERING. [*Conscience stricken*] Perhaps we were a little inconsiderate. Is she very angry?

MRS. HIGGINS. [*Returning to her place at the writing-table*] Well, I'm afraid she wont go back to Wimpole Street, especially now that Mr. Doolittle is able to keep up the position you have thrust on her; but she says she is quite willing to meet you on friendly terms and to let bygones be bygones.

HIGGINS. [*Furious*] Is she, by George? Ho!

MRS. HIGGINS. If you promise to behave yourself, Henry, I'll ask her to come down. If not, go home; for you have taken up quite enough of my time.

HIGGINS. Oh, all right. Very well. Pick: you behave yourself. Let us put on our best Sunday manners for this creature that we picked out of the mud. [*He flings himself sulkily into the Elizabethan chair.*]

DOOLITTLE. [*Remonstrating*] Now, now, Henry Higgins! have some consideration for my feelings as a middle class man.

MRS. HIGGINS. Remember your promise, Henry. [*She presses the bell-button on the writing-table.*] Mr. Doolittle: will you be so good as to step out on the balcony for a moment. I dont want Eliza to have the shock of your news until she has made it up with these two gentlemen. Would you mind?

DOOLITTLE. As you wish, lady. Anything to help Henry to keep her off my hands. [*He disappears through the window.*]

[*The parlor-maid answers the bell.* PICKERING *sits down in* DOO-LITTLE's *place.*]

MRS. HIGGINS. Ask Miss Doolittle to come down, please.

THE PARLOR-MAID. Yes, maam. [*She goes out.*]

MRS. HIGGINS. Now, Henry: be good.

HIGGINS. I am behaving myself perfectly.

PICKERING. He is doing his best, Mrs. Higgins.

[*A pause.* HIGGINS *throws back his head; stretches out his legs; and begins to whistle.*]

MRS. HIGGINS. Henry, dearest, you dont look at all nice in that attitude.

HIGGINS. [*Pulling himself together*] I was not trying to look nice, mother. 278

MRS. HIGGINS. It doesn't matter, dear. I only wanted to make you speak.

HIGGINS. Why?

MRS. HIGGINS. Because you cant speak and whistle at the same time.

[HIGGINS *groans. Another very trying pause.*]

HIGGINS. [*Springing up, out of patience*] Where the devil is that girl? Are we to wait here all day?

[ELIZA *enters, sunny, self-possessed, and giving a staggeringly convincing exhibition of ease of manner. She carries a little work-basket, and is very much at home.* PICKERING *is too much taken aback to rise.*]

LIZA. How do you do, Professor Higgins? Are you quite well?

HIGGINS. [*Choking*] Am I— [*He can say no more.*] 291

LIZA. But of course you are: you are never ill. So glad to see you again, Colonel Pickering. [*He rises hastily; and they shake hands.*] Quite chilly this morning, isn't it? [*She sits down on his left. He sits beside her.*]

HIGGINS. Dont you dare try this game on me. I taught it to you; and it doesn't take me in. Get up and come home; and dont be a fool.

[ELIZA *takes a piece of needlework from her basket, and begins to stitch at it, without taking the least notice of this outburst.*] 300

MRS. HIGGINS. Very nicely put, indeed, Henry. No woman could resist such an invitation.

HIGGINS. You let her alone, mother. Let her speak for herself. You will jolly soon see whether she has an idea that I havnt put into

her head or a word that I havnt put into her mouth. I tell you I have created this thing out of the squashed cabbage leaves of Covent Garden; and now she pretends to play the fine lady with me.

MRS. HIGGINS. [*Placidly*] Yes, dear; but youll sit down, wont you?

[HIGGINS *sits down again, savagely.*] 309

LIZA. [*To* PICKERING, *taking no apparent notice of* HIGGINS, *and working away deftly*] Will *you* drop me altogether now that the experiment is over, Colonel Pickering?

PICKERING. Oh dont. You mustnt think of it as an experiment. It shocks me, somehow.

LIZA. Oh, I'm only a squashed cabbage leaf—

PICKERING. [*Impulsively*] No.

LIZA. [*Continuing quietly*] —but I owe so much to you that I should be very unhappy if you forgot me.

PICKERING. It's very kind of you to say so, Miss Doolittle. 319

LIZA. It's not because you paid for my dresses. I know you are generous to everybody with money. But it was from you that I learnt really nice manners; and that is what makes one a lady, isn't it? You see it was so very difficult for me with the example of Professor Higgins always before me. I was brought up to be just like him, unable to control myself, and using bad language on the slightest provocation. And I should never have known that ladies and gentlemen didnt behave like that if you hadnt been there.

HIGGINS. Well!!

PICKERING. Oh, thats only his way, you know. He doesnt mean it. 329

LIZA. Oh, *I* didnt mean it either, when I was a flower girl. It was only my way. But you see I did it; and thats what makes the difference after all.

PICKERING. No doubt. Still, he taught you to speak; and I couldnt have done that, you know.

LIZA. [*Trivially*] Of course: that is his profession.

HIGGINS. Damnation!

LIZA [*Continuing*] It was just like learning to dance in the fashionable way: there was nothing more than that in it. But do you know what began my real education?

PICKERING. What? 340

LIZA. [*Stopping her work for a moment*] Your calling me Miss Doolittle that day when I first came to Wimpole Street. That was the beginning of self-respect for me. [*She resumes her stitching.*] And there were a hundred little things you never noticed, because they came naturally to you. Things about standing up and taking off your hat and opening doors—

PICKERING. Oh, that was nothing.

LIZA. Yes: things that shewed you thought and felt about me as if I were something better than a scullery-maid; though of course I know you would have been just the same to a scullery-maid if she had been let into the drawing room. You never took off your boots in the dining room when I was there.   353

PICKERING. You mustnt mind that. Higgins takes off his boots all over the place.

LIZA. I know. I am not blaming him. It is his way, isnt it? But it made *such* a difference to me that you didnt do it. You see, really and truly, apart from the things anyone can pick up (the dressing and the proper way of speaking, and so on), the difference between a lady and a flower girl is not how she behaves, but how she's treated. I shall always be a flower girl to Professor Higgins, because he always treats me as a flower girl, and always will; but I know I can be a lady to you, because you always treat me as a lady, and always will.   364

MRS. HIGGINS. Please dont grind your teeth, Henry.

PICKERING. Well, this is really very nice of you, Miss Doolittle.

LIZA. I should like you to call me Eliza, now, if you would.

PICKERING. Thank you. Eliza, of course.

LIZA. And I should like Professor Higgins to call me Miss Doolittle.

HIGGINS. I'll see you damned first.

MRS. HIGGINS. Henry! Henry!

PICKERING. [*Laughing*] Why dont you slang back at him? Dont stand it. It would do him a lot of good.   374

LIZA. I cant. I could have done it once; but now I cant go back to it. Last night, when I was wandering about, a girl spoke to me; and I tried to get back into the old way with her; but it was no use. You told me, you know, that when a child is brought to a foreign

country, it picks up the language in a few weeks, and forgets its own. Well, I am a child in your country. I have forgotten my own language, and can speak nothing but yours. Thats the real break-off with the corner of Tottenham Court Road. Leaving Wimpole Street finishes it.

PICKERING. [*Much alarmed*] Oh! but youre coming back to Wimpole Street, arnt you? Youll forgive Higgins? 385

HIGGINS. [*Rising*] Forgive! Will she, by George! Let her go. Let her find out how she can get on without us. She will relapse into the gutter in three weeks without me at her elbow.

[DOOLITTLE *appears at the centre window. With a look of dignified reproach at* HIGGINS, *he comes slowly and silently to his daughter, who, with her back to the window, is unconscious of his approach.*]

PICKERING. He's incorrigible, Eliza. You wont relapse, will you?

LIZA. No: not now. Never again. I have learnt my lesson. I dont believe I could utter one of the old sounds if I tried. [DOOLITTLE *touches her on her left shoulder. She drops her work, losing her self-possession utterly at the spectacle of her father's splendor*] A-a-a-a-a-ah-ow-ooh! 398

HIGGINS. [*With a crow of triumph*] Aha! Just so. A-a-a-a-ahow-ooh! A-a-a-a-ahowooh! A-a-a-a-ahowooh! Victory! Victory! [*He throws himself on the divan, folding his arms, and spraddling arrogantly.*]

DOOLITTLE. Can you blame the girl? Dont look at me like that, Eliza. It aint my fault. Ive come into some money.

LIZA. You must have touched a millionaire this time, dad.

DOOLITTLE. I have. But I'm dressed something special today. I'm going to St. George's, Hanover Square. Your stepmother is going to marry me.

LIZA. [*Angrily*] Youre going to let yourself down to marry that low common woman! 410

PICKERING. [*Quietly*] He ought to, Eliza. [*To* DOOLITTLE] Why has she changed her mind?

DOOLITTLE. [*Sadly*] Intimidated, Governor. Intimidated. Middle class morality claims its victim. Wont you put on your hat, Liza, and come and see me turned off?

LIZA. If the Colonel says I must, I—I'll [*Almost sobbing*] I'll demean myself. And get insulted for my pains, like enough.

DOOLITTLE. Dont be afraid: she never comes to words with anyone now, poor woman! respectability has broke all the spirit out of her.

PICKERING. [*Squeezing* ELIZA's *elbow gently*] Be kind to them, Eliza. Make the best of it.   421

LIZA. [*Forcing a little smile for him through her vexation*] Oh well, just to shew theres no ill feeling. I'll be back in a moment.
                                                                    [*She goes out.*]

DOOLITTLE. [*Sitting down beside* PICKERING] I feel uncommon nervous about the ceremony, Colonel. I wish youd come and see me through it.

PICKERING. But youve been through it before, man. You were married to Eliza's mother.

DOOLITTLE. Who told you that, Colonel?   430

PICKERING. Well, nobody told me. But I concluded—naturally—

DOOLITTLE. No: that aint the natural way, Colonel: it's only the middle class way. My way was always the undeserving way. But dont say nothing to Eliza. She dont know: I always had a delicacy about telling her.

PICKERING. Quite right. We'll leave it so, if you dont mind.

DOOLITTLE. And youll come to the church, Colonel, and put me through straight?

PICKERING. With pleasure. As far as a bachelor can.   439

MRS. HIGGINS. May I come, Mr. Doolittle? I should be very sorry to miss your wedding.

DOOLITTLE. I should indeed be honored by your condescension, maam; and my poor old woman would take it as a tremenjous compliment. She's been very low, thinking of the happy days that are no more.

MRS. HIGGINS. [*Rising*] I'll order the carriage and get ready. [*The men rise, except* HIGGINS.] I shant be more than fifteen minutes. [*As she goes to the door* ELIZA *comes in, hatted and buttoning her gloves.*] I'm going to the church to see your father married, Eliza. You had better come in the brougham with me. Colonel Pickering can go on with the bridegroom.   451

[MRS. HIGGINS *goes out.* ELIZA *comes to the middle of the room between the centre window and the ottoman.* PICKERING *joins her.*]

DOOLITTLE. Bridegroom! What a word! It makes a man realize his position, somehow. [*He takes up his hat and goes towards the door.*]

PICKERING. Before I go, Eliza, do forgive him and come back to us.

LIZA. I dont think papa would allow me. Would you, dad?

DOOLITTLE. [*Sad but magnanimous*] They played you off very cunning, Eliza, them two sportsmen. If it had been only one of them, you could have nailed him. But you see, there was two; and one of them chaperoned the other, as you might say. [*To* PICKERING] It was artful of you, Colonel; but I bear no malice: I should have done the same myself. I been the victim of one woman after another all my life; and I dont grudge you two getting the better of Eliza. I shant interfere. It's time for us to go, Colonel. So long, Henry. See you in St. George's, Eliza. [*He goes out.*] 466

PICKERING. [*Coaxing*] Do stay with us, Eliza. [*He follows* DOOLITTLE.]

[ELIZA *goes out on the balcony to avoid being alone with* HIGGINS. *He rises and joins her there. She immediately comes back into the room and makes for the door; but he goes along the balcony quickly and gets his back to the door before she reaches it.*]

HIGGINS. Well, Eliza, youve had a bit of your own back, as you call it. Have you had enough? and are you going to be reasonable? Or do you want any more? 476

LIZA. You want me back only to pick up your slippers and put up with your tempers and fetch and carry for you.

HIGGINS. I havnt said I wanted you back at all.

LIZA. Oh, indeed. Then what are we talking about?

HIGGINS. About you, not about me. If you come back I shall treat you just as I have always treated you. I cant change my nature; and I dont intend to change my manners. My manners are exactly the same as Colonel Pickering's.

LIZA. That's not true. He treats a flower girl as if she was a duchess.

HIGGINS. And I treat a duchess as if she was a flower girl. 487

LIZA. I see. [*She turns away composedly, and sits on the ottoman, facing the window.*] The same to everybody.

HIGGINS. Just so.

LIZA. Like father.

HIGGINS. [*Grinning, a little taken down*] Without accepting the comparison at all points, Eliza, it's quite true that your father is not a snob, and that he will be quite at home in any station of life to which his eccentric destiny may call him. [*Seriously.*] The great secret, Eliza, is not having bad manners or good manners or any other particular sort of manners, but having the same manner for all human souls: in short, behaving as if you were in Heaven, where there are no third-class carriages, and one soul is as good as another.

LIZA. Amen. You are a born preacher.   500

HIGGINS. [*Irritated*] The question is not whether I treat you rudely, but whether you ever heard me treat anyone else better.

LIZA. [*With sudden sincerity*] I dont care how you treat me. I dont mind your swearing at me. I dont mind a black eye: Ive had one before this. But [*standing up and facing him*] I wont be passed over.

HIGGINS. Then get out of my way; for I wont stop for you. You talk about me as if I were a motor bus.

LIZA. So you are a motor bus: all bounce and go, and no consideration for anyone. But I can do without you: dont think I cant.   510

HIGGINS. I know you can. I told you you could.

LIZA. [*Wounded, getting away from him to the other side of the ottoman with her face to the hearth*] I know you did, you brute. You wanted to get rid of me.

HIGGINS. Liar.

LIZA. Thank you. [*She sits down with dignity.*]

HIGGINS. You never asked yourself, I suppose, whether *I* could do without you.

LIZA. [*Earnestly*] Dont you try to get round me. Youll *have* to do without me.   520

HIGGINS. [*Arrogant*] I can do without anybody. I have my own soul: my own spark of divine fire. But [*with sudden humility*] I shall miss you, Eliza. [*He sits down near her on the ottoman.*] I have learnt something from your idiotic notions: I confess that

humbly and gratefully. And I have grown accustomed to your voice and appearance. I like them, rather.

LIZA. Well, you have both of them on your gramophone and in your book of photographs. When you feel lonely without me, you can turn the machine on. It's got no feelings to hurt. 529

HIGGINS. I cant turn your soul on. Leave me those feelings; and you can take away the voice and the face. They are not you.

LIZA. Oh, you *are* a devil. You can twist the heart in a girl as easy as some could twist her arms to hurt her. Mrs. Pearce warned me. Time and again she has wanted to leave you; and you always got round her at the last minute. And you dont care a bit for her. And you dont care a bit for me.

HIGGINS. I care for life, for humanity; and you are a part of it that has come my way and been built into my house. What more can you or anyone ask? 539

LIZA. I wont care for anybody that doesnt care for me.

HIGGINS. Commercial principles, Eliza. Like [*reproducing her Covent Garden pronunciation with professional exactness*] s'yollin voylets [*selling violets*], isnt it?

LIZA. Dont sneer at me. It's mean to sneer at me.

HIGGINS. I have never sneered in my life. Sneering doesnt become either the human face or the human soul. I am expressing my right-eous contempt for Commercialism. I dont and wont trade in affection. You call me a brute because you couldnt buy a claim on me by fetching my slippers and finding my spectacles. You were a fool: I think a woman fetching a man's slippers is a disgusting sight: did I ever fetch *your* slippers? I think a good deal more of you for [551 throwing them in my face. No use slaving for me and then saying you want to be cared for: who cares for a slave? If you come back, come back for the sake of good fellowship; for youll get nothing else. Youve had a thousand times as much out of me as I have out of you; and if you dare to set up your little dog's tricks of fetching and carrying slippers against my creation of a Duchess Eliza, I'll slam the door in your silly face.

LIZA. What did you do it for if you didnt care for me?

HIGGINS. [*Heartily*] Why, because it was my job. 560

LIZA. You never thought of the trouble it would make for me.

HIGGINS. Would the world ever have been made if its maker had been afraid of making trouble? Making life means making trouble. Theres only one way of escaping trouble; and thats killing things. Cowards, you notice, are always shrieking to have troublesome people killed.

LIZA. I'm no preacher: I dont notice things like that. I notice that you dont notice me. 568

HIGGINS. [*Jumping up and walking about intolerantly*] Eliza: youre an idiot. I waste the treasures of my Miltonic mind by spreading them before you. Once for all, understand that I go my way and do my work without caring twopence what happens to either of us. I am not intimidated, like your father and your stepmother. So you can come back or go to the devil: which you please.

LIZA. What am I to come back for?

HIGGINS. [*Bouncing up on his knees on the ottoman and leaning over it to her*] For the fun of it. Thats why I took you on.

LIZA. [*With averted face*] And you may throw me out tomorrow if I dont do everything you want me to? 579

HIGGINS. Yes; and you may walk out tomorrow if I dont do everything *you* want me to.

LIZA. And live with my stepmother?

HIGGINS. Yes, or sell flowers.

LIZA. Oh! if I only *could* go back to my flower basket! I should be independent of both you and father and all the world! Why did you take my independence from me? Why did I give it up? I'm a slave now, for all my fine clothes.

HIGGINS. Not a bit. I'll adopt you as my daughter and settle money on you if you like. Or would you rather marry Pickering? 589

LIZA. [*Looking fiercely round at him*] I wouldnt marry *you* if you asked me; and youre nearer my age than what he is.

HIGGINS. [*Gently*] Than he is: not "than what he is."

LIZA. [*Losing her temper and rising*] I'll talk as I like. Youre not my teacher now.

HIGGINS. [*Reflectively*] I dont suppose Pickering would, though. He's as confirmed an old bachelor as I am.

LIZA. Thats not what I want; and dont you think it. Ive always

had chaps enough wanting me that way. Freddy Hill writes to me
twice and three times a day, sheets and sheets.   599

HIGGINS. [*Disagreeably surprised*] Damn his impudence! [*He recoils and finds himself sitting on his heels.*]

LIZA. He has a right to if he likes, poor lad. And he does love me.

HIGGINS. [*Getting off the ottoman*] You have no right to encourage him.

LIZA. Every girl has a right to be loved.

HIGGINS. What! By fools like that?

LIZA. Freddy's not a fool. And if he's weak and poor and wants
me, may be he'd make me happier than my betters that bully me
and dont want me.   609

HIGGINS. Can he *make* anything of you? Thats the point.

LIZA. Perhaps I could make something of him. But I never thought
of us making anything of one another; and you never think of
anything else. I only want to be natural.

HIGGINS. In short, you want me to be as infatuated about you as
Freddy? Is that it?

LIZA. No I dont. Thats not the sort of feeling I want from you.
And dont you be too sure of yourself or of me. I could have been
a bad girl if I'd liked. Ive seen more of some things than you, for
all your learning. Girls like me can drag gentlemen down to make
love to them easy enough. And they wish each other dead the next
minute.   621

HIGGINS. Of course they do. Then what in thunder are we quarrelling about?

LIZA. [*Much troubled*] I want a little kindness. I know I'm a
common ignorant girl, and you a book-learned gentleman; but I'm
not dirt under your feet. What I done [*correcting herself*] what I
did was not for the dresses and the taxis: I did it because we were
pleasant together and I come—came—to care for you; not to want
you to make love to me, and not forgetting the difference between
us, but more friendly like.   630

HIGGINS. Well, of course. Thats just how I feel. And how Pickering feels. Eliza: youre a fool.

LIZA. Thats not a proper answer to give me. [*She sinks on the
chair at the writing-table in tears.*]

HIGGINS. It's all youll get until you stop being a common idiot. If youre going to be a lady, youll have to give up feeling neglected if the men you know dont spend half their time snivelling over you and the other half giving you black eyes. If you cant stand the coldness of my sort of life, and the strain of it, go back to the gutter. Work til you are more a brute than a human being; and [640 then cuddle and squabble and drink til you fall asleep. Oh, it's a fine life, the life of the gutter. It's real: it's warm: it's violent: you can feel it through the thickest skin: you can taste it and smell it without any training or any work. Not like Science and Literature and Classical Music and Philosophy and Art. You find me cold, unfeeling, selfish, dont you? Very well: be off with you to the sort of people you like. Marry some sentimental hog or other with lots of money, and a thick pair of lips to kiss you with and a thick pair of boots to kick you with. If you cant appreciate what youve got, youd better get what you can appreciate. 650

LIZA. [*Desperate*] Oh, you *are* a cruel tyrant. I cant talk to you: you turn everything against me: I'm always in the wrong. But you know very well all the time that youre nothing but a bully. You know I cant go back to the gutter, as you call it, and that I have no real friends in the world but you and the Colonel. You know well I couldn't bear to live with a low common man after you two; and it's wicked and cruel of you to insult me by pretending I could. You think I must go back to Wimpole Street because I have no-where else to go but father's. But dont you be too sure that you have me under your feet to be trampled on and talked down. I'll marry Freddy, I will, as soon as he's able to support me. 661

HIGGINS. [*Sitting down beside her*] Rubbish! you shall marry an ambassador. You shall marry the Governor-General of India or the Lord-Lieutenant of Ireland, or somebody who wants a deputy-queen. I'm not going to have my masterpiece thrown away on Freddy.

LIZA. You think I like you to say that. But I havnt forgot what you said a minute ago; and I wont be coaxed round as if I was a baby or a puppy. If I cant have kindness, I'll have independence.

HIGGINS. Independence? Thats middle class blasphemy. We are all dependent on one another, every soul of us on earth. 671

LIZA. [*Rising determinedly*] I'll let you see whether I'm dependent on you. If you can preach, I can teach. I'll go and be a teacher.

HIGGINS. Whatll you teach, in heaven's name?

LIZA. What you taught me. I'll teach phonetics.

HIGGINS. Ha! ha! ha!

LIZA. I'll offer myself as an assistant to Professor Nepean.

HIGGINS. [*Rising in a fury*] What! That impostor! that humbug!
that toadying ignoramus! Teach him *my* methods! *my* discoveries!
You take one step in his direction and I'll wring your neck. [*He
lays hands on her.*] Do you hear?   681

LIZA. [*Defiantly non-resistant*] Wring away. What do I care? I
knew youd strike me some day. [*He lets her go, stamping with
rage at having forgotten himself, and recoils so hastily that he
stumbles back into his seat on the ottoman.*] Aha! Now I know
how to deal with you. What a fool I was not to think of it before!
You cant take away the knowledge you gave me. You said I had
a finer ear than you. And I can be civil and kind to people, which
is more than you can. Aha! Thats done you, Henry Higgins, it has.
Now I dont care *that* [*snapping her fingers*] for your bullying and
your big talk. I'll advertize it in the papers that your duchess is only
a flower girl that you taught, and that she'll teach anybody to be a
duchess just the same in six months for a thousand guineas. Oh,
when I think of myself crawling under your feet and being trampled on and called names, when all the time I had only to lift up
my finger to be as good as you, I could just kick myself.   696

HIGGINS. [*Wondering at her*] You damned impudent slut, you!
But it's better than snivelling; better than fetching slippers and
finding spectacles, isnt it? [*Rising*] By George, Eliza, I said I'd
make a woman of you; and I have. I like you like this.

LIZA. Yes: you turn round and make up to me now that I'm not
afraid of you, and can do without you.

HIGGINS. Of course I do, you little fool. Five minutes ago you
were like a millstone round my neck. Now youre a tower of
strength: a consort battleship. You and I and Pickering will be
three old bachelors together instead of only two men and a silly girl.
[MRS. HIGGINS *returns, dressed for the wedding.* ELIZA *instantly becomes cool and elegant.*]   708

MRS. HIGGINS. The carriage is waiting, Eliza. Are you ready?

LIZA. Quite. Is the Professor coming?

MRS. HIGGINS. Certainly not. He cant behave himself in church. He makes remarks out loud all the time on the clergyman's pronunciation.

LIZA. Then I shall not see you again, Professor. Good-bye. [*She goes to the door.*]

MRS. HIGGINS. [*Coming to* HIGGINS] Good-bye, dear.

HIGGINS. Good-bye, mother. [*He is about to kiss her, when he recollects something.*] Oh, by the way, Eliza, order a ham and a Stilton cheese, will you? And buy me a pair of reindeer gloves, number eights, and a tie to match that new suit of mine, at Eale & Binman's. You can choose the color. [*His cheerful, careless, vigorous voice shows that he is incorrigible.*]   722

LIZA. [*Disdainfully*] Buy them yourself. [*She sweeps out.*]

MRS. HIGGINS. I'm afraid youve spoiled that girl, Henry. But never mind, dear: I'll buy you the tie and gloves.

HIGGINS. [*Sunnily*] Oh, dont bother. She'll buy em all right enough. Good-bye.

[*They kiss.* MRS. HIGGINS *runs out.* HIGGINS, *left alone, rattles his cash in his pocket; chuckles; and disports himself in a highly self-satisfied manner.*]

.   .   .   .

The rest of the story need not be shewn in action, and indeed, would hardly need telling if our imaginations were not so enfeebled by their lazy dependence on the ready-mades and reach-me-downs of the ragshop in which Romance keeps its stock of "happy endings" to misfit all stories. Now, the history of Eliza Doolittle, though called a romance because the transfiguration it records seems exceedingly improbable, is common enough. Such transfigurations have been achieved by hundreds of resolutely ambitious young women since Nell Gwynne set them the example by playing queens and fascinating kings in the theatre in which she began by selling oranges. Nevertheless, people in all directions have assumed, for no other reason than that she became the heroine of a romance, that she must have married the hero of it. This is unbearable, not only because her little drama, if acted on such a thoughtless assump-

tion, must be spoiled, but because the true sequel is patent to anyone with a sense of human nature in general, and of feminine instinct in particular.

Eliza, in telling Higgins she would not marry him if he asked her, was not coquetting: she was announcing a well-considered decision. When a bachelor interests, and dominates, and teaches, and becomes important to a spinster, as Higgins with Eliza, she always, if she has character enough to be capable of it, considers very seriously indeed whether she will play for becoming that bachelor's wife, especially if he is so little interested in marriage that a determined and devoted woman might capture him if she set herself resolutely to do it. Her decision will depend a good deal on whether she is really free to choose; and that, again, will depend on her age and income. If she is at the end of her youth, and has no security for her livelihood, she will marry him because she must marry anybody who will provide for her. But at Eliza's age a good-looking girl does not feel that pressure: she feels free to pick and choose. She is therefore guided by her instinct in the matter. Eliza's instinct tells her not to marry Higgins. It does not tell her to give him up. It is not in the slightest doubt as to his remaining one of the strongest personal interests in her life. It would be very sorely strained if there was another woman likely to supplant her with him. But as she feels sure of him on that last point, she has no doubt at all as to her course, and would not have any, even if the difference of twenty years in age, which seems so great to youth, did not exist between them.

As our own instincts are not appealed to by her conclusion, let us see whether we cannot discover some reason in it. When Higgins excused his indifference to young women on the ground that they had an irresistible rival in his mother, he gave the clue to his inveterate old-bachelordom. The case is uncommon only to the extent that remarkable mothers are uncommon. If an imaginative boy has a sufficiently rich mother who has intelligence, personal grace, dignity of character without harshness, and a cultivated sense of the best art of her time to enable her to make her house beautiful, she sets a standard for him against which very few women can struggle, besides effecting for him a disengagement of his affections,

his sense of beauty, and his idealism from his specifically sexual impulses. This makes him a standing puzzle to the huge number of uncultivated people who have been brought up in tasteless homes by commonplace or disagreeable parents, and to whom, consequently, literature, painting, sculpture, music, and affectionate personal relations come as modes of sex if they come at all. The word passion means nothing else to them; and that Higgins could have a passion for phonetics and idealize his mother instead of Eliza, would seem to them absurd and unnatural. Nevertheless, when we look round and see that hardly anyone is too ugly or disagreeable to find a wife or a husband if he or she wants one, whilst many old maids and bachelors are above the average in quality and culture, we cannot help suspecting that the disentanglement of sex from the associations with which it is so commonly confused, a disentanglement which persons of genius achieve by sheer intellectual analysis, is sometimes produced or aided by parental fascination.

Now, though Eliza was incapable of thus explaining to herself Higgins's formidable powers of resistance to the charm that prostrated Freddy at the first glance, she was instinctively aware that she could never obtain a complete grip of him, or come between him and his mother (the first necessity of the married woman). To put it shortly, she knew that for some mysterious reason he had not the makings of a married man in him, according to her conception of a husband as one to whom she would be his nearest and fondest and warmest interest. Even had there been no mother-rival, she would still have refused to accept an interest in herself that was secondary to philosophic interests. Had Mrs. Higgins died, there would still have been Milton and the Universal Alphabet. Landor's remark that to those who have the greatest power of loving, love is a secondary affair, would not have recommended Landor to Eliza. Put that along with her resentment of Higgins's domineering superiority, and her mistrust of his coaxing cleverness in getting round her and evading her wrath when he had gone too far with his impetuous bullying, and you will see that Eliza's instinct had good grounds for warning her not to marry her Pygmalion.

And now, whom did Eliza marry? For if Higgins was a pre-

destinate old bachelor, she was most certainly not a predestinate old maid. Well, that can be told very shortly to those who have not guessed it from the indications she has herself given them.

Almost immediately after Eliza is stung into proclaiming her considered determination not to marry Higgins, she mentions the fact that young Mr. Frederick Eynsford Hill is pouring out his love for her daily through the post. Now Freddy is young, practically twenty years younger than Higgins: he is a gentleman (or, as Eliza would qualify him, a toff), and speaks like one; he is nicely dressed, is treated by the Colonel as an equal, loves her unaffectedly, and is not her master, nor ever likely to dominate her in spite of his advantage of social standing. Eliza has no use for the foolish romantic tradition that all women love to be mastered, if not actually bullied and beaten. "When you go to women," says Nietzsche, "take your whip with you." Sensible despots have never confined that precaution to women: they have taken their whips with them when they have dealt with men, and been slavishly idealized by the men over whom they have flourished the whip much more than by women. No doubt there are slavish women as well as slavish men: and women, like men, admire those that are stronger than themselves. But to admire a strong person and to live under that strong person's thumb are two different things. The weak may not be admired and hero-worshipped; but they are by no means disliked or shunned; and they never seem to have the least difficulty in marrying people who are too good for them. They may fail in emergencies; but life is not one long emergency: it is mostly a string of situations for which no exceptional strength is needed, and with which even rather weak people can cope if they have a stronger partner to help them out. Accordingly, it is a truth everywhere in evidence that strong people, masculine or feminine, not only do not marry stronger people, but do not shew any preference for them in selecting their friends. When a lion meets another with a louder roar "the first lion thinks the last a bore." The man or woman who feels strong enough for two, seeks for every other quality in a partner than strength.

The converse is also true. Weak people want to marry strong people who do not frighten them too much; and this often leads

them to make the mistake we describe metaphorically as "biting off more than they can chew." They want too much for too little; and when the bargain is unreasonable beyond all bearing, the union becomes impossible: it ends in the weaker party being either discarded or borne as a cross, which is worse. People who are not only weak, but silly or obtuse as well, are often in these difficulties.

This being the state of human affairs, what is Eliza fairly sure to do when she is placed between Freddy and Higgins? Will she look forward to a lifetime of fetching Higgins's slippers or to a lifetime of Freddy fetching hers? There can be no doubt about the answer. Unless Freddy is biologically repulsive to her, and Higgins biologically attractive to a degree that overwhelms all her other instincts, she will, if she marries either of them, marry Freddy.

And that is just what Eliza did.

Complications ensued; but they were economic, not romantic. Freddy had no money and no occupation. His mother's jointure, a last relic of the opulence of Largelady Park, had enabled her to struggle along in Earlscourt with an air of gentility, but not to procure any serious secondary education for her children, much less give the boy a profession. A clerkship at thirty shillings a week was beneath Freddy's dignity, and extremely distasteful to him besides. His prospects consisted of a hope that if he kept up appearances somebody would do something for him. The something appeared vaguely to his imagination as a private secretaryship or a sinecure of some sort. To his mother it perhaps appeared as a marriage to some lady of means who could not resist her boy's niceness. Fancy her feelings when he married a flower girl who had become déclassée under extraordinary circumstances which were now notorious!

It is true that Eliza's situation did not seem wholly ineligible. Her father, though formerly a dustman, and now fantastically disclassed, had become extremely popular in the smartest society by a social talent which triumphed over every prejudice and every disadvantage. Rejected by the middle class, which he loathed, he had shot up at once into the highest circles by his wit, his dustmanship (which he carried like a banner), and his Nietzschean transcendence of good and evil. At intimate ducal dinners he sat on

the right hand of the Duchess; and in country houses he smoked in the pantry and was made much of by the butler when he was not feeding in the dining room and being consulted by cabinet ministers. But he found it almost as hard to do all this on four thousand a year as Mrs. Eynsford Hill to live in Earlscourt on an income so pitiably smaller that I have not the heart to disclose its exact figure. He absolutely refused to add the last straw to his burden by contributing to Eliza's support.

Thus Freddy and Eliza, now Mr. and Mrs. Eynsford Hill, would have spent a penniless honeymoon but for a wedding present of £500 from the Colonel to Eliza. It lasted a long time because Freddy did not know how to spend money, never having had any to spend, and Eliza, socially trained by a pair of old bachelors, wore her clothes as long as they held together and looked pretty, without the least regard to their being many months out of fashion. Still, £500 will not last two young people for ever; and they both knew, and Eliza felt as well, that they must shift for themselves in the end. She could quarter herself on Wimpole Street because it had come to be her home; but she was quite aware that she ought not to quarter Freddy there, and that it would not be good for his character if she did.

Not that the Wimpole Street bachelors objected. When she consulted them, Higgins declined to be bothered about her housing problem when that solution was so simple. Eliza's desire to have Freddy in the house with her seemed of no more importance than if she had wanted an extra piece of bedroom furniture. Pleas as to Freddy's character, and the moral obligation on him to earn his own living, were lost on Higgins. He denied that Freddy had any character, and declared that if he tried to do any useful work some competent person would have the trouble of undoing it: a procedure involving a net loss to the community, and great unhappiness to Freddy himself, who was obviously intended by Nature for such light work as amusing Eliza, which, Higgins declared, was a much more useful and honorable occupation than working in the city. When Eliza referred again to her project of teaching phonetics, Higgins abated not a jot of his violent opposition to it. He said she was not within ten years of being qualified to meddle with his pet

subject; and as it was evident that the Colonel agreed with him, she felt she could not go against them in this grave matter, and that she had no right, without Higgins's consent, to exploit the knowledge he had given her; for his knowledge seemed to her as much his private property as his watch: Eliza was no communist. Besides, she was superstitiously devoted to them both, more entirely and frankly after her marriage than before it.

It was the Colonel who finally solved the problem, which had cost him much perplexed cogitation. He one day asked Eliza, rather shyly, whether she had quite given up her notion of keeping a flower shop. She replied that she had thought of it, but had put it out of her head, because the Colonel had said, that day at Mrs. Higgins's, that it would never do. The Colonel confessed that when he said that, he had not quite recovered from the dazzling impression of the day before. They broke the matter to Higgins that evening. The sole comment vouchsafed by him very nearly led to a serious quarrel with Eliza. It was to the effect that she would have in Freddy an ideal errand boy.

Freddy himself was next sounded on the subject. He said he had been thinking of a shop himself; though it had presented itself to his pennilessness as a small place in which Eliza should sell tobacco at one counter whilst he sold newspapers at the opposite one. But he agreed that it would be extraordinarily jolly to go early every morning with Eliza to Covent Garden and buy flowers on the scene of their first meeting: a sentiment which earned him many kisses from his wife. He added that he had always been afraid to propose anything of the sort, because Clara would make an awful row about a step that must damage her matrimonial chances, and his mother could not be expected to like it after clinging for so many years to that step of the social ladder on which retail trade is impossible.

This difficulty was removed by an event highly unexpected by Freddy's mother. Clara, in the course of her incursions into those artistic circles which were the highest within her reach, discovered that her conversational qualifications were expected to include a grounding in the novels of Mr. H. G. Wells. She borrowed them in various directions so energetically that she swallowed them all within two months. The result was a conversion of a kind quite

common today. A modern Acts of the Apostles would fill fifty whole Bibles if anyone were capable of writing it.

Poor Clara, who appeared to Higgins and his mother as a disagreeable and ridiculous person, and to her own mother as in some inexplicable way a social failure, had never seen herself in either light; for, though to some extent ridiculed and mimicked in West Kensington like everybody else there, she was accepted as a rational and normal—or shall we say inevitable?—sort of human being. At worst they called her The Pusher; but to them no more than to herself had it ever occurred that she was pushing the air, and pushing it in a wrong direction. Still, she was not happy. She was growing desperate. Her one asset, the fact that her mother was what the Epsom greengrocer called a carriage lady, had no exchange value, apparently. It had prevented her from getting educated, because the only education she could have afforded was education with the Earlscourt greengrocer's daughter. It had led her to seek the society of her mother's class; and that class simply would not have her, because she was much poorer than the greengrocer, and, far from being able to afford a maid, could not afford even a housemaid, and had to scrape along at home with an illiberally treated general servant. Under such circumstances nothing could give her an air of being a genuine product of Largelady Park. And yet its tradition made her regard a marriage with anyone within her reach as an unbearable humiliation. Commercial people and professional people in a small way were odious to her. She ran after painters and novelists; but she did not charm them; and her bold attempts to pick up and practice artistic and literary talk irritated them. She was, in short, an utter failure, an ignorant, incompetent, pretentious, unwelcome, penniless, useless little snob; and though she did not admit these disqualifications (for nobody ever faces unpleasant truths of this kind until the possibility of a way out dawns on them) she felt their effects too keenly to be satisfied with her position.

Clara had a startling eyeopener when, on being suddenly wakened to enthusiasm by a girl of her own age who dazzled her and produced in her a gushing desire to take her for a model, and gain her friendship, she discovered that this exquisite apparition had graduated from the gutter in a few months time. It shook her

so violently, that when Mr. H. G. Wells lifted her on the point of his puissant pen, and placed her at the angle of view from which the life she was leading and the society to which she clung appeared in its true relation to real human needs and worthy social structure, he effected a conversion and a conviction of sin comparable to the most sensational feats of General Booth or Gypsy Smith. Clara's snobbery went bang. Life suddenly began to move with her. Without knowing how or why, she began to make friends and enemies. Some of the acquaintances to whom she had been a tedious or indifferent or ridiculous affliction, dropped her: others became cordial. To her amazement she found that some "quite nice" people were saturated with Wells, and that this accessibility to ideas was the secret of their niceness. People she had thought deeply religious, and had tried to conciliate on that tack with disastrous results, suddenly took an interest in her, and revealed a hostility to conventional religion which she had never conceived possible except among the most desperate characters. They made her read Galsworthy; and Galsworthy exposed the vanity of Largelady Park and finished her. It exasperated her to think that the dungeon in which she had languished for so many unhappy years had been unlocked all the time, and that the impulses she had so carefully struggled with and stifled for the sake of keeping well with society, were precisely those by which alone she could have come into any sort of sincere human contact. In the radiance of these discoveries, and the tumult of their reaction, she made a fool of herself as freely and conspicuously as when she so rashly adopted Eliza's expletive in Mrs. Higgins's drawing room; for the newborn Wellsian had to find her bearings almost as ridiculously as a baby; but nobody hates a baby for its ineptitudes, or thinks the worse of it for trying to eat the matches; and Clara lost no friends by her follies. They laughed at her to her face this time; and she had to defend herself and fight it out as best she could.

When Freddy paid a visit to Earlscourt (which he never did when he could possibly help it) to make the desolating announcement that he and his Eliza were thinking of blackening the Largelady scutcheon by opening a shop, he found the little household already convulsed by a prior announcement from Clara that she also

was going to work in an old furniture shop in Dover Street, which had been started by a fellow Wellsian. This appointment Clara owed, after all, to her old social accomplishment of Push. She had made up her mind that, cost what it might, she would see Mr. Wells in the flesh; and she had achieved her end at a garden party. She had better luck than so rash an enterprise deserved. Mr. Wells came up to her expectations. Age had not withered him, nor could custom stale his infinite variety in half an hour. His pleasant neatness and compactness, his small hands and feet, his teeming ready brain, his unaffected accessibility, and a certain fine apprehensiveness which stamped him as susceptible from his topmost hair to his tipmost toe, proved irresistible. Clara talked of nothing else for weeks and weeks afterwards. And as she happened to talk to the lady of the furniture shop, and that lady also desired above all things to know Mr. Wells and sell pretty things to him, she offered Clara a job on the chance of achieving that end through her.

And so it came about that Eliza's luck held, and the expected opposition to the flower shop melted away. The shop is in the arcade of a railway station not very far from the Victoria and Albert Museum; and if you live in that neighborhood you may go there any day and buy a buttonhole from Eliza.

Now here is a last opportunity for romance. Would you not like to be assured that the shop was an immense success, thanks to Eliza's charms and her early business experience in Covent Garden? Alas! the truth is the truth: the shop did not pay for a long time, simply because Eliza and her Freddy did not know how to keep it. True, Eliza had not to begin at the very beginning: she knew the names and prices of the cheaper flowers; and her elation was unbounded when she found that Freddy, like all youths educated at cheap, pretentious, and thoroughly inefficient schools, knew a little Latin. It was very little, but enough to make him appear to her a Porson or Bentley, and to put him at his ease with botanical nomenclature. Unfortunately he knew nothing else; and Eliza, though she could count money up to eighteen shillings or so, and had acquired a certain familiarity with the language of Milton from her struggles to qualify herself for winning Higgins's bet, could not write out a bill without utterly disgracing the establishment. Fred-

dy's power of stating in Latin that Balbus built a wall and that Gaul was divided into three parts did not carry with it the slightest knowledge of accounts or business: Colonel Pickering had to explain to him what a cheque book and a bank account meant. And the pair were by no means easily teachable. Freddy backed up Eliza in her obstinate refusal to believe that they could save money by engaging a bookkeeper with some knowledge of the business. How, they argued, could you possibly save money by going to extra expense when you already could not make both ends meet? But the Colonel, after making the ends meet over and over again, at last gently insisted; and Eliza, humbled to the dust by having to beg from him so often, and stung by the uproarious derision of Higgins, to whom the notion of Freddy's succeeding at anything was a joke that never palled, grasped the fact that business, like phonetics, has to be learned.

On the piteous spectacle of the pair spending their evenings in shorthand schools and polytechnic classes, learning bookkeeping and typewriting with incipient junior clerks, male and female, from the elementary schools, let me not dwell. There were even classes at the London School of Economics, and a humble personal appeal to the director of that institution to recommend a course bearing on the flower business. He, being a humorist, explained to them the method of the celebrated Dickensian essay on Chinese Metaphysics by the gentleman who read an article on China and an article on Metaphysics and combined the information. He suggested that they should combine the London School with Kew Gardens. Eliza, to whom the procedure of the Dickensian gentleman seemed perfectly correct (as in fact it was) and not in the least funny (which was only her ignorance), took his advice with entire gravity. But the effort that cost her the deepest humiliation was a request to Higgins, whose pet artistic fancy, next to Milton's verse, was calligraphy, and who himself wrote a most beautiful Italian hand, that he would teach her to write. He declared that she was congenitally incapable of forming a single letter worthy of the least of Milton's words; but she persisted; and again he suddenly threw himself into the task of teaching her with a combination of stormy intensity, concentrated patience, and occasional bursts of interesting disquisition on the beauty

and nobility, the august mission and destiny, of human handwriting. Eliza ended by acquiring an extremely uncommercial script which was a positive extension of her personal beauty, and spending three times as much on stationery as anyone else because certain qualities and shapes of paper became indispensable to her. She could not even address an envelope in the usual way because it made the margins all wrong.

Their commercial schooldays were a period of disgrace and despair for the young couple. They seemed to be learning nothing about flower shops. At last they gave it up as hopeless, and shook the dust of the shorthand schools, and the polytechnics, and the London School of Economics from their feet for ever. Besides, the business was in some mysterious way beginning to take care of itself. They had somehow forgotten their objections to employing other people. They came to the conclusion that their own way was the best, and that they had really a remarkable talent for business. The Colonel, who had been compelled for some years to keep a sufficient sum on current account at his bankers to make up their deficits, found that the provision was unnecessary: the young people were prospering. It is true that there was not quite fair play between them and their competitors in trade. Their week-ends in the country cost them nothing, and saved them the price of their Sunday dinners; for the motor car was the Colonel's; and he and Higgins paid the hotel bills. Mr. F. Hill, florist and greengrocer (they soon discovered that there was money in asparagus; and asparagus led to other vegetables), had an air which stamped the business as classy; and in private life he was still Frederick Eynsford Hill, Esquire. Not that there was any swank about him: nobody but Eliza knew that he had been christened Frederick Challoner. Eliza herself swanked like anything.

That is all. That is how it has turned out. It is astonishing how much Eliza still manages to meddle in the housekeeping at Wimpole Street in spite of the shop and her own family. And it is notable that though she never nags her husband, and frankly loves the Colonel as if she were his favorite daughter, she has never got out of the habit of nagging Higgins that was established on the fatal night when she won his bet for him. She snaps his head off on the

faintest provocation, or on none. He no longer dares to tease her by assuming an abysmal inferiority of Freddy's mind to his own. He storms and bullies and derides: but she stands up to him so ruthlessly that the Colonel has to ask her from time to time to be kinder to Higgins; and it is the only request of his that brings a mulish expression into her face. Nothing but some emergency or calamity great enough to break down all likes and dislikes, and throw them back on their common humanity—and may they be spared any such trial!—will ever alter this. She knows that Higgins does not need her, just as her father did not need her. The very scrupulousness with which he told her that day that he had become used to having her there, and dependent on her for all sorts of little services, and that he should miss her if she went away (it would never have occurred to Freddy or the Colonel to say anything of the sort) deepens her inner certainty that she is "no more to him than them slippers"; yet she has a sense, too, that his indifference is deeper than the infatuation of commoner souls. She is immensely interested in him. She has even secret mischievous moments in which she wishes she could get him alone, on a desert island, away from all ties and with nobody else in the world to consider, and just drag him off his pedestal and see him making love like any common man. We all have private imaginations of that sort. But when it comes to business, to the life that she really leads as distinguished from the life of dreams and fancies, she likes Freddy and she likes the Colonel; and she does not like Higgins and Mr. Doolittle. Galatea never does quite like Pygmalion: his relation to her is too godlike to be altogether agreeable.

Thomas Stearns Eliot

MURDER IN THE CATHEDRAL

I n its original form, *Murder in the Cathedral* was written for the 1935 Canterbury Festival in England. It contains considerable history or legend, so that we may piece together from it an outline of the life and martyrdom of Thomas à Becket, the twelfth-century archbishop of Canterbury. The action of the play begins just before Becket's return from the Continent, where he had been in exile for seven years as a result of his opposition to Henry II's measures against the Church. We learn further from the play that Becket had once been Henry's intimate adviser and Chancellor, and that he had turned against the secular policies of the government after he became archbishop. Finally the play presents the murder, which occurred historically December 29, 1170, and various comments on it.

Despite the historical element in the play, the reader will soon feel that it is not a memorial in the usual sense, not a historical costume play or a dramatized murder story. It is in fact a poetic drama, which means for Eliot, as he has explained in various places, not merely a play in verse but a deliberate revolt against the surface realism of the modern problem play, with the aim of presenting a truer or deeper reality. The deeper reality sought for in this play is obviously not further information about the historical Becket, but rather the significance of his martyrdom. To get at that deeper reality, Eliot felt justified in using characters and devices that violate the conventions of "true-to-life" drama.

One departure from realism is the use of characters that are more

abstract than individual. Instead of providing pleasure through their closeness to life, they are chiefly interesting because of their function in an intellectual scheme. The first three Tempters, for example, personify the worldly attractions and achievements which Becket renounced when he left the Chancellorship for the Church. They help to tell us who Becket was and what he is trying to become. The First Tempter is his old political amiability with its easy judgments of men; the second, more subtle, is the opportunity to serve society by returning to the Chancellorship; the third is the possibility of getting supreme power by forming a "happy coalition of intelligent interests" against the King. The Fourth Tempter is not from the past; he has not been rejected already but is present in Becket's subconscious mind, and therefore his appearance is unexpected. He is spiritual pride, the desire of martyrdom for the wrong reason. The organization here and at other places is reminiscent of that in *Oedipus at Colonus* or Milton's *Samson Agonistes* (to whom Becket is compared). The central character defines himself and what he represents by rejecting various lower values. The resemblance is even closer to the medieval morality play, such as *Everyman,* in which mankind wrestles with the personified temptations of the world and the flesh. It is significant that Eliot has called *Everyman* the last English play written within the limitations of art, drama thereafter turning away, in his opinion, from art toward photographic realism.

A second departure from realism is the grouping of characters to dramatize a concept rather than to individualize them as human beings. Becket, the chorus of Canterbury women, and the group composed of the Priests, Tempters, and Knights represent three distinct orders of being. Even if the reader does not know that the three orders have their basis in theology, he will see that they correspond to the divine, the natural, and the worldly or rationalistic. This grouping emphasizes important questions: How are the three orders unlike each other? How are they related? Does the highest order, the divine or saintly, evolve from the lower orders, or is it altogether separate and other-worldly?

Such questions are answered explicitly or abstractly in Becket's sermon and elsewhere, but the fullest answers are presented indirectly through a third departure from realism, the widespread use of imagery and symbolism. A principal image is that of the seasons. We are soon aware that the Chorus' opening description of rural life as it passes from harvest to winter is more than a clue to their character and manner of living or to the fact that Becket was murdered in December. The stubble of November, "brown sharp points of death in a waste of mud and water," has moral overtones; the emphasis on seasonal change suggests a hard necessity forcing us to go through a sequence of experiences that are more than physical. The blurring of seasons implies spiritual insensitivity. With the Chorus we are faced toward the cathedral, "we are forced to bear witness"; and the thing we are implicated in is a sharpening of the seasons caused by the return of Becket. As the reader follows the elaboration of the seasonal imagery, he will observe that it is tied in with other devices (the amiable First Tempter, for example, represents desire for perpetual summer), and that it brings into the play the seasonal ritual behind Greek tragedy.

Another and equally important image is that of Fortune's wheel. It is introduced by the Third Priest in the speeches following the opening chorus, and its connection with the seasonal imagery is at once clear. The wheel like the seasons has been seemingly quiet for seven years, but now with the approach of Becket it must turn. Everyone seeks peace; the problem is to reach true peace, the stillness at the hub of the turning wheel. One by one the kinds of peace offered by the Chorus, the Priests, and the Knights are exposed as limited or delusive, until finally the whole play looks toward the single still point, the one moment of timelessness in time, Becket's martyrdom. By it all lesser values are measured. In it alone what is partial is made whole and satisfying. Mortality with all its degradation and disvalue is redeemed by the blood of the Christ-like martyr. The final truth of the play, then, is the divine illumination which comes to the saint.

The attempt to base a play on a point of reality outside of the

actual world may be beyond the scope and powers of drama, and it may be philosophically unacceptable to some readers, but it is still possible to admire the skill with which Eliot has satirized the materialism and moral inattention of modern society. The martyrdom of a twelfth-century bishop is revitalized for the twentieth-century skeptic not necessarily by effecting the skeptic's conversion but by forcing him to see himself as he is mirrored in the Priests and the Knights. That disturbing and educational sight is brought into focus by the spiritual values of the saint and above all by the play's poetic technique. Eliot's poetic language is a reminder of what had been slowly lost to the theater since Greek and Elizabethan drama and of what the future may hold.

MURDER IN THE CATHEDRAL

PART I

Characters

A CHORUS OF WOMEN OF CANTERBURY

THREE PRIESTS OF THE CATHEDRAL

A HERALD

ARCHBISHOP THOMAS BECKET

FOUR TEMPTERS

ATTENDANTS

*The Scene is the Archbishop's Hall,
on December 2nd, 1170.*

CHOR. Here let us stand, close by the cathedral. Here let us wait.
Are we drawn by danger? Is it the knowledge of safety, that
draws our feet
Towards the cathedral? What danger can be
For us, the poor, the poor women of Canterbury? what tribu-
lation
With which we are not already familiar? There is no danger
For us, and there is no safety in the cathedral. Some presage of
an act
Which our eyes are compelled to witness, has forced our feet
Towards the cathedral. We are forced to bear witness.

Since golden October declined into sombre November   9
And the apples were gathered and stored, and the land became
    brown sharp points of death in a waste of water and mud,
The New Year waits, breathes, waits, whispers in darkness.
While the labourer kicks off a muddy boot and stretches his
    hand to the fire,
The New Year waits, destiny waits for the coming.
Who has stretched out his hand to the fire and remembered the
    Saints at All Hallows,
Remembered the martyrs and saints who wait? and who shall
Stretch out his hand to the fire, and deny his master? who
    shall be warm
By the fire, and deny his master?

Seven years and the summer is over
Seven years since the Archbishop left us,
He who was always kind to his people.   20
But it would not be well if he should return.
King rules or barons rule;
We have suffered various oppression,
But mostly we are left to our own devices,
And we are content if we are left alone.
We try to keep our households in order;
The merchant, shy and cautious, tries to compile a little for-
    tune,
And the labourer bends to his piece of earth, earth-colour, his
    own colour,
Preferring to pass unobserved.
Now I fear disturbance of the quiet seasons: 30
Winter shall come bringing death from the sea,
Ruinous spring shall beat at our doors,
Root and shoot shall eat our eyes and our ears,
Disastrous summer burn up the beds of our streams
And the poor shall wait for another decaying October.
Why should the summer bring consolation

For autumn fires and winter fogs?
What shall we do in the heat of summer
But wait in barren orchards for another October?
Some malady is coming upon us. We wait, we wait,   40
And the saints and martyrs wait, for those who shall be mar-
    tyrs and saints.
Destiny waits in the hand of God, shaping the still unshapen:
I have seen these things in a shaft of sunlight.
Destiny waits in the hand of God, not in the hands of statesmen
Who do, some well, some ill, planning and guessing,
Having their aims which turn in their hands in the pattern of
    time.
Come, happy December, who shall observe you, who shall pre-
    serve you?
Shall the Son of Man be born again in the litter of scorn?
For us, the poor, there is no action,
But only to wait and to witness.   50
                 [*Enter* PRIESTS.]

IST PR. Seven years and the summer is over.
Seven years since the Archbishop left us.

2ND PR. What does the Archbishop do, and our Sovereign Lord the
    Pope
With the stubborn King and the French King
In ceaseless intrigue, combinations,
In conference, meetings accepted, meetings refused,
Meetings unended or endless
At one place or another in France?

3RD PR. I see nothing quite conclusive in the art of temporal govern-
    ment,
But violence, duplicity and frequent malversation.   60
King rules or barons rule:
The strong man strongly and the weak man by caprice.
They have but one law, to seize the power and keep it,
And the steadfast can manipulate the greed and lust of others,
The feeble is devoured by his own.

ıst pr. Shall these things not end
     Until the poor at the gate
     Have forgotten their friend, their Father in God, have for-
          gotten
     That they had a friend?

[*Enter* HERALD.]

her. Servants of God, and watchers of the temple,   70
     I am here to inform you, without circumlocution:
     The Archbishop is in England, and is close outside the city.
     I was sent before in haste
     To give you notice of his coming, as much as was possible,
     That you may prepare to meet him.

ıst pr. What, is the exile ended, is our Lord Archbishop
     Reunited with the King? what reconciliation
     Of two proud men? what peace can be found
     To grow between the hammer and the anvil? Tell us,
     Are the old disputes at an end, is the wall of pride cast down
     That divided them? Is it peace or war? Does he come   81
     In full assurance, or only secure
     In the power of Rome, the spiritual rule,
     The assurance of right, and the love of the people,
     Contemning the hatred and envy of barons?

her. You are right to express a certain incredulity.
     He comes in pride and sorrow, affirming all his claims,
     Assured, beyond doubt, of the devotion of the people,
     Who receive him with scenes of frenzied enthusiasm,
     Lining the road and throwing down their capes,   90
     Strewing the way with leaves and late flowers of the season.
     The streets of the city will be packed to suffocation,
     And I think that his horse will be deprived of its tail,
     A single hair of which becomes a precious relic.
     He is at one with the Pope, and with the King of France,
     Who indeed would have liked to detain him in his kingdom:
     But as for our King, that is another matter.

ıst pr. But again, is it war or peace?

HER.   Peace, but not the kiss of peace.
A patched up affair, if you ask my opinion.
And if you ask me, I think the Lord Archbishop   100
Is not the man to cherish any illusions,
Or yet to diminish the least of his pretensions.
If you ask my opinion, I think that this peace
Is nothing like an end, or like a beginning.
It is common knowledge that when the Archbishop
Parted from the King, he said to the King,
My Lord, he said, I leave you as a man
Whom in this life I shall not see again.
I have this, I assure you, on the highest authority;
There are several opinions as to what he meant   110
But no one considers it a happy prognostic.   [*Exit.*]

1ST PR. I fear for the Archbishop, I fear for the Church,
I know that the pride bred of sudden prosperity
Was but confirmed by bitter adversity.
I saw him as Chancellor, flattered by the King,
Liked or feared by courtiers, in their overbearing fashion,
Despised and despising, always isolated,
Never one among them, always insecure;
His pride always feeding upon his own virtues,
Pride drawing sustenance from impartiality,   120
Pride drawing sustenance from generosity,
Loathing power given by temporal devolution,
Wishing subjection to God alone.
Had the King been greater, or had he been weaker
Things had perhaps been different for Thomas.

2ND PR. Yet our Lord is returned. Our Lord has come back to his
    own again.
We have had enough of waiting, from December to dismal
    December.
The Archbishop shall be at our head, dispelling dismay and
    doubt.
He will tell us what we are to do, he will give us our orders,
    instruct us.

Our Lord is at one with the Pope, and also the King of France.
We can lean on a rock, we can feel a firm foothold   131
Against the perpetual wash of tides of balance of forces of
    barons and landholders.
The rock of God is beneath our feet. Let us meet the Arch-
    bishop with cordial thanksgiving:
Our Lord, our Archbishop returns. And when the Archbishop
    returns
Our doubts are dispelled. Let us therefore rejoice,
I say rejoice, and show a glad face for his welcome.
I am the Archbishop's man. Let us give the Archbishop wel-
    come!

3RD PR. For good or ill, let the wheel turn.
The wheel has been still, these seven years, and no good.
For ill or good, let the wheel turn.   140
For who knows the end of good or evil?
Until the grinders cease
And the door shall be shut in the street,
And all the daughters of music shall be brought low.

CHOR. Here is no continuing city, here is no abiding stay.
Ill the wind, ill the time, uncertain the profit, certain the danger.
O late late late, late is the time, late too late, and rotten the
    year;
Evil the wind, and bitter the sea, and grey the sky, grey grey
    grey.
O Thomas, return, Archbishop; return, return to France.
Return. Quickly. Quietly. Leave us to perish in quiet.   150
You come with applause, you come with rejoicing, but you
    come bringing death into Canterbury:
A doom on the house, a doom on yourself, a doom on the
    world.

We do not wish anything to happen.
Seven years we have lived quietly,
Succeeded in avoiding notice,
Living and partly living.

There have been oppression and luxury,
There have been poverty and licence,
There has been minor injustice.
Yet we have gone on living,   160
Living and partly living.
Sometimes the corn has failed us,
Sometimes the harvest is good,
One year is a year of rain,
Another a year of dryness,
One year the apples are abundant,
Another year the plums are lacking.
Yet we have gone on living,
Living and partly living.
We have kept the feasts, heard the masses,   170
We have brewed beer and cyder,
Gathered wood against the winter,
Talked at the corner of the fire,
Talked at the corners of streets,
Talked not always in whispers,
Living and partly living.
We have seen births, deaths and marriages,
We have had various scandals,
We have been afflicted with taxes,
We have had laughter and gossip,   180
Several girls have disappeared
Unaccountably, and some not able to.
We have all had our private terrors,
Our particular shadows, our secret fears.

But now a great fear is upon us, a fear not of one but of many,
A fear like birth and death, when we see birth and death alone
In a void apart. We
Are afraid in a fear which we cannot know, which we cannot
    face, which none understands,
And our hearts are torn from us, our brains unskinned like
    the layers of an onion, our selves are lost lost   189

In a final fear which none understands. O Thomas Archbishop,
O Thomas our Lord, leave us and leave us be, in our humble
and tarnished frame of existence, leave us; do not ask us
To stand to the doom on the house, the doom on the Archbishop, the doom on the world.
Archbishop, secure and assured of your fate, unaffrayed among
the shades, do you realise what you ask, do you realise
what it means
To the small folk drawn into the pattern of fate, the small
folk who live among small things,
The strain on the brain of the small folk who stand to the
doom of the house, the doom of their Lord, the doom of the
world?
O Thomas, Archbishop, leave us, leave us, leave sullen Dover,
and set sail for France. Thomas our Archbishop still our
Archbishop even in France. Thomas Archbishop, set the
white sail between the grey sky and the bitter sea, leave
us, leave us for France.

2ND PR. What a way to talk at such a juncture!
You are foolish, immodest and babbling women.
Do you not know that the good Archbishop
Is likely to arrive at any moment?   200
The crowds in the streets will be cheering and cheering,
You go on croaking like frogs in the treetops:
But frogs at least can be cooked and eaten.
Whatever you are afraid of, in your craven apprehension,
Let me ask you at the least to put on pleasant faces,
And give a hearty welcome to our good Archbishop.

[*Enter* THOMAS.]

THOM. Peace. And let them be, in their exaltation.
They speak better than they know, and beyond your under-
standing.
They know and do not know, what it is to act or suffer.
They know and do not know, that acting is suffering   210
And suffering is action. Neither does the actor suffer
Nor the patient act. But both are fixed

In an eternal action, an eternal patience
To which all must consent that it may be willed
And which all must suffer that they may will it,
That the pattern may subsist, for the pattern is the action
And the suffering, that the wheel may turn and still
Be forever still.

2ND PR.   O my Lord, forgive me, I did not see you coming,
Engrossed by the chatter of these foolish women.   220
Forgive us, my Lord, you would have had a better welcome
If we had been sooner prepared for the event.
But your Lordship knows that seven years of waiting,
Seven years of prayer, seven years of emptiness,
Have better prepared our hearts for your coming,
Than seven days could make ready Canterbury.
However, I will have fires laid in all your rooms
To take the chill off our English December,
Your Lordship now being used to a better climate.   229
Your Lordship will find your rooms in order as you left them.

THOM.   And will try to leave them in order as I find them.
I am more than grateful for all your kind attentions.
These are small matters. Little rest in Canterbury
With eager enemies restless about us.
Rebellious bishops, York, London, Salisbury,
Would have intercepted our letters,
Filled the coast with spies and sent to meet me
Some who hold me in bitterest hate.
By God's grace aware of their prevision
I sent my letters on another day,   240
Had fair crossing, found at Sandwich
Broc, Warenne, and the Sheriff of Kent,
Those who had sworn to have my head from me.
Only John, the Dean of Salisbury,
Fearing for the King's name, warning against treason,

242. Broc, Warenne: Ranulf de Broc and Reynold de Warenne were bitter
foes of Becket in his struggle with King Henry II.

Made them hold their hands. So for the time
We are unmolested.

1ST PR.   But do they follow after?

THOM. For a little time the hungry hawk
Will only soar and hover, circling lower,
Waiting excuse, pretence, opportunity.   250
End will be simple, sudden, God-given.
Meanwhile the substance of our first act
Will be shadows, and the strife with shadows.
Heavier the interval than the consummation.
All things prepare the event. Watch.

[*Enter* FIRST TEMPTER.]

1ST TEM. You see, my Lord, I do not wait upon ceremony:
Here I have come, forgetting all acrimony,
Hoping that your present gravity
Will find excuse for my humble levity
Remembering all the good time past.   260
Your Lordship won't despise an old friend out of favour?
Old Tom, gay Tom, Becket of London,
Your Lordship won't forget that evening on the river
When the King, and you and I were all friends together?
Friendship should be more than biting Time can sever.
What, my Lord, now that you recover
Favour with the King, shall we say that summer's over
Or that the good time cannot last?
Fluting in the meadows, viols in the hall,
Laughter and apple-blossom floating on the water,   270
Singing at nightfall, whispering in chambers,
Fires devouring the winter season,
Eating up the darkness, with wit and wine and wisdom!
Now that the King and you are in amity,
Clergy and laity may return to gaiety,
Mirth and sportfulness need not walk warily.

THOM. You talk of seasons that are past. I remember
Not worth forgetting.

TEM.   And of the new season.
     Spring has come in winter. Snow in the branches
     Shall float as sweet as blossoms. Ice along the ditches   280
     Mirror the sunlight. Love in the orchard
     Send the sap shooting. Mirth matches melancholy.
THOM. We do not know very much of the future
     Except that from generation to generation
     The same things happen again and again.
     Men learn little from others' experience.
     But in the life of one man, never
     The same time returns. Sever
     The cord, shed the scale. Only
     The fool, fixed in his folly, may think   290
     He can turn the wheel on which he turns.
TEM. My Lord, a nod is as good as a wink.
     A man will often love what he spurns.
     For the good times past, that are come again
     I am your man.
THOM.   Not in this train.
     Look to your behaviour. You were safer
     Think of penitence and follow your master.
TEM. Not at this gait!
     If you go so fast, others may go faster.
     Your Lordship is too proud!   300
     The safest beast is not the one that roars most loud.
     This was not the way of the King our master!
     You were not used to be so hard upon sinners
     When they were your friends. Be easy, man!
     The easy man lives to eat the best dinners.
     Take a friend's advice. Leave well alone,
     Or your goose may be cooked and eaten to the bone.
THOM. You come twenty years too late.
TEM. Then I leave you to your fate.
     I leave you to the pleasures of your higher vices,   310
     Which will have to be paid for at higher prices.
     Farewell, my Lord, I do not wait upon ceremony,

I leave as I came, forgetting all acrimony,
Hoping that your present gravity
Will find excuse for my humble levity.
If you will remember me, my Lord, at your prayers,
I'll remember you at kissing-time below the stairs.

THOM. Leave-well-alone, the springtime fancy,
So one thought goes whistling down the wind.
The impossible is still temptation.   320
The impossible, the undesirable,
Voices under sleep, waking a dead world,
So that the mind may not be whole in the present.

[*Enter* SECOND TEMPTER.]

2ND TEM. Your Lordship has forgotten me, perhaps. I will remind
you.
We met at Clarendon, at Northampton,
And last at Montmirail, in Maine. Now that I have recalled
them,
Let us but set these not too pleasant memories
In balance against other, earlier
And weightier ones: those of the Chancellorship.
See how the late ones rise! The master of policy   330
Whom all acknowledged, should guide the state again.

THOM. Your meaning?

TEM.   The Chancellorship that you resigned
When you were made Archbishop—that was a mistake
On your part—still may be regained. Think, my Lord,
Power obtained grows to glory,
Life lasting, a permanent possession,
A templed tomb, monument of marble.
Rule over men reckon no madness.

THOM. To the man of God what gladness?

TEM.   Sadness
Only to those giving love to God alone.   340
Fare forward, shun two files of shadows:
Mirth merrymaking, melting strength in sweetness,
Fiddling to feebleness, doomed to disdain;

And godlovers' longings, lost in God.
Shall he who held the solid substance
Wander waking with deceitful shadows?
Power is present. Holiness hereafter.

THOM. Who then?

TEM.   The Chancellor. King and Chancellor.
King commands. Chancellor richly rules.
This is a sentence not taught in the schools.   350
To set down the great, protect the poor,
Beneath the throne of God can man do more?
Disarm the ruffian, strengthen the laws,
Rule for the good of the better cause,
Dispensing justice make all even,
Is thrive on earth, and perhaps in heaven.

THOM. What means?

TEM.   Real power
Is purchased at price of a certain submission.
Your spiritual power is earthly perdition.
Power is present, for him who will wield.   360

THOM. Whose was it?

TEM.   His who is gone.

THOM. Who shall have it?

TEM.   He who will come.

THOM. What shall be the month?

TEM.   The last from the first.

THOM. What shall we give for it?

TEM.   Pretence of priestly power.

THOM. Why should we give it?

TEM.   For the power and the glory.

THOM. No!

TEM.   Yes! Or bravery will be broken,
Cabined in Canterbury, realmless ruler,
Self-bound servant of a powerless Pope,
The old stag, circled with hounds.

THOM. No!

TEM.   Yes! men must manoeuvre. Monarchs also,   370
    Waging war abroad, need fast friends at home.
    Private policy is public profit;
    Dignity still shall be dressed with decorum.

THOM. You forget the bishops
    Whom I have laid under excommunication.

TEM. Hungry hatred
    Will not strive against intelligent self-interest.

THOM. You forget the barons. Who will not forget
    Constant curbing of petty privilege.

TEM. Against the barons   380
    Is King's cause, churl's cause, Chancellor's cause.

THOM. No! shall I, who keep the keys
    Of heaven and hell, supreme alone in England,
    Who bind and loose, with power from the Pope,
    Descend to desire a punier power?
    Delegate to deal the doom of damnation,
    To condemn kings, not serve among their servants,
    Is my open office. No! Go.

TEM. Then I leave you to your fate.
    Your sin soars sunward, covering kings' falcons.   390

THOM. Temporal power, to build a good world,
    To keep order, as the world knows order.
    Those who put their faith in worldly order
    Not controlled by the order of God,
    In confident ignorance, but arrest disorder,
    Make it fast, breed fatal disease,
    Degrade what they exalt. Power with the King—
    I *was* the King, his arm, his better reason.
    But what was once exaltation
    Would now be only mean descent.   400
        [*Enter* THIRD TEMPTER.]

3RD TEM. I am an unexpected visitor.

THOM.   I expected you.

TEM. But not in this guise, or for my present purpose.

THOM. No purpose brings surprise.

TEM.   Well, my Lord,
I am no trifler, and no politician.
To idle or intrigue at court
I have no skill. I am no courtier.
I know a horse, a dog, a wench;
I know how to hold my estates in order,
A country-keeping lord who minds his own business.
It is we country lords who know the country   410
And we who know what the country needs.
It is our country. We care for the country.
We are the backbone of the nation.
We, not the plotting parasites
About the King. Excuse my bluntness:
I am a rough straightforward Englishman.

THOM. Proceed straight forward.

TEM.   Purpose is plain.
Endurance of friendship does not depend
Upon ourselves, but upon circumstance.
But circumstance is not undetermined.   420
Unreal friendship may turn to real
But real friendship, once ended, cannot be mended.
Sooner shall enmity turn to alliance.
The enmity that never knew friendship
Can sooner know accord.

THOM.   For a countryman
You wrap your meaning in as dark generality
As any courtier.

TEM.   This is the simple fact!
You have no hope of reconciliation
With Henry the King. You look only
To blind assertion in isolation.
That is a mistake.

THOM.   O Henry, O my King!

TEM.   Other friends
May be found in the present situation.
King in England is not all-powerful;

King is in France, squabbling in Anjou;
Round him waiting hungry sons.
We are for England. We are in England.
You and I, my Lord, are Normans.
England is a land for Norman
Sovereignty. Let the Angevin
Destroy himself, fighting in Anjou.
He does not understand us, the English barons.
We are the people.

THOM. To what does this lead?

TEM.　　　　　　　　　　To a happy coalition
Of intelligent interests.

THOM.　　　　　　　　　　But what have you—
If you do speak for barons—

TEM.　　　　　　　　　　For a powerful party
Which has turned its eyes in your direction—
To gain from you, your Lordship asks.
For us, Church favour would be an advantage,
Blessing of Pope powerful protection
In the fight for liberty. You, my Lord,　　　　　　　450
In being with us, would fight a good stroke
At once, for England and for Rome,
Ending the tyrannous jurisdiction
Of king's court over bishop's court,
Of king's court over baron's court.

THOM. Which I helped to found.

TEM.　　　　　　　　　　Which you helped to found.
But time past is time forgotten.
We expect the rise of a new constellation.

THOM. And if the Archbishop cannot trust the King,
How can he trust those who work for King's undoing?　　460

TEM. Kings will allow no power but their own;
Church and people have good cause against the throne.

THOM. If the Archbishop cannot trust the Throne,
He has good cause to trust none but God alone.

It is not better to be thrown
To a thousand hungry appetites than to one.
At a future time this may be shown.
I ruled once as Chancellor
And men like you were glad to wait at my door.
Not only in the court, but in the field   470
And in the tilt-yard I made many yield.
Shall I who ruled like an eagle over doves
Now take the shape of a wolf among wolves?
Pursue your treacheries as you have done before:
No one shall say that I betrayed a king.

TEM. Then, my Lord, I shall not wait at your door;
And I well hope, before another spring
The King will show his regard for your loyalty.

THOM. To make, then break, this thought has come before,
The desperate exercise of failing power.   480
Samson in Gaza did no more.
But if I break, I must break myself alone.

[*Enter* FOURTH TEMPTER.]

4TH TEM. Well done, Thomas, your will is hard to bend.
And with me beside you, you shall not lack a friend.

THOM. Who are you? I expected
Three visitors, not four.

TEM. Do not be surprised to receive one more.
Had I been expected, I had been here before.
I always precede expectation.

THOM.   Who are you?

TEM. As you do not know me, I do not need a name,   490
And, as you know me, that is why I come.
You know me, but have never seen my face.
To meet before was never time or place.

THOM. Say what you come to say.

TEM..   It shall be said at last.
Hooks have been baited with morsels of the past.
Wantonness is weakness. As for the King,
His hardened hatred shall have no end.

You know truly, the King will never trust
Twice, the man who has been his friend.
Borrow use cautiously, employ   500
Your services as long as you have to lend.
You would wait for trap to snap
Having served your turn, broken and crushed.
As for barons, envy of lesser men
Is still more stubborn than king's anger.
Kings have public policy, barons private profit,
Jealousy raging possession of the fiend.
Barons are employable against each other;
Greater enemies must kings destroy.

THOM. What is your counsel?

TEM.   Fare forward to the end.   510
All other ways are closed to you
Except the way already chosen.
But what is pleasure, kingly rule,
Or rule of men beneath a king,
With craft in corners, stealthy stratagem,
To general grasp of spiritual power?
Man oppressed by sin, since Adam fell—
You hold the keys of heaven and hell.
Power to bind and loose: bind, Thomas, bind,
King and bishop under your heel.   520
King, emperor, bishop, baron, king:
Uncertain mastery of melting armies,
War, plague, and revolution,
New conspiracies, broken pacts;
To be master or servant within an hour,
This is the course of temporal power.
The Old King shall know it, when at last breath,
No sons, no empire, he bites broken teeth.
You hold the skein: wind, Thomas, wind
The thread of eternal life and death.   530
You hold this power, hold it.

THOM.   Supreme, in this land?

TEM. Supreme, but for one.
THOM.   That I do not understand.
TEM. It is not for me to tell you how this may be so;
    I am only here, Thomas, to tell you what you know.
THOM. How long shall this be?
TEM. Save what you know already, ask nothing of me.
    But think, Thomas, think of glory after death.
    When king is dead, there's another king,
    And one more king is another reign.
    King is forgotten, when another shall come: 540
    Saint and Martyr rule from the tomb.
    Think, Thomas, think of enemies dismayed,
    Creeping in penance, frightened of a shade;
    Think of pilgrims, standing in line
    Before the glittering jewelled shrine,
    From generation to generation
    Bending the knee in supplication.
    Think of the miracles, by God's grace,
    And think of your enemies, in another place.
THOM. I have thought of these things.
TEM.   That is why I tell you.
    Your thoughts have more power than kings to compel you.
    You have also thought, sometimes at your prayers,   552
    Sometimes hesitating at the angles of stairs,
    And between sleep and waking, early in the morning,
    When the bird cries, have thought of further scorning.
    That nothing lasts, but the wheel turns,
    The nest is rifled, and the bird mourns;
    That the shrine shall be pillaged, and the gold spent,
    The jewels gone for light ladies' ornament,
    The sanctuary broken, and its stores   560
    Swept into the laps of parasites and whores.
    When miracles cease, and the faithful desert you,
    And men shall only do their best to forget you.
    And later is worse, when men will not hate you
    Enough to defame or to execrate you.

But pondering the qualities that you lacked
Will only try to find the historical fact.
When men shall declare that there was no mystery
About this man who played a certain part in history.

THOM. But what is there to do? what is left to be done?   570
Is there no enduring crown to be won?

TEM. Yes, Thomas, yes; you have thought of that too.
What can compare with glory of Saints
Dwelling forever in presence of God?
What earthly glory, of king or emperor,
What earthly pride, that is not poverty
Compared with richness of heavenly grandeur?
Seek the way of martyrdom, make yourself the lowest
On earth, to be high in heaven.
And see far off below you, where the gulf is fixed,   580
Your persecutors, in timeless torment,
Parched passion, beyond expiation.

THOM.   No!
Who are you, tempting with my own desires?
Others have come, temporal tempters,
With pleasure and power at palpable price.
What do you offer? what do you ask?

TEM. I offer what you desire. I ask
What you have to give. Is it too much
For such a vision of eternal grandeur?

THOM. Others offered real goods, worthless   590
But real. You only offer
Dreams to damnation.

TEM.   You have often dreamt them.

THOM. Is there no way, in my soul's sickness,
Does not lead to damnation in pride?
I well know that these temptations
Mean present vanity and future torment.
Can sinful pride be driven out
Only by more sinful? Can I neither act nor suffer
Without perdition?

TEM. You know and do not know, what it is to act or suffer.   600
 You know and do not know, that acting is suffering,
 And suffering action. Neither does the actor suffer
 Nor the patient act. But both are fixed
 In an eternal action, an eternal patience
 To which all must consent that it may be willed
 And which all must suffer that they may will it,
 That the pattern may subsist, that the wheel may turn and still
 Be forever still.

CHOR. There is no rest in the house. There is no rest in the street.
 I hear restless movement of feet. And the air is heavy and thick.
 Thick and heavy the sky. And the earth presses up beneath my
  feet.   611
 What is the sickly smell, the vapour? the dark green light from
  a cloud on a withered tree? The earth is heaving to parturi-
  tion of issue of hell. What is the sticky dew that forms on
  the back of my hand?

THE FOUR TEMPTERS.
 Man's life is a cheat and a disappointment;
 All things are unreal,
 Unreal or disappointing:
 The Catherine wheel, the pantomime cat,
 The prizes given at the children's party,
 The prize awarded for the English Essay,
 The scholar's degree, the statesman's decoration.
 All things become less real, man passes   620
 From unreality to unreality.
 This man is obstinate, blind, intent
 On self-destruction,
 Passing from deception to deception,
 From grandeur to grandeur to final illusion,
 Lost in the wonder of his own greatness,
 The enemy of society, enemy of himself.

THE THREE PRIESTS.
 O Thomas my Lord do not fight the intractable tide,
 Do not sail the irresistible wind; in the storm,

Should we not wait for the sea to subside, in the night
Abide the coming of day, when the traveller may find his way,
The sailor lay course by the sun?   632

[CHORUS, PRIESTS *and* TEMPTERS *alternately*.]

C. Is it the owl that calls, or a signal between the trees?

P. Is the window-bar made fast, is the door under lock and bolt?

T. Is it rain that taps at the window, is it wind that pokes at the door?

C. Does the torch flame in the hall, the candle in the room?

P. Does the watchman walk by the wall?

T. Does the mastiff prowl by the gate?

C. Death has a hundred hands and walks by a thousand ways.

P. He may come in the sight of all, he may pass unseen unheard.

T. Come whispering through the ear, or a sudden shock on the skull.

C. A man may walk with a lamp at night, and yet be drowned in a ditch.   642

P. A man may climb the stair in the day, and slip on a broken step.

T. A man may sit at meat, and feel the cold in his groin.

CHOR. We have not been happy, my Lord, we have not been too happy.

We are not ignorant women, we know what we must expect and not expect.

We know of oppression and torture,

We know of extortion and violence,

Destitution, disease,

The old without fire in winter,   650

The child without milk in summer,

Our labour taken away from us,

Our sins made heavier upon us.

We have seen the young man mutilated,

The torn girl trembling by the mill-stream.

And meanwhile we have gone on living,

Living and partly living,

Picking together the pieces,

Gathering faggots at nightfall,

Building a partial shelter, 660
For sleeping, and eating and drinking and laughter.

God gave us always some reason, some hope; but now a new
    terror has soiled us, which none can avert, none can avoid,
    flowing under our feet and over the sky;
Under doors and down chimneys, flowing in at the ear and
    the mouth and the eye.
God is leaving us, God is leaving us, more pang, more pain,
    than birth or death.
Sweet and cloying through the dark air
Falls the stifling scent of despair;
The forms take shape in the dark air:
Puss-purr of leopard, footfall of padding bear,
Palm-pat of nodding ape, square hyaena waiting
For laughter, laughter, laughter. The Lords of Hell are here.
They curl round you, lie at your feet, swing and wing through
    the dark air.
O Thomas Archbishop, save us, save us, save yourself that we
    may be saved; 672
Destroy yourself and we are destroyed.

THOM. Now is my way clear, now is the meaning plain:
Temptation shall not come in this kind again.
The last temptation is the greatest treason:
To do the right deed for the wrong reason.
The natural vigour in the venial sin
Is the way in which our lives begin.
Thirty years ago, I searched all the ways
That lead to pleasure, advancement and praise.
Delight in sense, in learning and in thought, 682
Music and philosophy, curiosity,
The purple bullfinch in the lilac tree,
The tiltyard skill, the strategy of chess,
Love in the garden, singing to the instrument,
Were all things equally desirable.
Ambition comes when early force is spent

And when we find no longer all things possible.
Ambition comes behind and unobservable.   690
Sin grows with doing good. When I imposed the King's law
In England, and waged war with him against Toulouse,
I beat the barons at their own game. I
Could then despise the men who thought me most contemptible,
The raw nobility, whose manners matched their fingernails.
While I ate out of the King's dish
To become servant of God was never my wish.
Servant of God has chance of greater sin
And sorrow, than the man who serves a king.
For those who serve the greater cause may make the cause
     serve them,   700
Still doing right: and striving with political men
May make that cause political, not by what they do
But by what they are. I know
What yet remains to show you of my history
Will seem to most of you at best futility,
Senseless self-slaughter of a lunatic,
Arrogant passion of a fanatic.
I know that history at all times draws
The strangest consequence from remotest cause.
But for every evil, every sacrilege,   710
Crime, wrong, oppression and the axe's edge,
Indifference, exploitation, you, and you,
And you, must all be punished. So must you.
I shall no longer act or suffer, to the sword's end.
Now my good Angel, whom God appoints
To be my guardian, hover over the swords' points.

INTERLUDE

THE ARCHBISHOP. [*Preaches in the Cathedral on Christmas Morning*, 1170.] "Glory to God in the highest, and on earth peace, good will toward men." *The fourteenth verse of the second chapter of the*

Gospel accoraing to Saint Luke. In the Name of the Father, and of the Son, and of the Holy Ghost. Amen.

Dear children of God, my sermon this morning will be a very short one. I wish only that you should ponder and meditate the deep meaning and mystery of our masses of Christmas Day. For whenever Mass is said, we re-enact the Passion and Death of Our Lord; and on this Christmas Day we do this in celebration of His Birth. So that at the same moment we rejoice in His coming for [11 the salvation of men, and offer again to God His Body and Blood in sacrifice, oblation and satisfaction for the sins of the whole world. It was in this same night that has just passed, that a multitude of the heavenly host appeared before the shepherds at Bethlehem, saying, "Glory to God in the highest, and on earth peace, good will toward men"; at this same time of all the year that we celebrate at once the Birth of Our Lord and His Passion and Death upon the Cross. Beloved, as the World sees, this is to behave in a strange fashion. For who in the World will both mourn and rejoice [20 at once and for the same reason? For either joy will be overborne by mourning, or mourning will be cast out by joy; so it is only in these our Christian mysteries that we can rejoice and mourn at once for the same reason. But think for a while on the meaning of this word "peace." Does it seem strange to you that the angels should have announced Peace, when ceaselessly the world has been stricken with War and the fear of War? Does it seem to you that the angelic voices were mistaken, and that the promise was a disappointment and a cheat? 29

Reflect now, how Our Lord Himself spoke of Peace. He said to His disciples, "My peace I leave with you, my peace I give unto you." Did He mean peace as we think of it: the kingdom of England at peace with its neighbours, the barons at peace with the King, the householder counting over his peaceful gains, the swept hearth, his best wine for a friend at the table, his wife singing to the children? Those men His disciples knew no such things: they went forth to journey afar, to suffer by land and sea, to know torture, imprisonment, disappointment, to suffer death by martyrdom. What then did He mean? If you ask that, remember then

that He said also, "Not as the world gives, give I unto you." So then, He gave to His disciples peace, but not peace as the world gives.   42

Consider also one thing of which you have probably never thought. Not only do we at the feast of Christmas celebrate at once Our Lord's Birth and His Death: but on the next day we celebrate the martyrdom of His first martyr, the blessed Stephen. Is it an accident, do you think, that the day of the first martyr follows immediately the day of the Birth of Christ? By no means. Just as we rejoice and mourn at once, in the Birth and in the Passion of Our Lord; so also, in a smaller figure, we both rejoice and mourn in the death of martyrs. We mourn, for the sins of the world that has martyred them; we rejoice, that another soul is numbered among the Saints in Heaven, for the glory of God and for the salvation of men.   54

Beloved, we do not think of a martyr simply as a good Christian who has been killed because he is a Christian: for that would be solely to mourn. We do not think of him simply as a good Christian who has been elevated to the company of the Saints: for that would be simply to rejoice: and neither our mourning nor our rejoicing is as the world's is. A Christian martyrdom is no accident. Saints are not made by accident. Still less is a Christian martyrdom the effect of a man's will to become a Saint, as a man by willing and contriving may become a ruler of men. Ambition [63 fortifies the will of man to become ruler over other men: it operates with deception, cajolery, and violence, it is the action of impurity upon impurity. Not so in Heaven. A martyr, a saint, is always made by the design of God, for His love of men, to warn them and to lead them, to bring them back to His ways. A martyrdom is never the design of man; for the true martyr is he who has become the instrument of God, who has lost his will in the will of God, not lost it but found it, for he has found freedom in submission to God. The martyr no longer desires anything for himself, not even the glory of martyrdom. So thus as on earth the Church [73 mourns and rejoices at once, in a fashion that the world cannot understand; so in Heaven the Saints are most high, having made

themselves most low, seeing themselves not as we see them, but in the light of the Godhead from which they draw their being.

I have spoken to you today, dear children of God, of the martyrs of the past, asking you to remember especially our martyr of Canterbury, the blessed Archbishop Elphege; because it is fitting, on Christ's birthday, to remember what is that Peace which He [81 brought; and because, dear children, I do not think I shall ever preach to you again; and because it is possible that in a short time you may have yet another martyr, and that one perhaps not the last. I would have you keep in your hearts these words that I say, and think of them at another time. In the Name of the Father, and of the Son, and of the Holy Ghost. Amen.

PART II

Characters

THREE PRIESTS

FOUR KNIGHTS

ARCHBISHOP THOMAS BECKET

CHORUS OF WOMEN OF CANTERBURY

ATTENDANTS

The first scene is in the Archbishop's Hall,
the second scene is in the Cathedral,
on December 29th, 1170.

CHOR. Does the bird sing in the South?
  Only the sea-bird cries, driven inland by the storm.

80. **Elphege:** Aelfheath or St. Elphege (954-1012) was born of noble English parents, became a monk when a young man, and was made archbishop of Canterbury in 1006. In 1011 Canterbury was burned by the Danes, and Aelfheath died a martyr the following year when he refused to allow his people to sacrifice their property to pay his ransom. In 1023 King Cnut moved his body from London to Canterbury.

What sign of the spring of the year?
Only the death of the old: not a stir, not a shoot, not a breath.
Do the days begin to lengthen?
Longer and darker the day, shorter and colder the night.
Still and stifling the air: but a wind is stored up in the East.
The starved crow sits in the field, attentive; and in the wood
The owl rehearses the hollow note of death.
What signs of a bitter spring?   10
The wind stored up in the East.
What, at the time of the birth of Our Lord, at Christmastide,
Is there not peace upon earth, goodwill among men?
The peace of this world is always uncertain, unless men keep
    the peace of God.
And war among men defiles this world, but death in the Lord
    renews it,
And the world must be cleaned in the winter, or we shall have
    only
A sour spring, a parched summer, an empty harvest.
Between Christmas and Easter what work shall be done?
The ploughman shall go out in March and turn the same
    earth
He has turned before, the bird shall sing the same song.   20
When the leaf is out on the tree, when the elder and may
Burst over the stream, and the air is clear and high,
And voices trill at windows, and children tumble in front of the
    door,
What work shall have been done, what wrong
Shall the bird's song cover, the green tree cover, what wrong
Shall the fresh earth cover? We wait, and the time is short
But waiting is long.

                    [*Enter the* FOUR KNIGHTS.]

IST KNI. Servants of the King.
IST PR.   And known to us.
    You are welcome. Have you ridden far?
IST KNI. Not far today, but matters urgent   30
    Have brought us from France. We rode hard,

Took ship yesterday, landed last night,
Having business with the Archbishop.

2ND KNI. Urgent business.

3RD KNI.   From the King.

4TH KNI. By the King's order.

1ST KNI.   Our men are outside.

1ST PR. You know the Archbishop's hospitality.
We are about to go to dinner.
The good Archbishop would be vexed
If we did not offer you entertainment
Before your business. Please dine with us.   40
Your men shall be looked after also.
Dinner before business. Do you like roast pork?

1ST KNI. Business before dinner. We will roast your pork
First, and dine upon it after.

2ND KNI. We must see the Archbishop.

3RD KNI.   Go, tell the Archbishop
We have no need of his hospitality.
We will find our own dinner.

1ST PR. [*To* ATTENDANT] Go, tell His Lordship.

4TH KNI.   How much longer will you keep us waiting?
[*Enter* THOMAS.]

THOM. [*To* PRIESTS] However certain our expectation
The moment foreseen may be unexpected   50
When it arrives. It comes when we are
Engrossed with matters of other urgency.
On my table you will find
The papers in order, and the documents signed.
[*To* KNIGHTS]
You are welcome, whatever your business may be.
You say, from the King?

1ST KNI.   Most surely from the King.
We must speak with you alone.

THOM. [*To* PRIESTS]   Leave us then alone.
Now what is the matter?

1ST KNI.   This is the matter.   59

THE FOUR KNIGHTS.

> You are the Archbishop in revolt against the King; in rebellion
>   to the King and the law of the land;
> You are the Archbishop who was made by the King; whom he
>   set in your place to carry out his command.
> You are his servant, his tool, and his jack,
> You wore his favours on your back,
> You had your honours all from his hand; from him you had
>   the power, the seal and the ring.
> This is the man who was the tradesman's son: the backstairs
>   brat who was born in Cheapside;
> This is the creature that crawled upon the King; swollen with
>   blood and swollen with pride.
> Creeping out of the London dirt,
> Crawling up like a louse on your shirt,
> The man who cheated, swindled, lied; broke his oath and be-
>   trayed his King.

THOM. This is not true.   70

> Both before and after I received the ring
> I have been a loyal vassal to the King.
> Saving my order, I am at his command,
> As his most faithful vassal in the land.

1ST KNI. Saving your order! let your order save you—

> As I do not think it is like to do.
> Saving your ambition is what you mean,
> Saving your pride, envy and spleen.

2ND KNI. Saving your insolence and greed.

> Won't you ask us to pray to God for you, in your need?   80

3RD KNI. Yes, we'll pray for you!

4TH KNI.   Yes, we'll pray for you!

THE FOUR KNIGHTS.

> Yes, we'll pray that God may help you!

THOM. But, gentlemen, your business

> Which you said so urgent, is it only
> Scolding and blaspheming?

1ST KNI.   That was only
 Our indignation, as loyal subjects.
THOM. Loyal? to whom?
1ST KNI.   To the King!
2ND KNI.   The King!
3RD KNI. The King!
4TH KNI.   God bless him!
THOM. Then let your new coat of loyalty be worn
 Carefully, so it get not soiled or torn.   90
 Have you something to say?
1ST KNI.   By the King's command.
 Shall we say it now?
2ND KNI.   Without delay,
 Before the old fox is off and away.
THOM.   What you have to say
 By the King's command—if it be the King's command—
 Should be said in public. If you make charges,
 Then in public I will refute them.
1ST KNI.   No! here and now!
 [*They make to attack him, but the* PRIESTS *and* ATTENDANTS
   return and quietly interpose themselves.]
THOM. Now and here!
1ST KNI. Of your earlier misdeeds I shall make no mention.
 They are too well known. But after dissension
  Had ended, in France, and you were endued   100
  With your former privilege, how did you show your gratitude?
  You had fled from England, not exiled
  Or threatened, mind you; but in the hope
  Of stirring up trouble in the French dominions.
  You sowed strife abroad, you reviled
  The King to the King of France, to the Pope,
  Raising up against him false opinions.
2ND KNI. Yet the King, out of his charity,
  And urged by your friends, offered clemency,
  Made a pact of peace, and all dispute ended   110
  Sent you back to your See as you demanded.

3RD KNI. And burying the memory of your transgressions
        Restored your honours and your possessions.
        All was granted for which you sued:
        Yet how, I repeat, did you show your gratitude?
4TH KNI. Suspending those who had crowned the young prince,
        Denying the legality of his coronation;
        Binding with the chains of anathema,
        Using every means in your power to evince
        The King's faithful servants, everyone who transacts   120
        His business in his absence, the business of the nation.
1ST KNI. These are the facts.
        Say therefore if you will be content
        To answer in the King's presence. Therefore were we sent.
THOM. Never was it my wish
        To uncrown the King's son, or to diminish
        His honour and power. Why should he wish
        To deprive my people of me and keep me from my own
        And bid me sit in Canterbury, alone?
        I would wish him three crowns rather than one,   130
        And as for the bishops, it is not my yoke
        That is laid upon them, or mine to revoke.
        Let them go to the Pope. It was he who condemned them.
1ST KNI. Through you they were suspended.
2ND KNI.   By you be this amended.
3RD KNI. Absolve them.
4TH KNI.   Absolve them.
THOM.   I do not deny
        That this was done through me. But it is not I
        Who can loose whom the Pope has bound.
        Let them go to him, upon whom redounds
        Their contempt towards me, their contempt towards the Church
           shown.
1ST KNI. Be that as it may, here is the King's command: 140
        That you and your servants depart from this land.
THOM. If that *is* the King's command, I will be bold
        To say: seven years were my people without

My presence; seven years of misery and pain.
Seven years a mendicant on foreign charity
I lingered abroad: seven years is no brevity.
I shall not get those seven years back again.
Never again, you must make no doubt,
Shall the sea run between the shepherd and his fold.

1ST KNI. The King's justice, the King's majesty,   150
You insult with gross indignity;
Insolent madman, whom nothing deters
From attainting his servants and ministers.

THOM. It is not I who insult the King,
And there is higher than I or the King.
It is not I, Becket from Cheapside,
It is not against me, Becket, that you strive.
It is not Becket who pronounces doom,
But the Law of Christ's Church, the judgement of Rome.
Go then to Rome, or let Rome come   160
Here, to you, in the person of her most unworthy son.
Petty politicians in your endless adventure!
Rome alone can absolve those who break Christ's indenture.

1ST KNI. Priest, you have spoken in peril of your life.
2ND KNI. Priest, you have spoken in danger of the knife.
3RD KNI. Priest, you have spoken treachery and treason.
4TH KNI. Priest! traitor confirmed in malfeasance.

THOM. I submit my cause to the judgement of Rome.
But if you kill me, I shall rise from my tomb
To submit my cause before God's throne.   170

KNIGHTS. Priest! monk! and servant! take, hold, detain,
Restrain this man, in the King's name;
Or answer with your bodies, if he escape before we come,
We come for the King's justice, we come again.   [*Exeunt.*]

THOM. Pursue those who flee, track down those who evade;
Come for arrest, come with the sword,
Here, here, you shall find me ready, in the battle of the Lord.
At whatsoever time you are ready to come,
You will find me still more ready for martyrdom.

CHOR. I have smelt them, the death-bringers, senses are quickened
    By subtile forebodings; I have heard   181
    Fluting in the nighttime, fluting and owls, have seen at noon
    Scaly wings slanting over, huge and ridiculous. I have tasted
    The savour of putrid flesh in the spoon. I have felt
    The heaving of earth at nightfall, restless, absurd. I have heard
    Laughter in the noises of beasts that make strange noises:
        jackal, jackass, jackdaw; the scurrying noise of mouse and
        jerboa; the laugh of the loon, the lunatic bird. I have seen
    Grey necks twisting, rat tails twining, in the thick light of
        dawn. I have eaten
    Smooth creatures still living, with the strong salt taste of living
        things under sea; I have tasted
    The living lobster, the crab, the oyster, the whelk and the
        prawn; and they live and spawn in my bowels, and my
        bowels dissolve in the light of dawn. I have smelt
    Death in the rose, death in the hollyhock, sweet pea, hyacinth,
        primrose and cowslip. I have seen   190
    Trunk and horn, tusk and hoof, in odd places;
    I have lain on the floor of the sea and breathed with the breath-
        ing of the sea-anemone, swallowed with ingurgitation of
        the sponge. I have lain in the soil and criticised the worm.
        In the air
    Flirted with the passage of the kite, I have plunged with the
        kite and cowered with the wren. I have felt
    The horn of the beetle, the scale of the viper, the mobile hard
        insensitive skin of the elephant, the evasive flank of the
        fish. I have smelt
    Corruption in the dish, incense in the latrine, the sewer in the
        incense, the smell of sweet soap in the woodpath, a hellish
        sweet scent in the woodpath, while the ground heaved. I
        have seen
    Rings of light coiling downwards, leading
    To the horror of the ape. Have I not known, not known
    What was coming to be? It was here, in the kitchen, in the
        passage,

In the mews in the barn in the byre in the market place
In our veins our bowels our skulls as well   200
As well as in the plottings of potentates
As well as in the consultations of powers.
What is woven on the loom of fate
What is woven in the councils of princes
Is woven also in our veins, our brains,
Is woven like a pattern of living worms
In the guts of the women of Canterbury.

I have smelt them, the death-bringers; now is too late
For action, too soon for contrition.
Nothing is possible but the shamed swoon   210
Of those consenting to the last humiliation.
I have consented, Lord Archbishop, have consented.
Am torn away, subdued, violated,
United to the spiritual flesh of nature,
Mastered by the animal powers of spirit,
Dominated by the lust of self-demolition,
By the final utter uttermost death of spirit,
By the final ecstasy of waste and shame,
O Lord Archbishop, O Thomas Archbishop, forgive us, forgive
    us, pray for us that we may pray for you, out of our shame.
THOM. Peace, and be at peace with your thoughts and visions.
These things had to come to you and you to accept them.   221
This is your share of the eternal burden,
The perpetual glory. This is one moment,
But know that another
Shall pierce you with a sudden painful joy
When the figure of God's purpose is made complete.
You shall forget these things, toiling in the household,
You shall remember them, droning by the fire,
When age and forgetfulness sweeten memory
Only like a dream that has often been told   230
And often been changed in the telling. They will seem unreal.
Human kind cannot bear very much reality.

PRIESTS. [*Severally*] My Lord, you must not stop here. To the minster. Through the cloister. No time to waste. They are coming
back, armed. To the altar, to the altar. They are here already.
To the sanctuary. They are breaking in. We can barricade the
minster doors. You cannot stay here. Force him to come. Seize
him.

THOM. All my life they have been coming, these feet. All my life
I have waited. Death will come only when I am worthy,
And if I am worthy, there is no danger.   241
I have therefore only to make perfect my will.

PRIESTS. My Lord, they are coming. They will break through presently.
You will be killed. Come to the altar.

THOM. Peace! be quiet! remember where you are, and what is hap-
pening;
No life here is sought for but mine,
And I am not in danger: only near to death.

PRIESTS. Make haste, my Lord. Don't stop here talking. It is not
right.
What shall become of us, my Lord, if you are killed; what
shall become of us?

THOM. That again is another theme   250
To be developed and resolved in the pattern of time.
It is not for me to run from city to city;
To meet death gladly is only
The only way in which I can defend
The Law of God, the holy canons.

PRIESTS. My Lord, to vespers! You must not be absent from vespers.
You must not be absent from the divine office. To vespers.
Into the cathedral!

THOM. Go to vespers, remember me at your prayers.
They shall find the shepherd here; the flock shall be spared.
I have had a tremor of bliss, a wink of heaven, a whisper,
And I would no longer be denied; all things   260
Proceed to a joyful consummation.

PRIESTS. Seize him! force him! drag him!
THOM. Keep your hands off!
PRIESTS. To vespers! Take his feet! Up with him! Hurry.

> [*They drag him off. While the* CHORUS *speak, the scene is changed to the cathedral.*]

CHOR. [*While a* Dies Irae *is sung in Latin by a choir in the distance*]
Numb the hand and dry the eyelid,
Still the horror, but more horror
Than when tearing in the belly.

Still the horror, but more horror
Than when twisting in the fingers,
Than when splitting in the skull.   270

More than footfall in the passage,
More than shadow in the doorway,
More than fury in the hall.

The agents of hell disappear, the human, they shrink and dissolve
Into dust on the wind, forgotten, unmemorable; only is here
The white flat face of Death, God's silent servant,
And behind the face of Death the Judgement
And behind the Judgement the Void, more horrid than active shapes of hell;
Emptiness, absence, separation from God;
The horror of the effortless journey, to the empty land
Which is no land, only emptiness, absence, the Void,   281
Where those who were men can no longer turn the mind
To distraction, delusion, escape into dream, pretence,
Where the soul is no longer deceived, for there are no objects, no tones,
No colours, no forms to distract, to divert the soul
From seeing itself, foully united forever, nothing with nothing,
Not what we call death, but what beyond death is not death,

We fear, we fear. Who shall then plead for me,
Who intercede for me, in my most need?

Dead upon the tree, my Saviour,　　　　　　　　　　　290
Let not be in vain Thy labour;
Help me, Lord, in my last fear.

Dust I am, to dust am bending,
From the final doom impending
Help me, Lord, for death is near.
　　　　　　　[*In the cathedral*. THOMAS *and* PRIESTS.]
PRIESTS. Bar the door. Bar the door.
　　　The door is barred.
　　　We are safe. We are safe.
　　　The enemy may rage outside, he will tire
　　　In vain. They cannot break in.　　　　　　　　　300
　　　They dare not break in.
　　　They cannot break in. They have not the force.
　　　We are safe. We are safe.
THOM. Unbar the doors! throw open the doors!
　　　I will not have the house of prayer, the church of Christ,
　　　The sanctuary, turned into a fortress.
　　　The Church shall protect her own, in her own way, not
　　　As oak and stone; stone and oak decay,
　　　Give no stay, but the Church shall endure.　　　　309
　　　The church shall be open, even to our enemies. Open the door!
PRIESTS. My Lord! these are not men, these come not as men come,
　　　　but
　　　Like maddened beasts. They come not like men, who
　　　Respect the sanctuary, who kneel to the Body of Christ,
　　　But like beasts. You would bar the door
　　　Against the lion, the leopard, the wolf or the boar,
　　　Why not more
　　　Against beasts with the souls of damned men, against men
　　　Who would damn themselves to beasts. My Lord! My Lord!

THOM. Unbar the door!
    You think me reckless, desperate and mad. 320
    You argue by results, as this world does,
    To settle if an act be good or bad.
    You defer to the fact. For every life and every act
    Consequence of good and evil can be shown.
    And as in time results of many deeds are blended
    So good and evil in the end become confounded.
    It is not in time that my death shall be known;
    It is out of time that my decision is taken
    If you call that decision
    To which my whole being gives entire consent. 330
    I give my life
    To the Law of God above the Law of Man.
    Those who do not the same
    How should they know what I do?
    How should you know what I do? Yet how much more
    Should you know than these madmen beating on the door.
    Unbar the door! unbar the door!
    We are not here to triumph by fighting, by stratagem, or by
        resistance,
    Not to fight with beasts as men. We have fought the beast
    And have conquered. We have only to conquer 340
    Now, by suffering. This is the easier victory.
    Now is the triumph of the Cross, now
    Open the door! I command it. OPEN THE DOOR!
        [*The door is opened. The* KNIGHTS *enter, slightly tipsy.*]
PRIESTS. This way, my Lord! Quick. Up the stair. To the roof. To
    the crypt. Quick. Come. Force him.
KNIGHTS. [*One line each*]
    Where is Becket, the traitor to the King?
      Where is Becket, the meddling priest?
    Come down Daniel to the lions' den,
      Come down Daniel for the mark of the beast.

Are you washed in the blood of the Lamb?
Are you marked with the mark of the beast?   350
Come down Daniel to the lions' den,
Come down Daniel and join in the feast.

Where is Becket the Cheapside brat?
Where is Becket the faithless priest?
Come down Daniel to the lions' den,
Come down Daniel and join the feast.

THOM. It is the just man who
Like a bold lion, should be without fear.
I am here.
No traitor to the King. I am a priest,   360
A Christian, saved by the blood of Christ,
Ready to suffer with my blood.
This is the sign of the Church always,
The sign of blood. Blood for blood.
His blood given to buy my life,
My blood given to pay for His death,
My death for His death.

KNIGHTS. Absolve all those you have excommunicated.
Resign the powers you have arrogated.
Restore to the King the money you appropriated.   370
Renew the obedience you have violated.

THOM. For my Lord I am now ready to die,
That His Church may have peace and liberty.
Do with me as you will, to your hurt and shame;
But none of my people, in God's name,
Whether layman or clerk, shall you touch.
This I forbid.

KNIGHTS. Traitor! traitor! traitor! traitor!

THOM. You, Reginald, three times traitor you:
Traitor to me as my temporal vassal,   380
Traitor to me as your spiritual lord,
Traitor to God in desecrating His Church.

1st KNI. No faith do I owe to a renegade,
     And what I owe shall now be paid.
THOM. Now to Almighty God, to the Blessed Mary ever Virgin, to
     the blessed John the Baptist, the holy apostles Peter and Paul,
     to the blessed martyr Denys, and to all the Saints, I commend
     my cause and that of the Church.

          [*While the* KNIGHTS *kill him, we hear the* CHORUS]

CHOR. Clear the air! clean the sky! wash the wind! take stone from
     stone and wash them.
     The land is foul, the water is foul, our beasts and ourselves
          defiled with blood.   390
     A rain of blood has blinded my eyes. Where is England?
          where is Kent? where is Canterbury?
     O far far far far in the past; and I wander in a land of barren
          boughs: if I break them, they bleed; I wander in a land of
          dry stones: if I touch them they bleed.
     How how can I ever return, to the soft quiet seasons?
     Night stay with us, stop sun, hold season, let the day not come,
          let the spring not come.
     Can I look again at the day and its common things, and see
          them all smeared with blood, through a curtain of falling
          blood?
     We did not wish anything to happen.
     We understood the private catastrophe,
     The personal loss, the general misery,
     Living and partly living;
     The terror by night that ends in daily action,   400
     The terror by day that ends in sleep;
     But the talk in the market-place, the hand on the broom,
     The nighttime heaping of the ashes,
     The fuel laid on the fire at daybreak,
     These acts marked a limit to our suffering.
     Every horror had its definition,
     Every sorrow had a kind of end:
     In life there is not time to grieve long.

But this, this is out of life, this is out of time,

An instant eternity of evil and wrong.   410

We are soiled by a filth that we cannot clean, united to super-
natural vermin,

It is not we alone, it is not the house, it is not the city that is
defiled,

But the world that is wholly foul.

Clear the air! clean the sky! wash the wind! take the stone
from the stone, take the skin from the arm, take the muscle
from the bone, and wash them. Wash the stone, wash the
bone, wash the brain, wash the soul, wash them wash
them!

[*The* KNIGHTS, *having completed the murder, advance to the
front of the stage and address the audience.*]

1ST KNI. We beg you to give us your attention for a few moments.
We know that you may be disposed to judge unfavourably of
our action. You are Englishmen, and therefore you believe in
fair play: and when you see one man being set upon by four,
then your sympathies are all with the under dog. I respect [419
such feelings, I share them. Nevertheless, I appeal to your sense
of honour. You are Englishmen, and therefore will not judge
anybody without hearing both sides of the case. That is in ac-
cordance with our long established principle of Trial by Jury.
I am not myself qualified to put our case to you. I am a man
of action and not of words. For that reason I shall do no more
than introduce the other speakers, who, with their various
abilities, and different points of view, will be able to lay before
you the merits of this extremely complex problem. I shall call
upon our youngest member to speak first. William de [429
Traci.

2ND KNI. I am afraid I am not anything like such an experienced
speaker as Reginald Fitz Urse would lead you to believe. But

430. Traci: Tracy (d. 1173), Morville (d. 1200), Fitsurze, and Brito or le
Breton were the historical murderers of Becket and had been his men when
he was Chancellor. They fled to Scotland after the murder and were finally
banished to the Holy Land by the Pope.

there is one thing I should like to say, and I might as well say it at once. It is this: in what we have done, and whatever you may think of it, we have been perfectly disinterested. [*The other* KNIGHTS: "Hear! hear!"] *We* are not getting anything out of this. We have much more to lose than to gain. We are four plain Englishmen who put our country first. I dare say that we didn't make a very good impression when we [439 came in. The fact is that we knew we had taken on a pretty stiff job; I'll only speak for myself, but I had drunk a good deal—I am not a drinking man ordinarily—to brace myself up for it. When you come to the point, it does go against the grain to kill an Archbishop, especially when you have been brought up in good Church traditions. So if we seemed a bit rowdy, you will understand why it was; and for my part I am awfully sorry about it. We realised that this was our duty, but all the same we had to work ourselves up to it. And, as I said, *we* are not getting a penny out of this. We know per- [449 fectly well how things will turn out. King Henry—God bless him—will have to say, for reasons of state, that he never meant this to happen; and there is going to be an awful row; and at the best we shall have to spend the rest of our lives abroad. And even when reasonable people come to see that the Archbishop *had* to be put out of the way—and personally I had a tremendous admiration for him—you must have noticed what a good show he put up at the end—they won't give *us* any glory. No, we have done for ourselves, there's no mistake about that. So, as I said at the beginning, please give us at least the [459 credit for being completely disinterested in this business. I think that is about all I have to say.

IST KNI. I think we will all agree that William de Traci has spoken well and has made a very important point. The gist of his argument is this: that we have been completely disinterested. But our act itself needs more justification than that; and you must hear our other speakers. I shall next call upon Hugh de Morville.

3RD KNI. I should like first to recur to a point that was very well
    put by our leader, Reginald Fitz Urse: that you are Eng- [469
    lishmen, and therefore your sympathies are always with the
    under dog. It is the English spirit of fair play. Now the worthy
    Archbishop, whose good qualities I very much admired, has
    throughout been presented as the under dog. But is this really
    the case? I am going to appeal not to your emotions but to
    your reason. You are hard-headed sensible people, as I can see,
    and not to be taken in by emotional clap-trap. I therefore ask
    you to consider soberly: what were the Archbishop's aims? and
    what are King Henry's aims? In the answer to these questions
    lies the key to the problem.   [479
The King's aim has been perfectly consistent. During the reign of
    the late Queen Matilda and the irruption of the unhappy
    usurper Stephen, the kingdom was very much divided. Our
    King saw that the one thing needful was to restore order: to
    curb the excessive powers of local government, which were usu-
    ally exercised for selfish and often for seditious ends, and to
    systematise the judiciary. There was utter chaos: there were
    three kinds of justice and three kinds of court: that of the
    King, that of the Bishops, and that of the baronage. I must
    repeat one point that the last speaker has made. While the [489
    late Archbishop was Chancellor, he wholeheartedly supported
    the King's designs: this is an important point, which, if neces-
    sary, I can substantiate. Now the King intended that Becket,
    who had proved himself an extremely able administrator—no
    one denies that—should unite the offices of Chancellor and
    Archbishop. No one would have grudged him that; no one
    than he was better qualified to fill at once these two most im-
    portant posts. Had Becket concurred with the King's wishes,
    we should have had an almost ideal State: a union of spiritual
    and temporal administration, under the central govern- [499
    ment. I knew Becket well, in various official relations; and I
    may say that I have never known a man so well qualified for
    the highest rank of the Civil Service. And what happened?
    The moment that Becket, at the King's instance, had been

made Archbishop, he resigned the office of Chancellor, he became more priestly than the priests, he ostentatiously and offensively adopted an ascetic manner of life, he openly abandoned every policy that he had heretofore supported; he affirmed immediately that there was a higher order than that which our King, and he as the King's servant, had for so [509 many years striven to establish; and that—God knows why—the two orders were incompatible.

You will agree with me that such interference by an Archbishop offends the instincts of a people like ours. So far, I know that I have your approval: I read it in your faces. It is only with the measures we have had to adopt, in order to set matters to rights, that you take issue. No one regrets the necessity for violence more than we do. Unhappily, there are times when violence is the only way in which social justice can be secured. At another time, you would condemn an Archbishop by vote of [519 Parliament and execute him formally as a traitor, and no one would have to bear the burden of being called murderer. And at a later time still, even such temperate measures as these would become unnecessary. But, if you have now arrived at a just subordination of the pretensions of the Church to the welfare of the State, remember that it is we who took the first step. We have been instrumental in bringing about the state of affairs that you approve. We have served your interests; we merit your applause; and if there is any guilt whatever in the matter, you must share it with us. [529

1ST KNI. Morville has given us a great deal to think about. It seems to me that he has said almost the last word, for those who have been able to follow his very subtle reasoning. We have, however, one more speaker, who has I think another point of view to express. If there are any who are still unconvinced, I think that Richard Brito will be able to convince them. Richard Brito.

4TH KNI. The speakers who have preceded me, to say nothing of our leader, Reginald Fitz Urse, have all spoken very much to the point. I have nothing to add along their particular lines of

argument. What I have to say may be put in the form of [539 a question: *Who killed the Archbishop?* As you have been eye-witnesses of this lamentable scene, you may feel some surprise at my putting it in this way. But consider the course of events. I am obliged, very briefly, to go over the ground traversed by the last speaker. While the late Archbishop was Chancellor, no one, under the King, did more to weld the country together, to give it the unity, the stability, order, tranquillity, and justice that it so badly needed. From the moment he became Archbishop, he completely reversed his policy; he showed himself to be utterly indifferent to the fate of the country, to [549 be, in fact, a monster of egotism, a menace to society. This egotism grew upon him, until it became at last an undoubted mania. Every means that had been tried to conciliate him, to restore him to reason, had failed. Now I have unimpeachable evidence to the effect that before he left France he clearly prophesied, in the presence of numerous witnesses, that he had not long to live, and that he would be killed in England. He used every means of provocation; from his conduct, step by step, there can be no inference except that he had determined upon a death by martyrdom. This man, formerly a [559 great public servant, had become a wrecker. Even at the last, he could have given us reason: you have seen how he evaded our questions. And when he had deliberately exasperated us beyond human endurance, he could still have easily escaped; he could have kept himself from us long enough to allow our righteous anger to cool. That was just what he did not wish to happen; he insisted, while we were still inflamed with wrath, that the doors should be opened. Need I say more? I think, with these facts before you, you will unhesitatingly render a verdict of Suicide while of Unsound Mind. It is the only [569 charitable verdict you can give, upon one who was, after all, a great man.

1st KNI. Thank you, Brito. I think that there is no more to be said; and I suggest that you now disperse quietly to your homes.

Please be careful not to loiter in groups at street corners, and
do nothing that might provoke any public outbreak.

[*Exeunt* KNIGHTS.]

1ST PR. O father, father, gone from us, lost to us,
How shall we find you, from what far place
Do you look down on us? You now in Heaven,
Who shall now guide us, protect us, direct us?
After what journey through what further dread   580
Shall we recover your presence? when inherit
Your strength? The Church lies bereft,
Alone, desecrated, desolated, and the heathen shall build on
     the ruins,
Their world without God. I see it. I see it.

3RD PR. No. For the Church is stronger for this action,
Triumphant in adversity. It is fortified
By persecution: supreme, so long as men will die for it.
Go, weak sad men, lost erring souls, homeless in earth or heaven.
Go where the sunset reddens the last grey rock
Of Brittany, or the Gates of Hercules.   590
Go venture shipwreck on the sullen coasts
Where blackamoors make captive Christian men;
Go to the northern seas confined with ice
Where the dead breath makes numb the hand, makes dull the
     brain;
Find an oasis in the desert sun,
Go seek alliance with the heathen Saracen,
To share his filthy rites, and try to snatch
Forgetfulness in his libidinous courts,
Oblivion in the fountain by the date-tree;
Or sit and bite your nails in Aquitaine.   600
In the small circle of pain within the skull
You still shall tramp and tread one endless round
Of thought, to justify your action to yourselves,
Weaving a fiction which unravels as you weave,
Pacing forever in the hell of make-believe
Which never is belief: this is your fate on earth

And we must think no further of you. O my Lord
The glory of whose new state is hidden from us,
Pray for us of your charity; now in the sight of God
Conjoined with all the saints and martyrs gone before you, 610
Remember us. Let our thanks ascend
To God, who has given us another Saint in Canterbury.

CHOR. [*While a* Te Deum *is sung in Latin by a choir in the distance*]

We praise Thee, O God, for Thy glory displayed in all the
creatures of the earth,

In the snow, in the rain, in the wind, in the storm; in all of
Thy creatures, both the hunters and the hunted.

For all things exist only as seen by Thee, only as known by
Thee, all things exist

Only in Thy light, and Thy glory is declared even in that
which denies Thee; the darkness declares the glory of light.

Those who deny Thee could not deny, if Thou didst not exist;
and their denial is never complete, for if it were so, they
would not exist.

They affirm Thee in living; all things affirm Thee in living;
the bird in the air, both the hawk and the finch; the beast
on the earth, both the wolf and the lamb; the worm in the
soil and the worm in the belly.

Therefore man, whom Thou hast made to be conscious of
Thee, must consciously praise Thee, in thought and in
word and in deed.

Even with the hand to the broom, the back bent in laying the
fire, the knee bent in cleaning the hearth, we, the scrubbers
and sweepers of Canterbury,   620

The back bent under toil, the knee bent under sin, the hands
to the face under fear, the head bent under grief,

Even in us the voices of seasons, the snuffle of winter, the song
of spring, the drone of summer, the voices of beasts and of
birds, praise Thee.

We thank Thee for Thy mercies of blood, for Thy redemption
by blood. For the blood of Thy martyrs and saints

Shall enrich the earth, shall create the holy places.

For wherever a saint has dwelt, wherever a martyr has given
his blood for the blood of Christ,

There is holy ground, and the sanctity shall not depart from it

Though armies trample over it, though sightseers come with
guide-books looking over it;

From where the western seas gnaw at the coast of Iona,

To the death in the desert, the prayer in forgotten places by
the broken imperial column,   629

From such ground springs that which forever renews the earth

Though it is forever denied. Therefore, O God, we thank Thee

Who hast given such blessing to Canterbury.

Forgive us, O Lord, we acknowledge ourselves as type of the
common man,

Of the men and women who shut the door and sit by the fire;

Who fear the blessing of God, the loneliness of the night of
God, the surrender required, the deprivation inflicted;

Who fear the injustice of men less than the justice of God;

Who fear the hand at the window, the fire in the thatch, the
fist in the tavern, the push into the canal,

Less than we fear the love of God.

We acknowledge our trespass, our weakness, our fault; we acknowledge

That the sin of the world is upon our heads; that the blood of
the martyrs and the agony of the saints   640

Is upon our heads.

Lord, have mercy upon us.

Christ, have mercy upon us.

Lord, have mercy upon us.

Blessed Thomas, pray for us.

I	3
J	4
K	5
L	6
M	7
N	8
O	9
P	0
Q	1